This recently discovered detailed architect's drawing of Swimbridge station building is interesting in that it bears no relationship to the structure actually built – or indeed to any other station on the line. The building that was constructed, which features on pages 375-379 of Volume 2, was far simpler and more austere than the delightful design shown here. It is likely that this plan was simply discarded for something cheaper after the finances had run dry during construction in the late 1860s but the plan is undated so we cannot say for certain. *Courtesy Network Rail Archives*

ELEVATION TOWARDS LINE.

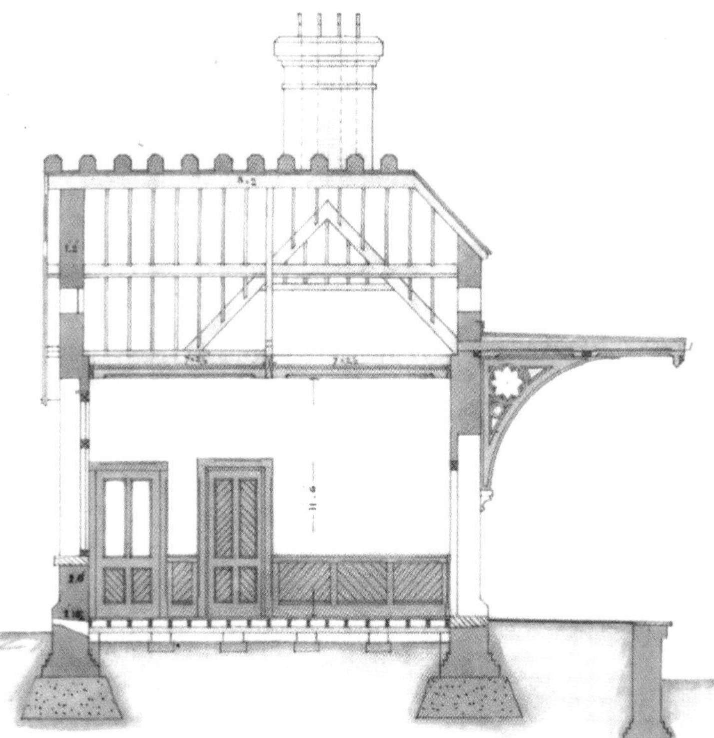

SECTION ON LINE A. B.

SECTION ON LINE C.D.

THE TAUNTON TO BARNSTAPLE LINE

A HISTORY OF THE DEVON & SOMERSET RAILWAY

VOLUME 3

'Mogul' No. 7304 heads an Up train away from Wiveliscombe towards Milverton and Taunton in 1963. The buildings of Wiveliscombe Brewery can be seen in the left background; latterly a part of Usher's Wiltshire Brewery Ltd, brewing here had ceased four years earlier in 1959 but the buildings still stand today. *John Carter, Neil Parkhouse collection*

FRONT COVER: No. 6343 drifts through Swimbridge with a short Up goods on 24th April 1960. *Roy Denison*

BACKGROUND: The brickwork which forms the cover background is a close-up of the office extension to the otherwise stone-built Barnstaple goods shed, which has been refurbished and converted for use as a church. *Author*

REAR COVER: Watched by the Barnstaple Victoria Road signalman, No. 6375 in seen in the process of running round its train on 24th April 1960. The junction for the Barnstaple Branch can be seen in the background, with the line to Barnstaple Junction station curving off to the right and there is a glimpse of the petrol depot on the right edge of the picture. *Roy Denison*

Collett 0-6-0 No. 2266 slows for the token exchange with the Morebath Junction signalman on 3rd August 1953. Bound for Taunton with an Up passenger train, No. 2266 would not have been travelling at any great speed in any case, having just called at Morebath Junction Halt, visible in the background. On the left, the Exe Valley Branch swings away southwards towards Bampton and Tiverton. *Roger J. Sellick, courtesy National Railway Museum*

Published by LIGHTMOOR PRESS

Designed by Neil Parkhouse

www.devonandsomersetrailway.co.uk

British Library Cataloguing-in-Publication Data. A catalogue record for this book is available from the British Library.

ISBN: 9781911038 73 3

LIGHTMOOR PRESS
Unit 144B, Lydney Trading Estate, Harbour Road, Lydney, Gloucestershire GL15 4EJ
www.lightmoor.co.uk
Lightmoor Press is an imprint of Black Dwarf Lightmoor Publications Ltd

Printed in Poland
www.lfbookservices.co.uk

THE TAUNTON TO BARNSTAPLE LINE

A HISTORY OF THE DEVON & SOMERSET RAILWAY

Volume 3: Locomotives, Operations & Recollections

FREDDIE HUXTABLE

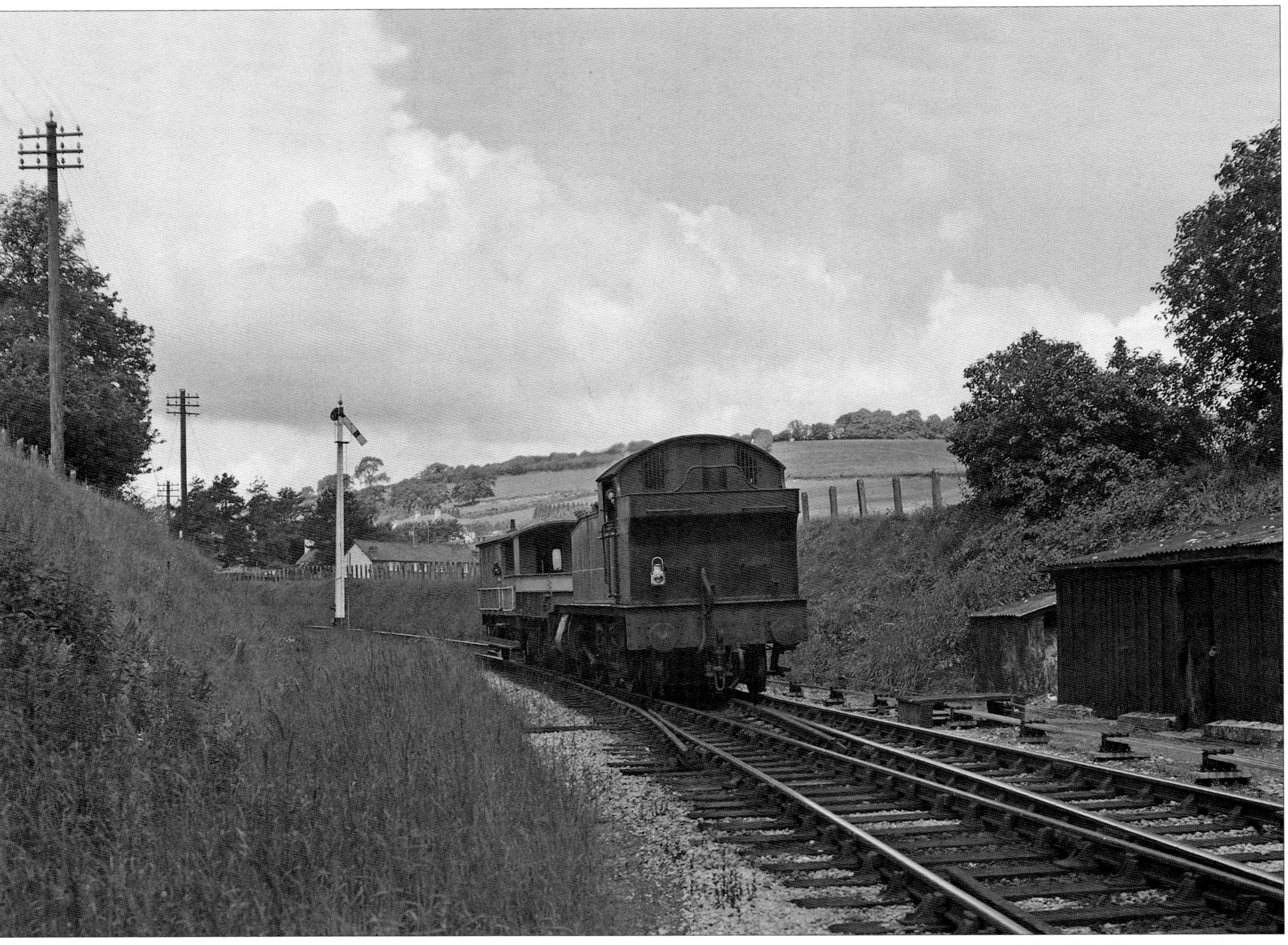

'Prairie' tank No. 5521 coasts into Dulverton running bunker first with a very light load comprising a low-sided ballast wagon and a 'Toad' brake van on 8th June 1961. This was most likely the South Molton pick-up goods returning to Taunton. *Michael J. Fox, courtesy Rail Archive Stephenson*

Contents – Volume 3
Locomotives, Operations & Recollections

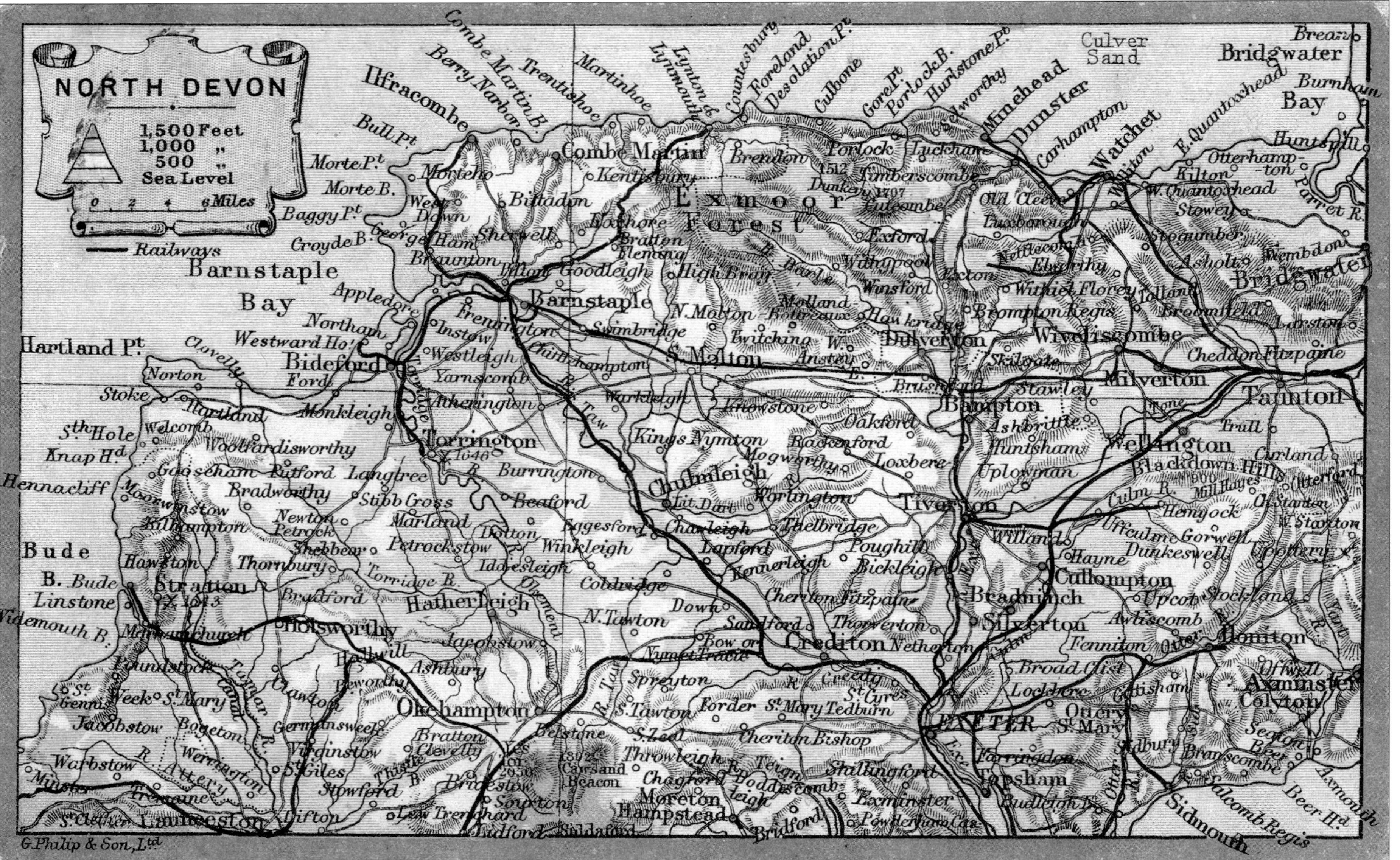

This unusual map postcard of the North Devon area was posted to a Mrs Kerslake at 39 Bear Street, Barnstaple in July 1905; the house is still there but is now a picture framers shop, Gallery Three Nine, next door to the Ebberley Arms pub. The railways serving the area are prominently shown as thick black lines, the early date meaning that the then recently opened (May 1898) narrow gauge Lynton & Barnstaple Railway is included but not the standard gauge North Devon & Cornwall Junction Light Railway, from Torrington to Halwill on the Bude Branch, which did not open until July 1925. As well as showing the full length of the GWR Barnstaple Branch from Taunton, the map also includes the Minehead Branch, the Exe Valley line and Tiverton Branch, the Culm Valley Branch and the GWR's main line south to Exeter. Running south up on to the Brendon Hills from Watchet is the line of the West Somerset Mineral Railway, which had closed by this date but was shortly (in 1907) to enjoy a brief reopening lasting a mere three years. The lower half of the map is mostly occupied with the lines of the L&SWR, their main line heading from Exeter via Okehampton to Plymouth, the branches to Barnstaple, Torrington and Ilfracombe, and the branches to Bude, and to Wadebridge and Padstow via Launceston. Bottom right are further L&SWR branches, to Exmouth, Sidmouth and Seaton. Finally, the narrow gauge Bideford, Westward Ho! & Appledore Railway is shown as part completed, having opened to Westward Ho! in April 1901, the section on to Appledore not being completed and opened until May 1908; it closed completely in 1917, whilst the L&BR was also an early closure, in 1935. *Neil Parkhouse collection*

INTRODUCTION TO VOLUME 3

Firstly, I would like to thank those readers who have been patient and have waited for this third and final volume on the history of the Devon & Somerset Railway. Readers have been most complementary about volumes 1 and 2, and therefore I hope that after reading this final part of the series you feel that it has been worth the wait. This volume covers the missing topics of locomotives and rolling stock, an analysis of the passenger and goods services over the ninety-five year life of the line, accidents and mishaps, and some of the recollections of those who worked on and that knew the railway; these stories bring it to life again. These recollections are as much about recording a by-gone age and showing how different life was in the 1940s, 1950s and 1960s, compared with the present day. This comparison can apply to railway operations or just how things generally were done then – a very different era. Furthermore, I have taken some writer's licence and included selected photographs of relevant GWR trains and locomotives at Barnstaple Junction and on the stretch to Ilfracombe. This is justified on the basis that we discuss through trains in Chapter 11.

Once again we are in the 'black & white period'. All three volumes have been devoid of colour photographs (bar the front covers) but the decision to leave the colour shots out was a practical one from the publishing and printing perspective. However, during my research I have collected a number of colour photographs. Neil and I have discussed putting together a colour album of the line (perhaps with some other local lines also featured). This will not be Volume 4 but a stand alone work that may well appear in the next few years.

During the compilation of this third volume I read the sad news that Peter Barnfield had passed away in mid-2018. For those of you who have volumes 1 and 2, you will be aware that Peter's collection of photographs enhanced them, whether it was station views or trains in the landscape. I am grateful to him for being so helpful in my project. Peter was not only a photographer, he was also an artist and one example of his work is reproduced right, based on a photograph which also appears in this volume, on page 680. Also, Charlie Fennamore, who kindly provided the Morebath train register for Volume 2, sadly passed away late in 2018.

There are two final points. Firstly, I again must thank Neil, Ian and Heather of Lightmoor Press for their support and commitment to my project over the last four years and the professional products that have resulted. They must surely be the primary railway publishers. Secondly, I am pleased to report that the Hope for Tomorrow Charity (www.hopefortomorrow.org.uk) will benefit from the proceeds of sales of the 'film of the book'. Passing reference was made to this film project getting underway in my introduction to Volume 2. Geoffrey Bray has been tireless in managing and motivating those involved in the production. It started as a plan to have a virtual journey down the line but developed in to a film with a story, a love story, which took place on an hypothetical journey down the line in the late 1950s. There is an element of poetic (or is it film maker's) licence with the result, especially given the line no longer exists and there is a scarcity of suitable locomotives on heritage lines but, nonetheless, the D&SR has inspired the project and a copy of the DVD is recommended viewing for all those interested in the line. The film, *A Chance Encounter*, was premiered at the Regal Cinema in Minehead on 18th May 2019 and has been well received. By June 2019 a total of £26,540 was raised for the charity. DVDs and further information can be found on www.chanceencounterfilm.co.uk or www.hopefortomorrow.org.uk. It is now hoped that another *A Chance Encounter* special will be run on 30th May 2020.

It is now just left for me to 'sign off' from this mammoth project which has so enjoyably taken up quite a part of my adult life and to say that I hope you all enjoy reading this third and final volume in the series.

Freddie Huxtable
Ealing
Spring 2020

Acknowledgements

This now series of books would not have been possible without significant help from many people. Following publication of the first volume, a number of people came forward to provide further research information and materials. Thus, in this regard, I would like first of all to thank John Jenkins, Jonathan Lomas, Charlie Fennamore, Philip Cox, Geoffrey Bray, Mike Kick and Ian Harrison. Additionally, Blake Patterson, Richard Gibbs, Brian Conyard and Mike Roach have very kindly made further photographs available for Volumes 2 and 3.

Special thanks should go to Ian Coleby, author of *The Minehead Branch 1848-1971* (Lightmoor Press 2006 & 2011) for his excellent work on the station track plans that appear in Volume 2.

In adition, Volume 3 has been greatly enhanced by the specialist assistance provided by others, notably from the Reverend Canon Brian Arman on broad gauge matters, both in regards to the text and sourcing additional photographs. In addition, John Lewis, has substantially supplemented my comments and captions in regards to GWR carriage stock used on the line. Mike Fenton also provided assistance on the GWR/BR camp/camping coaches. I am especially grateful therefore to these gentlemen for their kind support.

The list as now follows is as given in the previous volumes but I felt it only right, as some folk may only purchase this third part of the series, to repeat that *verbatim* here. Where possible and appropriate, I have also credited those mentioned in the body of the book.

So my thanks go to the railwaymen whose stories enthralled me – Jim Elson (signalman), Brindley Prust (driver), Dennis Bending (parcels), Harry Kirkland (fireman), Melvyn Baker (fireman), John Howard (signal & telegraph engineer) and Mrs Joyce Stone (widow of Eric Stone, signalman). Other authors, especially Ian Coleby, who gave me such great guidance and encouragement at the start, but also Sue Farrington, Richard Derry, Richard Antliff, Mike Christensen OBE (who did a sterling job reviewing and providing technical input on the signalling chapter in Volume 2), Amyas Crump and Kevin Robertson. My long-standing friend Thomas Hayes, who amongst other things explored the closed Dulverton station with me in the late 1960s and walked those parts of the line with me that could be traversed in the 2007-15 period. My long-standing friend Martin Bending, for promising to finish the book if I didn't and who provided useful guidance on railway matters and modelling. Special thanks are due to Lady Arran for agreeing to write the foreword, thereby creating that link between her family and the origins of the railway with my book. Credit is due to Karina Varma for designing the website (www.devonandsomersetrailway.co.uk). Also to my mother, for her memories and Alison for her patience.

The photographers and those who have supplied pictures: Peter Gray, Peter Barnfield, John Spencer Gilks, the late Owen Mogg (Peter Triggs), the late Peter Treloar, Tim Stephens, Roy Denison, Gordon Bray, James G. Tawse, Stephen Derek, Hugh Davies, Roger Joanes, the late Michael J. Fox (Brian Stephenson), the late Ron Lumber (David Mitchell), Colin Caddy, Stephen Linney, Richard Antliff, David Burgess and John Alsop.

The modellers: Chris Nelder, Martin Bird, Mark Henshaw, Derek Garrett, Tony Hiscock, Douglas Grindlay, Jose Kimber, Maurice Sandell, Brian Morgan, Ian Harrison, Martin Tester and Norman Solomans.

Those who have helped generally, such as William Hancock, Wesley Wyatt, Graham Robertson, John B. Perkin, Mary Proffitt, Toni & Francois Jones, Rob Doidge, Derek Goodwin, Ken Morrish of the Grosvenor Church, Max Perry, Sylvia Manley, Stephen Jervis, Mr & Mrs Anning (Venn Cross, goods shed), Mr & Mrs Wilson (Venn Cross booking office), Roddy Kane (Bathealton Tunnel) and Dr Sarah Blackburn (Dulverton goods shed), and also once again not forgetting my English teacher, the late Hilary Binding.

Those who have helped at a number of museums: Peter Treharne, at the West Somerset Railway Museum, Blue Anchor; Jenny Yendall, Alison Ricks, Andy Hedges and Phil Tonkin at the South Molton Museum; Ruth Spiers at the North Devon Museum, Barnstaple; North Devon Athenaeum, Barnstaple; Judith Elsdon and Patrick at Tiverton Museum; Elaine Arthurs at STEAM, the Museum of the Great Western Railway at Swindon; Laurence Waters of the Great Western Society at Didcot; Braunton Museum; Jan Ross OBE of the Dulverton Heritage Centre; and David Bird and others of the Railway Correspondence & Travel Society.

Significant research was carried out at the National Archives, Kew, the National Railway Museum, York, the Wiltshire Records Office at Chippenham, Somerset Archives & Local Studies at Taunton, at the Barnstaple Athenaeum and North Devon Records Office. The National Railway Museum proved invaluable for research and access, and the use of images from its photographic collection. Also Mr Warwick Burton of the Brunel University, Mowat Collection (3 Fairway, Clifton, York, YO30 5QA), the Lens of Sutton Association; Roger Carpenter; Robert Blencowe; Stephen Edge and David Holmes of the West Somerset Railway Association Journal; the Industrial Railway Society; and the Lynton & Barnstaple Railway and its associated magazine.

I am also indebted to the Signalling Record Society, the Great Western Study Group (and its Yahoo group members) and the Great Western Society, in particular Adrian Knowles and Lawrence Waters.

Whilst every effort has been made to make the appropriate credits, it is not the intention to miss out anyone, so if it transpires there is an omission please let the author or publisher know so the matter can be put right in the future. Every effort has been made to identify and credit images wherever possible. Where there is no credit it will be the author's own, where it belongs to a collection this too is noted. Should an error have occurred this is entirely unintentional and if notified will be corrected in any subsequent edition.

Chapter 10

The Locomotives and Rolling Stock of the Taunton to Barnstaple Line

Locomotives

There is little firm evidence in regards to the locomotives that worked the Devon & Somerset Railway (D&SR) for the first twenty years of its existence. Few photographs have been found showing trains on the line in that period and surviving GWR engine shed allocation records commence in 1902. Consequently, any picture that we can provide of the motive power that operated the line during this period is based on supposition. Ironically, we know more about the contractors' engines used in building the line than we do about the locomotives that worked it subsequently. The D&SR itself never owned any locomotives or rolling stock.

Contractors' Locomotives (1865-1873)

A summary of locomotives used by the two contractors who were involved in building the D&SR is given in **Appendix 2** of Volume 1, and pages 56 and 57 carry an illustration of one of these engines. However, a brief summary of the locomotives used is set out below.

Messrs W.&J. Pickering, the initial contractors (19th July 1865 to 13th December 1867) made use of a standard gauge locomotive named *Fortescue*, an 0-6-0 saddle tank built by the Hunslet Engine Co. in 1865 (Works No. 3), and this was used from new in constructing the line. It later moved to John Aird & Sons, working on the Nottingham to Melton Mowbray line of the Midland Railway.

John Langham Reed had the contract to finish the railway from 11th May 1870 and he used a number of broad and standard gauge engines for completing the line. Broad gauge engines included *Defiance*, an 0-6-0 built by Vulcan Foundry in 1844 for the Bristol & Gloucester Railway. Purchased by Thomas Brassey in 1857, he used it to help build and then operate the North Devon Railway. *Defiance* was used in the construction of the Taunton to Wiveliscombe section of the line.

Next was *Venus*, a broad gauge 2-4-0 built by Stothert & Slaughter in 1844 again for the Bristol & Gloucester Railway, which became a part of the Midland Railway in 1845. It too was on hire from Brassey and, renamed *Industry*, was used for ballasting work on the western section of the line. One other broad gauge locomotive was purchased from the GWR in March 1873 and was used for ballasting the eastern section of the line but it remains unidentified.

Reed's standard gauge fleet numbered five locomotives and two rail-mounted steam cranes. Three of the engines were 0-6-0 saddle tanks that were probably bought new from the manufacturers Fox, Walker & Co. in 1870, Works No's 16, 18 and 19; No. 16 was named *Taunton* but the others were not graced with names. The 5-ton steam cranes also came from Fox, Walker, again probably from new in 1870, Works No's 15 and 18. Finally, there was a 4-wheeled 12hp chain locomotive built by Aveling & Porter in 1870 and a vertical boilered 0-4-0 built by Alexander Shanks & Son circa 1872, which later in the 1870s was used on the construction of the Malmesbury Railway.

The Alexander Shanks vertical boiler 0-4-0 in use by the contractors Budd & Holt on the construction of the Malmesbury Railway circa 1876. Bought from Reed after being put up for sale in January 1873, it was up for sale again in July 1877 but nothing is known of its subsequent history. ***Oliver Pike collection***

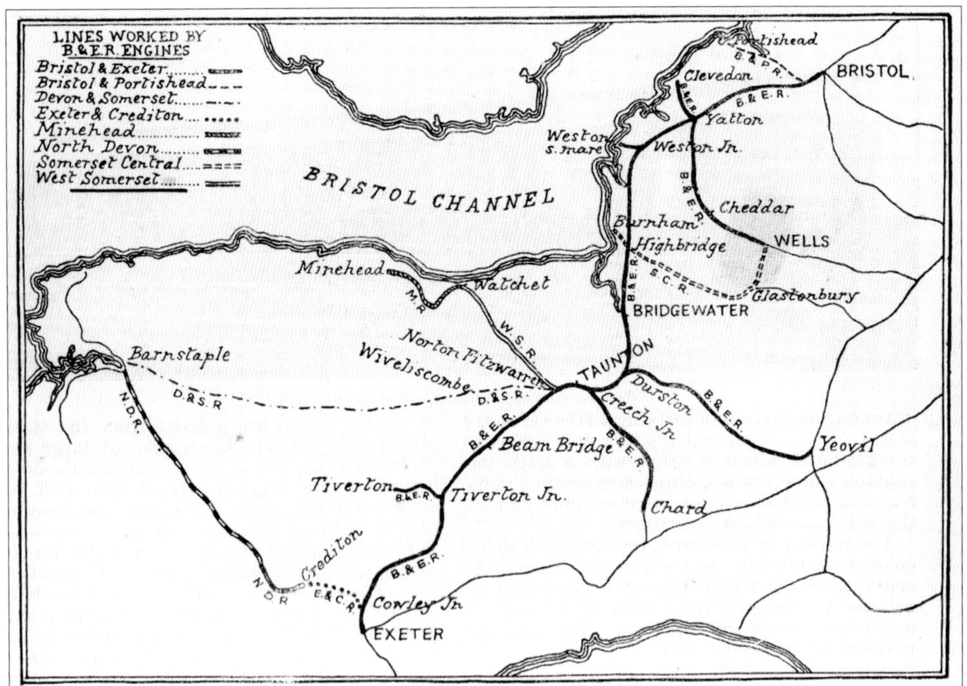

Left: This map of the Bristol & Exeter Railway system showing the lines that the company's engines also worked appeared in Volume III of *The Locomotive Magazine* in 1898.

Below: A fairly well known view of B&ER No. 52, one of first batch of six of the 4-4-0 saddle tanks (No's 47-52) built by Rothwell & Co. The first five were built in 1855 with No. 52 being completed in January 1856. This first batch were slightly smaller than the twenty further engines of this type that were built for the B&ER. Seen here at Exeter circa 1860, it is not known if this particular engine worked on the D&SR but it is likely to be one of this batch which appears in the photograph taken at Wiveliscombe in 1871 (Vol. 1, page 61). They performed much useful work on main and branch lines but led relatively short lives as the broad gauge system contracted. This engine became GWR No. 2033 after takeover in January 1876 and was withdrawn in July 1880. ***Neil Parkhouse collection***

Broad Gauge (1871-1881)

The D&SR never built and owned any locomotives or rolling stock. As was seen in Chapter 3 (Vol. 1), the operations of the company were leased to the Bristol & Exeter Railway (B&ER) and then, following the takeover, by the GWR. The B&ER had operational responsibility for other railways in the area; namely the West Somerset Railway, the Exeter & Crediton Railway (until 1862), the Somerset Central Railway (until 1861) and some lines around Bristol. In addition, it had its own branch lines to Tiverton, Chard, Yeovil, Cheddar and Clevedon to operate. So in this initial broad gauge period it is the B&ER locomotives we need to study.

However, specific locomotive records pertaining to the D&SR for this period are hard to come by. There is limited photographic evidence available, some of which can be seen in Volume 1 (pages 61, 76 and 80, for example). From this evidence it is not really possible to draw any firm conclusions but, bearing in mind the length of the line and of the trains, it would seem likely that B&ER 0-6-0 tender locomotives provided the staple motive power. The view of a saddle tank 4-4-0 at Wiveliscombe when that was the terminus may indicate they were replaced by tender engines when the line opened fully but, equally, they may have continued working longer distance trains too. Another of the photographs shows a GWR saddle tank rebuild of an ex-B&ER 0-6-0 on a goods train.

The 4-4-0 saddle tanks worked on the WSR and were one of the most numerous class of passenger tank engines on the B&ER, with many allocated at Taunton. They had a leading bogie with the driving wheels coupled and the footplate was placed high over the rear axle, necessitating a ladder-like footstep over the wheels to gain access to the footplate. The cylinders were 17ins diameter by 24ins stroke, the coupled wheels were 5ft 6ins in diameter and placed 8ft 6ins apart (centre to centre) in the earlier series but 9ft 4ins apart in the later series. There were twenty-six in the class built in four distinct batches. No's 47-52 were built by Rothwell & Co. in 1855-56 and were renumbered as No's 2028 to 2033 by the GWR. No 51 was the first to work the WSR. These earlier engines were $13^{1}/_{2}$ inches shorter in the wheelbase and had smaller boilers than the later batches. The second batch, No's 61-64 and renumbered as No's 2034-2037, were from Beyer, Peacock of the Gorton Foundry in Manchester. In 1867, Vulcan Foundry at Warrington supplied ten more, No's 65-74, renumbered as No's 2038-2047, and the final batch were produced by the Avonside Engine Co. (formerly Stothert & Slaughter) in the 1872-73 period; No's 85-90, they became No's 2048-2053 under the GWR.

Stothert & Slaughter also built eight 0-6-0 goods engines for the

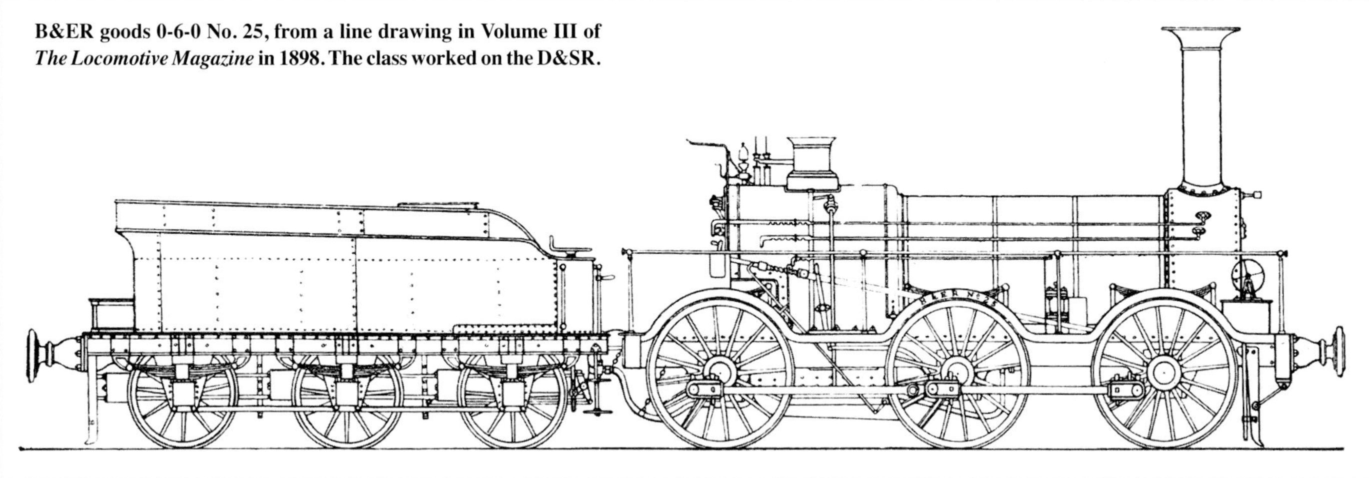

B&ER goods 0-6-0 No. 25, from a line drawing in Volume III of *The Locomotive Magazine* in 1898. The class worked on the D&SR.

B&ER in 1849, No's 21-28, to a design by Daniel Gooch and thus similar to locomotives built by Swindon. Rebuilt at the B&ER's locomotive works at Bristol between 1858 and 1863, they had distinctively tall chimneys. The picture on page 76 (Vol. 1) is thought to show one of these on a passenger train at South Molton.

Four more 0-6-0 goods engines to a similar design to these rebuilds were built by Stothert & Slaughter (or Slaughter, Grüning & Co. as the firm became around this time) in 1856, which carried B&ER No's 53-56 and a further two followed in 1860 from Rothwell & Co., No's 59-60. Two of the first batch, No's 54 and 56, were rebuilt at Bristol in 1870 as 0-6-0 saddle tanks, one of which is seen on a goods train at South Molton circa 1880 on page 80 (Vol. 1). Both are believed to have been shedded at Taunton.

The B&ER engines were painted black all over, even to chimney caps and buffer beams, without any lining. The company initials and number were in brass. The GWR assumed responsibility for the line when they leased the B&ER from January 1876, followed by the absorption of the company in August of that year.

Florence Mine

As noted on page 22 (Vol. 1), it is recorded that a narrow gauge locomotive operated at the D&SR end of the Florence Mine tramway. Furthermore, the *South Molton Gazette* of 26th June 1880 stated '*a locomotive engine last week ran over the tram-rail-way* [sic] *from South Molton to the iron mines for the first time.*'.

That locomotive was a John Fowler of Leeds 2ft 6ins gauge 0-4-2 tank engine, one of a batch apparently built on spec in 1880 and bought by the mine company for £450. A loan of £200 was raised on the security of the locomotive by the liquidators in 1886 (so it must have still been at the tramway then). Following its sojourn at Florence Mine, it was bought back by Fowlers circa 1886-87 for £170 (per the liquidators accounts) and was re-gauged to 2ft 8ins. It was then sold to Pike Bros in 1889 and moved to their clay pits at Furzebrook in Dorset, where it was named *Quartus*. It was scrapped in 1934.

Above and Right: Two rare views of the narrow gauge Fowler 0-4-2 tank engine that worked on the Florence Mine tramway, both taken at Furzebrook circa 1890, soon after it had arrived there. In the picture on the right it is coupled to what looks to be some new 4-wheeled clay wagons and there is no sign that it had yet been named *Quartus*. Fowlers had re-gauged it from 2ft 6ins to 2ft 8ins prior to re-selling it to Pike Bros but it otherwise had probably changed little in appearance from its days working to the transhipment siding with the D&SR.
Both courtesy Twelveheads Press

TABLE 10.1: BARNSTAPLE SHED – Locomotives as at Jan. 1902, with later movements that year.

No.	Class	Wheel Arr.	Comments. Note: The build date is given for each locomotive on its first appearance in the table
739	'Buffalo'	0-6-0ST	Built 1873. Moved to Bristol 02/02
1368	ex-B&ER 'Goods'	0-6-0	Standard gauge, built Sharp, Stewart 1875, B&ER No. 118, rebuilt Swindon 1896. Taunton engine transferred to Barnstaple on 18/10/02
1371	ex-B&ER 'Goods'	0-6-0	Standard gauge, built Sharp, Stewart 1875, B&ER No. 121, rebuilt Swindon 1895. Taunton engine, also transferred on 18/10/02
1369	ex-B&ER 'Goods'	0-6-0	Standard gauge, built Sharp, Stewart 1875, B&ER No. 119, rebuilt Swindon 1895. At Barnstaple until 13/12/02 then to Bristol
1493	'Metro Tank'	0-4-2T	Built 1892. At Barnstaple until 06/02
1454	'Metro Tank'	0-4-2T	Built 1882. Transferred Bristol to Barnstaple 28/06/02 (probably taking over from No. 1493) and transferred back to Bristol 23/08/02
1458	'Metro Tank'	0-4-2T	Built 1882. Transferred to Barnstaple on 23/08/02 from Swindon (to replace No. 1454)

1881-1902

No records exist detailing the motive power that appeared on the line in the two decades after conversion to standard gauge in May 1881 and there are no known photographs to assist us either, prior to the advent of the postcard era in the early years of the 20th century. We must therefore rely on supposition but we can base this on the locomotives allocated to Barnstaple shed in 1902, which we can presume would reflect to an extent the situation pertaining over the previous twenty years. It should also be noted that the 1860-built B&ER two-road shed at Taunton was only replaced by a much larger GWR facility in 1896

For the first six and a half years of this period, there was no through connection at Barnstaple either, as the GWR's terminus station was not joined to the London & South Western Railway's line on the other side of the River Taw until the opening of the Barnstaple Loop or West Chord on 1st June 1887.

The January 1902 table above shows a 'Buffalo' Class 0-6-0 saddle tank, a 'Metro Tank' 0-4-2T (three are shown but only one of them was out-stationed there at any point throughout that year) and three ex-B&ER 0-6-0 'Goods' engines, only one of which was actually allocated to Barnstaple for most of the year, the other two being Taunton engines. The likelihood is that these handled most of the goods services, with the two tank engines and other Taunton-based locomotives covering passenger workings and providing the balance of the motive power.

We can extrapolate from the early years of the 1903-1923 table, in which the ex-B&ER 'Goods' engines and 'Metro Tanks' are dominant, that members of these two classes had largely been in charge of services through the 1890s at least. The early 1870s-built

GWR No. 1369, an ex-B&ER standard gauge 'Goods' 0-6-0 built by Sharp, Stewart & Co. in 1875, poses with its driver and fireman outside the old Bristol & Exeter works at Bristol circa 1900. This engine spent several periods based at Barnstaple shed, the last time being for the first quarter of 1905; it was also the last of the class to be withdrawn, in March 1911, the others nine having all gone between 1905 and 1909. *John Alsop collection*

Table 10.2: BARNSTAPLE SHED – Locomotives 1903 to 1922			
No.	**Class**	**Wheel Arr.**	**Comments. Note: The build date is given for each locomotive on its first appearance in the table**
As at January 1903 with later movements			
818	'806'	2-4-0	Built 1873. To Barnstaple 25/07/03
814	'806'	2-4-0	Built 1873. To Barnstaple from Taunton on 25/07/03
1368	ex-B&ER 'Goods'	0-6-0	Transferred to Taunton 04/03
1369	ex-B&ER 'Goods'	0-6-0	Transferred from Bristol to Barnstaple 03/03
1375	ex-B&ER 'Goods'	0-6-0	Built 1875, B&ER No. 118. Barnstaple 01/03 until 08/03 (transferred to Weymouth)
1440	'517'	0-4-2T	Built 1877. Barnstaple 01-02/03 only
1459	'Metro Tank'	2-4-0T	Built 1882. To Barnstaple 7/02/03 (to replace No. 1440)
2346	'Dean Goods'	0-6-0	Built 1884. To Barnstaple 26/07/03.
As at January 1904 with later movements			
824	'806'	2-4-0	Built 1873. Bristol to Barnstaple 23/07/04 then to Taunton 15/10/04
1369	ex-B&ER 'Goods'	0-6-0	Barnstaple until 10/12/04 then to Bristol
1366	ex-B&ER 'Goods'	0-6-0	Built 1875, B&ER No. 116. Swindon to Barnstaple 23/03/04
1434	'517'	0-4-2T	Built 1877. Only allocated for 09/04
1458	'Metro Tank'	2-4-0T	Barnstaple 01/04 until 25/06/04 then to Swindon Works
1459	'Metro Tank'	2-4-0T	Allocated throughout year
2346	'Dean Goods'	0-6-0	Moved to Bristol 04/04
As at January 1905 with later movements			
823	'806'	2-4-0	Built 1873. To Barnstaple 1/04 and to Taunton 29/04/05
824	'806'	2-4-0	To Barnstaple 27/5/05 from Taunton then to Bristol 22/07/05
930	'Coal Engine'	0-6-0	Built 1874. Barnstaple 01/05 (only) then to Bristol
1369	ex-B&ER 'Goods'	0-6-0	To Barnstaple 7/01/05 until 1/04/05
1366	ex-B&ER 'Goods'	0-6-0	Barnstaple all year
1375	ex-B&ER 'Goods'	0-6-0	To Barnstaple 11/04/05 (from Swindon) for remainder of year
1435	'517'	0-4-2T	Built 1877. Barnstaple 7/01/05 (from Bristol) until 14/10/05 transferred to Minehead
1451	'Metro Tank'	2-4-0T	Built 1881. Barnstaple 19/08/05 then to Swindon 16/09/05
1456	'Metro Tank'	2-4-0T	Built 1882. Barnstaple 01/05-24/06/05 to Taunton, then 07/05 Barnstaple and back to Taunton 19/08/05 and back to Barnstaple 1/10/05
1459	'Metro Tank'	2-4-0T	Barnstaple until 1/04/05 then to Swindon Works
1463	'Metro Tank'	2-4-0T	Built 1882. Barnstaple 29/04/05-24/06/05 to Minehead
As at January 1906 with later movements			
1366	ex-B&ER 'Goods'	0-6-0	Transferred to Bristol 18/08/06
1375	ex-B&ER 'Goods'	0-6-0	Transferred to Bristol 18/08/06
1456	'Metro Tank'	2-4-0T	At Barnstaple all year except 18/10-10/11/06
1445	'Metro Tank'	2-4-0T	Built 1881. Barnstaple 10/06 (to substitute No. 1456)
As at January 1907 with later movements			
630	'Metro Tank'	2-4-0T	Built 1871. Barnstaple 20/07/06 for remainder of year
624	'Metro Tank'	2-4-0T	Built 1871. Barnstaple January until 2/02/07 to Swindon, back to Barnstaple 17/08/07 for remainder of year
794	'Standard Goods'	0-6-0	Built 1873. Barnstaple January until 14/09/07 then Bristol, then Barnstaple 9/11/07-7/12/07 then Taunton
1456	'Metro Tank'	2-4-0T	Barnstaple until 2/2/07 then to Swindon

Armstrong '806' Class 2-4-0s which appear in the table for a short period between the summer of 1903 and the summer of 1905 – but with gaps therein – may have also been used on passenger trains prior to 1900 and probably odd members of the '517' Class 0-4-2 tanks as well, although the 'Metro Tanks' were clearly preferred.

Although it might seem unlikely that the 'Dean Goods' 0-6-0 that arrived at Barnstaple shed in July 1903 was the first of the class to be seen on the line, only one was allocated to Taunton shed in 1902. It is notable, too, that none of the 'Standard Goods' 0-6-0s appear until January 1907, which suggests that the ex-B&ER 'Goods' were the mainstay for much if not all of these two decades, performing sterling service and not needing to be supplemented. It should also be noted that 0-6-0 saddle tanks barely feature after 1902, so whether they were largely unsuited to the line or the 'Buffalo' Class engine above is a pointer to other 19th century motive power that was used is impossible to say. It would therefore not be unreasonable to assume that the small range of types built in the 1870s-1880s and shown in **Table 10.1** was fairly representative of the motive power used on the line after its conversion from broad to standard gauge.

1903-1922

From 1903, a slightly wider variety of engines began to be seen on the line. In that year, a Class '517' 0-4-2T, a 'Dean Goods' 0-6-0 and two Armstrong '806' Class 2-4-0s spent time allocated to Barnstaple shed, supplementing the 'Metro Tanks' and ex-B&ER 'Goods' engines. The 'Dean Goods', No. 2346, was probably the single example allocated to Taunton in 1902, being sent to Barnstaple on 26th July 1903 apparently to replace ex-B&ER 'Goods' No. 1375, which was then sent to Weymouth. No. 1369 replaced No. 1368 in the Spring, so there was only one of the class stationed here for most of this year, whilst the two 2-4-0s No's 814 and 818, both arrived at the end of July and were probably used on passenger duties. No. 1440, the '517' Class tank, was only there for January and February, being replaced by 'Metro Tank' No. 1459. It can be seen therefore that at any one time throughout this year there was usually one small tank engine and two 0-6-0 goods tender engines stationed at Barnstaple, with the two small passenger 2-4-0s also on the roster from the last week of July.

The advent of the picture postcard, which first appeared in Britain in 1896 but which mushroomed into a collecting craze from the early

Table 10.2 (Cont.): As at January 1908 with later movements			
496	'Standard Goods'	0-6-0	Built 1870. Barnstaple 18/07/08-7/11/08 (to Bristol) 5/12/08 back to Barnstaple
624	'Metro Tank'	2-4-0T	Barnstaple until 5/12/08 then to Taunton
630	'Metro Tank'	2-4-0T	Barnstaple throughout year
629	'Metro Tank'	2-4-0T	Built 1871. Barnstaple 18/07-12/09/08 (allocated for summer period)
794	'Standard Goods'	0-6-0	Barnstaple throughout year
837	'517'	0-4-2T	Built 1874. Barnstaple 28/03-25/04/08
886	'Standard Goods'	0-6-0	Built 1874. Barnstaple 29/02-28/03/08
1076	'Buffalo'	0-6-0ST	Built 1870. Barnstaple 15/08-19/09/08
1205	'Standard Goods'	0-6-0	Built 1876. Barnstaple 01-02/08 (then Taunton), 28/03-18/07/08 Barnstaple.
1451	'Metro Tank'	2-4-0T	Built 1881. Barnstaple 5/12/08 onwards
1496	'Metro Tank'	2-4-0T	Built 1892. Barnstaple until 28/03/08 to Taunton, then Barnstaple 25/04-15/08/08 (back to Taunton), then Barnstaple 12/09-10/10/08
As at January 1909 with later movements			
496	'Standard Goods'	0-6-0	Barnstaple until 27/03, then Bristol. Barnstaple 24/04-11/09/09
458	'Metro Tank'	2-4-0T	Built 1869. Barnstaple 11/09 for remainder of year
624	'Metro Tank'	2-4-0T	Barnstaple throughout year
629	'Metro Tank'	2-4-0T	Barnstaple throughout year
630	'Metro Tank'	2-4-0T	Barnstaple throughout year (allocated to Yeovil at end of year)
632	'Metro Tank'	2-4-0T	Built 1871. Barnstaple 6/11-4/12/09
791	'Standard Goods'	0-6-0	Built 1873. Barnstaple 11/9-9/10/09
1076	'Buffalo'	0-6-0ST	Barnstaple 30/01-27/02/09
1451	'Metro Tank'	2-4-0T	Allocated to Taunton and Chard during the year
2385	'Dean Goods'	0-6-0	Barnstaple 14/08-11/09/09
2388	'Dean Goods'	0-6-0	Barnstaple 17/07-14/08/09
3590	'Metro Tank'	2-4-0T	Built 1899. Barnstaple 17/07-14/08/09
As at January 1910 with later movements			
458	'Metro Tank'	2-4-0T	Barnstaple 1/01-29/01/10
624	'Metro Tank'	2-4-0T	Barnstaple throughout (but at Swindon 18/06-30/09/10)
629	'Metro Tank'	2-4-0T	Barnstaple until 29/01/10 then to Taunton
626	'Metro Tank'	2-4-0T	Built 1871. Barnstaple 14/02/10 remainder of year (except 23/04-21/05/10 at Bristol)
623	'Metro Tank'	2-4-0T	Built 1871. Barnstaple 17/04 for remainder of year
1496	'Metro Tank'	2-4-0T	Barnstaple 29/01-23/04/10 and again 18/06-8/10/10
1629	'Buffalo'	0-6-0ST	Built 1880. Barnstaple 1/03-16/07 (then transferred to Minehead) Barnstaple 5/11/10
3285	'Duke'	4-4-0	*St. Erth*. Built 1897. Barnstaple 11/07-13/08/10. Renumbered 3275 in 1912.
3288	'Duke'	4-4-0	*Isle of Tresco*. Built 1897. Barnstaple 13/08-8/10/10. Renumbered 3277 in 1912.
3590	'Metro Tank'	2-4-0T	Barnstaple 29/01-26/02/10 and again 13/08-5/11/10
As at January 1911 with later movements			
463	'Metro Tank'	2-4-0T	Built 1869. Barnstaple 15/07-12/08/11 then Minehead
551	'517'	0-4-2T	Built 1869. Barnstaple 22/04-20/05/11
623	'Metro Tank'	2-4-0T	Barnstaple until 4/11/11 then Swindon works
624	'Metro Tank'	2-4-0T	Barnstaple throughout
626	'Metro Tank'	2-4-0T	Barnstaple 20/5/11 for remainder of year
629	'Metro Tank'	2-4-0T	Barnstaple 17/06-15/07/11
1629	'Buffalo'	0-6-0ST	Barnstaple until 15/07/11
3279	'Bulldog'	4-4-0	*Exmoor*. 'Duke' built 1897, rebuilt as 'Bulldog' 12/07. Barnstaple 15/07-7/10/11
3590	'Metro Tank'	2-4-0T	Barnstaple 12/08-7/10/11 then 2/12-30/12 (to Swindon)

1900s, saw local communities and their railway stations amongst the myriad of subjects to be featured. Whilst the locomotives seen in some of these merely confirm what we know from the table in terms of the motive power that appeared on the line, they do also indicate that the goods engines were regularly used on passenger trains and that the small 2-4-0 and 0-4-2 tank engines worked through passenger services over the 43½ mile route. Also, whilst the table lists the locomotives stationed at Barnstaple shed, some of Taunton's much larger allocation would have regularly appeared as well. For instance, whilst there was one 'Dean Goods' allocated to Taunton in 1902, there were nine in 1909 and five in 1913, some of which would undoubtedly have worked to Barnstaple and back from time to time.

The '806' Class 2-4-0s disappear from Barnstaple after July 1905, so may have proved unsuitable. In addition, most of the ex-B&ER 'Goods' engines were coming to the end of their working lives, with all bar one of the ten strong class being withdrawn between 1905 and 1909, No's 1366 and 1375 being the last two to be allocated to Barnstaple, moving away to Bristol in mid-August 1906. Replacement motive power then seems to have been supplied from Taunton until January 1907, when the first of the 'Standard Goods' 0-6-0s, No. 794, was allocated to Barnstaple.

By the following year, duties from Barnstaple were in the hands of the 'Standard Goods' 0-6-0s, with at least two members of the class allocated there throughout the year, and 'Metro Tank' 2-4-0s, with at least three based there at all times. A solitary '517' 0-4-2T, No. 837, spent a month at Barnstaple in the spring, whilst the visit of a 'Buffalo' Class 0-6-0 saddle tank for a month in late summer 1908 looks like an aberration until one notes that other members of the class visited

Table 10.2 (Cont.): As at January 1912 with later movements			
458	'Metro Tank'	2-4-0T	Barnstaple 15/06-13/07/12 and 7/09/12 onwards
551	'517'	0-4-2T	Barnstaple 27/01-24/02
623	'Metro Tank'	2-4-0T	Barnstaple 27/01-24/02
624	'Metro Tank'	2-4-0T	Barnstaple until 28/02 then Taunton
626	'Metro Tank'	2-4-0T	Barnstaple 24/02 to 5/10/12 (to Swindon)
629	'Metro Tank'	2-4-0T	Barnstaple allocations; 24/02-23/03,18/07-10/08, 2/11-30/11/12
986	'Metro Tank'	2-4-0T	Built 1874. Barnstaple 23/03 onwards
1496	'Metro Tank'	2-4-0T	Barnstaple 28/12 onwards
2348	'Dean Goods'	0-6-0	Built 1884. Barnstaple 15/06-13/07/12 then to Taunton
2394	'Dean Goods'	0-6-0	Built 1890. Barnstaple 10/08-7/09/12 then to Taunton
3533	'3521'	4-4-0	Built 1887 as 0-4-2T, as 4-4-0T 1892, rebuilt 1901. Barnstaple 13/07-5/10/12
As at January 1913 with later movements			
422	'Standard Goods'	0-6-0	Built 1887. Barnstaple 12/07-4/10/13
458	'Metro Tank'	2-4-0T	Barnstaple 22/02-22/03/13
463	'Metro Tank'	2-4-0T	Barnstaple 9/08-6/09/13
600	'Standard Goods'	0-6-0	Built 1871. Barnstaple 22/03-19/04/13 then to Taunton
620	'Metro Tank'	2-4-0T	Built 1871. Barnstaple 1/11-27/12/13 then to Taunton
624	'Metro Tank'	2-4-0T	Barnstaple 22/03-19/04/13 then Taunton until 9/08/13 to Barnstaple
967	'Metro Tank'	2-4-0T	Built 1874. Barnstaple 14/06-12/07/13
986	'Metro Tank'	2-4-0T	Barnstaple until 4/10 then to Bristol works and 29/11 back to Barnstaple
1185	'Buffalo'	0-6-0ST	Built 1875. Barnstaple 27/12/13 onwards
1457	'Metro Tank'	2-4-0T	Built 1882. Barnstaple 14/07-1/11/13
1496	'Metro Tank'	2-4-0T	Barnstaple 11/09-4/11/13 then to Taunton
1499	'Metro Tank'	2-4-0T	Built 1892. Barnstaple 1/11-29/11/13
1587	'Buffalo'	0-6-0ST	Built 1879. Barnstaple until 17/05 and again 1/11-27/12/13
2348	'Dean Goods'	0-6-0	Barnstaple until 22/02/13 then to Taunton
3558	'3521'	4-4-0	Built 1888 as BG 0-4-2T, as 4-4-0T 1890, SG 1892, rebuilt 1901. Barnstaple 16/06-4/10/13 (Gloucester loco)

As rebuilds of rebuilds which began life as tank engines, the '3521' Class lacked the natural goods looks of other 4-4-0s such as the 'Bulldogs'. No. 3558, which had a short spell at Barnstaple in the Summer/Autumn of 1913, began life as a broad gauge convertible 0-4-2 saddle tank built in June 1889 but was altered to a 4-4-0 tank in September the following year. In May 1892 it was converted to standard gauge but was then rebuilt to the form seen here with a large 'D0' boiler in December 1901. Surprisingly, perhaps, it carried the same number through all these changes. It is seen here at an unknown location circa 1905, posed with its footplate crew and having been given a good polish by the shed staff. A note in the table indicates that it was a Gloucester-based engine at the time it was sent down to Barnstaple and it was still there in 1921. Superheated in 1910, it was withdrawn in September 1923. *John Alsop collection*

TABLE 10.2 (CONT.): As at January 1914 with later movements			
626	'Metro Tank'	2-4-0T	Barnstaple throughout year
986	'Metro Tank'	2-4-0T	Barnstaple until 21/02/14 then Taunton
967	'Metro Tank'	2-4-0T	21/02/14 to Barnstaple
1185	'Buffalo'	0-6-0ST	Barnstaple 24/01 then Taunton. Barnstaple 8/08/14 for remainder of year
3551	'3521'	4-4-0	Built 1889 as BG 0-4-2T, as 4-4-0T 1890, SG 1892, rebuilt 1900. Barnstaple 5/08-3/10/14
3533	'3521'	4-4-0	Barnstaple 11/07-5/09/14
As at January 1915 with later movements			
626	'Metro Tank'	2-4-0T	Barnstaple throughout year
967	'Metro Tank'	2-4-0T	Barnstaple until 17/04 (Taunton until) 15/05-25/12/15 then Swindon works
1185	'Buffalo'	0-6-0ST	Barnstaple until 4/09/15 then Taunton
1496	'Metro Tank'	2-4-0T	Barnstaple 4/09-25/12/15 then Taunton
2385	'Dean Goods'	0-6-0	Barnstaple 7/08-2/10/15
3532	'3521'	4-4-0	Built 1887 as 0-4-2T, as 4-4-0T 1892, rebuilt 1901. Barnstaple 7/08-2/10/15 (Gloucester loco)
As at January 1916 with later movements			
626	'Metro Tank'	2-4-0T	Barnstaple until 13/05 and then to Taunton. Barnstaple 10/06-5/08/16 and again 30/09-23/12/16
628	'Metro Tank'	2-4-0T	Built 1871. Barnstaple 30/09-25/11/16
456	'Metro Tank'	2-4-0T	Built 1869. Barnstaple 22/01-30/09 then to Taunton. Barnstaple 28/10 onwards
459	'Metro Tank'	2-4-0T	Built 1869. Barnstaple 13/05-5/08/16 to Taunton. Barnstaple 28/10/16 for remainder
1496	'Metro Tank'	2-4-0T	Barnstaple until 10/06 to Taunton. Barnstaple 8/07-2/09/16
1499	'Metro Tank'	2-4-0T	Barnstaple 15/04-13/05 (then to Swindon works)
2394	'Dean Goods'	0-6-0	Barnstaple 5/08-30/09/16
3539	'3521'	4-4-0	Built 1888 as 0-4-2T, as 4-4-0T 1892, rebuilt 1900. Barnstaple 5/08-28/10/16
As at January 1917 with later movements			
456	'Metro Tank'	2-4-0T	Barnstaple until 9/06. Taunton 9/06-7/07/17. Barnstaple 7/07-4/08/17. Taunton 4/08-1/09/17. Barnstaple 1/09
626	'Metro Tank'	2-4-0T	From Taunton to Barnstaple 20/01 for remainder of year
981	'Metro Tank'	2-4-0T	Built 1874. To Barnstaple 1/09 until 24/11 then Taunton until 22/12/17 back to Barnstaple
As at January 1918 with later movements			
456	'Metro Tank'	2-4-0T	Barnstaple in January then Taunton until 3/08/18 and back to Barnstaple
626	'Metro Tank'	2-4-0T	Barnstaple until 19/01 then Taunton
1496	'Metro Tank'	2-4-0T	Barnstaple 16/02-16/03/18 then Taunton
470	'Metro Tank'	2-4-0T	Built 1869. 23/11/18 to Barnstaple
981	'Metro Tank'	2-4-0T	Barnstaple throughout except 16/02-16/03/18
As at January 1919 with later movements			
456	'Metro Tank'	2-4-0T	Barnstaple until 25/10/19 then to Taunton
470	'Metro Tank'	2-4-0T	Barnstaple 15/02-15/03/19 (then works)
981	'Metro Tank'	2-4-0T	Barnstaple until 18/01/19 then to Swindon
The 1920 records were not available			

over the following three years to 1911 and 1913-15

January 1910 saw the appearance of probably the first named engines to be allocated to Barnstaple shed, although possibly not the first to work over the line, when 'Duke' Class 4-4-0s No. 3285 *St. Erth* and No. 3288 *Isle of Tresco* spent a month and two months there respectively. They were followed by the first 'Bulldog' 4-4-0 the year after, appropriately No. 3279 *Exmoor*, which was at Barnstaple for three months. All these were summer months allocations, so presumably to cater for increased tourist traffic. In the following years, odd members of the less glamorous, un-named '3521' Class 4-4-0s appeared in the summer months. These engines had all been rebuilt in 1899-1902 from a mixture of 19th century broad gauge convertible and standard gauge tank engines.

Meanwhile, during 1910 and 1911, no 0-6-0 goods tender engines were out-stationed at Barnstaple, two of the 'Dean Goods' Class finally reappearing in the summer of 1912. Looking at the table, it is quite clear that during this period, Barnstaple was essentially a 'Metro Tank' shed, with the occasional '517' or 'Buffalo' class tank engine thrown in. The 0-6-0s would still have featured regularly on the line but working from Taunton shed.

In July 1912, the first allocation of one of the '3521' Class 4-4-0s, No. 3533, was made to Barnstaple. Clearly intended for the summer traffic, they were a less glamorous alternative to the 'Duke' and 'Bulldog' 4-4-0s, having gone through various rebuilds and not being graced with names. Half of the class started out life in 1889-89 as broad gauge convertible 0-4-2 saddle tanks, which were rebuilt as 0-4-4 side tanks in 1890-91 and then converted to standard gauge in 1892. The other half were built as standard gauge 0-4-2 side tanks in 1887-88 and were rebuilt as 0-4-4Ts in 1891-92. They had a reputation for derailing and consequently all were rebuilt as 4-4-0 tender engines between 1899 and 1902 but some with small boilers and some with large. No. 3539 which appeared at Barnstaple shed in August 1916 for ten weeks was the only small boilered version to be allocated there, the others all being from the large boiler sub-class.

Variety almost completely disappeared from Barnstaple shed during the later years of the First World War, with 'Metro Tanks' only being stationed there during 1917, 1918 and 1919, whilst the records for 1920 were not given. Indeed, 1919 appears to end with the shed having no allocation at all. However, 1921 was the precursor to a decade of lots of comings and goings and also provided plenty of variety, with a '517' Class 0-4-2T, a 'Buffalo' Class saddle tank, a 'Standard Goods' and two 'Dean Goods' 0-6-0s, and no less then three '3521' Class 4-4-0s making appearances there alongside the 'Metro Tanks'. August 1921 was also to see the first allocation to the shed of a locomotive built in the 20th century (discounting the '3521' rebuilds), in the form of '45XX' Class 'Prairie' tank No. 4505; two more followed in 1922.

Table 10.2 (Cont.): As at January 1921 with later movements			
456	'Metro Tank'	2-4-0T	Barnstaple 27/02-27/03/21, 24/04-17/07/21, 14/08-9/10/21 and 6/11-4/12/21
461	'Metro Tank'	2-4-0T	Built 1869. Barnstaple 30/01-24/04 (then Minehead). Barnstaple 17/07-9/10/21 to Taunton
704	'Standard Goods'	0-6-0	Built 1872. Barnstaple 17/07-14/08/21 to Taunton
985	'Metro Tank'	2-4-0T	Built 1874. Barnstaple January to 30/01 then Taunton then Barnstaple 22/5-17/07/21
975	'Metro Tank'	2-4-0T	Built 1874. Barnstaple 30/01-27/02 and 27/03-22/05/21
959	'Buffalo'	0-6-0ST	Built 1874. Barnstaple 27/02-27/03/21, 24/04-17/07/21, 14/08-9/10/21 and 6/11-4/12/21
1496	'Metro Tank'	2-4-0T	Barnstaple 5/10-6/11/21 then returning 1/01/22
1430	'517'	0-4-2T	Built 1877. Barnstaple 17/07-14/08
2467	'Dean Goods'	0-6-0	Built 1896. Barnstaple 17/07-14/08 then to Bristol
2460	'Dean Goods'	0-6-0	Built 1895. Barnstaple 9/10-6/11/21 then to Taunton
3539	'3521'	4-4-0	Barnstaple 14/08-11/09/21 then Bristol
3547	'3521'	4-4-0	Built 1888 as BG 0-4-2T, as SG 4-4-0T 1891, rebuilt 1902. In factory (Swindon) 9/09/20, Barnstaple 14/08-9/10/21 then to Taunton
3548	'3521'	4-4-0	Built 1888 as BG 0-4-2T, as 0-4-4T 1891, SG 1892, rebuilt 1901. Barnstaple 24/04 to 14/08/21 then to Taunton
4505	'45XX'	2-6-2T	Built 1907. Barnstaple 14/08-11/09/21. The first 20th century-built locomotive allocated to Barnstaple
As at January 1922 with later movements			
461	'Metro Tank'	2-4-0T	Barnstaple 26/03-23/04 and 10/09-5/11/22
469	'Metro Tank'	2-4-0T	Built 1869. Barnstaple 5/11-3/12/22 then Taunton 31/12 back to Barnstaple
511	'Standard Goods'	0-6-0	Built 1870. Barnstaple 26/02-26/03/22 (Condemned in June)
1496	'Metro Tank'	2-4-0T	Barnstaple but to Taunton 29/01/22
1500	'Metro Tank'	2-4-0T	Built 1892. Barnstaple 01 until 26/03 to Taunton. Barnstaple 23/04-13/08/22 to Taunton. Barnstaple 3/12-31/12/22
2320	'Dean Goods'	0-6-0	Built 1883. Barnstaple until 23/04 then Taunton
2327	'Dean Goods'	0-6-0	Built 1884. Barnstaple 8/06-16/07/22
2467	'Dean Goods'	0-6-0	Barnstaple from 31/12/22
2470	'Dean Goods'	0-6-0	Built 1896. Barnstaple 26/06-8/10/22
3307	'Bulldog'	4-4-0	*Exmoor*. Renumbered from 3279 in 1912. Barnstaple 29/01-26/03/22 and 18/07-13/08/22.
3335	'Bulldog'	4-4-0	*Tregothnan*. Built 1900. Renumbered from 3347 in 1912. Barnstaple 13/08-8/10/22
4505	'45XX'	2-6-2T	Barnstaple until 10/09/22
4525	'45XX'	2-6-2T	Built 1910. Barnstaple 23/04-21/05, 18/06-13/08, 10/09-5/11/22

Although four 'Metro Tanks' spent time at Barnstaple shed in 1922, there were occasions when only one was on the allocation, whilst the variety saw a 'Standard Goods, four 'Dean Goods', and two 'Bulldogs' allocated here for spells, along with the two '45XX' 2-6-2Ts. The 'Bulldogs' included *Exmoor* for the second time, although now with a different number, No. 3307, acquired in the GWR renumbering scheme of 1912, along with No. 3335 *Tregothnan*.

From the early 1920s, tender engines began to take over the main D&SR line services, with the role of the 'Metro Tanks' reducing, as illustrated by the relevant shed allocations. Taunton in 1920 had an allocation of thirty-nine locomotives, including two 'Metro Tanks' (No's 975 and 1500), five 'Dean Goods' (No's 2381, 2382, 2435, 2460 and 2473) and two of the '3521' Class (No's 3532 and 3548). Churchward Class '43XX' 2-6-0 No. 6300 was also allocated there. In 1917, the shed got its first allocation of these 'Moguls' which were later to become a common sight on the D&SR line but they did not venture onto it until the mid 1920s as far as can be ascertained, as their initial duties for the GWR were primarily on main line passenger and goods workings.

By May 1922, No. 5348 was shedded at Taunton, along with 'Bulldogs' No's 3307 *Exmoor*, 3318 *Vulcan* and 3363 *Alfred Baldwin*. By December, meanwhile, the allocation of 'Dean Goods' locomotives at Taunton was as follows: No's 2316, 2320, 2381, 2405, 2435, 2460, 2467 and 2543.

1923-1947

During 1923 and 1924, local passenger trains continued to be operated by 'Metro Tanks' some based at Barnstaple and some at Taunton, the latter including No's 461, 621 and 632. However, this era then came to an abrupt end, with none of the class allocated to Barnstaple in 1925 and 1926, although there was to be one last hurrah in 1927, when No. 632 was sent there from 23rd January to 12th June. Its departure ended a forty-year association of the class with the D&SR.

By this time, the regular passenger trains were largely being operated by Class '3521' 4-4-0s, No's 3529 (with a parallel boiler) and 3547 (with tapered boiler) being regulars working from Taunton shed, until their withdrawal around the end of that decade. They were now being supplemented by 'Bulldog' Class 4-4-0s during the summer and autumn months, whilst '45XX' Class 'Prairie' tanks began to appear more frequently on the line also, again often on passenger trains. The most notable of these was No. 4567, which was only two months old when it arrived at Barnstaple shed for a three month stay on 25th January 1925, almost certainly the newest locomotive ever to feature on the D&SR up to that date and possibly since.

Goods services in the mid-1920s were mostly in the hands of 'Dean Goods' engines but this was also soon to change. No less than seven of the class featured at Barnstaple shed in 1924 but only two in 1925, one in 1926 and 1927, and none thereafter. They were superceded by Churchward's Class '43XX' 2-6-0s, the first of which to be shedded at Barnstaple was March 1923-built No. 6343 in 1925. They also began to make appearances on through trains to Barnstaple and Ilfracombe, made possible by the installation of a new 65ft turntable at the latter place which was of adequate length to turn them. All GWR locomotives working to Ilfracombe had their steps cut back to keep them within an overall engine width of 8ft 4ins, to negotiate the River Taw viaduct between Barnstaple Junction and Barnstaple Town stations. Incidentally, the 'Moguls' had a total wheelbase exceeding 48ft and as a consequence were unable to turn on the Barnstaple GWR turntable, which had a diameter of only 42ft. Therefore, they had

Along with the ex-B&ER 'Goods' 0-6-0s, the 'Metro Tank' 2-4-0Ts formed the staple motive power on the D&SR probably from soon after the line's conversion to standard gauge. As this era finally drew to a close, No. 632 was photographed shrouded in steam and producing a fine plume of smoke, leaving Barnstaple in 1927, the last year it was allocated there. By this date something of an anachronism, built at Swindon in 1871 and still fitted with a half-cab, the engine was in the twilight of its career, being withdrawn in November 1929. This Taunton-bound train comprises a diagram E116 B-set with a clerestory coach at the front and two vans at the rear. ***Arthur Halls, courtesy National Railway Museum***

to use the one at the Southern's engine shed at Barnstaple Junction which was of 50ft diameter; alternatively they could use the triangle when it was open.

By the end of the 1920s, the 'Moguls' had become commonplace but were still outnumbered, certainly at Barnstaple, by members of the 'Bulldog' class and it was not until the early 1930s that the '43XX' Class began to work more regular turns. As the table shows, the 'Bulldogs' remained the predominant motive power on passenger trains well into the 1930s. Initially it had been the earlier members of the class that were allocated to D&SR duties, including curved-framed No. 3335 *Tregothnan* and straight framed No. 3348 *Launceston*. Other 'Bulldogs' regularly allocated included No. 3364 *Frank Bibby*, No. 3371 *Sir Massey Lopes*, No. 3376 *River Plym*, No. 3377 *Penzance*, No. 3403 *Trinidad*, No. 3416 *John W. Wilson* and No. 3417 *Lord Mildmay of Flete*.

It was in or around 1928 that the first of the deep-framed 'Bulldogs' arrived, such as No. 3444 *Cormorant* and No. 3453 *Seagull*, remaining then on the line into the 1930s. These two had been built in 1909 and 1910 respectively and were part of a fifteen-strong sub-class known as 'Birds'. In 1930, there were three 'Bulldogs' allocated to Taunton (No. 3362 *Albert Brassey*, No. 3377 *Penzance* and No. 3344 *Dartmouth*) and three to Barnstaple (No. 3335 *Tregothnan*, No. 3348 *Launceston*, No. 3453 *Seagull*). These were reduced further by 1934 as only one was allocated to Taunton and two to Barnstaple, a result of Class '43XX' locomotives then becoming the mainstay of services. However, by 1938, with 'Hall' Class locomotives coming into traffic on the main line, some 'Bulldogs' were reallocated to Taunton (including No. 3361 *Edward VII*, No. 3443 *Chaffinch* and No. 3444 *Cormorant*). In 1939, the *Railway Observer* reported the fact that the 'Bulldogs' were being used less on the Barnstaple line and were instead appearing more frequently on the 'stopper' services from Taunton to Bristol and Exeter. After the Second World War, two 'Bulldogs' remained allocated to Taunton in 1947 but none were diagrammed to work Barnstaple services. The last 'Bulldogs' were withdrawn in 1951 (*Seagull* and *Cormorant* amongst them) but their time on the D&SR had ceased a while before their ultimate demise.

Freight trains in the 1920s were usually worked by 'Dean Goods' engines, the following being allocated at Taunton: No's 2313, 2355, 2435, 2467 and 2526. They were supplemented by '45XX' Class 2-6-2Ts, which also made appearances on passenger workings too, including No's 4502, 4507, 4516, 4567, 4568 and 5502. Examples were also regularly out-stationed at Barnstaple between 1924 and

Table 10.3: BARNSTAPLE SHED – Locomotives 1923 to 1948			
No.	Class	Wheel Arr.	Comments. Note: The build date is given for each locomotive on its first appearance in the table
As at January 1923 with later movements			
469	'Metro Tank'	2-4-0T	Barnstaple to Taunton on 28/01/23 for remainder of year
975	'Metro Tank'	2-4-0T	Barnstaple 15/07-12/08 then to Minehead. Barnstaple 4/11-2/12
1496	'Metro Tank'	2-4-0T	Barnstaple 9/09-7/10/23
2470	'Dean Goods'	0-6-0	Barnstaple 25/03-22/04/23
2467	'Dean Goods'	0-6-0	Barnstaple until 28/01/23 then Taunton
2522	'Dean Goods'	0-6-0	Built 1897. Barnstaple 20/05-17/06/23
2526	'Dean Goods'	0-6-0	Built 1897. Barnstaple to 25/03 then to Taunton. Barnstaple 22/04-20/05/23, then 17/06-2/12 and from 30/12/23
3380	'Bulldog'	4-4-0	*River Yealm*. Built 1903. Barnstaple 15/07-12/08 and 9/09-7/10/23
3416	'Bulldog'	4-4-0	*John W. Wilson*. Built 1906. Barnstaple 12/8-9/09/23
3403	'Bulldog'	4-4-0	*Trinidad*. Built 1904. Barnstaple 6/07-7/10/23
4505	'45XX'	2-6-2T	Barnstaple 17/06-15/07, 12/08-7/10 and 4/11-30/12/23. Moved to St Blazey in 1924
4525	'45XX'	2-6-2T	Barnstaple 25/3-17/06, 7/10-4/11 and 2/12-30/12/23
As at January 1924 with later movements			
469	'Metro Tank'	2-4-0T	Barnstaple 5/10-2/11/24 (then to Swindon Works)
1446	'Metro Tank'	2-4-0T	Built 1881. Barnstaple until 22/09/24 then to Taunton
1448	'Metro Tank'	2-4-0T	Built 1881. Barnstaple 10/08-5/10/24
2305	'Dean Goods'	0-6-0	Built 1883. Barnstaple 27/01-24/02/24
2470	'Dean Goods'	0-6-0	Barnstaple 10/08-5/10/24
2467	'Dean Goods'	0-6-0	Barnstaple 30/11-28/12/24
2456	'Dean Goods'	0-6-0	Built 1895. Barnstaple 5/10-2/11/25
2526	'Dean Goods'	0-6-0	Barnstaple until 27/01 then Taunton. Barnstaple 24/02-18/05/24
2543	'Dean Goods'	0-6-0	Built 1897. Barnstaple15/06-13/07/24
2522	'Dean Goods'	0-6-0	Barnstaple 13/07-10/08/24
3424	'Bulldog'	4-4-0	Un-named. Built 1906. Barnstaple 13/07-2/11/24
4502	'45XX'	2-6-2T	Built 1906. Barnstaple then Taunton 27/01-23/03/24 Barnstaple 13/07-28/12/24
4525	'45XX'	2-6-2T	Barnstaple 15/06-10/08/24 and back again on 28/12/24
As at January 1925 with later movements			
2467	'Dean Goods'	0-6-0	Barnstaple to 22/03/25 (to Bridgewater).
2526	'Dean Goods'	0-6-0	Barnstaple 17/05-14/06/25
3335	'Bulldog'	4-4-0	*Tregothnan*. Barnstaple 17/05-14/06/25 to Taunton. Barnstaple 12/07-6/09/25, back on 4/10/25 for rest of year
3380	'Bulldog'	4-4-0	*River Yealm*. Barnstaple 14/06-12/07/25
3377	'Bulldog'	4-4-0	*Penzance*. Built 1903. Barnstaple 18/05-12/07/25
3376	'Bulldog'	4-4-0	*River Plym*. Built 1903. Barnstaple 6/09-4/10/25
3371	'Bulldog'	4-4-0	*Sir Massey Lopes*. Built 1903. Barnstaple 3/07-9/08 and 6/09-4/10/25
3417	'Bulldog'	4-4-0	*Lord Mildmay of Flete*. Built 1906. Barnstaple 9/08-6/09/25
4502	'45XX'	2-6-2T	Barnstaple 17/05-14/06/25
4525	'45XX'	2-6-2T	Barnstaple until 25/01 then to Taunton. Barnstaple 19/04-17/05/25
4567	'45XX'	2-6-2T	Built 1924. Barnstaple 25/01-19/04/25, 17/05-12/07/25 and 6/09/25 for remainder of the year
6343	'43XX'	2-6-0	Built 1923. Barnstaple from 1/11/25. First 'Mogul' allocated
As at January 1926 with later movements			
2526	'Dean Goods'	0-6-0	Barnstaple 28/11 until end of year
3335	'Bulldog'	4-4-0	*Tregothnan*. Barnstaple until 21/02/26 then to Taunton
3371	'Bulldog'	4-4-0	*Sir Massey Lopes*. Barnstaple 21/02-3/10/26 then to Swindon
3417	'Bulldog'	4-4-0	*Lord Mildmay of Flete*. Barnstaple 24/01-13/06/26 and 8/08-3/10/26
3364	'Bulldog'	4-4-0	*Frank Bibby*. Built 1903. 3/10/26 for remainder of the year
3403	'Bulldog'	4-4-0	*Trinidad*. Barnstaple 24/01-21/02/26 and 21/03-28/11/26
3547	'3521'	4-4-0	Barnstaple 21/02-21/03 then Taunton and Barnstaple 28/11/26 for remainder of year
3348	'Bulldog'	4-4-0	*Launceston*. Built 1900. Barnstaple 23/11/26 to the end of year
4507	'45XX'	2-6-2T	Built 1907. 01/26
4567	'45XX'	2-6-2T	Barnstaple until 24/01/26, then 13/06-3/10/26 and 31/10-28/11/26
6343	'43XX'	2-6-0	Barnstaple until 24/01 then Taunton

1929, although only for a few weeks or months at a time, never the whole year. Notable amongst these was No. 4589 which was only seven months old when allocated to Barnstaple shed on 30th October 1927.

Although other classes of locomotives appeared on the line regularly over the four decades from when Churchward's 'Mogul' 2-6-0s first appeared, these useful mixed traffic engines were to become synonymous with the D&SR up until the early 1960s. It is thus perhaps appropriate here to examine them in a little more detail.

They were the first British 2-6-0s to be built in substantial numbers, the first, No. 4301, emerging from Swindon in 1911. It is believed that Churchward got his design inspiration from the USA, following a visit there by Henry Holcroft, one of his principal assistants. Similarities existed in the USA such as Stephenson valve gear, tapered boilers, horizontal cylinders with integral cast steam chests and saddle, superheating, 200lbs working pressure and a modest axle-loading

TABLE 10.3 (CONT.): As at January 1927 with later movements			
632	'Metro Tank'	2-4-0T	Built 1871. Barnstaple 23/01-12/06/27 then to Taunton
2526	'Dean Goods'	0-6-0	Barnstaple until 23/01/27 then Taunton
3335	'Bulldog'	4-4-0	*Tregothnan*. Barnstaple 23/01-17/04, then 12/06-7/08 and 2/10-25/12/27 (to factory)
3348	'Bulldog'	4-4-0	*Launceston*. Barnstaple until 23/01 then factory
3371	'Bulldog'	4-4-0	*Sir Massey Lopes*. Barnstaple until 23/01 then Swindon and Barnstaple 12/06-2/10/27
3364	'Bulldog'	4-4-0	*Frank Bibby*. Barnstaple until 23/01 then Taunton and Barnstaple 7/08-25/12/27
3417	'Bulldog'	4-4-0	*Lord Mildmay of Flete*. Barnstaple 17/04-12/06 then Taunton then Barnstaple 2/10-30/10 and again from 25/12/27
3403	'Bulldog'	4-4-0	*Trinidad*. Barnstaple 25/12/27 onwards
3547	'3521'	4-4-0	Barnstaple until 20/02 to Taunton. Barnstaple 20/03-17/04/27 to Taunton. Barnstaple 12/06-13/09/27 to Swindon
5346	'43XX'	2-6-0	Built 1918. Barnstaple 7/08-2/10/27
5309	'43XX'	2-6-0	Built 1917. Barnstaple 2/10-30/10/27. Number and rebuilt to No. 8309 in 1928
4589	'45XX'	2-6-2T	Built 1927. Barnstaple 30/10-December 1927
As at January 1928 with later movements			
3335	'Bulldog'	4-4-0	*Tregothnan*. Barnstaple 5/08-25/11/28
3398	'Bulldog'	4-4-0	*Montreal*. Built 1904. Barnstaple 19/02-30/07/28
3362	'Bulldog'	4-4-0	*Albert Brassey*. Built 1902. Barnstaple 30/09-28/10/28
3371	'Bulldog'	4-4-0	*Sir Massey Lopes*. Barnstaple until 18/03/28 then Swindon works
3377	'Bulldog'	4-4-0	*Penzance*. Barnstaple until 30/09/28 then to Taunton
3364	'Bulldog'	4-4-0	*Frank Bibby*. Barnstaple 28/10/28 until end of year
3403	'Bulldog'	4-4-0	*Trinidad*. Barnstaple until 19/02/28 then Taunton
3444	'Bulldog'	4-4-0	*Cormorant*. Built 1909. Barnstaple 13/05-5/08/28 and again 28/10/28 until end of year
4323	'43XX'	2-6-0	Built 1913. Barnstaple 18/03-13/05/28
4302	'43XX'	2-6-0	Built 1911. Barnstaple 15/04-13/05/28
4344	'43XX'	2-6-0	Built 1914. Barnstaple 2/09-30/09/28
4304	'43XX'	2-6-0	Built 1911. Barnstaple 25/11/28 to end of year
4590	'45XX'	2-6-2T	Built 1927. Barnstaple until 18/03/28 then Taunton
5346	'43XX'	2-6-0	Barnstaple 13/05-2/09/28 to Taunton. Barnstaple 30/09/28 until end of year
As at January 1929 with later movements			
3335	'Bulldog'	4-4-0	*Tregothnan*. Barnstaple until 17/03 returning 29/09/29
3348	'Bulldog'	4-4-0	*Launceston*. Barnstaple from 17/03/29 (one month at Taunton)
3364	'Bulldog'	4-4-0	*Frank Bibby*. Barnstaple until 17/03 then Taunton and back 12/05-9/06/29 and 7/07-22/07/29
3398	'Bulldog'	4-4-0	*Montreal*. Barnstaple 9/06-7/07/29
3377	'Bulldog'	4-4-0	*Penzance*. Barnstaple 12/05-4/06/29
3444	'Bulldog'	4-4-0	*Cormorant*. Barnstaple until until 20/01 then Taunton. Barnstaple 17/03-12/05/29 then Taunton
3453	'Bulldog'	4-4-0	*Seagull*. Built 1910. Barnstaple from 27/10/29 for remainder of year
4302	'43XX'	2-6-0	Barnstaple 4/08-24/11/29
4304	'43XX'	2-6-0	Barnstaple until 14/04 and again 4/08-27/10/29
4323	'43XX'	2-6-0	Barnstaple 4/08-27/10/29
4325	'43XX'	2-6-0	Built 1913. Barnstaple from 24/11 for remainder of year
4591	'45XX'	2-6-2T	Built 1927. Barnstaple 12/05-9/06/29
5502	'45XX'	2-6-2T	Built 1927. Barnstaple 9/06-7/07/29
As at January 1930 with later movements			
3348	'Bulldog'	4-4-0	*Launceston*. Barnstaple until 12/04/30 and again 7/06-22/11/30
3335	'Bulldog'	4-4-0	*Tregothnan*. Barnstaple until 10/05/30
3362	'Bulldog'	4-4-0	*Albert Brassey*. Barnstaple 7/06-5/07/30 and 2/08-27/09/30
3453	'Bulldog'	4-4-0	*Seagull*. Barnstaple until 10/05/30 then Taunton. Barnstaple 5/07-25/10/30
4325	'43XX'	2-6-0	Barnstaple until 12/04/30 again 7/06-5/07/30
4327	'43XX'	2-6-0	Built 1913. Barnstaple 2/08-22/11/30
4380	'43XX'	2-6-0	Built 1915. Barnstaple 7/06-5/07/30 and 27/11/30 for remainder of year
As at January 1931 with later movements			
3350	'Bulldog'	4-4-0	*Newlyn*. Built 1900. Barnstaple 14/02-14/03/31 and 11/04-26/09/31
3348	'Bulldog'	4-4-0	*Launceston*. Barnstaple 14/02-14/03/31
3331	'Bulldog'	4-4-0	*Pegasus*. Built 1900. Barnstaple 14/02-6/06/31 then 26/09 until end of year
3362	'Bulldog'	4-4-0	*Albert Brassey*. Barnstaple 6/06-4/05/31
3453	'Bulldog'	4-4-0	*Seagull*. Barnstaple until 14/02 then 14/03-11/04/31 then Swindon
3443	'Bulldog'	4-4-0	*Chaffinch*. Built 1909. Barnstaple 14/03-6/06/31 and 4/07-26/09/31
4325	'43XX'	2-6-0	Barnstaple 6/06/31 until end of year
4380	'43XX'	2-6-0	Barnstaple until 11/04/31 then Swindon
6341	'43XX'	2-6-0	Built 1921. Barnstaple 26/09/31 onwards
6358	'43XX'	2-6-0	Built 1923. Barnstaple until 14/02/31
2268	'22XX'	0-6-0	Built 1930. Barnstaple 6/06-4/07/31

for maximum route availability. However, the GWR locomotives were built to a higher standard, including a Swindon No. 4 boiler with trapezoidal section, Belpaire firebox and top feed, a continuous running plate, splashers and a cut-away cab. The frame was increased by 9 inches after the first twenty locomotives had been built to give more accommodation to the crew. This extra frame-length design was reflected in the '53XX', '63XX' and '73XX' series when built, which also incorporated other modifications such as inside or outside steam pipes, two patterns of boiler/frame stay-plate, different splasher arrangements, chimneys, buffers, lamp irons and pipework detail. The wheels originally used by Churchward were replaced by the more substantial Collett designs in the 1930s. These locomotives weighed 62 tons, with a tender weight of 40 tons full, giving an overall weight of 102 tons. The class had driving wheels measuring 5ft 8ins and their nominal tractive effort was 25,860lbs. The water capacity of the tender was 3,500 gallons, either flush-sided (counter sunk rivets) or rivetted. Overall length was 58ft $1^{1}/_{4}$ins, with a length from front wheel to tender rear wheel of 48ft $6^{3}/_{4}$ins (earlier versions were slightly shorter). There were 342 built in total, with production ceasing in 1934.

The class carried a variety of liveries over the years, including GWR plain and lined green but with most then being painted black during the Second World War. Many ended their days in that livery but one example, No. 7313, was subsequently lined out by BR and then, in 1956, two were painted BR green and fully lined out for working the Royal Train to Barnstaple on 8th May. By the end of the year it had been decided to adopt this for the entire class but, later, some were turned out in unlined green, whilst the programme was never completed, many being withdrawn before they could be treated. The first withdrawals were of the '43XX' Series in 1936 and by Nationalisation the class numbered 241. The final few survived until 1964 and continued to work on the D&SR until that time. Whilst replacing the 'Dean Goods' on mixed traffic duties, the route availability of the 'Moguls' was not as wide. The maximum load for the class was 280 tons (eight or nine coaches) and D&SR timings were based on maximum loads of 230 tons.

As already noted, the locomotives that were to work direct to Ilfracombe had to have their footsteps cut back to clear the tightly curved Taw River Bridge and their 25ins vacuum release valve altered to 21ins in order to comply with the SR's requirements for double-heading, as GWR and SR engines were normally prohibited from working in tandem. All of the '63XX' series achieved more than one million miles in service (other than No. 6315 which was withdrawn early in 1945), with No. 6340 achieving the most, a total of 1,558,713 miles at an average of 38,017 per year. No. 7337, a regular on the D&SR (built in March 1932 as No. 9315 but renumbered in May 1959), was the most travelled of the Collett versions of the class, accumulating just over one million miles before being withdrawn in September 1964.

Another new class, which was to see use on the D&SR, was brought in to service by the GWR in 1930, Collett's Class '22XX' 0-6-0 locomotives. The April 1930 edition of the *Great Western Magazine* introduced them to its readership, the locomotives coming into service in March of that year. With a maximum axle loading of $15^{3}/_{4}$ tons,

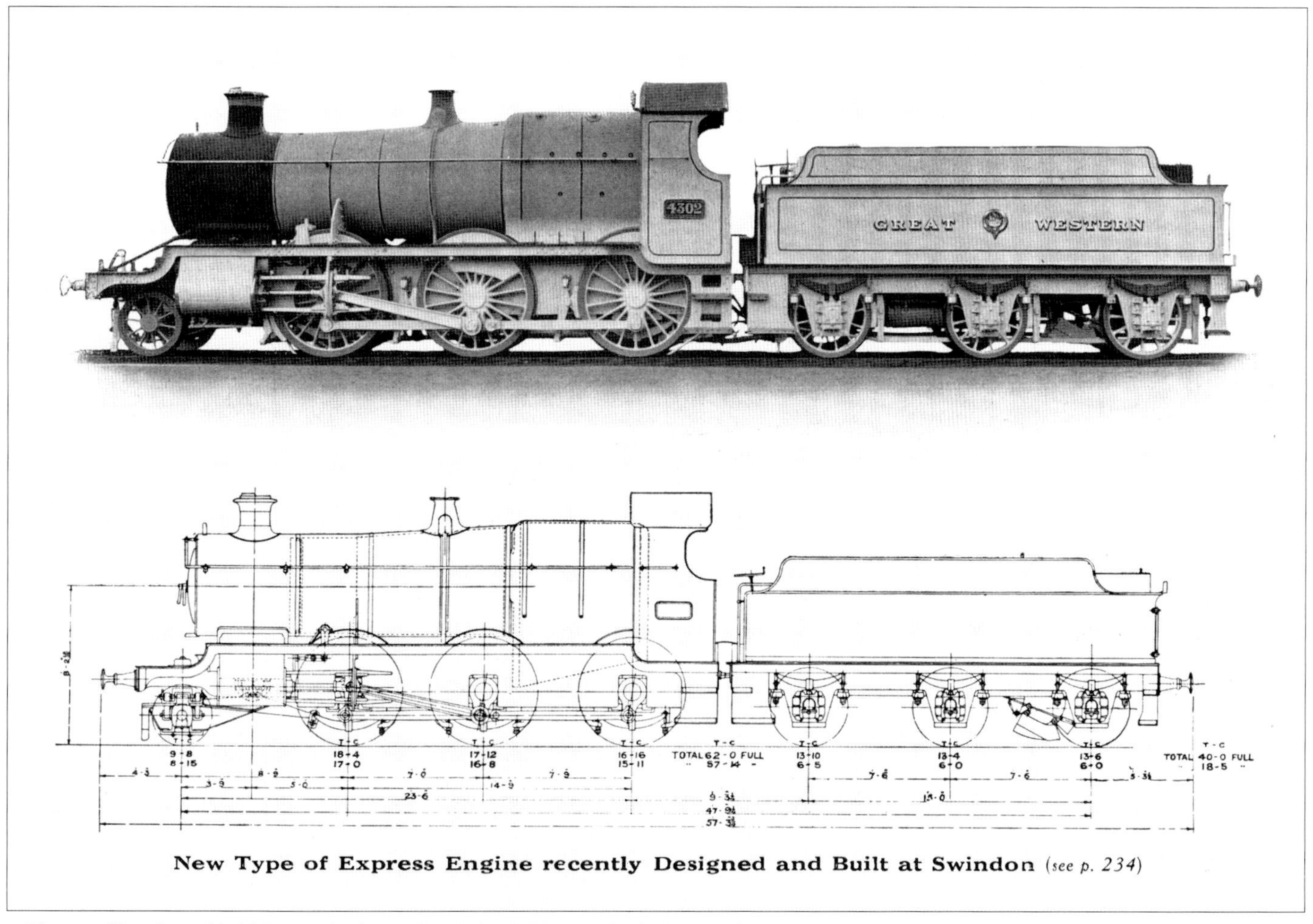

4302
GREAT WESTERN
New Type of Express Engine recently Designed and Built at Swindon (see p. 234)

The new Churchward 2-6-0 locomotive is unveiled in the *GWR Magazine* in August 1911.

Straight-framed '3521' Class No. 3529 stands just off the turntable alongside Barnstaple shed circa the early 1930s. Note the water tower in the background, with the apex of the shed roof left of and behind that. Although rebuilt from tank engines built in the 1800s, the similarity with the 'Bulldog' design is apparent. No. 3529 was built in 1887, converted to a 4-4-0 in April 1900 and allocated to Salisbury. Its final home was Kidderminster, from where it was withdrawn in April 1931, having completed 1,092,648 miles in service. ***Arthur Halls, courtesy National Railway Museum***

Right: The first of a short series of pictures of GWR engines on the Southern at Barnstaple Junction and the line to Ilfracombe in 1931, which illustrate the close co-operation between the two companies in this part of north Devon. Under the watchful eye of the Barnstaple Junction signalman, '43XX' Class 2-6-0 No. 4356 eases out of the yard having been turned on the larger 52ft diameter turntable located here. The locomotive was one of the fourth batch of the class to be built, at Swindon Works in March 1914. Whilst the class generally had quite a long life, with numbers of later builds in the '53XX, '63XX', 73XX' and '93XX' series, the majority of the '43XX' series were withdrawn in the later 1930s, with No. 4356 going in November 1936.
Brian Perkes, courtesy Leslie Walker

Left: 'Bulldog' No. 3443 *Chaffinch* waits at Barnstaple Junction, having arrived over the Devon & Somerset line from Taunton with a train bound for Ilfracombe. This engine, one of the final batch of 'Bird' series of 'Bulldogs', was originally built in May 1909 as No. 3733, becoming No. 3443 under the GWR 1912 renumbering scheme. Superheated in January 1911, *Chaffinch* was fortunate to be one of the longer lived 'Bulldogs', surving in to early BR days to be withdrawn in May 1949.
Brian Perkes, courtesy Leslie Walker

Right: 'Bulldog 'No. 3350 at the Up platform at Barnstaple Junction, the train it had brought in having been taken on to Ilfracombe by a Southern engine. Built in November 1900 as No. 3362 *Newlyn*, it was renumbered in 1912 as No. 3350. From the late 1920s, the GWR began to have a concern that the names of certain engines were being confused with train destinations by passengers and a number of the 'Bulldogs' had their names removed as a result, No. 3350 losing its *Newlyn* plates in July 1930. Fitted with superheating in February 1912, No. 3350 was nearing the end of its career, withdrawal taking place in July 1935.
Brian Perkes, courtesy Leslie Walker

Collett '22XX' 0-6-0 No. 2268 pilots 'N' Class No. A826 over Caen Street crossing, Braunton, with a through summer Saturday train returning from Ilfracombe. The locomotive combination is unusual but the train includes a mix of SR and GWR stock and would be split at Barnstaple Junction for onward travel to Taunton (GWR) and Exeter (SR). No. 2268 was one of the first batch of the '22XX' Class built in 1930, completed at Swindon in June of that year and allocated to Taunton, so was probably only a year old when seen here. It was still at Taunton in 1948 but had migrated to the Cambrian line at Machynlleth by the time withdrawal occurred in May 1965. The SR 'Mogul' was new in June 1924 and worked until September 1963. *Brian Perkes, courtesy Leslie Walker*

A GWR train for Ilfracombe passes over Braunton Gates crossing, with '45XX' Class 2-6-2T No. 5535 in charge. These trains would not stop to pick up passengers but would halt if a banker were required. Through GWR workings – as opposed to the carriages simply being worked forward by the SR – had begun in 1925, coinciding with the upgrading of the route to main line status and the provision of a larger turntable at Ilfracombe. At busy times the Southern would allow GWR engines and drivers to work the line, thereby saving their own motive power for SR needs or banking duties from Braunton. No. 5535 may indeed be stopping here for a banker to be attached to help with the climb to Mortehoe. One of the penultimate batch of the class built at Swindon in 1928, these engines had the sloping 1,300 gallon capacity side-tanks. It was an early withdrawal, succumbing in June 1957. *Brian Perkes, courtesy Leslie Walker*

they were classified as 'yellow' engines for route availability and were the perfect mixed traffic locomotive for the D&SR. Barnstaple shed was an early recipient of one these new locomotives, when twelve months-old No. 2268 was allocated there for a month in the summer of 1931 but there was then a six year hiatus before any more arrived, with No. 2268 finally returning in June 1937. It was to be followed by classmates No's 2261, 2266 and 2267 in late 1937-1938, and then No's 2211, 2212, 2213, 2214, and 2215 between 1939 and 1941, all of which were regularly allocated to Barnstaple shed throughout the war and up to Nationalisation in 1948. Most of these were Taunton-based when not allocated to Barnstaple and primarily worked the freight duties on the D&SR and also on the Minehead Branch. However, they also worked passenger services from time to time.

In 1934, Taunton shed had amongst its complement, two 'Bulldogs' (No. 3331 *Pegasus* and No. 3453 *Seagull*) and four 'Moguls', No's 4304, 4313, 4321 and 6309. Four '22XX' Class 0-6-0s were also based there, No's 2261, 2265, 2266 and 2267, whilst several 'Dean Goods' locomotives also remained, No's 2410, 2416, 2482, 2517 and 2527, all fitted with ATC apparatus. These were additionally supplemented by eleven Class '45XX' 2-6-2Ts, No's 4531, 4537, 4569, 4571, 4581, 5503, 5521, 5537, 5542, 5543 and 5571.

By the late 1930s, the '43XX' 2-6-0s had become the most common engines on the D&SR, with 'Bulldog' 4-4-0s, '22XX' 0-6-0s and '45XX' 2-6-2Ts making up the remainder of the locomotives that appeared. As the accompanying photographs show, all of these classes were permitted to work though to Ilfracombe and frequently did so on summer Saturdays. A 'Dean Goods' occasionally worked the line on a summer Saturday when no other engine was available to take the few goods services which were run. An example of Class '43XX' members working the line in the early to mid-thirties is extracted with permission from *Great Western Journal* No. 19 (1996) and reproduced below:

Date	No.	Notes
24/03/1931	6384	5.40pm Taunton to Barnstaple passenger
30/12/1932	4304	10.55am Barnstaple to Taunton passenger
10/07/1934	6326	1.50pm Barnstaple to Taunton goods
16/12/1935	6309	5.48am Taunton to Barnstaple goods
17/05/1936	6345	6.10am Barnstaple to Taunton passenger

As the decade progressed, the 'Bulldogs' began to be used less often and by the end of the 1930s they were being phased out altogether, the last one to be out-stationed at Barnstaple shed being No. 3443 *Chaffinch* for the first three months of 1940.

With the introduction of Whitaker automatic token exchange on the line in 1938, a number of Taunton engines were fitted with the token catchers. These included the following locomotives so fitted in 1937 and 1938, as noted in the *Railway Observer*: '22XX' No's 2261, 2266-2268; 'Dean Goods' No's 2410, 2418, 2472, 2527, 2537 and 2578; 'Bulldogs' No's 3361, 3443 and 3444, '43XX' No's 4339, 4361, 4379, 6305, 6323, 6354, 6363, 6372, 6383 and 6398; '45XX' No's 4581, 5501-5504, 5521, 5522, 5525, 5537, 5542 and 5571; and '51XX' 2-6-2Ts No's 4117 and 5172. The last two were 'Large Prairie' engines, built in 1936 and 1930 respectively, the fitting of

TABLE 10.3 (CONT.): As at January 1932 with later movements			
3350	'Bulldog'	4-4-0	*Newlyn*. Barnstaple 16/01-13/02/32 and 2/07/32 until end of year
3321	'Bulldog'	4-4-0	*Brasenose*. Built 1899. Barnstaple to 16/01 then factory. Barnstaple 13/02-2/07/32 then Taunton
3362	'Bulldog'	4-4-0	*Albert Brassey*. Barnstaple 12/03-9/04/32
3444	'Bulldog'	4-4-0	*Cormorant*. Barnstaple 9/04-7/05/32 then to Taunton
3453	'Bulldog'	4-4-0	*Seagull*. Barnstaple 4/06/32 for remainder of the year
4304	'43XX'	2-6-0	Barnstaple 7/05-24/09/32
4313	'43XX'	2-6-0	Built 1911. Barnstaple 22/10/32 for remainder of year
4323	'43XX'	2-6-0	Barnstaple 2/07-22/10/32
4325	'43XX'	2-6-0	Barnstaple until 9/04 then Taunton
4391	'43XX'	2-6-0	Built 1916. Barnstaple 22/10/32 to end of year
6341	'43XX'	2-6-0	Barnstaple until 9/04 and then back 4/06-2/07/32
There were no records available for 1933			
As at January 1934 with later movements			
3444	'Bulldog'	4-4-0	*Cormorant*. Barnstaple until 5/05/34
3453	'Bulldog'	4-4-0	*Seagull*. Barnstaple 5/05-28/07/34
4313	'43XX'	2-6-0	Barnstaple 5/05-28/07/34
4321	'43XX'	2-6-0	Built 1913. Barnstaple 20/10-17/11/34
4391	'43XX'	2-6-0	Barnstaple until 28/07 then to Swindon and back 17/11/34
5503	'45XX'	2-6-2T	Built 1927. Barnstaple 17/11-15/12/34
6309	'43XX'	2-6-0	Built 1921. Barnstaple 20/10-17/11/34
6326	'43XX'	2-6-0	Built 1921. Barnstaple 28/07-17/11/34
6343	'43XX'	2-6-0	Barnstaple 28/07-20/10/34
6377	'43XX'	2-6-0	Built 1921. Barnstaple 28/07-20/10/34
As at January 1935 with later movements			
3383	'Bulldog'	4-4-0	*Ilfracombe*. Built 1903. Barnstaple 9/02-9/03/35 and 6/04-29/06/35 then to Taunton
3453	'Bulldog'	4-4-0	*Seagull*. Barnstaple 9/03-6/04/35
3416	'Bulldog'	4-4-0	*John W. Wilson*. Built 1906. Barnstaple 29/06-24/08 and 16/11-14/12/35 (then to scrap)
3401	'Bulldog'	4-4-0	*Vancouver*. Built 1904. Barnstaple 14/12/35 to end of year
4304	'43XX'	2-6-0	Barnstaple 9/03-27/07 then Taunton. Barnstaple 19/10-16/11/35
4313	'43XX'	2-6-0	Barnstaple 9/02-9/03 and 6/04-1/06 and 27/07-21/09 and 19/10-16/11/35 then condemned 02/36
4314	'43XX'	2-6-0	Built 1911. Barnstaple 27/07-24/08/35
4321	'43XX'	2-6-0	Barnstaple 29/06-27/07/35
4330	'43XX'	2-6-0	Built 1913. Barnstaple 24/08-19/10/35
4391	'43XX'	2-6-0	Barnstaple until 9/02 then 9/03-6/04, 24/08-16/11/35 and 14/12 to end of year
6343	'43XX'	2-6-0	Barnstaple 1/06-29/06 and 27/07-24/08 and 16/11-14/12/35
6309	'43XX'	2-6-0	Barnstaple 12/01-9/03 then Taunton. Barnstaple 16/11/35 for remainder of year
6383	'43XX'	2-6-0	Built 1921. Barnstaple 21/09-19/10/35 Taunton
As at January 1936 with later movements			
3383	'Bulldog'	4-4-0	*Ilfracombe*. Barnstaple 8/02-4/04/36
3401	'Bulldog'	4-4-0	*Vancouver*. Barnstaple until 8/02/36
3427	'Bulldog'	4-4-0	Un-named. Barnstaple 25/07-22/08 and 17/10-12/12/36
3441	'Bulldog'	4-4-0	*Blackbird*. Built 1909. Barnstaple 4/04-25/07 then to Taunton. Barnstaple 22/08-17/10 then to Taunton. Barnstaple 14/11-12/12/36
3443	'Bulldog'	4-4-0	*Chaffinch*. Barnstaple 4/04-30/05 and 22/08-19/09/36
4314	'43XX'	2-6-0	Barnstaple 12/12/36 until end of year (condemned 06/37)
4348	'43XX'	2-6-0	Built 1914. Barnstaple 11/01-8/02/36
4330	'43XX'	2-6-0	Barnstaple from 12/12/36
4391	'43XX'	2-6-0	Barnstaple until 11/01 then to Taunton and Barnstaple 30/05-17/10/36
5542	'45XX'	2-6-2T	Built 1928. Barnstaple 30/05-27/06/36
6343	'43XX'	2-6-0	Barnstaple 11/01-4/04 , 27/06-22/08 and 19/09 onwards
6398	'43XX'	2-6-0	Built 1921. Barnstaple 17/10-12/12/36
6383	'43XX'	2-6-0	Barnstaple 7/03-30/05/36

ABOVE: One of *Seagull*'s nameplates now resides at the Gauge Museum Bishops Lydeard.

LEFT: One each of Chaffinch's name and numberplates at Kidderminster Railway Museum. A regular performer on the D&SR, the locomotive (originally No. 3733) was built in May 1909 and withdrawn in May 1949 with recorded mileage of 1,199,214. *Both author*

'Bulldog' No. 3453 *Seagull* inches its way off the turntable at Barnstaple shed in the early 1930s. Built in January 1910 as No. 3743, No. 3453's first allocation was to Neyland shed in west Wales. It was withdrawn in November 1951 from Reading shed, having long-since been moved away from D&SR duties. *Arthur Halls, courtesy National Railway Museum*

'Bulldog' No. 3335 on Barnstaple shed in the early 1930s, standing on the short road leading to the turntable. Built in 1900 as No. 3347 *Tregothnan* and first allocated to Plymouth shed, the nameplates were removed in December 1930, one of those engines to lose its name due to passengers confusing them with train destinations. When withdrawn in October 1948 it was allocated to Exeter and had accumulated a total of 1,397,566 miles in service. *Arthur Halls, courtesy National Railway Museum*

RIGHT: A Down train with through coaches for Ilfracombe arriving at South Molton behind 'Bulldog' No. 3441 *Blackbird*, a member of the class that we have not seen before. In 1936, this engine had three spells allocated to Barnstaple shed, totalling seven months, so this view is likely to date from that year. The train is just about to pass the Down side token apparatus. *Courtesy, Great Western Railway Society*

BELOW: 'Bulldog' No. 3453 *Seagull* looks splendid and a good advert for the class as it passes Acland Woods heading east towards Taunton with a five-coach train in 1935. *Donovan E.H. Box, R.J. Sellick Collection, courtesy National Railway Museum*

the token apparatus apparently indicating that this was yet another class which featured on the D&SR but which we have yet to see a photograph of working the line so they may have been only trialled briefly. However, the RC&TS's *The Locomotives of the Great Western Railway Part Nine* (1962) recorded that '*No. 5172 was noted in 1956 with tablet changing apparatus for use on the Minehead and Barnstaple branches*'. At the time they were built they were intended for suburban passenger duties and most went new to the Wolverhampton Division.

The early morning Bristol (West Depot) to Barnstaple goods was, by 1939, a regular turn of the '43XX' Class, as was the 7.30pm Barnstaple to Bristol goods, the locomotive of which worked at least as far as Taunton. In 1941, the '43XX' diagram for the Bristol goods was as follows – the locomotive would work the 6.35pm passenger from Taunton to Bristol Temple Meads, arriving at 8.20pm; it would then work the 1.15am Bristol West Depot goods to Barnstaple arriving at 10.00am, the return working for the locomotive being the 11.35am Barnstaple to Taunton passenger service.

Between June and December 1940, a further twenty Collett 0-6-0s, No's 2211-30, entered service and the first five of those numerically were transferred to Taunton. They were replacing the earlier '43XX' number series 'Moguls', of which few were left in service and none allocated to Taunton. Having been built at Swindon in May 1940,

A pleasing portrait of Churchward 'Mogul' No. 5309 in immaculate condition coming off the connecting line from Barnstaple GWR at Barnstaple Junction circa 1926. This is clearly a posed shot, as the three crew members are all focused on the photographer. Built in February 1917, it was one of sixty-five of the class that were rebuilt at the front end between January and March 1928, having their buffer beams extended forward by a foot and a heavy weight placed behind, to counteract heavy flange wear on the leading pair of driving wheels on the sharply curving lines that abounded in the West Country. All were renumbered in to the '83XX' series, with No. 5309 becoming No. 8309. The modification was successful but had the effect of turning the '83XX' in to red route engines. The engine was restored to original condition and reverted back to its old number in July 1944 and was withdrawn in January 1953. ***Arthur Halls, courtesy National Railway Museum***

Table 10.3 (Cont.): 1937 and 1938 (records combined) and movements (all locos with Whitaker apparatus fitted except *)			
2268	'22XX'	0-6-0	Built 1930. Barnstaple Dec. 1937-Feb. 1938, Dec. 1938
2261	'22XX'	0-6-0	Built 1930. Barnstaple March-April 1938, Oct.-Nov. 1938
2267	'22XX'	0-6-0	Built 1930. Barnstaple Aug. 1938
3361	'Bulldog'	4-4-0	*Edward VII*. Built 1902. Barnstaple July-Aug. 1937. Oct.1937-Jan. 1938. April-June 1938
3401*	'Bulldog'	4-4-0	*Vancouver*. Barnstaple May-July 1937
3443	'Bulldog'	4-4-0	*Chaffinch*. Barnstaple May-June 1937. Aug.-Sept. 1937. Oct.-Dec. 1937. Jan.-April 1938, May-June 1938
3444	'Bulldog'	4-4-0	*Cormorant*. Barnstaple July-Oct. 1937. June-Aug. 1938
4339	'43XX'	2-6-0	Built 1913. Barnstaple Sept.-Oct. 1937. April-May 1938. July-Sept. 1938. Oct.-Dec. 1938. Condemned Swindon Jan. 1939
4361	'43XX'	2-6-0	Barnstaple Nov.-Dec. 1937. June-Aug. 1938. Oct.-Nov. 1938
5522	'45XX'	2-6-2T	Built 1927. Barnstaple June-July 1938
5502	'45XX'	2-6-2T	Built 1927. Barnstaple July-Aug. 1938
5504	'45XX'	2-6-2T	Built 1927. Barnstaple Sept.-Oct. 1938
5525*	'45XX'	2-6-2T	Built 1928. Barnstaple May 1937
6323	'43XX'	2-6-0	Built 1921. Barnstaple Sept.-Oct. 1938
6354*	'43XX'	2-6-0	Built 1923. Barnstaple Dec. 1938
6363	'43XX'	2-6-0	Built 1925. Barnstaple July-Aug. 1938
6372	'43XX'	2-6-0	Built 1921. Barnstaple July-Sept.1937. Feb.-March 1938
6383	'43XX'	2-6-0	Barnstaple Feb. 1937-March 1937. Sept.-Nov. 1937. April-May 1938
6398*	'43XX'	2-6-0	Built 1921. Barnstaple Jan.-Feb. 1937. May-July 1937. Dec. 1937-May 1938. Aug.-Oct. 1938. Nov. onwards
1939 and 1940 (records combined) and movements (all locos with Whitaker apparatus fitted except *)			
2211	'22XX'	0-6-0	Built 1940. Barnstaple July-Aug. 1940. Nov.-Dec. 1940
2213	'22XX'	0-6-0	Built 1940. Barnstaple Oct.-Nov. 1940
2214	'22XX'	0-6-0	Built 1940. Barnstaple Aug.-Oct. 1940
2215*	'22XX'	0-6-0	Built 1940. Barnstaple July-Aug. 1940
2261	'22XX'	0-6-0	Barnstaple July-Aug.1939
2267	'22XX'	0-6-0	Barnstaple Aug.-Oct. 1939. Dec. 1939-Jan. 1940. March 1940
2266	'22XX'	0-6-0	Barnstaple March-Aug. 1939
2268	'22XX'	0-6-0	Barnstaple June-July 1939, Sept. 1939, Dec. 1939-June 1940. Dec. 1940
2275	'22XX'	0-6-0	Built 1934. Barnstaple Feb.-March 1939. April-May 1939. Oct.-Nov. 1940
3361	'Bulldog'	4-4-0	*Edward VII*. Barnstaple March-April 1939. Oct.-Dec. 1939
3443	'Bulldog'	4-4-0	*Chaffinch*. Built 1900. Barnstaple Jan.-March 1940
4361	'43XX'	2-6-0	Barnstaple Jan. 1939. Condemned at Swindon Feb. 1939
5503	'45XX'	2-6-2T	Barnstaple Feb.-March 1940
5522	'45XX'	2-6-2T	Built 1927. Barnstaple Oct.-Dec. 1939. Jan.-Feb. 1940
5537	'45XX'	2-6-2T	Built 1928. Barnstaple Feb.-March 1939. July-Sept. 1939.
6305	'43XX'	2-6-0	Built 1920. Barnstaple Aug.-Oct. 1940
6323	'43XX'	2-6-0	Barnstaple April 1939. March-April 1940
6354	'43XX'	2-6-0	Barnstaple March-April 1939. April-May 1940
6363	'43XX'	2-6-0	Barnstaple March-May 1939. Aug.-Nov. 1939
6364	'43XX'	2-6-0	Built 1925. Barnstaple June-Aug. 1939
6372	'43XX'	2-6-0	Barnstaple Jan.-Feb. 1939. May-July 1939
6383	'43XX'	2-6-0	Barnstaple April 1939-June 1939
6398*	'43XX'	2-6-0	Barnstaple Feb.-March 1939. Sept.-Oct. 1939. March-May 1940
1941 and 1942 (records combined) and movements (all locos with Whitaker apparatus fitted except *)			
2211	'22XX'	0-6-0	Barnstaple March 1941, Aug. 1941, Dec. 1941
2212	'22XX'	0-6-0	Built 1940. Barnstaple Jan. 1941, Nov. 1941, Feb. 1942
2213	'22XX'	0-6-0	Barnstaple March 1941, June 1942, July 1942
2214	'22XX'	0-6-0	Barnstaple Aug. 1941 March-June 1942. Nov. 1942
2215*	'22XX'	0-6-0	Barnstaple June 1941. Dec. 1942
2266	'22XX'	0-6-0	Barnstaple April 1941, June 1942
2267	'22XX'	0-6-0	Barnstaple Feb.-June 1942. Spark arrester fitted
2268	'22XX'	0-6-0	Barnstaple June 1941. July 1942-Aug. 1942
5542	'45XX'	2-6-2T	Built 1928. Barnstaple April-June 1941. Jan.-April 1942
6323	'43XX'	2-6-0	Barnstaple Feb. 1941. Oct. 1941-Feb. 1942
6305	'43XX'	2-6-0	Barnstaple Oct. 1942
6372	'43XX'	2-6-0	Barnstaple Jan. 1941
6364	'43XX'	2-6-0	Barnstaple March 1941. Sept. 1941
7314*	'43XX'	2-6-0	Built 1921. Barnstaple Nov.-Dec. 1942

TABLE 10.3 (CONT.): 1943 and 1944 (records combined) and movements (all locos with Whitaker apparatus except *)			
2211	'22XX'	0-6-0	Barnstaple March-April 1943. July-Aug. 1943 (then Taunton for remainder of year and 1944)
2212	'22XX'	0-6-0	Barnstaple June-Aug. 1943. Sept.-Oct. 1944. Nov. 1944 to Taunton then Newton Abbot for repairs
2213	'22XX'	0-6-0	Barnstaple Sept. 1943-Jan. 1944. Sept.-Oct. 1944
2214	'22XX'	0-6-0	Barnstaple April-May 1943. April-June 1944
2215*	'22XX'	0-6-0	Barnstaple Jan.-Feb. 1943. May-June 1943 (then to Newton Abbot) back to Taunton 1944
2261	'22XX'	0-6-0	Barnstaple Aug.-Sept. 1943. May-July 1944. Nov.-Dec. 1944
2266	'22XX'	0-6-0	Barnstaple Aug.-Sept. 1943. Nov. 1943-Jan. 1944
2267	'22XX'	0-6-0	Barnstaple Feb.-March 1943 and Oct. to Nov. 1943 (then Swindon). Feb.-April 1944. July-Sept. 1944 (then to Minehead). Barnstaple Oct.-Nov 1944. Spark arrester fitted
2268	'22XX'	0-6-0	Barnstaple Jan.-Feb. 1944
2275	'22XX'	0-6-0	Barnstaple June-July 1943. Oct.-Nov. 1943. Jan.-Feb. 1944
3361	'Bulldog'	4-4-0	*Edward VII*. At Taunton
3443	'Bulldog'	4-4-0	*Chaffinch*. At Taunton
3444	'Bulldog'	4-4-0	*Cormorant*. At Taunton
6305	'43XX'	2-6-0	Barnstaple April-June 1943. July-Sept. 1943. May-June 1944. Sept. 1944
6364	'43XX'	2-6-0	Barnstaple Jan.-March 1943. June-July 1943. Sept.-Oct. 1943, then Taunton and throughout 1944
6398	'43XX'	2-6-0	Barnstaple Feb.-June 1944
7314*	'43XX'	2-6-0	Barnstaple March-April 1943
1945 and 1946 (records combined) and movements (all locos with Whitaker apparatus except *)			
2211	'22XX'	0-6-0	Barnstaple May 1946
2212	'22XX'	0-6-0	Barnstaple May-July 1945. Aug. 1945. May 1946. Sept. 1946
2213	'22XX'	0-6-0	Barnstaple Feb. 1945
2214	'22XX'	0-6-0	Barnstaple Sept. 1945. Nov. 1945. June 1946 for remainder of year
2215	'22XX'	0-6-0	Barnstaple Nov. 1946
2230	'22XX'	0-6-0	Built 1940. Barnstaple May 1945 (then to Exeter)
2261	'22XX'	0-6-0	Barnstaple Jan. 1945 (fitted with spark arrester)
2266	'22XX'	0-6-0	Barnstaple Jan. 1945. March 1946. June 1946. Dec. 1946
2267	'22XX'	0-6-0	Barnstaple Feb. 1945 (fitted with spark arrester)
2268	'22XX'	0-6-0	Barnstaple March-June 1945. Dec. 1945. Feb. 1946. July-Aug. 1946
2275	'22XX'	0-6-0	Barnstaple Oct. 1946
6305	'43XX'	2-6-0	Barnstaple Jan. 1946
6328*	'43XX'	2-6-0	Built 1921. Barnstaple Oct. 1945. Jan. 1946. April 1946
6364	'43XX'	2-6-0	Barnstaple April 1945. Aug. 1945. April 1946
6372	'43XX'	2-6-0	Built 1921. Barnstaple June 1945-July 1945. Sept. 1945. Dec. 1945
6398*	'43XX'	2-6-0	Barnstaple Feb. 1946
7304	'43XX'	2-6-0	Barnstaple March 1945. Oct.-Nov. 1945. March 1946
7314*	'43XX'	2-6-0	Barnstaple July 1945. Dec. 1945
1947 and 1948 (records combined) and movements (all locos with Whitaker apparatus fitted except *)			
2211	'22XX'	0-6-0	Barnstaple April-May 1947
2212	'22XX'	0-6-0	Barnstaple May-June 1947. April 1948
2213	'22XX'	0-6-0	Barnstaple Aug.-December 1947. Sept. 1948
2214	'22XX'	0-6-0	Barnstaple Jan.-Aug. 1947
2215	'22XX'	0-6-0	Barnstaple Jan. 1947
2266	'22XX'	0-6-0	Barnstaple Jan. 1947. June 1948
2267	'22XX'	0-6-0	Barnstaple Nov. 1947. June 1948. Oct. 1948
2261	'22XX'	0-6-0	Barnstaple June 1948. Oct. 1948
6343	'43XX'	2-6-0	Barnstaple Oct. 1948
6328	'43XX'	2-6-0	Barnstaple July 1948
6317	'43XX'	2-6-0	Built 1921. Barnstaple Aug. 1948
6364	'43XX'	2-6-0	Barnstaple Sept. 1948

No's 2211, 2213, 2214 and 2215 were all allocated to Barnstaple between July and December when virtually brand new. By December 1941, Taunton shed had No's 2212, 2213, 2214, 2215, 2230, 2267 and 2268 on its allocation, whilst Barnstaple had No's 2211 and 2261; at this time both Barnstaple engines had Whitaker's apparatus fitted, as did No's 2212-14 and 2267 at Taunton. Indeed, No. 2212 would spend most of its career at Taunton, finally departing in 1958. In the early 1950s, it had a ROD tender attached rather than the usual, smaller 3,000 gallon tender.

By January 1942, Taunton's allocation of 'Moguls' comprised No's 6305, 6354, 6364, 6372 and 6398, all fitted with Whitaker automatic token apparatus, and No's 7304 and 7314 that were not fitted. Barnstaple shed had No. 6323 on its allocation. Also by this time, whilst the '45XX' 2-6-2Ts were still abundant at Taunton, none were allocated to Barnstaple after No. 5542 departed in April 1942.

As previously noted, by the early war years the frequency of 'Bulldog' workings had declined dramatically and most Barnstaple line duties were now in the hands of the '22XX' and '43XX' classes. The heavy use of the latter on main line goods trains during the war years meant the Collett 0-6-0s appeared in greater numbers on the D&SR throughout this period. The last 'Bulldog' allocated to Barnstaple was No. 3443 *Chaffinch* during the first three months of 1940. They were presumably still working the line after this, however, as No. 3443, along with classmates No. 3361 *Edward VII* and No. 3444 *Cormorant*, are shown in the table as still allocated to Taunton in 1943-44, after which they disappear from the D&SR completely.

In January 1946, Taunton's allocation of 'Moguls' comprised No's 6364, 6372, 6398, 7304 and 7316, whilst Barnstaple shed had No's 6305 and 6328. As can be seen from the photographs in these volumes, a number of these were becoming regulars and were clearly the branch engines for some time.

Locomotives allocated to Taunton at January 1947 were reported in the *GWR Magazine* as follows:

0-6-0: 2211, 2212, 2213, 2214, 2215, 2261, 2266, 2267, 2268, 2275
2-6-2T: 5501, 5503, 5504, 5521, 5522, 5533, 5542, 5543, 5571
2-6-0: 6305, 6323, 6328, 6364, 6372, 6398, 7304, 7314
0-6-0PT: 1338, 1760, 1909, 2038, 2127, 2194, 2708, 2748, 2755, 6420, 7421, 8440, 9718, 9757

In addition there were three 'Bulldogs', No. 3361 *Edward VII*, No. 3443 *Chaffinch* and No. 3444 *Cormorant*. However, in 1946 the *Railway Observer* had reported that *Chaffinch* was appearing less on Barnstaple duties.

On 29th May 1947, Collett No. 2214 was recorded on the 4.00pm Barnstaple Junction to Taunton passenger service and on the 9.10pm Taunton to Barnstaple return working. In December 1947, No's 2211, 2212, 2214, 2215, 2261 and 2267, all equipped with Whitaker's apparatus, were still allocated to Taunton shed. No's 2266 and 2275 were still sub-shedded at Barnstaple and No. 2213 was at Minehead.

It is apparent from the table that fewer locomotives were allocated throughout 1947 and 1948 to Barnstaple shed. Collett 0-6-0s No's 2214 and 2213 covered the January to July and August to December period of 1947 respectively, whilst there was no full cover from 1948. This presumably resulted from Nationalisation with all locomotives being allocated at Taunton and then occasional engines out-stationed at Barnstaple.

Table 10.4 below, again taken from *Great Western Railway Journal* No. 19 (1996), shows some recorded Class '43XX' workings in the 1946 to 1948 period.

Table 10.4: Some Class '43XX' Workings on the D&SR 1946-48

Date	No.	Notes
10th July 1946	6398	8.15pm Barnstaple to Bristol – goods
19th July 1946	6328	2.30pm Taunton to Barnstaple – passenger
20th Dec. 1946	6361	12.30pm Taunton to Barnstaple – goods
14th Feb. 1947	6328	12.30pm Taunton to Barnstaple – goods
29th Mar. 1947	6305	1.30pm Barnstaple to Taunton – goods
14th Apr. 1947	6328	8.30pm Taunton to Barnstaple – passenger
5th July 1947	6328	9.25am Ilfracombe to Taunton – passenger
14th Aug. 1947	6332	1.15am Bristol to Barnstaple – goods
6th Dec. 1947	6377	11.34am Barnstaple to Taunton – passenger
5th Jan. 1948	7314	4.05am Taunton to Barnstaple – goods
9th Mar. 1948	7304	4.05am Taunton to Barnstaple – goods
1st Apr. 1948	6305	8.15pm Barnstaple to Bristol – goods
1st Apr. 1948	6394	6.40pm Barnstaple to Taunton – passenger
24th May 1948	6372	1.30pm Barnstaple to Taunton – goods
28th July 1948	6317	11.35am Barnstaple to Taunton – passenger
5th Aug. 1948	7304	5.30am Taunton to Barnstaple – goods
30th Aug. 1948	6305	12.50pm Taunton to Barnstaple – goods
23rd Oct. 1948	6394	12.30pm Taunton to Barnstaple – goods

'Bulldog' No. 3417 *Lord Mildmay of Flete* was a regular on the D&SR line during the 1920s and is pictured leaving Barnstaple with an Up train circa 1930 in Volume 1 (page 147). It was built as No. 3707 Francis Mildmay in June 1906, being renumbered in 1912 and renamed with Mildmay's new title in July 1923. Seen here with an empty tender and devoid of lettering, the view may well be on Swindon dump shortly after withdrawal from Wellington (Salop) shed in April 1948. It had travelled 1,142,888 miles. *Jim Elson collection*

TABLE 10.5: BARNSTAPLE SHED – Locomotives 1949-1952			
No.	**CLASS**	**WHEEL ARR.**	**COMMENTS. NOTE: The build date is given for each locomotive on its first appearance in the table**
1949 and 1950 (records combined) and movements			
2267	**'22XX'**	**0-6-0**	**Barnstaple Jan.-July 1949,then to Swindon returning to Taunton Sept. 1949**
2261	**'22XX'**	**0-6-0**	**Barnstaple Jan.-May 1949. July 1949-July 1950. Nov. 1950 onwards**
2268	**'22XX'**	**0-6-0**	**Barnstaple Jan.-Aug. 1949. Sept. 1949-December 1950**
1951 and 1952 (records combined) and movements			
2261	**'22XX'**	**0-6-0**	**Barnstaple 1951-1952 (Oct.) then to St. Philip's Marsh**
2268	**'22XX'**	**0-6-0**	**Barnstaple 1951-1952 (Sept.) then to Swindon, returning to Taunton**
			Barnstaple WR shed officially closed on 1st January 1951

1948-1963

By the late 1940s, the '43XX' Class were running the majority of the services, supplemented by members of the '22XX' Class. However, although the 'Moguls' maintained their stranglehold on most services right through the 1950s until 1964, the last year of steam on the line, these faithful Great Western locomotives were also joined by interlopers from the Southern Railway after Nationalisation.

With Barnstaple GWR station having been renamed Barnstaple Victoria Road by British Railways in 1949, the first major change under the new regime occurred when the shed there was closed on 1st January 1951, the intention being for all locomotives to use the ex-Southern shed (72E) at Barnstaple Junction. However, the *Railway Observer* recorded at the ex-GWR shed on 2nd January 1951 No's 2211 and 2212, two of the Collett 0-6-0s from Taunton shed. 'Mogul' No. 6343 was shunting, whilst No. 6377 (again both of Taunton shed) ran in from Barnstaple Junction tender-first.

Barnstaple shed had been coded 'Barn' by the GWR from circa 1900 onwards. In the later GWR era it became a part of the Newton Abbot Division ('NA') and a sub-shed of Taunton ('TN', code '203'), Barnstaple being code '23'. Under BR it had remained a sub-shed to Taunton, which was recoded 83B.

An 'M7' 0-4-4 tank, No. 30252 of Exmouth Junction shed, was recorded at Taunton on 8th May 1951 in the *Railway Observer*, perhaps the first of the class ever to visit there. These locomotives were from around this time permitted over the Taunton to Barnstaple line, albeit restricted to 25mph throughout, so it is possible it had worked a train up from Barnstaple but that was not recorded so there is no proof of this. The 'M7' subsequently worked an empty coaching stock train in the Down direction but it is not known whether this was to Exeter or along the D&SR to Barnstaple.

The *Railway Observer* went on to note in February 1952 that Southern Region 'N' Class 'Moguls' were more regularly working the trains on the branch, No. 31842 (of Exmouth Junction shed) being a regular performer. On 23rd January, 'T9' Class 4-4-0 No. 30712 was also seen, the engine having recently been re-allocated from Basingstoke to Exmouth Junction shed. A popular roster for these locomotives was the 4.00pm Barnstaple Junction to Taunton and the 9.10pm return Taunton to Barnstaple Victoria Road, the 1950s Working Time Tables stipulating their diagramming on these trains. A photograph of 'T9' No. 30710 heading an Up train near Castle Hill on 3rd July 1953 can be found in Volume 2 (page 357).

The 1952 allocation of Class '43XX' engines at Taunton shed comprised No's 6305, 6317, 6323, 6328, 6343, 6364, 6372, 6394, 6398 and 7304. These engines were the mainstay of branch services during the final years of steam.

Although Barnstaple shed was closed at the start of 1951, the turntable was left in place for a couple of years. However, the only scheduled daily use of it in the early 1950s was by a Class '22XX' engine on a goods turn and this ceased in early 1953, with the sidings and turntable being removed in the July and the pit filled in. Thereafter engines were sent to Barnstaple Junction. The shed here would also have the locomotives stabled overnight that worked the two final Down trains of the day.

The roster for 1953 required that six Class '43XX' locomotives worked the line on weekdays, increasing to nine on summer Saturdays. Mostly supplied by Taunton, they were supplemented from Exeter and Newton Abbot sheds, one locomotive working light engine from Exeter to Taunton on the Friday night in preparation for the next day's duties. These would broadly be a Taunton-Ilfracombe-Barnstaple-Ilfracombe-Taunton turn, with locomotive changes at Victoria Road or Barnstaple Junction. A '22XX' Class 0-6-0 was scheduled to work the 7.24am Taunton to Barnstaple passenger and, following a quick turn around, would work back on the 9.35am Barnstaple to Taunton goods. A '45XX' 2-6-2T was rostered for the 6.15pm Taunton to Barnstaple passenger and the 8.55pm return from Barnstaple Junction. A Southern Region engine was allocated to the 4.00pm Barnstaple Junction to Taunton departure and the 9.10pm return (this being the same turn as that for No. 2214 in 1947 as referred to in the previous section). As this was the last train of the day, the locomotive would then run light engine back to Barnstaple Junction shed for servicing. The 7.40am Taunton to Dulverton goods was scheduled

Class '45XX' No 5522 arrives at Dulverton just after 7.00pm with the 6.15pm train from Taunton to Barnstaple on 4th July 1952. Built in December 1927, the 'Prairie' was withdrawn on 3rd March 1959, having spent its BR years allocated to Taunton shed. ***Peter Treloar Collection***

'Prairie' tank No. 5503 takes on water at Dulverton on 28th July 1951, whilst working a Barnstaple-bound train, as indicated by the large red 'B' in a white disc carried on the buffer beam. This was a leisurely stop and the driver looks to have refreshed the tea can whilst the fireman does the work! Several young lads lean from the windows of the front carriage to watch progress The locomotive, built in May 1927 and withdrawn in May 1961, was a Taunton engine throughout the 1950s. *R.J. Sellick, courtesy National Railway Museum*

for a '22XX' 0-6-0, which would return to Taunton on the 12.05pm goods departure from Dulverton.

Appendix 16 shows the scheduled workings of the '43XX' Class on the branch on a typical Summer Saturday in 1953 and also includes rosters for '22XX' Class engines in 1953, the roster for winter 1955-56, Saturdays only in 1957 and August 1961.

Looking at the weekday Summer Time Table for 1954, **Table 10.6** traces the movements of one busy locomotive (Diagram TN72 in **Appendix 16**) over the branch.

TABLE 10.6: LOCOMOTIVE DIAGRAM TN72, SUMMER 1954

TYPE	TIME AND LOCATION(D)	TIME AND LOCATION (A)
Light engine	5.10am Taunton shed	Taunton
Goods	5.30am Taunton to BVR	BVR 8.26am
Goods	10.40am BVR to BJ trip	BJ 10.45am
Passenger	11.25am BJ to BVR	BVR 11.30am
Passenger	11.36am BVR to Taunton	Taunton 1.14pm
Light engine	1.20pm Taunton	Taunton shed 1.25pm
Passenger	5.00pm Taunton to BVR	BVR 6.36pm
Passenger	6.50pm BVR to BJ	BJ 6.55pm
Goods	7.30pm BJ to BVR trip	BVR 7.35pm
Goods	8.00pm BVR to Bristol	Taunton 10.24pm
Light engine	10.30pm Taunton to Shed	Taunton Shed 10.35pm

In the winter 1955-56 period, the line had six Down and seven Up passenger services, with four Down and three Up goods trains. Two pairs of engines each worked three trips between Taunton and Victoria Road daily, each turn being a two-day schedule, one engine running four sectors and two more turns running two trips each. A number of turns ran passenger and goods trip workings to Barnstaple Junction. Given that it was the Winter Time Table, there were no through services to Ilfracombe so they did not need to be accommodated into the workings. From June 1956, all the '93XX' series 'Moguls' passing through the factory for heavy repairs were renumbered as No's 7322-7341. Of these, No's 7333 and 7337 were reallocated to Taunton and worked the line.

From 1957 there was a run down of the Collett '22XX' Class and by January 1958 Taunton only had No. 2212 allocated to it, whilst No. 2211 was the only one of the class allocated to Exeter. At March 1959, Taunton shed had No. 2235.

By the summer of 1959, the rosters had changed and, in summary, three '43XX' Class locomotives worked a three-four-three trip schedule over a three day period; one engine was on a four-trip day and two others on two-trip turns each. The most popular members of the class on the route at this period were No's 6323, 6337, 6343, 6364, 6372, 6375, 7304, 7305, 7319 and 7337 (ex-No. 9315), all Taunton based. At this time Taunton had seven turns for 'Moguls' with ten engines allocated. **Appendix 16** summarises this. By January 1960, there were only thirty-three of the class still in use, so Taunton had a good number and they enjoyed a substantial role in working the D&SR passenger services at this time.

In the period from 1950 to 1964, Barnstaple Junction shed (72E at August 1950 and 83F at September 1963 when it was transferred to WR control) had the following Southern Region locomotives stabled there that may have worked the line:

'T9' 4-4-0 No. 30717 (allocated from June 1956 to July 1959)

'N' Class 2-6-0s No. 31840 (06/52-09/52), No. 31841 (06/52-09/52), No. 31842 (08/50-05/51, 06/52-11/52, 06/54-02/55 and 06/55-11/56), No. 31843 (11/52-11/56), No. 31844 (07/53-09/53) and No. 31845 (07/53-09/53).

In addition, No. 31406, an Eastleigh engine transferred to Exmouth Junction, was caught on camera by Peter W. Gray working the 9.25am Ilfracombe to Taunton train on 25th July 1964. No. 31846 of Exmouth Junction, also worked the line. By the time the 'T9's appeared on the branch they were in their final years and only worked

ABOVE: 'Mogul' No. 6340 rests between duties at Taunton Shed on 14th April 1962. Note the Whitaker token collection apparatus visible on the tender. Built in July 1921, the locomotive was fitted with outside steam pipes in January 1950 and was withdrawn in July 1962. ***Jim Elson collection***

LEFT: Classmate No. 7304 photographed at Taunton Shed, its home throughout the 1950s, a few days later on 20th April 1962. Built in February 1922 by Robert Stephenson & Co. Ltd, Darlington, it had outside steam pipes fitted in November 1947 and was withdrawn in December 1963. Again the Whitaker apparatus is clearly visible on the tender. ***Jim Elson collection***

occasional turns, certainly not as frequently as the 'N' Class.

The 'West Country'/ 'Battle of Britain' Class Bullied 'Light Pacific' locomotives weighing-in at 86/90 tons had route availability on the branch and examples apparently occasionally hauled the trip workings between Barnstaple Junction and Victoria Road.

Table 10.7 shows Taunton shed's allocation of '43XX' Class engines between 1950 and 1964.

Table 10.7: Class '43XX' Allocated to Taunton Shed 1950-1964

Number	Dates
5321	Sept. 1953-July 1958
5325	Sept. 1954-July 1955
5336	Oct. 1963-Sept. 1964
5344	Sept. 1956-Aug. 1958
6301	Sept. 1955-June 1956
6305	Aug. 1950-Oct. 1952
6312	Mar. 1961-June 1961
6317	Aug. 1950-Dec. 1953
6322	Sept. 1954-Dec. 1954
6323	Aug. 1950-Mar. 1958; May 1958-Oct. 1959
6326	Dec. 1963-Sept. 1964 – then withdrawn
6327	July 1962-Sept. 1963 – then withdrawn
6328	Aug. 1950-June 1956
6337	Sept. 1956-July 1958; Oct. 1958-Oct. 1959; Nov. 1959-May 1962
6340	Apr. 1961-June 1962 – then withdrawn
6343	Aug. 1950-Aug. 1960 – then withdrawn
6345	Dec. 1963-Sept. 1964 – then withdrawn
6363	June 1964-Sept. 1964 – then withdrawn
6364	Aug. 1950-Oct. 1959
6372	Aug. 1950-Dec. 1963 – then withdrawn
6375	June 1956-Sept. 1960
6377	Aug. 1950-July 1958
6390	Sept. 1953-May 1962 – then withdrawn
6394	Aug. 1950-Nov. 1953
6398	Aug. 1950-Sept. 1960 – then withdrawn
7303	Nov. 1963-Sept. 1964 – then withdrawn
7304	Aug. 1950-Nov. 1963 – then withdrawn
7305	Nov. 1960-Aug. 1962 – then withdrawn
7311	Oct. 1952-May 1958
7317	Sept. 1963-Dec. 1963 – then withdrawn
7319	June 1960-Sept. 1960
7320	Aug. 1964-Sept. 1964
7326	Mar. 1961-Sept. 1963 – then withdrawn
7332	Sept. 1963-Mar. 1964 – then withdrawn
7333	June 1960-Oct. 1963 – then withdrawn
7337	1962-Sept. 1964 – then withdrawn

Also during the 1950s period, Class '45XX' 2-6-2Ts and various 0-6-0PTs were deployed on the line, largely on goods workings, especially the more local Taunton/Dulverton/South Molton pick-up goods. Indeed, pannier tanks were used on the occasional passenger train, presumably when larger motive power was not available. 'Prairie' tanks at Taunton shed in 1955 were No's 5501, 5503, 5504, 5522, 5533, 5558 and 5571. By 1958 the allocation comprised No's 5501, 5503, 5504, 5515 (previously at Truro), 5522, 5525 (previously at Bristol Bath Road), 5543 (previously at Newton Abbot) and 5571. No's 5533 and 5558 had moved to Newton Abbot. In 1960, the '45XX' fleet at Taunton constituted No's 5503, 5504, 5521 (previously at St. Blazey), 5525, 5554 (previously at Westbury), 5562 (previously at Truro) and 5571. No's 5501, 5522 and 5533 were withdrawn in 1959-60 and scrapped soon after. No. 5515 was back at Truro shed along with No. 5543 and No. 5558 was at Newton Abbot.

Class '57XX' 0-6-0PT No. 9670 on an Up four-coach train at Filleigh in 1964. This was a Taunton-based engine for most of its BR life, which may have been rostered on this occasion due to the lack of an available 'Mogul'. ***Courtesy Roger Joanes***

As new BR-designed steam locomotives appeared, they also ventured onto the D&SR. The BR 'Standard' Class '3MT' 2-6-2s ('82XXX') supplemented the 'Moguls' in the late 1950s and early 1960s on passenger and goods duties. Also used were the Ivatt-designed Class '2MT' 2-6-2Ts ('41XXX') on both passenger and goods duties. The first Ivatt to arrive at Barnstaple Junction shed was No. 41298 in July 1953.

In the early 1960s, '43XX' 2-6-0s continued to operate the Bristol to Barnstaple goods and the return working but only over the D&SR section, as diesels had taken over on the main line. The Bristol goods was included in the Working Time Table for 12th June 1961 to 10th September 1961 but was then shown as '*suspended*' in the period after (from 11th September 1961) at which point it ceased to run for good; this is explored further in Chapter 11.

In 1961-62, BR 'Standard' Class '3MT' 2-6-2Ts began to be allocated from the LMR to Taunton and **Table 10.8** shows those of the class that were shedded there in the early 1960s.

In December 1962, the following Ivatt Class '2MT' 2-6-2Ts were at Barnstaple Junction; No's 41290, 41294, 41297, 41298, 41310, 41312, 41313 and 41314. By this date these locomotives had been transferred to Western Region stock.

Table 10.8: BR Class '3MT' Allocated to Taunton Shed 1961-1962

Number	Dates
82001	Dec. 1963-June 1964
82008	Nov. 1961-Feb. 1964 – then withdrawn
82030	Nov. 1961-June 1964
82042	Nov. 1961-June 1964
82043	Jan. 1962-Feb. 1962
82044	Nov. 1961-June 1964

It is believed the first visit of a diesel over the line was on 7th May 1963, when a North British Type '2' ran from Plymouth to Halwill Junction, Torrington and Barnstaple, and then traversed the D&SR line to Taunton. Sadly, its number appears not to have been recorded but it is likely that the trip was to assess route availability, for future use on summer Saturday services for example. Morebath Junction and the route to Dulverton also saw Class '22' North British diesel-hydraulics on the final day of the Exe Valley service on 5th October 1963, much to the disappointment of those travelling who expected the usual Collett 0-4-2T steam haulage.

At the start of 1963, the '43XX' Class allocated at Taunton were No's 6327, 6372, 7304, 7326, 7333 and 7337. By the end of the year, the only members of the class left in the West Country were all at Taunton shed, being No's 6372, 7304, 7317, 7332 and 7337.

ABOVE: Pannier tank No. 9670 outside the shed at Taunton on 20th April 1962, awaiting its next turn out duty. ***Jim Elson Collection***

LEFT: Classmate No. 3794 poses between duties on the loop line beyond the Exe Valley bay at Dulverton, most likely having worked a Taunton to Dulverton goods. It was an Exeter allocated engine for most of its BR life but was withdrawn from Oxford shed in December 1964. ***Peter Barnfield***

BELOW: Completing this trio of Class '57XX' pannier tanks, No. 9635 is seen shunting the Down side yard at Dulverton on 22nd July 1963 (the author's seventh birthday!). This engine was not well liked by Taunton-based footplatemen, having a reputation as a poor steamer and with slow injectors, as recounted by fireman Roger Sellick on page 671.
Owen Mogg collection, courtesy Peter Triggs

1964-1966

The year 1964 was to see not just the end of the ex-GWR 'Mogul's hauling trains on the D&SR but, indeed, the end of steam on the line altogether, well over a year before steam operations on the Western Region of British Railways ceased completely. No's 6363 and 7306 from Taunton shed were regulars at this time but were now looking much the worse for wear. No. 7306 showed the remains of its green livery on the firebox and tender but lacked a number plate. No. 6363 meanwhile was still in faded green but the *Railway Observer* noted that it looked '*quite smart*' compared with other Taunton 'old stagers' of the same class.

BR 'Standard' Class '3' 2-6-2T No. 82001 was noted on the 16.20pm Taunton to Barnstaple passenger service on 30th May 1964, just before its withdrawal. Ex-LM&SR Ivatt Class '2MT' 2-6-2Ts were also rostered on some of the turns from Barnstaple shed in 1964, No. 41216 from Plymouth Friary shed being seen on 27th June, for example.

Steam traction ceased on the D&SR with the end of the Summer Time Table on 5th September 1964, when Barnstaple Junction shed was closed. However, the last steam locomotive over the D&SR was to be now preserved '22XX' Class No. 3205 in March 1965 with the Exmoor Ranger enthusiasts special (referred to further in Chapter 12).

From 6th September, diesel multiple units (DMUs) and railcars

ABOVE: Ex-SR 'N' Class 'Mogul' No. 31846 of Exmouth Junction shed arrives at Morebath on the Up loop line circa 1962, passing an unidentified ex-GWR counterpart working to Barnstaple.
Courtesy Lens of Sutton Association

RIGHT: A twin-car Birmingham RC&WC DMU (later Class '118'), in green livery with yellow whiskers and comprising Driving Motor Seconds (DMS) No's W51329 and W51324, is seen here at Silk Mills having just come off the Barnstaple branch on 3rd April 1965. The unit is now heading along the WR main line towards Taunton on the final stage of its journey.
Owen Mogg collection, courtesy Peter Triggs

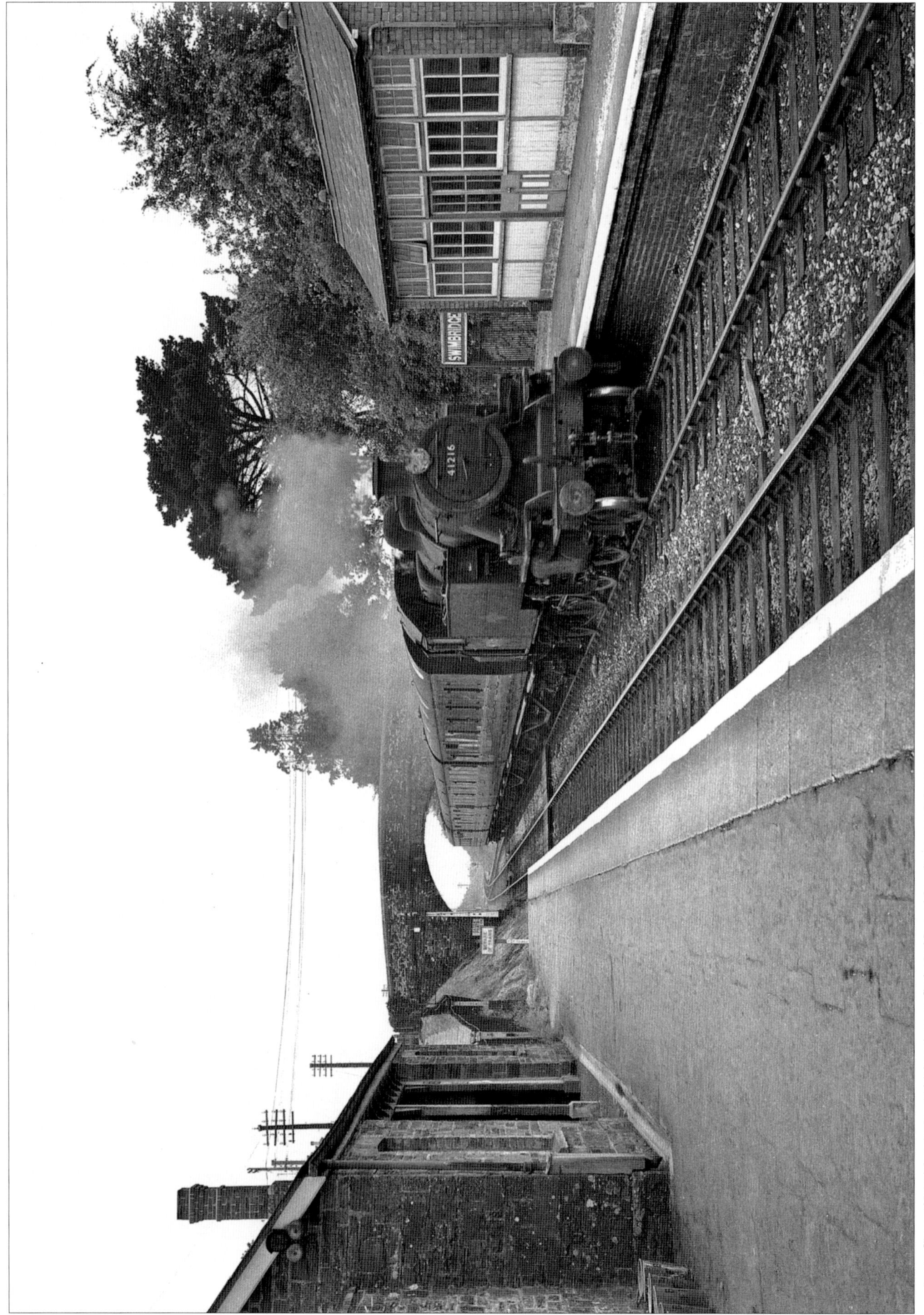

Ivatt Class '2MT' 2-6-2 No. 41216 arrives at Swimbridge with a four-coach Taunton-bound train on 27th June 1964, just over two months before steam operation on the branch ceased altogether. An LM&SR design but built by British Railways at Crewe Works in September 1948, No. 41216 was withdrawn from Plymouth Friary shed in March 1966. *R.A. Lumber, courtesy Dave Mitchell*

Left: **An unidentified single 'bubble car' DMU passes the sad remains of Norton Fitzwarren station on 13th February 1965, heading east with a Barnstaple Junction to Taunton service.**
Owen Mogg collection, courtesy Peter Triggs

Below: **North British Type '2' No. D6331, a regular performer on the D&SR on summer Saturdays, pulls away from Milverton on 4th September 1965 with an Ilfracombe-bound Saturdays only service. These diesel-hydraulic locomotives were not the most attractive or reliable but as far as is known, they were the only diesel locomotives to work the line. North British went bankrupt shortly after the last of class was delivered in 1962.**
Owen Mogg collection, courtesy Peter Triggs

became the main passenger service providers. Types that appeared on the line included the Pressed Steel Company single units (later Class '121') numbered in the W550XX series but most services had two- or three-car units built circa 1957 by BR's Derby Works (later Class '116') and the Birmingham Railway Carriage & Wagon Company (later Class '118'), both introduced circa 1960. Gloucester Railway Carriage & Wagon Company Cross-Country units (later Class '119') also featured. In 1965, only the remaining summer Saturday through trains (and the unusual Torrington milk service that year – see Chapter 11, page 582) would be locomotive hauled trains and it seems that only Class 'D63XX' (later Class '22') North British diesel-hydraulics worked these. In 1965, summer Saturday trains such as the Wolverhampton to Ilfracombe working were hauled over the route by members of this class, No. D6332 of Newton Abbot shed being recorded on 28th August 1965. These trains would have been steam hauled to Taunton, the diesel-hydraulic taking over from there. Finally, there has been little authoritative evidence discovered of a 'Hymek' diesel-hydraulic ('D70XX', later Class '35') making the journey along the line, even though they had route capability and regularly worked to Minehead. People who knew the line just before closure state that a 'Hymek' was seen on the Torrington milk train on one occasion, whilst someone else related that a 'Hymek' worked a demolition train on one occasion.

LINE CLASSIFICATION

The Taunton to Barnstaple line was nominally limited to 'Yellow' engines, with the '43XX' Class specially permitted onto the route but were not allowed to take an assisting engine over the line. The maximum passenger loading was 280 tons in either direction (being eight or nine coaches) and train timings were normally based on a 230-ton maximum loading.

For 'D Group' engines the permitted goods loads were twenty-six loaded coal wagons but with a restriction of twenty-one wagons up the banks. With general merchandise, thirty-nine wagons were permitted westbound and forty-two eastbound but again with a restriction of thirty-two on the banks. However, the normal maximum was twenty-eight loaded wagons, due to a combination of the inclines, and the lengths of the passing loops and refuge sidings.

The twenty Churchward '93XX' series engines of the '43XX' Class were built in 1932 and are distinguishable by their side window cabs. With a heavy weight behind the front buffer beam and extended frames, they were eleven tons heavier and classified as 'Red' engines for route availability. The scrapping of some of the early '43XX' locomotives in the 1950s created a shortage of 'Blue' engines, so the '93XX' had their weights removed in 1956-59 and were renumbered in to the '73XX' group. Two of the regulars on the line, No's 7326 and 7337, were originally No's 9304 and 9315 respectively. The 280-ton maximum passenger train load restriction on the line applied to the 'Moguls', with the '45XX' 'Prairie' tanks restricted to 220 tons, whilst the Collett Class '22XX' 0-6-0s and '57XX' pannier tanks were restricted to 190 tons.

It seems odd that the 4-4-0s were prohibited at this point but it suggests that none then traversed the line as nothing, other than some engineering trains and a shuttle service for a period, went only as far as Wiveliscombe (as discussed in Chapter 11). It may well be that the state of the viaducts west of Wiveliscombe at this time caused the restriction. Also, it is evident 'Small Prairie' tanks worked the line up until the early 1960s.

There has been no evidence, photographic or otherwise, of any members of the '78XXX', 'West Country' or 'M7' classes, along with diesel shunters or 'Hymeks' working the line. However, some diesel shunters and 'M7' tanks did visit Victoria Road on trip workings

TABLE 10.9: CLASSIFICATION ENGINE TYPES ON D&SR FROM 1950S

CLASS	ROUTE RESTRICTION	POWER CLASS	TRACTIVE EFFORT (LBS)
43XX	Blue	D	25,001-33,000
45XX	Yellow	C	20,501-25,000
57XX	Yellow	C	20,501-25,000
14XX	–	–	below 16,000

TABLE 10.10: ENGINE PROHIBITIONS NORTON FITZWARREN-BARNSTAPLE

ENGINES AUTHORISED	PROHIBITION
All Yellow types	South Molton-Oil Co's siding/Vickery's siding: engines not to pass stop board
Blue types 2-6-0 43XX, 53XX, 63XX, 73XX	Dulverton-goods shed
Blue types 4-4-0 33XX, 34XX, 2-6-2T	Not beyond Wiveliscombe

TABLE 10.11: ENGINES PERMITTED ON THE D&SR 1960S

TYPE	LOCOMOTIVE	COMMENTS
2-6-0	43XX	43XX Blue engines with concession to travel over the yellow D&SR route
2-6-0	Southern N	
2-6-0	78XXX	BR standard-uncoloured route availability*
4-4-0	T9	
4-6-2	West Country	Un-rebuilt restricted to 20mph
2-6-2T	82XXX	BR Standard 3MT
2-6-2T	Ivatt 41200 Class	
2-6-2T	45XX Prairie	Small Prairie
0-4-4T	M7	Restricted to 25mph
0-6-0T	57XX Pannier	
D2000	shunter	
D3000	shunter	
D63XX	North British	No's D6300-6305 were registered as blue route engines but they could travel over yellow routes not exceeding 40mph*
D7XXX	Hymek	These were badged red engines but were permitted over most blue routes as long as speed was restricted to 60mph*

*as added from *BR(WR) Locomotive Route Availability June 1963*

TABLE 10.12: ENGINE RESTRICTIONS, BR(WR) LOCOMOTIVE ROUTE AVAILABILITY, JUNE 1963

SECTION OF LINE	ROUTE COLOUR	ENGINES AUTHORISED	LOCAL PROHIBITIONS
Norton Fitzwarren to Barnstaple Junction	Yellow	All 'uncoloured' and 'yellow' types. 73XX SR M7 SR 'N' SR West Country Class (except rebuilt engines)	South Molton-Back Road Siding. All beyond stop board. Speed restricted to 25mph. Not to be assisted by any other engine. In emergency may work between Morebath Junction and Barnstaple Junction Speed 20mph. All Permanent Speed Restrictions of less than 20mph to be rigidly observed, particularly Castle Hill Viaduct at 199m 75ch near Filleigh, 15mph. West Country engines not to be coupled to any other engine. Filleigh-Crossover to Goods Yard. Barnstaple (Victoria Road)-Engine Escape Crossover at Stop Block end of arrival and departure platform. Barnstaple East Loop- All sidings except No. 2-Run. Around Siding at Barnstaple (Victoria Road).
Barnstaple Junction to Ilfracombe	Yellow	55XX, 32XX, 73XX	55XX, 73XX, 32XX must have steps cut back to width of 8ft 4in. This to apply to all footsteps occurring between rail level and 1ft 9in above rail level. Engines fitted with AWS apparatus not to work Barnstaple Junction (SR) Yard East and West of Goods Shed unless shoes clipped up.

from Barnstaple Junction in addition to some of the usual motive power. 'Hymeks' were regular Taunton engines but were a Type '3' diesel-hydraulic and weighed 75 tons 8cwt, whilst the North British engines were a Type '2' diesel-hydraulic weighing only 65 tons. A 'Mogul' weighed 62 tons plus a 40-ton tender when full. The coupling of GWR and Southern engines was usually prohibited but the GWR 'Mogul' 2-6-0s on the Ilfracombe route had to have their ejectors set to work at 21 inches of vacuum to comply with the Southern's requirements for double-heading. However, the picture on page 492, showing a Collett 0-6-0 piloting a Southern 'N' Class 'Mogul' at Braunton in 1931, suggests that the prohibition was either not strictly adhered to or that other types had to have their ejectors set to match as well.

Drivers' and Firemen's Duties 1961

By way of illustration, drivers' and firemen's duties at Barnstaple Junction (SR) shed in the summer 1961 are set out in **Table 10.13** below.

Table 10.13: Loco. Crew Duties, Barnstaple Summer 1961

Duty 1			
Location	**Time (a)**	**Time (d)**	**Duty/Loco**
Shed – on duty	12.32pm		Walk to Station
Barnstaple		12.48pm	TN74(43XX) Taunton Passenger
Taunton	2.29pm		Light to Taunton loco
Taunton		6.18pm	Passenger
Barnstaple	8.02pm	8.05pm	light to shed
Shed	8.10pm	8.32pm	off duty
Duty 2			
Location	**Time**	**Time**	**Duty/Loco**
Shed	6.30am	7.30am	TN76(43XX) on duty and light to station
Barnstaple	6.35am	7.45am	to Taunton Passenger
Swimbridge	8.05am	8.11am	Exchange with TN74(43XX) on down goods
Victoria Road	8.31am		arrive and shunt yard
Victoria Road		10.50am	goods to Jnc
Barnstaple	11.00am	11.10am	light to shed
Shed	11.15am	12.30pm	light to Station
Barnstaple	12.35pm		leave TN74
Barnstaple		12.40pm	take TN77 on shed
Shed	12.45pm	2.30pm	and off duty
Duty 3			
Location	**Time**	**Time**	**Duty/Loco**
Shed – on duty	5.25am	6.25am	TN77 (43XX) light to Jnc
Barnstaple	6.30am	6.43am	TN77 Departure to Taunton
Taunton	8.30am		To Taunton loco on arrival
Taunton		10.25am	Off loco shed and on 10.25am departure
Barnstaple	12.16pm	1.25pm	Off duty
Duty 4			
Location	**Time**	**Time**	
Shed	2.00pm	2.15pm	On duty and light TN77 (43XX)
Victoria Road	2.23pm	3.05pm	Goods to Taunton
Taunton	7.34pm		to shed
Taunton		8.42pm	off shed and Passenger to Jnc
Barnstaple	10.24pm	10.30pm	to shed
Shed	10.35pm	10.45pm	and off duty

A Trip Behind No. D6333 on 28th August 1965

Table 10.14 is an extract from an article on the Class '22' North British diesel-hydraulics, reproduced with permission from *Modern Locomotives Illustrated No. 197* (October/November 2012). It summarises a timed run from Ilfracombe to Taunton and is taken from the logs of senior operational officer G.J. Aston (whose logs are now retained in the Railway Performance Society digital archive). Locomotive No. D6333 was in charge of six coaches (weighing 197 tons) on the 11.10am Ilfracombe to Wolverhampton Low Level (Saturdays only) train on 28th August 1965. This would have been one of the last locomotive hauled summer Saturday trains on the branch. No. D6333 would have coped easily with its relatively light load over the 63 miles of the line from Ilfracombe, with eight intermediate stops, reaching 54mph on a number of stretches. On departing from Ilfracombe, No. D6333 was helped up the fearsome Mortehoe Bank by No. D6342.

Table 10.14: Ilfracombe to Barnstaple 28/08/65

Miles	Timing Point	WTT	Mins/Secs	MPH
0.00	Ilfracombe (d)	0	0.00	1/2L-/22
2.25	Milepost 224		6.54	20/31
3.13	Mortehoe (a)	12	9.06	
0.00	(d)	15	14.20	
1.13	Milepost 222		2.19	54
4.72	Braunton (a)	10	9.25	
0.00	(d)	12	11.05	
0.95	Wrafton (a)	2	2.51	20 (average)
0.00	(d)	4	3.37	
2.32	Milepost 214		4.29	48 and 50
4.31	Barnstaple Town (a)	7	7.58	
0.00	(d)	9	11.37	
0.70	Barnstaple Junction (a)	3	3.30	12 (average)
0.00	(d)	10	10.31	2L
7.26	Swimbridge	11	11.01	39.8 (average)
10.65	Filleigh		18.09	28.2 (average)
13.94	South Molton (a)	25	25.24	27.4 (average)
0.00	(d)	27	26.51	-/53
4.35	Bishops Nympton	6	7.38	
7.75	Yeo Mill Halt		14.32	28 and 37
9.38	East Anstey		18.08	22 and 54
13.15	Dulverton (a)	22	24.04	
0.00	(d)	25	25.00	
1.76	Morebath Jnc		4.09	45
3.29	Morebath		6.04	54
6.91	Venn Cross	15	12.32	
11.66	Wiveliscombe (a)	24	21.08	
0.00	(d)	25	23.53	
2.93	Milverton	5	5.23	32.3 (average)
7.46	Norton Fitzwarren	11	11.24	45.2 (average)
9.43	Taunton (a)	16	15 .15	30.6T (average)

As can be seen, the locomotive gave a good account of itself traversing the D&SR line with its six coach train in about 90 minutes. Its time tabled departure from Barnstaple Junction was 12.00 noon, with registered stops at South Molton, Dulverton and Wiveliscombe only and arrival at Taunton at 1.33pm – a planned journey time of 93 minutes.

ROLLING STOCK

1870s – THE BRISTOL & EXETER RAILWAY PERIOD

There are no records of what rolling stock specifically worked on the line other than from photographs and to date there are only three from broad gauge days which show a train, one of which is a goods train. Enlargements from these, showing the rolling stock, are included below. The D&SR opened to Wiveliscombe on 8th June 1871 and throughout on 1st November 1873, and was worked by the Bristol & Exeter Railway from the outset, the Devon & Somerset Railway possessing no rolling stock of its own.

Over the years the B&ER purchased its coaching stock from many different private building companies and built some vehicles at its own works in Bridgwater. In addition, vehicles were re-built at Bridgwater with new bodies fitted to old underframes. This latter observation is especially relevant to the B&ER practice of using old underframes for their brake vans, which were fitted with 'Bird Cage' lookouts on the roof – one of which is visible in the photograph below.

Vehicles were built in small batches by various manufacturers and because of this there was little standardisation. Consequently, what few photographs there are of B&ER passenger trains present a truly varied image and therefore, one can only give a generalised description of contemporary carriage dimensions.

First Class: These varied in length from 24ft to 27ft 3ins and were generally of four compartments, each well upholstered with arm rests etc. Heights varied between 6ft and 6ft 6ins.

A broad gauge passenger train posed at Wiveliscombe circa June 1871, with a B&ER 4-4-0 saddle tank at the head. The first coach is a B&ER vehicle but the one behind, in the two-tone livery is, like those in the picture below, of uncertain origin. ***John Spencer Gilks collection***

Another cruel enlargement, of the Down mixed passenger and perishables train at South Molton around the time of opening in 1873, hauled by a B&ER 0-6-0 goods engine. The first vehicle is a 6-wheeled, iron-sided B&ER luggage or parcels van with guard's lookout in the roof, whilst the three two-tone liveried carriages comprise two Thirds and a First/Second Composite respectively but their provenance otherwise is not certain. They might be B&ER coaches in the cinnamon & coffee bean livery but they might also be GWR carriages in chocolate & cream or even ex-West Cornwall Railway. The fifth vehicle is a carriage truck complete with load and then, with the cupola on the roof, is a meat van and possibly another behind. ***Courtesy South Molton Museum***

Second Class: These vehicles were often a little longer but do not seem to have exceeded 28ft in length. There were generally five compartments, fitted with padded bench seats and backrests.

Third Class: These were of similar lengths to the Second Class coaches but had six compartments with wooden bench seats.

Composites: A number of coaches were built with First and Second Class accommodation – usually two First Class compartments and two Second Class, though vehicles incorporating all three classes were not unknown. These vehicles generally incorporated a luggage compartment in the middle of the coach. In fact, this was a common practice and is equally relevant to the types of vehicles already mentioned, especially those of Second or Third classes where the luggage compartment replaced one of the seated compartments.

With the exception of a few iron luggage vans, later B&ER coaches were built with timber bodies mounted on 6-wheeled iron chassis. Earlier vehicles had 4ft diameter wheels, whilst later ones were fitted with 3ft 6ins wheels and improved springing. One of the peculiarities of later B&ER designs was the incorporation of elliptical windows and a coach of this type is visible in the photograph of a B&ER train at Portishead, below.

Towards the end of its independent existence, the B&ER became increasingly financially challenged and as a result maintenance suffered. In this context, the GWR Carriage Registers throw some disquieting light on the company's difficulties, because very few ex-B&ER coaches survived in service much beyond 1880.

Initially the B&ER, was worked by the GWR but the company assumed responsibility for its own services in 1849. At first, coaches were painted in a dark crimson colour which, when weathered, gave the appearance almost of black. In October 1867, a change was made to dark brown but in 1870, at the suggestion of the Locomotive, Carriage & Waggon Superintendent, James Pearson, a two-tone livery was adopted. The upper panels were painted a lighter brown colour which had a distinctive 'pinky' hue, whilst the lower panels remained dark brown – this is often referred to as the 'cinnamon & coffee bean' livery. However, in 1874, the board of the B&ER directed that a revision to the all-over brown livery should be made. The wording of this instruction is slightly ambiguous, however, for it states '*a single shade of brown now relieved with black*'. Presumably this implies that the raised beading on the coach sides should be picked out in black? Lettering, at least from 1874, was executed in gold.

Therefore, for the very short time that the B&ER worked the Devon & Somerset Railway, before absorption by the GWR in 1876, coaching stock might have been seen sporting either the cinnamon & coffee bean or the dark brown & black liveries.

A pair of B&ER coaches in cinnamon & coffee bean livery, photographed at Plymouth Millbay circa 1870. ***Brian Arman collection***

Without doubt the best photograph of what would be a representative B&ER passenger train of the period during which they operated the D&SR is this superb circa 1875 view at Portishead. With B&ER 4-4-0 tank No. 48 at the head, the first vehicle is a five-compartment Second in all over brown livery, with the luggage compartment in the centre. Next is a four-compartment First of 1849 vintage, in the two-tone livery, which has been modified with a second roof over the original and grab handles on the doors. This is followed by a five-compartment Second of 1853-56, again in two-tone livery and with a central luggage compartment, and then we have a short, five-compartment Third possibly converted from a coach of very early construction originally. Finally, the last vehicle is a 28ft First/Second Composite of 1866-67, with the two First Class compartments in the centre, flanked by luggage and then Second Class compartments either side. This coach, too, has a double roof and the louvres visible in the doors of several of these carriages indicate the presence of dog lockers behind. Pulley wheels and eyelets for the communication cord can be seen fixed to the edge of the carriage roofs. No. 48 was one of the first batch of six of these engines built for the B&ER by Rothwell & Co. between October 1855 and January 1856, which were smaller than later members of the class from other manufacturers. It became GWR No. 2029 and was the first of the class withdrawn in March 1879. ***Brian Arman collection***

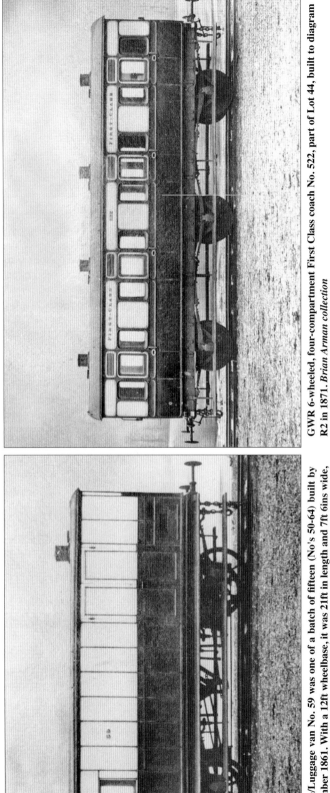

GWR 4-wheeled Brake/Luggage van No. 59 was one of a batch of fifteen (No's 50-64) built by Wright & Son in December 1861. With a 12ft wheelbase, it was 21ft in length and 7ft 6ins wide, and was condemned in January 1900. *Brian Arman collection*

GWR 6-wheeled, four-compartment First Class coach No. 522, part of Lot 44, built to diagram R2 in 1871. *Brian Arman collection*

GWR 6-wheeled Brake Third coach No. 1278 was part of Lot 149, built to diagram T38 in 1877. *Brian Arman collection*

GWR 6-wheeled four-compartment Third Class coach No. 1098 was part of Lot 205, built to diagram S3 in 1880. *Brian Arman collection*

1881-1900

It is not possible to be specific about the types of coaching stock in use on the line in the early narrow or standard gauge era. The GWR owned a large quantity of 4-wheeled carriages, some of which were of considerable vintage, many having been acquired from railways previously taken over by the company, such as the West Midland Railway and the two Shrewsbury companies. The Bristol & Exeter Railway also had a small stock of standard gauge vehicles which might well have found their way on to Devon & Somerset metals. Regrettably, no photographic evidence is available to us but it is suspected that a typical train of the 1881-85 period would have presented a quite antiquated appearance.

Towards the end of the 1880s, newer 4- and 6-wheeled coaches would have become available, as they were replaced on main line duties by more modern stock. These would have provided higher levels of comfort, a much smoother ride and would also have presented a much more uniform appearance, whilst gas lighting replaced oil. The GWR owned a large number of coaches of these types of many different 'diagrams', so once again due to the lack of photographic evidence, it is impossible to be specific. Coaches of all three classes, *i.e.* First, Second and Third, would have been found in most, if not all, trains. Some would be Composites and tri-Composites were not unknown. In this era, brake vehicles would normally be found at both the front and rear of each train, though as the vacuum brake was progressively fitted to older stock the necessity to provide braking at each end of the train declined. A selection of coaches likely to have been seen on the line is shown on page 514, opposite.

In terms of passenger comfort, coaches built in the mid-19th century, unless a First Class fare could be afforded, might be termed basic for Second Class passengers and downright spartan for those in Third Class, where a wooden bench seat lit by one or, if you were lucky, two dim oil lamps per coach was all that you could hope to expect.

By the 1880s, newer vehicles offered better passenger facilities in Third Class, an upholstered bench seat in red moquette being the norm, whilst Second Class passengers were offered greater leg room and deeper padding. Upholstery was a dark emerald green. First Class travellers could luxuriate in deeply padded seating with individual armrests, all finished in royal blue plush. Toilets, however, were still a provision of the future, unless one was rich enough to afford a Family Saloon, which had to be booked in advance.

The GWR was slow to abolish Second Class accommodation on its trains, unlike some of its competitors and it lingered on routes to the north of Shrewsbury until May 1910. It disappeared in South Wales and the West of England in October 1909, having been in decline for many years.

1901-1922

By the turn of the century, old 4-wheeled passenger stock had largely been phased out and 6-wheeled coaches in five-vehicle formations usually worked local services on the line during this period, with additional coaches, often bogie clerestories, as required. At this time all coaches on the branch were normally non-corridor, even the through coaches from Paddington, all of which were detached at Taunton and went through to Ilfracombe.

Whilst the local services were still utilitarian, new coaching stock designs, especially for main line routes, became more elegant. These better carriages would have appeared on the through trains, which usually comprised Brake tri-Composite coaches or gangwayed-corridor stock. For some of this period, 4-wheeled coaches were still in use, some with side lamps, but Swindon had stopped building them at the end of 1902. Through coach workings between 1902 and 1905 can be summarised as follows.

In the summer of 1902, for example, there was the 9.00am to Penzance, which carried two coaches for Ilfracombe – a luggage tri-Composite and a Brake Third with four compartments; the 11.35am to Kingswear, which did not stop at Taunton, instead slipped there a slip tri-Composite and a luggage tri-Composite for Ilfracombe plus, on Saturdays only, a Third for Taunton; and the 3.00pm to Plymouth which conveyed one Brake tri-Composite for Ilfracombe that returned on the 7.20am the next day. The coaches from the 9.00 and 11.35 trains were returned to Paddington on the 11.20am from Ilfracombe. At Taunton, the slip coach was detached to be added to the rear of the 11.42am from Newton Abbot to Paddington, from which it was then slipped at Reading.

In addition to the above, the 1.10pm from Paddington to Plymouth had a Second and Third Class Composite and a four-compartment Brake Third detached at Taunton, which the next day were sent to Ilfracombe on the 3.15pm train, returning to Paddington on the third day on the 11.20am. So the 11.20 from Ilfracombe consisted of at least five bogie clerestory coaches as far as Taunton. In the winter of 1902-03, there were no through coaches to or from London.

For the 1903 summer time table, the main change was the introduction of through coaches, a Brake tri-Composite and a three-compartment Brake Third which had left Birkenhead at 8.55am bound for Ilfracombe. The 11.35am to Kingswear now carried one slip tri-Composite from Paddington and another attached at Bath, both for Ilfracombe and slipped coupled together at Taunton. The Brake tri-Composite on the 1.10pm was sent on to Ilfracombe on the 7.06pm that day. The slip coach from Bath was sent back as far as Barnstaple on the 7.25pm and then on to Taunton on the 7.30am the next day, while the slip coach from Paddington left Ilfracombe on the 7.30am for Taunton. The Ilfracombe to Paddington train now left at 12.10pm and conveyed the two Birkenhead coaches as far as Bristol, along with the two coaches off the 9.00am and the Brake tri-Composite off the 1.10pm.

Few photographs exist showing passenger services on the line in the Edwardian era, prior to 1914. This enlargement from a view that appeared in Volume 1 shows a '517' Class 0-4-2T at Dulverton circa 1905, with a six coach train of 4-wheeled stock. ***Courtesy Great Western Society***

It is likely that the 'Dean Goods' at the head of these two coaches at Barnstaple GWR station circa 1911 had brought them back from South Junction, where they had been detached from an Ilfracombe-bound train. Nearest the camera is a Diagram H2 Dining car, whilst the other coach is a 70ft Brake Composite, to diagram E78, unable to go beyond Barnstaple Junction due to its length. ***Courtesy National Railway Museum***

There were some minor changes in 1904, with the 11.35am reverting to a slip tri-Composite plus a Second/Third Composite and there were no coaches for Ilfracombe on the 1.10pm from Paddington. The through train from Ilfracombe to Paddington now left at 12.15pm and consisted of the two Birkenhead coaches – which were now deposited at Taunton for collection by the 8.30am from Penzance to Crewe – the Composite off the 11.35am and the two coaches off the 9.00am train. Also starting in October 1904 and continuing until the 1905 July summer time table, the 11.35am Kingswear train slipped a tri-Composite at Taunton for Ilfracombe, which then departed Taunton at 3.57pm. It returned the next day on the 9.15am from Ilfracombe and was attached to the 1.00pm from Taunton, being slipped at Reading.

In 1905, there was a time table shake up: the 'Cornish Riviera Express Limited' started running, whilst the Ilfracombe line got a through train from Paddington at 10.15am instead of the coaches on the 9.00am train. The 1905 'CRE' did not convey any slip coaches, being a six-coach train which left Paddington at 10.10am. However, there was a new through train to Ilfracombe leaving Paddington five minutes later which included corridor coaches, the first time they were programmed to appear on the Barnstaple Branch. The 'CRE' first carried a slip coach for Ilfracombe in October 1906, when it began running all year round, but this facility did not operate in the summer when the 10.15am through train to Ilfracombe ran.

The formation of the new through train on leaving Taunton was (all 8-wheeled stock): a non-corridor Third (attached at Taunton), with corridor coaches from Paddington comprising a Third, a Composite, a passenger Brake van for Ilfracombe and a non-corridor Brake tri-Composite for Barnstaple. In addition, from Taunton to Barnstaple, 6-wheeled stock added comprised a Composite, a Third and a passenger Brake van. The 11.35am, as the previous summer, slipped a slip tri-Composite and for Ilfracombe at Taunton, whilst the 12.25pm Penzance and the 3.03pm to Taunton each conveyed a Brake tri-Composite also for Ilfracombe, the latter at its head.

In addition there were a Brake Third (three-compartments) and a Brake tri-Composite from Birkenhead (8.15am) to Ilfracombe; a

A GWR 'Coupé' coach at Barnstaple GWR in 1926 – note the elliptical main roof and arc-roofed clerestory. The coach does not have lower step boards but has steps mounted on the outer end of each bogie. ***Courtesy National Railway Museum***

GWR Brake tri-Composite from Manchester (8.35am) for Barnstaple and a GWR Brake tri-Composite from Liverpool (7.05pm) for Ilfracombe.

Trains on the branch returning through coaches from Ilfracombe to Paddington were:

8.00am – Brake tri-Composite.

9.15am – Brake tri-Composite, slip tri-Composite for 1.00pm Taunton.

9.55am – Brake tri-Composite (for Manchester).

12.17pm – Brake tri-Composite, Brake Third (for Birkenhead), Second/Third Composite (from 11th July), plus corridor coaches: Third, Composite passenger Brake van. Plus, from Barnstaple, Brake tri-Composite for Paddington and Brake tri-Composite for Liverpool.

Dining cars seem first to have appeared on the branch in summer 1907, when the 11.50am from Paddington to Kingswear slipped three coaches at Taunton: a corridor slip tri-Composite for Ilfracombe and a Dining car plus a corridor Brake Third for Barnstaple. In 1908, a three- or four-coach portion was slipped at Taunton, comprising a slip Composite (a 56ft First/Third), a Dining car, a First/Third Composite (when required) and a van Third, all for Ilfracombe, the last two coaches being worked back to Barnstaple on the 6.15pm train.

The GWR abolished Second Class entirely in October 1909, so after that date all Brake Composites were First/Third; what had been Second/Third Composites became all Thirds and were renumbered.

All of the through coaches between Paddington and Ilfracombe/Barnstaple had been 8-wheelers since the summer of 1892 at least. All 'Toplight' coaches were 8-wheeled and, except for slip coaches and some London and Birmingham suburban stock, all were also corridor coaches. Steel underframes had been introduced with the 'Dreadnought' carriages and were used on all subsequent stock, except for the 70ft Sleeping cars of 1907. Steel panelling (on wooden framing) appeared circa 1914 on the 'Toplight' coaches and after the First World War it began to be used for repairs to wooden panelled carriages.

Toplight coaches built between 1907 and 1920 of 56ft, 57ft and 70ft length were used on the line on the more prominent trains. A clerestory Dining car (Diagram 'H2') was used on the Paddington to Ilfracombe train in the early 1900s, along with a 70ft Brake Composite coach (Diagram 'E78'), these being detached at South Junction (these operations are discussed in the next chapter) and shunted in to Barnstaple GWR, where they were stabled until being collected by the return service.The 70ft steel-panelled stock (with roof boards) were introduced and these would also run as far as Barnstaple GWR or SR. The route beyond Barnstaple SR to Ilfracombe was unable to accommodate these longer coaches, mainly due to the radius and confines of the curved iron bridge crossing the River Taw leading to Barnstaple Town station.

Two predominant slip coaches working the line at the time were the Bars 1 (referring to the underframe bracing) single-ended Composite Toplights. Constructed in 1908 to Lot No. 1150, No's 7101 and 7102 were thought to have been built specifically for the Paddington to Barnstaple and Ilfracombe service and they were working that route by 1911. They were 57ft in length and were equipped with 8ft bogies and six vacuum reservoirs. The guard's end was equipped with a foot-operated motor horn, which would have been replaced in the mid-1920s by an auto-gong similar to that used on auto coaches. They also had electric lighting and steam heating.

As passengers travelling in slip coaches were isolated from the rest of the train, this was countered on the Ilfracombe slip before the Second World War with a four-coach slip portion including a Restaurant car, whilst a Brake Third was also included in the formation. The 11.50am Paddington departure, the 'Torbay Express', contained this four-coach unit and the slipped set would go forwards on the 2.40pm Taunton to Ilfracombe and return the following day on the 9.48am Ilfracombe to Paddington. Slip coaches were identified by the signalman by double tail lamps, with one lens surrounded by a red disc and the other by a white one (this description replaced the earlier lamp identification at the turn of the 20th century). Slip apparatus on coaches No's 7101 and 7102 was removed in 1918 and restored in 1921. However, when the slip apparatus was removed subsequently (No. 7101 in May 1942 and No. 7102, in October 1940), it was never replaced. No. 7102 was condemned in December 1954 and No. 7101 in November 1957.

SLIP COACHES

Slip coaches were first operated in 1858, the concept being that one or more coaches could be detached from a speeding express train, thus enabling it to operate non-stop but still serve the main intermediate stations and certain branch lines without passengers having to change trains. Each slip portion (of which there may have been several in a train) was controlled by a guard and was isolated from the rest of the train, as they had no gangway communication.

In order to separate the portion to be slipped from the main train a special coupling connection was required, in the form of a hinged drawhook on the slip coach. The screw coupling of the normal coach would be placed in the hinged drawhook, which would be closed by hand and kept closed by a bolt. This bolt was connected to a slip lever, the upper end of which was in the guard's compartment.

In addition to the modification to the couplings, the brake attachments had to be modified to enable the brake pipes to separate and be closed without the automatic brakes coming on. Various developments took place to improve the separation of the brake pipes, which usually required the guard to lean out of the slip coach and physically detach them with a handle. Once the slip had been detached, the application of the brake on the slip portion by the guard was originally by handbrake and then vacuum brake using vacuum reservoirs attached to the underframe of the slip coaches, which enabled more control to be exercised.

Steam heating also posed a challenge; the pressurised steam heating pipes between the main train and the slip coach were located lower down between carriages so the guard could not reach down to detach them. In addition, without some form of seal, the steam would escape out of the open pipe. In 1906, a valve was developed and patented which enabled the steam pipes to separate and automatically seal. This was also adapted to enable the brake pipes to self-seal, removing the need for the guard to lean out to separate the pipes.

In order to slip the coach, the guard would raise a catch (lock) on the drawhook lever in his compartment and then would then pull the lever towards him as far as possible. The bolt on the coupling would be withdrawn, the slip hook would open, the coupling on the main coach drop away and the two coaches separate, with the brakes also being applied to the slip portion. This would slow the separated slip portion and the guard would then move the drawhook lever back to a central position, which would activate the vacuum reservoirs, the brakes would release and the slip would start to coast. The guard would bring the coach to a halt at the required place using the slip lever. This new slip apparatus was introduced in 1909.

Slip coach operation ceased during both world wars. In 1914, the GWR operated seventy slip services daily but this had reduced to thirty-five by 1931. Some coaches were single slips, with the guard's operating compartment at only one end, double slips being introduced subsequently for more flexibility of operation. Surplus slip coaches were often employed on branch line duties after their main line use diminished.

In 1905, the 'Cornish Riviera Limited' express appeared in time tables with slips for Weymouth, Taunton and Exeter – the Taunton portion carried on to Ilfracombe. By 1939, coaches were slipped at Taunton for Minehead and Ilfracombe. Slip coach operation ceased on BR in 1960.

1923-1947

From the early 1920s through to 1930, there was still a four-coach, 4-wheeled, close-coupled set working the line on two return trips per day. These sets had a Brake at both ends, each with a guard's ducket in the middle of the coach. Passenger running boards also were fitted along the side of the coach between the sets of wheels. However, the majority of the branch trains were now formed of a pair of Brake Composites (8-wheeled stock), to which were added any through slip coaches, additional coaches when required or other vans, including horse boxes or stores vans. Clerestory coaches would be added to a set of four 4-wheeled coaches and 8-wheeled Collett corridor stock, forming a train of seven-plus coaches, for example. Some trains would be comprised of only clerestory coaches (usually four, of which two would be Brake Composites). A corridor train of three coaches operated the 7.55am from Taunton to Barnstaple Junction, returning as part of the 9.55am Ilfracombe to Paddington service. Ilfracombe to Paddington trains were often comprised of 8-wheeled corridor coaches. Toplight 8-wheeled bogie coaches were also used at this time, usually in a set of six with two Brake Thirds as part of the consist. Toplights would also be mixed in with clerestory coaches on some services. Photographs of various of these coaches in use on the line can be found on pages 139, 147 and 149-156 of Volume 1, as well as in this and the following chapter, which also, along with **Appendix 17**, covers the stock that was used on through services, including coaches from other railway companies which worked along the line from up-country (including the LM&SR, Great Central Railway and others).

RIGHT: 'Bulldog' No. 3371 *Sir Massey Lopes* comes off Castle Hill Viaduct circa 1927, hauling a set of four 4-wheeled wooden coaches with running boards and the guard's duckets in the centre of the first and last vehicles.

BELOW: Seen near Acland Woods, an unidentified Class '45XX' tank heads towards Barnstaple with a train of mixed passenger stock circa 1927.
Both Arthur Halls, courtesy National Railway Museum

A very smart looking 'Mogul' 2-6-0 approaches Ackland Cross with a Barnstaple bound train circa 1926; the locomotive is almost certainly No. 5309 again, which we saw at Barnstaple a little earlier (page 498). The leading 4-wheeled van has oil lamps, so at this date it is probably a hounds van, almost certainly No. 86. This ancient vehicle had been built in 1877 and comprised a new body on an old underframe, being intended for the transport of a hunt's hounds. However, there are no horse boxes on the train, so it may be empty, or being used for other purposes, whilst it also appears to still be in the lake livery of 1912-22. It had two compartments, one for the dogs and the other for a guard and, presumably, for the lads looking after the hounds. There was another like it, No. 46, which was allocated to Badminton. Behind the van is a four-coach, 4-wheeled set, a bogie clerestory coach and three elliptical-roofed bogie coaches. *Arthur Halls, courtesy National Railway Museum*

'Bulldog' No. 3371 *Sir Massey Lopes* again, shunting a clerestory corridor Brake Third coach at Barnstaple Junction in the late 1920s. *Arthur Halls, courtesy National Railway Museum*

'Mogul' No. 6344 heads another mixed coaching stock train illustrating the variety of stock in use. The two clerestory coaches leading are followed, probably, by two Toplights (they have canvas covered roofs) with passenger boards, then another clerestory, along with a further four or five probably Collett coaches at the rear. The train has just passed through the arch of Newport Bridge on the Barnstaple Branch, heading towards Barnstaple Junction. *Arthur Halls, courtesy National Railway Museum*

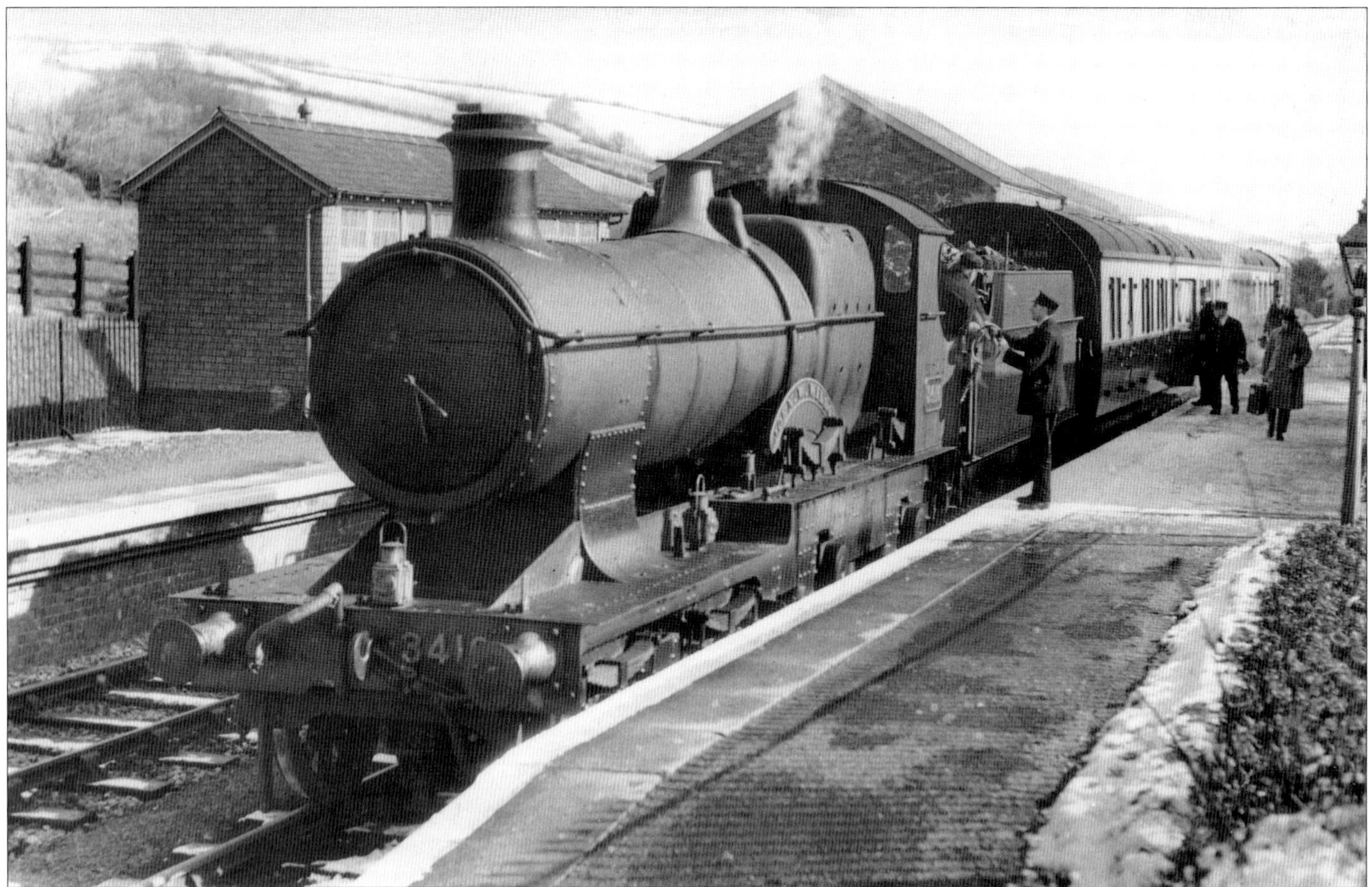

'Bulldog' No. 3416 *John W. Wilson* on a Down train comprised of a 'B-set' and what appears to be a horse box on the rear, at Swimbridge in the mid-1930s. The locomotive was originally No. 3706 but was renumbered in 1912 and withdrawn in May 1936, not long after this photograph was taken. The signalman is exchanging the token with the fireman and the steam heating is evident from the coaches in this snowy scene. *Courtesy National Railway Museum*

During this era, steel underframes were incorporated into newly built coaches but they still had wooden bodies. However, steel sided coaches were also being developed and, in the late 1920s, the Collett 56ft stock began appearing from Swindon and in time these would be used on the line. Clerestory coaches were still regularly seen on the D&SR, usually being added to other coaches such as an E116 'B-set' (as shown in the photograph earlier in this chapter on page 486).

The staple coaching stock on branch lines in this period became the 'B-set'. Between the wars, it became GWR policy to provide two-coach sets of modern, non-gangwayed, close-coupled, Brake Composite coaches. They were between 57ft and 61ft in length (depending on the construction lot) and of all-steel construction. The 'B-set' was the designation in Bristol and other south-west divisions, which was in accordance with the GWR policy of identifying standard formations. These sets were to be mainly used on branch line and secondary rural stopping services. The sets had two First Class compartments, giving a total of sixteen seats and ten or twelve Third Class compartments, giving another 100 or 120 seats. They were ideal for use where there was a significant demand for luggage accommodation and a modest requirement for First Class seating. Equally, they were suited to longer runs, where most of the stations were staffed and where reversals of trains were infrequent, and, accordingly, the Taunton to Barnstaple route fitted these requirements. There were no lavatories in the sets, which was just about acceptable for the meandering journey all the way to Barnstaple for those starting at Taunton.

They were steel-panelled in Collett style, with a steel roof and close-coupled. They were brought in to use in the period 1924-1936 but it has not been established with any certainty when they first started appearing on D&SR, although the picture on page 486 indicates that

TABLE 10.15: TAUNTON 'B-SET' ALLOCATION 1930-31

TAUNTON NO.	COACH NO'S	TARE (T-CWT)	DATE WRITTEN
1	6979-80	30-10	13th Sept. 1930
2	6986-87	30-10	13th Sept. 1930
3	6995-96	30-10	13th Sept. 1930
4	6999-7000	30-10	13th Sept. 1930
5	6240-41	30-10	2nd May 1931
6	6261-62	30-10	2nd May 1931
7	6365-66	30-10	2nd May 1931
8	6371-72	30-10	2nd May 1931

TABLE 10.16: TAUNTON/BARNSTAPLE THROUGH COACHES 1936

STOCK	TIME	TRAIN
Brake Compo X	1.30pm	Paddington to Taunton
(London)	4.30pm	Taunton to Barnstaple Jct.
	6.37pm	Barnstaple Jct. to Ilfracombe
	9.50am	Ilfracombe to Paddington (next day)
Siphon G	10.35pm	Paddington to Taunton SX
(London)	7.50am	Taunton to Barnstaple MX
	6.12pm	Barnstaple to Taunton SX
	8.40pm	Taunton to Paddington SX
Van Third X	6.30pm	Paddington to Plymouth
Compo X	4.25pm	Plymouth to Taunton (next day)
Van Third X	7.50am	Taunton to Barnstaple Jct. (next day)
(London)	10.39am	Barnstaple Jct. to Paddington (attached to 9.50am Ilfracombe to Paddington)

Table 10.17: Taunton to Barnstaple Line Coaching Diagrams Sept. 1937

No. 17	
5.40pm	Taunton to Barnstaple Junction
7.50pm SX	Barnstaple Junction to Barnstaple (to form next day diagram 18, see below)
8.35pm SO	Barnstaple Junction to South Molton
9.45pm SO	South Molton to Barnstaple
Notes	The stock comprises Van Third X, Compo X, Third X which arrived on the 1.05pm Swindon to Taunton service (part of diagram 15). See diagram 18 below.
No. 18	
6.55am	Barnstaple to Taunton
Notes	Stock as diagram 17 above (return working). Will form part of diagram 19, 10.15am Taunton to Swindon.
No. 92 ('B-set'), set 100 previous day	
12.30pm	Barnstaple Junction to Ilfracombe*
1.40pm	Ilfracombe to Taunton*
6.30pm	Taunton to Minehead
8.10pm	Minehead to Taunton
Notes	Will form set 93 next day. *Compo X attached
No. 93 ('B-set'), set 92 previous day	
Notes	The set did not work the Barnstaple branch but started by working the 7.20am Taunton to Minehead and 9.20am return, then to Yeovil (returning to Langport and back to Yeovil SO), then back to Taunton and Minehead, return to Taunton and back to Yeovil. It formed set 100 the following day (see below).
No. 94 ('B-set'), set 99 previous day	
8.45am	Barnstaple to Taunton*
2.50pm	Taunton to Minehead
4.25pm	Minehead to Taunton
5.58pm	Taunton to Yeovil
7.33pm	Yeovil to Taunton
Notes	Forms set No. 99 next day. * Compo X attached for 1.10pm Taunton Down train.
No. 99 ('B-set'), set 94 previous day	
7.10am	Taunton to Yeovil
9.20am	Yeovil to Taunton
1.10pm	Taunton to Barnstaple Junction Y, *, $
3.58pm	Barnstaple Junction to Taunton *$
8.17pm	Taunton to Barnstaple $
Notes	Forms set 94 next day. Y= Slip Paddington to Ilfracombe arriving off 10.30am Paddington, returning 9.50am from Ilfracombe *= Van SX, Third SO, Taunton to Barnstaple Junction and back, next engine leaving Taunton. $ = Compo X arriving and returning at 8.45am (see 94 above)
No. 100 ('B-set'), Set 93 previous day	
7.38am	Yeovil to Taunton
10.45am	Taunton to Minehead
1.15pm	Minehead to Taunton
4.30pm	Taunton to Barnstaple *
Notes	Forms set 92 next day (see above). * Brake Compo X, 1.30pm Paddington to Ilfracombe for 6.37pm Barnstaple Junction to Ilfracombe, returning 9.50pm Ilfracombe to Paddington. Compo X, Taunton to Barnstaple Junction, next set (101), arriving 1.40pm Ilfracombe for 12.30pm Barnstaple Junction (see below)
No. 101 ('B-set')	
7.20am	Taunton to Langport West
8.00am	Langport West to Taunton
10.35am	Taunton to Barnstaple Junction *
5.40pm	Barnstaple Junction to Taunton E, *
Notes	E= Siphon G, SX, Barnstaple to Paddington, arriving 7.50am Taunton (see below, 111) for 8.40pm Taunton to Paddington. *= Compo X, Taunton to Barnstaple Junction and back.
No. 111	
7.50am	Taunton to Barnstaple Junction
Notes	Siphon G MX, Paddington to Barnstaple arriving 10.35pm Paddington returning 6.12pm Barnstaple. Comprising Van Third X, Compo X, Van Third 70 ft stock, arrving 4.25pm Plymouth, returning 10.39am Barnstaple Junction to Paddington.

THE 'B-SET' DESIGNATION

Divisional books of local coach workings had lists of common (local) coach formations, each of which was denoted by a letter. The listed formations could vary between divisions and from time to time in individual divisions. It just so happens that when the pairs of Brake Composites became common they were usually designated with the letter 'B' and the expression has become common knowledge and generally adopted, but in the Birmingham and Worcester District books they actually appeared as 'D-sets'.

they were in use on the line by 1927. Whilst all sets appeared outwardly very similar, there were six different designs, the earliest (1924-1929) being of 57ft-58ft length, the 1930 to 1933 productions of 61ft 2ins length and slightly wider at 9ft 3ins and the latter ones from 1933 being 57ft long and 9ft wide. By the late 1930s, all local services were formed of 'B-sets', sometimes supplemented by an additional coach.

Most of the regular branch services were lightly loaded, with two or three coaches thus giving a relatively easy task for a 'Mogul' or similar locomotive to haul. At this time, the 'B-sets' worked the circuit of branches around Taunton (Minehead, Chard, Yeovil and Barnstaple) but were strengthened with other coaching stock as necessary, as well as being used on local main line services. **Table 10.15** shows the 'B-sets' allocated to Taunton in the 1930s (from Diagram 140).

A summary of through coaches on the branch in this period is given in **Table 10.16.** The *GWR Rule Book* (1936) stated that 60ft by 9ft were the maximum permitted dimensions of coaches allowed over the line to Ilfracombe and no coaches with lower centre-step boards would be accepted. As 70ft carriages were prohibited, the slip on the Ilfracombe portion of the 'Cornish Riviera' was a 60ft coach.

A review of the programme for the Exeter and Plymouth Divisions showing the working of passenger coaches from 27th September 1937, reveals the following information. There were nine coaching diagrams that involved the branch, as set out in **Table 10.17**. The bulk of the workings were 'B-sets', comprising a Van Composite 'A' and Van Composite 'B', with sixteen First Class seats and one hundred Third Class. Brake Thirds had a brake compartment in the centre, whilst those with Van ends are described as Van Thirds. Those marked 'X' are corridor stock and all vehicles were 8-wheeled unless otherwise indicated. Spare coaches to meet contingencies were kept at Barnstaple. Incidentally, the 'A' and 'B' designations applied to van/brake ended coaches in the coach programmes: 'B' meant

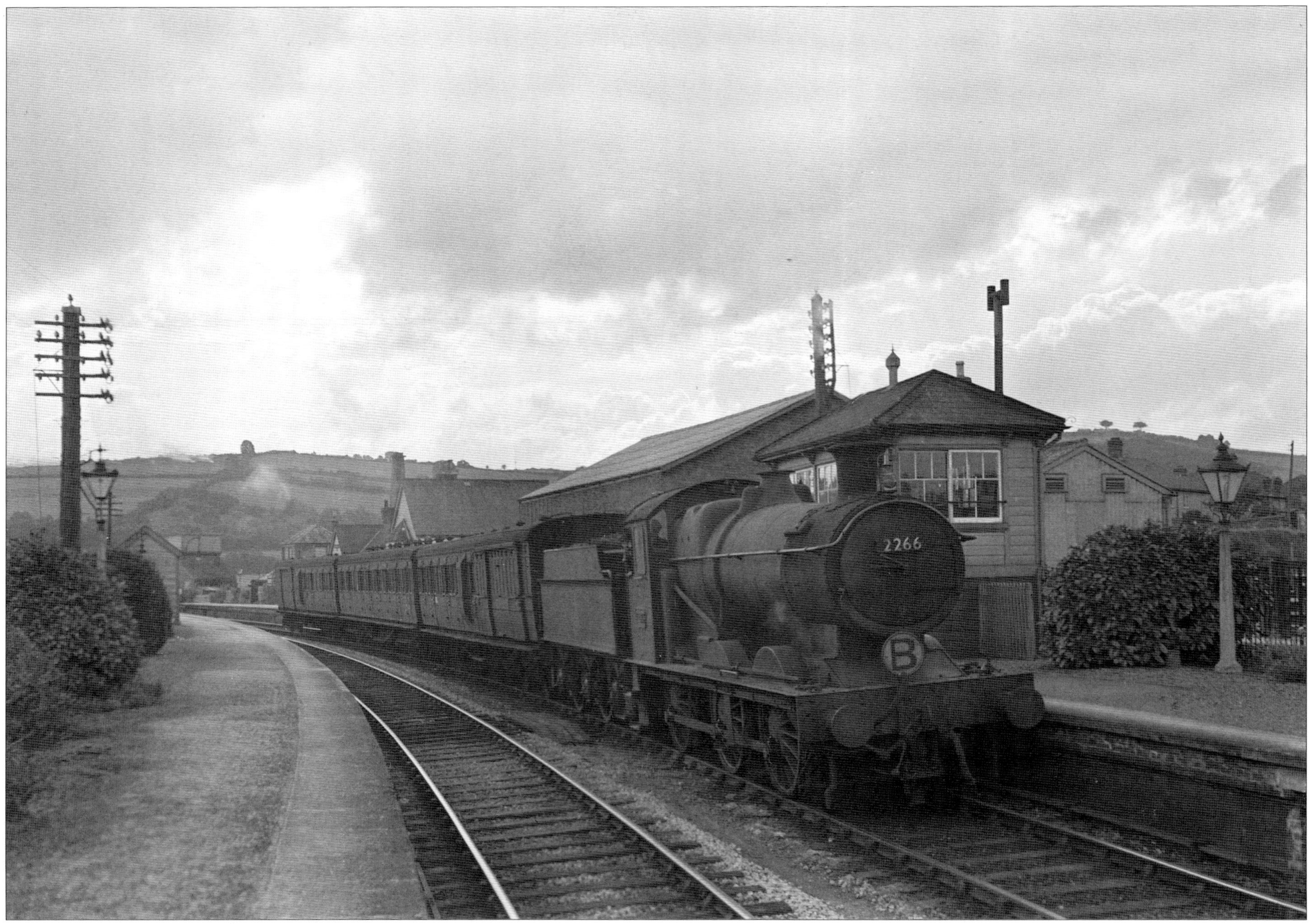

Collett 0-6-0 No. 2266 pauses at Wiveliscombe on 13th September 1952 with a Taunton-bound train, comprised of an ex-London & South Western Railway three-coach set. Note the red 'B' in a white disc on the front of the locomotive, providing an indication to the Norton Fitzwarren signalman when No. 2266 reached that complicated three-way junction that it was a Barnstaple line train.
Roger J. Sellick, courtesy National Railway Museum

No. 7333 heads towards the Tone Viaduct and Taunton with the 12.25pm from Ilfracombe to Taunton on Saturday 7th September 1963, with a five-coach train that includes a Gresley Brake Third nearest the engine, followed by three BR Mk 1 coaches and, possibly, a passenger Brake van bringing up the rear. Based at Taunton from June 1960, the 'Mogul' was just weeks away from withdrawal in the October. ***R.A. Lumber, courtesy Dave Mitchell***

the van/brake end was to be leading, whilst 'A' meant the passenger compartments were to be leading and the letters only applied to the journey being undertaken.

Set 104 ('B-set'), which worked between Taunton and Chard/ Chard Junction most of the day was used on Saturdays only for the 11.05pm Taunton to Wiveliscombe and 11.45pm return services. Also, a Taunton auto-trailer was diagrammed to work the 1.35pm Taunton to Wiveliscombe, Thursdays and Saturdays only working. It returned at 2.05pm from Wiveliscombe.

In the period after the Second World War, Bulleid-designed and built his classic SR coaching stock, which would eventually also be seen in use on the Taunton to Barnstaple line from time to time.

1948-1964

By the mid-1950s, 'B-sets' continued to be the basic coaching stock programmed to work the line on the local services. They were often supplemented by an additional coach, a Hawksworth Brake Third or Brake Composite for example. Alternatively, the train might comprise a Van Second/Second/Brake Composite combination. In the late 1950s, 60ft bow-ended sets were popular but, by 1963, the later 57ft 'B-sets' were in evidence. Occasional workings in the early 1950s were comprised of ex-L&SWR wooden, non-corridor, bogie coaching stock, with green-liveried Bulleid 64ft 6ins carriages appearing in the late 1950s and early 1960s. Some trains, especially on summer Saturdays, could be comprised entirely of SR coaches or mixed in with WR stock – see pages 263 and 281 of Volume 2, for example. Collett and Hawksworth main line stock would also be used on summer Saturday through trains.

Of the 613 Hawksworth carriages constructed from 1946, most were built post-Nationalisation and up to 1951. The advent of BR Mark 1 coaches led to the Hawksworth stock being relegated to secondary line work relatively quickly (circa 1956). At 64ft, the coaches were 4ft longer than the Collett 1938 coaching stock, which enabled the vestibules to be enlarged and, with flat sides and sloping roof ends, they were distinctive. They were mounted on 9ft wheelbase, double-bolster, pressed-steel bogies of the type introduced by Collett in the early 1930s. The corridor Thirds (later redesiganted Seconds) had eight compartments to a coach, with two toilets at either end. The third and sixth compartments had external access doors and two small windows, the remaining compartments had picture windows. The Hawksworth corridor Thirds had eight compartments, whilst the Brake Thirds and slip Brakes had seven, Composite Brakes had six and Brake vans only four. All Thirds were later redesignated Seconds.

The main liveries carried were GWR chocolate and cream for the early builds, followed by BR brown and cream, carmine and cream and maroon, whilst two were overhauled in the mid-1960s and reappeared in BR blue and grey.

The BR Mark 1 coaches were built in the 1950s and established a standard length of 63ft 6ins and a width of 8ft 8½ins. They were constructed of steel cladding attached to steel frames built on a steel sub-frame and started to appear on the line on summer Saturday trains in the late 1950s. The last ordinary main line clerestories were withdrawn in 1953 but had not been used on the line some time prior to this.

When the WR discontinued slip coach working in 1960, three redundant Hawksworth slip vehicles were converted back to Brake Composites. No's 7374, 7375 and 7376, were allocated to Taunton from early 1961 and then appeared on the Barnstaple line, as well as the Minehead and Chard branches. No. 7375 remained in BR brown and cream livery but No. 7376 had been painted maroon by 1963. The Western Region ended the use of all non-corridor stock

TABLE 10.18: SUMMARY OF CARRIAGE WORKINGS – SATURDAYS ONLY 16TH JULY-13TH AUGUST 1955

TRAIN	FORMATION	PREVIOUS SERVICE
8.25am Ilfracombe to Manchester	7 LMS corridor coaches	Berthed at Ilfracombe
9.25am Ilfracombe to Cardiff	6 WR corridor coaches	Formed of 5.20am Taunton departure to Ilfracombe (arrives 8.12am)
10.12am Ilfracombe to Taunton	4 WR corridor coaches	Formed of 6.20am Taunton to Ilfracombe service (arrives 9.10am)
10.55am Ilfracombe to Wolverhampton	6 WR corridor coaches	Formed of 7.15am Taunton to Ilfracombe (arrives 9.58am)
5.10pm Ilfracombe to Taunton	4 WR corridor coaches	Formed of 12.50pm Taunton to Ilfracombe (arrives 3.56pm)
5.45pm Ilfracombe to Barnstaple Jct.	2 SR Thirds + 4 WR corridor coaches	8.30am Taunton to Ilfracombe (arrives 11.18am)
6.30pm Ilfracombe to Taunton	6 WR corridor coaches	2.26pm Taunton to Ilfracombe (arrives 5.10pm)
8.00pm Ilfracombe to Taunton	6 WR corridor coaches	3.36pm Taunton to Ilfracombe (arrives 6.16pm)
8.45pm Ilfracombe to Barnstaple Jct.	4 WR corridor coaches	4.35pm Taunton to Ilfracombe (arrives 7.37pm)

(including the 'B-sets') by the end of 1963, so the line's passenger trains then usually comprised three gangwayed ex-GWR coaches, Hawksworth and Collett designed vehicles, including No's 7071 and 7074, 1938-built slip coaches.

The summer Saturday through trains comprised corridor coaches, usually a six-coach set on the Paddington services. Seven LMR coaches (generally of Stanier design) usually made up the Manchester summer Saturdays (only) service from Ilfracombe. From the 1960s, maroon Mark 1 coaches appeared more regularly on the summer Saturday services as the older stock was retired. Table 10.18, above, presents a summary of carriage workings and train formations on the Taunton to Barnstaple line through the summer of 1955, whilst Table 10.19, below, compiled from the *District Controller's View (North Devon)*, summarises summer Saturday carriage workings in the 1960s.

Also classed as passenger stock and attached to certain passenger trains on the line were parcels stock, such as 4- and 6-wheeled Siphons and the 8-wheeled, bogie Siphons G and H. Covered carriage trucks (CCT) and general utility vans (GUVs) also appeared, and horse boxes were regularly conveyed, GWR designs originally but then the more modern BR (WR) design in the latter years from 1958, when No's 96355-96358 were allocated to the WR. With the 'Rabbit Special', racehorses, and hunting horses and hounds, also being transported, a variety of vans could be observed and this is covered further in the relevant sections of Chapter 11 and 12.

Although dedicated milk trains did not run on the line (unlike other local branches), the ubiquitous 6-wheeled milk tank wagons could be seen attached occasionally to passenger services in the 1950s, usually coupled next to the locomotive.

TABLE 10.19: SAMPLE SUMMER SATURDAY CARRIAGE WORKINGS 1960S

LOCATION	TIME (A)	TIME (D)	LOCATION	TIME (A)	TIME (D)
CW4 – Three Western coaches			CW 38 Five Western coaches		
Barnstaple Jct.		6.43am	Taunton		8.30am
Taunton	8.30am	10.25am	Ilfracombe	11.22am	12.25pm
Barnstaple Jct.	12.16pm	12.30pm	Paddington	6.25pm	
Torrington	1.03pm	2.46pm	CW48 – Four Western coaches		
Barnstaple Jct.	3.20pm	3.55pm	Taunton		8.16am
Taunton	6.01pm	8.40pm	Minehead	9.27am	10.05am
Bristol	10.24pm		Taunton	11.19am	12.50pm
CW8 – Four Western coaches			Ilfracombe	3.56pm	5.10pm
Barnstaple Jnc		7.45am	Taunton	7.51pm	
Taunton	9.36am	12.35pm	CW51 – Six Western coaches		
Yeovil	1.54pm	2.32pm	Paddington		11.30am
Taunton	3.42pm	6.15pm	Ilfracombe	5.10pm	6.37pm
Barnstaple Jct.	8.02pm		Taunton	9.21pm	
CW11 – Three Western coaches			CW55 – Six Western coaches		
Barnstaple Jct.		8.13am	Wolverhampton		10.50am
Torrington	8.46am	11.48am	Ilfracombe	6.35pm	8.05pm
Barnstaple Jct.	12.25pm	12.48pm	Taunton	10.30pm	
Taunton	2.30pm		CW56 – Four Western coaches		
CW25 – Nine Midland corridor coaches			Taunton		4.35pm
Ilfracombe		8.30am	Ilfracombe	7.37pm	8.30pm
Manchester Exch.	6.54pm		Ilfracombe*	9.09pm	
CW33 – Eight Western coaches			CW66 – PMV**		
Taunton		5.50am	Yeovil Town***		6.25am
Ilfracombe	7.58am	9.22am	Barnstaple Jct.	10.03am	10.12am
Cardiff	3.37pm		Torrington	10.45am	2.46pm
CW35 – Six Western coaches			Barnstaple Jct.	3.20am	3.55pm
Taunton		6.20am	Taunton/Bristol	6.01pm	
Ilfracombe	9.04am	10.12am	CW84 – Five Western coaches		
Wolverhampton	6.20pm		Taunton		7.25am
CW 37 Eight Western coaches			Minehead	8.32am	9.05am
Taunton		7am	Taunton	10.11am	1.48pm
Ilfracombe	9.42am	11am	Barnstaple	3.36pm	5pm
Wolverhampton	6.40pm		Taunton	6.55pm	

NOTES: *Berthed; **PMV – Parcels & Miscellaneous Van; ***via Exeter

WAGONS

In the early days of the line, the variety of wagons were limited, so some of the broad types available at that time are easily described. Wagons were usually 4-wheeled and although timber was used in construction, iron was also popular. Open wagons were plentiful but box wagons developed. There was a 21ft 8ins iron-sided box wagon, for example, which had doors at each end. There was a smaller 17ft version of all iron construction with side doors and there were also tilting wagons, 17ft long, of all iron construction, with side doors, 4ft wheels and 7ft in width. Such wagons at this time usually had no brakes. The B&ER livery at this early stage was grey, with the initials and wagon number on the bottom left-hand side of the wagon, as well as on the ends.

After the line had been converted from broad to standard gauge, wagons lettered for other railway companies began to be regularly seen, through the pre-Grouping and 'Big Four' eras and especially later on as the common user method of increasing the efficient utilisation of wagons developed.

The nature of the goods wagons used on the D&SR clearly reflects the type of merchandise carried and the fact that the line served what was an almost exclusively agricultural area. As can be seen from the tonnages carried (see each station's summary in Chapters 6, 7 and 8 of Volume 2) the traffic at the stations varied widely. Most would receive coal in wooden open

Right: The only glimpse we have of a broad gauge goods train on the line is this view of GWR 0-6-0ST No. 2060 or 2062 (both were rebuilds of B&ER 0-6-0 tender engines) at South Molton circa 1880. The train is in fact a mixed working, with a carriage visible towards the rear but none of the wagons are positively identifiable, although they look to be of a mix, with possibly a carriage truck at the front and a selection of opens behind.
Courtesy South Molton Museum

wagons, which were superceded in later years by 16-ton steel open wagons. General merchandise for delivery and despatch would be loaded in wooden box vans and the occasional GW 'Iron Mink'. Agricultural provisions such as feedstuffs and fertiliser would be transported in box vans. Most stations received such goods but Wiveliscombe, Dulverton and South Molton dealt with the largest tonnages. Dulverton would see the despatch of tree trunks on bogie flat wagons, along with pit props and sawn timber in open wagons. South Molton also received 4-wheeled tank wagons for the Shell Mex private siding and Barnstaple had a substantial oil depot which, over the years it was in use, was served by tank wagons belonging to the Anglo-American Oil Co., Pratts Oils, Shell-Mex, BP, Esso and National Benzole. Agricultural equipment would occasionally be delivered on short wheelbase 4-wheeled flat wagons.

Below: Pictures of B&ER wagons are rare but here we see an example of a sheeted hooped open wagon at Plymouth Millbay station circa 1870. Note the end lettering.
Brian Arman collection

Below: Southern Railway 'E1R' Class 0-6-2T No. B94 looks immaculate in lined condition as it shunts the yard at Barnstaple Junction circa 1930. Built in November 1883 at the London, Brighton & South Coast Railway's Brighton Works as 'E' Class No. 94 *Shorwell*, the locomotive returned there for rebuilding to 'E1R' Class in May 1927, one of ten 'E' Class that were to be so treated specifically for working in the West Country. The rebuilding involved lengthening the frames at the rear to incorporate an enlarged bunker and an additional 348-gallon water tank but also provided sufficient space for an improved South Eastern & Chatham Railway-style cab to be fitted as well. The locomotive lost its B-prefix when it was renumbered in 1931, becoming SR No. 2094, and was withdrawn in April 1955 carrying BR No. 32094. Although apparently a Southern scene, No. B94 is shunting Taunton-based GWR 'Toad' brake van No. 17852, which would have arrived here via the D&SR. *Brian Perkes, Lesley Walker collection*

LEFT: **W. Sanders & Son of South Molton purchased their first wagon new from the Gloucester Railway Carriage & Wagon Company in September 1898. A seven-year payment plan was agreed, which included repairing the wagon when required. The livery was plain black with white lettering. William Sanders was a local man, born in 1846 and was also a coucillor and, for a time Mayor of South Molton. The business was still trading in 1944.**
Courtesy Gloucestershire Archives

BELOW: **A poor quality but rare view of two Goodlands wagons being unloaded at an unknown location probably around 1890; note that both wagons have dumb buffers.**
Courtesy Martin Bird

Cattle markets were located adjacent to some of the stations, such as Dulverton and Molland, which along with South Molton and Wiveliscombe thus saw substantial requirements for cattle wagons. Barnstaple, being the major station for goods arrival and despatch of products from local industry, is covered in Chapter 13, Recollections, which gives a good flavour of what wagons would be needed to facilitate transport of those items.

During the GWR standard gauge era, from the late 1880s and up to Nationalisation, a variety of private owner wagons would also have been seen, although only a few belonged to users based at stations on the line, such as William Sanders & Son, a builder and contractor based at South Molton and the coal and builders' merchants Henry Shapcott & Co., who had depots at Bishops Nympton & Molland and at South Molton.

C. Goodland & Sons, who became Goodlands Ltd in 1912 and had several depots in the area, including one at Dulverton on the D&SR line. Although Goodlands had their own fleet of wagons, coal from the collieries at Parkend and Foxes Bridge in the Forest of Dean was delivered in wagons belonging to these pits, as seen in the picture on page 134 of Volume 1. House coal from the small Forest of Dean coalfield was in fact well known in the North Devon/West Somerset area, being delivered coastwise for approaching 150 years from Lydney to numerous West Country harbours, including Bridgwater, Watchet, Barnstaple, Combe Martin and Ilfracombe. Such was Goodlands' connection with the Forest of Dean that they had five wagons built there in 1886 but as output from this area declined in the 1930s, the company looked elsewhere for their coal, to collieries near Stoke on Trent. The company took over several other small coal factors and general merchants over the years and traded as builders merchants up to around 2012. Photographs of their wagons are extremely scarce.

Over the years, the wagons regularly seen on the line comprised: wooden ventilated box vans, 'Mica' vans (for meat), 'Iron Mink' vans, cattle wagons, 10/12-ton wooden-sided coal wagons and 16-ton steel-sided opens, a range of wooden open wagons from 2-planks up to 7-planks, 'Con-flat' wagons carrying containers (both types A and B), 4-wheeled oil tank wagons (Esso, Shell-Mex, National Benzole, etc), 6-wheeled, 3,000 gallon, glass-lined milk tanks (usually conveyed in passenger trains), horse boxes (again, usually conveyed in passenger trains), and 'Siphon G' and 'Siphon H' parcels wagons.

As the wagons were largely unbraked (or some wagons braked such that goods trains were partially fitted) there would be a GWR 'Toad' brake van attached at the rear, whilst there is photographic evidence of the use of the BR 'Standard' brake van on the line in 1965, on an engine and brake van working to Torrington, as described in Chapter 11 (page 582). Note also, page 249 of Volume 2 does illustrate what appears to be an ex-LM&SR brake van on a short goods train off the branch in the early 1960s.

A summary of standard loads (in tons) of passenger, parcels, milk, and fish trains for engine working purposes, extracted from the GWR Exeter Division Service Time Table July 5th to September 26th (inclusive) 1937, is given in Table 10.20, below.

TABLE 10.20: STANDARD LOADS, IN TONS, FOR PASSENGER, PARCELS, MILK & FISH TRAINS 1937

	43XX, 53XX, 63XX, 73XX	3300-3455 4500-4599 5500-5574	3252-3291 2251-2290	0-6-0 & 0-6-0T	3210 to 3223	2-4-0T 'Metro' 0-4-2T 48XX, 58XX
Taunton to Barnstaple	280*	220	190	190	176	120
Barnstaple to Taunton	280*	220	190	190	176	120

* The timing of passenger trains on this branch is based on a maximum load of 230 tons.

Chapter 11

Passenger and Goods Services

Introduction

This chapter sets out to review the provision of both passenger and goods services over the ninety-five years of the Taunton to Barnstaple line's existence. For convenience we look at matters decade by decade and Part 1 deals with passenger services, whilst Part 2 looks at goods operations. This is only a broad review outlining the nature of these services, a regular pattern of which existed for passenger and goods over several years. Unsurprisingly, staple services were occasionally re-timed, perhaps only by a few minutes, and this detail is deliberately not always covered. As was noted previously in Volume 1 (Chapter 3), the Bristol & Exeter Railway entered into an agreement with the D&SR to work the line. As a consequence, the Company never ran its own services but relied on the B&ER from opening on 8th June 1871 through to 1st January 1876, when the GWR leased the B&ER and with it the responsibility for the train services on the D&SR (the B&ER was amalgamated in to the GWR from 1st August 1876). However, the D&SR remained an independent concern through this and was not officially taken over by the GWR until 1901, although this had no direct impact on services. Nationalisation in 1948 brought the line in to the preserve of British Railways (Western Region) until closure.

Part 1: Passenger Services – 1870s

The first passenger train on the D&SR ran on Thursday 8th June 1871, departing Wiveliscombe at 7.00am and commencing a service that was to be maintained for over ninety-five years. For the first two years Wiveliscombe was the terminus, meaning a short run of just over 9 miles from Taunton, the branch seemingly being operated on the 'one engine in steam' principle.

An extract from the B&ER public time table for January 1872 is reproduced below.

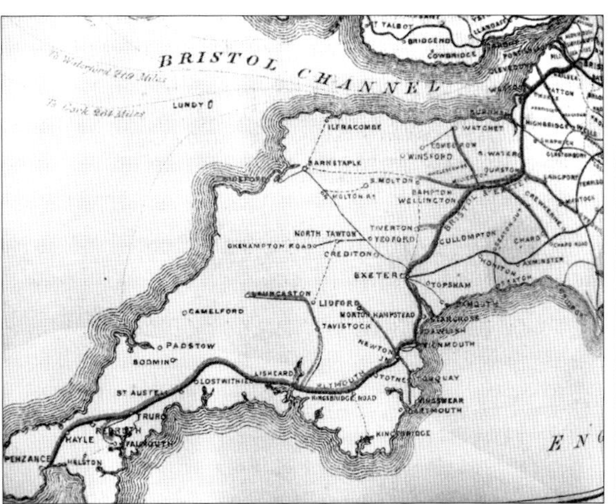

Above: Map of the B&ER from the 1872 public time table, the thicker lines marking their routes. Note the dotted line for the continuation of the railway on from Wiveliscombe to Barnstaple, then still under construction. ***Courtesy National Archives***

DOWN						
Taunton (d)	8.30am*	11.15am	1.20pm	3.25pm	5.00pm	8.15pm*
Milverton	8.50am	11.35am	1.40pm	3.41pm	5.20pm	8.35pm
Wiveliscombe (a)	9.00am	11.45am	1.50pm	3.50pm	5.30pm	8.45pm
UP						
Wiveliscombe (d)	7.00am	10.10am	12.15pm	4.00pm	6.25pm	8.55pm
Milverton	7.10am	10.20am	12.25pm	4.10pm	6.35pm	9.05pm
Taunton (a)	7.30am	10.40am	12.45pm	4.30pm	6.55pm	9.25pm
*by July 1872 the first Down train was retimed to start at 7.55am, the last Down train at 8.10pm						

As can be seen, carrying on from the precedent of the opening day, the first passenger train ran Up from Wiveliscombe. With the last passenger train terminating at Taunton, therefore, the coaching stock needed to get back to Wiveliscombe in the early morning. One can surmise that the Down goods, being the first train (see Part 2 of this Chapter, page 564), would convey the coaches and provide the locomotive to work the first Up passenger service. The journey over the line usually took a leisurely thirty minutes, at an average of about 18mph. The provision of six Up and six Down trains in this first time table broadly set the trend for the life of the branch most years for weekday services. The timings set out above were subject to only minor changes until November 1873, when the line opened through to Barnstaple.

The early afternoon period makes interesting reading. There were two consecutive Down trains (leaving Taunton at 1.20pm and 3.25pm). Again, this unbalanced movement can be explained by reference to the goods time table – the Up goods departing at 2.10pm and arriving at 3.00pm, in good time therefore for the return passenger working at 3.25pm. The first train of the day included First, Second and Third Class carriages (the Parliamentary train).

The line from Wiveliscombe to Barnstaple was opened for passenger traffic from Saturday 1st November 1873, station stops including Norton Fitzwarren which had just opened to passengers. A review of the November 1873 passenger time

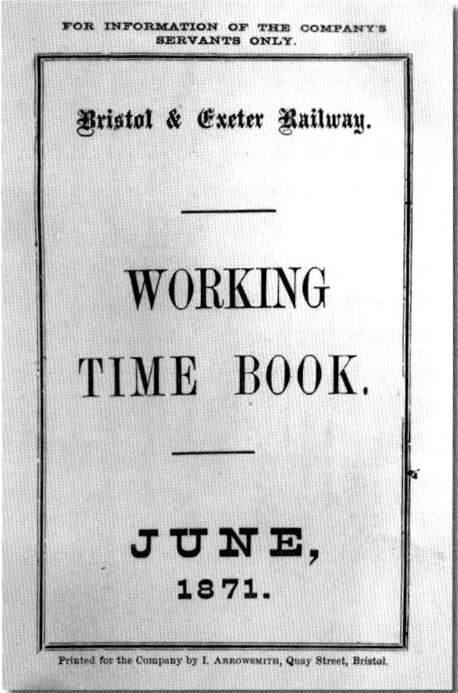
FOR INFORMATION OF THE COMPANY'S SERVANTS ONLY.

Bristol & Exeter Railway.

WORKING TIME BOOK.

JUNE, 1871.

Printed for the Company by I. Arrowsmith, Quay Street, Bristol.

Above: The cover sheet of the B&ER Working Time Book for June 1871. ***Courtesy National Archives***

DEVON AND SOMERSET BRANCH.

The 7.50a.m. Train from Taunton will cross the 7.40a.m. Train from Barnstaple at Dulverton, and the 9.15a.m. Train from Barnstaple at South Molton

The 9.15a.m. Train from Barnstaple will cross the 10.45a.m. Train from Taunton at Norton Fitzwarren.

The 10.30a.m. Train from Barnstaple will cross the 10.45a.m. Train from Taunton at Dulverton, and the 12.40p.m. Train from Taunton at Norton Fitzwarren.

The 12.40p.m. Train from Taunton will cross the 2.0p.m. Train from Barnstaple at South Molton.

The 2.0p.m. Train from Barnstaple will cross the 3.30p.m. Train from Taunton at Wiveliscombe.

The 3.30p.m. Train from Taunton will cross the 3.30p.m. Train from Barnstaple at Dulverton.

The 5.20p.m. Train from Barnstaple will cross the 5.35p.m. Train from Taunton at Dulverton.

The 5.30p.m. Goods Train from Barnstaple will cross the 8.15p.m. Train from Taunton at Wiveliscombe.

The 8.40p.m. Goods Train from Barnstaple will cross the 8.15p.m. Train from Taunton at South Molton, and the 11.5p.m. Goods Train from Taunton at Wiveliscombe.

ABOVE: The working time table specified the crossing of trains, as this extract from the November 1873 edition shows.

THE SPECIAL FAST EXPRESS TRAINS

BETWEEN

LONDON

AND

THE WEST OF ENGLAND

RUN AS UNDER:–

DOWN			UP		
Paddington	dep	11.45am	Plymouth	dep	8.35am
Taunton	arr	3.18pm	Torquay	"	9.15am
South Molton	"	4.55pm	Exeter	"	10.30am
Barnstaple	"	5.15pm	Barnstaple	"	9.15am
Exeter	"	4.00pm	South Molton	"	9.47am
Torquay	"	5.20pm	Taunton	"	11.09am
Plymouth	"	6.00pm	Paddington	arr	2.45pm

ABOVE: An example of B&ER propaganda as displayed in the public time table for 1874. Note that this and other documents that follow are reproduced from originals held at the National Archives, Kew but they are tightly bound and difficult to copy, so have been recreated for publication here.

table shows that there were six Down trains and six Up trains running the length of the branch. The first Down train was the 7.50am from Taunton, arriving at Barnstaple at 10.20am, thus taking two and a half hours for the 44¾ miles, an average speed of about 18mph. The fastest Down train was the 3.30pm departure, which took 'only' an hour and three-quarters (averaging about 25mph). This working, like the 9.15am Up train, only stopped for passengers at the main stations of South Molton, Dulverton and Wiveliscombe. The last Down train departed Taunton at 8.15pm, arriving at Barnstaple at 10.45pm. The last four trains of the day connected with Down trains from London, the quickest possible trip being a respectable five and a half hours (leaving London at 11.45am, arriving Barnstaple at 5.15pm). The other services would take passengers up to nine hours to reach Barnstaple, leaving London at 6.00am for instance and arriving at Barnstaple at 3.10pm. In the Up direction, the first train was the 7.40am departure from Barnstaple, arriving at Taunton at 10.15am. The last Up train left at 5.20pm, arriving at 8.07pm, a long and rather arduous journey at two hours and forty-seven minutes.

It is understood that it was B&ER practice for station staff to ring a hand bell to alert awaiting passengers when the train was known to be arriving.

Despite the time it took to traverse the branch, the B&ER lost no opportunity in highlighting the benefits of the line running through to Barnstaple and its impact in opening up the attractions of North Devon.

The train services as described above were broadly maintained during 1874 but by June of that year, the 9.00pm Barnstaple to South Molton local service had appeared for the first time. It took thirty-one minutes for the 10 miles 40 chains journey, arriving at 9.31pm. In this early period it only worked one way, returning to Barnstaple as empty stock.

Although the B&ER ran rail services only as far as Barnstaple, this did not stop them opening up Ilfracombe as a destination for travellers. A coach service was inaugurated to connect Barnstaple station to Ilfracombe on Monday 2nd November 1874. Taking nearly two hours, someone leaving Ilfracombe at 7.15am would have been able to catch the 9.05am departure from Barnstaple and get to Taunton by 10.58am. The ability to transport their passengers elsewhere was not lost on the B&ER either, as from 1st June 1876 a well-appointed four-horse coach service, 'The Flying Dutchman', commenced running for the summer season between Bude and Barnstaple. It went via Stratton, Kilkhampton, Hartland Cross, Clovelly Cross and Bideford, leaving from the Falcon Hotel in Bude at 9.45am on Mondays, Wednesdays and Fridays, and returning at 5.30pm on Tuesdays, Thursdays and Saturdays. The coach would connect for trains to Bristol, Bath and Paddington (changing at Taunton). Whilst a similar service operated the previous year, it did not carry the flamboyant, if somewhat curious, name.

The fares to and from Bristol, from the 1875 public time table, are set out in **Table 11.1** below. Note that at this time all services catered

TABLE 11.1: FARES TO BRISTOL IN 1875

	FIRST	SECOND	THIRD	FIRST RETURN	SECOND RETURN
Milverton	11s 0d	8s 5d	4s 2½d	17s 9d	13s 7d
Wiveliscombe	11s 8d	8s 10d	4s 5½d	18s 6d	14s 2d
Venn Cross	12s 7d	9s 8d	4s 10½d	20s 0d	15s 5d
Morebath	13s 5d	10s 4d	5s 2 d	21s 3d	16s 5d
Dulverton	14s 3d	11s 0d	5s 5½d	22s 6d	17s 5d
East Anstey	14s 11d	11s 6d	5s 9 d	23s 6d	18s 2d
BN & Molland	15s 11d	12s 4d	6s 2 d	25s 0d	19s 5d
South Molton	16s 11d	13s 2d	6s 6½d	26s 6d	20s 8d
Castle Hill	17s 7d	13s 8d	6s 9½d	27s 6d	21s 5d
Swimbridge	18s 3d	14s 2d	7s 1 d	28s 6d	22s 2d
Barnstaple	19s 0d	14s 10d	7s 5 d	29s 8d	23s 2d

New and Shortest Route between

LONDON

AND

ILFRACOMBE

(Via Taunton and the Devon and Somerset Railway)

The BRISTOL AND EXETER COMPANY'S well-appointed NEW CARRIAGES run three times in each direction daily (Sundays excepted) between the Clock Tower Office, High Street, **ILFRACOMBE**, and the Station of the **Devon and Somerset Railway at BARNSTAPLE.**

By this new and shortest route Passengers and Parcels can now be booked through from **ILFRACOMBE** to **LONDON** (Paddington Station) and to all the principal towns in the Kingdom.

Orders given for the collection of Luggage, Parcels and Goods will receive prompt attention.

Full particulars as to Times, Fares, and Rates can be obtained on application to MR. HOLCOMBE, Clock Tower Office, Ilfracombe or the undersigned,

J. C. WALL,
General Manager

BRISTOL, 1874

BRISTOL AND EXETER RAILWAY.

The New and Shortest Route between

LONDON

AND

BARNSTAPLE

Via the DEVON & SOMERSET RAILWAY

IS NOW OPEN FOR

PUBLIC TRAFFIC.

THIS LINE ALSO FORMS THE

DIRECT & SHORTEST ROUTE

FROM

YEOVIL AND CHARD

TO THE

NORTH OF DEVON

AT

REDUCED FARES.

THROUGH COMMUNICATION

BETWEEN

LONDON, SOUTH MOLTON BARNSTAPLE, and ILFRACOMBE.

DOWN.	1 & 2 Class a.m.	3rd Class a.m.	1 & 2 Class a.m.	1 & 2 Exp. a.m.	1, 2 & 3 Class p.m.
PADDINGTON ... dep.	6 45	9 0	10 30	11 45	1 50
WESTBOURNE PARK ...	...	...	...	...	1 53
SOUTH MOLTON ... arr.	2 38	4 55	7 15	4 55	10 12
BARNSTAPLE	3 10	5 15	7 45	5 15	10 45
ILFRACOMBE BY COACH...	...	7 15	...	7 15	...

UP.	1 & 2 Class a.m.	1 & 2 Exp. a.m.	3rd Class a.m.	1 & 2 Class a.m.	1 & 2 Class p.m.	3rd Class p.m.	1 & 2 Class p.m.
ILFRACOMBE BY COACH	...	...	...	8 30	...	...	...
BARNSTAPLE ... dep.	7 40	9 15	9 15	10 30	2 00	3 30	5 25
SOUTH MOLTON	8 18	9 47	9 47	11 08	2 38	3 57	5 56
WESTBOURNE PARK ar.	5 00	...	...	5 55	10 15	10 15	... ...
PADDINGTON	5 15	2 45	5 15	6 00	10 20	10 20	3 55 4 35

ABOVE LEFT: The 'New and Short Route' to Ilfracombe, an extract from an 1874 public time table. ABOVE RIGHT: The 1874 time table also included a summary of the fastest trains facilitating travel to North Devon and encompasses the horse-drawn coach service between Ilfracombe and Barnstaple GWR.

for all classes of passengers and most were also mixed passenger and goods trains.

By 1876, omnibus services met the trains at the various stations on the line, as summarised below:

- Wiveliscombe – An omnibus met the 7.45am and 11.00am, and the 1.40pm, 3.30pm and 5.35pm trains from Taunton, and the 1.15pm train from Barnstaple. The fare to any part of the town was 6d.
- Morebath – Conveyances could be had on application at the White Horse, Bampton
- Dulverton – An omnibus from the Lion Hotel met the Up and Down trains due at Dulverton at 8.51am, 11.58am, 4.27pm and 6.36pm. The single journey was 1 shilling.
- South Molton – An omnibus met every train except the 8.15pm from Taunton. The fare to the town was 6d and conveyances could also be hired from the George Hotel.
- Barnstaple – The Company's carriages left Barnstaple daily (except Sundays) upon the arrival of the 2.26pm train from Bristol and the 11.45am train from London. They returned to the Company's offices, under the clock tower in the High Street, Ilfracombe at 8.30am daily (Sundays excepted), in time for the train leaving Barnstaple at 10.30am, due in London at 6.00pm. To facilitate the transfer of passengers and luggage at Barnstaple, omnibuses ran daily (Sundays excepted) from the D&SR station at Barnstaple to the L&SWR station at Barnstaple and vice versa.

During the period January 1877 to October 1878, there were consistently six Up and six Down trains daily. The first Up train departed Barnstaple at 7.25am, with the first Down train leaving Taunton at 7.45am. The time taken to traverse the line was between 1 hour 40 minutes and 2 hours for all-stations stopping services, so the average speed had increased to 22mph for these trains. The last Up train was at 5.35pm from Barnstaple, with the last Down train departing Taunton at 8.25pm. These services were subsequently retimed to depart at 5.45/5.55pm (the Up train) and at 8.40pm for the Down train (it was retimed for 9.40pm in the summer period of 1878). The 9.00pm Up goods from Barnstaple to Taunton was noted in the time table as conveying passengers as far as South Molton, where it arrived at 9.31pm, replacing the specific local service that had previously operated. This goods train was retimed to depart Barnstaple at 9.20pm in October 1877, running as a goods and passenger train to Dulverton where it arrived at 10.24pm. This combined service continued until the commencement of the October 1879 time table, at which point the local passenger service to South Molton resumed.

In the summer of 1878, there were two Up and Down stopping passenger trains introduced on Sundays. The Up trains left Barnstaple at 8.45am (arriving at Taunton at 10.52am) and 2.10pm (Taunton

BRISTOL AND EXETER RAILWAY

NOTICE AS TO CONVEYANCE OF HORSES, CATTLE, &c.

The Company will not be responsible for any Loss or Injury to any Horse, Cattle, or other Animal in the receiving, forwarding, or delivery, if the damage be occasioned by the kicking, plunging or unruliness of the same.

WHEREAS, by an Act of 1854 (17 and 18 Vic., cap 31, section 7), entitled "An Act for the better Regulation of the Traffic on Railways and Canals," it is provided in reference to the liability of Railway and Canal Companies for the loss or injury done to any Horse, Cattle, or other Animals, that no greater damages shall be recovered for the loss of, or for any injury done to, any Animals, beyond the sums hereinafter mentioned; that is to say,

For any Horse £50,
For any Neat Cattle, per head. £15
For any Sheep or Pigs, per head . . . . £2 ;

unless the person sending or delivering the same to such Company shall, at the time of such delivery, have declared them to be respectively of higher value than as above-mentioned; in which case it shall be lawful for such Company to demand and receive, by way of compensation for the increased risk and care thereby occasioned, a reasonable per centage upon the excess of the value so declared above the respective sums so limited as aforesaid, and which shall be paid, in addition to the ordinary Rate of Charge:

NOTICE is therefore hereby given, that from and after the date hereof, a per centage of Five per cent. will be charged by THE BRISTOL AND EXETER RAILWAY COMPANY, in addition to its usual charge for conveyance, upon any excess in the declared value of Horses, Cattle, or other Animals, over and above the amounts fixed by the Act aforesaid, as above-mentioned.

And NOTICE is hereby further given, that all declarations of the value of Horses, Cattle, or other Animals, where such value exceeds the above sums respectively, must be signed by the Sender thereof, or by the person delivering the same for carriage, before they can be received by the Company for transmission by the Railway.

Bristol, 28th October, 1868

The 1874 B&ER public time table included provision for those wishing to transport livestock too.

passengers as far as Dulverton (arriving at 10.24pm). On Fridays, the Down goods from Taunton (leaving at 3.00am) could convey passengers from South Molton and Castle Hill to Barnstaple (leaving South Molton at 6.09am, arriving at 6.45am). This may well have been for market day traffic.The 2 hour 10/15 minutes journey times were consistent throughout the day, even for those trains not booked to stop at every station, thus maintaining an average speed of circa 20 mph.

By October 1879, the five Up and Down trains were supplemented by a re-introduction of the daily Barnstaple to South Molton stopping service and its return, although this was a replacement for the passenger carriages conveyed on the late goods, which had been removed. It left Barnstaple at 9.20pm, arriving South Molton at 9.50pm and returning at 10.05pm, getting back at 10.30pm.

4.17pm), whilst the Down trains departed Taunton at 8.30am (Barnstaple 10.35am) and 5.35pm (Barnstaple 7.40pm). These were the only Sunday passenger services at this time and when discontinued, they were not reintroduced until July 1936 but again only in the July to September summer period.

The February 1879 time table showed only five weekday Up and Down trains, the first Up train departing at 7.25am and the first Down train at 7.55am. The mid-day Barnstaple train was discontinued along with the 8.40pm Down train. This would have been an inconvenience to passengers travelling down from London, as they would have had to catch the 10.30am from Paddington to connect at Taunton for the late afternoon train to Barnstaple, rather than catch the 1.50pm from Paddington which would have connected with the later Barnstaple-bound train.

In the summer period of 1879, there were six Down and six Up passenger trains, the first Down service leaving Taunton at 7.55am (arriving at Barnstaple at 10.16am) and the last leaving at 9.40pm (arriving at 11.25pm). In the Up direction, the first was the 7.25am from Barnstaple (arriving at Taunton at 9.30am). Although the last passenger train set off from Barnstaple at 4.50pm (arriving at 6.56pm), the 9.20pm Barnstaple to Taunton goods continued to convey

TO DULVERTON,

BY TRAINS LEAVING	TIME. A.M	TIME. A.M.	FARES TO & FRO 1ST CLASS.	FARES TO & FRO 3RD CLASS.
EXETER . . . . . at	6 0	9 20	9/0	4/0
Tiverton	. .	9 47	7/6	3/9
Wellington	7 14	10 22	5/0	2/6
Chard	6 0	9 45	8/0	3/6
Barnstaple	7 40	10 30	5/0	2/6
Swimbridge	7 53	10 43	4/6	2/3
Castle Hill	8 5	10 55	3/6	2/0
South Molton	8 18	11 8	3/0	1/6
Bishop's Nympton and Molland . .	8 33	11 23	2/0	1/0
East Anstey	8 49	11 39	0/9	0/6
Morebath (for Bampton)	8 54	11 40	0/9	0/6
Venn Cross	8 41	11 29	1/6	0/9
Wiveliscombe	8 26	11 15	2/6	1/6
Milverton	8 14	11 5	3/0	1/9
Norton Fitzwarren . .	7 59	10 52	4/0	2/0
Taunton	7 50	10 45	4/6	2/0
BRIDGWATER	7 11	10 4	7/6	3/9

These Tickets will also be issued on the first TUESDAY in every Month by the same Trains.

This final extract from the 1874 public timetable shows the designated 'market trains' to Dulverton, along with the fares.

MARKET TRAINS

The B&ER were keen to encourage passengers onto their network. Livestock markets were prevalent in this era and almost every day of the week there was a local town that held such event. Local market days in the 1870s (and beyond) were held on Mondays at Chard, Tuesdays at Tiverton, Wednesdays at Bridgwater, Thursdays at Bristol and Wellington, and Fridays at Exeter and Barnstaple, and those living along the D&SR could benefit and travel to those markets.

The market trains were not specially laid on excursions as such but normal time tabled trains so designated with special (cheap) fares. As can be seen for the Barnstaple destination, above, the 7.50am from Taunton was a normal service train, with a fare of 10s First Class or 5s Third Class. The public time table stated '*For the accommodation of persons attending the following Markets special tickets as cheap fares by special trains will be issued for the return journey.*'

1880s

The last broad gauge time tables, for 1880 and 1881, showed a significant consistency in services, with five Down and five Up trains on weekdays. The first Down train still departed from Taunton at 7.55am and still took until 10.16am to get to Barnstaple, an average of 19mph. By January 1881, this train arrived at 9.50am, increasing the average speed to about 22mph. The last Down train was scheduled at 6.55pm from Taunton, arriving at 9.03pm (improved to 8.50pm by January 1881), having been retimed to run earlier than in prior years. The first Up train was at 7.25am from Barnstaple and took two hours to reach Taunton. The last Up train, at 5.50pm, was later than in prior periods, arriving at 7.48pm. The additional stopping service from Barnstaple to South Molton now only ran on Tuesdays and Fridays but to broadly the same time as before but it then became a Fridays only train in October 1883. The summer period of 1881 had an additional (faster) Up train, leaving Barnstaple at 2.30pm and not stopping until South Molton, then passing straight through Milverton and arriving at Taunton at 4.25pm, its average speed being just over 22mph.

The last broad gauge passenger train ran on Saturday, 14th May 1881 and the 'narrow' (standard) gauge era for the line began on Wednesday, 18th May, when one goods and two passenger trains ran. The normal time tabled services resumed the following day.

A similar pattern of trains and timings as described above ran in the 1881-1884 period following the conversion to standard gauge. However, from October 1884, the number of services between Taunton and Barnstaple was reduced to only four per day, the first Up train of the day being cut out along with the 3.35pm train to Barnstaple. There was an additional Down train at 3.35pm on Saturdays only from Taunton to Dulverton (arriving at 4.32pm), which returned empty at 5.00pm (arriving at Taunton at 6.45pm). It was held up at certain points en route to allow other trains to cross.

By January 1885, services had been returned to five Up and five Down trains daily, with similar timings to the beginning of the decade. This pattern of services continued through to 1886 but the first Up train was retimed from 7.25am to depart at 7.35am (arriving at 9.25am). In the summer periods of 1886 and 1887, there were six Up and Down passenger trains, with the additional services inserted in the middle of the day: the 1.40pm Down from Taunton and the 11.45am Up from Barnstaple, both only stopping at South Molton and Dulverton.

On 1st June 1887, the chord line to Barnstaple L&SWR station opened and this inevitably expanded passenger services. Trains were then able to run through to this station, with through coaches (and later through trains) carrying on to Ilfracombe. During the weekday time table, whether summer or winter, there was a provision for through coaches from Taunton to Ilfracombe. Using an illustration from the October 1887 time table, below, there were three trains each way to Barnstaple L&SWR from Taunton via Barnstaple GWR, with coaches on each train continuing to Ilfracombe.

In the summer period of 1888, for example, the second Up train of the day started from the L&SWR station but this first necessitated an empty stock working from the GWR station at 8.00am, arriving at 8.05am for an 8.15am departure. The train then arrived at Barnstaple GWR station at 8.20am, with the onward departure to Taunton at 8.50am. Four of the five daily trains at that time would work through to and from the L&SWR station.

	am (A)	pm (C)	pm (B)		am (B)	pm (D)	pm (A)
Taunton dep.	**11.20**	**1.30**	**3.35**	**Ilfracombe SW dep.**	**10.10**	**2.25**	**3.54**
Barnstaple GW arr.	**1.13**	**3.06**	**5.30**	**Barnstaple SW arr.**	**10.53**	**3.09**	**4.36**
Barnstaple SW dep.	**1.35**	**3.29**	**6.00**	**Barnstaple GW dep.**	**11.25**	**3.49**	**5.50**
Ilfracombe SW arr.	**2.23**	**4.15**	**6.47**	**Taunton arr.**	**1.15**	**5.30**	**7.52**

A – These coaches leave Taunton at 11.20am. Return from Ilfracombe 3.54pm same day
B – These coaches leave Ilfracombe at 10.10am. Return from Taunton 3.35pm same day
C – These coaches leave Taunton at 1.30pm. Return from Ilfracombe 2.25pm next day
D – These coaches leave Ilfracombe at 2.25pm. Return to Taunton 1.30pm next day.

EXCURSIONS

The line did have its fair share of excursion traffic and research has uncovered a few examples in the 1888 and 1889 period to illustrate this. On Saturday, 9th June 1888, in connection with a return excursion from Cardiff to Exeter, a late train was added to the D&SR route leaving Taunton at 8.05pm, arriving at Barnstaple at 9.55pm after stopping at all stations. The engine and guard to work this travelled up on the 5.50pm normal service train from Barnstaple.

On Saturday. 8th June 1889, the 1.30pm train from Taunton was to run in two parts, the first taking passengers from a London excursion, leaving Taunton at 1.10pm and arriving at Barnstaple at 2.50pm. Through coaches to Ilfracombe could be arranged by Mr Lailey, Mr Gray at Barnstaple was to arrange with Mr Heather in regards to the train running over to the Junction, and the engine and guard were to return on the 3.40pm Up service.

In those days, the Whitsuntide weekend was in June, so on Whit-Monday, 10th June 1889, there was an excursion from Barnstaple to Exeter (via Dulverton and the Exe Valley). The train was to be formed of one First and ten Third Class coaches and two Brakes. An extract of the running times is set out below (the train stopped at all stations):

FORWARD TRAIN	ARRIVE	DEPART
Barnstaple		8.30am
South Molton	8.56am	8.58am
Dulverton	9.31am	9.34am
Bampton..	9.45am	9.47am
Tiverton...	10.01am	10.04am
Exeter	10.52am	
RETURN TRAIN	**ARRIVE**	**DEPART**
Exeter		7.00pm
Tiverton...	7.43pm	7.46pm
Bampton..	8.00pm	8.03pm
Dulverton	8.17pm	8.20pm
South Molton	8.56pm	8.58pm
Barnstaple	9.24pm	

The Barnstaple to South Molton (Fridays only) service was reintroduced for this Whit Monday and there was also a 'picnic' note as follows in the instructions:

PICNIC AT DULVERTON

Willis' Party, about 150, Tiverton to Dulverton and Back, will travel forward by 7.15am ex Exeter, and return by 8.05pm ex Dulverton. Mr Mears, Exeter, to arrange accommodation.

A further example came to light, later in 1889. Cross Street Sunday School ran a special for 150 adults and 250 children from Barnstaple (departing at 1.40pm) to South Molton (arriving at 2.16pm), on Wednesday, 17th July 1889. It returned at 8.45pm from South Molton to Barnstaple, arriving at 9.35pm. This Sunday School train may well have been for the South Molton Agricultural Show as, on the same day, somewhat unusually, three coaches were to be attached at South Molton to the 7.00pm Bristol goods, which was retimed to leave South Molton at 8.40pm, then stopping at all stations to arrive at Taunton at 10.14pm, earlier than usual. These coaches were sent down from Taunton. Instructions stated that the guard was to record in his journal the number of passengers in the special on leaving South Molton, Dulverton and arriving at Taunton.

Returning to normal services, by summer 1889 there were seven Down and seven Up trains daily including Saturdays. The first trains were the same as previously, namely 7.35am Up and 7.55am Down. The last Up train was retimed to depart at 5.55pm and the last Down service at 7.10pm. The 1.45pm departure from Taunton was only scheduled to stop at Dulverton, arriving at Barnstaple at 3.10pm, but the 6.40pm Taunton departure ran non-stop to arrive at Barnstaple at 7.57pm. In the Up direction, it was the 11.45am departure which only stopped at South Molton and Dulverton, arriving at Taunton at 1.15pm before travelling on to Paddington. The fastest Down train took only 1 hour 17 minutes (approaching an average speed of 30mph), which contrasted with the 1 hour 55 minutes of the stopping services. Whilst the second train of the day started at Barnstaple L&SWR, leaving at 8.15am as in earlier years, this required a GWR locomotive to work across 'light engine' from the GWR shed at 8.00am, arriving at 8.05am to join the coaching stock which had been stabled there overnight. The Friday's only train to South Molton and back still ran.

In the summer period, unsurprisingly, the through coach services to Ilfracombe increased to five each way. Also, services were expanded beyond the local area for the first time. For example, the 10.10am from Ilfracombe ran daily through to London, whilst the 1.45pm Taunton Down departure included a through coach from London (arriving Ilfracombe at 4.15pm). In addition, the 7.15am Ilfracombe departure had a daily through coach to the surprising destination of Birkenhead. The return through coach from Birkenhead was on the 3.35pm Taunton departure, arriving at Ilfracombe at 6.47pm. These improvements appear to have arisen from an initiative by Mr N.J. Burlinson, the new GWR superintendent for the region.

The opening of the chord line to the L&SWR had therefore clearly increased the potential for passenger traffic travelling down the line, as well as potential and actual destinations of services. Indeed, at this time, the fastest GWR Paddington to Ilfracombe service took 4 hours 55 minutes, quicker than the L&SWR route from Waterloo via Exeter.

1890s

The early (winter) 1890 time table showed five Up and five Down trains, with the first and last of them being the same scheduled departure times as generally in the 1880s. The 1.30pm Down train made fewest stops, avoiding Venn Cross, Morebath and Molland, arriving at Barnstaple at 3.06pm and, as a result, was the fastest Down train of the day (the others taking broadly 1 hour and 55 minutes). There was no equivalent fast Up service, whilst the evening Barnstaple to South Molton train still ran on Fridays only. There was little change in the summer of 1890 but there there was an Up train leaving Barnstaple at 3.40pm, which made few stops and arrived at Taunton at 5.30pm.

The April 1891 time table was similar to 1890 – five trains each way with the 1.30pm Down train being the fastest. The last Down train was retimed to leave Taunton at 7.00pm (not 6.55pm) and there were three trains with through coaches to and back from Ilfracombe during the day: the 11.20am, 1.30pm (from London) and 3.35pm departures from Taunton and the 10.25am (to London), 2.05pm and 4.45pm from Ilfracombe. There was also a curious note to the summer time table, namely that a Brake Third Class coach was to go from Barnstaple to South Molton by the 7.55am departure on Fridays, to be returned attached to the 5.20am ex-Taunton (Bristol) Down goods at South Molton – another accommodation for market day in Barnstaple perhaps.

The pattern of five Up and Down trains daily continued during the non-summer months throughout the decade. The first Down train in 1891 was 8.50am but this was retimed by the summer of 1892 to depart at 8.00am. The 7.05pm continued to be the last Down train, whilst the first Up service was consistently the 7.35am from Barnstaple GWR but, by May 1896, it had been retimed to 7.30am. The last Up train was 5.55pm throughout the period. There were three Up and Down trains with through coaches to Ilfracombe each day and, by October 1895, one coach was through from London (on the 3.38pm from Taunton) and one from Ilfracombe (on the 9.15am departure). The Fridays only Barnstaple to South Molton (and return) evening train continued to run.

In the summer period of the 1890s, there was consistently seven Up and Down trains daily, six of which conveyed through coaches to Ilfracombe. Depending on the year in question, four or five through coach train services would return from Ilfracombe but, by July 1896, the through coaches had increased to seven trains Down and six in the Up direction. In the summer period the last trains both Down and Up ran at later times than the winter period. The 7.20pm departure from Taunton was the last Down. In the 1892 and 1893 summer periods, there was a 9.45pm Fridays only departure from Barnstaple which arrived at Taunton at 11.35pm. Accordingly, the number of Up trains increased to eight when this train ran. As a consequence, the South Molton Fridays only 'shuttle' did not run but the late Up train had ceased running by 1895 and the shuttle recommenced. Two of the Down trains were fast (3.15pm and 6.55pm from Taunton) and did not stop at any intermediate stations other than the first of them at Dulverton. Likewise, two Up trains made limited stops, the 11.17am from Ilfracombe to Paddington service only stopping at Dulverton. This train reached London in 6 hours 43 minutes and was formed of five coaches from four Down services. A later Up train, the 4.10pm from Barnstaple, only stopped at South Molton on the first part of the journey until Dulverton, from where it then stopped all stations.

In the summer time table (July onwards) of 1897, there were seven through coach trains, that is all services, from Taunton to Ilfracombe, with six working back from Ilfracombe (only the first train of the day did not work through from Ilfracombe in this summer period).

Over the Easter period in 1899 (28th March to 9th April), cheap Third Class rail fares were on offer and these are illustrated below:

RETURN FARES TO PADDINGTON FROM	PRICE
Dulverton	..22s
East Anstey....	..22s 6d
Bishops Nympton & Molland	..23s
South Molton	..24s 6d
Barnstaple	..26s 6d
Ilfracombe	..28s

A detailed summary of through coaches for selected years between 1892 and 1938, along with related information, is included in **Appendix 17**.

1900s

In January 1900, the line offered five Up and Down passenger trains on weekdays, the first Down service leaving Taunton at 7.55am (arriving at Barnstaple at 10.05am). The last Down train was the 7.20pm, arriving at 9.27pm. In the Up direction, the first departure from the GWR station was the 7.30am (arriving at 9.28pm), the last up being at 6.10pm (arriving at 8.25pm). The three trains that ran in the middle of the day from Taunton had through coaches to Ilfracombe and the last three trains had coaches back from Ilfracombe to Taunton. However, the journey time to Ilfracombe was over an hour (and up to an hour and 10 or 20 minutes) despite the time tabled quick turnaround at the GWR station of five minutes in the quickest case (this being the 1.25pm departure from Taunton arriving at 3.13pm and departing at 3.18pm). The 3.40pm Down train arrived at Barnstaple GWR at 5.40pm and then departed at 5.50pm for the L&SWR station, after the arrival from there at 5.48pm of the 6.10pm departure to Taunton. This would have clearly necessitated a quick turnaround and shunting of the Down train into the bay platform. On Fridays (only), the stopping train from Barnstaple GWR to South Molton continued but there were no through coaches beyond Taunton to London and the north until the July to September period of 1900.

In the summer period (from July 1900), there were seven Down and Up trains, the regular services being supplemented by two fast passenger workings in both directions. The 7.55am departure from Taunton was the first weekday Down train (arriving at 10.05am) and the last was the 7.20pm (as for the earlier period). In the Up direction, the 7.30am was the first with 6.10pm the last. The 3.15pm and 6.55pm from Taunton were the fast trains (taking 1 hour 40 minutes and 1 hour 35 minutes respectively). In the Up direction, the fast trains were the 12.15pm from Barnstaple (arriving at Taunton at 1.53pm) and the 4.10pm departure (arriving at 6.02pm). The South Molton evening service also ran as before.

On summer Saturdays only, there was a Down train at 5.00am from Taunton to Barnstaple (arriving at 6.50am) and on to Ilfracombe (arriving at 7.52 am) badged 'London Excursion'. These coaches worked back empty (ECS) to Taunton leaving Ilfracombe at 8.15am, arriving at Barnstaple GWR at 9.05am, where they crossed with the 7.55am Down train before departing at 10.07am. Travelling east, the ECS only stopped to exchange the electric train staff at stations other than at Dulverton, where there was a 23 minute wait, and Morebath with a 19 minute wait to pass a Down train, arriving Taunton at 12.58pm. Also on Thursdays only, there was a 'Northern Excursion' from Ilfracombe at 7.25pm, departing Barnstaple GWR at 9.50pm and arriving at Taunton at 11.40pm. It too only stopped at stations, other than South Molton and Dulverton, to exchange the staff. These trips were run along the branch to connect with main line excursions and did not work beyond Taunton, so passengers needed to change trains to proceed on their journey. The badges 'London Excursion' or 'Northern Excursion' were thus a marketing exercise it seems.

The through coach workings of 1902 register the first slip coach at Taunton for the Barnstaple Branch. The 11.35am Paddington to Kingswear had an 8-wheeled tri-Composite (luggage body) coach and an 8-wheeled tri-Composite slip coach, which were slipped at Taunton to work forwards to Ilfracombe.

In 1903, through coaches only ran in the summer months. There was a pair of through coaches from Birkenhead which, on the Down journey, were worked forward from Crewe on the 9.35am to Kingswear and detached at Taunton, working on to Ilfracombe with a local service. The return working had these coaches on the 12.10pm Ilfracombe to Paddington, from which they were detached at Bristol, then going forwards on the 4.10pm Bristol to Crewe. Services were improving. In addition to the seven Up and Down trains (two of which were fast trains in the Down direction, one in the Up), there were also two Saturdays only Down trains. The 'London Excursion' (Taunton departure 4.55am, arriving at Barnstaple at 6.35am and Ilfracombe at 7.47am) and the 'Northern Excursion' (Taunton depart 5.45am, arriving Barnstaple at 7.20am and Ilfracombe at 8.45am). In the Up direction, the 'London Excursion' ran on Mondays and Fridays only, departing from Ilfracombe at 7.08am and Barnstaple GWR at 8.18am. The 'Northern Excursion' ran Thursdays only in the summer period, departing Barnstaple L&SWR at 9.50am and GWR at 10.05am.

BRIEF FACT

Foot-warmers were supplied on or around 20th October 1900/1901 to Barnstaple for use in trains which were not steam heated. It was the responsibility of the Superintendents from time to time to regulate the working between different points. ***GWR Study Group No. 125, Autumn 2013***

By 1904, the slip coaches employed on the D&SR were double-ended, whilst from October of that year there was one through coach working. A slip coach on the 11.35am Paddington to Kingswear was detached at Taunton and went to Ilfracombe on the 3.57pm Taunton departure. It returned the next day to Taunton and was attached to the 10.50am Kingswear to Paddington to be slipped at Reading.

July of 1904 saw the first through train from London. The 10.15am Paddington to Ilfracombe comprised twelve coaches when it left London but two were slipped at Bath and Bridgwater, and two worked to Minehead. The remainder were destined for Barnstaple (four) and Ilfracombe. Other Down trains had through coaches from London. In the Up direction, in addition to the 12.17pm Ilfracombe to Paddington, there was an 11.00am Barnstaple to Paddington service. The former conveyed two through coaches from Ilfracombe to Birkenhead and one to Liverpool, the latter also conveying a through coach from Ilfracombe to Manchester.

By the summer of 1904, the excursions had been varied. There was one Saturdays only Down excursion (Taunton departure at 5.30am, Barnstaple GWR arrival 7.08am and Ilfracombe 8.07am). The notes indicated it was a combined 'London & Northern Excursion'. In the Up direction, there were two excursions to supplement the seven regular services: the 8.50am Ilfracombe 'London Excursion' (Mondays and Fridays), which ran as a 'Northern Excursion' on Thursdays, and the Friday's only evening 'London Excursion' (departing Ilfracombe at 10.00pm). These trains had a locomotive change at Barnstaple L&SWR, where a GWR locomotive took over to work to Taunton, necessitating the working of a light engine from the GWR shed.

In the summer of 1905, the east curve had opened and this enabled trains to avoid Barnstaple GWR station, with the time consuming process of running around and travelling tender-first to/from L&SWR, as described in Chapter 8 of Volume 2. Of the seven Down passenger services, four by-passed the GWR station and two of the seven Up trains did the same. Passengers for Barnstaple GWR were accommodated by coaches being detached at South Junction and taken back there. Also, Taunton-bound trains had coaches added at East Junction (as described on page 395 of Volume 2). These routine services were supplemented by two Down excursions, one in the early morning (Saturdays only) and one early afternoon on Thursdays and Fridays. These trains did reverse at the GWR station. The Up excursions were morning ('London' on Mondays and Fridays, 'Northern' on Thursdays) and late evening (Fridays only to London).

In October 1905, the slip coaches did not run but there was one through coach (a Brake tri-Composite) to Ilfracombe on the 12.25pm Paddington to Penzance, which returned the next day at 9.15am to Taunton and then on to Paddington.

In the 1906 summer period, the number of regular services increased to eight Up and Down trains, six of the Down workings taking the East Curve and avoiding the GWR station but only two Up services did likewise. These were supplemented by three Down excursions (two early morning Saturdays only and one early afternoon). In the Up direction, the morning Mondays and Fridays'London Excursion', and the Thursdays 'Northern Excursion' were supplemented by the Fridays only late evening excursion.

In 1907, the 11.50am Paddington to Kingswear had a slip tri-Composite, a Dining car and a Van Third all from Paddington to Ilfracombe being slipped at Taunton. This was the first example of a Dining car working from Paddington through to Ilfracombe, whch would then return at 6.15pm to Barnstaple and the next day be attached to the 1.05pm Barnstaple to Paddington (the 12.17pm Ilfracombe to Paddington service). In October 1907, there were five Up and Down trains, supplemented by a 1.31pm Taunton to Dulverton service (returning at 2.50pm).

In 1908, the GWR ran a flagship express from Wolverhampton to Penzance, which commenced on 1st July of that year. When it arrived at Bristol Temple Meads, a slip coach was added for Ilfracombe; this was continued in 1909. Departing at 1.10pm, once the coach had been slipped at Taunton it went forward to Ilfracombe on the 2.40pm stopping service; in the winter months, the slip was for Taunton only. The Fridays only South Molton evening shuttle continued to run throughout this decade, up until October 1909.

The May 1909 *Appendix to the GW Service Time Table* summarised engine whistles as follows:

STATIONS AND JUNCTIONS	WHISTLES
Norton Fitzwarren Jnc-Main line	1
Norton Fitzwarren-Barnstaple Branch	2
Morebath Junction-D&SR	1
Morebath Junction-Exe Valley	2
Barnstaple Junction-GW Main line trains	1
Barnstaple Junction-to L&SWR	2

1910-1919

The pattern of five Up and Down trains continued as the mainstay of weekday services outside of the summer period from 1910 to 1914. The summer time table of 1910 showed eight Up and seven Down trains, along with the Fridays only South Molton local, which had recommenced by July 1910 (for the summer period only). The 'London' and 'Northern' excursions also ran on summer Fridays and Saturdays only, the two Friday services leaving Ilfracombe at 9.10pm and 11.00pm. There was also a late afternoon Mondays and Fridays only Up excursion. In the Down direction, there were two early morning excursions (at 3.32am and 5.40am) and one at 12.10pm, and this pattern broadly reflected services through to 1914. However, the 1914 time table is more explicit with the excursions. There was a Saturdays only Wolverhampton to Ilfracombe (which left Taunton at 2.05pm), along with the curiously labelled 'Lancashire & Yorkshire and Great Central and Midland Excursion'. This is understood to have run from Manchester, via Sheffield, Nottingham, Loughborough, Banbury, Swindon and Bristol to Taunton, which it then departed at 5.10pm, arriving Ilfracombe at 7.55pm.

Not surprisingly, during the war years the number of passenger train services was reduced and through coaches were removed. However, the October 1914 time table revealed the usual five Up and Down trains but this was then reduced from July 1915 to four in each direction, through and until April 1917, although the summer period from July 1916 was an exception, as it had five Up and Down trains time-tabled.

The Ilfracombe slip was continued to the summer of 1914 but by 1916, with services affected by the war, the slip coach only went from Bristol to Taunton on Saturdays. The Wolverhampton to Penzance services were withdrawn in the 1916/17 time table and when they resumed in 1919 there was no Ilfracombe portion. However, by the summer of 1920, the 10.40 am Wolverhampton to Penzance had the slip coach for Ilfracombe being added at Bristol again.

From the autumn of 1917, there was a reduction to three Up and Down passenger trains daily, providing a basic service of morning, lunchtime and early evening services. All the Down services ran through to Barnstaple L&SWR station, whilst the two later Up services also worked from there. This pattern continued until July 1919, when the number of passenger services increased to four in each direction. The early morning 7.00am up service from the GWR station had been reinstated, with two Down services at 12.15pm and 1.25pm. The 12.10 Ilfracombe to Taunton (and Paddington) service ran on Mondays, Wednesdays and Fridays in this summer period. Four Down services ran through to the L&SWR station but only two Up services started there, although an ECS train ran from the L&SWR station to the GWR at 2.45pm. The winter service of 1919 reverted to three Up and Down services.

1920-29

The early part of 1920 had four Up and Down passenger services but, by the July, this had been increased back to six each way. Two Up trains, the 9.40am and 11.55am from Ilfracombe, were destined for Paddington, so through trains were running again. These used the East Curve, with coaches being attached from Barnstaple GWR and departing at 10.43am and 12.45pm; the time table allowed ten minutes to attach the coaches at East Junction. Five of the Down trains used the East Curve, with only the final train of the day terminating at Barnstaple GWR but coaches were detached at South Junction from the other

A Barnstaple line departure from the bay platform at Taunton rather unusually in the hands of an unidentified 'Buffalo' Class saddle tank 0-6-0, which is having a final inspection before setting off. The date is circa 1910, with the locomotive having a round top firebox and an S4 boiler, and with a worksplate visible on the frame just above the centre driver; these were removed in 1912. The number 7 is just discernible on the buffer beam, so one candidate could be No. 1187, which was based at Taunton at this time, whilst the carriages in the picture would all thus be in the all-over brown livery. *Jim Elson collection*

five Down trains for the GWR station. With the advent of the winter time table in October 1920, there were five Up and Down trains, whilst the East Curve was closed, so services ran into and reversed at the GWR station. There was one Paddington Up through train, the 9.40am from Ilfracombe, departing Barnstaple GWR at 11am.

In the summer of 1921, the number of Up and Down trains was maintained at six, including the two Ilfracombe to Paddington through trains (9.20am and 11.45am ex-Ilfracombe) but these services were supplemented in the peak period by the excursions again. There was one early departure on Fridays (at 5.30am) and Saturdays (4.10am) from Taunton, one at 11.30am (Saturdays) and another at 4.40pm (Fridays). The corresponding Up workings on Saturdays at 8.30am and 11.20am from Ilfracombe were 'London Excursions', whilst the Fridays only evening service worked Up at 9.50pm from Ilfracombe. In the autumn, the usual five Up and Down trains had resumed, with an additional 1.33pm departure from Taunton to Dulverton but there appeared to be no corresponding return service for public use. The through service to Paddington (departing Ilfracombe at 9.30am) continued to run.

For summer of 1922 (from 10th July), there were seven Up and Down trains, including two from Ilfracombe to Paddington, and a Saturdays only Taunton to Wiveliscombe service (departing at 11.15pm, arriving at 11.38pm) commenced running, working back as empty stock. These services were supplemented by two Saturdays only Down excursions (4.20am and 5.30am) from Taunton to Ilfracombe and a Fridays only 4.02pm departure. The coaches for the two Saturday Down trains worked back empty at 8.25am and 10.45am. In the Up direction, the Fridays only 1.05pm Ilfracombe to Paddington excursion departure had its stock worked down empty from Taunton at 8.50am. The two later Up excursions were the 7.45pm and 9.50pm from Ilfracombe, the coaches for the earlier train working down as empty stock at 3.25pm. A similar pattern applied for summer 1923.

In October 1922, services reverted to five Up and Down trains, with the Saturdays only Wiveliscombe train continuing, as did the daily 9.30am Ilfracombe to Paddington which, by this time, departed from Barnstaple GWR by 10.49am, a little earlier.

The summer of 1924 had eight Down and Up trains but there was a ninth that left Barnstaple GWR for Dulverton at 10.50am, arriving at 11.46am. It then departed at 12.05pm for Taunton, arriving at 12.57pm. The corresponding return working formed the 5.35pm Taunton to Dulverton, where it arrived at 6.33pm and then formed the 7.15pm Dulverton to Barnstaple GWR, arriving at 8.06pm. The purpose of this train was to provide an additional daytime stopping service between the faster services, as four of the Down trains and three Up trains did not stop at all stations. The 3.07pm from Taunton (12.05pm ex-Paddington through train) and the 11.40am ex-Ilfracombe (12.35pm Barnstaple GWR) were designated 'luncheon and tea car train'. The Down train was a seven-coach through portion, which was strengthened on Saturdays. The 9.00am departure was badged the 'Ilfracombe, Minehead and Torbay Express'. There was a Saturdays only 8.50am Ilfracombe to Bath, along with three extra Down services, whilst Fridays saw three Up trains, with two empty stock trains working down to form these. The Saturdays only Taunton to Wiveliscombe late evening service continued.

The 3.30pm from Paddington also conveyed a slip coach, which was attached to the 6.05pm Taunton departure. There were two additional services on Saturdays in the summer, including an Up through train from Ilfracombe to Bristol and Bath (departing Ilfracombe at 8.50pm), which used the East Curve. The 11.15pm local departure from Taunton to Wiveliscombe (arriving 11.37pm) continued.

From the 1924 public time table (14th July to 21st September). the noted through coaches were Ilfracombe to Bristol and Bath (on the 8.50am and 9.15am), to Manchester London Road (on the 9.15am) and to Paddington (on the 9.15am, 11.40am, and 2.55pm). In that year, it took 5 hours 22 minutes to travel from Paddington to Ilfracombe on the 3.30pm departure, with the slip coach.

The 1924 winter timetable showed five Up and Down trains on weekdays, plus the Saturdays only Taunton to Wiveliscombe evening local train. There was a slip carriage off the 10.30am Paddington train, the 'Cornish Riviera Express', which worked through to Ilfracombe on the 1.10pm departure from Taunton. The 9.30am from Ilfracombe formed the 'Ilfracombe, Minehead, Bristol and Bath Spa Express', as referred to in the public time table. This train reached Paddington at 4.05pm, being the only through train in this winter period.

The summer of 1925 (13th July to 20th September) continued with eight Up and Down weekly services. The 7.00am was the first Up train, with the 9.55am and 12 noon Ilfracombe to Paddington services still running. Saturdays provided four extra Down trains, including the 10.50am Wolverhampton to Ilfracombe and the 12.06pm Paddington to Ilfracombe, which replaced a weekdays Taunton to Ilfracombe train. There were four extra Up trains, with the two Paddington services being maintained. Fridays also had supplementary services, with three Down ECS trains from Taunton to Ilfracombe and four Up passenger services: a 1.15pm excursion and three late evening Ilfracombe to Taunton excursions at 8.45pm, 9.45pm and 10.45pm. The Taunton to Dulverton service continued.

The winter time table of 1925 showed six Up and Down trains, including the 9.55am Ilfracombe to Paddington service. Similarly, from September 1926, the six Up and Down passenger services continued, along with the usual two Paddington departures from Ilfracombe and the Saturdays only Wiveliscombe service.

For the summer of 1928, there were eight Up and Down weekday services supported by three Saturdays only Down Ilfracombe excursions, departing Taunton at 3.50am, 4.30am and 5.30am, and the 10.50am from Wolverhampton (this replaced one of the regular services). In addition, there was a Saturdays only 12.06pm train from Paddington through to Ilfracombe. The Saturdays only evening Wiveliscombe service continued but there was also a Thursdays and Saturdays only 2.55pm departure from Taunton to Wiveliscombe, arriving at 3.15pm. In the Up direction, the Ilfracombe departures at 9.55am, 11.50am and 1.15pm (Fridays only) were for Paddington but there were also three additional Up Ilfracombe excursions leaving Barnstaple GWR at 9.10pm, 10.25pm and 11.25pm on Fridays only. Three sets of empty coaches would work Down earlier in the day (8.50am, 3.45pm and 7.05pm from Taunton) for these excursions. There was also a Taunton to Dulverton and return service, departing Taunton at 5.40pm and returning from Dulverton at 7.00pm. Four Down and three weekly up Ilfracombe services by-passed Barnstaple GWR by using the East Curve, whilst on Saturdays, eight Down and five Up services, including the Paddington and Wolverhampton trains, took this route. The September 1928 time table had six Up and Down trains, whilst the 9.55am Ilfracombe to Paddington ran on Saturdays only.

The summer service of 1928 was broadly repeated in 1929 but one change was the extension on Saturdays only of the 5.42pm Taunton to Dulverton train. Arriving at 6.34pm, it would depart for Barnstaple at 7.20pm and arrive at 8.11pm; there was no equivalent return working. The lunchtime Thursdays and Saturdays only Taunton to Wiveliscombe service was suspended in this summer period but returned in the autumn.

A superb panorama of an Ilfracombe to London train passing over Castle Hill Viaduct behind a 'Mogul' 2-6-0 in the late 1920s. Composed mostly of 'Toplight' corridor carriages, most appear to be painted in the 1922-27 lined brown and cream livery, with the garter emblem centrally on each coach. The leading vehicle is a Brake Composite with two First, four Third and a guard's and luggage compartments at the end; it appears to be a Bars II type of Diagram E95 and is the only coach showing its compartment side. The second coach is a Bars I type Brake Third with four compartments, a guard's compartment and a separate luggage compartment, with two double doors each side, probably Diagram D45. Third is a Bars II type Composite with three Third and four First compartments, which appears to be of Diagram E88 or E98 – steel panelled if the latter. Coach four is a Brake Third with three passenger compartments, plus guard's and luggage compartments, to Diagram D52. Next is another Composite which appears to be the same type as coach three, whilst the last coach is a Brake Third which does not have any toplights and appears to have a steel roof (the other coaches all have rain strips), so is probably one of Collett's bow-ended designs. It has three passenger compartments, plus guard's and luggage, and is probably to Diagram D94 but might possibly be a rebuilt 'Toplight' that had been used in an ambulance train during the First World War, in which case it might be of Diagram D88. It is hard to see any lining on the cream on this coach, so it may be in the simplified brown and cream livery of 1927. The roof boards on the leading three carriages read 'PADDINGTON AND ILFRACOMBE'. It is likely that the last three coaches were added at Barnstaple GWR. *Arthur Halls, courtesy National Railway Museum*

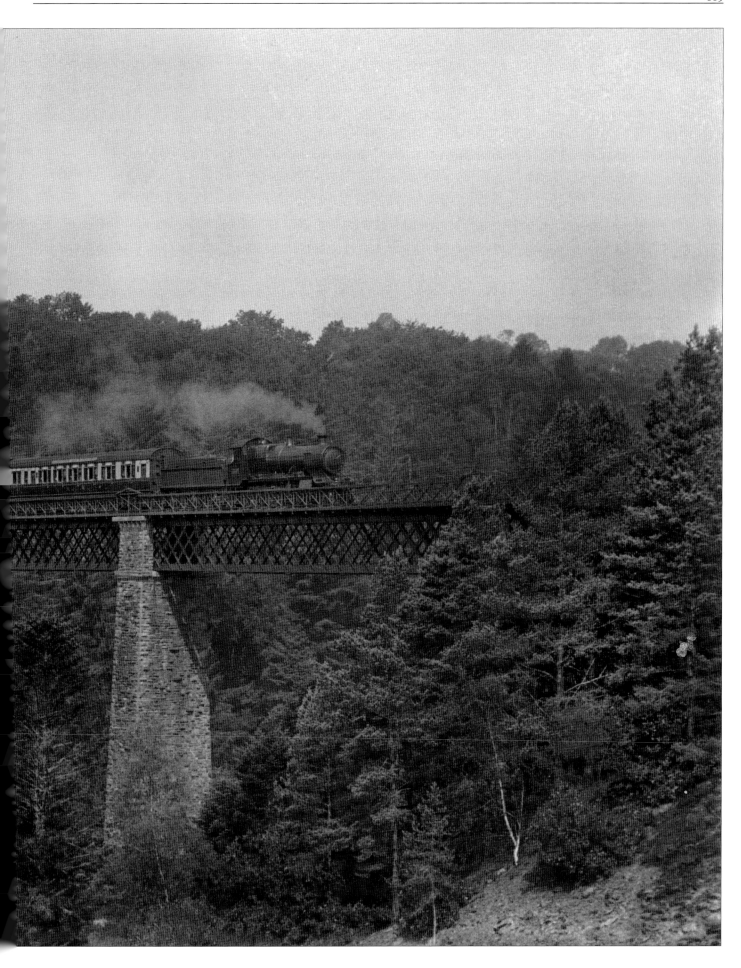

Manoeuvres at Barnstaple South Junction circa 1926. The locomotive has a two-word nameplate which is not quite readable but would be either No. 3376 *River Plym* or No. 3364 *Frank Bibby* and is on a Down train that has arrived via the East Curve (to the right but out of the picture). It has come to a halt at the South Junction Starting signal but beyond the South Junction Signal Box, the roof of which is just visible over the second coach. Note the arrangement of the signals, the East Curve being subsidiary to the route into the GWR station, whilst the Distant arms are red with white chevrons – it was not until 1928 that yellow with black chevrons was adopted instead. The leading coach is a low roof Brake Third which had been built as a 6-wheeled, four-compartment coach with a centre guard's and luggage compartment. The luggage area had double external doors with no windows which can be seen next to the guard's lookout. This was a standard design and over 150 were built between 1876 and 1884 and were eventually illustrated by Diagram T38. This particular coach has had its luggage compartment extended to include the two compartments nearest the camera, leaving the two on the far side of the guard's compartment for passengers. There are horizontal bars on the inside of the windows at the near end and it had been rebuilt so that there is no sign of doors or any handles below the windows. It has also had the centre wheels removed, so is now 4-wheeled, in which state it was covered by Diagram T27. The second coach, which seems to be down a little on its springs, is a more modern design, a four-compartment 4-wheeled Composite, originally with Second, First, First, Second Class compartments, the Seconds being reclassified Third by 1909. It has taller windows than the leading coach and has a 3-arc (elliptical) roof profile, as opposed to the single arc profile of the first coach. The coach was illustrated by Diagram U4 and 113 were built between 1891 and 1902. Next is a five compartment Third of the same style as the leading coach, originally 6-wheeled but now four and of a type that was the most numerous built by the GWR (636 built between 1872 and 1884) Diagrams S3 with six wheels and S4 with four. Fourth is another two-compartment Brake Third, the same as the first coach, except that it is still 6-wheeled and the far end has been repanelled, so that there are no windows in the enlarged luggage compartment and it only has its original doors. The last coach is a 46ft 6¾ins long clerestory, double-ended slip, which can be indentified as either No. 7071 or 7072 of Diagram F2. These two coaches were built in September 1886 and their accommodation comprised a guard's and luggage compartment with double doors, Third, Second, First, First, Second, Third, guard plus luggage, the Seconds being Third Class by this date. The coach has an arc plus elliptical roof profile and its sides are in a transitional style with tall fixed windows (lights) and smaller door droplights, with a deeper panel and ventilator above, and is mounted on Dean's 8ft 6ins bogies. Unusually for a clerestory slip, the vacuum reservoirs on these coaches (and the similar Diagram F1s) were slung fore and aft from the underframe instead of being mounted on the roof. The locomotive in the background has ventured out from Barnstaple GWR to collect this vehicle and deliver to the GWR station, whilst the rest of the train will then continue on to Ilfracombe. *Arthur Halls, courtesy National Railway Museum*

RIGHT: An unusual combination in 1931, showing Southern Railway 'M7' Class 0-4-4T No. E36 of Barnstaple Junction shed passing the Wrafton Down Distant signal with a train of modern GWR express stock, the roof boards of which most likely read 'PADDINGTON AND ILFRACOMBE' again. The view is looking south-east, with the expanse of the Taw Estuary in the background. ***Lesley Walker, Brian Perkes collection***

BELOW: The first of three average quality but extremely rare views around East Junction and the East Curve. Looking towards Taunton in 1933, the addition of coaches here is referred to in the text – the locomotive propelling carriages out from Barnstaple GWR station is out of shot to the left. Once coupled to the 12.20pm Barnstaple to Taunton service, it will be ready to leave. ***Courtney Card Collection, courtesy Ian Huxtable***

1930-1939

During this decade, there was a significant expansion of traffic in the holiday season in comparison to the previous ten years and there were regular services working to Ilfracombe, with through coaches to and from Paddington. In the Up direction they were the 9.55am and 11.50am from Ilfracombe, the latter also conveying a Dining car from Barnstaple. These trains were formed from the through coaches of four Down trains, whilst the Dining car arrived off the 9.00am Paddington to Kingswear service and was put on the 12.25pm Taunton departure. The Paddington, Wolverhampton and Manchester trains were normally scheduled for four to six coaches but the 9.45am Ilfracombe to Manchester consisted of nine carriages in the mid-1930s.

In 1931-32, the 10.30am departure from Paddington, the 'Cornish Riviera Express', carried a slip coach for Ilfracombe and a Brake Composite coach for Minehead. The Ilfracombe slip coach went forward on the 1.10pm Taunton departure, arriving at 4.27pm. At Taunton, the coaches would be left on the Down main line platform, with the branch train moving out of the bay and reversing on to the slip coaches to couple up; it would then depart from the Down main. The slip coach was stabled overnight at Ilfracombe before returning the next day on the 9.55am departure for Paddington. This train also included a Brake Composite corridor coach from Ilfracombe and was joined by three more carriages (two corridor Brake Thirds and a corridor Composite) from Barnstaple GWR. On arrival at Taunton, the five coaches from Ilfracombe and Barnstaple then joined up with a Composite coach from Minehead to be taken forward, arriving at Paddington (via Bristol and Bath) at 4.05pm. The three Barnstaple coaches for Paddington had arrived at 9.05am on the first Down working, which left Taunton at 7.50am earlier that morning. However, they had reached Taunton via Plymouth the previous day! The three coaches off the 4.05pm arrival would then leave on the 6.30pm Paddington to Plymouth departure. Arriving at Plymouth at 00.45am the next day, they would then work back to Taunton later that day, therefore making it a three day trip for the coaches to complete the diagram.

The Ilfracombe Brake Composite corridor coach had worked down the previous day on the 1.15pm departure from Paddington, arriving at Ilfracombe at 6.08pm. The Down Barnstaple parcels van left Paddington at 10.35pm and the Full Brake was detached at Taunton (at 3.01am) to go forward to Barnstaple on the 7.50am stopping service. The Full Brake from this Down train then left Barnstaple that evening on the 6.15pm stopping service to Taunton, where it joined the 6.20pm Plymouth to Paddington parcels, leaving Taunton at 8.43pm and arriving back at Paddington at 2.40am the next day.

In the summer of 1932, there were seven Up and Down services, supplemented by the Taunton to Dulverton return evening train, plus on Saturdays only three additional services and a Wolverhampton to Ilfracombe train. On Fridays only there was an 8.25pm Ilfracombe to Manchester excursion, whilst the 9.55am and 11.50am were the Ilfracombe to Paddington trains. The first Up train was retimed to depart Barnstaple GWR at 6.55am. In the 1932-33 winter period, six Up and Down trains provided the services, with no Taunton to Dulverton and the 9.55am being the only departure to Paddington.

The summer period of 1933 (17th July to 10th September) had seven Up and Down trains, including the two Ilfracombe to Paddington services. The Taunton to Dulverton evening service ran but was extended to Barnstaple on Saturdays only. Summer Saturdays had five additional Down trains (eight working through to Ilfracombe, including the 10.25am from Birmingham) and four additional Up trains, six of which worked back from Ilfracombe – the East Curve was in full use.

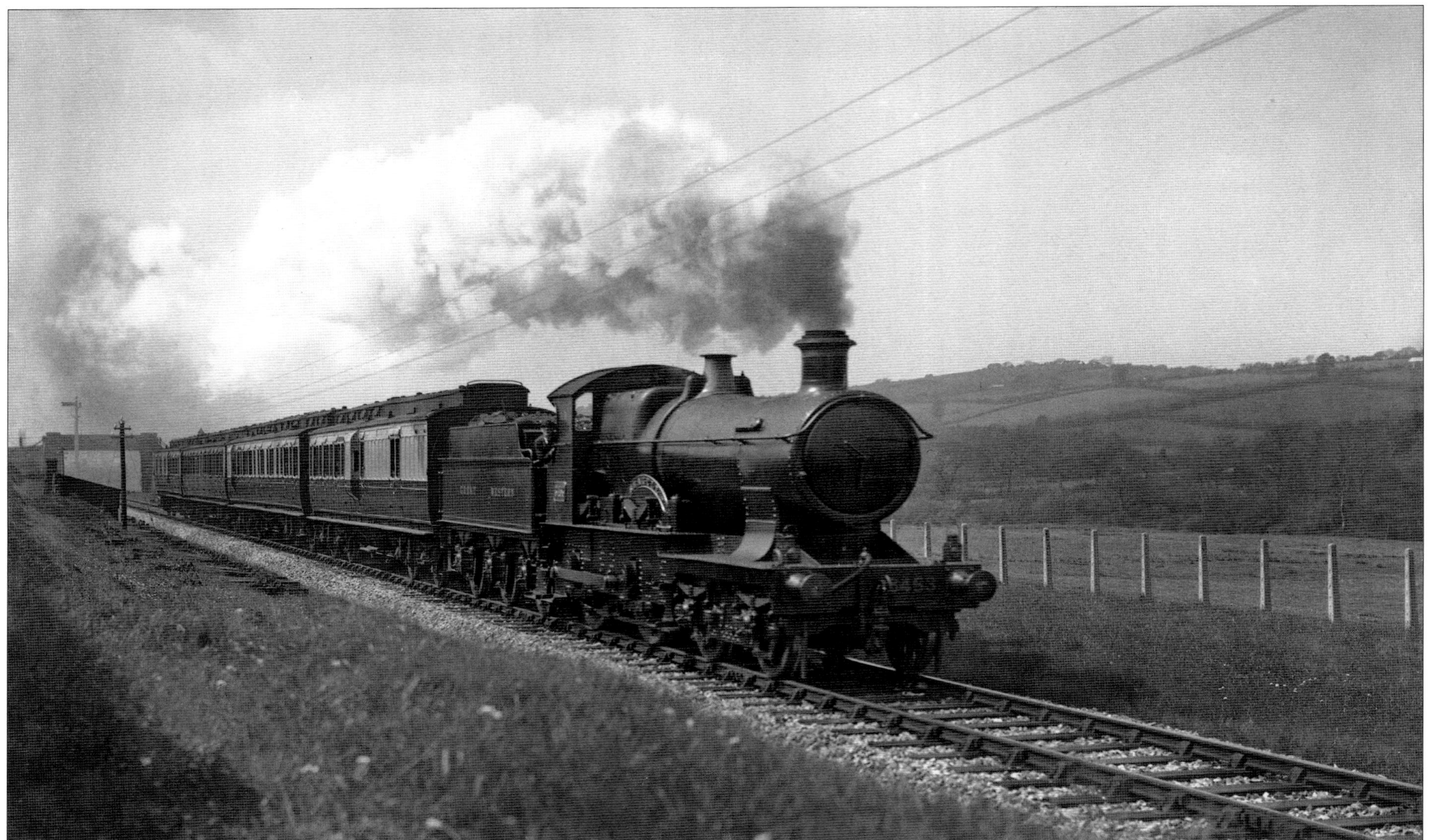

'Bulldog' No. 3453 *Seagull* near Westcott Lane Bridge, shortly after leaving Barnstaple GWR with a four-coach train of clerestory stock, bound for Taunton at an unknown date in the early 1930s. This is an interesting train – four clerestory coaches, all with brake compartments with the lookouts still intact and running with Class 'A' headlamps! The leading two coaches seem to be in the simplified brown and cream livery introduced in mid-1927, the first being a four-compartment Brake Third (or Van Third as the GWR would call it), which appears to be to Diagram D14. It has elliptical profile clerestory and main roofs and Dean 8ft 6in bogies, is 50ft 0¾ins long and 8ft 0¾ins wide and was built sometime between 1894 and 1896. The second coach appears to be wider than the first one (*i.e.* 8ft 0¾ins) and looks as if it was built as a Brake tri-Composite – the doors seem to be grouped into three, possibly two Seconds, two Firsts and three Third Class compartments with toilets between each group. Then there is the guard's lookout which could be concealing a pair of doors for the guard's and luggage compartment. Diagram E72 would be an example but there were other similar designs. The third coach seems to be a similar ex-Brake tri-Composite, except the guard's door(s) seem to be this side of the lookout which appears to be at the end of the coach. Lastly is a Brake Third with three double doors each side to the luggage compartment. This may be a corridor coach –there were several diagrams of these plus at least one for a non-corridor version. Based throughout this period mostly at Taunton, the 4-4-0 spent time allocated to Barnstaple, mostly during the summer months but occasionally in to the autumn, every year between 1929 and 1935. As noted in the previous volumes, this section of line is now buried beneath the A361 North Devon Link Road, whilst Westcott Lane is also no more, having been subsumed on the north (right) side of the line by an industrial estate and a golf course to the south. *Arthur Halls, courtesy National Railway Museum*

Above: A distant view of a seven-coach train leaving Barnstaple GWR station and heading towards the East Box, providing an impressive view of the triangle in 1933.

Below: From a similar viewpoint, the 4.30pm Taunton to Ilfracombe is seen approaching South Junction. The locomotive on the West Curve patiently waits to couple up and draw the rear two coaches back to the GWR station. *Both the Courtney Card Collection, courtesy Ian Huxtable*

The Taunton to Wiveliscombe evening service ran but the lunchtime Thursdays and Saturdays only was suspended during the summer, running again in the winter period.

Three digit train identification codes were introduced by the GWR on 14th July 1934, to minimise delays and assist in the handling of trains during the busy summer Saturday periods. The system made it possible to tell at a glance the starting time and place of an express train and its destination, and where a train was comprised of a number of parts, which part it was. The numbering was composed of three 16ins white numerals on a 20ins black plate, which were slotted into a 3ft wide frame on the smokebox door. The first number gave the originating area, the other two numbers identifying the train itself. Trains originating in the Paddington area were 100-199, those from Exeter 500-599.

On the August 1939 Bank Holiday Saturday, the 9.35am Paddington to Minehead and Ilfracombe train was No. 130; the 12.06pm for the same destinations had No. 165 as its reporting number, whilst the 2.15pm to Minehead and Ilfracombe was No. 190 but also had a relief train which carried No. 197. In the Up direction, the 12-noon Ilfracombe to Paddington carried No. 520, the 9.50am Ilfracombe to Manchester (London Road) No. 575 and the 10.40am Wolverhampton to Ilfracombe No. 745.

Thus the regular trains were numbered with a 0 or 5 at the end, with the relief trains being numbered 1 to 4 or 6 to 9. This numbering was particularly helpful at busy locations such as Taunton and the junction at Norton Fitzwarren but trains did not always carry them throughout; Minehead and Ilfracombe-bound trains would only carry the numbers as far as Taunton and Up trains might only put them on at Norton or, more likely, Taunton. On the weekend of 4th/5th August 1939, a special ran from Wolverhampton at 9.45pm to Ilfracombe on the Friday night with reporting No. 076. On the Saturday afternoon of that weekend, there was a 'Guaranteed Excursion', which ran from Leicester (LM&SR) to Ifracombe under reporting No. 043. The numbering system continued into the early years of the war and was in operation again in 1946 but the coding was different from the pre-war identification and many more regular trains were numbered. In summer 1949 for example, the 9.25am Ilfracombe to Cardiff carried No. 588 from Taunton.

The winter period of 1934 (1st October to 7th July 1935), showed five Up and Down trains. There were no Down through trains and two Up through trains from Ilfracombe, including the 9.50am to Paddington, the other just running to Taunton. The Taunton to Wiveliscombe Thursdays and Saturdays only auto train service still ran.

Weekdays in summer 1934 had seven regular Up and Down trains, including the 9.45am and 11.50am Ilfracombe to Paddington. There was also an extension to the Exe Valley service with, on weekdays only, the 6.10pm Exeter auto train arriving at Dulverton at 7.18pm and then departing at 7.21pm for South Molton (arriving 7.45pm). It would return, departing at 8.00pm, arriving at Dulverton at 8.26pm and leaving for Exeter at 8.35pm. Summer Saturdays in 1934 had twelve Up and eleven Down trains, including the 10.25am Birmingham to Ilfracombe, the 9.45am Ilfracombe to Manchester and the 10.48am Ilfracombe to Paddington.

A similar pattern of services applied to 1935. In August, for example, the Saturdays only 10.48am Ilfracombe to Paddington train had a scheduled formation of Third, Van Third, Composite, Third and Van Third (all 60ft stock) from Ilfracombe and a Brake Composite from Barnstaple (added at East Junction). This was combined with a seven-coach set (including a Dining car) from Minehead on arrival at Taunton, the train being scheduled to arrive at Paddington at 4.00pm.

In the mid-1930s, Down summertime trains left Paddington at 9.35am and 12.05pm (the latter Fridays/Saturdays only) and in the Up direction at 9.45am (retimed to 10.48am Saturdays) and 11.50am from Ilfracombe. On Saturdays, the 9.45am Ilfracombe departure ran to Manchester, whilst a Wolverhampton to Ilfracombe service ran in the Down direction and there was an Ilfracombe to Birmingham service in the Up direction.

In the period September 1935 to July 1936, the regular services comprised six Up and Down trains, the 9.50am Ilfracombe to Paddington continuing to run, as did the Taunton to Wiveliscombe

Class '45XX' 'Prairie' tank No. 4581 heads a Barnstaple to Taunton train near Swimbridge in 1935. The locomotive, which was new in February 1927, looks in smart condition here, the pristine condition of its livery suggesting it may have recently returned from a Heavy General overhaul. It was, however, to be an early withdrawal for members of this class, in April 1958. The leading carriage is a Diagram F16 Toplight, double-ended slip; note the window in the end, this type had three, a central droplight and a fixed window either side. The ends of the vacuum cylinders can be glimpsed under the coach, together with the flat 'bars' underframe truss and the 8ft 'American' bogies. This was a Bars I coach with a guard's and luggage compartment at the end nearest the camera, four Third and two First Class passenger compartments, separated by a toilet and a small guard's compartment at the far end with single doors. The second coach is one of Collett's Brake Composite designs, probably with four Third and two First compartments. The other three coaches appear to be two Brake Thirds at each end, with the one in between them not identifiable. ***Arthur Halls, courtesy National Railway Museum***

Saturdays only evening service. There were excursion trains booked to commence before the July summer period and to run on certain other public holidays. Being winter, the East Curve was closed to through services, so all trains reversed at Barnstaple GWR. The service time table referred to certain trains having their GWR engine and guard working through from Ilfracombe, in the summer period when the East Curve was open to avoid any tender-first working. Curiously, a footnote was included in the 1934 summer time table which stated '*If engines require turning they must run around the triangle*'. One surmises that if locomotives had to be changed at Barnstaple GWR, and there was limited time for engines to be turned at Barnstaple SR, given the GWR turntable was too small for a 'Mogul' the only practical option was to run around the triangle. GWR engines would be turned on the 65ft turntable installed at Ilfracombe shed in 1925 on arrival there.

By the summer of 1936, on Saturdays there were thirteen Down and twelve Up trains, the 10.40am departure from Wolverhampton referred to above becoming a Minehead and Ilfracombe service on those days. The weekday services remained the same, with seven Up and Down services. Passenger trains ran again on Sundays from the summer time table of 1936, up to and including the summer of 1939. In 1936 (6th July to 27th September), they commenced with one Down train, the 2.15pm departure from Taunton, which used the East Curve to arrive at Barnstaple SR at 3.45pm, and one Up, which departed Ilfracombe at 4.20pm.

One Saturday morning in the summer of 1937, as reported in the *GWR Magazine*, the third portion of the down 'Cornish Riveria Express' conveyed nine coaches, four of which were slipped at Westbury (for Weymouth). Five more were to be slipped at Taunton, three for Minehead and two for Ilfracombe, but the apparatus failed, so the train had to stop so that they could be detached and then be taken forwards on the usual branch passenger services.

The GWR had issued instructions for the holding up of branch line trains if there were main line delays. The guidelines for the Barnstaple Branch from September 1937 are shown in **Table 11.2**, below.

In the summer of 1937, on weekdays there were seven Up and six

TABLE 11.2: LENGTH OF TIME TRAINS TO BE HELD TO MAKE CONNECTIONS

TRAIN	MINS HELD	NOTES
7.50am Taunton to Barnstaple Jnc	10	If connection not maintained special to be run if required
10.35am Taunton to Barnstaple Jnc	20	
1.10pm Taunton to Barnstaple Jnc	15	
4.30pm Taunton to Barnstaple Jnc	15	If connection not maintained special to be run if required
5.40pm Taunton to Barnstaple Jnc	15	If connection not maintained special to be run if required
8.17pm Taunton to Barnstaple	30	If connection not maintained special to be run if required
11.05pm (SO) Taunton to Wiveliscombe	30	If connection not maintained special to be run after arrival of the 11.45pm Wiveliscombe

Down trains, plus the early evening Taunton to Dulverton and return service. These included the daily Ilfracombe to London services (9.50am and 12.00pm from Ilfracombe), although there was no equivalent through return service. On summer Saturdays, the services were enhanced, with the thirteen Down trains including two early trains from Taunton to Ilfracombe (4.30am and 5.30am), the 12.06pm Paddington to Ilfracombe and the 10.40am Wolverhampton to Ilfracombe – most additional trains ran through to the terminus at the Devon resort. There were eleven Up trains, including the 9.50am Ilfracombe to Manchester, whilst the 12 noon departure was the London through train. The Saturdays only Taunton to Wiveliscombe evening service ran but the Taunton to Dulverton service did not run on summer Saturdays. A similar pattern was repeated for the summer of 1939.

The working of through coaches in the periods 27th September 1937 to 3rd July 1938 and 4th July to 25th September 1938 are reviewed in **Appendix 17**. This shows the contrast between the winter period and the busier summer months. In 1938, the fastest train from Paddington to Ilfracombe was 5 hours 10 minutes, just a little quicker than the comparison for 1924, above. However, on Fridays and Saturdays only, the time accelerated to 4 hours 35 minutes, most of this saving coming from the largely non-stop D&SR section of the journey.

A review of the summer 1939 time table (3rd July to 24th September) showed seven Down trains on weekdays, excluding Saturdays, four of which ran through to Ilfracombe. The first Down train left Taunton at 7.50am (arriving at Barnstaple Junction at 9.51am, where it terminated), the last at 8.17pm arriving at Barnstaple GWR at 9.56pm, where it too terminated. It is worth highlighting that the 12.02pm (to Ilfracombe), the 1.50pm (to Junction only), the 4.32pm and 6.15pm from Taunton (both to Ilfracombe) all used the East Curve and by-passed Barnstaple GWR station completely. However, the station was served by these trains stopping at South Junction and uncoupling a coach or more, with a locomotive waiting on the loop to couple up and then hauling them in to Barnstaple GWR; from the departure time at South Junction, 3 minutes was time-tabled for the arrival into the GWR station. There was an additional passenger service that ran from Taunton to Dulverton on weekdays only (5.45pm, arriving at 6.32pm).

In the Up direction, there were also seven trains. The first two (the 6.55am and 8.45am departures) started at Barnstaple GWR (albeit the coaches for the second departure worked over from the Junction empty) and reached Taunton at 8.31am and 10.31am respectively. The next two were the 9.50am and 12 noon Ilfracombe to Paddington through services. These avoided the GWR station but passengers from there boarded coaches standing in the platform which were shunted out to East Junction, where they were coupled to the Up train for the onward journey. The remaining three weekday trains ran between the Junction and Taunton but called en route in the usual manner at the GWR station, the last Up train being the 5.48pm departure from the Junction. The Dulverton return service back to Taunton left at 6.55pm (weekdays only).

Summer Saturdays in this period generally had twelve Down and thirteen Up services, although not all of them ran every Saturday. The first Down train was 4.30am from Taunton through to Ilfracombe, this being followed by the 5.30am. There was one through train from Paddington (the 12.06pm departure from London) and one from Wolverhampton (the 10.40am departure, leaving Taunton at 3.02pm). Eight of these Down services avoided Barnstaple GWR but, as with the weekday through services, two of them had coaches detached at South Junction for that station. In the Up direction, the 9.50am departure from Ilfracombe ran to Manchester and the noon departure to Paddington, both of them having coaches attached from the GWR station at East Junction, but five Up trains by-passed Barnstaple GWR completely.

In most instances with the Down trains, the service time table indicated that the GWR engine and guard were to work through to Ilfracombe. There was also a Fridays only Up train leaving Ilfracombe at 9.20pm, running to Taunton to arrive at 11.56pm; this also ran on Saturdays and was the final Up train of the day.

On Sundays through this period, there were two departures from Ilfracombe, at 11am and 4.35pm. These services by-passed Barnstaple GWR but stopped at major stations en route to Taunton. There was a Down working at 2.15pm from Taunton, which ran through to Ilfracombe, the stock from which most likely formed the later departure in the Up direction. The locomotive for the first train worked light engine from Barnstaple GWR to Ilfracombe at 9.20am.

In addition to these main services, there was a local Saturdays only (on two weekends in September only) Barnstaple Junction to South Molton service, leaving at 8.55pm, arriving at 9.33pm and returning empty at 9.45pm to Barnstaple GWR. There was a Fridays only 10.15pm departure for the Junction, arriving at 10.20pm, the stock returning empty at 10.30pm. At the other end of the line, there was an 11.05pm that left Taunton for Wiveliscombe, arriving at 11.27pm; this too returned empty, at 11.45pm.

In the summer of 1939, the 9.00am Paddington to Paignton passenger carried a Restaurant car for Barnstaple. It was detached at Taunton, added to the next local service – most likely the 12.02pm SO Taunton to Ilfracombe – and returned on the 12.02pm Ilfracombe to Paddington departure the following day. On 15th July 1939, records show that Dining car No. 9672 was used on the 9.50am Ilfracombe to Manchester train, being attached at the rear along with a Brake Composite coach at Barnstaple East Junction, departing at 10.44am. The carriage for this Saturday train would work up locally from Plymouth on the previous Friday and travel to Barnstaple on the 8.17pm from Taunton. It would return to the GWR on the Sunday on the 11.55am Crewe to Plymouth.

On 12th August 1939, the following locomotives were recorded arriving at Paddington on Ilfracombe trains, having taken over at Taunton:

No.	Class	Shed	Train	No.	Load
4026	'Star'	TN	11.00am Ilfracombe	516	11
5038	'Castle'	PDN	12.00pm Ilfracombe	521	11
5036	'Castle'	PDN	12.00pm Ilfracombe	520	12
4016	'Castle'	BRD	2.15pm Ilfracombe		15

The public time table from 25th September 1939 until 30th June 1940 shows six Down and six Up trains, the 1.10pm departure from Taunton conveying the slip coach from Paddington (off the 10.30am departure). The first Down train was the 7.50am off Taunton (arriving 9.45am), whilst the first Up was the 6.55am (arriving at 8.35am). Last trains were the 8.15pm Down (arriving 9.57pm at Barnstaple) and the 6.10pm departure Up (arriving at Taunton at 8.15pm). In addition, there was a a train that ran on Thursdays and Saturdays only, leaving Taunton at 1.34pm, arriving at Wiveliscombe at 1.55pm and returning from there at 2.10pm, arriving back at Taunton at 2.30pm. On Saturdays only there was an 11.05pm departure from Taunton to Wiveliscombe, arriving at 11.27pm. There was no corresponding public return working. A number of extra trains were published to run on 23rd-24th December and the Easter public holidays. These connected with London Down trains, the last of them departing Taunton at 3.00am, arriving at Barnstaple at 4.45am.

1940-1949

There were no further Sunday trains after this time. In addition, the East Curve was closed at the end of the summer season of 1939 and did not reopen again until June 1960, when Barnstaple Victoria Road, as it by then been renamed, closed to all passenger traffic.

From 1940 through to 1945, there was a certain consistency in the passenger train services, with five Up and five Down trains each weekday throughout this period. The first Down train left Taunton at 8.55am (later retimed to 8.50am), arriving at 10.55am at the Junction. The first Up train left Barnstaple GWR at 8.10am and arrived at Taunton at 9.55am. The last Up train left Barnstaple Junction at 6.42pm (retimed to 6.40pm from May 1943) and arrived at Taunton at 8.35pm (retimed to 8.30pm). The last train Down did vary depending on the year and time of year but in winter 1940 it departed Taunton at 8.55pm arriving at Barnstaple GWR at 10.42pm. It was then retimed to depart earlier but in May 1943 and subsequent years the last Down train left Taunton at 9.25pm, arriving at Barnstaple GWR at 11.10pm. Also in the summer months (late June to late September) throughout this period, there was a 9.30am Ilfracombe to Bristol and a 1.00pm Taunton to Ilfracombe passenger, these being the only through services at this time. Until 1942, the service time table stated that the GWR locomotive and crew would take this train through to Ilfracombe but from 1943 they only worked as far as the Junction, at which point a Southern crew and locomotive would take over. In addition, there was an unusual working that operated throughout the period. In 1941, an auto-train departed Bridgwater at 7.10am, Taunton at 7.36am and ran to Venn Cross, arriving at 8.07am. It is understood that this was a workmen's train and operated by a Class '54XX' locomotive turn. It departed Venn Cross at 8.12am for Taunton (arriving at 8.38am) and then went on to Castle Cary, no doubt conveying school children and folk working in Taunton on the return journey. The service was retimed to run slightly earlier in 1942 and for the remainder of the war years to beyond October 1945 but had stopped operating by 1947. In essence, this auto-train had replaced the early morning departures from Barnstaple and Taunton during the war years but ceased when the normal early trains started to run again.

A time table supplement for October 1941 introduced a new parcels service from Barnstaple GWR to Taunton, departing at 4.45pm and arriving at 7.42pm. It was not incorporated into the 1942 time table and from October May 1943 onwards ran only from South Molton to Taunton. This parcels service was the 'Rabbiter' and is covered in more detail in Chapter 12.

In the October 1946 to May 1947 period, there were six Up and six Down passenger trains, the first Down working being the 7.24am from Taunton (arriving and terminating at Barnstaple GWR at 9.15am). The first Up train was at 6.55am, whilst the last train Down was at 9.10pm (arriving at Barnstaple GWR at 10.53pm). The last Up train departed the Junction at 6.40pm. The 'Rabbiter' was incorporated into the time table, running when required at 3.20pm from Taunton and returning from South Molton at 5.45pm to arrive Taunton at 8.05pm.

In the summer Saturday period of 1947 (June to October), the regular six Down trains were supplemented by four additional services. The first Down service was the 5.25am from Taunton to Ilfracombe, whilst the last was the usual 9.10pm departure. All four additional Saturday Down trains ran through to Ilfracombe. In the Up direction there were eight fare-earning services, three of which started from Ilfracombe. The 9.25am departure was for Cardiff, whilst the 10.45am to Taunton would join with the Minehead service to run onto Paddington. These were the only two services to run beyond Taunton at this time. Some – but not all – of these through trains were stated as running with GWR locomotive and crew throughout. The last Up train was the 6.50pm from Ilfracombe, arriving at Taunton at 9.31pm, but either side of this, at 6.25pm and 7.25pm from Ilfracombe, ran Up ECS trains back to Taunton with a GWR engine and crew throughout the journey.

By 1947, the trend was being set for the time tabling of trains for the remainder of the line's life. The period commencing 6th October showed six Up and Down trains. The first Up service was the now established 6.55am from Barnstaple GWR, arriving at Taunton at 8.32am, the second being the 8.45am also from the GWR station. The first Down train was at 7.24am from Taunton, arriving at 9.15am, whilst the last was at 9.10pm, terminating at Barnstaple GWR at 10.53pm. The last Up train was at 6.40pm, arriving at Taunton at 8.38pm. These services were broadly repeated in 1948 post-Nationalisation.

Table 11.3 below illustrates ticket prices taken from October 1947 public time table.

Following Nationalisation of the railway network on and from 1st January 1948, Barnstaple GWR became Barnstaple Victoria Road under British Railways (Western Region) control. In the first time table issued under the regime, on summer Saturdays in 1948 the regular services were supplemented by four additional Down trains running through to Ilfracombe, the first at 5.25am from Taunton, the last at 3.30pm. In the Up direction there were four additional services starting at Ilfracombe, including the 9.25am departure that ran through to Cardiff. There was also an ECS train at 7.25pm from Ilfracombe to Taunton. The Down through trains and all but one Up train were usually worked by a Western region engine and crew throughout.

The weekday train pattern continued in to the winter of 1948 and early 1949 but a seventh train was added in both directions, the last Up train at 8.55pm being the extra service and the return working of the additional Down train. The other first and last trains retained broadly the same timings. In the summer of 1949, on weekdays there were still seven Up and Down trains but the 6.15pm from Taunton ran through to Ilfracombe, with a Southern Region engine and crew taking over at the Junction. These were supplemented by the four Up and Down Saturday's only Ilfracombe trains, including the service to Cardiff (9.25am departure), plus the ECS train back at 7.25pm.

Table 11.3: Ticket Prices Oct. 1947

Station	Single 1st	Single 3rd	Monthly Return 1st	Monthly Return 3rd
Barnstaple	54s 11d	32s 11d	66s 2d	44s 1d
Dulverton	47s 11d	28s 8d	57s 11d	38s 7d

Destination Roof Label Boards

The GWR introduced roof label boards (or destination boards) that were fitted to carriage roofs to help passengers select the right train. These were originally 17ft 10¾ins overall length, 8¾ins high and ⅞ inch thick. They were considerably reduced in size when

BARNSTAPLE

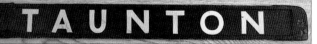

Destination boards for the two ends of the line. ***Amyas Crump collection***

TAUNTON

Hawksworth stock was introduced, this smaller destination board being 2ft 8ins long by 3½ins high and ⅞ inch thick. These were clipped into small brackets on the coach side, below the gutter. Two were fitted to 57ft-plus stock on the platform side.

Roof label boards existed for Paddington and Barnstaple, Paddington and Barnstaple Junction, and Paddington and Ilfracombe. There were also boards for Ilfracombe, Taunton, Bristol, Shrewsbury and Manchester (London Road).

1950-1959

The impact of the war was slowly beginning to fade and holiday traffic began to pick up again during the 1950s, something which was reflected in the number of trains and their loadings during the summer season.

The first winter period of this decade had seven Up and Down trains time tabled. The 6.55am was the first Up service and the 7.24am the first Down train, whilst the last were at 9.05pm Up and 9.10pm Down. In the summer period, the weekday service of seven Up and Down trains were supplemented by five additional Down trains, including the 8.20am Preston to Ilfracombe, which departed from Taunton at 3.41pm. There were four extra Up trains, including the 9.25am Ilfracombe to Cardiff.

Summer Saturdays in 1951 saw eleven Up and Down workings, including the 9.25am Ilfracombe to Bristol/Cardiff and the 10.52am Ilfracombe to Birmingham Snow Hill. In the Down direction were the 11.30am Paddington to Ilfracombe, and the Wolverhampton and Birmingham to Ilfracombe. This latter train left Snow Hill at 11.25am and after travelling via the former GWR Honeybourne line, would depart from Taunton at 3.35pm.

With the engine shed at Barnstaple Victoria Road being closed in January 1951, locomotives would work to and from the Junction shed for the first and last train services which started and terminated at Victoria Road. Through services continued to change engines at Barnstaple Junction or Victoria Road.

The summer of 1952 had seven Down but only six Up trains. There was a working time table note that referred to the 4.00pm from Barnstaple Junction and the 9.10pm Taunton to Barnstaple Victoria Road being worked by a Southern Region locomotive and train crew. Now that Nationalisation had taken hold, boundaries became blurred and with Barnstaple being both BR(WR) and BR(SR), there was inevitably some integration, not least of which was for maintaining alternative route knowledge for crew, in case of emergencies.

On summer Saturdays there were three extra services including the Ilfracombe to Cardiff and Birmingham trains, and more trains worked through to and from Ilfracombe. The 10.12am departure from Ilfracombe combined with a train from Minehead at Taunton to run through to Paddington.

The winter period had the seven Up and Down services and this continued into the summer period (8th June to 20th September) of 1953. These were supplemented by an additional five Down and four

Ex-GWR 'Mogul' No. 6364 starts away from Mortehoe & Woolacombe station on the Southern Region branch to Ilfracombe on 28th July 1951, with a Saturday's only Wolverhampton to Ilfracombe train that is embarking on the final leg of its journey. These trains had travelled down the D&SR line to join the Ilfracombe Branch at Barnstaple Junction. ***Roger J, Sellick, courtesy National Railway Museum***

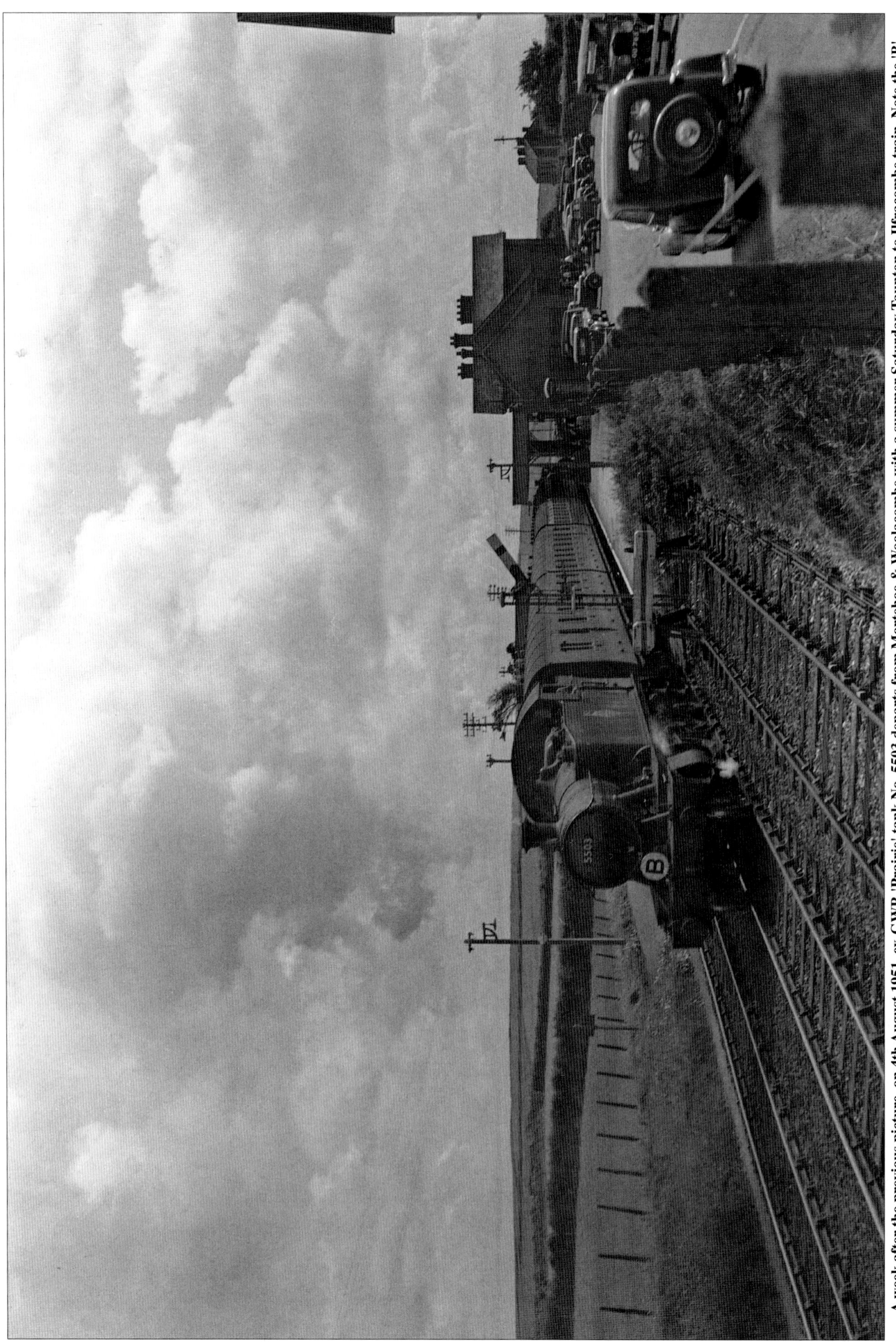

A week after the previous picture, on 4th August 1951, ex-GWR 'Prairie' tank No. 5503 departs from Mortehoe & Woolacombe with a summer Saturday Taunton to Ilfracombe train. Note the 'B' disc mounted on the buffer beam, an aid to the Taunton and Norton Fitzwarren signalmen on the main line as to the where the train was bound. There is a fine selection of period motor cars on the right, many meeting the train, probably collecting holidaymakers and their luggage who would be booked in to local bed & breakfast houses or hotels. As an aside, Lightmoor Press publisher Neil Parkhouse spent the first three years of his life in a house called 'Bella Vista' on Mortehoe Station Road, just behind the photographer and about 200 yards off picture to the right, so this was his local station of which he does have vague memories. The station building has recently been renovated and now forms the entrance to a holiday home development called Tarka Lane, whilst a terrace of new properties has been built on the trackbed in the foreground. ***Roger J. Sellick, courtesy National Railway Museum***

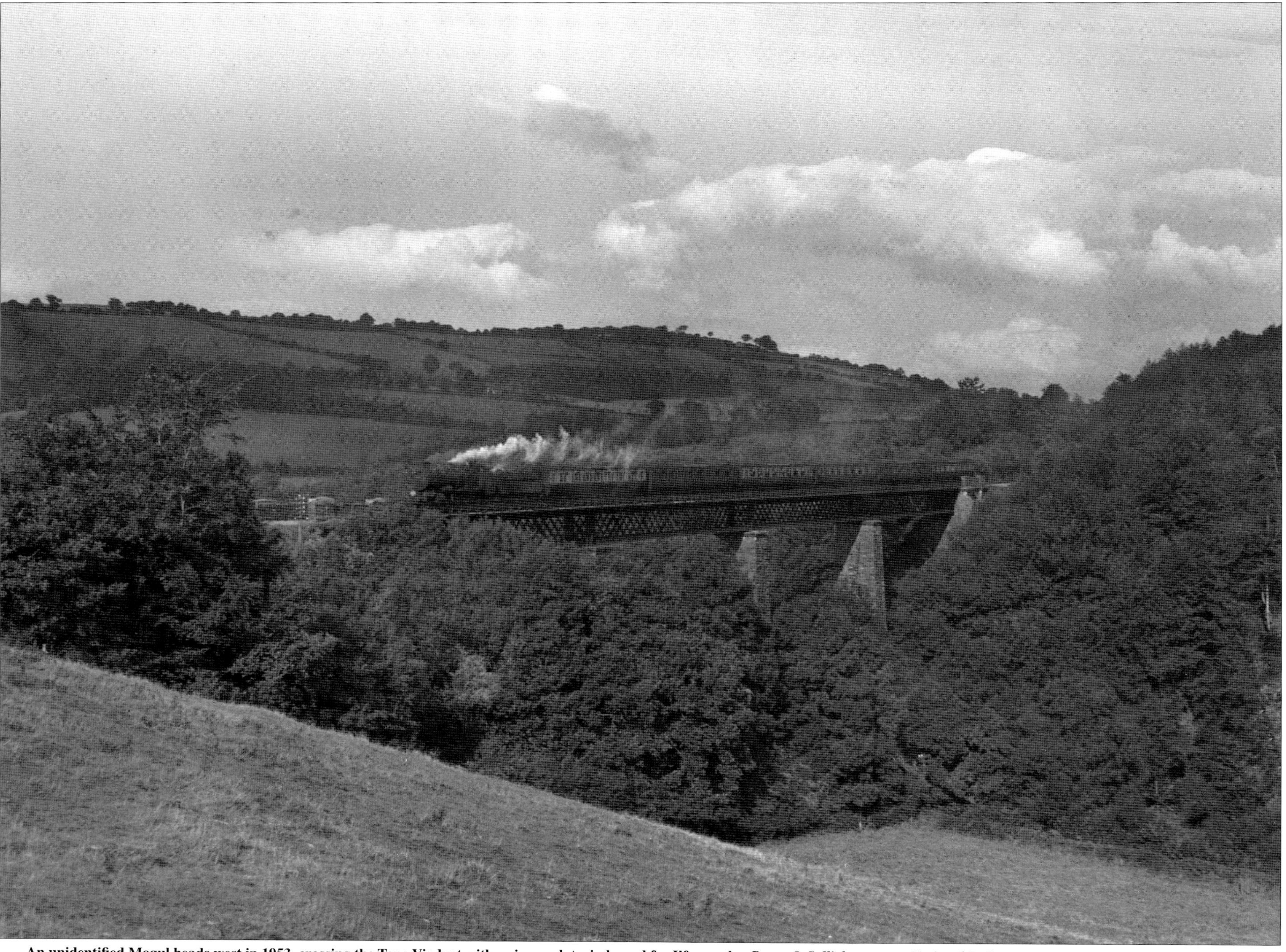

An unidentified Mogul heads west in 1953, crossing the Tone Viaduct with a six-coach train bound for Ilfracombe. *Roger J. Sellick, courtesy National Railway Museum*

A Southern Region interloper! 'N' Class 'Mogul' No. 31842 arrives at Dulverton with a Taunton-bound train on 13th September 1952. New in August 1924, the 2-6-0 was based at Barnstaple Junction shed at the date of this view, so may have made this journey a few times. It flitted between Barnstaple and Exmouth Junction sheds through the mid-1950s, with further allocations to North Devon in 1954-55 and 1955-56. It was withdrawn from Guildford shed in early September 1965. Note the Exe Valley auto service in the bay platform on the left. *Roger J. Sellick, courtesy National Railway Museum*

LEFT: The fireman of No. 6317 receives the token from the Dulverton signalman whilst paused at the station on Saturday 4th August 1951. Note the automatic token exchange post by the signalman and the token catcher apparatus for Down trains on the left. The picture is not quite sharp but does provide a rare glimpse of the rail entrance to the goods yard from this end of the station, on the right. ***Roger J. Sellick, courtesy National Railway Museum***

BELOW: Collett 0-6-0 No. 2275 pauses at Dulverton with a four-coach Up train in the mid 1950s. The date is prior to April 1956, when the locomotive moved north to Oswestry shed and then to Machynlleth, from where it was withdrawn early in 1960. Dulverton Signal Box was rebuilt on a brick base at a so far unascertained date in the early 1950s. ***Roger Carpenter, Lens of Sutton Association***

Up services, including the destinations of Manchester, Cardiff and Birmingham. With unbalanced Saturday workings there would be a light engine time tabled to depart Victoria Road at 9.30pm and arrive at Taunton at 11.07pm. Also, the working time table made reference to a Southern Region light engine departing Barnstaple Junction at 6.05am, arriving at Victoria Road at 6.10am to pick up coaches and work to Ilfracombe at 6.20am, with a Southern Region driver. This engine would then work the 8.25am Ilfracombe to Manchester as far as Barnstaple Junction, where there would be a locomotive and crew change and the WR would take over. The 'Rabbiter' from South Molton was still time-tabled to run at this time.

By the winter of 1954-55, services were back to six trains each way, the 6.55am being the first Up departure from Victoria Road, with the first Down the 8.05am from Taunton, arriving at 9.57am at the Junction.

The last Up train was the 6.40pm and the last Down at 8.15pm from Taunton, terminating at Victoria Road. In addition, there was a 5.25pm Up parcels departure from Victoria Road taking almost three hours to get to Taunton (arrival time 8.10pm) but this was not matched by a corresponding Down train. This six-train service was maintained for the remainder of the decade in winter periods but with a variation to the Up parcels service. **Appendix 18** shows, for 1954, the summer period normal weekday carriage workings along with those for summer Saturdays.

In the summer of 1955, on weekdays there were eight Up and seven Down trains. The 5.25pm Victoria Road departure was designated 'Third Class only' and although it replaced the parcels train, it was retimed to reach Taunton at 7.28pm, a more respectable two hours journey time; it remained the unbalanced working. In addition, there was an evening (5.45pm departure) Taunton to Dulverton train, which returned departing at 7.05pm but did not run on Saturdays. There were no through trains to or from Ilfracombe, London or other destinations during the normal weekday service.

ABOVE: No. 9670 at the head of a Barnstaple-bound train on 1st August 1959, showing that the 'Moguls' did occasionally relinquish their hold on passenger services in the 1950s. Perhaps there was a shortage of the normal motive power. The crew have a chat whilst they wait for departure and note the collection of bottles on the bay platform on the right. ***Jim Elson collection***

BELOW: 'Mogul' No. 6343 shows that normal service had been resumed, however, as it waits with a Barnstaple-bound train on the same day. ***Jim Elson collection***

Turning to the summer Saturday period for 1955 (27th June to 19th September), there were twelve Down and thirteen Up trains, eight of which were through trains between Taunton and Ilfracombe. In the return direction, seven of the thirteen Up trains started at Ilfracombe and three of those ran beyond Taunton to Manchester Exchange (8.25am ex-Ilfracombe), Cardiff (9.25am ex-Ilfracombe) and Wolverhampton Low Level (10.55am ex-Ilfracombe), the latter being designated as through carriages in the public time table. There were no direct train services between Ilfracombe and Paddington or *vice versa* but through carriages ran on the 11.30am departure from Paddington to Minehead and Ilfracombe, reaching the latter at 5.10pm. In this period, as Victoria Road was still open, no Western engines worked straight through from Taunton to Ilfracombe as they would have required turning at Barnstaple Junction (the East Chord being closed). The manoeuvres at Victoria Road meant it could take thirty minutes from arrival there to reach Barnstaple Town, also on the north side of the River Taw, running via the chord line and Barnstaple Junction. With the through trains running in to Victoria Road, locomotive changes often took place there in this period, necessitating light engine movements between the Junction shed and the terminus (and *vice versa*), to avoid a tender-first run to the Junction followed by a change. The 1955 carriage workings for summer and winter periods are shown in **Appendix 18**.

Weekdays in summer 1956 (11th June to 16th September) had seven Up and Down trains between Taunton and Barnstaple but there was an additional 5.45pm Taunton to Dulverton (arrival 6.30pm) and return (at 7.05pm), and the 5.25pm departure from Barnstaple was now designated a 'Second Class only' service.

On summer Saturdays in 1956, there were thirteen Up and twelve Down trains as per the previous summer and this pattern now continued until the end of the decade (1959 summer period; 15th June to 13th September) with little variation on timings or destinations. With the post-war economy boom and the general feel-good factor, the holiday heyday period for the line had returned but it was to be its swan-song.

Notable features for this exceptionally busy period showed the first Down train leaving Taunton at 5.20am for Ilfracombe, which would usually comprise six coaches. There were three more Down

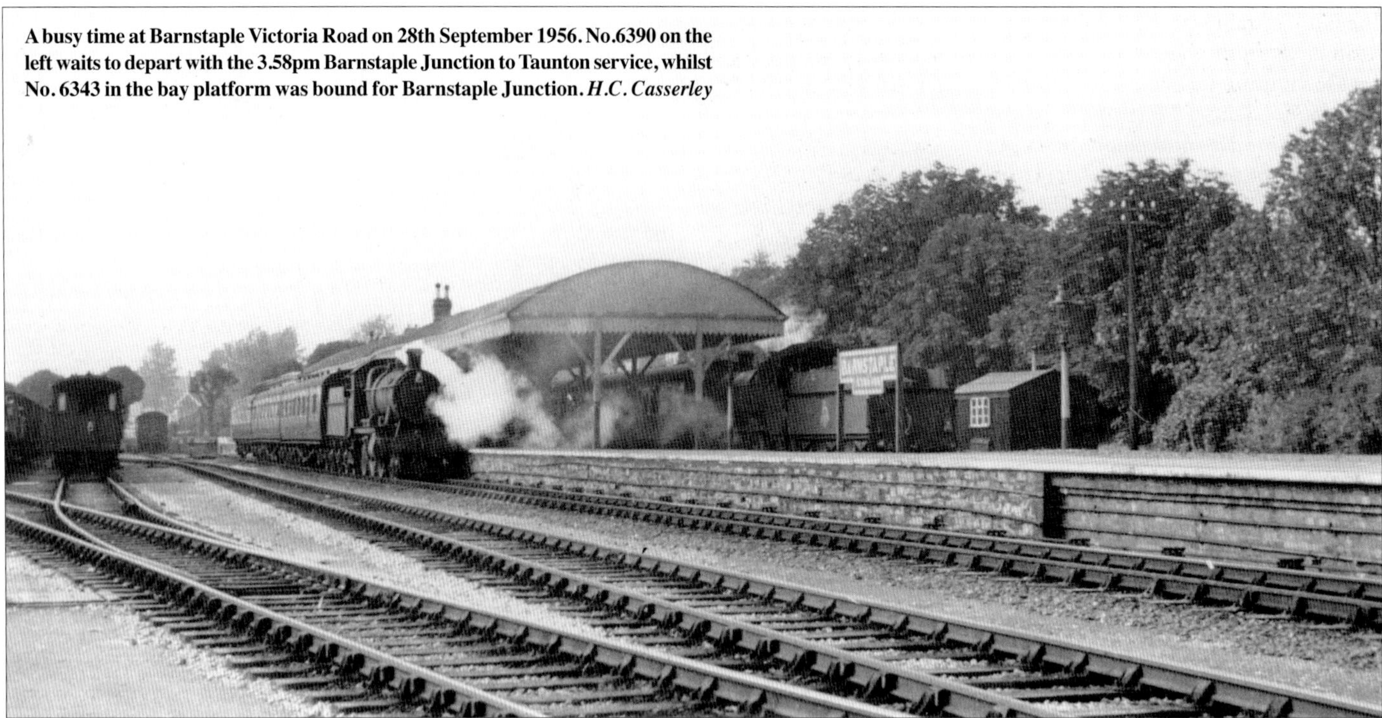

A busy time at Barnstaple Victoria Road on 28th September 1956. No.6390 on the left waits to depart with the 3.58pm Barnstaple Junction to Taunton service, whilst No. 6343 in the bay platform was bound for Barnstaple Junction. ***H.C. Casserley***

trains leaving Taunton by 8.30am, all working to Ilfracombe and usually comprising four coaches on the 6.20am and six coaches on the 7.00am. In the Up direction, the first train was the 6.55am from Victoria Road to Taunton. There were four Up through trains: the 8.25am Ilfracombe to Manchester, usually comprising seven LMR coaches (this train terminated at Bristol until 20th June); the 9.25am Ilfracombe to Cardiff, usually comprising six WR coaches (terminating at Taunton until 20th June) and two trains for Wolverhampton. One, the 10.55am from Ilfracombe (usually comprising six WR coaches), worked throughout the period but there was an extra train at 10.12am from Ilfracombe in the period 11th July to 5th September (although it terminated at Taunton on 11th, 18th and 25th July). The stopping train to Taunton that left Victoria Road at 12.54pm started from Torrington at 11.50am.

In the Down direction, the first through train was the 11.30am from Paddington leaving Taunton at 2.26pm, getting to Ilfracombe by 5.10pm. This train would work back as the 6.30pm Ilfracombe to Taunton. The next Down through train left Taunton at 3.36pm.

No. 6377 passes Blinkhorn Depot with the 8.00am Taunton to Ilfracombe Saturday's only service on 28th August 1954. The six chocolate & cream liveried coaches were being worked down to Ilfracombe to form a return service, to either Cardiff or Wolverhampton. ***Owen Mogg collection, courtesy Peter Triggs***

The last Up train was the 8.00pm from Ilfracombe, leaving Victoria Road at 8.55pm and arriving at Taunton at 10.30pm, whilst the last Down train was the 8.35pm from Taunton which terminated at Victoria Road at 10.17pm.

The locomotive movements on these summer Saturdays were very interesting, as some engine changes took place at Victoria Road. For example, the Manchester, Cardiff and Wolverhampton through trains had their engines detached at Victoria Road, which would then work back 'light engine' to the Junction. The replacement locomotive for the onward departure would have worked over to Victoria Road from the Junction earlier. Given the number of trains being dealt with, there was inevitably some crossing movements at Victoria Road requiring the use of the bay platform, with the arriving train being shunted in to there before departure. This can be illustrated by the 8.30am from Taunton to Ilfracombe, which arrived at Victoria Road at 10.12am. It had eighteen minutes before it had to depart but had eleven minutes to shunt into the bay, as the 9.25am Ilfracombe to Cardiff arrived at 10.23am. This working's turnaround was rapid, as it was due to depart at 10.28am but the engine for the Up service had worked light from the Junction at 9.55am (arriving at Victoria Road at 10.00am), so this facilitated the swiftness of the manoeuvres. Once the Cardiff train had departed, the 10.30am to Ilfracombe could leave behind a fresh Southern Region locomotive, which had worked from the Junction at 10.02am, getting to Victoria Road five minutes later. The released locomotives would then work back to the Junction for servicing/turning.

By September 1956, the 5.25pm Up passenger had the stock for this service worked over from the Junction at 10.25am; the extra stock presumably having worked down on the first (8.05am) Taunton Down service as this would balance the workings.

Consistency remained on weekday services. By the summer of 1959, there were six Up and Down trains on weekdays, the Dulverton service no longer running and neither did the 5.25pm Barnstaple service; both appear to have ceased in 1958. If we look at this period in detail, the first three Up trains departed from Barnstaple between 6.50am and 10.00am. There was then a gap until the 1.11pm service and then the 3.58pm service, whilst the 6.40pm was the last Up train. In the Down direction, the first arrival was at 9.57am, being followed by the 12.10pm, 2.22pm, 6.31pm, 7.39pm and 10.06pm services.

1960-1966

Barnstaple Victoria Road closed to all passenger traffic on 11th June 1960, the last Saturday of the winter time table. The chord line between East Junction and South Junction was therefore re-opened, allowing direct and thus more efficient running to Barnstaple Junction. At the start of the 1960 summer time table (13th June), the four-character headcodes that were a symbol of the early diesel era across all regions were published in the *Exeter District Working Time Table*. The branch stopping trains were all designated 2C84 in which ever direction they travelled. The steam locomotives of course never displayed them but the diesel multiple units and certain diesels with headcode boxes did. The Saturday through services to Cardiff initially carried code 1F36, the Wolverhampton Low Level services 1H26 and 1H28, and the Manchester through train 1M14. Steam

'Mogul' tug-of-war! No. 7319 on the nearer end has presumably recently arrived here at Barnstaple Junction with a train from Taunton, whilst a classmate is attached at the Taunton end, most likely to take the train back east. The direction each locomotive is facing suggests that the photograph was taken after Victoria Road had closed in June 1960 and trains then ran direct around the East Curve to and from the Junction. ***S.V. Blencowe***

LEFT: The 6.37pm Barnstaple Junction to Taunton train passing the Filleigh Down Distant signal whilst running 19 minutes late on Saturday 18th July 1964. On this occasion, the train comprised six coaches and one milk tank and it was photographed slowing for the 25mph speed restriction over Castle Hill Viaduct. No. 7303 of Taunton shed was withdrawn from service six weeks after the picture was taken. ***Michael L. Roach***

BELOW: 'Mogul' No. 6363 with a six-coach summer Saturday train on the double track section of line near Oake, between Norton Fitzwarren and Milverton, on 8th August 1964.
Owen Mogg collection, courtesy Peter Triggs

working on the D&SR line ceased with the end of the summer period on 5th September 1964, diesel multiple units then taking over all services, other than on the summer Saturdays long-distance through trains, which were diesel locomotive hauled.

The pattern of normal weekday services was consistent throughout the final seven years. The start of the final part-decade summer time table showed six Down and six Up weekday services. As this was the first period following closure of Victoria Road to passenger traffic, the first Up train started at 6.40am from Barnstaple Junction, arriving at Taunton at 8.29am. The first Down train was the 8.05am from Taunton, arriving at the Junction at 9.51am. The last Up train of the day was at 6.45pm, arriving at 8.36pm, with the final Down train starting at 8.25pm, arriving at 10.13pm at the Junction. This broad time table was maintained through summer and winter periods until 1965. From 11th September 1961, the last Down train was retimed to depart from Taunton at 9.12pm, arriving at 10.54pm. Later on, this late evening train only ran at this time on Fridays and Saturdays, and the remainder of the week the last Down train left Taunton at between 7.15 and 7.50pm, depending on the year.

Turning now to the summer Saturdays, the decline in these services

No. 7320 passes Oake on Saturday 5th September 1964, with a four-coach Up train bound for Taunton. *Owen Mogg collection, courtesy Peter Triggs*

becomes evident. In the steam era, as many Taunton 'Moguls' as possible would be made available to work the line, because of their automatic token exchange capabilities and the cut-back cab steps to clear the Taw Bridge in Barnstaple. Using the East Curve, without the reversal at Victoria Road, meant that these WR engines could work right through to Ilfracombe again but this only occurred on the summer Saturday services by this stage.

The summer Saturday period (13th June to 11th September) 1960 saw twelve Down and twelve Up trains. Eight of the Down trains ran through to Ilfracombe, including the earliest leaving Taunton at 5.20am, followed by another three until 8.30am. These early trains were effectively working stock down to Ilfracombe to form the morning long distance Up trains referred to below. Four later trains just went to the Junction, including the last at 8.35pm from Taunton arriving at 10.26pm. In the Up direction, the first two left from the Junction (6.43am and 7.45am) and two others would start from there. The next three Up trains were the 8.30am Ilfracombe to Manchester (Exchange), which was at the Junction at 9.20am, the 9.22am Ilfracombe to Cardiff, and the 10.12am/11.00am Ilfracombe to Wolverhampton Low Level services. The Manchester and second Wolverhampton trains did not stop at all stations on the D&SR. The 12.48pm from Barnstaple had the distinction of being the only Up train to start from Torrington at 11.50pm, running through to Taunton to arrive at 2.39pm. Of the twelve trains, four would start from Ilfracombe and run to Taunton. The 6.37pm departure from Ilfracombe was designated to be worked by a WR engine and trainmen throughout. The last Up train was the 8.05pm from Ilfracombe, which left the Junction at 8.50pm. The 12.25pm ex-Ilfracombe joined the service from Minehead at Taunton to reach Paddington, whilst in the Down direction, the 2.26pm from Taunton had departed Paddington at 11.30am.

This pattern of services was broadly repeated in 1961 but, by 1962, the heyday of twelve trains Up and Down was over. In the summer period for that year (22nd July to 2nd September) there were five through trains from Taunton to Ilfracombe, commencing with the 6.20am Down service and three trains terminating at Barnstaple Junction. The 3.45pm Taunton service was the train from Wolverhampton to Ilfracombe There were nine Up trains, starting with the 6.45am from Barnstaple to Taunton. One other train originated at Barnstaple and four others started from Ilfracombe, including the 8.05pm departure, which left Barnstaple at 8.50pm and arrived at Taunton at 10.28pm, the last Up train of the day. The remaining three Up trains were reporting number 1M14, the 8.35am Ilfracombe to Manchester Exchange (this only ran as far as Bristol Temple Meads until 23rd June), the 10.12am Ilfracombe to Taunton (which went from Taunton as a portion of the 12.05pm Minehead to Cardiff) and the 11.15am Ilfracombe to Wolverhampton Low Level (which joined up with the 12.45pm Minehead to Wolverhampton train). These latter trains carried the 2C34 headcode. With eight Down and nine Up trains, there had to be a balancing of locomotives and coaching stock, which was achieved with a light engine (code 0A05) time-tabled to leave Taunton at 12.20pm and run all the way down the branch to Barnstaple, arriving there at 2.25pm. This locomotive would have worked up on the 9.22am Ilfracombe to Taunton train earlier that day. Similar services ran in 1963.

The summer period in 1964 (20th June to 5th September) had nine

Up and Down trains. Five of the Down trains worked through to Ilfracombe, including the 8.02am from Wolverhampton Low Level (1V53), which travelled the line between 12.55pm from Taunton and 2.46pm at Barnstaple Junction. The 1.28pm departure from Taunton to Ilfracombe was a portion off the 7.50am from Llanelli (2C87). In the Up direction, all bar the 6.48am and the 3.50pm departures started from Ilfracombe. The 10.12am from Ilfracombe (2C34) went forwards on the 12.07pm Minehead to Cardiff train at Taunton. The 11.15am Ilfracombe to Wolverhampton Low Level (now 1M35) left Barnstaple Junction at noon and stopped only at the major stations to Taunton. These were the only two long distance trains on the line by this stage, the Manchester service no longer running.

The time table for the period 14th June 1965 to 17th April 1966 showed six Up and six Down trains on weekdays (excluding Saturdays 19th June to 4th September). By now, the twenty-four hour clock was in use in BR time tables, so this period's working time table indicated that the 08.37 departure from Barnstaple Junction originated as the 08.00 from Torrington, as did the 17.55 departure, which left Torrington at 17.20. This would go some way to explaining the almost three hours between the arrival at Barnstaple Junction of the 15.06 Down service and its departure at 17.55.

In that 1965 summer period, there were nine Down trains, the first six of which went through to Ilfracombe. Two of these were the 08.00 Wolverhampton to Ilfracombe service and the 08.00 Carmarthen to Ilfracombe (1C59). In addition, there was an ECS train (3C87) that left Taunton at 07.50 for Ilfracombe to form one of the ten Up services, eight of which started from Ilfracombe. The 10.20 Ilfracombe to Cardiff (1T33) still ran, along with the 11.10 to Wolverhampton (1M35). The working time table annotated the Cardiff train as '*D70XX 325 tons*' but no photographic or other evidence of a 'Hymek' locomotive ever appearing on the line has been found and this train was usually worked by a 'D63XX' North British locomotive (later Class '22'). However, a 'Hymek' would have been the most likely motive power beyond Taunton to Cardiff. This was also to be the final year of through services on the line to and from destinations beyond Taunton.

The public time table when initially published for the period 18th April 1966 to 5th March 1967 had no tabling for trains along the branch, which inevitably caused some consternation. However, a supplement was later published for the period and this showed six Up and six Down trains on weekdays and Saturdays outside of the 18th June to 3rd September summer period. The first Up train departed Barnstaple Junction at 06.40, arriving at Taunton at 08.17. The first Down train left Taunton at 07.52, arriving at the Junction at 09.26. The last trains of the day were the 19.04 from Barnstaple, arriving at Taunton at 20.42. From Mondays to Thursdays, the last Down train was at 19.45 from Taunton, which arrived Barnstaple at 21.17. On Fridays (and Saturdays in the 'winter' period), the last train left Taunton at 21.10 and arrived at 22.42. There were significant gaps between services, amounting to almost three hours in the morning, and early and late afternoon in the Up direction. A couple of similar gaps existed in the Down direction. This clearly did not help to encourage the travelling passenger, whilst a number of trains were only two or single car units, so passenger comfort was compromised. As with the other earlier time tables, there were two Up trains before the first Down train arrived, necessitating a stabling of two units at Barnstaple Junction overnight.

Summer Saturdays in the 18th June to 3rd September 1966 period had nine Up and nine Down trains between Taunton and Barnstaple. The first Up service was at 06.48, with arrival at Taunton booked for 08.33, whilst the last was at 20.45, arriving at Taunton at 22.24. In the Down direction, the first was the 06.10 from Taunton arriving Barnstaple at 07.50, and the last was at 21.25, arriving at 23.06. Two of the nine trains

ABOVE: On 5th September 1964, the final summer Saturday of that year, No. 6326 is seen near Wiveliscombe with six coaches from Ilfracombe. Most likely bound for Wolverhampton, this was one of the last steam-hauled passenger trains on the line; soon it would be all diesels and DMUs. ***Michael J. Fox, courtesy Rail Archive Stephenson***

RIGHT: A single 'bubble car' unit stands at Bishop's Nympton & Molland station in 1966. The 2C84 head code was carried by all branch trains in both Up and Down directions. Railway staff clearly out-number passengers. ***Roger Joannes***

in both directions did not stop at some stations. The 06.10 Down service avoided Milverton, Venn Cross, both Morebath's, East Anstey and Yeo Mill, whilst the 13.15 Down train did not stop at the two halts. In the Up direction, the 08.49 only stopped at Dulverton and Wiveliscombe after leaving South Molton, arriving at Taunton at 10.28, and the 09.48 from Barnstaple called at South Molton, East Anstey, Dulverton and Wiveliscombe, arriving at Taunton at 11.12. There were no through services to or from Ilfracombe.

The service of six Up and Down trains was resumed for the remaining month of the line's existence, until the official closure on and from Monday 3rd October 1966, although as with most such events at this period, the last trains ran on the preceeding Saturday.

Some Passenger Service Details From the 1960s

Having reviewed the train services over the decades, the running of certain of them is now further illustrated, the research having uncovered more details behind certain of these workings.

On 9th July 1960, the 8.30am Ilfracombe to Manchester (train No. 1M14) was worked by 'Mogul' No. 6343 from Barnstaple Junction and was then taken over at Taunton by Class No. 1005 *County of Devon*, which took the train on to Bristol. No. 6343 returned to Ilfracombe on the 10.50am from Wolverhampton (2C34), which left Taunton at 3.26pm and arrived back there on the 8.05pm from Ilfracombe. On the same day, the 11.00am Ilfracombe to Wolverhampton (1H28) was taken to Taunton by No. 5376 of St. Philip's Marsh shed and then on from there by No. 4985 *Allesley Hall*. No. 6337 from Taunton shed worked the 5.20am Taunton to Ilfracombe (2C34), and worked back on the 9.22am Ilfracombe to Cardiff (1F36). Having been detached at Taunton in favour of No. 6859 *Yiewsley Grange*, which took the train on, its next working was back to Ilfracombe, taking over the 11.30am from Paddington (2C34) at 2.26pm from No. 5034 *Corfe Castle*. The train had left Paddington with thirteen or fourteen coaches, six of which were detached for the trip to Ilfracombe, the remainder going forwards to Minehead. There were no restaurant facilities on the Ilfracombe portion. No. 6337 would finally work back to Taunton on the 6.37pm from Ilfracombe. On this long day, No. 6337 would cover about 243 miles and work about a sixteen hour day. No. 7319 of Taunton shed worked the 8.30am Taunton to Ilfracombe (2C84) and then returned on the 12.25pm Ilfracombe to Paddington (1A95) train, running into Platform 8 (the usual arrival bay) at Taunton. Once the Minehead portion (the 2.15pm departure) arrived – on this day behind 2-6-2T No. 6155 – the stock was coupled together and went forwards behind No. 5034 *Corfe Castle*, returning to Paddington from where it had come that morning. **Table 11.4** below summarises the 'Mogul' locomotive movements described above.

Table 11.4: 'Mogul' Trips from Taunton on 9th July 1960

6337	6343	7319
5.20am Taunton to Ilfracombe	8.30am Ilfracombe to Manchester, from Barnstaple to Taunton	8.30am Taunton to Ilfracombe
9.22am Ilfracombe to Cardiff as far as Taunton	3.26pm Taunton departure on 10.50am Wolverhampton to Ilfracombe	12.25pm Ilfracombe to Paddington as far as Taunton*
2.26pm departure Taunton on 11.30am Paddington to Ilfracombe*	8.05pm Ilfracombe to Taunton	
6.37pm departure Ilfracombe to Taunton		

* These trains were not shown as through trains in the working time table

The *Railway Observer* noted that, on 29th April 1961, 'Moguls' No's 7305, 7325 and 7333 were seen on trains, which were usually of three or four coaches at this time. The passenger traffic on the branch fell into two categories: the through travellers, largely on summer Saturdays, and locals journeying between Wiveliscombe, Milverton and Taunton. Only Dulverton, South Molton and occasionally Swimbridge provided passengers in significant numbers out of the other stations.

On Saturday 30th June 1962, the 10.56am Wolverhampton Low Level to Ilfracombe service was hauled by No. 6975 *Capesthorne Hall* as far as Taunton, at which point the train divided, one portion going to Minehead, the other to Ilfracombe, with 'Mogul' No. 7337 at its head. This train was time tabled to make only three stops before Barnstaple, at Wiveliscombe, Dulverton and South Molton.

On 27th July 1963, the 1.07pm departure from Taunton was the Wolverhampton Down train, with 'Mogul' No. 7333 at the head; the train was split at Taunton, a portion going to Minehead behind 'Hymek' No. D7045. On the same date, No. 6327 took the 1.58pm departure from Taunton to Ilfracombe forwards.

The Ilfracombe to Manchester service travelled via the Severn Tunnel and the Maindee Curve at Newport, then through Craven Arms, Chester and Warrington to Manchester Exchange. The Wolverhampton service worked up the former GWR Honeybourne line and then ran via Birmingham Snow Hill.

Coaching stock movements for the summer Saturday services were reasonably complex. Set out below in **Table 11.5** is an illustration as to how the nine LM&SR coaches got to Ilfracombe for the Saturday's only Ilfracombe to Manchester Exchange service in the 1950s. It also shows that one set of coaches spent most of the week idle – the sort of waste and inefficiency that British Railways sought to cut out under the Beeching plan.

Appendix 19 has a review of certain services on the line in the period 1962-1965.

Table 11.5: Movements of LM&SR Coaching Stock to Ilfracombe

Train	Coaches	Comments
07.43 (Saturday) Nottingham to Plymouth (4.36pm (a))	9	
Plymouth to Exeter	7	Monday local service; these go from St. Davids to Central for berthing and are split into 4- and 3-coach sets. The set is split because of locomotive restrictions over the Ilfracombe line (no bankers on weekdays)
Plymouth to Taunton	2	Monday local service; these are then berthed until Friday (see below)
07.50 Yeovil to Ilfracombe (Tuesdays)	4	attached and work through to Ilfracombe where they are berthed
07.50 Yeovil to Ilfracombe (Wednesdays)	3	Attached and work through to Ilfracombe where they are berthed
2.33pm Taunton to Barnstaple (Fridays)	2	See above (Plymouth to Taunton)
5.25pm Barnstaple to Ilfracombe (Fridays)	2	

Table 11.6 showing ticket prices has been constructed from the *British Railways Western Region Passenger Time Table (Plymouth Division)* for 14th June 1965 to 17th April 1966 (inclusive) and gives the Second Class return fares.

At this time it was also possible to purchase 'Holiday Runabout' tickets. These were available until 30th October 1965, were issued on any day for seven days travel in a defined area and were not valid for

No. 7320 near Milverton with the 3.50pm Barnstaple Junction to Taunton service on Saturday 27th June 1964. The van at the front is a General Utility Vehicle (GUV), most likely carrying Passenger Luggage in Advance (PLA) and general parcels. Note too that two of the four carriages are in the chocolate and cream livery which by this date had largely been replaced by BR maroon.
Michael J. Fox, courtesy Rail Archive Stephenson

TABLE 11.6: SECOND CLASS RETURN TICKET PRICES 1965

To ☞ From ☜	Barnstaple	South Molton	Dulverton	Wiveliscombe	Taunton	Paddington
Barnstaple Jnc		4s 3d	7s 9d		11s 6d	51s 0d
Bishops Nympton	5s 7d	1s 10d	3s 5d		8s 6d	
Dulverton	7s 9d	4s 6d		4s 0d	6s 4d	47s 0d
East Anstey	7s 0d	3s 5d	1s 10d		7s 3d	
Filleigh	3s 2d	1s 10d	5s 10d		9s 6d	51s 0d
Milverton	10s 0d		4s 9d		2s 11d	
Morebath	8s 6d	5s 10d		3s 5d	5s 3d	
Morebath Jnc Halt	8s 3d	4s 9d		3s 9d	5s 10d	
South Molton	4s 3d		4s 6d		9s 0d	50s 0d
Swimbridge	2s 5d		6s 9d		10s 0d	
Venn Cross	9s 6d	6s 4d	2s 11d	2s 2d	4s 6d	
Wiveliscombe	9s 6d	7s 3d	4s 0d		3s 5d	43s 0d
Yeo Mill	6s 4d	3s 2d	2s 8d		7s 9d	

travel before 8.30am. Area No. 5 covered parts of Devon and Somerset and the D&SR line from Taunton to East Anstey. Area No. 6 covered from Ilfracombe east to Taunton and Weston-Super-Mare, and the Minehead Branch. These two areas were priced at 27s 6d each. Area No. 7 covered just Devon, including the D&SR from Barnstaple to Morebath Junction, for 30s.

PASSENGER LUGGAGE IN ADVANCE

With a substantial amount of holiday traffic to the West Country and other destinations, the GWR developed a procedure known as Passenger Luggage in Advance (PLA). This was to cater for the substantial volumes of trunks, portmanteaus and other luggage which travelled with the holidaying public. PLA might be conveyed in special trains or in Brake vans or 'Siphon G's on normal passenger trains. However, the key point was that these items were collected from passengers' homes, conveyed in advance to the destination station and then to where they were staying. In 1938-39, the charge for PLA was 2s per package, whilst in the summer of 1939 for example, the PLA from Paddington to Ilfracombe was conveyed in a regular 8-wheeled Brake van on the trains shown in **Table 11.7**.

TABLE 11.7: PASSENGER LUGGAGE IN ADVANCE, PADDINGTON-ILFRACOMBE 1939

DAYS ON WHICH RUN	DEPARTURE TIME	FROM	TO	ARRIVAL TIME
Saturdays excepted	10.35pm	Paddington	Taunton	3.21am
Mondays excepted	7.50am	Taunton	Ilfracombe	10.44am
Saturdays excepted	4.45pm	Ilfracombe	Taunton	8.15pm
Saturdays excepted	8.40pm	Taunton	Paddington	2.40am

The loading arrangements of the Brake van were as shown in the top diagram below (leading end to the right). Ilfracombe parcels were at the left-hand side and Ilfracombe PLA to the right. The second diagram shows the loading for the reverse direction (trailing end right).

Barnstaple, Taunton and transfer	Milverton	Venn Cross Wiveliscombe
	Morebath East Anstey	Dulverton Bishops Nympton South Molton
Barnstaple Jct and transfer	Filleigh	Swimbridge

P A D D N T	Swindon	Bristol and transfer	Bath	P A D D N T
	(This van not to be used for Bristol and transfer traffic on Fridays when the Ilfracombe to Manchester Van runs)			
	Chippenham Didcot	Reading		

PASSENGER RATED TRAFFIC

Reference has been made above to parcels services (including the 'Rabbiter' which is looked at further in Chapter 12). The passenger rated parcels traffic peaked in the late 1930s, when between 70,000 and 72,000 items were handled each year, on average, at Barnstaple (see **Appendix 10** of Volume 2 for total parcels dealt with on the line in the 1920s and 1930s). Also, horse traffic was carried in special wagons on passenger services and again Chapter 12 covers these matters in more detail.

As can be seen from the photographs below, milk tanks were occasionally added to passenger services. Usually coupled next to the engine, they were sometimes added as tail traffic. It is not entirely certain from where the milk traffic conveyed along the line originated but it is most likely to be Torrington, which had a dairy, rather than any of the stations on the branch, which only generated the carriage

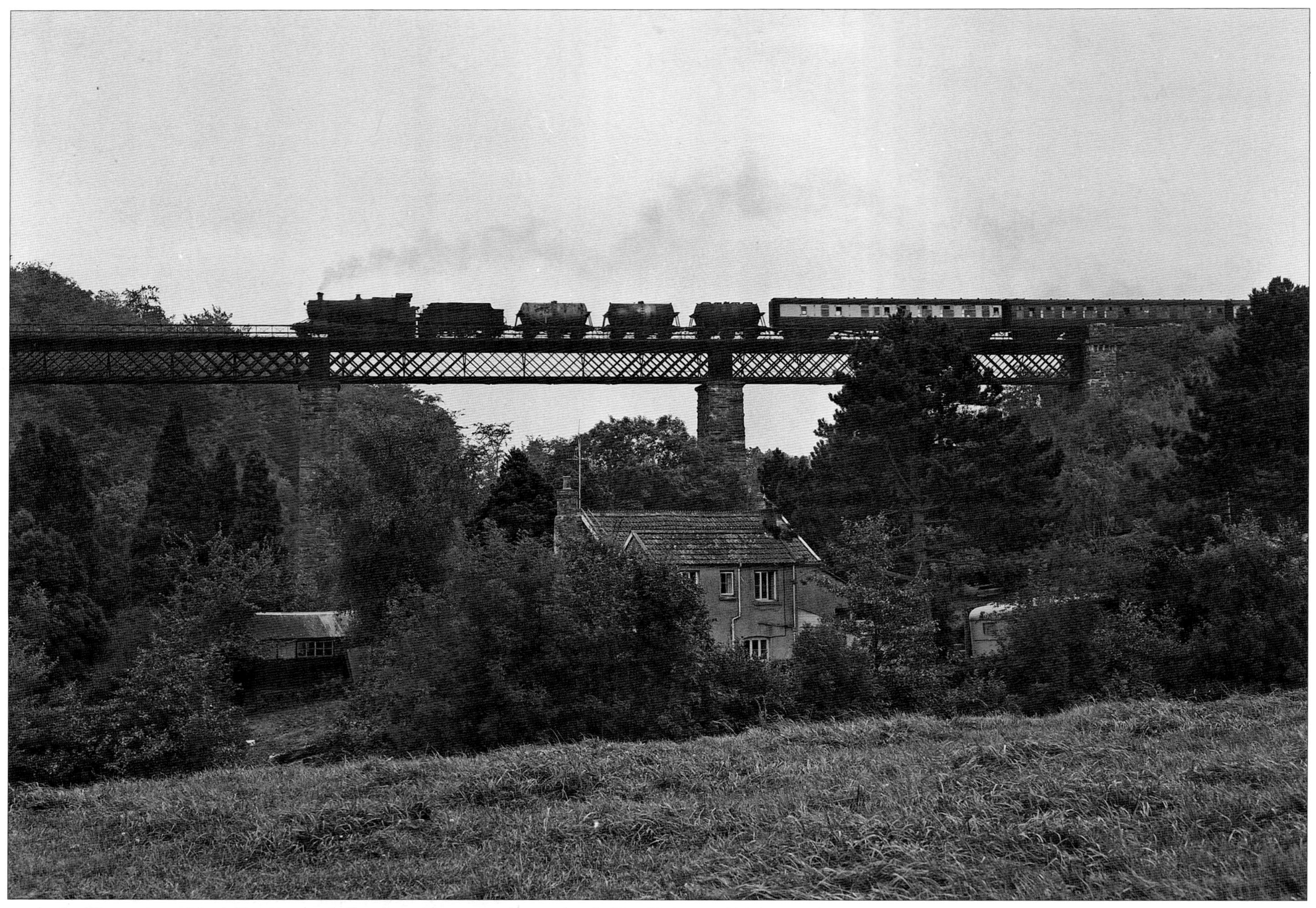

A splendid panorama of the 1.17pm Barnstaple Junction to Taunton service crossing the Tone Viaduct on 30th August 1961, hauled by an unidentified 'Mogul', which included three 6-wheeled glass-lined milk tanks at the head of the train. Sadly the tanks are too dirty to make out any lettering but they are almost certainly from the dairy at Torrington and would more commonly have been routed via the Southern Region line from Barnstaple Junction to Exeter. However, from time to time they were added to Taunton line trains, although the exact reasons for this have not yet been ascertained. ***Michael J. Fox, courtesy Rail Archive Stephenson***

Right: No. 5336 enters the Up loop at Wiveliscombe with the 4.10pm from Barnstaple Junction to Taunton on 1st September 1964. Note the two milk tanks at the head of the consist. ***Steve Linney, courtesy Richard Derry***

Below: An unidentified 'Mogul' heads west away from a stop at Dulverton station on 26th February 1960. The train is passing Brushford village, where the station was situated, about a mile away from Dulverton itself, with the rectory in the centre background. The three coach train is supplemented at the rear by two parcels wagons and a flat wagon with a container on board. ***John Spencer Gilks***

of milk churns. The Up trains thus carried full milk tanks and Down trains the returning empties, milk being given priority as perishable goods, hence the association with passenger services. The only 'official' time tabled milk traffic was that referred to in the goods section (in 1965 only) below and this was a Torrington service.

A photograph has also been seen that showed a passenger train conveying three loaded open wagons attached to the rear but what they contained is not clear.

In the 1940s, two or three 'D' containers of ice cream arrived each week from Acton in the summer. The wagons were fully fitted and attached to the rear of the 11.00am service from Taunton. On arrival at Barnstaple the locomotive would run around its train, cut off the wagons and put them by the crane in the mileage siding, so they could be loaded onto lorries and transported to their final destination.

Appendix 20 shows a summary of minutes lost on the 9.55am Ilfracombe to Paddington service for August 1930 and **Appendix 21** shows the counting of passengers for a variety of dates between 1913 and 1937.

Part 2: Goods Services

As the area which the line served was primarily agricultural, incoming traffic for farms and local businesses was predominately of that nature, comprising commodities such as fertiliser, slag (waste from South Wales iron ore smelting) and animal feeds, along with occasional deliveries of farm equipment. These items tended to be stocked at the local goods depots and warehouses at the various stations. The farmers would then either collect their merchandise or have it delivered by the local station lorry. Coal was also brought in to locations such as Wiveliscombe, Dulverton, Molland and South Molton, along with oil to South Molton and Barnstaple. More specific details for each station are provided in Volume 2, Chapters 6-8.

The line had a regular number of goods services over the decades, usually four per weekday in its heyday. These were sometimes supplemented by shorter pick-up goods services from Taunton to Dulverton and South Molton, whilst the Bristol to Barnstaple goods and its return service operated for most years. Latterly, however, with increasing competition from road hauliers and BR's focus on larger goods and coal concentration depots instead of local yards, all through freight loads to Barnstaple were diverted via Exeter and the former North Devon Railway. As a result, all goods facilities on the D&SR line were withdrawn by September 1964.

1870s

The initial goods time table is shown below. One goods each way sufficed in the beginning, taking 50 minutes to travel between Taunton and Wiveliscombe including 10 minutes to service Milverton. Reference back to the passenger services time table of this period (page 529) will show how it was integrated with the goods services.

There was a variation to the time table by May 1872, when an extra five minutes was allowed at Milverton; this was accompanied by the note '*Stops at Thomas and Co's siding*', which is shown as an extract from the working time book below. The future stations were indicated even though the line through to Barnstaple had yet to be opened and note, too, that the Up direction at this stage was to Wiveliscombe.

With the opening of the Wiveliscombe to Barnstaple section on Saturday 1st November 1873, it was then possible for goods traffic to run throughout but this only commenced nine days later on Monday 10th November. The notice below top is from the working time book, whilst the first goods time table for the whole line is shown here at the top of the next page. Note that Up and Down had now been reversed so that the Up direction was now correctly shown as towards Taunton and therefore London.

There was an additional service notice which stated that the '*First goods train will leave Taunton for Barnstaple at 12.40am and the second at 2.40am on Tuesday morning 11 November. But goods trains from Barnstaple will not commence running until Tuesday night, 11 November*'.

As can be seen, there were two Down and two Up goods services, taking over four hours to work the branch. With only three crossing places available on the branch at this early stage of the line's life – at Wiveliscombe, Dulverton and South Molton – the timely running of three of these goods trains would have been crucial.

In March 1874, there was inserted in the time table a note that the 8.40pm Barnstaple to Taunton goods was to be given a fifteen minute stop at Florence Siding, South Molton between 10.15pm and 10.30pm; a track plan of this siding, which at this date formed the southern terminus of a four-mile, horse-worked branch to iron ore mines at North Molton, also appears on the next page. In July 1874, a service notice indicated that there was a 10.12pm goods from South Molton, which was effectively a 'continuation' of the Barnstaple to South Molton passenger working but as a goods train only, with the same motive power.

By 1877, the trend had been set for three weekday Down goods, the first starting from Taunton at 12.05am and arriving at Barnstaple at 4.30am. This was followed on Tuesdays to Saturdays by the 2.20am departure, arriving at 6.55am. However, these early departure services were slightly retimed after 1877, so that the late morning Down goods left Taunton at 11.20am, arriving at 5.00pm, spending about ten minutes at most stations, with the exception of East Anstey where it was held for fifty minutes to enable the 1.15pm ex-Barnstaple to pass (this train later being retimed to depart at 1.30pm). There were two Down goods on Sundays in the early months of 1877, the 2.20am Taunton departure arriving at 6.55am and a 12.05am departure arriving at 4.30am; neither called all stations, some stops being alternated between the two. The second Down goods had ceased by April 1877, so just one Sunday Down goods ran until October 1879.

On weekdays, there were three Up goods from Barnstaple. The 5.00am, which arrived at Taunton at 10.30am, and the 5.55pm which arrived at 10.30pm and did not stop at the smaller stations. In this period this goods ran on to Bristol, terminating at Pylle Hill at 3.55am the following day. The

WORKING TIME BOOK.

The Goods Trains between Taunton and Barnstaple will not commence running until MONDAY, November 10th, 1873.

J. C. WALL,
General Manager.

DEVON & SOMERSET BRANCH.

UP					DOWN				
Miles	STATIONS.	ARR.	DEP.	REMARKS.	Miles	STATIONS.	ARR.	DEP.	REMARKS.
		a.m.	a.m.				p.m.	p.m.	
	Taunton		6 00			Wiveliscombe ...		2 10	
6¼	Milverton	6 25	6 35		2¾	Milverton	2 25	2 35	
9¼	Wiveliscombe ...	6 50	...		9¼	Taunton	3 00	...	

DEVON & SOMERSET BRANCH.

UP					DOWN				
Miles	STATIONS.	ARR.	DEP.	REMARKS.	Miles	STATIONS.	ARR.	DEP.	REMARKS.
		a.m.	a.m.				p.m.	p.m.	
	Taunton	...	6 0			Barnstaple ...	...	...	
2	Nrtn. Fitzwarren	...	6 7		3¾	Swimbridge ...	...	...	
6¼	Milverton	6 25	6 40	Stops at Thomas & Co.'s	7	Castle Hill ...	...	...	
9¼	Wiveliscombe ...	6 50	...	Siding.	10	South Molton ...	...	...	
14	Venn Cross ...	...	...		14¾	Molland	...	...	
17½	Morebath (Bpton.)	...	...		19¾	East Anstey ...	...	...	
21	Dulverton	...	...		23½	Dulverton	...	...	
24¾	East Anstey ...	...	...		26¾	Morebath	...	...	
29¾	Molland	...	...		30¼	Venn Cross ...	...	...	
34¼	South Molton ...	...	...		35¼	Wiveliscombe ...	...	2 10	
37½	Castle Hill ...	...	...		38	Milverton	2 25	2 40	Stops at Thomas & Co.'s
40½	Swimbridge ...	...	...		42½	Nrtn. Fitzwarren	...	2 53	Siding.
44½	Barnstaple ...	...	...		44½	Taunton	3 0	...	

DEVON & SOMERSET BRANCH.

DOWN

Miles	Stations.	Arr.	Dep.	Remarks.
		a.m.	a.m.	
	Taunton	...	2 40	
2	Nrtn. Fitzwarren	2 50	2 53	
6¼	Milverton	3 13	3 28	
9¼	Wiveliscombe ...	3 42	3 57	
14	Venn Cross ...	4 19	4 24	
17½	Morebath (Bpton.)	4 40	4 50	
21	Dulverton	...	...	
24¾	East Anstey ...	...	...	
29¾	Molland	5 40	5 45	
34¼	South Molton ...	...	...	
37½	Castle Hill ...	6 2	6 7	
40¼	Swimbridge ...	6 19	6 34	
44½	Barnstaple ...	6 50	...	

UP

Miles	Stations.	Arr.	Dep.	Remarks.
		p.m.	p.m.	
	Barnstaple ...	...	5 30	
3¾	Swimbridge ...	...	...	
7	Castle Hill ...	...	...	
10¼	South Molton ...	6 15	6 30	
14¾	Molland	...	...	
19¾	East Anstey ...	7 10	7 20	
23½	Dulverton	7 35	7 50	
26¾	Morebath	...	...	
30¼	Venn Cross ...	...	...	
35¼	Wiveliscombe ...	8 30	8 55	Cross 8 15 p.m. from
38	Milverton	9 8	9 23	Taunton
42½	Nrtn. Fitzwarren	9 37	9 40	
44½	Taunton	9 50	...	

DOWN

Miles	Stations.	Arr.	Dep.	Remarks.
		p.m.	p.m.	
	Taunton	...	11 5	
2	Nrtn. Fitzwarren	11 16	11 19	
6¼	Milverton	11 38	11 53	
9¼	Wiveliscombe ...	12 7	12 40	Cross 8 40 p.m. from
14	Venn Cross ...	...	...	Barnstaple
17½	Morebath (Bpton.)	...	...	
21	Dulverton	1 30	1 45	
24¾	East Anstey ...	2 3	2 18	
29¾	Molland	...	...	
34¼	South Molton ...	2 50	3 5	
37½	Castle Hill ...	...	...	
40¼	Swimbridge ...	...	...	
44½	Barnstaple ...	3 40	...	

UP

Miles	Stations.	Arr.	Dep.	Remarks.
		p.m.	p.m.	
	Barnstaple ...	...	8 40	
3¾	Swimbridge ...	8 58	9 13	
7	Castle Hill ...	9 29	9 35	
10¼	South Molton ...	9 51	10 15	Cross 8 15 p.m. from
14¾	Molland	10 36	10 41	Taunton
19¾	East Anstey ...	...	...	
23½	Dulverton	...	...	
26¾	Morebath (Bpton.)	11 21	11 31	
30¼	Venn Cross ...	11 45	11 50	
35¼	Wiveliscombe ...	12 8	12 23	Cross 11 5 p.m. from
38	Milverton	12 36	12 51	Taunton
42½	Nrtn. Fitzwarren	1 7	1 10	
44½	Taunton	1 20	...	

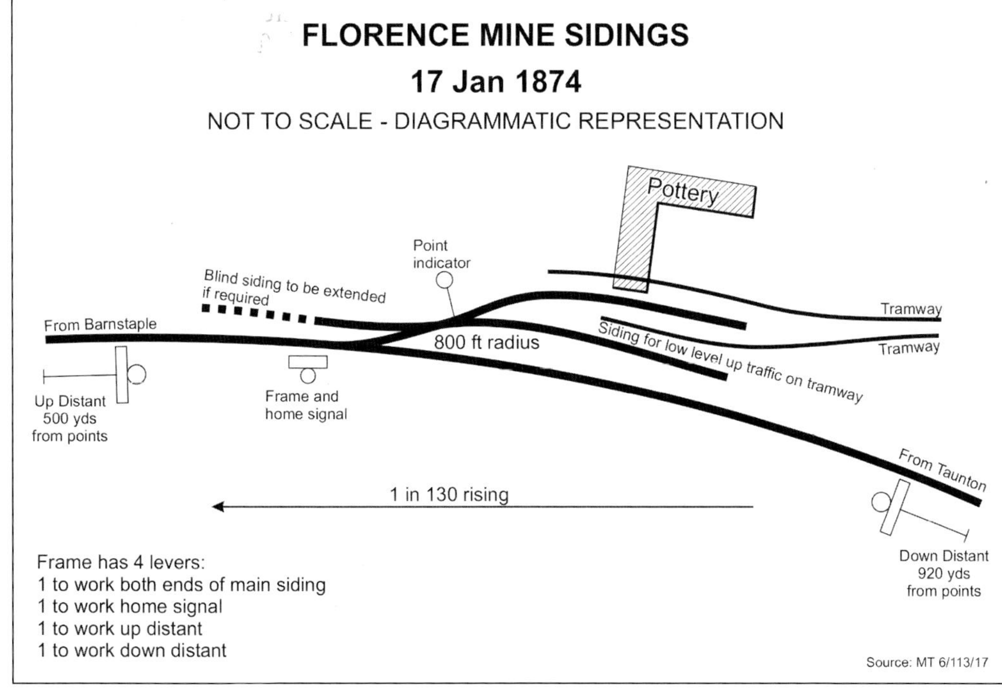

latter again carrying passengers to Dulverton (as referred to in Part 1 of this chapter).

A review of the July to December 1879 service time table shows that, with Mondays excepted, the first goods left Taunton at 12.30am. It had about ten minutes at most stations, calling (if required) at Thomas' Siding at Milverton, Venn Cross, Morebath and Bishops Nympton, arriving at Barnstaple at 4.40am. The second Down goods was the 3.00am departure from Taunton arriving at 6.45am, which also conveyed passengers on Fridays between South Molton, Castle Hill and Barnstaple. There were two corresponding Up goods: the first left Barnstaple at 6.20pm, taking five hours to get to Taunton, where it arrived at 11.25pm. This had eight minutes at Florence Siding near South Molton, to collect loaded wagons of ore extracted from the nearby mines from the transfer siding. Other station stops were again of about ten minutes duration with the exception of Wiveliscombe (twenty-five minutes), so time was clearly taken travelling the steeply graded line. The second Up goods left at 9.20pm, getting to Taunton at 12.35am. This continued to convey passengers for stations between Barnstaple and Dulverton. The third goods was the 10.30am Taunton to Dulverton, arriving there at 1.35pm, with one hour allowed for shunting at Wiveliscombe. The return working left Dulverton at 2.00pm, getting back to Taunton at 3.45pm. There was one Down goods on Sundays (replacing the first Down goods that did not run on Mondays), still leaving Taunton at 12.30am but arriving at Barnstaple at 4.55am. There was no corresponding return working on Sundays (this return working going back on the following Monday evening).

third working was the 9.00pm goods, which also ran as a passenger train to South Molton until October 1877, when the passenger portion was extended to Dulverton until October 1879.

In February 1879, there were only two Down and two Up goods: the 12.30am and 2.10am from Taunton, the latter conveying passengers on Fridays from South Molton and Castle Hill to Barnstaple, and the 6.20pm and 9.20pm from Barnstaple, with the

STATION TRUCKS

The working time table for July 1877 to 1885 (and beyond) refers to Station Trucks No's 45a and 45b being conveyed. An explanation of the concept of Station Trucks, which lasted in to the BR era, was given in the April 1935 issue of the *Great Western Railway Magazine*. They were goods wagons, sometimes referred to as a 'Pick-up wagon', normally attached to a slow goods train or to a local stopping train, that catered for small consignments that were individually insufficient to form a full wagon load. At the date of the article, more than 600 were in operation daily on the GWR system.

They picked up and conveyed goods from smaller stations to transshipment depots, for transfer to other wagons for despatch and unloading at their destinations, and were a means of giving 'next morning' delivery of goods to small stations far away from their source of supply. Every station truck worked to a pre-determined regular schedule and its stops were pre-arranged, whilst a special label was printed for each truck. The label showed all the stations being called at and the position of goods in the truck for each.

1880s

There appear to be some inconsistencies between the B&ER time tables and the GWR ones in this period, so what follows is indicative of the service selected from the available information. There did not appear to be an Up or Down Bristol goods in the first part of the decade. However, references to a Swindon, Bristol and Barnstaple goods appear in the July 1883 GWR service time table.

In the period from 1880 to 1883, there were two Up and two Down goods that ran the length of the line. A third ran from Taunton, departing at 1.00pm, to East Anstey and back (in 1880) but later this left Taunton at 12.00pm and terminated at Dulverton. The 5.15am departure from Taunton arrived at Barnstaple at 8.35am but, from 1881, this early goods did not run on Mondays and was the only Down train on a Sunday, leaving Taunton at 8.00am and arriving at Barnstaple at 10.50am. The afternoon Down goods left Taunton at 2.00pm in 1880, whilst both the Down Dulverton goods and the afternoon Down goods to Barnstaple were retimed to noon and 4.00pm respectively after the conversion from broad to narrow gauge in 1881. In 1880, in the Up direction, the early goods left Barnstaple at 6.10am, arriving Taunton 12.50pm. This was retimed to a 10.00am departure in 1881 and was booked to stop at Florence Siding for ten minutes and Thomas' Siding, Milverton, as required. The Up evening goods left Barnstaple at 6.40pm in summer of 1880 but was retimed after that date to depart at 7.05pm. It arrived at Taunton at 9.45pm and then at 10.22pm after retiming.

Alteration of Goods Services

A notice issued from Mr Campfield (superintendent, Exeter Division on 11th June 1881) made minor changes to the 6.10am Barnstaple Up goods, the 1.00pm Taunton to Dulverton goods and the 2.00pm Taunton to Barnstaple goods.

However, it also stated '*If a goods train is so late that it will delay a passenger train 10 minutes, the train must be put away and the engine sent on with the staff to the next crossing place and then return to its train, the station master who sends the engine forward will be responsible for making all necessary arrangements for the working of train staffs beyond.*

Until further orders not more than two wagons are to be put on any passenger train.

Until further orders the loads of goods trains will be as follows:- from Taunton to Wiveliscombe, 22 wagons and 1 van. From Wiveliscombe to East Anstey, 18 wagons and 1 van.'

GWR Notice 167, issued on 12th October 1881, referred to an extension, on some days, of the 12 noon Taunton to Dulverton goods on to South Molton. This was '*in consequence of the large amount of lime and other traffic now being loaded at Milverton for stations on the Devon and Somerset branch*'. This extension was only to be done when '*absolutely necessary*'. The timings are shown below.

The notice from Mr Campfield (superintendent, Exeter Division) confirmed that '*Mr Burrows, of Dulverton, will arrange to wire all stations between South Molton and Taunton inclusive when the Goods*

DEVON & SOMERSET BRANCH.

UP

	Arr.	Dep.	Remarks
	p.m.	p.m.	
Dulverton	3 00	3 15	
East Anstey	3 32	3 40	
Molland	3 53	4 20	Cross 3 40pm up passenger
South Molton	4 33		

DOWN

	Arr.	Dep.	Remarks
	p.m.	p.m.	
South Molton		5pm	after 3 35pm down passenger arrives
Molland	5 15	5 19	
East Anstey	5 38	5 43	
Dulverton	5 55	6	
Morebath	6 12	6 17	cross 4pm down goods
Venn Cross		6 29	
Wiveliscombe	6 42	6 52	
Milverton	7 05	7 15	cross 6 55pm down passenger
Nrtn. Fitzwarren	7 28	7 30	
Taunton	7 36		

have to be sent on, so that the Train Staff Working on the Branch may be properly arranged. Mr Burrows will at the same time advise me by wire what has been done.'.

In the period from the end of 1881, the 2.00pm Taunton Down goods was retimed to 4.00pm, then in 1884 to 3.45pm and in 1885 to 7.25pm. In addition, the 10.00am Up goods was retimed to 2.20pm in 1885 but the other goods services broadly maintained their timings from earlier years. The time table stated that '*Every effort must be made to work the 2.20pm Barnstaple goods punctually. This is very important*'. It would seem the reason for this was to ensure the swift passage of perishable goods conveyed on that train, namely meat traffic.

On 14th August 1883, new sidings came in to operation at Norton Fitzwarren, resulting in time table amendments: '*All up Barnstaple branch goods will call at Norton Fitzwarren and all wagons for Bridgwater and Bristol containing iron ore, timber and all such traffic (including empties) must be put off at Norton Fitzwarren, but ordinary goods and cattle must be taken to Taunton as at present*'. As a consequence, new calls were inserted: the 10.00am Barnstaple to Taunton was booked to arrive at 2.18pm and depart at 2.25pm, the 3.50pm Dulverton to Taunton goods was booked to arrive at 6.23pm and depart at 6.30pm, and the 7.05pm Barnstaple to Bristol goods was booked to arrive at 10.15pm and depart at 10.30pm. The Down goods trains (7.00am and 4.00pm Taunton to Barnstaple and the 12 noon to Dulverton) were booked to stop there as well.

By August 1884, the Tiverton & North Devon Railway (the Exe Valley line) had opened from Morebath Junction to Tiverton and in addition to the initial four passenger services, the first Up train conveyed goods, arriving at Dulverton at 8.40am. The return passenger and goods departed at 4.45pm from Dulverton. With the opening of the Exe Valley Railway, which ran south from Tiverton to Stoke Canon, the Up goods commenced from Exeter at 6.30am, with the return working arriving back at 6.45pm, the Dulverton times remaining the same as above. This mixed goods was maintained until late 1885, when a specific D&SR and Exe Valley goods was introduced.

The July 1885 time table records a Swindon to Bristol and Barnstaple fast goods. Departing Swindon at 8.45pm, it reached Pylle Hill at 11.50pm, departing at 12.40am and arriving at Taunton at 3.05am.

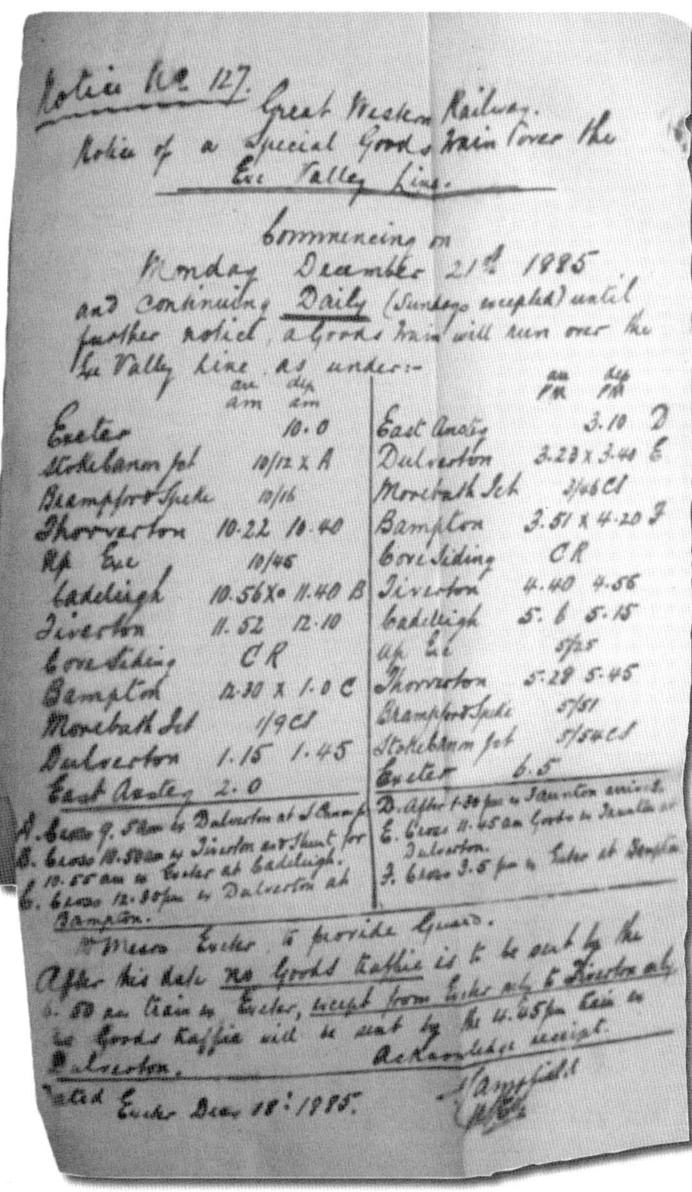

Notice No. 127. Great Western Railway.

Notice of a Special Goods Train over the Exe Valley Line.

Commencing on Monday December 21st 1885 and continuing Daily (Sundays excepted) until further notice, a Goods train will run over the Exe Valley Line as under:-

	arr am	dep am		arr pm	dep pm
Exeter		10.0	East Anstey		3.10 D
Stoke Canon Jct	10/12 X A		Dulverton	3.23 X	3.40 E
Brampford Speke	10/16		Morebath Jct	3/46 CS	
Thorverton	10.22	10.40	Bampton	3.51 X	4.20 F
Up Exe	10/45		Cove Siding	CR	
Cadeleigh	10.56 X	11.40 B	Tiverton	4.40	4.56
Tiverton	11.52	12.10	Cadeleigh	5.6	5.15
Cove Siding	CR		Up Exe	5/25	
Bampton	12.30 X	1.0 C	Thorverton	5.28	5.45
Morebath Jct	1/9 CS		Brampford Speke	5/51	
Dulverton	1.15	1.45	Stoke Canon Jct	5/54 CS	
East Anstey	2.0		Exeter	6.5	

A. Cross 9.5am ex Dulverton at Stoke Canon
B. Cross 10.50am ex Tiverton and shunt for 10.55am ex Exeter at Cadeleigh.
C. Cross 12.30pm ex Dulverton at Bampton.
D. After 1.30pm ex Taunton arrives [illegible]
E. Cross 11.45am Goods ex Taunton at Dulverton.
F. Cross 3.5pm ex Exeter at Bampton

Mr Mears Exeter to provide Guard.

After this date No Goods traffic is to be sent by the [illegible] pm train ex Exeter, except from Exeter only to Tiverton only. The Goods traffic will be sent by the 4.45pm train ex Dulverton.

Acknowledge receipt.

Dated Exeter Dec 18th 1885.

J. Campfield

A copy of a manuscript time table amendment dated December 1885, reflecting a new goods service running over the Exe Valley Line and on to East Anstey on the D&SR. ***Courtesy National Archives***

After a two hour stop over, it departed at 5.15am for Barnstaple arriving at 8.35am. It did not stop at the intermediate stations on the D&SR to pick up or drop off wagons. The train was not booked to stop at Morebath or Morebath Junction but a 'CS' annotation indicated that it did so for staff [token] exchange. The marshalling instructions of the Bristol goods stated that '*through traffic for the Barnstaple branch from Swindon, Bristol and stations above Taunton should as far as possible be forwarded by this train instead of being sent by local trains to Taunton*' and the time table further emphasised '*this is important*'. The instructions went on to state that station truck goods for Morebath in this train will be '*put out at Wiveliscombe* [there was six minutes in which to do this] *and sent forward on the 7.15am down goods*'. The Up Bristol goods left Barnstaple at 7.00pm.

From Monday 26th October 1885, the 11.35am Taunton to Dulverton goods was retimed to depart at 11.45am, arriving at 3.05pm and departing for the return at 3.50pm (originally 3.00pm), arriving at Taunton at 7.05pm. As a result of the retiming, it arrived at Wiveliscombe at 1.20pm and was booked to depart at 2.05pm, which meant that the Down goods had to shunt at Wiveliscombe to allow the 1.30pm ex-Taunton Down passenger to pass. On the return journey, the goods was to pass the 3.35pm Down passenger at Morebath and then shunt for the 3.40pm Up passenger to pass. At Wiveliscombe, the goods had to shunt to give priority for the 2.20pm fast goods from Barnstaple and then transfer the meat van on its train on to the 2.20pm goods. A footnote stipulated that '*the 2.20pm Barnstaple to Taunton goods will call at Milverton when required for Meat traffic only*' (Milverton was to wire Wiveliscombe when necessary).

A further notice issued by Mr Campfield, in October 1885, showed that a special goods would run from Taunton to Barnstaple when required: '*When this conditional train is to run, Inspector Price will advise Mr Gibson at 10am, and then he will notify all D&SR stations by 11.20am, which notification must be acknowledged at once by telegraph. Whenever this special is run it would not be necessary to continue the 11.45am Dulverton goods on to South Molton. On or after this date no Goods Train must be run with a double load over the branch from Taunton to Norton. The special is not to be detained at stations to do yard shunting, but will shunt to allow passenger trains to pass and must run to time. The engine, van and Guard are to return to Taunton with the 7pm up goods from Barnstaple unless otherwise ordered.*' The special was due to arrive at Barnstaple at 6.48pm, allowing twelve minutes before the Up goods departed.

In December 1885, a new goods service was introduced over the Exe Valley, leaving Exeter at 10.00am, arriving at Morebath Junction at 1.09pm and Dulverton at 1.15pm. At 1.45pm it went on to East Anstey, arriving at 2.00pm. It returned at 3.10pm, getting to Dulverton at 3.23pm, where it crossed the 11.45am ex-Taunton goods before leaving for Exeter at 3.40pm. By April 1886, *Notice 167* for the extension of the Dulverton goods to South Molton (12th October 1881, referred to above), was noted in the time table as '*cancelled*'.

A review of the service time table in April and October 1886, for example, shows there were two Up and two Down goods trains per day which ran the length of the line. The first of these was the Mondays excepted 5.20am from Taunton, arriving at Barnstaple at 8.35am – the fast goods from Swindon (8.45pm/Bristol). Extracts from the service time table regarding the marshalling of goods trains ran as follows:

'*1. The train must be formed before starting that wagons for each station shall be together, and this rule must be observed throughout the journey.*

2 The order of marshalling must be, that wagons for the stations at which the train terminates shall be next to the rear brake van and the wagons to come off at the next station next to the engine; this rule must be observed throughout; the object being to facilitate the work with the trains at stations by having as few wagons as possible attached to the engine when shunting.'

In October 1886, the 7.15 am ex-Taunton goods referred to above was labelled 'D&S & EV' [Exe Valley]. This train had time to shunt at intermediate stations, reaching Dulverton at 10.02am. It then left at 10.30am to go back to Morebath Junction to travel down the Exe Valley line, reaching Exeter at 12.55pm (again shunting at key intermediate stations). It returned from Exeter at 1.40pm, reaching Dulverton at 4.45pm and then at 5.15pm it worked its way back to Taunton, arriving at 6.55pm. Given the time allocated, there would be little, if any, shunting at stations other than Wiveliscombe on its return leg. The Exe Valley goods could, when required, be extended to East Anstey (and this would be disclosed in relevant traffic notices).

During 1886, the afternoon Down goods left Taunton at 3.45pm. There was limited time at stations, any extended stays at intermediate points being primarily to allow other trains to pass. It reached Barnstaple at 8.30pm, one hour of this long journey being spent at

Norton Fitzwarren.

The first Up goods train was the 10.00am Barnstaple to Taunton, arriving at 2.40pm. This had roughly ten minutes at most stations but over half an hour at East Anstey, to cross the 11.20am ex-Taunton Down passenger, and twenty minutes at Wiveliscombe, where the 1.30pm Down passenger train was passed. The time table also allowed ten minutes (11.02am to 11.12am) at Florence Siding, South Molton to pick up/drop off wagons. The 7.00pm Barnstaple departure was the returning Bristol and Swindon fast goods, which reached Taunton at 10.45pm. It ran on to Bristol at 11.30pm, where it was booked at North Somerset Junction at 2.20am, finally arriving at Swindon at 5.50am.

There was one Down goods on a Sunday, the 11.30pm Saturday night fast goods from Swindon. It arrived at Pylle Hill at 2.45am on Sunday morning and departed at 3.10am, arriving at Taunton at 5.25am. Leaving Taunton at 7.00am, it reached Barnstaple at 10.20am.This in effect was the balancing working given that the fast Bristol goods did not run down on a Monday.

A note was made in the service time table that, where there was an accumulation of wagons for the Minehead and Barnstaple branches blocking the yard at Taunton, they should be sent by narrow (standard) gauge* engine to Norton Fitzwarren, after it had been confirmed there was sufficient room for storage there. If there were goods wagons for the Barnstaple Branch from stations between Highbridge and Taunton, they would go forward on the 7.30am Highbridge to Tiverton Junction goods, being detached at Taunton for onwards transfer on the next branch goods.

Set out below is the shortened summary of the Taunton and Burlescombe ballast train that ran in 1888. The note said that the train would run every Monday, Wednesday and Friday until further notice and Mr Hammett was to provide the guard:

STATIONS	ARRIVE	DEPART	NOTES
Taunton	..	7.25am	
Burlescombe..	...7.50am	8.10am	
Norton Fitzwarren	...8.40am	8.45am	
Dulverton	. 10.12am	10.17am	Crosses the 10.30am goods
East Anstey....	. 10.32am	....	
East Anstey....		11.15am	
Dulverton	. 11.27am	11.32am	
Norton Fitzwarren	...1.00pm	1.05pm	
Burlescombe..	...1.30pm	1.45pm	
Taunton	...2.10pm	....	

Between 1887 and 1889, there were only minor changes to the goods services as set out above. The Exe Valley goods started a little earlier at 7.00pm from Taunton, whilst the afternoon goods, despite leaving Taunton at the same time of 3.45pm, arrived at Barnstaple at 9.25pm, even later than in previous years. This change occurred in 1889; one hour was spent at Norton Fitzwarren as before but the time at Dulverton and South Molton was extended.

With the chord line to Barnstaple L&SWR opening in 1887, this enabled the start of trip workings between the two Barnstaple goods yards. By way of example, in July 1888, there was a 9.30am departure from the GWR yard arriving at Barnstaple L&SWR at 9.35am. This would have carried wagons off the Down Bristol goods (8.35am arrival). The return working was at 9.50am from the L&SWR, a 9.55am arrival at the GWR yard, presumably to add wagons to and work the 10.00am Up goods. There was also a light engine (1.40pm L&SWR; 1.45pm GWR, returning 2.45pm GWR and to L&SWR at 2.50pm) which had brought in the Down passenger arriving at 1.25pm at the L&SWR station and departed for Taunton at 3.25pm. One surmises it may have done shunting in that hour at the GWR yard before returning to Barnstaple L&SWR to resume its passenger duties. There was a final trip working leaving the L&SWR at 6.15pm, arriving at Barnstaple GWR at 6.20pm, which would convey wagons for the 7.00pm Up goods. This was broadly the theme of the trip workings throughout the life of the line.

*Although the Barnstaple Branch had been converted from broad to narrow or standard gauge in 1881, the main line through Norton Fitzwarren remained mixed gauge at this date.

1890s

There was little significant change to goods services in this decade, so the Swindon/Bristol goods continued to run down in the early morning (and Sundays), with the return service in the evening at 7.00pm on weekdays. An interesting note appeared in the 1890 service time table. A Brake Third was to go from Barnstaple to South Molton by the 7.35am Barnstaple passenger departure on Fridays, to be attached to the 5.20am Down Bristol goods to return it to Barnstaple. The 7.35am was timed to get to South Molton at 8.01am, where it was time-tabled to cross the Down goods before departing at 8.03am; the goods arrived at 7.53am to depart at 8.05am. This requirement must have necessitated some quick and efficient shunting.

The second Taunton goods left at 3.45pm, arriving at Barnstaple at 8.40pm. From July 1892 this was displaced by the 3.40pm Down passenger and was thus retimed to run at 5.10pm – and retimed again in the non-summer periods to 4.15pm, arriving at 9.32pm; it conveyed station truck No. ST259 (Exeter to Barnstaple) from Dulverton, as noted in January 1895. In the Up direction in October 1891, there was a 9.00am goods departure which arrived at Taunton at 2.40pm but this was retimed by July 1892 to leave Barnstaple at 10.25am (arriving 3.47pm). It then got retimed again to a 10.00am departure and by July 1896 departed at 11.15am. At this time it conveyed station truck No. ST273 from Barnstaple to Taunton.

Thirdly was the D&SR and Exe Valley goods, that continued to run but was retimed, leaving Taunton at 7.00am and arriving at Dulverton at 10.15am, before travelling back to Morebath at 11.10am and down the Exe Valley. The Up working was timed to leave Dulverton at 5.00pm following arrival at 4.20pm. By July 1892, it had been retimed to depart at 5.20pm, after a later arrival time of 4.51pm. However, by May 1896, it had ceased to run from Taunton and was just an Exe Valley branch goods, leaving Dulverton at 9.10am and returning at 5.40pm.

By January 1895 there was provision in the service time table to run an additional Taunton to Barnstaple goods, running when required and timed to depart at 9.20am, arriving at 2.15pm. The corresponding Up working was timed to depart Barnstaple at 3.40pm, arriving at Taunton at 7.41pm. Also, there was an optional 2.00pm goods departure from Barnstaple to Dulverton, arriving at 5.10pm and returning at 5.30pm, getting back to at Barnstaple at 7.00pm. By May 1896, these two goods were not shown in the service time table but there was a '*runs when required*' 7.00am departure from Taunton to Dulverton (arriving 9.50am) and a 10.25am departure from Dulverton (arriving at Taunton at 12.20pm).

In this period, a couple of goods trip workings between the GWR station and the Junction were the norm. The Down workings were early (both by 9.15am), whilst the Up workings were at 9.30am (9.35am arrival) and 6.20pm (6.25pm arrival), in time for the Up Bristol goods.

In July 1897, the fast goods was running from Chippenham (and Bristol), the other two being the usual morning and afternoon goods from Taunton. As and when required there continued to be the additional goods running from Taunton to Dulverton and back (leaving Taunton at 8.05am and arriving 9.55am, then returning at 10.25am from Dulverton). There were three Up goods as previously, including the 7.00pm departure for Bristol. The Exe Valley goods still ran, arriving at Dulverton at 3.10pm and departing back to Exeter at 6.00pm. The Bristol goods worked down from Taunton on Sunday mornings and did not run on Mondays, and this pattern continued for the remainder of the decade.

There were three goods trips to Barnstaple L&SWR, one of which included empty coaches departing from the GWR station at 8.00am on Mondays only, for the second Up train, and three back from the Junction. The last one was at 6.25pm, conveying wagons for the Bristol goods, if required. At this time, the evening weekdays goods off Barnstaple at 7.00pm ran through to Chippenham as an express goods, rather than to Swindon or Bristol.

1900s

Reference is made to the January 1900 time table as a basis of the goods services through the 1900s and there are parallels with the previous decade. The Bristol goods left Taunton at 5.30am and arrived at Barnstaple GWR at 8.40am, followed by a trip working to the Junction at 9.10am. During the day, there would be three other trip workings back, the final one, arriving at 6.25pm, being just ahead of the departure of the Up Bristol goods at 7.00pm, which got to Taunton at 11.10pm. In addition, there was the 9.00am Taunton to Barnstaple goods, arriving at 2.53pm, and the 5.20pm from Taunton, arriving at 8.50pm. The latter conveyed the station truck (No. ST259) from Exeter to Barnstaple which was put on at Dulverton. The Up goods to Taunton left Barnstaple at 11.15am (arriving 4.17pm) and 3.35pm (arriving 6.55pm), the former also conveying the station truck (No. ST273) from Barnstaple to Taunton. The latter goods had a time table entry that indicated that it '*must not be detained for roadside work*'. In addition to the three Up and Down workings above, there was a Taunton to Dulverton goods that ran when required, leaving Taunton at 8.05am and arriving at 10.05am. This would work back from Dulverton at 10.25am, arriving at Taunton at 12.20pm. Dulverton also received the Exe Valley goods at 3.10pm, which shunted the yard and worked back to Exeter from Dulverton at 6.00pm. The Down Bristol goods also ran on a Sunday (not the Monday).

The July 1900 time table saw no change to these services, except the 5.20pm Down goods now arrived at 10pm, most of the surplus time being spent at Dulverton (7.10pm to 7.55pm). These services were broadly maintained (with some retiming) until July 1905, when an additional service was added departing Taunton at 7.15am to South Molton, where it arrived at 10.58am. This returned at 12 noon, arriving at 4.52pm, whilst the 12 noon Taunton to Dulverton goods (arriving at 1.45pm) was retimed, continuing as a 'runs when required' service, returning from Dulverton at 3.15pm. However, the late afternoon Down goods no longer ran. On Saturdays only there was an early Up goods departing Barnstaple at 8.20am and an additional weekday goods (running when required) was inserted, which departed Barnstaple at 11.30am for South Molton and returned at 12.50pm, arriving at 1.55pm. In July 1906, the Dulverton goods was retimed to depart from Taunton at 6.35pm, arriving at 8.20pm, with the return working leaving at 9.15pm and arriving at 10.55pm. This service ran when required and maintained this latter schedule for the remainder of the decade.

In 1905, the Taunton to Barnstaple goods conveyed station trucks as follows: No. ST19 (Paddington to Dulverton), No. ST236 (Bristol to Dulverton), No. ST213 (Taunton to Barnstaple) and No. ST315 (Taunton to Dulverton). The service time table noted that the 12.40am Bristol to Barnstaple goods on Sundays was to call when required at Venn Cross and Morebath to put out newspapers.

By October 1909, the former Sundays Down Bristol goods ran early on a Monday. Other than this, the services remained broadly consistent with prior years.

1910-1919

The May/June time table for 1910 indicates that the services had not significantly changed. In summary, the Down Bristol goods arrived at 8.15am (7.05am Mondays only) and the Up goods departed at 7.00pm. The Taunton to Barnstaple goods departed at 10.15am and a balanced Up working returned from Barnstaple at 3.40pm. The Taunton to South Molton morning Down goods was timed to depart at 7.10am, its return departure being at 12.10pm. There were two 'runs when required services'; the 11.50am Barnstaple to South Molton (and 12.50pm return) and the 6.35pm Taunton to Dulverton, which returned at 9.15pm. The Exe Valley goods arrived at Dulverton at 3.35pm and departed at 5.30pm. The Barnstaple trip workings were unbalanced; two to the Junction, departing at 9.20am and 5.25pm but with four returning to the GWR, being spread throughout the day. A similar pattern of goods ran through until the winter of 1910 and beyond.

In the period before the Great War the Bristol goods was worked by tender engine 0-6-0s. The locomotive would work up to Bristol from Taunton before working back in the early hours of the morning. **Table 11.8**, overleaf, illustrates the marshalling of some of the goods trains on the line at this time from GWR records.

As this table shows, in 1913 there were the Bristol to Barnstaple and Taunton to Barnstaple daily goods Down and Up. These were supplemented by the goods from Taunton to South Molton and Taunton to Dulverton, and the respective return services. In 1915, there was the potential for five goods trains to run daily on the branch, commencing with the Bristol goods, the 5.00am from Taunton to Barnstaple, arriving at 8.16am. This was followed down by the 6.10am branch goods to South Molton, arriving at 10.30am. Time was allowed for the engine to shunt at most stations, with Wiveliscombe and Dulverton having most time allocated. This goods returned at 11.40am from South Molton, arriving at Taunton at 4.15pm. At 10.15am, the Taunton goods departure also worked the branch to Barnstaple, arriving at 2.40pm. Sometimes following this was also a 'runs when required' goods to Dulverton, time-tabled to leave Taunton at 10.40am, arriving at Dulverton at 12.55pm. This would return at 2.20pm to reach Taunton at 4.27pm. The Up goods running the length of the branch were the 3.40pm Barnstaple to Taunton (arriving 7.25pm) and the 7.00pm from Barnstaple to Bristol, arriving at Taunton at 10.55pm. Finally, there was a further 'runs when required' goods, this being the 6.35pm Taunton to Dulverton, arriving at 8.25pm and returning at 9.00pm, to reach Taunton at 10.15am. The local goods from Barnstaple to South Molton and back also ran when required.

At this time, the trip workings between the Junction and Barnstaple GWR station were maintained. An L&SWR light engine would leave at 8.55am and return with a 9.20am departure from the GWR station (presumably with wagons off the 8.16am goods arrival). There was a reverse goods working from the L&SWR at 3.50pm, arriving at the Barnstaple GWR at 3.55pm and returning at 5.25pm back to the Junction. At 6.50pm, the departure from Barnstaple Junction was labelled '*coaches and goods*'; this is curious as the last Up train of the day was the 7.00pm goods, the last Up passenger having left at

TABLE 11.8: MARSHALLING FOR GOODS TRAINS (JANUARY 1913)	
TRAIN	**NOTES**
3.40pm Barnstaple to Taunton	**0-6-0 engine. Load 24 wagons Barnstaple to Wiveliscombe; 28 wagons Wiveliscombe to Taunton. This train must not be detained to do roadside work. Station truck traffic from Cadeleigh [on the Exe Valley line] to London to be sent to Dulverton by 3.18pm passenger ex-Exeter to connect with the 3.40pm goods ex-Barnstaple. Station trucks 335 and 357a.**
7pm Barnstaple to Bristol	**0-6-0 engine. Load 21 wagons Barnstaple to Wiveliscombe, 25 wagons Wiveliscombe to Taunton, 60 wagons (30 loaded 30 empties) Taunton to Bristol, restricted to 45 from Taunton for destinations beyond Bridgwater (50 wagons in summer). To reach West Depot, Bristol, marshalled as follows: Engine; Pylle Hill, Canon's Marsh, East Depot van. To convey South Wales traffic from Dunball to Bristol on Saturday nights. Highbridge to advise Bridgwater what traffic they have for this train. Bridgwater to load train to clear Highbridge. Station Trucks 311, 323, 326, 354, 355, 356, 357 and 360.**
12.40am Bristol to Barnstaple (1.20am MO)	**0-6-0 engine. Load 50 wagons Bristol to Taunton, 21 Taunton to Barnstaple. Through traffic for the Barnstaple branch must be sent by this train, not by local trains to Taunton. Goods not to convey traffic for Exeter or below. Traffic for Tiverton Junction and stations to Stoke Cannon to be kept together. To convey parcels van from Taunton to Barnstaple. Dulverton to advise Taunton what traffic they have for this train, Taunton to load accordingly. This train must always be worked with a 20-ton brake van. Station trucks 20, 234, 236, 237, 239, 289 and MO 312 and 334.**
6.15pm Dulverton to Exeter	**0-6-0 tank engine. Load 18 wagons to Bampton, 37 wagons beyond. Station truck 353.**
11.45am Exeter to Dulverton	**0-6-0 tank engine. Load 30 wagons, Exeter to Tiverton, 21 Tiverton to Dulverton. Station trucks 334 and 335.**
11.05am South Molton to Taunton	**0-6-0 tank engine. Load 24 wagons, South Molton to Wiveliscombe, 28 beyond.**
6.10am Taunton to South Molton	**0-6-0 tank engine. Load 26 wagons to Milverton, 24 beyond. Station truck 19.**
10.15am Taunton to Barnstaple	**0-6-0 tank engine. Load 26 wagons to Milverton, 24 beyond. Station trucks 236, 313 and 315.**

6.33pm, so was presumably returning stock for working the first Up passenger train of the following day.

By the summer of 1914 there is no reference to the through running of a goods from or to Bristol, which does not appear to have resumed until the 1920s. In January 1917, there were three goods in each direction, two to/from Barnstaple and one to/from South Molton. By April 1919, there were two Down Taunton to Barnstaple goods and a Taunton to Dulverton goods, with respective Up workings. This pattern continued for the remainder of the decade.

It is likely that during the war years a number of special goods services ran. No evidence of this has been found but given comments in Chapter 12, with Barnstaple being a railhead for military purposes, it would seem likely.

1920-1929

In July 1920, there were two Down goods from Taunton to Barnstaple, at 6.00am and 10.50am, with an 8.00am Taunton to South Molton goods and a 11.15am Taunton to Dulverton goods (on Tuesdays, Thursdays, Fridays and Saturdays). The corresponding Up goods were at 9.15am and 2.50pm from Barnstaple, 1.30pm from South Molton and 2.10pm from Dulverton. The Exe Valley goods arrived at Dulverton at 3.25pm and departed at 4.50pm but there appears to be no Bristol goods in this period. There was an early trip goods to Barnstaple Junction and a return in the evening of goods and coaches. A similar pattern of goods ran in the October period through to summer 1921, with an additional 5.45am Taunton to Barnstaple which ran when required.

July 1921 saw a similar pattern of goods to and from Barnstaple but the 8.40am Taunton ran only as far as Dulverton daily, departing back at 1.55pm and with no South Molton service. In October 1921, there was a Down goods departing Taunton at 5.45am, running when required. In addition, there were the 6.40am (arriving 11.30am) and the 11.40am (arriving 4.45pm) departures from Taunton to Barnstaple. An 8.40am departure from Taunton ran to South Molton, arriving at 1.03pm and returning at 1.35pm, whilst on Tuesdays, Thursdays, Fridays and Saturdays, a Taunton to Dulverton goods, departing at 10.35am and arriving at 12.30pm, was reinstated. In the Up direction, there were two Barnstaple to Taunton goods departing at 9.15am and 2.15pm, along with the returning South Molton and Dulverton goods (at 1.35pm). The Exe Valley goods arrived at Dulverton at 3.35pm and departed at 4.55pm. There were two trip goods workings at this time to and from the Junction, the 5.00pm departure from Barnstaple GWR and the 8.00pm from the L&SWR both labelled '*goods and coaches*'.

By the summer of 1922, there was a 5.00am Down goods from Taunton and a 5.45am additional goods which operated when required. The South Molton and Dulverton goods ran, along with a further Down Barnstaple goods at 11.35am. The Up goods from Barnstaple were timed at 9.15am and 1.40pm and these services were broadly maintained through the winter of 1922 and beyond to the middle of the decade, with three Down and three Up goods, plus the Taunton to Dulverton service. The L&SWR became part of the Southern Railway from 1923.

It would seem the Bristol goods resumed running on weekdays in the summer period of 1925 but did not appear in the winter time table of 1925 to 1927.

By the summer of 1928, the Down Bristol goods had resumed again, leaving Taunton at 4.15am and arriving Barnstaple at 7.30am, continuing into the winter period and beyond. In addition, there were the 5.45am and 11.46am Taunton to Barnstaple goods, arriving at 9.15am and 5.05pm respectively. The earlier goods would not stop for any shunting until Dulverton and there was also limited time beyond this point for shunting. This service was supplemented by a Taunton to Dulverton goods, which was a Saturdays excepted 9.20am departure, arriving at 12.15pm, with time for shunting at most stations. The return service departed at 2.25pm, arriving at 4.30pm. The Up goods were the 9.18am and 2.15pm Barnstaple to Taunton, arriving at 2.50pm and 8pm respectively, and the 8.00pm Bristol goods which arrived at Taunton at 11.12pm. At this stage, the only time-tabled trip workings were the 8.30am departure from GWR to Barnstaple Junction SR, returning at 6.30pm and connecting with the Down and Up Bristol goods respectively.

1930-1939

In the period before 1932, goods traffic for Dulverton and the Barnstaple line also came by way of the Exe Valley goods. This traffic would arrive at Tiverton Junction at 4.40am on the 4.00am departure from Exeter (the Exeter to Tiverton pick-up goods, via the main line), conveying traffic that had arrived at Exeter during the night. Having shunted the yard at Tiverton Junction, the service would

'Small Prairie' tank No. 5502 heads an Up goods at Westcott Lane bridge, near Landkey, hauling a train of in the region of twenty goods wagons and a brake van circa 1930. Note the open wagons loaded with timber in the middle of the train. *Arthur Halls, courtesy National Railway Museum*

run to Tiverton at 6.30am and the relevant wagons would then be taken forward to Dulverton on the up Exe Valley goods later that day.

The '43XX' Class 'Mogul' 2-6-0s were the regular motive power on the Bristol goods in the 1930s and 1940s. The engine would work to Bristol on an evening passenger train and then return with the 1.15am goods to Barnstaple. Having reached its destination, the engine would work back on an early morning Up passenger train to Taunton.

During this decade there were three freight services each way that ran the length of the line. The Down Bristol goods arrived at 7.20am for most of the period and was followed by the 6.00am and 12.20pm from Taunton, due at 9.15am and 4.35pm respectively. The Up goods departed at around 9.40am and 2.15pm, with the Up Bristol goods at 8.00pm/8.15pm in the early part of the period, to 7.20pm by summer 1939. In addition, there was a pick-up goods from Taunton to Dulverton, departing at 8.45am, arriving at 11.05am and returning at 12.20pm. The Exe Valley goods ran to Dulverton in this period, where it arrived at 1.30pm and departed at 3.10pm.

There were the usual trip workings each way between Barnstaple GWR and the Junction; two in the morning and one late evening (to the Southern), and two late afternoon and evenings back to the GWR yard.

From 4th November 1935, a 2.55pm Barnstaple to Taunton goods was introduced by a notice which, in effect, was a retiming of the early afternoon goods. The train was stated not to exceed fifteeen wagons on leaving Barnstaple and was due to arrive at Taunton at 7.45pm, having stopped at most stations en route but only for urgent traffic or station truck items. However, stops at South Molton, East Anstey and Dulverton were to shunt to allow a train to pass or to perform work.

By the summer of 1937, the usual Barnstaple workings were supplemented by a Taunton to South Molton goods (6.30am/8.44am) but this did not run on Saturdays. There was a goods that ran when required from Dulverton to South Molton, departing at 1.25pm to 2.00pm; it was worked by the engine off the 10.15am Exe Valley goods, which then arrived a little earlier at 1.20pm. It returned at 2.10pm from South Molton as just an engine and van, and did not run on Fridays and Saturdays. **Table 11.9** below is an extract from a 1930s service time table regarding the working of goods trains on the branch.

Trip workings in the period were of a similar pattern, with a goods from Barnstaple GWR to the Junction at 8.30am following arrival of the Bristol goods and a later service, after the departure of the Up Bristol goods, which left the Junction at 8.50pm. By the winter of 1935, there was an additional afternoon trip working from the Junction at 4.45pm.

TABLE 11.9: WORKING OF GOODS AND MINERAL TRAINS DOWN INCLINES (1930s)

Incline upon which 'Stop Board' is fixed	Down or Up Trains	Point where Train must stop to release brakes
Venn Cross	Down	Morebath Starting signal
Venn Cross	Up	Wiveliscombe station
East Anstey	Down	Bishops Nympton & Molland Starting signal
East Anstey	Up	Dulverton station
Swimbridge	Down	Barnstaple Home signal

The power of this unidentified Class '45XX' 2-6-2T is in evidence as it nears Castle Hill Viaduct with a typical mixed goods circa 1927. Note the 'Mica' van directly behind the locomotive. Although its exact identity is not known, the engine can be pinned down as one of the final batch built with flat-topped tanks, No's 4555 to 4574, completed at Swindon Works between September and November 1924. They were the first of the class to be fitted with outside steam pipes and cast iron chimneys. *Arthur Halls, courtesy National Railway Museum*

Watched by the signalman, this 'Dean Goods' 0-6-0 is paused at Milverton in the 1930s, whilst running tender first on a short goods bound for Taunton. The first van next to the locomotive is an 'Iron Mink'. ***Roger Carpenter/Lens of Sutton Association***

1940-1949

Goods time tables have been difficult to come by for the early years of the Second World War. However, one suspects that the services were broadly similar throughout the period and were most likely supplemented by unpublished special troop and military trains, especially around the 1943-44 period ahead of the D-Day landings (see Chapter 12 on Special Trains and Special Events). In the October 1944 time table, there were four goods trains that ran the length of the line in both directions. Downwards were the 4.15am, 7.00am and 12.30pm Taunton (East Yard Down sidings) to Barnstaple goods and the 1.55am Bristol goods, which left Taunton at 6.05am and arrived at Barnstaple at 10.00am. In the Up direction, the departures were at 9.00am, 11.00am and 1.30pm, all to Taunton, and the 8.15pm to Bristol. The 9.00am departure arrived at Taunton at 3.25pm, a journey of six hours and twenty-five minutes. There was also the 7.45am Taunton West Yard departure for Dulverton, arriving at 10.30am, which returned departing at 12 noon for an arrival at Taunton of 2.50pm. Dulverton also saw the Exe Valley goods arriving at 12.14pm and departing at 1.15pm. Traffic off the Exe Valley destined for stations to Barnstaple would be shunted to await the next Down goods, most likely the 12.30pm ex-Taunton. Traffic from Bampton on the Exe Valley line which was eastbound would also be shunted at Dulverton to await the next Up goods – the exchange siding beyond the bay platform on the Down side was used for this purpose. Goods for Dulverton would be shunted into the Up side goods yard, whilst the Exe Valley locomotive would shunt wagons for that line which had come off the earlier Down goods from Taunton.

In the Barnstaple area, there were three trip workings to the Junction from the GWR station (two being associated with the first three goods arrivals) and two return workings, one late afternoon and the other in the evening. By summer 1945, the 7.00am Down goods was removed from the time table and the 11.00am Up departure was also taken out. The trip workings and the Dulverton goods remained consistent though.

By 1942, it seems the Bristol goods was being worked by larger engines between Bristol and Taunton, probably as a result of increased war-time loadings, with a Class '43XX' being attached at Taunton to work the branch.

In the winter of 1946-47, there were three goods trains (now labelled '*freight*' in the service time table) daily between Taunton and Barnstaple, including the Bristol goods, plus the Dulverton goods and the Exe Valley goods. At this time there were three trip goods workings from Barnstaple GWR to the Junction and two (in the evening) from the Junction to the GWR. This goods pattern continued through the summer months until the end of the decade.

The first few months of Nationalisation, from January to May 1948, saw two goods that ran down the length of the line, the 1.15am Bristol goods, arriving at 8.36am, and the 12.50pm Taunton to Barnstaple, arriving at 5.13pm. There was also a Saturdays excepted Taunton to Dulverton goods, which departed at 7.50am and arrived at 10.23am. The return working left at 11.45am, after a goodly time spent shunting the yard, arriving at Taunton at 1.43pm. The three Up goods were the 9.35am Barnstaple to Taunton, arriving 2.25pm, and the 1.25pm departure from Barnstaple which arrived at Taunton at 5.13pm. The Bristol goods left at 8.30pm. There were a couple of trip workings from Victoria Road to the Junction and one back in the evening prior to the departure of the Bristol goods. The Exe Valley goods stayed broadly on its same schedule.

By summer 1949 (23rd May to 25th September), on weekdays there were four Down goods to Barnstaple (one did not run on Saturdays) and four Up (again, one did not run on Saturdays). In addition, the Taunton to Dulverton goods still ran with Saturdays excepted. Freight loadings were good in this period. For example, it was recorded that the 12.30pm Taunton to Barnstaple goods on 20th December 1946 pulled by 'Mogul' No. 6361 comprised twenty-four wagons and a 20-ton brake van. Similarly, the 1.30pm Barnstaple to Taunton goods hauled by No. 6305 on 29th March 1947 had a load of twenty-seven wagons plus the 'Toad' brake van. This load was repeated on 14th August 1947, with the 1.15am Bristol to Barnstaple goods behind by No. 6332.

1950-1959

The summer of 1951 had three Up and four Down goods (one not running on Saturdays). In addition, the Taunton to Dulverton and Taunton to South Molton goods both ran but again Saturdays excepted. In the winter of that year there were four goods each way to and from Barnstaple including the Bristol goods, plus a Taunton West Yard to South Molton and a Taunton to Dulverton goods. This pattern continued for the early part of the decade.

In 1952 and beyond, these workings left Taunton at 4.05am (Bristol goods), 5.00am (Saturdays excepted), 5.30am and 11.40am. Arrival times at Barnstaple were 6.43am, 7.58am, 8.20am and 3.38/3.55 (Saturdays excepted).

In the summer period of 1954, there were five weekday trip workings between Victoria Road and Barnstaple Junction, along with four in the reverse direction, two of which did not run on Saturdays in the summer season. There were two light engine movements to the Junction and three light engine movements coming back, one of which was in respect of the unbalanced goods working.

Moving to the middle of the decade, the weekdays goods services were broadly as follows (from the 20th September 1954 to 12th June 1955 time table). The Down Bristol goods arrived at 7.20am and was followed by the 5.20am, the 6.10am and 11.40am from Taunton to Barnstaple (arriving respectively at 8.01am, 9.06am and 3.38pm). In addition, the 6.55am ran from Taunton to South Molton, arriving at 9.10am, and there was the 8.25am from Taunton to Bampton, which arrived at Dulverton at 11.15am. In the Up direction, the workings were balanced: Up goods departed Barnstaple at 9.10am (although this was suspended in this period), 9.55am, 2.20pm and 7.35pm for Bristol. The South Molton and Bampton goods worked back at 11.35am and 12.26pm (from Dulverton) respectively. In the summer weekday period, the services were broadly the same. On summer Saturdays only three freights ran, the Down Bristol and the 4.45am and 10.30am from Taunton to Barnstaple. Five freights worked Up on summer weekdays, with two only operating on summer Saturdays, namely the 3.05pm Barnstaple departure and the 8.00pm to Bristol; the 9.55am Barnstaple to South Molton and the Bampton goods had to make way for additional passenger services.

GOODS TRAIN OPERATION ON THE D&SR

With the various steep gradients, goods train operation over the D&SR was a skill and required good team work between driver, fireman and guard. There were written rules to adhere to, which were designed to ensure safety at all times. Goods trains were required to stop and pin down their brakes at key points on the route; this was a manual job for the guard but one which required some skill and he would also operate the brake in his van as the train descended the gradient. The guard had to judge the number of handbrakes on the wagons he should pin down, given the length of the train and tonnage being conveyed. The start of the 1 in 59 downgrade at East Anstey running to Dulverton was a case in point. At the Taunton end of Dulverton's Up platform there was a sign stating 'GOODS AND MINERAL TRAINS TO STOP HERE TO PICK UP BRAKES', meaning that on arrival at the bottom of the gradient, the process was reversed before the train went on its way. Special care was required when shunting. 'Sprags' – essentially a plug of wood – were used to put in between the spoked wheels of the wagons to prevent inadvertent movement. Rules stipulated that in shunting on a rising gradient the sprags should be placed on wagons near the brake van (at the rear) but on a falling gradient they were to be placed on those at the front. The number of sprags to be used was determined by the steepness of the gradient, the number of vehicles, their loads, and the state of the weather and the rails. Sprags were usually kept handy at certain locations between the Up and Down running lines and were particularly useful, if not essential, at Venn Cross and East Anstey stations. A photograph showing sprags lying between the lines at Swimbridge appears in Volume 2, page 377.

An unidentified 'Mogul' powers its way along the line with a goods train in the 1950s. The location has to date defied positive identification but is thought to be just out of Barnstaple; confirmation would be welcome. ***Courtesy National Railway Museum***

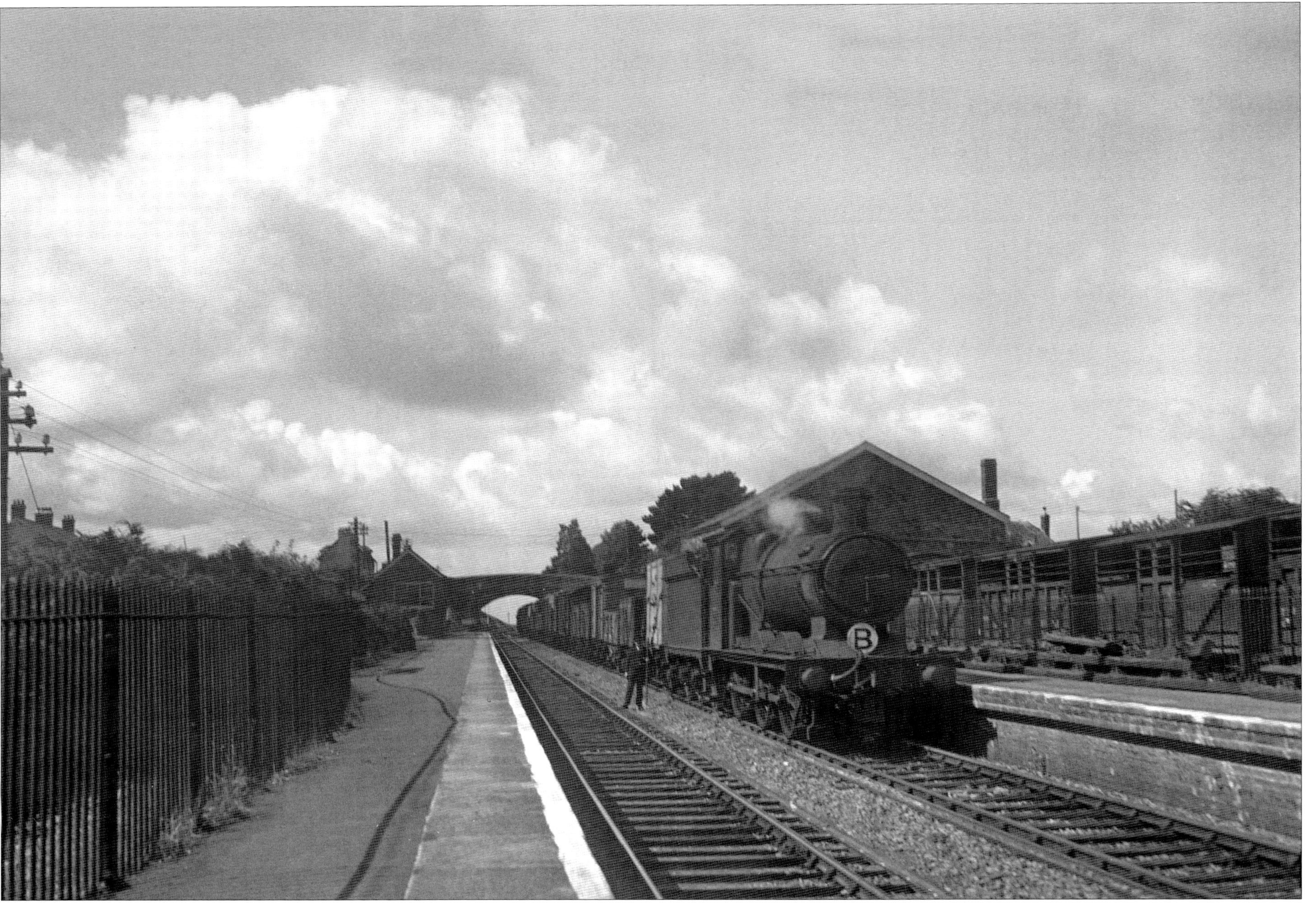

An unknown Collett 0-6-0 poses with an Up goods at Swimbridge in 1950 (note the same train appears on page 435 of Volume 2). The guard is standing with shunter's pole in hand so the train may have stopped to drop off a wagon or two or collect some, perhaps the cattle wagons in the goods shed road. Swimbridge was at the summit of a climb almost all of the way from Barnstaple but the drop down from here eastwards was short, with the ascent starting again after just half a mile and continuing all the way past Filleigh and Castle Hill. Consequently, some of the wagon wheels in Up trains stopping here to drop off or collect wagons were 'spragged' to guard against a runaway. Note that the 'B' disc was not just reserved for passenger workings. *Roger J. Sellick, courtesy National Railway Museum*

By summer 1956, weekdays saw the South Molton goods running only on Tuesdays and Thursdays, whilst the Taunton to Bampton goods ran only on Mondays, Wednesdays and Fridays. There were three Down goods to Barnstaple, leaving Taunton at 4.35am (from Bristol), 6.10am and 11.40am. There were only two Up goods, at 2.45pm and 7.35pm from Barnstaple, with the latter going to Bristol; the 9.55am Up goods had been suspended. The 1958 period also broadly reflected these services.

BRISTOL ST. PHILIP'S MARSH DEPOT TURNS, SUMMER 1957

Turn 415 was one '68XX' or 'Grange' Class on Tuesdays to Fridays, which would come off Taunton shed at 12.30am and at 12.50am would work the 7.30pm Barnstaple to Bristol West Depot goods, arriving at 2.14am and then going on shed. On Saturdays it would leave the depot at 12.10am and work the Barnstaple goods to Bristol at 12.30am, arriving at 2.05am and then going on shed.

Turn 417 was two '43XX' locomotives, which would work the 8.00pm Saturdays only Barnstaple to Bristol goods from Taunton. Coming off shed at 12.30am, they left at 2.50am on Sundays and having arrived at West Depot at 2.14am, would then go on shed.

Turn 425 was two '22XX' 0-6-0s on Tuesdays and Thursdays, which would work the Bristol West Depot to Barnstaple goods to Taunton. Leaving the shed at 1.25am and West Depot at 1.50am, on arrival at Taunton at 3.26am they would go on shed. On Fridays they would take the 10.50pm West Depot to Barnstaple goods to Taunton. Off shed at 10.25pm, they would leave West Depot at 10.50pm and arrive at Taunton at 3.26am, where they would then go on shed.

The winter 1956-57 period reverted to four Down goods plus the South Molton and Bampton services that ran every day. There were three Up goods plus the return services from South Molton and Bampton. The period from 15th September 1958 to 14th June 1959 showed three Down goods plus the South Molton service but the Bampton goods had ceased. However, also running when required was an 11.50am Dulverton to Bampton local trip, returning at 12.26pm with a turn-round time of eight minutes at Bampton. In the Up direction there were three workings and all this was repeated in the 2nd September to 12th June 1960 winter period.

The Bampton goods did not run in the summer period of 1959 but there were three Down goods to Barnstaple on weekdays and summer Saturdays, and the South Molton goods, which did not run on Saturdays. There were only two Up goods from Barnstaple, the 2.10pm and 7.35pm (Bristol) departures. Trip workings to and from the Junction continued in the familiar pattern of previous years but the end of the decade had started to see the decline of goods services. The trip working from Dulverton to Bampton remained but running only when required, which was usually for coal and a stores truck. The motive power for this service was off the South Molton to Taunton goods.

1960-1966

It is interesting to review the freight working time tables in the early 1960s and see the transition from the service that had more or less been in place for some decades to a very skeleton offering and then closure. With Victoria Road closing to passengers on 13th June 1960 and the East Chord reopening, the direct running of Down trains into Victoria Road was suspended. Furthermore, photograph evidence points to the track between East Junction and Victoria Road as having been lifted by circa May 1961. Certain Down goods were still time-tabled to arrive at the ex-GWR yard and it would therefore seem that these would traverse the East Chord to the South Junction ground frame and then shunt back into Victoria Road. This manoeuvre has not been substantiated but no other alternative seems practicable unless the goods ran to Barnstaple Junction, ran around and came back to Victoria Road but this seems unlikely. Victoria Road was still served by trip workings from the Junction in any event and, as is commented elsewhere, remained open until March 1970. All tender locomotives arriving at Victoria Road would also have had to work to the Junction for turning and servicing.

At the start of the summer time table (13th June 1960), there were four Down freights. The 1.50am Bristol goods (now with headcode 8C54) still ran, leaving Taunton at 4.35am on weekdays and arriving at Victoria Road at 7.20am. This was followed by 9A06, the 6.04am Taunton to Victoria Road, which arrived at 9.06am, then 9A61, the 6.15am departure Taunton to South Molton pick-up goods, arriving 9.10am. The last Down goods, 9A06, departed Taunton at 11.40am and arrived Victoria Road at 3.40pm. The timings of the three main workings were slightly different on Saturdays and the South Molton goods did not run. In the Up direction there were only three freight services; 9A38 to Fairwater Sidings, departing at 10.25am, was suspended, as was 8C94 at 2.20pm but retimed at 2.10pm, stopping only at certain stations for livestock and urgent traffic. The South Molton pick-up goods left at 10.42am for Fairwater Sidings. This was the first instance of the time table mentioning the Taunton goods as only working to Fairwater Yard. The Bristol goods (8B75) left Victoria Road at 7,45pm (8.00pm on Saturdays). There were four freight trip workings from the Junction, one working only when required, and four working back.

Taunton-based 'Pannier' tank No. 3736 alongside the Down platform at Milverton, whilst in the process of shunting some empty wooden-bodied coal wagons, on 7th July 1959. ***Roger Carpenter, Lens of Sutton Association***

On 26th February 1960 a '57XX' Class 0-6-0PT trundles a short eastbound freight towards Nightcott Tunnel, near West Knowle, about half way between East Anstey and Dulverton. The consist includes a single empty coal wagon, five box vans and a couple of cattle wagons, with a 'Toad' brake van bringing up the rear. ***John Spencer Gilks***

In this period there was also, when required, the weekdays Dulverton to Bampton goods, leaving at 11.50am and returning at 12.26pm. This continued to be worked by the the locomotive off the South Molton to Taunton goods.

The 12th September 1960 to 11 June 1961 winter period showed the three Saturdays only goods (one from Bristol and two from Taunton) as suspended. However, four weekday services remained, broadly as illustrated for the earlier period. In the Up direction, there were also three goods suspended, two being Saturday's only including the Up Bristol. The first Up goods was the 10.25am Victoria Road to Fairwater Sidings (9A38), where it arrived at 1.51pm but did not have significant time at the stations on route. The 10.42am departure from South Molton to Fairwater Sidings (9A38) spent fifty-two minutes at Dulverton. This was to allow for, if required, the locomotive to work a goods to Bampton on the Exe Valley line, leaving Dulverton at 11.50 am, returning at 12.26pm, which was allocated headcode 9A04 on the way out and 9A26 on the return. The goods would then proceed and reach Fairwater at 2.13pm. At 2.05pm, a goods would leave Barnstaple Junction (8C94) to reach Taunton at 5.06pm. It avoided Victoria Road and was time-tabled to spend about half an hour at South Molton, otherwise it was only to stop at other stations for livestock and urgent traffic. The final Up goods of the day was 8B75, the 7.50pm Victoria Road to Bristol, which got to Taunton at 10.27pm and was not time-tabled to shunt at stations.

There were a number of trip workings between the Junction and Victoria Road – four Down and three Up, one of which was formed in part from the Down Bristol goods (the 8.15am departure) and another from the 9.05am arrival, leaving at 10.15am. A trip would also come over in the evening at 7.15pm to take wagons for the Up Bristol goods.

In the summer period 12th June to 10th September 1961, the four weekday Down goods (as referred above) remained in the time table, as did the three Saturday's only Down workings. In the Up direction, the 10.35am to Fairwater Yard was suspended but the South Molton goods, the 2.05pm departure from Barnstaple Junction to Fairwater Yard and the 7.50pm Bristol goods were still time-tabled. On Saturdays only, the Down Bristol goods ran through to the Junction, by-passing Victoria Road and starting back at 8.10pm. The 10.30am from Taunton arrived at Victoria Road at 2.04pm, before leaving at 3.15pm to travel to the Junction, where it arrived at 3.25pm. The Saturday's only 4.35am Taunton to Barnstaple terminated at Victoria Road and there was a 3.03pm departure for Fairwater Yard. The Bampton trip was still run as required.

The winter period of 11th September 1961 to 17th June 1962 showed a consistency of services. The weekday Bristol goods still ran but had an extended stay at Swimbridge of thirty-two minutes. At this time the 10.35am Barnstaple to Fairwater goods was not suspended and as a consequence caught up and overtook the South Molton goods at Dulverton at 12.06pm. The Saturday's only goods were all marked as suspended.

There were regular trip workings between the Junction and Victoria Road at this time, as summarised in **Table 11.10** below.

There were a couple of unbalanced workings. It appears that the 10.20am departure was served by a light engine running over from the Junction at just after 9.00am, whilst it is likely the locomotive from the 7.05/7.15pm trip worked the 7.50pm Bristol goods.

Table 11.10: Barnstaple Trip Workings

	9A06	9A05	9A05	9A06	9A05	9A06	9A05	9A06
Jct (d)	7.10a			11.25a		5.16p		7.05p
Victoria Road (a)	7.20a			11.35a		5.26p		7.15p
Victoria Road (d)		8.30a	10.20a		12.40p		5.53p	
Jct (a)		8.40a	10.30a		12.50p		6.03p	
Notes: (d) – depart; (a) – arrive; a – morning; p – afternoon								

In the next time table, for the period 18th June to 9th September 1962, there were radical changes. The through Bristol goods had ceased, whilst there were two Down goods but only one in the Up direction. The 4.35am ran from Taunton to Victoria Road arriving at 8.31am, with the most booked time on route (eighteen minutes) being spent at South Molton. There was also a Saturdays excepted

6.04am Taunton departure to Swimbridge, arriving at 10.00am, which would run when required on to Barnstaple Junction. It was booked at South Molton for twenty-five minutes and a number of other stations for about ten minutes each. In practice and based on comments from those who worked the line this service frequently took most goods to South Molton and only 'tripped' to Filleigh or Swimbridge if required with the odd wagon. The isolated Up working was the 10.22am Swimbridge to Fairwater Sidings (9A38). Again, when required, this could work from Barnstaple Junction. If indeed it did this, it would presumably have to leave the Junction about fifteen minutes earlier than the 10.22am booked time from Swimbridge to maintain its schedule. Assuming the goods did not extend to Barnstaple, there was a turnround time of twenty-two minutes at Swimbridge. Given the simple track layout at that station, there was a limit to what, if any, shunting took place. By this time it is likely that most goods trains were limited to modest loads, with Dulverton and South Molton being the main destinations for the supplies.There were four trip workings to the Junction and two back, with light engine movements balancing those workings.

A review of the working time table for the period 9th September 1963 until further notice designates Fairwater Yard to Swimbridge and back as a trip working from Taunton under the charge of Plymouth locomotive turn 833, which was booked for a Class '57XX' 0-6-0PT. The Taunton enginemen clocked on at 5.00am to 1.05pm and the Barnstaple men 10.30am to 6.30pm. The times are illustrated in **Table 11.11** below.

TABLE 11.11: LOCO TURN 833 (1963)

LOCATION	ARRIVE (AM)	DEPART (AM)	LOCATION	ARRIVE (AM/PM)	DEPART (AM/PM)
Taunton shed		5.45	Swimbridge (9A37)		10.22
Taunton	5.50	6.04	Filleigh		
Milverton	6.25	6.35	South Molton	10.37	11.25
Wiveliscombe	6.49	7.02	Bishops Nympton & Molland		
Venn Cross			East Anstey		
Morebath			Dulverton	12.04	
Dulverton	7.56	8.10	Bampton SX Q	12.22	12.41
East Anstey	8.25	8.30	Dulverton	12.56	1.02
Bishops Nympton & Molland	8.46	8.56	Venn Cross	1.31	1.36
South Molton	9.08	9.33	Wiveliscombe	1.52	2.00
Filleigh	9.47	9.52	Milverton		
Swimbridge	10.00		Fairwater Sidings	2.25	2.30
			Taunton shed	2.35	

Notes: SX – Saturdays Excepted
Q is runs when required (headcode 9A03 to Bampton, 9A26 on return). Loco from Taunton shed to Taunton (0A71) and on return Fairwater to Taunton shed is light engine (0A66)

The time allowance for goods trains hauled by steam locomotives over the line at this time, as extracted from the working time table, is set out in **Table 11.12** below.

The local trip workings between the Junction and Victoria Road continued. There were two to Victoria Road, one arriving at 7.30am, the other at 4.25pm, and four out to the Junction.

Two of these were balanced workings, whilst of the others, the 10.20am departure would be the locomotive off the 8.31am goods arrival from Taunton. The 12.35am goods trip would be worked by the locomotive coming light engine from the Junction at 11.33am. There were also certain light engine movements, the first of which was to Victoria Road at 6.25am, returning at 7.00am, presumably for shunting the yard. There is also reference to a Saturday's excepted light engine working from Victoria Road to the Junction (1.38pm departure, arriving at 1.48pm), which appears to be a typing error in the time table, as the balanced working is a Saturday's only light engine arriving at 12.33pm, again most likely to shunt the yard. At this time, the 12.10pm departure from Dulverton to Bampton goods still ran, returning at 12.56pm, with the Swimbridge to Fairwater Sidings service providing the locomotive.

TABLE 11.12: TIME ALLOWANCES GOODS TRAINS (1963)

LOCATION	STOP BOARD	LOCATION	STOP BOARD
Taunton	–	Yeo Mill Halt	-
Norton Fitzwarren	5	Bishops Nympton & M	14
Milverton	11	South Molton	10
Wiveliscombe	10	Filleigh	9
Venn Cross	13	Swimbridge	8
Stop Board	–	Stop Board	4
Morebath	8	Barnstaple East Jct	-
Morebath Jct	–	Stop Board	-
Morebath Jct Halt	–	Barnstaple Victoria Rd	6
Dulverton	8	Barnstaple South Jct	-
East Anstey	13	Barnstaple Jct	3
Stop Board	–		

Table 11.13 below shows the destination descriptions for local light engines and local freight movements to stations and yards in the Exeter District only, as extracted from the working time table for September 1963 and from June 1964 to June 1965; curiously, they are different.

The same time table showed that the time allowed for banking engines to return from East Anstey to Dulverton was eight minutes. As there was no provision for a spare engine at Dulverton, one presumes that this duty would have been performed by the Exe Valley train locomotive, before that line closed and assuming that there was sufficient time between services to allow for this supporting role. In terms of working goods trains to Anstey, the 1960 edition of *The Sectional Appendix to the Working Time Table and Books of Rules and Regulations* stated that the load was not to exceed thirty-two 10-ton

TABLE 11.13: BARNSTAPLE BRANCH HEADCODES 1963-65

HEADCODE (1963 WTT)	DESTINATION	HEADCODE (1964-65 WTT)
A03	Bampton	Closed
A04	Barnstaple Junction	Southern WTT
A05	Barnstaple Victoria Road	D02
A25	Dulverton	D21
A28	East Anstey	D25
A37	Fairwater Sidings	D33
A38	Filleigh	–
A57	Milverton	D60
A67	South Molton	D71
A71	Swimbridge	D76
A72	Taunton	D77
A84	Venn Cross	D87
A93	Wiveliscombe	D97

In 1964-65, the codes for light engines to running and maintenance depots was Z34 for Taunton and Z99 for Barnstaple Junction

On a warm early summer's day in beautiful countryside near the Devon and Somerset border, having just exchanged tokens with the Morebath Junction signalman, 2-6-2T No. 5521 exits the Up loop on its way to Taunton. This is a later view on 8th June 1961, the same day as the frontispiece picture and can be seen to that the engine has now picked up an additional half dozen wagons at Dulverton. The consist now included wooden and steel bodied opens, two 4-wheeled container flats and a pair of ventilated box vans. The junction with the Exe Valley line can just be seen in the left distance, opposite the signal box. ***Michael J. Fox, courtesy Rail Archive Stephenson***

RIGHT: No. 6337 slows to carry out a token exchange as it passes through Morebath with an Up goods bound for Taunton. This train did not call here in the Up direction but the down Dulverton goods would occasionally stop to service the yard, as evidenced by the 1959-60 signal box train register (see Volume 2 page 460).
Roger J. Sellick, courtesy National Railway Museum

Below: On 29th September 1962, Class '57XX' 0-6-0PT No. 4663 trundles past Blinkhorn depot and Silk Mills near Norton Fitzwarren with an Up goods off the Barnstaple Branch. The volume of traffic on this occasion was low, comprising two ventilated vans, a mineral wagon loaded with stone ballast and a BR standard brake van.
Owen Mogg collection, courtesy Peter Triggs

wagons with this assisting locomotive, which had to be coupled at the rear.

In the period 15th June 1964 to 13th June 1965, the only timetabled goods was the 6.04am Taunton to Swimbridge, which was shown as running daily. The train was scheduled to spend twenty minutes at Wiveliscombe, thirty-five minutes at Dulverton, thirty-seven minutes at Bishops Nympton & Molland and twenty-four minutes at South Molton. It worked back at 10.32am, spending fifty-three minutes at South Molton but much less at the other stations.

The working time table supplement No. 5 for the period 7th September 1964 to 13th June 1965, showed that the 6.04am Taunton to Swimbridge goods (9D76), which by then had been restricted to Mondays, Wednesdays and Fridays only, as withdrawn from 31st July 1964. Unsurprisingly, the same fate applied to the corresponding 10.32am Up working (9D33).

The 15th June 1964 to 13th June 1965 working time table showed the time allowances (point to point times in minutes) for freight trains hauled by steam locomotives, which is given in **Table 11.14**, overleaf.

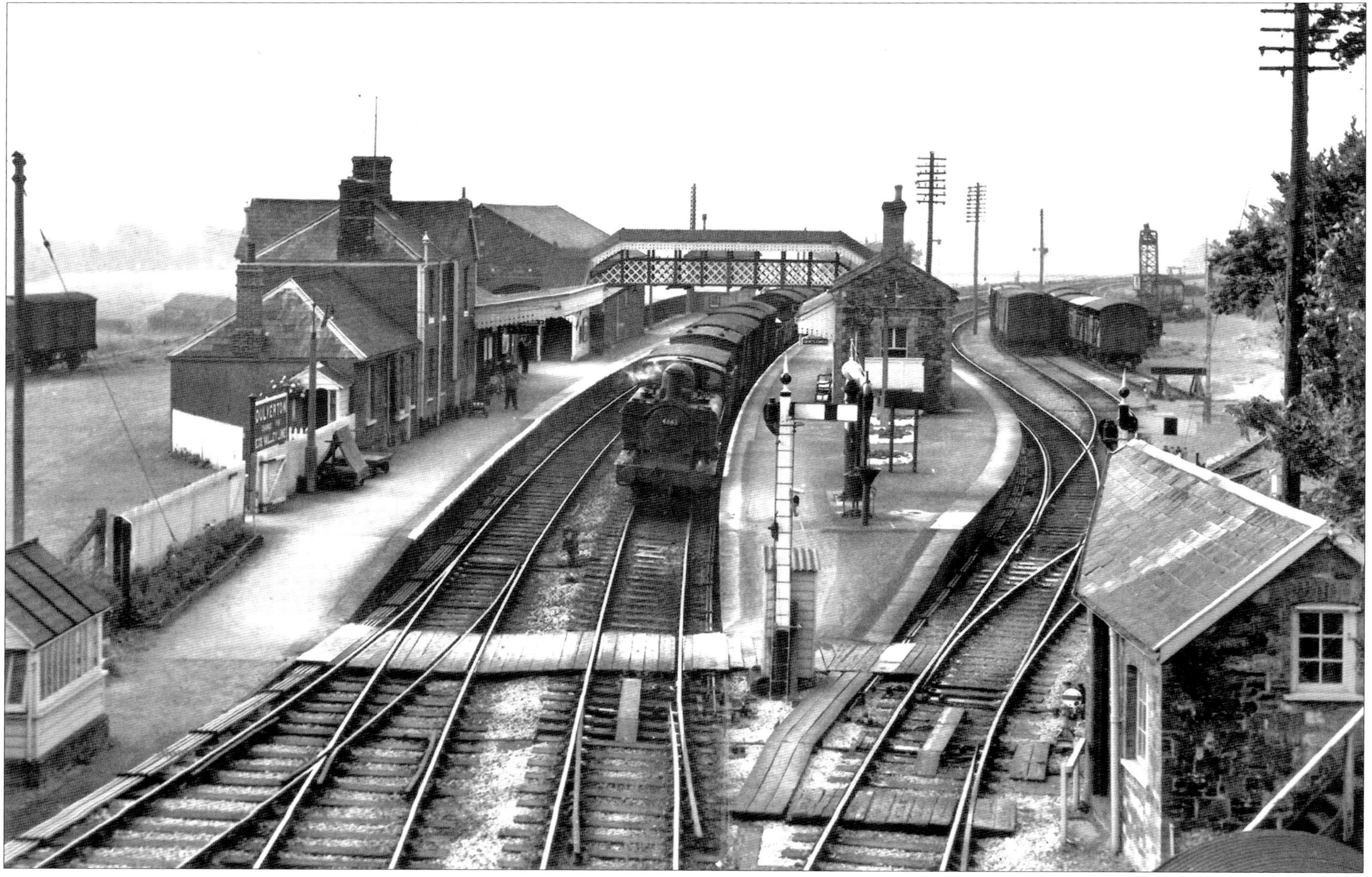

Pannier tank No. 4663 with a westbound goods at Dulverton on 9th July 1962. The sidings here were clearly still seeing plenty of use at this date and No. 4663 will spend some time here dropping off wagons and shunting the Down side yard. The classic view of the station, from the B3222 road bridge, the picture should be compared with the similar panoramic photograph taken from the same spot around fifty-five years earlier on page 134 of Volume 1. The building in the right foreground was the pump house for the water supply here, which had its corner 'shaved' off when the Exe Valley bay was extended to form a loop behind the Down platform in 1910. *C.J. Gammell, courtesy Roger Joannes*

TABLE 11.14: TIME ALLOWANCES GOODS TRAINS 1964-65		
STATION	TIME – DOWN	TIME – UP
Norton Fitzwarren	5	11
Milverton	11	7
Wiveliscombe	10	13
Venn Cross	13	11
Morebath	8	12
Dulverton	8	15
East Anstey	13	13
Bishop's Nympton & Molland	14	10
South Molton	10	10
Filleigh	9	9
Swimbridge	8	–
Barnstaple Victoria Road	–	–
Barnstaple Victoria Road Ground Frame	–	-
Barnstaple Junction	–	–

The total time Down was 109 minutes, whilst the total time Up was 111 minutes. At this point the freights were terminating at Swimbridge, hence the lack of times to Barnstaple but in practice the goods traffic had ceased at the end of July 1964.

The working time table for the period 14th June 1965 to 17th April 1966 showed one freight diagram. It was a curious one because freight had ceased on the line in the previous year and sidings had been taken out of use. However, at 12.30pm on weekdays, an engine and brake van (3C94) would depart from Taunton and work down the line. With only a seven minute stop at Venn Cross to allow the 11.55am from Barnstaple Junction to cross, it would trundle to Barnstaple, arriving at 2.07pm and then work on to Torrington. It returned on the 4.12pm Torrington milk (3C84), departing the Junction at 6.32pm and arriving at Taunton at 8.03pm. This was an odd movement, as the milk from Torrington usually travelled over the SR line to Exeter and this is an isolated period in the life of the Barnstaple Branch when this train worked along it. The diagram was usually the preserve of a Class 'D63XX' (later Class '22') diesel-hydraulic, No. D6337 being captured on camera at Venn Cross on 23rd June 1965 on one such occasion. However, no photographic evidence of the return working with the tanks has been seen to date.

Leaving aside the 1965 milk train, it might be argued that the last goods trains to work the line were the demolition trains in 1967. More can be read about them in Volume 1, Chapter 4, Decline and Closure.

STORES VANS AND STATION TRUCKS

In the summer of 1922, the 6.35pm Birmingham to Taunton train conveyed a stores van for Barnstaple from Birmingham. It would return on the 11.00pm Taunton to Birmingham stores train the following day. By the 1950s, the stores van would be run down the branch on Tuesdays only, attached to the 'B-set' and Brake Composite coach forming the 10.15am Taunton departure for Barnstaple Junction.

Mentioned earlier, Station Trucks were used on the line for many years. Usually ventillated vans, they were attached to local goods services to deliver or pick up small consignments along a determined route. As one wagon might convey traffic for a number of stops, it was important the contents were packed and stowed in some structured order to enable easy and quick loading and unloading. There was usually a map or diagram in the truck to facilitate this. The loading and unloading often took place at the passenger platforms, as the goods service might only have a limited stopping time with no provision for shunting. The guard would be responsible for monitoring the consignments and the receiving station would have to sign for the delivery. The trucks were separately numbered, usually with a large label prominently displaying the number and the number in use changed annually.

GOODS OPERATIONS AT VICTORIA ROAD

(Courtesy *Great Western Journal* No. 42)

The goods trains would arrive in the main platform line. The locomotive would then uncouple and run around the train and couple up to the rear of the goods. The locomotive would then draw the whole train back out of the station towards south loop, making sure the last vehicle was clear of the points into the yard. Cuts were then made in the wagons by the shunter and they were allowed to gravitate into the required sidings; the shunter would instruct the porters who were manually operating the yard points. Ideally the engine would be tender first when shunting so the driver would be on the shunter's side but this was rarely the case [*given that the locomotive usually would have arrived smokebox first and would not be turned before shunting*]. Priority in shunting was given to the goods shed traffic, which was usually perishable in nature (especially on the Bristol goods). Wagons of Lyons tea were placed alongside a warehouse outside the Taunton end of the goods shed. The remaining wagons were positioned in the mileage roads, cattle pens and end docks as required. Those wagons destined for the Southern were placed aside, usually in the middle road, and later attached to the brake van. Oil wagons made for interesting operations; tanks were berthed at both ends of the back road. Esso and Pratts wagons were positioned at the far end of the back road for discharge. The main oil depot siding which served Shell-Mex, BP and National Benzole was a 'kick-back' from the back road. Wagons would be detached from the locomotive whilst moving and fly shunted into the depot (this was an unofficial manoeuvre!).

The back road was usually left clear (aside from the tank wagons berthed there) as the Up Bristol goods was made up in that siding in the latter part of the day. In making the cuts the discharged oil tank wagons would be drawn out first to give access to the 27-wagon road (at which point when full of wagons the locomotive would just foul the road crossing into the oil depot). The Bristol goods was formed in a strict order. The Bristol traffic and Bristol local transfers (such as Wapping Wharf) went on the brake van, then the Bristol mixed, South Wales and Taunton wagons next, with cattle wagons always on the engine. Later in the morning the yard would be shunted and wagons for the afternoon Taunton bound goods be made up wherever convenient, sometimes in the back road. The 9.35am Up goods to Taunton (in 1930s) was usually made up in and for departure from the carriage siding. Even the bay platform could have been used if they were pressed for space.

TRIP WORKINGS

(As recounted by those that worked at Victoria Road and again taken from *Great Western Journal* No. 42)

There were regular numbers of transfer freights between the GWR station and the Southern. They were formed in the goods yard and in the late 1930s left at 7.35am, largely with traffic off the Down Bristol goods. The 11am took wagons from the 6am from Taunton. The final one was at 8.35pm. The return workings were 4.45pm and 8.50pm. By the 1940s a branded 'Toad' brake van was allocated for the transfer traffic. However it seems that the 11am used the brake van off the Bristol goods. When this came back the men cleared out the empty oil tanks and placed the brake at the end of the back road

A fine study of No. 7333 exiting the tight bore of Venn Cross Tunnel with a well-laden Down goods bound for Barnstaple on 30th August 1961. As well as the usual assortment of box vans and loaded mineral wagons, there are two 4-wheeled flats at the head of the train carrying containers, which are followed by a 4-wheeled carriage wagon carrying what looks to be a motor vehicle, possibly a van. The sign on the left indicated that all Up goods trains had to stop here to pin down brakes before beginning the descent through the tunnel which, apart from the occasional short rise, saw the line dropping all the way down to Norton Fitzwarren. Note that the fireman is leaning ou of the cab with the token in his hand, ready to make the exchange with the Venn Cross signalman as the train crested the rise and rumbled slowly through the station. ***Michael J. Fox, courtesy Rail Archive Stephenson***

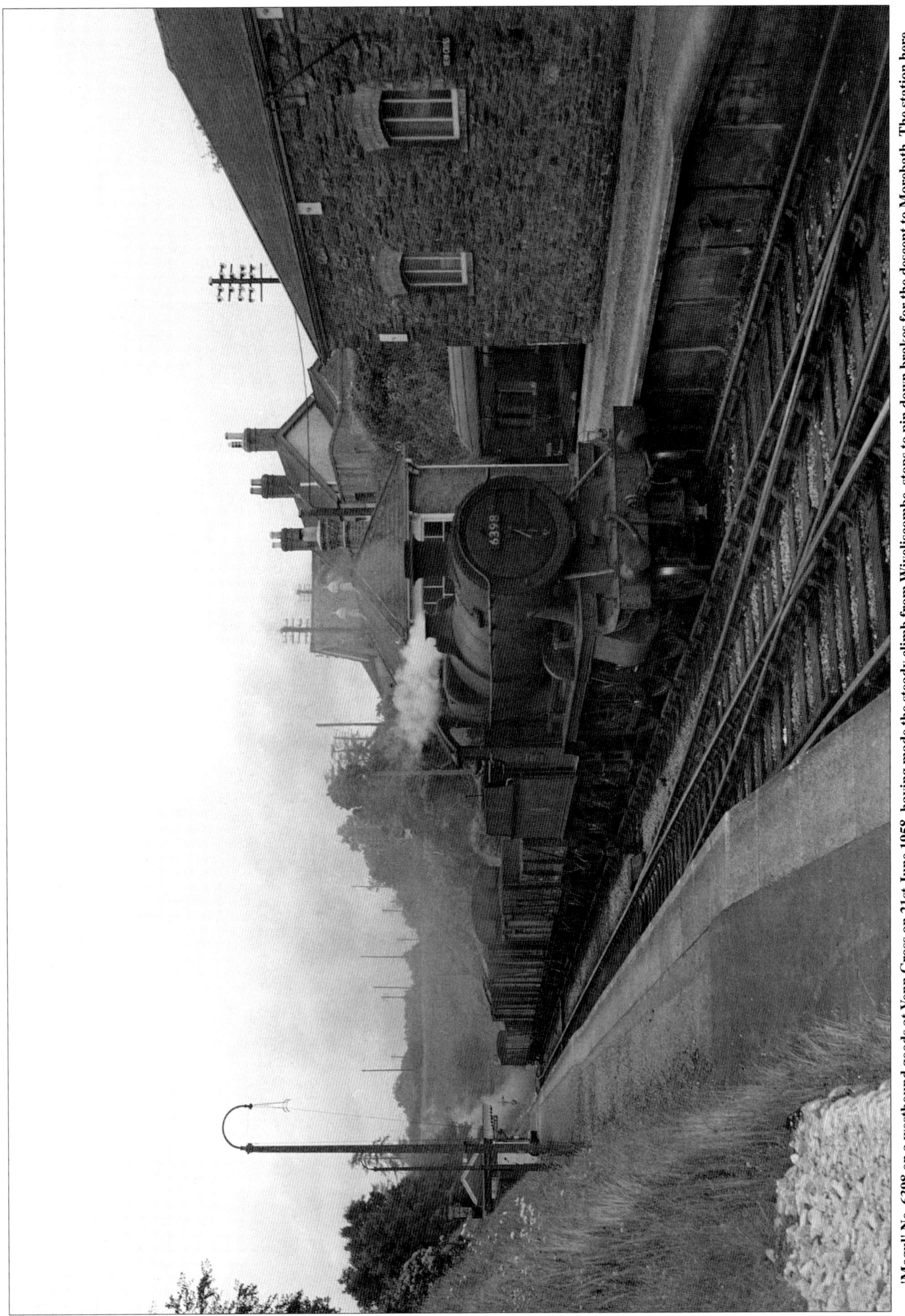

'Mogul' No. 6398 on a westbound goods at Venn Cross on 21st June 1958, having made the steady climb from Wiveliscombe, stops to pin down brakes for the descent to Morebath. The station here being at the summit of climbs in each direction, both Up and Down goods trains had to stop to pin down brakes. In the background, the smoke and steam emitted by the engine on the steep climb through the tunnel is still drifting out of the portal, giving an indication of how unpleasant the journey through the bore in the Down direction could be for footplate crews. Note the parcels van behind the signal box, at the end of the goods shed siding, no doubt parked here to facilitate loading and also the small station nameboard mounted on the goods shed wall – most of the D&SR line stations were never supplied with BR totems. ***Roger J. Sellick, courtesy National Railway Museum***

A very wet Wednesday at Wiveliscombe, on 17th July 1963, and a variation in motive power as BR 'Standard' Class '3MT' 2-6-2T No 82008 pauses at Wiveliscombe with the 10.22am Swimbridge to Taunton (Fairwater Sidings) goods. New from Swindon Works and in to service at Tyseley shed on 5th June 1952, the locomotive was on the final posting of its short career, having been reallocated from Neyland to Taunton in October 1961; it was withdrawn from there in early February 1964, a service life of just eleven years and eight months. Note the impressive floral display at this end of the Up platform, which disguised the rag-tag assortment of sheds, one of which was the brick base of the original signal box. ***Stephen P. Derek***

to work back to Bristol. There were two branded brakes being used on the Bristol goods by this time. By nature of these trip workings, they would contain 'odds and sods', like fish vans normally returning to Exeter via the Southern going to Taunton instead. The 4.45pm trip would convey traffic for the 7.30 Bristol goods. This might include loaded cattle wagons which would then have to be forwarded immediately, so if the train was already loaded to the maximum certain wagons would have to be taken off for transit the next day, giving the cattle priority.

WORKING THE LINE

Given the nature of the line, with its steep inclines, some of which were at either end of the stations along it, special instructions were issued to staff. These shown in Volume 2 at each relevant station section in Chapters 6 to 8 and are reproduced from the *Appendix to No. 5 Section of the Service Time Tables* issued by the GWR (in respect of the period February 1947 and until further notice).

MAXIMUM LOADS FOR FREIGHT TRAINS ON THE GWR

Taken from the 1908 service time table, the figures in **Table 11.15** represent maximum loads in fine weather for one engine (unless otherwise stated), with the engine and wagons in good order. In calculating the loads, one and a half empty wagons was deemed equivalent to one loaded goods wagon and two empty wagons equivalent to one loaded coal wagon. The guard was to inform the engineman of the number of loaded and empty wagons comprising the train, and how many were vacuum fitted and coupled up to the engine before leaving the station or goods yard.

The maximum loads calculated for engines may have exceeded the

TABLE 11.15: MAXIMUM LOADS BARNSTAPLE BRANCH 1908

FROM/TO	TENDER ENGINES			TANK ENGINES		
	COAL	GOODS	EMPTY	COAL	GOODS	EMPTY
Norton Fitzwarren to Milverton	15	23	30	17	26	34
Milverton to Wiveliscombe	14	21	28	16	24	32
Wiveliscombe to Barnstaple	14	21	28	16	24	32
Barnstaple to Barnstaple Junction	12	18	24	14	21	28
Barnstaple to Wiveliscombe	14	21	28	16	24	32
Wiveliscombe to Norton Fitzwarren	16	25	40	18	28	44
Barnstaple Junction to Barnstaple	16	24	32	18	27	36
EXE VALLEY LINE						
Tiverton to Dulverton				14	21	28
Dulverton to Bampton				12	18	24

TABLE 11.16: MAXIMUM LOADS BARNSTAPLE BRANCH 1947						
FROM	TO	MAX NO OF WAGONS	CLASS 1	CLASS 2	CLASS 3	EMPTIES
For Group A Engines						
Norton Fitzwarren	Milverton	32	15	19	24	32
Milverton	Wiveliscombe	32	15	18	23	30
Wiveliscombe	East Anstey	32	14	17	21	28
East Anstey	South Molton	-	16	19	24	32
South Molton	Barnstaple	-	14	17	21	28
Barnstaple	Barnstaple Junction	32	14	17	21	28
Barnstaple Junction	Barnstaple	32	18	22	27	36
Barnstaple	Wiveliscombe	32*	14	17	21	28
Wiveliscombe	Norton Fitzwarren	32	18	22	27	36
For Group B Engines						
Norton Fitzwarren	Milverton	32	17	20	26	34
Milverton	Wiveliscombe	32	16	19	24	32
Wiveliscombe	East Anstey	32	15	18	23	30
East Anstey	South Molton	-	18	22	27	36
South Molton	Barnstaple	-	15	18	23	30
Barnstaple	Barnstaple Junction	32	15	18	23	30
Barnstaple Junction	Barnstaple	32	19	23	29	38
Barnstaple	Wiveliscombe	32*	15	18	23	30
Wiveliscombe	Norton Fitzwarren	32	19	23	29	38
For Group C Engines						
Norton Fitzwarren	Milverton	32	19	23	29	38
Milverton	Wiveliscombe	32	17	20	28	34
Wiveliscombe	East Anstey	32	17	20	26	34
East Anstey	South Molton	-	22	26	33	44
South Molton	Barnstaple	-	17	20	26	34
Barnstaple	Barnstaple Junction	32	17	20	26	34
Barnstaple Junction	Barnstaple	32	21	25	32	42
Barnstaple	Wiveliscombe	32*	17	20	26	34
Wiveliscombe	Norton Fitzwarren	32	21	25	32	42
For Group D Engines						
Norton Fitzwarren	Milverton	32	25	30	35	50
Milverton	Wiveliscombe	32	23	28	35	46
Wiveliscombe	East Anstey	32	21	25	35	42
East Anstey	South Molton	-	26	31	35	52
South Molton	Barnstaple	-	21	25	35	42
Barnstaple	Barnstaple Junction	32	21	25	35	42
Barnstaple Junction	Barnstaple	32	28	34	35	56
Barnstaple	Wiveliscombe	32*	21	25	35	42
Wiveliscombe	Norton Fitzwarren	32*	26	34	35	56

*42 from Dulverton on 7.30pm ex-Barnstaple (Bristol goods). Note there were slight variations on these wagon loads in certain periods.

refuging accommodation, so such loads could only be worked when they could be done so without interfering unduly with the working of other trains. **Table 11.16** above gives the maximum loads on the branch for engines of Groups A, B, C and D, with Class 1, 2 and 3 freights and trains of empties in 1947.

BELOW: An 0-6-0PT (possibly No. 9670 – a Taunton engine) shunts the yard at Dulverton in the early 1960s. The locomotive is Taunton-bound, most likely Fairwater Yard. The siding it is on leads to the rear food store at the back of the goods siding, with the goods shed and siding to the left and just beyond the signal box. Note the BR standard brake van eight wagons back, a type of vehicle not often photographed on this line. ***Courtesy Martin Bird***

Chapter 12

Special Trains, Events, Accidents and Mishaps

'Mogul' No. 6326 takes the Barnstaple line as it heads through Norton Fitzwarren on 5th August 1964, with a four-coach train that also includes a horse box marshalled at the front. The footbridge remained in place as it carried a right of way but trains no longer stopped here, the station having closed to traffic on 30th October 1961. The tall posts on the bracket signal were to enable sighting of the arms above the bridge. *Owen Mogg collection, courtesy Peter Triggs*

Horse and Related Traffic

As the line skirted Exmoor and cut through the hunting country of at least three packs from Dulverton and beyond, it is no surprise to learn that horse traffic was common. This was broadly local in nature, involving the movement of hunting horses between various stations but in addition there is evidence of longer distance transportation, whether privately owned or racehorses used for stud. Special horse loading docks were provided at Wiveliscombe and Dulverton, whilst at South Molton the dock in the goods yard was also used for this purpose. At Barnstaple Victoria Road horses were loaded and unloaded at the passenger platform or end dock, whilst despite the lack of special facilities, they could also be loaded and unloaded at the other stations on the line, either at the platform or alongside loading docks in the goods yards.

Horses were transported in specially designed box vans which were usually attached to passenger trains, so the animal spent the minimum amount of time in transit. In addition, there was a small compartment at the end of the wagon for the groom to be accommodated, with a hatch to look through so the horse could be checked during the journey. The general rule (*BR(WR) Regional Appendix to the Working Timet Table, Rules and Regulations*) about marshalling of vehicles containing livestock was that they should be placed in such a position in the train so as to reduce any shunting to a minimum. In addition, the location of relevant sidings and docks for loading/unloading would play a part and this is best illustrated by looking at certain locations on the D&SR. The *Appendix to the Service Time Tables, Exeter Division (1947)* is a good starting point, although the coverage in relation to horse transportation is minimal. There is a general instruction and a starting point, that '*No vehicle must be detached and allowed to stand on the main line*' (this applied to Dulverton, East Anstey, Bishop's Nympton & Molland and South Molton stations). The instructions for East Anstey go on to state:

'*Vehicles attached to down passenger trains must be formed next to the engine, except as shewn below, and placed in the siding by the engine.*

Unless absolutely necessary, non-vacuum vehicles must not be used for passenger train traffic. In the event of non-vacuum stock being loaded the traffic must be unloaded on the platform, the vehicle remaining on the train.

Unless horses for up trains can be loaded or unloaded at the loading bank, the vehicle must be formed in the up train at the rear and the horses dealt with at the down platform.'

'Bulldog' No. 3361 places a horse box in the cattle dock siding at Dulverton in the early 1930s, a view which supports the likelihood that such vehicles on Down trains were shunted into this dock rather than the horse dock siding on the Up side. Note the original weighbridge shed in the left background, which was later replaced by a stone-built hut at some point (Volume 2, see page 323). No. 3361, which when built in 1902 was originally No. 3413 *Edward VII*, was withdrawn in September 1947. *Courtesy Stephenson Locomotive Society*

Above: This pre-First World War GWR poster showed that the company encouraged the transportation of hunting horses (and grooms) by rail.

Below: Extract from the B&ER public time table of 1872, outlining the price structure for hunting personnel, horses and hounds travelling by rail. ***Courtesy National Archives***

HUNTING ARRANGEMENTS.—Hunting Gentlemen, Huntsmen, and Grooms, are charged single fares for the double journey, according to the class by which they travel. Huntsmen and Grooms attending the hunt, who travel in the Boxes with the Horses or Hounds, are charged Third Class Fares each way.

For Horses, the charge is a fare and a half for the double journey to all Stations, Local and Foreign, for which the ordinary Horse rates have been supplied. The Horses are conveyed at the owner's risk, and must return the same day.

Packs of Hounds are conveyed at the risk of the owner, and are charged at the option of the sender, either at the rate for Horses, according to the number of Horse Stalls occupied, or singly, at the scale of charges for Dogs. If the Hounds return the same day, the rate for a single journey and a half for the double journey is charged.

This latter point presumably meant that an Up train was required to run into the Down platform to facilitate this, even though the signalling did not allow for that. The Up platform had no road access but the Down platform did so horses were not required to cross the lines to use it, which would be both dangerous and potentially injurious to the horse and maybe the handler as well. Presumably, too, advance warning would be given by telephone to the East Anstey signalman of the need for the train to run in to the Down platform, otherwise it would have to run in to the Up platform and then reverse. Similar instructions applied for loading/unloading at Bishops Nympton & Molland and South Molton, although excluding the third one.

The role of the train engine in shunting such vehicles is problematic, given the delays this would give to the timing of services, as most passenger trains were only booked to call at intermediate stations for one or two minutes. However, a review of procedures at Dulverton, for example, will bring the marshalling and shunting of horse boxes to life.

If the horse box was on a Down train for detaching at Dulverton it would usually be coupled next to the engine. On arrival, it would be uncoupled from the train, and engine and horse box would draw forward into the cutting beyond the bridge before shunting back, most likely into the dock platform behind the cattle pens on the Down side. It is unlikely that horse boxes on a Down train would have been deposited at the Up platform, at the west end of which the horse dock was located, as regulations sought to prevent vehicles being left on the main line and in this case there was a 1 in 660 falling gradient through the station. If the box was placed on the cattle dock siding, the engine could return to the train with minimal disruption to the service and the horse could be unloaded there.

The option of the train engine shunting a horse box to the bay platform and then running round to collect it, reverse and shunt it into the horse dock, all via the Up line, before rejoining its passenger train and continuing the journey westwards seems unlikely; such an operation would take time and Dulverton was frequently used as a passing station. One other practical option at this location, however, would have been to leave the horse box in the Down side yard for the engine of a passing pick-up goods or that off the Exe Valley auto train to then shunt it into the Up side horse dock siding. However, if the Exe Valley locomotive was commandeered for this (or any) shunting duty, the regulations specified that the auto coach had to be uncoupled from the locomotive, which would have been quite an involved procedure. Of course, there was always the application of 'local practice' where on occasion the rule book may have been ignored.

Trains travelling in the Up direction with a horse box to be detached at Dulverton would usually have it on the rear and having stopped for passengers, the whole train would then shunt back to drop the box in the siding at the Barnstaple end of the Up platform. Manually propelling the horse box in to the dock seems unlikely, due to the falling gradient eastwards through the station of 1 in 660. However, Up trains collecting a horse box from the siding may have waited for it to be pushed out manually, assisted by the gradient, to be attached to the rear of the train (as was done at Dunster and Crowcombe on the West Somerset line). Photographic evidence of an Up train backing into the horse dock to either drop off or attach a horse box is shown in Volume 2 (page 309), with No. 7332 set back into the horse dock siding with its Taunton-bound train in October 1963.

Some of the time-tabled trains were specifically prohibited from taking horse traffic, usually the more important services including through workings sich as the Ilfracombe to Paddington train that ran in the early part of the 20th century. This was presumably to prevent any delay.

The transportation of horses by rail for hunting was a regular occurrence in the first half of the 20th century. Horses were often taken down the D&SR and then un-boxed at a station local to the meet for a day's hunting on the moor.

Richard Stapleton brought the role of the railway and hunting to life in his book *Exmoor; Elegance and Rhythm*. During Captain Amory's tenure of the Tiverton Staghounds in the 1920s there was a meet at South Molton and a special train was chartered, complete with a passenger coach, horse boxes and hound van. The train presumably started at Tiverton, as the hounds were kennelled at Fordlands Farm, four miles north-east of there, then worked its way down the Exe Valley, picking up hunt subscribers and their horses at East Anstey and Molland, before they all disembarked at South Molton. On this particular day the hounds drew White Hill, just south of the South Molton to Barnstaple road. Having found their quarry, they hunted up to Shallowford and up the River Bray towards and under Castle Hill Viaduct. The hounds continued on up the valley between Goodleigh and Stoke Rivers and then on to Loxore and Arlington Court. The stag was accounted for just below Arlington Court, nine miles north of Barnstaple. They finished in isolated countryside, so in order to return home the Field then trotted back to Barnstaple GWR, where the special train had been summoned from South Molton to pick them up. Thus they were able to complete their journey home in relative comfort on the train – truly a local railway service!

Whilst it is known that the railways generally would be used from time to time to transport the huntsmen, horses, hunt staff and hounds to meets in other parts of the country, this was predominately before the First World War. It is not known if any of the local packs regularly used the D&SR in these early days or to what extent. Given the location of the various kennels and the hunting country of each pack, the line would most likely only be used for this purpose irregularly. It would seem that only those that rode to hounds and could afford the luxury of train travel (as described above) would use this facility.

There was an increase in the deer population in the area north of Barnstaple in the late 19th/early 20th century, which necessitated the importation of a number of staghound packs into the district. The Devon & Somerset Staghounds, Sir John Amory's Staghounds and Peter Omerod's Staghounds all helped out, whilst in 1901 the Barnstaple Staghounds were formed, hunting the area until 1910 (with some breaks), when the Minehead Staghounds took over. It is recorded that the Lynton & Barnstaple Railway was used from time to time to transport hounds and hunt followers of the Barnstaple Staghounds but the L&BR being a narrow gauge line, it would not have been practicable for horses to have been transported. However, for the meet on 4th September 1902 at South Molton, it was reported that the Master arrived with twenty couple of hounds (forty hounds) by train. The ensuing hunt passed close to Filleigh station and also Swimbridge before heading away from the railway line and up towards Stoke Rivers. The same report stated that the staghounds would regularly hunt the district, including Bremridge (around Castle Hill Tunnel) and Hacche Woods, so the association with the line was there, albeit tenuous. In another hunting link, Mr William Ashton, the Honorary Secretary of the Barnstaple & North Devon Harriers, wrote to the editor of the *North Devon Herald* on 28th June 1898 to make it known that the hound pack had been moved to new kennels near the Great Western Railway station, so that all kennel-flesh should in future be sent to the station for collection by the hunt.

Indeed, the rural railway lines and their operations co-existed with hunting, the British Railways operating instructions for 1963 acknowledging this when stating that '*every care must be taken to avoid running over a pack of hounds, which during the hunting season may cross the line, consistent with due regard being paid to the proper working of the line and trains*'. In the book *Stag-Hunting* by the Hon. John Fortescue, there was a hunting report dated 18th January 1876 that referred to a meet at Exe Bridge (just south of Dulverton station), which had hounds on occasions close to and crossing the railway line as far west as Mornacott, just east of South Molton. The hind was eventually accounted for at Bottreaux Mill just down from Yeo Mill but as the report states '*Hounds had a narrow escape from a train, but the engine-driver stopped in time*'. The railway was not accepted that easily by certain members of the hunting fraternity. Indeed Mr Bisset (Master of the Devon & Somerset Staghounds in 1874) was hunting hounds in April of that year when they went under the viaduct at Castle Hill and with the stag at bay, a train passed over the viaduct. Mr Bisset noted the event with some horror – '*a clashing of two distinct ages, indicating but too surely what must be here long-the ancient occupant of the primeval forest being trampled under by the Juggernaut representative of advancing civilisation.*'. At this early date, this would have been a B&ER broad gauge train, which had only commenced running over this section of the line the previous year.

The work ethic (if that is the right phrase) of the country railway is no better illustrated than from this extract from *Hounds Magazine* (Volume 23, No 3, page 43): '*The Barnstaple train was once a little late because the hounds had marked in the railway embankment. That in itself was not the cause of the delay but the fireman and the guard had disembarked the train to help dig out the fox.*'.

If a train driver pulled up for hounds in Lord Fortesque's country, he would write a letter of thanks and usually enclose a financial reward for the driver, fireman and guard.

Trains would also bring stallions into the area from 'up country' when required. Such animal would arrive at Dulverton, for example, and then be taken off to the Lion Stables in the town for a few weeks before returning home by train. This may well explain the reason for the conveyance of a horse box from Market Rasen, in Lincolnshire, to Dulverton on 16th July 1946. The box commenced its travels on 15th July by being attached at the rear of the 8.10pm from Sheffield, then onto the rear of the 5.30am Paddington Down train from Swindon Junction to Taunton, thence on to Dulverton by local service. On the very same day, it seems that Dulverton despatched two horse boxes – one for Cheltenham, put on to the rear of the 11.35am departure from Taunton, the other going to Ashbourne in Derbyshire on the 9.00pm Penzance perishables from Taunton. Records show that a box was despatched from Dulverton at 7.49pm on Wednesday 10th September 1947 for Wolverhampton, on the rear of the 6.40pm Barnstaple Junction to Taunton local service and then on the 11.20pm Taunton to Wolverhampton parcels train, this journey taking a little over twelve hours. John Howard remembers that there was a regular trip up from South Molton for a stallion to go by train to Dulverton and then to carry out his 'duties' in the area, before being taken by road to Exford and then back to South Molton. John remembers the horse as '*a nasty begger*'.

For illustration, the 1901 passenger time table showed the following fares for conveyance

A meet of hounds – most likely the Devon & Somerset Staghounds – at South Molton Station just prior to the First World War. These were exciting events for locals, particularly children, as well as for the hunt and its followers, hence the turnout. ***Courtesy South Molton Museum***

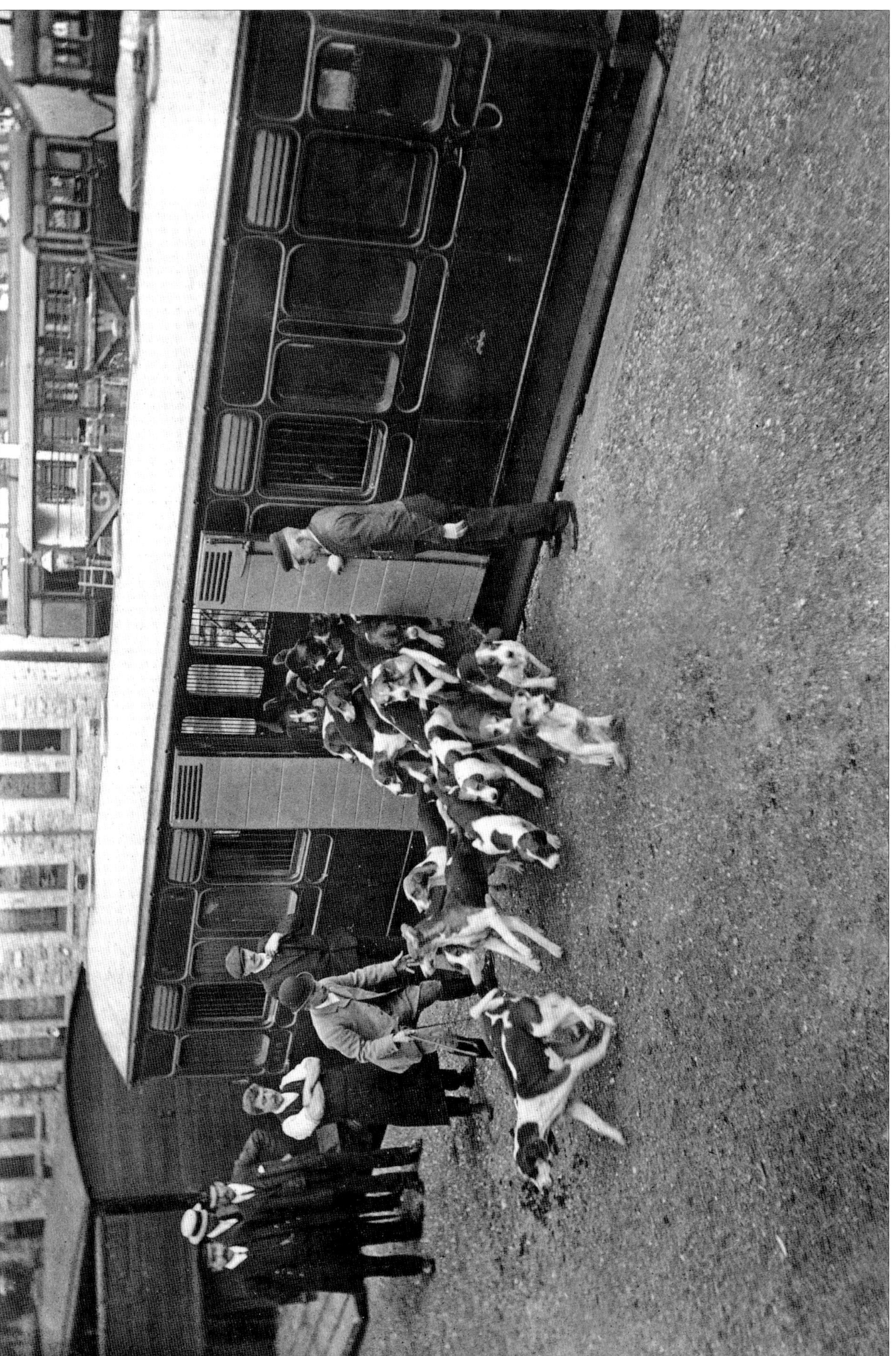

A pack of hounds (possibly the Tiverton Staghounds) being un-boxed at Dulverton station circa 1912. The van is parked in the cattle dock, with a horse box with its doors open on the left, the station behind and the carriages of an Exe Valley train visible in the bay. Note too the empty lime-washed GWR cattle wagon. The Hounds van is a unique and interesting vehicle, having been built originally in 1874 as a 28ft, 6-wheeled, four-compartment Third with central luggage compartment, one of a batch of twenty-four to diagram S5 (No's 875-890 and 893-900). No. 885 was subsequently converted at an unknown date for use as a Hounds van, probably not long before this photograph was taken judging by its clean condition here, and was renumbered as No. 949; the number is just discernible in the waist high panels at each end of the vehicle. The end compartment to the right was retained as accommodation for the huntsman, who here shepherds the excited hounds as they burst out of the double doors of the van in what may well have been an official GWR photograph. *Courtesy Chris Nelder*

An unidentified 'Mogul' heads west at Acland Cross in the 1920s, on its way to Barnstaple with a horse box as the first vehicle next to the locomotive, followed by a mix of clerestory and elliptical roofed coaching stock. ***Arthur Halls, courtesy National Railway Museum***

of horses from Barnstaple and Dulverton to Paddington.

FROM	1 HORSE	2 HORSES*	3 HORSES*	4-WHEELED CARRIAGE	2-WHEELED CARRIAGE
Barnstaple	63s	94s 6d	133s 9d	87s	62s 6d
Dulverton	55s	82s	115s	74s 6d	54s 6d

* If same property and loaded in same box

The 1889 time table *Notice of Trains and Special Arrangements* showed the running of a special train for a horse show at Taunton on Thursday 18th July. Special trains carrying horses would run as set out below.

FORWARD TRAIN	ARR. AM	DEP. AM	RETURN TRAIN	ARR. PM	DEP. PM
Barnstaple		5.00	Taunton		9.05
Swimbridge	5.10	5.14	Norton Fitz'n	9.11	9.12
Filleigh	5.24	5.28	Milverton		9.25
South Molton	5.38	5.43	Wiveliscombe	9.38x	9.43C
Molland		5.55	Venn Cross		9.55
East Anstey		6.08	Morebath	10.06	10.08
Dulverton	6.20	6.23	Morebath Jct	CS	
Morebath Jct	CS		Dulverton	10.20	10.23
Morebath	6.35x	6.38A	East Anstey		10.35
Venn Cross	CR		Molland		10.47
Wiveliscombe	7.05	7.10	South Molton	10.59	11.02
Milverton	7.20	7.23	Filleigh	11.12	11.15
Norton Fitz'n	7.34x	7.36B	Swimbridge	11.25	11.28
Taunton	7.41		Barnstaple	11.38	

Notes: A – crosses 5.20am Down goods at Morebath
B – crosses 7.00am Down goods at Norton Fitz'n
C – crosses 7.00pm Up goods at Wiveliscombe
CS – change staff/token

It was noted that, on the return journey, this special train would convey passengers.

Hounds Magazine of October 2018 (Volume 34, No. 8), made reference to an entry in Mr Ludic Cameron's 'An Otterhunters Diary' for 1910, *viz.* Regulation 73 of the *Railway Clearing House (Coaching Arrangements) Book of April 1909.* This stated that return tickets available for the day of issue were '*issued to gentlemen travelling for hunting purposes ... also to huntsmen in charge of hounds ... at a single fare and a half for the double journey, minimum charge one shilling per passenger.*'. When the holders of hunting return tickets were unable to return the same day, their tickets may be available for return on the following day on payment of the difference between the two single journey fares and the fare and a half. Hounds carried in hound vans (*i.e.* cattle trucks, owners vans or carriage trucks) were charged for a single journey at the usual rate for two horses. For a return journey the rate was one journey and a half – at the owners risk! Packs of hounds were charged at the option of the sender – either at the rate for horses according to the number of stalls occupied or at a 'per hound' rate under the scale of charges for dogs, with a minimum charge as for the horse. If the hounds returned the same day, the charge was one rate and a half at owners risk.

There were a number of sheep and cattle fairs in the district and as Dulverton Fair died away at the turn of the 20th century, the fair at Bampton, one stop down the Exe Valley line, gained in prominence. From the late 1800s, after that line had opened, horses and ponies previously driven 'on the hoof' to the market, often over a not inconsiderable distance, began to go by train instead. Taken down to the nearest station, they would then be transported to Bampton and once sold moved on again also by rail.

The 'Rabbiter'

It seems that the rabbit train service (or 'Rabbiter' as it became known) initially started in 1940, as the *West Somerset Free Press* reported at that time under the heading '*GWR start a service believed to be unique in railway circles*'. The journalist expanded on this stating: '*Every evening on weekdays a special train leaves Barnstaple for Taunton calling en route at about a dozen stations to pick up either additional vans already filled, or a consignment in crates of rabbits, packed in boxes or tied together in batches of a dozen. The arrival of the train at the larger centres such as Dulverton affords onlookers a revelation of the great contribution which the district covered by the branch line is making towards the nations' food supply. Here some evenings there may be seen as much as three tons of 'bunnies' crowded into a large covered van and packed together almost as tightly as the proverbial sardine. Similar scenes at Wivvey [sic] and elsewhere such that full train loads carrying from 16 to 20 tons of rabbits on a single evening were taken to cities for sale next morning.*'

Looking at this service from an operational perspective, the supplement to the October 1941 working time table referred to the 4.45pm (new parcels train) from Barnstaple to Taunton to run on weekdays (Saturdays excepted), commencing on 6th October 1941. It carried 'C' headlamps and was time-tabled as follows:

Station	Arr. (pm)	Dep. (pm)	Station	Arr. (pm)	Dep. (pm)
Barnstaple		4.45	Morebath Jct	CS.	
Swimbridge	4.52	5.00	Morebath	6.42	6.47
Filleigh	5.07	5.15	Venn Cross	6.54	7.04
South Molton	5.22	5.42	Wiveliscombe	7.13	7.23
Bishops N&M	5.49	5.57	Milverton	7.28	7.30
East Anstey	6.06	6.14	Norton Fitzwarren	7.37	7.37
Dulverton	6.20x	6.35	Taunton	7.42	

It would cross the 5.32pm Taunton to Barnstaple train at Dulverton (x) and stop at Morebath Junction only to change the train staff (CS). There was no indication of the relevant Down working in the early days from the working time table. One explanation (not confirmed) may have been that an earlier Down passenger train took additional vans to be detached and later used for this Up parcels service. Potentially in support of this are the observations by Walter King, who was at Barnstaple Victoria Road in the 1930s and 40s. He remembers from the winter months of 1945 the 7.24am Taunton to Barnstaple GWR Down train arriving with two vans attached at the front. On arrival the stock would be shunted to the bay and the surplus vans uncoupled and left there whilst the coaches worked a later departure to Taunton. These vans subsequently left Barnstaple on an evening train to Taunton, with oversized parcels that could not be taken on normal passenger trains in the luggage compartment of the Brake coach; this may well have formed the 'Rabbiter' in the early 1940s as it started from Barnstaple By the mid-1940s, the 'Rabbiter' was running up from South Molton (with a corresponding time-tabled Down empties from Taunton to form the Up working). Certainly in the war years, rabbits were a staple part of the nation's diet and the connections at Taunton fed the conurbations of London, Birmingham and the North. Up to 400 hampers could be handled in a single night, with a combined weight of 20 tons and containing up to 15,000 rabbits.

The parcels train did not feature in the 1942 working time table but was incorporated in the October 1943 edition. However, by then it ran only from Taunton to South Molton and back on an 'as and when required' basis.

When required, the Down empty rabbit special was time-tabled to run from Taunton to South Molton in the early afternoon. The working time table in 1947 (6th October until further notice) indicated, in the notes under the 'Passenger Trains' heading, that commencing 6th October on weekdays (Saturdays excepted) empty vans left Taunton at 3.20pm when required. Arrival at South Molton was booked for 4.41pm and this timing appears to be consistent throughout the life of the service. It is understood from Jim Elson, a former Venn Cross signalman, that the train was often hauled by a 'Prairie' tank locomotive and would usually comprise two bogie parcels vans, most likely 'Siphons', although a 'Mica B' or horse box substituted on occasion instead. The locomotive would usually run down from Taunton boiler first, thus enabling the use of the automatic token apparatus if it was fitted and possibly a non-stop run. As there were no locomotive turning facilities at South Molton, it would return bunker first but given that it would then stop at most stations on the return journey to Taunton, this reverse running was not a disadvantage, as the token exchange would of necessity and convenience be done by hand, rather than automatically. A review of the same period of the 1947 time table shows the path of the train working back to Taunton as set out below.

Station	Time (Arr.)	Time (Dep.)
South Molton		5.45pm
Bishops Nympton	5.53	6.03
East Anstey	6.15X	6.37
Dulverton	6.43	7.00
Morebath	7.08	7.15
Venn Cross	7.22	7.30
Wiveliscombe	7.39	7.45
Milverton	7.50	7.53
Taunton	8.05	

On arrival at Taunton, the vans would be detached to await the 4.10pm Plymouth to Paddington parcels, which was time-tabled to arrive at 8.15pm and leave at 8.55pm. The train would go via Bristol, where it would arrive at 11.00pm and leave at 1.15am. It is not clear whether the rabbit vans were worked to London on this train, which is most likely, or be detached and go to Birmingham. The 2.00pm Penzance to Crewe perishables was booked to arrive at Taunton at 9.00pm and go forward at 9.20pm, so any rabbits for the Midlands would most likely have been attached to this train. John Howard, who worked at Dulverton station (and whose memories are noted in Chapter 13, page 657) believes the rabbits usually went to Smithfield Market in London. It is known that rabbits despatched from South Devon (Kingsbridge, for example) usually went to Birmingham on the back of the 6.35pm express passenger train from Taunton in this same period.

John Howard remembers local trappers such as 'Trapper Jack' Thomas from Brushford, who would source the rabbits, with permission, from farmland around Dulverton. Some of these would go to the local butcher, others would be crated up for transport to the cities and on a good day, as many as thirty crates would be despatched just from Dulverton station on the 'Rabbiter'. There were of course similar individuals plying the same trade at other stations on route who would bring their 'bag' to the nearest station in time to load the 'Rabbiter'. Richard Rawle, who lived at East Nightcott Farm in the 1950s, recalls Jim Wyne, who lived in a cottage opposite his farm and took rabbits to Dulverton as well.

In order to catch the rabbits and make sure they remained edible (and not peppered with lead shot!), it is understood they were snared after ferrets had been deployed to 'flush' them out of their holes. Once caught the rabbit carcus commanded one shilling, then the equivalent to the rent per week for a cottage. In addition to the meat, the skins were also useful in those austere times.

The rabbits were stored in the vans in wooden crates, each weighing $1^1/_4$cwt (63kg) and each holding about forty rabbits, hung over two poles by the tendons of their hind legs and therefore head down; usually they were joined in pairs. There were no lids on the crates and so after a time the smell of the dead rabbits inevitably permeated the railway vans!

This special parcels service continued until myxomatosis decimated the rabbit population and trade in 1954. Sadly, no photographs of this unusual working have been located to date.

Cattle and Livestock Specials

Given the link of the line to the local farming community and the number of cattle auctions based along the line, such as South Molton, Molland, East Anstey and Wiveliscombe, it will be no surprise to learn that on market days cattle or livestock special trains would be run. Livestock was brought to market either by rail or driven on foot, depending on the location. Following their sale, the animals would then been sent by rail to abattoirs in towns and cities around much of the country, usually by express freight from Taunton.

In the period 1888 to 1904, the GWR built 1,250 8-ton 'Mex' cattle wagons, supplemented by a further 240 similar vehicles between 1929 and 1933. They were 18ft long with a moveable partition inside to change the layout and to enable mixed livestock loads to be carried.

The service time table for September 1930 published '*Standard Arrangements in connection with Cattle Auctions and Markets*'. Essentially, the arrangements set out below were subject to be modified or supplemented by instructions in a weekly notice. The service below covered auctions at East Anstey, Molland, Wiveliscombe and South Molton:

Station	Arr. am/pm	Dep. am/pm	Station	Arr. pm	Dep. pm
Taunton		U10.50	South Molton		3.15
Norton Fitz'n	CS		Molland	CS	3.20
Milverton	CS		East Anstey	CS	3.35
Wiveliscombe	11.15		Dulverton	3.50P	4.00
Venn Cross	11.25	P11.27	Morebath Jct	CS	
Morebath	P CS		Morebath	CS	
Morebath Jct	CS		Venn Cross	4.20	P 4.23
Dulverton	11.45	x 11.55	Wiveliscombe	3.48x	P4.50
East Anstey	12.10	P12.18	Mlverton	CS	
Molland	CSx		Norton Fitz'n	CS	
South Molton	12.55		Taunton	5.20	

Notes: U – empty cattle wagons
P – train must stop dead at that point
CS – change staff/token
x – crosses another train

The table shows the South Molton timings but the trains for the other auction locations would have broadly covered a similar path. Bampton livestock wagons would also be worked up the Barnstaple line to Taunton, where, along with other wagons off the branch, they would be re-marshalled for onward transport.

Transporting livestock was not like moving other commodities by rail. The Ministry of Agriculture set out regulations for the transport of animals, and for the cleaning and disinfection of cattle wagons, cattle pens and platforms, etc, to prevent transmission of diseases such as foot-and-mouth. Every time that livestock was unloaded and before the wagons were re-used, the floor and other parts coming into contact with the animals had to be scraped, swept and washed. The interiors were then coated with lime wash in earlier years, which leaked through to the outside leading to the distinctive white-washed appearance of these wagons, until it was found that lime was not as effective at preventing disease as first thought, whilst it also damaged the hooves, so its use was banned with the passing of the Animals (Transit & General) Order in 1927. A phenol-based disinfectant (known as 'white cyllin') was then used instead, along with sawdust as bedding. Cattle wagons from local stations were cleaned in Taunton West Yard near Forty Steps, where certain rails were set in concrete with drainage channels, to facilitate cleaning and avoid ballast getting wet and displaced. Hydrants were set at specific locations and effluent washed out with a high powered hose. Wagons were then swept clean with a special brush and then disinfected, and station cattle pens and lorries used for transport also had to be cleaned and treated. Transportation required movement orders issued by local authorities and relevant station staff were required to check the validity of licences and paperwork presented by the farmers.

The farmers benefitted from the railways, shipping their livestock away from local areas with a view to obtaining better prices. Transport by rail also meant that there was less driving of livestock from farms to markets, the railway taking some of the burden away of the animals moving on the hoof. It helped the livestock maintain their condition and well-being prior to sale, thus potentially improving the price the farmers would receive but care had to be taken by the railways in transporting the animals to avoid injury and claims from their owners.

The animals also had to be tended to, fed and watered over lengthy journeys, whilst cows of course had to be milked, if that was appropriate. In addition, pigs were not allowed to be loaded with sheep and calves, to avoid fights! Laid out in the *GWR Rules and Regulations* were the means of dealing with livestock in transit.

If loaded cattle wagons were attached to a routine freight service, rather than run as a special, they were required by regulations to be attached at the front of the consist, next to the locomotive.

By 1st January 1963, livestock facilities had been curtailed to just 232 goods stations and yards nationally and it was at this time that such traffic ceased on the D&SR, although it did continue at Barnstaple for a little longer. This decision no doubt precipitated the closure of the goods yards at some, but not all, of the D&SR stations from 30th September 1963.

Table 12.1 below sets out the peak receiving and forwarding of wagons at the various stations but detailed year by year information on a station by station basis can be found in Volume 2.

Table 12.1: Peak Years per Station for Wagon Traffic

Station	Best Year	Wagons Forwarded & Received
Milverton	1925	160
Wiveliscombe	1930	531
Venn Cross	1929	142
Morebath	1935	133
Dulverton	1926	487
East Anstey	1923	320
Bishops Nympton & Molland	1931	289
South Molton	1950	626
Filleigh	1931	214
Swimbridge	1913	97
Barnstaple GWR	1951	1,597

At four stations the traffic peaked in the late 1920s/early 1930s, whilst it is no surprise that Barnstaple dealt with the most wagons, followed by South Molton and Wiveliscombe. Traffic was very light at Swimbridge, the total of ninety-seven in 1913 being exceptional

– thirty-six wagons were dealt with in 1936, the next best year, and only one in 1933!

A special notice published for Thursday 20th March 1941 referred to South Molton Grading Market: '*A special with 10 empty Mex to leave Taunton at 11.15am for South Molton. To shunt as required and return working loaded Cattle Special as ordered*'.

Farm Specials

It was not uncommon for farm removals to take place by rail during the first half of the 20th century. Special trains comprising of cattle and horse trucks, flat wagons for farm implements, parcels vans and a passenger coach would be assembled to move the entourage. Given that the D&SR was a lifeline to the farming community throughout its length and most of its existence, it will be no surprise to learn that farmers used the railways to move house and home. An example of these was a Mr L.C. Fuller, who chose to bring all his livestock (including pedigree Friesian cattle) and farm machinery by rail from Kendal in Westmoreland to North Devon in March of 1954, alighting at Molland.

Barnstaple Great Fair 1875

Barnstaple Great Fair took place on 23rd September 1875 and was attended by more than 12,000 people, most of whom arrived by train from all directions. The broad gauge early train on the D&SR comprised fifteen carriages and conveyed around 1,000 passengers but hundreds were left behind on platforms back along the line and had to take a later train. Needless to say there were difficulties for passengers in getting home and at the next fair on 21st September 1877, the 9.00pm train ran to Dulverton and an extra train ran at 11.00pm to South Molton.

The Funeral of Parson Jack Russell

The funeral of Parson Jack Russell was held on Thursday, 3rd May 1883 at Swimbridge, his former parish, following his death on 28th April. He had lived latterly, and died, at Black Torrington near Hatherleigh. The hearse travelled by road to Great Torrington and then by rail to Swimbridge, a special train being laid on by the D&SR for those wishing to attend the funeral. The *North Devon Journal* recorded the occasion: '*The scene at the grave was a most impressive one. Hundreds of persons pressed forward in rotation to have a last look at the coffin which contained the mortal remains of one who was universally esteemed and beloved.*'. Mourners included Lord Ebrington and many Masters of Hounds. Russell had begun breeding dogs in his early twenties, developing the distinctive type of fox terrier which now bares his name, the Parson Jack Russell Terrier being officially recognised as a breed by the Kennel Club on 9th January 1990.

The Reverend John 'Jack' Russell (21st December 1795-28th April 1883) in a portrait photograph taken circa 1870.

Bad Weather - the Blizzard of 1891

The so called 'Great Blizzard' of 1891 played havoc with the railway, the 7.35am train from Barnstaple getting stuck in a snow drift near Filleigh on 10th March. A snow plough was to be brought from Barnstaple to clear the line but there was no engine available to which it could be fitted. A gang from Barnstaple released the stranded locomotive after three hours and the train eventually made it to Taunton. The 9.20am Down train failed to get through and the Divisional Superintendent (Mr Campfield) declared that no further trains should run. The line was cleared on 11th March but no trains ran as the main line was still blocked.

Visit of the Duke of Cambridge 1895

Barnstaple GWR station was hastily decorated with flags, bunting and a red carpet on Monday 20th May 1895, for the pending arrival of the Duke of Cambridge. He was due to travel from Waterloo to Barnstaple L&SWR station but had missed the 11.00am departure and had to rush to Paddington instead, to take the GWR route and arrive, later than planned, at the GWR station. Mr Withy, the Barnstaple GWR stationmaster, organised matters, the welcoming party having to abandon their plans at the L&SWR station and travel across town to meet their special guest. Prior to his arrival, lively music was played by a volunteer band and as the Duke disembarked, he was greeted by a guard of honour comprising the 4th Volunteer Battalion of the Devonshire Regiment, seventy-seven members of 'A' and 'B' Companies and thirty-three bandsmen, who played '*God Save the Queen*'. The purpose of his visit was to carry out an extensive list of engagements in Devon and during his time at Barnstaple he stayed at Broadgate, the home of Colonel Hibbert.

A New Telephone Line 1895

Also in 1895, telephone poles and cables were delivered to Dulverton station in the June for the start of a scheme to erect a telephone line to Exford.

A Well Respected Guard 1897

In November 1897, the Dulverton station master, Mr Burrows, presented Mr William Snell, a guard, with £14 14s 6d donated by the public towards his retirement after thirty-nine years – a large sum in those days.

The Wild West Show 1903

Colonel William F. Cody – 'Buffalo Bill' – brought his Wild West Show to Barnstaple via the GWR and its station on Sunday 26th July 1903. There were three train loads of horses, performers and related equipment, totalling some 500 passengers and 400 horses transported in around a hundred wagons and carriages. They were greeted by hordes of curious locals who had waited most of the day for the trains to arrive, the first eventually pulling in at 7.00pm.

There were to be two shows on the Monday at Sticklepath, so on arrival the entourage paraded (with most on horseback) to the showground where they set up their base. Mr Withy was still the station master and he welcomed the party, the third train conveying 'foreigners' – Red Indians, Chinese, Mexicans, Arabs, Turks, Cossacks and Egyptians – arousing the most interest. 'Buffalo Bill' himself was delayed for five hours at Wiveliscombe station as the result of a broken 'crawbar'. After the shows, the entourage packed up and went on to Exeter but the spectacle apparently returned to Barnstaple on other occasions.

FROM LEFT TO RIGHT: A.V. Dimond, aged 28, pw labourer at Wiveliscombe; Arthur G. Pierce, aged 26 and with the GWR since June 1906, clerk at Torre but previously at Taunton, Cullompton, Exeter and South Molton; Alfred J. Beer, porter, South Molton (all killed in 1916); F. Sloman, signal porter, South Molton 1918; E.H. Harford, porter, Norton Fitzwarren (both killed in 1918). ***Great Western Railway Magazine***

THE FIRST WORLD WAR

When the First World War broke out the railway would have played its part although little appears to be recorded. However, the West Somerset Yeomanry trained near Dulverton and would have almost certainly been transported by the railway.

The army put into action its mobilisation plan to acquire horses to serve in the conflict with the cavalry and hauling artillery, along with mules as pack animals. Horses were purchased on the open market from farmers and others but demand exceeded supply, so in addition to the domestic procurement of animals, the Horse Purchasing Commission went to the United States and Canada to purchase wild horses and mules. Between August 1914 and February 1919, 428,608 horses and 275,097 mules were purchased. A separate mule commission was established in Kansas (later moving to Montreal), the price per mule being set at $175. These animals offered sure-footedness, endurance, intelligence and speed, and they were imported from the USA to Avonmouth (and other docks), from where they were sent to rehabilitation depots such as at Shirehampton, near Bristol. However, smaller mules depots were needed to supplement the main locations; the Somerset or Taunton depot comprised a number of farms in the area which collectively could take 6,000 mules. One such location was Wiveliscombe (and also Minehead in the region), where the army mule depot was established to the north and west of the town. The mules were brought in by rail, usually on Sundays when other traffic did not run, for acclimatisation, conditioning and feeding-up in the farmers' fields, before being transported to France for service at the Western Front. It is understood cattle wagons were used for the purpose of transporting the mules, being unloaded at Wiveliscombe station.

The *Great Western Railway Magazine*, throughout the war, noted the deaths of employees killed in action, with three men associated with the line killed in 1916 and another two in 1918 (there may have been others); they are pictured above, South Molton seemingly being particularly unlucky. On a happier note, Mr J. Stone, (left) in peacetime a leading packer on the permanent way based at Norton Fitzwarren, was awarded the Military Medal for continuing to work whilst under heavy fire on 6th October 1917.

CIRCUS TRAINS

The *GWR Magazine* reported in 1933 that as a result of his successful experience last year, Mr Bertram Mills, the famous circus proprietor, had again asked the four main line railway companies to undertake conveyance by railway of his travelling circus throughout the summer. The nature of the task can be visualised by the fact that, apart from the conveyance of artistes, circus staff, and their extensive baggage and equipment, over a hundred animals had to be transported, including elephants, tigers, zebras, horses, ponies and others. Altogether, forty-seven vehicles were utilised, including an elephant truck, a 45ft

Two views by a GWR official photographer of the Bertram Mills Circus train which visited Devon in 1933, showing elephants being end unloaded from a 'Monster' wagon at Exeter St. Davids station. ***Great Western Railway Magazine***

covered van for tigers, a similar vehicle for smaller wild beasts, seventeen horse boxes and five covered cattle trucks. In addition, suitable vehicles had to be provided to accommodate the circus equipment, including tents, seating accommodation, motor lorries, tractors and caravans, and, of course, convenient loading and unloading facilities had to be afforded.

The essential feature of such an extensive circus tour was the speed and reliability of transport between the places at which the shows were to be given. The fact that the railway companies had been asked to repeat the previous year's arrangements was an indication that their organisation had adequately carried out their somewhat unusual task.

In 1948, 16-year old Derek Goodwin joined Bertram Mills Circus as an animal helper and would be mainly responsible for the elephants and big cats. It was the second biggest touring circus in the world at that time (the largest being in the USA) and it moved by train. In total, four special trains were required to move the entourage and although not specific to the D&SR, an article in *Steam World* (based on a letter written to Chris Leigh by Cyril B. Mills) explained the role of railways in moving the circus. The four trains were made up as follows and there was a certain military precision about the whole operation, which of course also had to fit it with railway time tables:

Train 1: When on tour, this would be the first to leave the current venue, about the time of the interval and be unloaded on arrival at the new site. It carried the staff mess tent, cook-house, staff kitchens, staff catering department, store wagon, four wild animal wagons, saddler's shop, stable fittings wagon, cage wagon, private office, general office, two box offices, one road tractor and one train unloading tractor.

Train 2: This would leave one hour after the end of the performance and comprise two wardrobe wagons, one harness wagon, the catering bar, toilet wagon, a wagon with small tents, canvas and poles, ring fence wagon, six seating wagons, one diesel plant, two fencing wagons, and a stable canvas and poles wagon.

Train 3: This would depart thirty minutes after the 'Big Top' had been pulled down. The train would consist of the Big Top canvas, king pole/quarter pole wagon, side poles, stakes, tailor's workshop, diesel plant, switch room, two artists dressing wagons, four road tractors, three David Brown winching tractors and three staff sleeping coaches.

Train 4: This usually departed by 8.00am the following morning with the horse boxes, the elephant wagon, artistes baggage wagon and two passenger coaches for those artistes that did not have their own caravans (which would have gone by road) and usherettes.

As a result, the trains consisted mainly of flat bed trucks (usually of 21ft 6ins in length), horses in horse box wagons and elephants in a large baggage wagon that had been specially sprung. The horses and

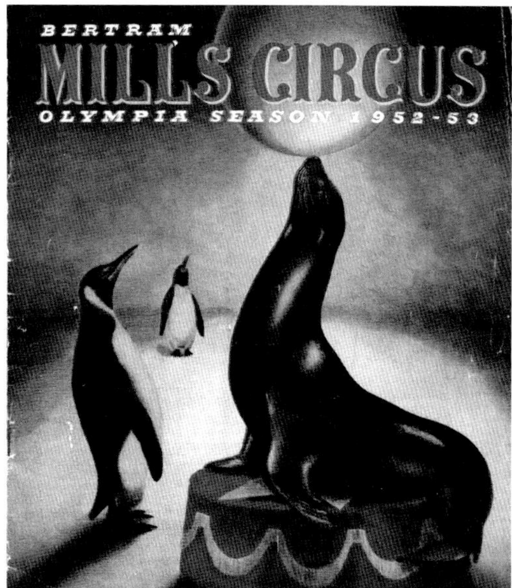

Left and Below: An advertisement for Bertram Mills Circus detailing the range of acts to be enjoyed and the cover of a programme, from the 1950s. ***Derek Goodwin collection***

elephants could either be side loaded from the platform or end loaded if a suitable bay (usually for motor vehicles) was available, and faced the direction of travel in their padded accommodation. The equipment trucks were end-loaded, so this required shunting manoeuvres at the destination.

In 1948, when Derek had just started with the circus, it toured the South West, starting at Bridgwater, then on to Taunton and Minehead. From Minehead, the four trains travelled back to Norton Fitzwarren and then down the D&SR to Barnstaple Victoria Road. Derek remembers the elephants being unloaded and walked in Rock Park (just a short distance from Victoria Road station and in full view of the line to Barnstaple Junction), where the circus was to be located. Three days later, once their shows were over in Barnstaple, the circus moved on to Bude and then Newquay by rail.

It is understood that these circus trains were turned complete at Victoria Road by using the triangle. As the junctions and the East Chord were out of use at this time – and indeed had not been used for some years – the points had to be unclipped. This has been confirmed by John Howard of the S&T department, who recalls going to unclip the points to enable the loaded train, including its elephants, to turn.

In 1951, the *Railway Observer* reported that the Bertram Mills Circus entourage that was on its way from Torquay to Barnstaple had to be diverted via Taunton and the D&SR line. This was because the North Devon Water Board were laying a new trunk main under the Exeter to Barnstaple line at Umberleigh during the night of 18th-19th August, scheduled so as to avoid interference to normal passenger workings. The diversion over the D&SR resulted in five trains rather than the usual three or four because of the steep gradients on the line. The first of these specials left Torquay on Saturday 18th August, arriving at Victoria Road on Sunday 19th August at 2.30am. The *Western Morning News* also reported that it was planned to march six elephants carrying road safety slogans from the station at 12.30pm on that Sunday and to go in procession along the Taw Vale and North Walk to the Braunton Road circus field. Sadly, no pictures have been located to date showing any of these trains in the area but a story involving a circus train is related by Bridley Prust in Chapter 13.

Camp Coaches

Whilst popular at a number of South West locations, it was only East Anstey station on the D&SR that was to have Camp Coaches, although there were a couple on the Exe Valley line at Bampton and Thorverton. In 1934, the first season for such coaches

East Anstey was the only recorded location on the D&SR for Camp(ing) Coaches both pre- and post-war but this photograph shows BR Camping Coach No. W9901W in the loading bay of the goods shed line at South Molton on 3rd April 1961. Built in May 1903 to Diagram E73 as No. 1492, a seven-compartment First/Second Composite with lavatories at each end, it was later renumbered as No. 7492 and condemned on 22nd March 1947, presumably then being stored as it was not altered to a Camping Coach until 17th May 1952. As No. 9901, it was sent first to St. Agnes on the Newquay to Chacewater branch but the following year is recorded in the register as having been sent to Congesbury, on 19th April 1953, the only other allocation for it recorded in the register. No Camping Coach was ever located at South Molton, so its appearance in this picture is something of a mystery. Mike Fenton suggests that it would have been here in some kind of departmental use, maybe providing accommodation for men employed by the signalling or pw department during a period of local repair work, or perhaps the station master's house was under repair and they needed to offer temporary accomodation. The coach was soon to be condemned again and was broken up at Swindon on 14th December 1963. *Michael L. Roach*

on the GWR, there was no D&SR location designated, most of them being positioned on lines near the coast. Initially, of the nineteen vehicles allocated, one was in Somerset and six in Devon. East Anstey first appeared in 1936, with six berths listed in what was called a Type 'B' coach (the classification reflecting the number of campers that could be accommodated). The first Camp Coaches were converted old 4- or 6-wheeled stock but these were joined by some bogie clerestory carriages when the scheme was expanded in 1935. The coaches were quite well appointed, with beds, bed and table linen, cutlery, glass, crockery, kitchen and cleaning utensils, lamps and a cooking stove.

The rent was £3 per week but a minimum of four rail tickets had to be taken. In addition, in 1936 special rail fares (for seven days) were stipulated for unlimited travel in area No. 5 at 15s for First Class and 10s for Second Class. The cost was reasonably inexpensive compared to local guest houses. The maintenance and servicing of the coaches was carried out by station staff as part of their normal duties, with laundry contracted out. The Camp Coaches returned to Swindon in the autumn for storage and were brought back again in the spring, most locations keeping the same vehicles. East Anstey was part of the scheme from 1936 through to 1939, most locations then being suspended due to the war and for the duration of it, although some were available for part of the 1940 season.

Area No. 5 referred to above covered to Taunton, Hemyock, Newton Abbott and Mortonhampstead. The published advertising made the following reference to East Anstey: '*This delightful Devonshire village is 800 feet above sea level within easy reach of Exmoor country where many charming walks may be enjoyed. The towns of Dulverton, Barnstaple and Taunton are all accessible by rail.*'.

With the Camp Coaches vehicles having been redesignated for various departmental uses during the war, none were in a fit condition for reuse immediately after hostilities ceased and consequently the scheme was slow to restart. Consequently, when the Western Region, under the newly formed British Railways, decided to bring the scheme back in 1952, it was necessary to fit out a whole new batch of vehicles, which the new regime now referred to as Camping Coaches. In the west, along with most of the other sites used pre-war, East Anstey was included again but only remained until 1955, after which it did not feature again. No other site on the line was ever used, the only other Camping Coach in close proximity in BR days being at Bampton on the Exe Valley route for one year in 1952. BR(WR) finally ended the Camping Coach scheme at the end of the 1964 summer season.

THE SECOND WORLD WAR

During the Second World War, the railways generally were in the front line of the war effort and essential to it, troop movements and the transport of munitions and supplies of goods taking priority. Railways moved goods, troops and equipment but, in addition, evacuees would arrive from London and other cities under siege to avoid the worst aspects of the conflict. For example, on Monday 4th September 1939, a train carrying 1,000 evacuees destined for the Exmoor area finally arrived at Dulverton five hours late, at 9.00pm in pitch darkness, delayed because of air raid alerts in the capital. Of those arriving, 750 disembarked at the station for Dulverton and Exmoor parishes, the balance being taken on to South Molton. However, a number of the evacuees could not settle and significant numbers of mothers and children returned home within a couple of months.

Despite its location away from major conurbations and the English Channel, the D&SR played its part in the war effort. Indeed it was during the preparation for the D-Day landings where the line played its most significant role. The beaches on the North Devon coast bore something of a resemblance to those in Normandy, so they were used for the practising of manoeuvres for 'Operation Overlord' – the D-Day landings – in 1944, American and British troops carrying out trial landing operations at Braunton Burrows, Saunton Sands, Woolacombe and Instow beaches. Over 100,000 troops trained in the area in one year. The US troops had landed at Liverpool and in Scotland and had to be transported down to the training grounds and camps in North Devon along with their equipment and provisions, this being a major logistical exercise. The line was used to transport troops and equipment primarily at night.

In a single day in May 1944, fifteen troop trains, each carrying a thousand US troops (GIs) and vast stores of food passed along the line to Dulverton, where they camped on Haddon Hill and South Hill. Arthur Saunders, the station master and at that time five years from retirement, was ready to receive the first train at 7.15am in the morning, the last arriving at 7.00pm in the evening. One of the trains carried the Supreme Commander of the Allied Expeditionary Forces, General Dwight D. Eisenhower, who had planned a visit to rally his troops prior to D-Day. This special train, assembled and modified by the GWR and codenamed 'Alive', comprised seven coaches including a Dining car, two Sleeping carriages, a Drawing Room car and a Cinema car, all liveried in British Army green. Saunders, who greeted Eisenhower on his arrival, had no idea who would be on the train – the American General was reported to have said "*I am very pleased to be here. Can I stay for two or three days?*". It is understood that the train was apparently stabled on the Down platform line, where it had arrived, and thus blocked it for the time he was there. Indeed, John Howard recalls the trains having to be diverted into the Exe Valley bay platform to keep services moving. It is understood that Saunders' wife, on hearing from her husband that the dining car was bare of flowers, gave the General Lilies of the Valley from her garden to brighten it up. After the formal troop inspections, Eisenhower hired a horse and for pleasure rode across Exmoor to Winsford and then Withypool, where he drank at the Royal Oak Inn. On returning back to Dulverton station, he stated that he had enjoyed Exmoor enormously and then said "*Now I must get back to work*". Although no report of Eisenhower's trip was made at the time, the *West Somerset Free Press* subsequently publicised things and a copy of the paper found its way to Eisenhower, who by then was ensconced back in the White House, as President. He wrote back stating "*It brought back memories. I very much enjoyed my few days on Exmoor and I wish they had been more*". It is recorded that Eisenhower's special train travelled 95,000 miles around the country before D-Day. John Howard also recalls troop trains of seven or more coaches, sometimes double-headed by 2-6-0 'Moguls' at their head, these engines being stalwarts in the war effort around the GWR and a number even got shipped to France.

One officer and six men were stationed at Dulverton, to assist with unloading provisions, such as supplies of fruit and vegetables, that arrived by rail. When the troops were mobilised at Saunton Sands prior to D-Day, extra goods trains conveyed stores and they would also run on Sundays. Troop trains would occasionally use the East Curve at Barnstaple and the shunting crew would have to collect coaches from time to time.

When the time came, the departure of troops from the area was sudden as they moved to the D-Day marshalling areas on the south coast, near the ports of Plymouth, Weymouth, Poole, Chichester, Southampton, Portsmouth and Newhaven. However, John Milton recalls a mass movement of troops out of the East Anstey area in June 1944. From time to time, farmers were told by the military to keep off the roads for twenty-four hours, for no apparent reason. On 4-5th June 1944, the reason for the empty roads became clear as American and British troops, along with their lorries and equipment, were loaded on to trains at East Anstey and Dulverton, leaving the area for good as they headed off to their destiny.

The Wiveliscombe Home Guard were given the task of guarding certain strategic points of the local transport network for months prior to D-Day, Waterrow Viaduct being the main object of their defence. A farmer living beside the line between Wiveliscombe and Venn Cross had US soldiers billeted at his farm, rehabilitating after being saved from a ship that was sunk a few weeks previously. One night four German planes came over to attack the line. The farm was a defence position with a search light and ack-ack guns, which the US soldiers manned, and there was a barrage of gunfire, rewarded when one plane went down near Hemyock to the east. The line survived intact.

It is also understood that, during the war, some of the waste ground in the centre of the triangle at Barnstaple was used for demonstrating various grenades and anti-tank bombs to the Home Guard.

During the war, several food storage depots were set up in and around Barnstaple, the Pannier Market and premises at Rolle Quay being commandeered by the Admiralty. It is understood that the former Lynton & Barnstaple Railway engine sheds at Pilton were also used for storage purposes. The food came in via the railway, thus increasing the goods traffic handled, and included bacon, cheese and tea. Some local factories were turned over to war production, such as Shapland & Petters (furniture manufacturers normally), who made camouflage nets and tents from hessian. In addition to the extra goods workings, there were Red Cross trains conveying wounded soldiers which ran through to Fremington. These would work into the GWR station and then run round in the normal way before proceeding to the Junction. These could run at almost any time and were given priority, regular shunting movements being suspended, whilst the shunting goods trains sometimes had to pull out of the way on the chord line to facilitate access to the yard.

The role of the railways in war-time operation come to light in the War Office papers, brief extracts from which as far as their impact on the D&SR are concerned, are set out below.

Referring to notes on the Southern Command draft letter on essential railways, it was indicated that the map of essential railways took account of Southern Command's requirements. However, the only recommendation of any consequence not accepted was '*the Taunton to Barnstaple line, which whilst being of little importance as a through route can easily be added as a local requirement if desired*'. There were clearly fears at this time of potential attacks on the North Devon coast and this led to the south coast lines being featured on the map, the aim being to provide as many alternative routes as possible. Whilst it was all very well to maintain railheads away from the main arterial routes, the benefit of keeping all terminal work off the main lines had to be balanced against the complication of train working and the maintenance of additional track mileage, which the use of a number of railhead spurs introduced.

In a letter of 8th December 1940 Lieutenant Neck wrote to Major A.H. Earley, RE, Movement Control, GHQ Home Forces, stipulating in relation to the map of 'essential railways':

'*Your view that the plan should envisage operations also on the northern shores of Devon and Somerset will necessitate revision of our railhead layout and so further delay publication* [of the map]: *nevertheless we are adopting the suggestion.*'

Clearly, the lines and key stations in North Devon and on the D&SR in particular had a role to play and a summary of the findings is set out below.

There was a meeting at HQ Southern Command on 4th February 1942 with MC Salisbury District, MC Exeter District and MC Oxford District also present. MC Exeter district was represented by Major E.J.H. Leighton and Captain H.T. Lake. In essence, the initial railheads selected were on predetermined lines for various commodities and to repel an invasion by sea but concerns then developed about possible attacks on inland areas by airborne troops. The additional railheads were to be selected in accordance with the following priorities:

- Ammunition – that was the forming of a certain number of

TABLE 12.2: SCHEDULE OF STATIONS ON THE BARNSTAPLE BRANCH AS SUITABLE RAILHEADS IN SOUTHERN COMMAND 1942				
NARRATIVE	BARNSTAPLE	SWIMBRIDGE	SOUTH MOLTON	DULVERTON
Map Ref	T0055	T9653	T1549	T3647
Telephone number	Barnstaple Goods 2425 Pass. 2630		South Molton 18	Dulverton 27
Recommend for Stores	PB	P	P	PB
Recommend for AFV	EL x		EL x	EL x
Recommend for Ambulance	Amb	Amb		
No. of wagons placed at one time for unloading to MT	40	15	15	40
No. of wagons stabled in addition to above	142	9	20	17
Road layout	Two-way approach roads good. Built-up area. No protection from the air	Single traffic, narrow winding roads. Condition of roads good. Hilly surroundings – good cover.	Good roads, two-way traffic. Traffic circuit could be arranged. Roads tree-lined, hilly surroundings	Good roads, two-way traffic; circuit can be arranged. Natural concealment. Hilly surroundings
MC district	E	E	E	E
Corps or district	8 Corps	8 Corps	8 Corps	8 Corps
Remarks	Single line x 1 WF only, but can place Sqn on blocking middle road. RTH for Cmd Sup & Pet depot RE Stores Dump	Single line	x 1WF only Alt RH for Cmd Sd. Barnstaple GW	x through goods shed. Single line. Alt RH for Wellington (Som) (62 Corps AD)

NOTES: Stores train: P – Pack train; B – Bulk train
AFV train: EL – End loading dock siding capacity less than 5 'Warflats' at one time; HQ – End Loading dock capacity 5 'Warflats' and complete HQ train; Sqn – End loading dock siding capacity 9 'Warflats' on a Squadron train
Amb – Ambulance train capacity
Movement Control District E – MC Exeter

trains and to ensure the rapid supply of ammunition in trains of about 250 tons.

• Supplies; maintenance by pack train would be deferred as long as fooding [*sic*] could be carried on by existing CSDs.

The additional stations to be recommended would be determined and these would be 'recc'ed' by 15th February 1942. If there were to be an invasion the railway lines remaining open for traffic would have been contracted and the railheads restricted accordingly.

In the war years the term 'Battery Train' was used to cover all rolling stock for a railway battery that is completely mobile and able to carry out strategical moves with its own transport. The Battery Train usually moved as one unit, comprising the fighting train – diesel engines, guns and rolling stock essential to their maintenance in action – and the living train, which carried personnel, the commissariat and non-essential stores.

In a letter of 15th September 1942, the Petroleum Board (South Western Region) asked for Barnstaple to be earmarked for use as an alternative railhead in the event this traffic was unable to reach its normal receiving point during active operations. Under such conditions, it was anticipated that trains of approximately thirty wagons would have to be dealt with at Barnstaple.

Table 12.2, above, was extracted from war records at the National Archives that were closed until 1972, as they were marked 'Top Secret'.

The regular time-tabled train service during the war years was reviewed in Chapter 11 but the number of passenger services was reduced to five Up and Down trains per day, thus giving some flexibility for running additional trains as and when required. It is understood the line was used a great deal to transport troops and equipment at night.

With the threat of a potential German invasion on the beaches near the mouth of the River Taw in 1940, an armoured train was deployed at Barnstaple Junction to patrol the line between Bideford and Braunton. It is not known if this train traversed the D&SR at any time but it comprised an LM&SR 20-ton steel-bodied loco coal wagon fitted with 6-pounder Hotchkiss Mk II gun, to defend against tank or armoured car attack at up to 800-1,000 yards. Another compartment contained rifles and three Bren guns and there was an armoured wagon for radio communication. Haulage was provided by L&NER 2-4-2T No. 7077, armoured and on loan to the War Department, whilst the crew of this special train numbered thirty-one.

A Special Train Notice in March 1941 referred to a '*Special Train – Manchester London Road to Barnstaple 'A' Headlamps*' and labelled No. 20.F.76. It was formed of seven LM&SR bogie vehicles and conveyed troops returning on leave. It departed from Taunton at 5.20pm, arriving at Barnstaple at 6.54pm and the stock was to be retained to form Special No. 21.F.1 on 21st March 1941.

THE WAR YEARS IN MILVERTON

Extracts from the letters of Nellie Clemens, who along with her daughter was evacuated from north London in the early days of the war, are recalled in '*Darlingest: Milverton in the War*', edited by by Elizabeth McDowell. The *Somerset County Gazette* reported on 15th June1940 that '*Sixteen thousand children are expected in Somerset this weekend*'.

Nellie left from Paddington in June 1940 and arrived by train at Wellington, ending up in Milverton where she stayed until December 1941. Some trains ended up in the wrong place and the Taunton to Barnstaple railway features in her letter writing, along with stories of bombings and the arrival of American soldiers into the area. Although Milverton was off the beaten track, there would be air raid warnings and bombs dropping '*horribly*' nearby, as the area was on a direct flight path from Cherbourg to Bristol and South Wales for German bombers. RAF and American aircraft were also spotted. In February 1941, eighty US soldiers stayed overnight and thousands of troops passed through the village in lorries, '*one long continuous stream since 9 o'clock this morning*', headed for Exmoor and manoeuvres there. The 8th Corps Field Firing exercise on Exmoor involved all rifle companies and this mass troop transportation was repeated in April of that year too.

Local Defence Volunteers (LDV – the 'Home Guard'), manned Venn Cross Viaduct in the run up to D-Day and Cyril Loram would go off at night with his rifle to undertake this duty. When Somerset emptied of troops as they headed off for the D-Day invasion, the Home Guard were fully responsible for defence of the town.

US soldiers arriving at Cardiff on 19th October 1943 were sent by train to Milverton, where they arrived at 8.00am. There they resumed training and garrison duties, including motor maintenance, covert operations, etc. Trucks and Jeeps arrived too and these may well have been transported by rail, whilst the GIs were billeted at Milverton.

East Anstey in the Movies

As mentioned in Volume 2 (page 336), East Anstey station was the location for some filming of the movie *The Halfway House*, which was an Ealing Studios production, filmed in 1944 in black and white. Other local filming for the movie was at Barlynch Abbey, just outside of Dulverton, north along the Exe Valley, which masqueraded as the Halfway House Hotel. It was a British drama directed by Basil Dearden (of *The Blue Lamp* fame) and starring amongst others were Tom Walls, Mervyn Johns and his daughter Glynis Johns. It told the story of ten strangers who were drawn to stay in an old hotel in a remote Welsh village and is a ghost story. East Anstey masqueraded as Ynysgwy, the station for Cymbach where the hotel was supposedly located. 'Mogul' No. 6364, with token apparatus on the tender, features for about two minutes of the ninety-two minute film (see stills right). The screenplay was written by Angus McPhail, Diane Morgan and T.E.B. Clarke (who also wrote *The Titfield Thunderbolt*), from the stage play by Denis Ogden.

The Winter of 1947

The first blizzards of this notorious winter came to the West Somerset area in late January 1947 but the Arctic conditions were not to relent until March. Everything froze, all transport ceased and villages were blocked off. The mining industry was unable to meet the demand for coal and this fuel crisis resulted in a reduction of services. The extent of the poor weather and how the railway coped is illustrated later in Chapter 13, from the memories of Jim Elson.

A Temporary Platform Between Milverton and Wiveliscombe

The *Railway Observer* reported in October 1951 on an extensive track drainage scheme that had been installed between Milverton and Wiveliscombe during the earlier part of that year. This resulted in a severe speed restriction along that section of the line for several months, which had finally been lifted on 13th August 1951. In addition, a temporary platform had been constructed of old sleepers, facilitating the movement of men and materials to and from the site.

The Royal Visit 1956

Her Majesty Queen Elizabeth II and Prince Philip visited North Devon on 8th May 1956, the middle day of a three day visit to the West Country that also included Launceston, Liskeard and Truro. The Royal Train ran the length of the Taunton to Barnstaple line to Victoria Road, arriving about 10.00am. The Earl of Fortescue, Lord Lieutenant Of Devon, and the Mayor of Barnstaple, Mr A.W. Clarke, welcomed the Queen and Prince along with a one hundred-strong guard of honour of the 4th Devonshire Regiment in the station forecourt, under their guard commander Major K.E. Wilkinson. The Queen, wearing a tailored pale blue coat and matching hat, inspected the regiment, along with equerry-in-waiting Squadron Leader C.C. Blount, before conducting official duties around the town. Although the skies were grey, the route of the entourage was lined with decorations and waving crowds. Later that day she was driven to Eggesford, where she and the Duke planted a tree to commemorate the one millionth acre of Forestry Commission land on which there had been plantings.

The locomotives in charge that day were Churchward 'Moguls' No's 6372 and 6385, with the former piloting the latter. Both were specially painted in BR lined green livery, with polished brass safety valve covers. Previously, only the first batch of these 2-6-0s had been so lined, so this was a departure from the normal liveries carried by them for this special occasion. However, by the autumn it had become official policy to repaint the whole class in unlined green and in February 1957 full lining was added to those that remained.

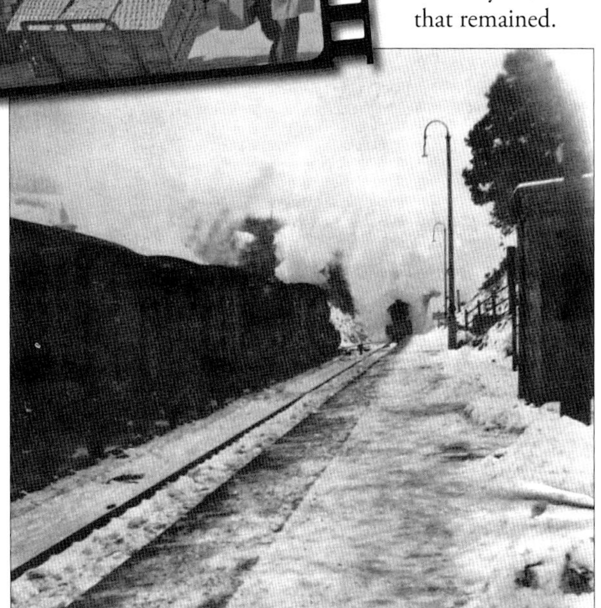

Looking east along the Down platform at Venn Cross, showing conditions here at the height of the winter of 1947. A goods train waits in the Up platform loop to cross the Down train arriving in the background. The snow had impacted on the platforms and turned to ice. Similar but worse conditions prevailed during the winter of 1963. *Jim Elson*

The platform and buildings at Barnstaple Victoria Road station are almost unrecognisable here, decked out ready for the Queen's and Prince Philip's arrival on 8th May 1956. The drapes and buntings were there to hide the basic and rundown structure of the station canopies and buildings. It is understood that the buntings were sold on after the visit to recoup some of the cost. Even the cattle wagons in the cattle dock line are neatly lined up! It was reported that it took staff five days working round the clock to get everything ready for the Royal party's arrival. The prevailing motif on the bunting was gold and white and apparently 600 yards of material had been fastened to the roof. The platform was flanked with trellis work and thirty boxes of hydrangeas.
Courtesy Terry Hatton

The coaches in the Royal Train were in maroon with pink lining and un-prefixed gold numbering, shaded in LM&SR block style; a new Royal Dining car was included in the set. The eleven-coach formation, as recorded by the *Railway Observer* in June 1956, was as follows (from the front as it traversed the D&SR-see below): Clerestory Brake First No. 5155, steel semi-Royal No. 2900, steel Royal Saloons No's 799 (the Queen's), and 798 (the Duke's), steel Royal Diner No. 499, Equerry's office Saloon No. 807 (clerestory), First Sleepers No's 495 and 477, clerestory semi-Royal Saloon No. 806 (the railway officials' coach), clerestory First Diner No. 77 and steel Power car No. 31209. The total load was 493 tons.

After arrival at Victoria Road, the locomotives then went separately to Barnstaple Junction for turning and servicing. On returning back, coupled together, they then worked the empty coaching stock back to Taunton, where ex-GWR 'Castle' Class 4-6-0s No. 7024 *Powis Castle* and No. 5044 *Earl of Dunraven* took the train on to Goodrington (Siding No. 4). 'Mogul' No. 6322 in plain black livery was the standby engine at Barnstaple and it too was turned out in pristine condition.

The Royal Train had arrived at Old Oak Common in the late morning of 7th May, being moved to Paddington where No. 7024 and No. 5044 were attached for the departure at 7.30pm. It went via the Berks & Hants line towards Westbury, arriving at Heywood Road Junction at 9.28pm after a number of speed restrictions. The train was reversed at Westbury, the Queen's coach being third from the rear at Paddington for ease of access from the roadside. The two 'Castles' were detached and ran to Westbury North box, after which 'Hall' Class No. 4927 *Farnborough Hall* was attached at the front and drew the train forward from Heywood Road Junction, through East Loop Junction and around the loop to Hawkeridge Junction, bringing it to a stand on the Up Main line to Trowbridge. The two 'Castles' then went around the west side of the loop to recouple at Hawkeridge, with No. 4927 being detached.

The train left Hawkeridge Junction at 9.58pm, stopping at Middle Box to allow the replenishment of gas and water for overnight stabling further on. The train departed Westbury at 10.30pm and was diverted into the

ABOVE AND RIGHT: HM Queen Elizabeth inspects the guard of honour in the station forecourt. Formed by a hundred men of the 4th Devonshire Regiment and accompanied by guard commander Major K.E. Wilkinson, the young Queen (then only 30 years of age) is seen making her way along the lines with equerry-in-waiting Squadron Leader C.C. Blount following behind. One of the 'Moguls' can be seen behind the Royal car in the top picture, along with one of the clerestory roofed Royal carriages, presumably Brake First No. 5155, which led the consist on the journey down the line to Barnstaple. Beyond the train is the roof of the goods shed, with the station building off to the left.
Both Courtney Card, courtesy Ian Huxtable

single line Durston Loop and moved just beyond Lyng Halt, where at 11.28pm it stabled for the night. No. 4971 *Stanway Hall* moved off from the goods shed road at Athelney and joined the rear of the train for heating and braking purposes, thus allowing the 'Castles' to detach and go to Taunton shed overnight. The two 'Moguls' came to collect the train at Lyng the next morning and departed at 8.05am.

It is worth noting that special trains were provided locally to bring school children into Barnstaple to see the Queen. One such train stabled at Barnstaple Town station comprised one of the latest Taunton 'B-sets' (No's 7392 and 7393), separated with four non-corridor Third coaches (No's 2682, 46060, 46167 and 46154) coupled between them. The school children played their part, 2,000 lining the Taw Vale waving their flags, growing to 5,000 by the time Her Majesty left the Queen's Hall and went to the Pannier Market.

The *North Devon Journal-Herald* carried a report of the event on 10th May, the only time the Queen has visited Barnstaple and the first by a reigning monarch.

A Special Train for the Lord Mayor of London

Sir Bernard Waley-Cohen Bart., whose country home was at Honeymead near Simonsbath, was elected as Lord Mayor of London in 1960. A special train was put on from Dulverton to London for friends and relatives to travel up for his inauguration ceremony. Included in the train was a restaurant car with full service.

The Winter of 1963

Sixteen years later came a second colder, even more bitter winter, the bad weather starting on 2nd November 1962. From Boxing Day, a fresh snowfall swept over south-west England and temperatures plummeted, blizzard conditions hitting southern England and Wales for two days. The cold snap lasted for three months and most of the country was frozen in the coldest winter since 1740, over 200 years earlier. Snow drifts of up to 20ft covered Exmoor and the surrounding areas, which resulted in many farms and villages being cut off. When temperatures dropped to -16 degrees celsius (3.2F), the snow was there for the long term and even the Bristol Channel had ice floes, whilst some harbours were frozen. The railway system was thrown into chaos by the ice and drifting snow, and roads were impassable. Outlying farms and villages were saved by RAF rescue teams, who received provisions at Dulverton station that arrived by train once the line was opened with help from the Taunton snow plough and then took them by helicopter to those people and animals most in need. Dulverton itself was cut off from road access (bus) for thirty-one days but those out on Exmoor relied on the helicopter for ten weeks.

The minor halt at Yeo Mill justified its existence in this bad winter. All roads were blocked in the area and the three year old daughter of an Exmoor farmer pierced her eye with a needle. Her father carried her to the halt, took the train to South Molton and she was treated at the cottage hospital.

The appropriately named Mr Fred Winter, formerly a signalman at Bishops Nympton & Molland, related his experience of that winter to Christopher Tull. One night Fred finished at 10.00pm and it took him three hours to walk home to Bishops Nympton, climbing hedges and walking through fields. He decided the next day it would be easier to walk to South Molton and catch the first train up to Molland from there. In all he did this for seven weeks, on occasion sleeping in the signal box to be ready for the first train.

'Flying Scotsman Coming to Devon'

An *Express & Echo* (the Exeter newspaper) report on 11th October 1963 was headlined 'Flying Scotsman *coming to Devon*'. The ex-L&NER Class 'A3' 'Pacific' locomotive No. 4472, which had just recently been saved in January 1963 from the scrapman by Alan Pegler, was scheduled to haul a ten-coach, all-Pullman Ian Allan excursion special titled 'The Western Belle'. The train left London behind No. 4472 at 8.33am on Saturday 19th October, travelling via Newbury and Devizes. Arrival at Taunton was planned for 12.30pm. There, *Flying Scotsman* was taken off and replaced by two Churchward 'Moguls', No's

No's 7332 and 7317 head the ten-coach 'Western Belle' up the bank out of Wiveliscombe station as they head towards Bathealton Tunnel and Waterrow viaduct where, strictly, the front locomotive should have uncoupled from the remainder of the train to make its own way over the viaduct due to weight restrictions. Ten coaches was probably a record for the line, whilst both locomotives were reported to be in a sorry state. *Peter W. Gray*

ABOVE AND BELOW: **The two 'Moguls' storm through South Molton station (scheduled through here at 1.55pm) in preparation for tackling the bank up to Filleigh and are then seen heading up through Hacche Cutting towards Castle Hill.** *Both Bryan Conyard*

7332 and 7317, neither of which were reportedly in good condition. The train was planned to depart from Taunton at 12.40pm to travel over the steeply graded D&SR to Dulverton and on to Barnstaple Junction where arrival was scheduled for 2.15pm.

From Barnstaple, the train went on to Ilfracombe (arrival planned at 3.10pm and departure at 4.25pm) and then to Exeter Central via the Southern/L&SWR route to arrive at 6.13pm, where it was reunited with *Flying Scotsman*. Departure from Exeter was booked for 6.35pm with a planned arrival at Waterloo at 9.52pm. Given the fact that locomotives were prohibited from traversing the D&SR viaducts in tandem, the time allowed over the route provided for the front locomotive to uncouple ahead of each structure and then work its way over, to then wait for the second 'Mogul' and coaches to cross before re-coupling for the onward journey. However, did that actually happen? The Six Bells Junction website carries only the booked timings for the trip, with no other details about what occurred on the day. The 95 minute schedule also still compared favourably with the 111 minutes allowed for in the 1964 time table for the through train from Wolverhampton, although on a summer Saturday this also provided for the crossing of more trains than on a dank October day!

THE BEATLES SPECIAL

The line was used in early March 1964 for the filming of scenes for the Beatles' first movie, *A Hard Days Night*, shot in black and white, which was released later that year. The band along with the actors – including Wilfred Brambell (aka 'Harold Steptoe'), Norman Rossington and Pattie Boyd (who later became Mrs George Harrison), director Richard Lester and the film crew travelled down from London to Taunton and planned to use both the West Somerset Railway and D&SR for shooting their train sequences. The location was supposed to be kept secret but the word got out!

The film, originally entitled *Beatlemania*, portrayed, in the form of a docu-drama, the Beatles' rather hectic pop-star work schedule. It was their first movie and it included a number of Beatles' soundtracks, one song of which was performed in the luggage compartment of the train. The train sequence commences at the beginning of the film at London's Marylebone station and lasts about twenty minutes, ending back there. In between, there are glimpses out of the carriage windows, some of which were shot in more urban areas but there is no obvious view in the film of any stretch of the D&SR! The special train was a big event locally and Beatlemania was at its height, so a number of 'Fab Four' fans turned out on the route to see if they could see their favourite Beatle or even get autographs. It was reported that when the train stopped at South Molton, George Harrison alighted to film his fellow Beatles through the carriage window and the watching crowds with his new movie camera.

The train comprised five Mark 1 coaches, four in maroon and one in carmine and cream or 'blood and custard' as it was nicknamed, and was hauled by North British locomotive No. D6336, displaying special train headcode No. 1Z48. Filming also took place on the Minehead Branch, where similar scenes of fan excitement were evidenced, the train being pulled on that line by 'Hymek' No. D7076.

The Beatles' special train heads east through Bishops Nympton & Molland. *John Spencer Gilks*

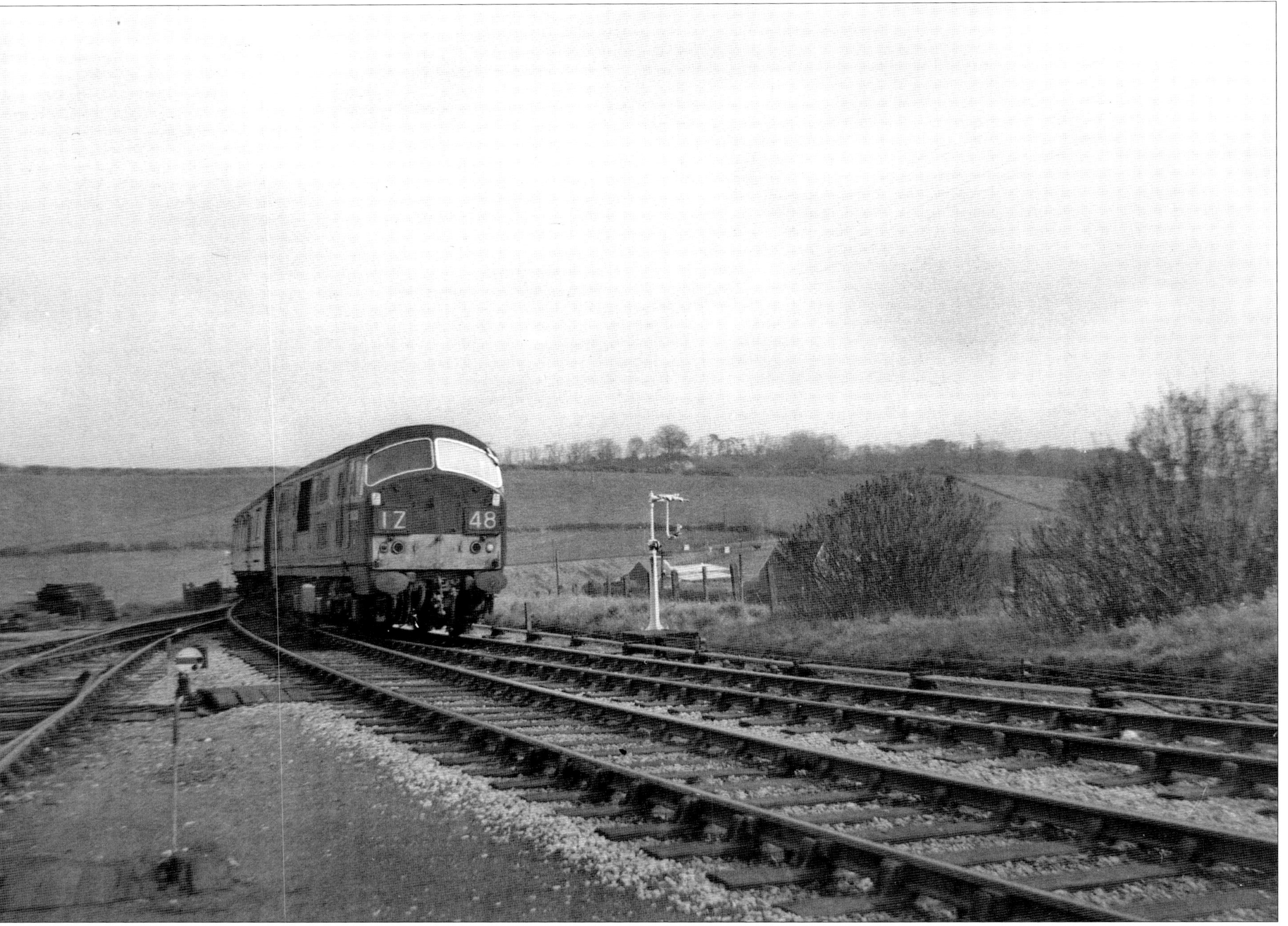

The Down Beatles special about to pass the token apparatus as it runs through Wiveliscombe station during the shooting of *A Hard Day's Night*, with North British Type '2' (later Class '22') No. D6336 in charge. Filming had begun at Marylebone station on Monday 2nd March 1964, with the following week being spent on the train on the Barnstaple and Minehead branches. *Brian Conyard*

LEFT: **The two Ivatts No's 41206 and 41291, coupled bunker to bunker, run round their train on the short visit to Victoria Road on 27th March 1965. Although the train stopped on the run-round loop, not the platform line, most passengers still disembarked for a picture opportunity!**
R.A. Lumber, courtesy Dave Mitchell

BELOW: **With the locomotives now facing the other way, one of the train staff ties the 'Exmoor Ranger' headboard to the smokebox door of No. 41291 in readiness for departure on the next leg of the tour to Ilfracombe.** *Michael Messenger*

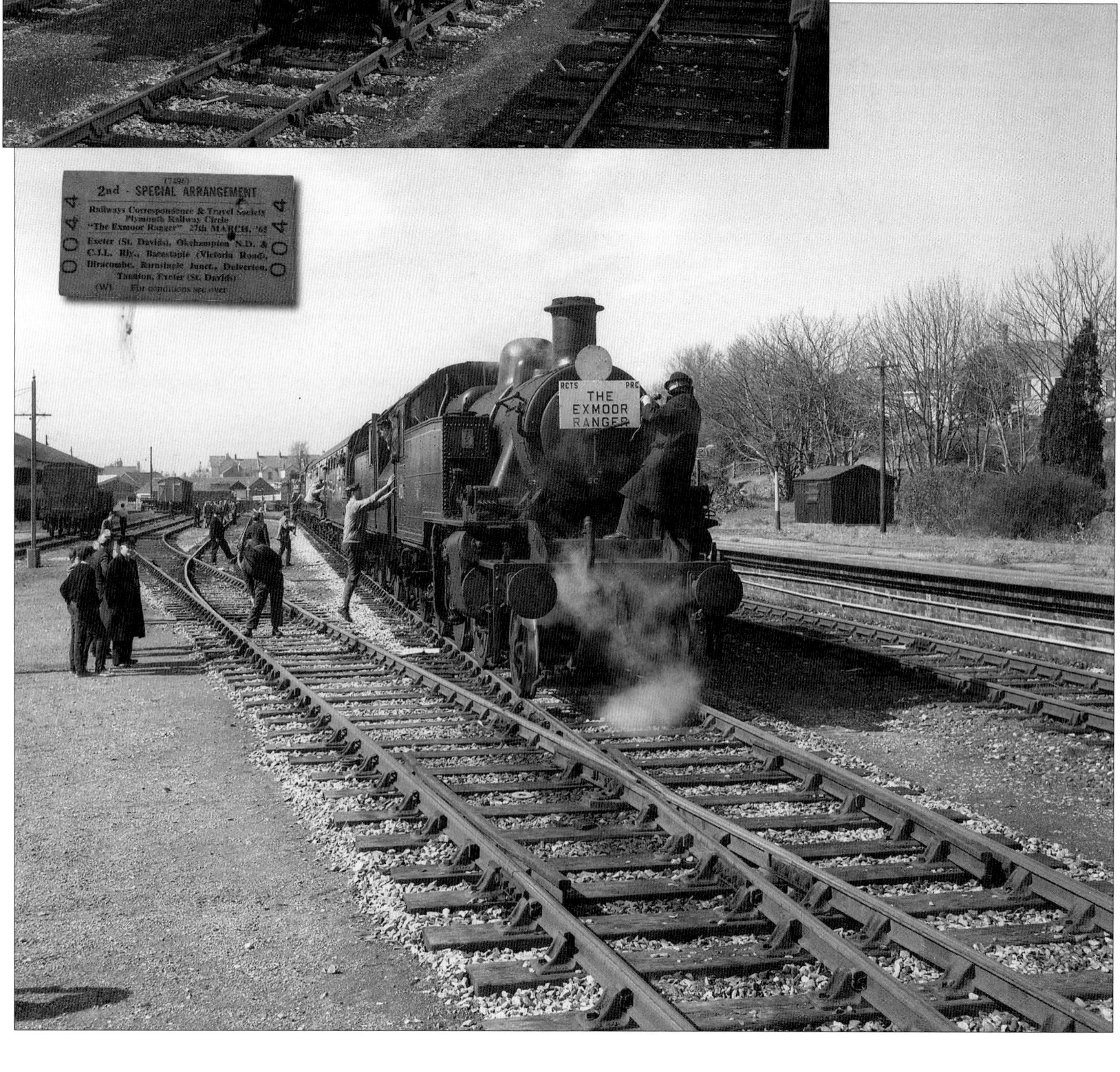

(7496)
2nd - SPECIAL ARRANGEMENT
0044
Railways Correspondence & Travel Society
Plymouth Railway Circle
"The Exmoor Ranger" 27th MARCH, '65
Exeter (St. Davids), Okehampton N.D. & C.J.L. Rly., Barnstaple (Victoria Road), Ilfracombe, Barnstaple Junct., Dulverton, Taunton, Exeter (St. Davids)
(W) For conditions see over
0044

RCTS PRC
THE
EXMOOR
RANGER

THE 'EXMOOR RANGER' RAIL TOUR

The 'Exmoor Ranger' was an enthusiasts' special organised by a joint committee of the Railway Correspondence & Travel Society and the Plymouth Railway Circle on Saturday 27th March 1965 (this was apparently a revised date). It comprised a train of five Mark 1 coaches both open and compartment stock, three in BR maroon livery, each separated by a chocolate and cream coach. There were about 200 enthusiasts on board the train on this warm and sunny spring day, making it ideal for photographers both on the train and by the lineside.

The tour started from Exeter St. Davids at 10.12am with two Ivatt Class '2' 2-6-2T locomotives from Exmouth Junction shed, No's 41206 and 41291, coupled bunker to bunker with No. 41291 at the front. The train ran via Crediton to Okehampton (the first stop where water was replenished), then to Halwill Junction and, after some manoeuvring on to the Bude Branch and setting back into the single platform line, it went up what had been the North Devon & Cornwall Junction Light Railway through Hatherleigh, Torrington and Bideford to Barnstaple. The lower part of this line from Halwill to Meeth had been closed to all traffic about four weeks earlier, so special permission to traverse it had to be granted. After a brief stop at Barnstaple Junction, the train proceeded to Victoria Road, now just a goods depot only. Here the Ivatts ran around the train, allowing time for photographers to take their pictures and also the passage of a DMU on a time-tabled service from Barnstaple Junction to Swimbridge. This was the last run of a steam-hauled passenger train over the D&SR and the last passenger train to visit the old GWR terminus, a joint LCGB/PRC/RCTS tour on 3rd October 1970, the 'Exmoor

PLYMOUTH DIVISION PASSENGER TRAIN ARRANGEMENTS WEEKLY NOTICE NO.13/S (CONTD).

SHEET 2.

SATURDAY 27th MARCH 1965

DOWN TRAINS.

10.12am EXETER ST. DAVIDS to ILFRACOMBE. via Okehampton and Torrington and Return via Taunton. "Exmoor Ranger" Excursion.

	Arr. am.		Dep. am.
As shown in M.M. Notice 73 to :			
Okehampton	10.58	W	11. 9
Meldon Quarry S.B.	11.13		11.22 J
Meldon Jn.	11.26		11.34 K
Ashbury		11/44	pm.
Halwill	11.50	W	12. 0
	pm.		
Hatherleigh	12.21		12.26
Petrockstow	12.39		12.44
Torrington	1.10		1.13
Bideford	1.23	X	1.26 V
Instow		1/31	
Fremington		1/38	
Barnstaple Jn.	1.43	W	1.53
Barnstaple Vic. Rd.	1.59	Z	2.15

	Arr. pm.		Dep. pm.
Barnstaple Jn.	2.21	W	2.29
Barnstaple Town		2/32	
Pottington Box		2/33	
Braunton		2/41	
Mortehoe & W.		2/53	
Ilfracombe	3. 3	Z	3.20
Mortehoe & W.		3/32	
Braunton		3/42	
Barnstaple Jn.	3.53	L	4. 3
South Molton		4/25	
East Anstey		Y	
Dulverton	4.49	X	5.10
Wiveliscombe		5/30	
Norton Fitzwarren		5/45	
Taunton	5.50	Z	6.30

Thence as shown in M.M. Notice 73.

J - Detach one 412XX to run "light" to Meldon Jn.
K - Re-attach 412XX.
V - 12. 5pm Torrington to Exeter Riverside Ft. 7C17 retimed.
W - Water
Y - 3.52pm Torrington Milk to be held to cross 4.20pm Taunton.
Z - Engine run round.

To be worked by 2 x 412XX Class engines Exeter St. Davids to Barnstaple Jn. via Okehampton and Torrington. Thence to Ilfracombe and return to Barnstaple Jn. 22XX Class engine Barnstaple Jn. to Exeter St. Davids via Taunton.

Formation : Set 57 strengthened to load 5 from Newton Abbot

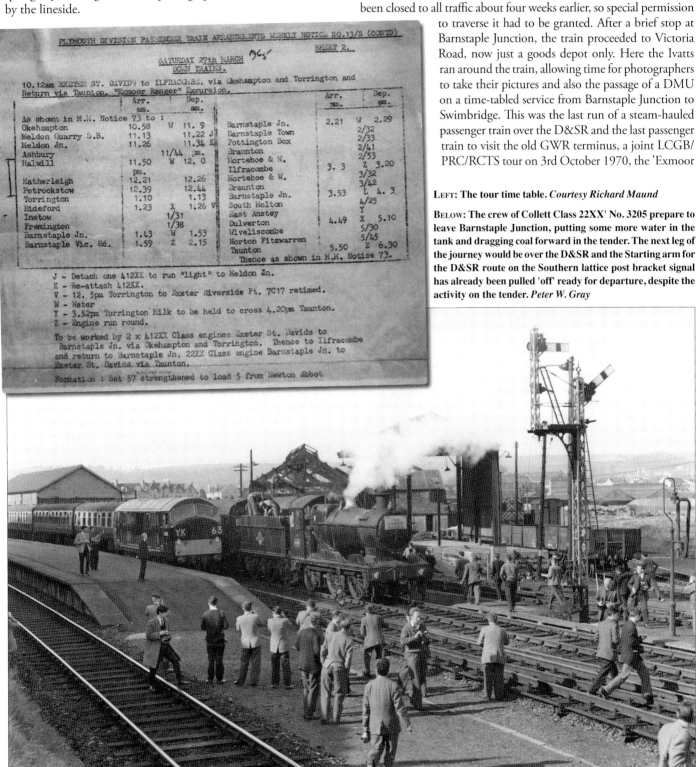

LEFT: The tour time table. ***Courtesy Richard Maund***

BELOW: The crew of Collett Class 22XX' No. 3205 prepare to leave Barnstaple Junction, putting some more water in the tank and dragging coal forward in the tender. The next leg of the journey would be over the D&SR and the Starting arm for the D&SR route on the Southern lattice post bracket signal has already been pulled 'off' ready for departure, despite the activity on the tender. ***Peter W. Gray***

A fine side study of No. 3205 at Dulverton, with the tender again being trimmed; more water was also taken here. With passenger services by this date now in the hands of DMUs and the single daily goods over the route also diesel hauled, No. 3205 is believed to be the last steam locomotive to travel over the D&SR. The course of the River Barle can be seen running across the picture just above and parallel with the engine's boiler, with the buildings of Perry Farm in the centre distance. ***Tim Stephens***

With all of the passengers back on board, the special is about to depart from Dulverton, having crossed with a two-car DMU which had arrived on a service to Barnstaple Junction and was now standing at the Down platform. ***Peter W. Gray***

Belle', taking place six months after Victoria Road goods depot was closed. Setting out from Exeter St. Davids to traverse the Ilfracombe Branch on its final day of operation, it ran as well to Meeth Siding beyond Torrington and would almost certainly have included the goods line to Barnstaple GWR too if it had still been open.

Returning to Barnstaple Junction, from there the special went to Ilfracombe. Having run on ahead light engine from the Junction, the two Ivatts were banked from Braunton by Collett 0-6-0 No. 3205 running tender first up to Mortehoe summit. It was detached at Mortehoe and then followed on light engine again to Ilfracombe, where it coupled-up and then hauled the train up the ferociously steep 1 in 36 incline out of the terminus back towards Barnstaple, with the two Ivatts now acting as bankers. Having been detached at Mortehoe, the two tank locomotives then ran light engine to Exeter, following in the wake of the 'Exmoor Ranger' as far as Barnstaple. After a brief water replenishment stop at Barnstaple Junction, by which time the train was about thirty minutes behind schedule, No. 3205 and its train headed for the D&SR via the East Chord, avoiding Victoria Road as the direct line out from there had by this date been lifted.

At Dulverton it passed another DMU on a regular branch service. No. 3205's tender was also topped-up with water and there was another photo-stop for the enthusiasts on board. On arrival at Taunton (now about twenty minutes behind schedule), the '22XX' was uncoupled and the stock shunted, thereby releasing the locomotive to Taunton shed for turning. It is believed this was the last steam locomotive to be turned here, as the connection to the depot was taken out after this, the shed having been closed in October 1964. No. 3205 then returned to its coaches, which had been repositioned to the Down side of the station ready for departure. The train then proceeded back to Exeter where it arrived at about 7.50pm, still twenty minutes down on the planned arrival time of 7.30pm. The adult fare for this 180-mile excursion, lasting more than nine hours, was £2 5s with children charged at £1 5s.

ANIMALS ON THE LINE

Being a country railway passing through agricultural and grazing pastures for virtually the whole of its length, there were numerous incidents of animals on the line. In such circumstances, it was the responsibility of the signalman to protect the line and the safety of travelling passengers and the animals causing the obstruction, as indicated in the Signalling chapter in Volume 2 (page 460).

In accordance with the GWR Regulations of 1936, the signalman in one box would be required to communicate with his counterpart in the adjoining box '*on a speaking instrument and take the necessary steps to have the line cleared. Until the line is cleared all trains allowed to proceed must be brought to a stand and the driver verbally informed of the circumstances and instructed to proceed cautiously.*'.

THE D&SR AS A DIVERSIONARY ROUTE

The D&SR, as far as Dulverton and in conjunction with the Exe Valley Railway, had the ability to take certain trains diverted off the main line from time to time. This could be when flooding of the main line occurred south of Cullompton in the Culm Valley, in the Hele & Bradnich area, for example, or where there were breakdowns or engineering works on the main line. In the case of emergency diversions, northbound trains would run up the Exe Valley as far as Tiverton and then rejoin the main line at Tiverton Junction, given that access to the Up main line there was straightforward. For southbound trains, access to the Tiverton Branch and thence the Exe Valley would have been more difficult, as this would necessitate a reversal from the Down Main line onto the Up Main at Tiverton Junction and on to the Tiverton Branch. As a consequence, southbound trains would more usually run via the D&SR to Dulverton, arriving at the Down platform there. The locomotive would then run round before the train would head back out to Morebath Junction and then down the Exe Valley. However, this posed its own problem, namely that of suitable motive power.

The Exe Valley was classified as a 'Yellow' route so only 'small Prairies', 0-6-0 Collets, and Pannier tanks could be rostered to work this leg; 'Moguls' (classified as 'Blue') would of course be able to work the D&SR section. What is clear is that the powerful main line express locomotives were unable to work either route, so substitute motive power had to be found when these diversions occurred.

The tank engines were underpowered for the heavy express loads, so special working arrangements had to apply. 'Large Prairie' locomotives were allowed on the Exe Valley (despite their Blue route availability) but they would work unassisted, whilst 'Mogul' 2-6-0s could also work down the Exe Valley under special circumstances. If double-heading was necessary, then it would be either two 'Small Prairies' together or a 'Small Prairie' and a 'Mogul'. These substitutes would usually be attached at Taunton or Exeter before traversing the branch.

When the D&SR and Exe Valley lines were used as a war-time diversionary route to keep the main line clear for military and essential traffic, all Up and Down trains would run via Dulverton. As indicated in the signalling section in Volume 2 (Chapter 9), the D&SR signal boxes, along with the Exe Valley ones, were manned continuously in the war years to facilitate this. In 1944, the main line was closed at Hele when a bomb was dropped on the line and all traffic was routed via the D&SR and Exe Valley. It is understood that on this occasion the Up and Down 'Cornish Riviera Express' trains crossed at Bampton; 'Small Prairies' were the respective train engines with 'Moguls' as pilots for both trains.

ACCIDENTS AND MISHAPS

As with all railway operation, safety is paramount but accidents and incidents do happen and in this respect the D&SR was no different. What is set out below is a selection of those which have been uncovered during research; it does not purport to be a complete list of all the incidents that occurred but, as far as the author is aware, all of the important ones have been noted.

1870 AND 1871

A young lad was clearing out the ash pan of a locomotive when a plug or valve in the boiler opened, causing boiling water to scald him to death. He was only 16 years of age. The accident occurred in September 1870, during construction of the line, so the lad would have been an employee of the contractor and this would have been one of the contractor's locomotives.

In January 1871, a brakesman from Crediton was coupling two wagons near Castle Hill, when some further loose wagons rolled down the grade and struck them. He did not have time to get clear and was caught between the buffers of the wagons he was coupling, dying from his injuries. This would again have been during construction of the line.

29TH MARCH 1873

Under the heading '*A Couple of Fast Runaways*', the *North Devon Journal* (NDJ) reported on 3rd April 1873 that, on Saturday 29th March, a couple of loaded ballast wagons set off on their own from Castle Hill and travelled back towards Barnstaple for seven miles, despite two adverse inclines en route. A new broad gauge contractor's locomotive (possibly *Venus*) had pushed the two laden wagons up to Castle Hill, where they were uncoupled and left after being 'trigged' – that is a large piece of wood being put between the spoked wheels of the wagons to act as a retarder. The locomotive had started on its return trip to Barnstaple but the wooden retarder broke and the wagons started to roll back to Barnstaple on their own. The workers at the station tried to stop them by throwing large sleepers in front of the wheels but these broke and the trucks continued on their way (for an idea of the sheer size of broad gauge wagons, see the view taken during construction on pages 70-71 of Volume 1).

They were eventually stopped at Barnstaple by colliding at great force with two wagons loaded with slate (the property of a Mr Dendle, builder) and a locomotive. The crew of the locomotive spotted the impending danger and jumped clear, prior to impact. Most of the slate was damaged, whilst the locomotive's buffers were twisted and the the pipe supplying water from the tender broken. In addition, another truck was pushed off the rails and onto a heap of coal. It was fortunate that no one was injured on this occasion. This was seven months before the opening of the line from Wiveliscombe on to Barnstaple, so presumably the slate had been destined for use in the construction of the roofs of the station building and goods shed.

23RD APRIL 1873

This accident occurred away from the railway but is connected with it. *Advance*, a road locomotive (or traction engine) that was employed to draw ballast waggons during construction of the line, was being transported away from the area following its sale by Messrs Crawley & Co of Bristol, a few weeks previously. As it approached the Barnstaple road bridge, the iron spokes of one of the rear wheels broke and the locomotive crashed to the ground, with the iron axle burying itself in the road. It was some hours before the locomotive could be moved, causing some disruption at a crucial area in the town. It would seem that the cast iron 'tire' (*sic*) had a serious crack and this had caused the break. A new wheel was eventually cast for it by a Mr J.D. Young.

21ST JULY 1873

Another accident reported which was linked to the construction of the railway was in the NDJ on 24th July 1873. A load of wagons for the D&SR were being horse-drawn by road from the L&SWR station to Victoria Road when, on the descent into the square from the bridge, a failure to apply the correct braking led to the horses drawing the load to lose control and the trucks ran into Mr Curtis' chemist shop. Fortunately, an iron post by the shop stopped the runaways from doing too much damage to property.

11TH NOVEMBER 1873

The NDJ reported on 13th November that the new railway had escaped a serious '*accident christening*'. The line having opened throughout just twelve days earlier on 1st of the month, a train left Barnstaple at 9.00pm and '*in shunting on the rather dangerous bit of metal outside the goods shed at Swimbridge, in some way or other left the metals, and caused a considerable obstruction of traffic, the down train being delayed nearly an hour in consequence.*'. This seems a very colourful way of describing a derailment, with the '*rather dangerous bit of metal*' referred to seemingly being the point for the siding at the east end of the goods loop! This was also the first full day of goods traffic on the D&SR.

6TH MARCH 1875

The *West Somerset Free Press* reported that the night goods train from Taunton to Barnstaple was derailed just west of Wiveliscombe. The 45-ton engine left the track and narrowly missed falling into a mill stream but the driver managed to jump clear after first shutting off steam. There was no information on the level of disruption and delays or for how long the line was closed. The locomotive involved sounds like one of the B&ER 4-4-0 saddle tanks built between 1855 and 1873, which weighed just shy of forty-five tons.

29th July 1875

A report in the *Chard & Ilminster News* for Saturday 7th August 1875 published details of an enquiry held by the district Coroner, Mr Munckton, at Pane's Golden Lion Inn, East Reach, Taunton. Mr Henry Frost* was the engine driver of the 1.15pm Barnstaple departure on the previous Thursday (28th July) and his fireman was 22 year old Mr Fred Stone, of Barnstaple. Frost reported that the train arrived at Milverton at about 3.00pm. On leaving that station, Stone said he had two or three potatoes which he would put in the safety valve of the engine to cook for his tea, so he climbed onto the boiler for that purpose. Immediately, Frost heard a blow on the watch-board as they passed under the Pig & Whistle bridge in the parish of Oake and he then saw Stone lying on the coal on the tender. Having pulled him up, Frost saw that Stone was injured and it would seem that his head had hit one of the girders of the bridge. On arrival at Norton Fitzwarren, the circumstances were related to Mr Chapman (the station master) and Mr Parsons, the guard on the train, who suggested that Stone should be taken to Taunton by the train, where at once he was driven in a cab to the hospital. Mr Farrant, the surgeon who attended Stone at the hospital shortly after his admission, found him suffering from a fractured skull and he died later that evening.

It seemed to be the custom of those on the engine to use the safety valve for the purpose of cooking and more specifically for warming tea. The Coroner stated (somewhat obviously) that it '*seems to be a dangerous practice*', to which Frost replied '*all things are dangerous to venturesome persons*'. Stone's back must have been towards the bridge when he met with the accident, and the Coroner stated that he had acted very foolishly and should have at least checked there was no bridge when he ventured onto the boiler. It appears that the accident was '*to be wholly due to Stone's folly*' and a verdict of 'accidental death' was returned. The proceedings were watched by Inspector Green of the B&ER and it was also reported in the *Somerset County Gazette*.

*** See Volume 1, Chapter 3, page 75, where it is recorded that Henry Frost was the driver of the first train to Barnstaple on 1st November 1873.**

11th November 1878

On 6th December 1878, Major R.E. Marindin, inspecting officer for the Railway Department of the Board of Trade, reported on the accident that had occurred at Bishops Nympton & Molland (which the Major referred to as Molland & Bishops Nympton in his report) four weeks earlier on 11th November.

The 8.40pm Down passenger train from Taunton, consisting of a 39-ton, 4-wheel coupled, bogie tank-engine, Composite carriage with brake compartment, ordinary Composite carriage and Third Class carriage with brake compartment, entered the passing loop at Bishops Nympton & Molland station at about 10.00pm at too high a speed. As a consequence, it ran through the station and came into collision with the 9.20pm Up mixed train from Barnstaple, on the single line just beyond the loop points. The Up train consisted of tender engine No. 2039, two wagons, a brake-van and one passenger carriage, and was drawing slowly up to the Up Home signal, which was at danger.

There were only three passengers on each train and just one of those was injured, a Mr Thomas Goulding, a bank clerk from Exeter, who broke a rib. However, the rolling stock incurred the following damage, albeit none of the vehicles were derailed:

- Down Train – leading bufferbeam, buffers, lifeguard and leading end of frame of the engine broken. Two buffers on Third Class and Composite carriage broken.
- Up Train – leading bufferbeam, both cylinder covers, right-hand cylinder, leading end of frame, buffers, lifeguard, bogie frame and leading axleboxes of engine broken, one buffer rod broken and one bent on brake van.

One rail and three sleepers were also damaged.

Evidence was taken from the driver of the Down train, one Henry Frost again, his fireman T. Tucker, William Pope the guard and James Elston, driver of the Up train, along with his guard, Henry Govier, and station master Walter Hole and porter Frank Pollard.

The adverse weather conditions were a significant factor that night, it being wild and stormy, with the Down train encountering sleet for most of its journey, which from Anstey had turned to snow. The Down train was on time (9.50 pm) at East Anstey but the 4½ mile down grade from Anstey to Molland, along with the slippery rails caused by the weather conditions, conspired against the driver. Frost had now been driving for sixteen years and had operated on the D&SR since it opened five years earlier, so he knew the line well. Steam was shut off and he had instructed the fireman to put on the handbrake (which manoeuvred a wooden block onto each of the coupled wheels) just after leaving East Anstey. The brakes were eased and tightened down the bank and put on fully about 1½ miles before Molland. He also tried to sand the rails but the pipes were choked with snow. About a mile from Molland, he blew the engine's whistle to attract the attention of the guard and to get him to apply the rear brake, which he duly did. Despite this, the train did not slow sufficiently and ran through the station at about 8-9 miles an hour, failing to stop at the platform. As it reached the Up Home signal some 30 yards west of the station, the driver tried to reverse the engine but it skidded and then ran into the slowly moving Up train at about 5mph, about 40 yards west of the signal, on a falling gradient of 1 in 155 and 70 yards outside the station loop. Driver Elston of the Up train admitted to not seeing the approaching Down train until it was within two engine lengths of him and neither did he hear a whistle, because of the appalling weather conditions. All evidence seemed to indicate that the signals were not at fault and their lights were burning brightly, and that the drivers and firemen were '*quite sober*'.

Despite Driver Frost's lengthy experience, Major Marindin blamed him for the accident for '*not having got his train under proper control when approaching Molland & Bishop's Nympton station, and so overrunning the station loop*'. Marindin acknowledged the severity of the weather conditions but felt that Frost, in view of his knowledge of the line, should have '*commenced to take all possible steps for stopping*

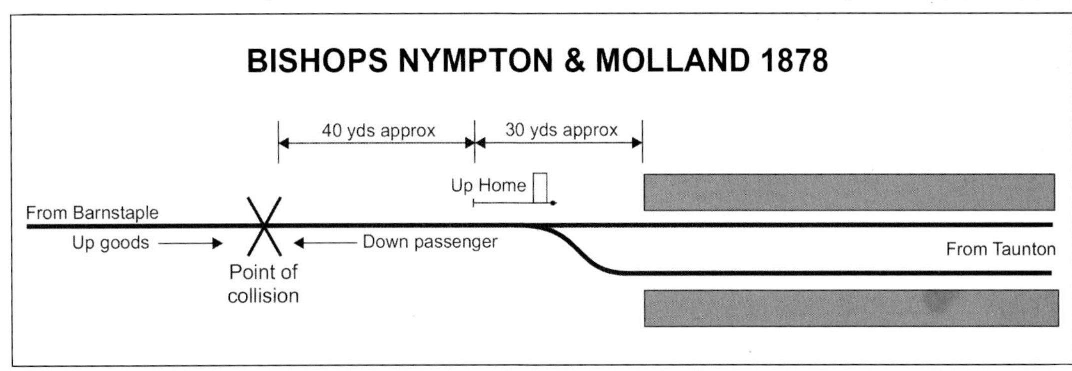

his train sooner in consequence'.

The breakdown gang was telegraphed at Barnstaple and Taunton. Mr Gibson, the divisional superintendent from Taunton, and that breakdown gang duly arrived, with Mr Keedwell, station master at Barnstaple and the gang from there arriving soon after. Working through the night, the line was clear by 10.00am the next morning. It is understood that the passengers on the trains stayed at the Black Cock Inn whilst the line was cleared.

Rail on the Line

Mr John Dodd was the station master at Castle Hill in 1879. His brother-in-law, a Mr John Tozer, was suspected of putting a length of rail across the track at Castle Hill Viaduct, with intent to derail a train. Dodd challenged Tozer over this accusation and an affray resulted where Tozer threatened to kill Dodd. The case was withdrawn when Tozer agreed to leave the area and pay costs.

Traffic Interruption on the Devon & Somerset Railway

A slight mystery has been solved with the discovery, by Toby Clempson, of an article in the *West Somerset Free Press* of 16th November 1889. Volume 2 (page 255) refers to the original stone bridge at Milverton potentially being replaced when the station had improvements made to it in 1880. However, this article not only confirms the date as 1889 but also the reason. The bridge had been showing signs of weakness for some time and, indeed, was cracked in several places, making '*ominous indications which rendered it imperative to stop the* [road] *traffic*'. By arrangement with the District Highway Board, Mr Hammett, the GWR locomotive and engineering superintendent at Taunton, made preparations to demolish it and have it rebuilt. A Sunday was originally chosen, when the line was closed to all traffic but the discovery of the cracking forced the line to close on a Friday, with the consequent interruption to rail traffic, so that the bridge could be replaced.

Accommodation rails had been laid to the side of the permanent way and some stone work removed in advance. Mr Campfield, the Exeter divisional passenger superintendent, was wired with the news of the emergency and arrived at Milverton by special train. He was followed by a breakdown train and sixty men, who set about demolishing the bridge. Several attempts were made to blow the bridge up with dynamite but it was found preferable to demolish it brick by brick, and by 6.00pm the task was accomplished and the line cleared.

During the blockage, train services to and from Barnstaple were diverted via Tiverton Junction, Tiverton and the then new Exe Valley line to Dulverton. There was also an unspecified service working on one side of the bridge, which may have been westwards to and from Dulverton or possibly a Milverton-Taunton shuttle. Mr Campfield was responsible for directing these special arrangements from Dulverton, which would suggest the former is more likely.

The Highway Board subsequently reported '*Main Roads – The Great Western Railway Company have erected the new iron girder bridge at Milverton station, and the road is now open for traffic.*'.

Helping the Barnstaple & Ilfracombe Railway

On Christmas Eve 1889, there was a derailment of the engine hauling the 3.54pm Ilfracombe departure, at Foxhunters Inn, between Mortehoe and Braunton. The L&SWR train had two GWR through coaches attached that were going to work on to Taunton. Although the GWR passengers on board were inconvenienced by this mishap, the D&SR put on a special train to get them to Taunton, as they had missed their planned connection because of the accident.

The First Norton Fitzwarren Accident, 11th November 1890

Although the accident did not occur on the D&SR, it should be observed that the branch played a part in the manoeuvres that led to it and is thus recorded here for completeness and as a mark of respect to the ten passengers that were killed.

On 11th November 1890, a standard gauge Down goods train bound for Exeter, which had departed from Bristol at 6.40pm the previous evening, arrived at Norton Fitzwarren at 12.36am to shunt. By this time, the train, which comprised thirty-eight wagons hauled by 'Standard Goods' 0-6-0 No. 1100 with a broad gauge pilot engine attached, was running an hour late from Taunton. With the final eradication of the broad gauge only eighteen months in the future, it should be noted that the line here was, and had been for many years by this date, dual gauge.

The broad gauge pilot engine was detached and initially placed on the Down main line whilst shunting was carried out. It was later sent on to either the West Somerset Railway or the Barnstaple Branch (reports are inconsistent) to be out of the way for shunting the goods. At 1.05am, shunting had been completed and the train was ready to proceed towards Tiverton Junction. However, the 9.55pm ex-Bristol fast Down goods was now due through and there was no siding space with which to temporarily store the 6.40pm train. It was therefore shunted on to the Up main line to allow the fast goods to pass on the Down main line, which it duly did at 1.17am. Meanwhile, the headlamps had been changed to warn Up trains of the presence of the stationary Down goods but once the fast train had gone though, Charles Noble, driver of the 6.40pm Bristol goods, assumed he would get the road, cross back onto the Down main, rejoin his pilot and be on their way. In preparation for this, he had the fireman change the front headlamp back from red to green, then the normal colour. Soon after they saw the lights and steam of an Up broad gauge train rapidly approaching at around 60mph. This was a special train from Plymouth to Paddington, with broad gauge saddle tank 4-4-0 No. 2051 hauling two 8-wheeled coaches and a van, carrying mostly miners travelling back to northern England, who had just arrived back from the Cape of Good Hope on the liner *Northam Castle*. This train ran head on in to the goods, the impact being of great violence and although both locomotives remained upright, debris piled 30ft into the air.

The changing back of the lamps on the Down goods had not helped matters, as the red lamp on the front may have warned the driver of the Up train, John Scott of Exeter, to take action to stop or slow his train. However, it was the signalman who was most culpable, as he had simply forgotten that he had put the goods on the Up line when he had given 'line clear' to the Up special. Scott and his fireman John Thomas were badly injured but survived.

It was suggested in the accident report that the Down goods should have been shunted onto the Barnstaple Branch, as no siding space was available that evening. Sadly, that did not happen and the result was the deaths of ten passengers (out of fifty on board), with nine others and the guard injured, along with the aforementioned driver and fireman. Signalman George Rice, aged 63 and a Norton signalman for twenty-seven years, was charged with the manslaughter of one of the passengers (Robert Walker). However, he had a previously unblemished record but had sustained an head injury earlier in the year, when he was knocked down by a light engine, resulting in a depressed fracture of the skull, broken ribs and fourteen weeks off work; his medicine had also made him drowsy. He was found guilty of negligence (but not criminally) at the inquest and committed to the assizes, where he was then acquitted by the jury. Driver Noble of the Bristol goods was found negligent for the early exchange of

The aftermath of the Norton Fitzwarren accident, with a lone policeman holding back onlookers and the roof of Norton Fitzwarren station building and a part of the footbridge visible in the left background. 'Standard Goods' No. 1100 has come off the rails and reared up somewhat but the solid squat broad gauge saddle tank remained resolutely on the track. Given the impact was at around 50-60mph, albeit the 4-4-0 was stationary, the fact that both crews survived although badly injured was a miracle. *Neil Parkhouse collection*

The remains of the two broad gauge carriages of the Up boat train prior to being hauled away. No. 302, which had originally been a 46ft 6ins six-compartment clerestory with a centre luggage compartment, built between 1876 and 1884, had been reduced to just half a compartment in length. Its near identical compatriot looks undamaged at a quick glance but had lost the nearer pair of axles, the coach now being supported on a trolley to be towed slowly back to Taunton; however, it would almost certainly have been scrapped as the broad gauge era was ending. The axles on these coaches were not on bogies but were fixed. A standard gauge box van can be glimpsed behind the second coach and note the 'PLYMOUTH' nameboards on the side near each end. The photograph does provide a rare glimpse of the roomy, 10ft 6ins wide interior of a broad gauge carriage compartment. ***Neil Parkhouse collection***

lamps and Guard Lowe was also negligent for failing to go to the box to remind the signalman that his train was held on the Up line.

Colonel Frederick Henry Rich RE, the investigating inspector, recommended the installation of refuge sidings where shunting could be carried out and lifting bars to lock the signals to protect a train standing on a running line. Ironically, the installation of these refuge sidings would play a part in the 1940 accident, as discussed below.

There was some confusion over which branch the broad gauge pilot locomotive was stabled on, the inspecting officer mentioning the D&SR but the guard referred to the WSR in the BoT report. In the event, the train was almost certainly stabled on the Minehead line, as although both had been converted to standard gauge (the D&SR in 1881 and the WSR in 1882), a few hundred yards of mixed gauge was left in place on the WSR as a refuge for broad gauge trains (as recounted by Ian Coleby in *The Minehead Branch 1848-1971*, page 141. Lightmoor Press 2006 & 2011). There is also a photograph of Norton Fitzwarren in 1892 (Volume 2, page 246) just prior to final conversion which shows this mixed gauge track on the first part of the Minehead Branch but standard gauge only on the Up section visible of the D&SR.

This accident resulted in the adoption of Rule 55 by all railways in Britain. Namely, that when a train had halted at a signal, the driver was to blow his whistle and if the signalman did not lower his board after three minutes in clear weather, or immediately if it were foggy or snowy, he must send a fireman, guard or shunter to the signal box to inform the signalman of the train's presence and not leave until a collar had been placed on the relevant signal levers to prevent a conflicting movement. The person sent was also to sign the train register.

The broad gauge locomotive, one of the class of twenty-six ex-B&ER passenger saddle tanks, originally No. 88 built in May 1873 by the Avonside Engine Company, was scrapped but 'Standard Goods' No. 1100 was repaired and put in a further twenty-six years of work before being sold to the War Department in 1916 and sent to Serbia to haul military trains for the Railway Operating Division.

1908

A fatal accident occurred at Filleigh on 8th June 1908 to Mr Samuel Beer, who was employed by the GWR as a driver. Beer was with the 7.40pm passenger service from Taunton to Barnstaple, which had two engines attached, he being in charge of the second of them, *i.e.*, the train engine rather than the pilot. On arrival at Filleigh, Beer got down from the footplate on the side away from the platform, apparently to look round the bearings, returning a few moments later to take away an oil feeder. Immediately afterwards, the guard gave the signal to start and fireman Hall, who was on the platform side of the engine, moved across the footplate to tell Beer that the right of way had been given. No sooner had he reached that side when the train started to move, because the fireman on the first engine had released the hand brake and they were on a falling gradient. Hall, seeing Beer on the ground, shouted to stop and applied the vacuum and steam brake, the train coming to a standstill after it had moved about 2ft. Hall jumped down to the ballast and found that Beer's right arm was caught between the spokes of the driving wheel and the connecting rod. It was subsequently amputated but, sadly, Beer died from his injuries.

It was found that the train was started in a regular manner, there being no instruction stipulating that signals must be exchanged between the engineman of an assisting engine (with whom the responsibility rests for the observance of signals and the working of the brake) and the engineman of the second engine, when a train is being drawn by two engines. The driver of the leading engine looked back before telling his fireman to release the brake and, seeing a figure through the spectacle glass of the second engine assumed that all was well; he could not be held to blame. Beer had informed no one of what he intended to do and being a driver of twenty-three years experience, he should have known that it was extremely risky to place his arm in such a position in the driving wheels. There did not appear to be a necessity to attend to the bearings at the time and the Inspector, Mr John P.S. Main, concluded that the accident was due to want of reasonable care on the part of Beer himself, who had been on duty eight hours when the accident occurred.

It was suggested that the GWR might consider laying down instructions to the effect that before starting a train drawn by two engines, signals must be exchanged between the driver of the leading engine and the driver of the second engine.

Later in the same year, Main reported on an accident at Venn Cross. On 28th October, Mr H. Gill was acting as assisting brakesman with the 7.10am Taunton to South Molton goods and had been on duty for two and a half hours when the incident happened. It was about 9.00am and some wagons loaded with timber and an open wagon were to be attached to the train. As they were in front of the engine, in what could be termed the headshunt siding, the only practicable way to get them to the rear was to tow-rope them along the goods shed line. The engine could then reverse into that siding to pick them up and attach them to the train for onward transportation. Gill placed the hook of the tow-rope (a steel wire hawser 53ft in length) into the hole in the solebar of the centre wagon, the other end being attached to the drawbar hook of the engine, which was run along a diverging connection from the siding. After the wagons had passed the engine and were entering the shed, Gill said he detached the hook and threw it to the ground but he thought it then caught on some part of the wagon. As he was applying the brake, the hawser broke and his right hand was caught and injured by it. None of the men there were clear on what happened but it would seem that, despite his experience at tow-roping, Gill was late trying to release the hook, which then turned right round. As the hawser, which was noted to be in good condition prior to the incident, tightened with the strain of the loaded wagons, it snapped when he was endeavouring to free it.

Main indicated that Gill was probably not as careful as he might have been in carrying out the shunt but the mishap may be classed as incidental to the method of working which '*at this pace is attended with considerable risk*'. Given the layout of the sidings, it was customary to tow-rope the wagons over the connections leading to the goods shed siding from one of the diverging roads. The result was that after the wagons had been started by a tug from the engine and the engine had been brought to rest, the rope slackened out and unless released quickly at that point, it would be carried past the engine and then either catch some obstruction whilst dragging along the ground or be restrained in pulling the wagons up. It was suggested that other arrangements be made so that the practice could be avoided in future.

This illustrates one of the dangers of the job and how shunting took place at remote locations when the track layout did not facilitate it in a particular direction.

The May 1909 *Appendix 5 to the GW Service Time Table* had a section on tow ropes and the places where they maybe used. As far as concerns the Barnstaple Branch, it stated:

'*The use of a Tow Rope is prohibited by the General Manager's Circular No. 1904 of 28th August 1902 unless specially authorised at certain places, where, owing to the formation of the sidings, it is absolutely necessary to use a Tow Rope. Stations at which the use of a Tow Rope is authorised until further notice are ... Wiveliscombe, Venn Cross, South Molton, Filleigh ...* [etc]'.

As can be seen, Venn Cross was on the authorised list.

1909 – Another Fatality

A GWR Accidents Report commented on an incident at Barnstaple locomotive yard on 5th May 1909. Mr F.J. Toms, a fireman, attempted to climb on engine No. 1496, a 'Metro' tank, as it was moving to the coaling stage. However, he failed to get onto the footplate before he was caught between the coal stage wall and the tank of the engine, suffering severe internal crushing from which he subsequently died. The inquest recorded a verdict of accidental death and there was a recommendation that the coal stage wall be set back to allow more clearance.

The breakdown gangs were an important part of keeping a railway running when an incident occurred and **Table 12.3** below, from the May 1909 *Appendix to Section 5 of the GW Service Time Table*, detailed the location and duties of those with responsibility for the D&SR.

Rerailing ramps were also kept in the goods yards at Dulverton and South Molton and at Barnstaple GWR in the breakdown van. Snow ploughs were kept ready for immediate use at Barnstaple and, as elsewhere, were the responsibility of the Locomotive Department there. Two loose screw couplings were kept at South Molton

Table 12.3: D&SR Breakdown Gangs 1909

Breakdown Gangs Stationed In	For the Undermentioned Stations
Taunton	Uphill Junction(inclusive) to Tiverton Junction (inclusive) including the Chard and Minehead Branches and Norton Fitzwarren to Dulverton ... [etc]
Barnstaple	Barnstaple to Dulverton (exclusive)
A Traffic Department Guard must in all cases accompany Breakdown trains	
When necessary to telegraph for the Breakdown gangs particulars must be given of the Train or Engine to which the mishap has occurred, what vehicles are off the line, whether Main Line or Siding, and if the Main Line is blocked or otherwise	In all cases of engine failures, or breakdowns, where Locomotive power or assistance's to be wired for, special care should be taken to advise the Station from which assistance is sought, of the nature of the failure, and the advice should state particularly whether the Engine can be moved or not, so that the Staff at the station receiving the message may clearly understand what has to be provided for, and be able to shape their arrangements accordingly. See Rule i General Rules and Regulations

MILVERTON ACCIDENT 1915

The *West Somerset Free Press* reported on 4th September that two trains collided at Milverton station. One was carrying 180 mules which were to be used for war purposes. Four livestock trucks were badly damaged and one mule was killed.

1931

The official accident reports in 1931 gave details of a small mishap at Barnstaple GWR, below, involving porter D.W. Helyar. One assumes that his injury was minor, as no mention is made of the unfortunate man's state of health but it goes to show how a moment's lapse in concentration could lead to an accident at any time on the railway, fortunately without any serious consequences in this instance.

1933

On the 5th September a Mr H. Boden was found lying in a wagon in the siding at Morebath with head injuries. It seems he was assisting the unloading of peat from a high sided wagon and when goods guard Mr W.G. Rogers, walked around the said wagon prior to shunting four more loaded ones against it, Boden was unobserved at this time. He was an old man and it seems he was resting in one of the corners of the wagon, out of sight of the guard and so was unaware of the shunt and consequently got injured.

GREAT WESTERN RAILWAY.

SIR,

I have the honour to report for the information of the Minister of Transport, in accordance with the Order of the 19th March, the result of my Inquiry into the circumstances attending the accident which occurred on the 6th March, 1931, to D. W. Helyar at Barnstaple on the Great Western Railway.

Helyar, who is employed as a porter, was assisting in shunting operations in the goods yard, his duty being to pin down brakes. About 12.20 p.m. certain trucks, which were being loaded from a motor lorry, were moved to an adjoining siding. Shunter Ebsworthy, with whom Helyar was working, told the latter to inform the man in charge of the lorry that he could continue his loading operations at the altered location. To reach the wagons the motor lorry had to be taken over a level crossing. As this was being done a shunt of three wagons was loose-shunted into the adjacent siding. Helyar, who had his pole under his arm, was caught by these wagons, the approach of which he had not observed, and his right arm was nipped between the buffers of the leading wagon and the first stationary wagon in the siding.

There was no necessity for Helyar to stand foul of the rails at all, and his lack of care in doing so was the cause of the occurrence.

He had been on duty 5¾ hours when the occurrence took place.

I have, etc.,

J. P. S. MAIN.

ABOVE: ***Courtesy National Archives***

BELOW: The plaque in East Anstey Church.

1935 – 'TRIPLE TRAGEDY AT DULVERTON STATION'

So ran the *West Somerset Free Press* headline on 16th April 1935. It was a normal day at Dulverton station, the Exe Valley train had just arrived at the bay platform and passengers were disembarking. Albert Tarr, a 54 year old local man who worked for Tom Miller, the tailors in the town, was waiting on the Down platform for the next train to East Anstey to go home to where he lived with his aged mother. Sadly he was deaf and dumb and had been since birth. The Exe Valley passengers often used the barrow crossing at the Barnstaple end as a shortcut over the tracks, rather than the footbridge. At the tail end of this group crossing the line was Mrs Ivy Ellen Thomas, aged 39, wife of a farm labourer of Higher Combe, Dulverton, and her 4 year-old son, Robert John. She was struggling to cross the tracks with him whilst laden with some parcels when, for some inexplicable reason, Robert suddenly ran back across the barrow crossing. With her attention diverted as she went back to get him, she was oblivious to the immediate arrival of the 4.10pm from Barnstaple (due at 4.51pm), which was coming down the grade from Anstey. Mr Tarr, from his location on the Down platform, could see the approaching train and therefore saw the potential danger to Mrs Thomas and the boy. He reacted quickly and leapt onto the tracks to try to push them to safety away from the train but it was too late and the engine hit all three of them. Tragically, all were killed and their bodies badly mutilated, Mr Tarr's being carried some distance along the track. The porter told the inquest that he shouted to Mrs Thomas to stand clear and that she tried to grab the child but hesitated for a second, at which point Mr Tarr tried to intervene. The engine driver, Mr F. Burridge from Barnstaple, saw the scene ahead but unfortunately too late to stop; he blew his whistle and applied his brakes but the momentum of the train meant that it carried on and caused the tragedy.

The inquest returned a verdict of misadventure, absolved the driver from any blame and recommended that passengers be stopped from using the barrow crossing. Mr Tarr got a tribute: '*We commend the presence of mind and gallant action of Mr Albert Tarr in his great effort to save the child and his mother, which cost him his life*'. A brass plaque was erected in East Anstey church to commemorate his bravery, which reads : ' *To the Glory of God and to perpetuate the memory of Albert William Tarr of this Parish who was accidentally killed at Dulverton 8 January 1935 at the age of 54. Although deaf and dumb, and so unable to raise an alarm, he threw himself in front of an approaching train in a valiant effort to save a mother and her child. This record is made by many friends in recognition of his sacrifice. The Bronze Medallion incorporated is the highest award of the Carnegie Hero Fund Trust on whose illuminated roll the heroic act is recorded*'.

It is a sad but ironic fact that this accident happened at Dulverton, the only station on the line with a footbridge and the whole catastrophe would have been avoided by properly using this bridge. Passengers wishing to cross the line at the other stations did not have the choice but as far as can be ascertained only one other such fatal accident occurred on the line at a barrow crossing. A Mrs Stacey was killed on the one at Wiveliscombe, when she was hit by a train coming down from Venn Cross. It is also understood that a red setter dog lost its hind legs when hit by a train there.

The triple tragedy at Dulverton was clearly the worst accident on the line in its 95-year life.

1939 – WRONG TRAIN, WRONG TRACK!

On 10th June 1939, the 11.00am departure from Taunton to Minehead was sent down the Barnstaple branch by mistake! The *Railway Observer* reported that a special train for Minehead had left Taunton earlier and the Norton Fitzwarren signalman clearly got confused when the regular service appeared. It reached Milverton before the error was reported and the locomotive ran round its train and took the service back to Norton, before reversing direction again to head to Minehead, where it arrived 90 minutes late.

The Second Norton Fitzwarren Accident, 4th November 1940

Again this accident did not occur on D&SR metals and has been well written up elsewhere but it should be mentioned here as it occurred close to the junction of the D&SR and Minehead branches and had an impact on them. It took place almost fifty years to the day after the first Norton accident.

In the early hours of Monday 4th November 1940, the 9.50pm Paddington to Penzance sleeping car express, which had departed from the capital on the previous evening and was hauled by one of the GWR's premier express engines, 'King' Class 4-6-0 No. 6028 *King George VI*, was directed onto the Down relief line from Taunton through to Norton Fitzwarren, unbeknownst to the driver. The normal route for this train was along the Down main line on departing from Taunton but this particular evening it was running sixty-eight minutes late, having left there at about 3.44am. W.J. Gardner, in his book *Cleaner to Controller*, relates a conversation some years after the event with the Taunton West Station Signal Box signalman, Mr H.J. (Jim) Wadham, who was on duty that fateful night. His account differs from the official report of 7th December1940 but perhaps brings further understanding to the events of that evening.

The express had arrived at Taunton at 3.30am, where it was normal practice for the point from the Down relief line (at Platform 1) to be switched to the main line for departures. Also the relevant Home signal (No. 3) could be pulled 'off' without reference to Taunton West Junction Signal Box, as it was protected by the West Station Signal Box Starting signal on the gantry a few yards further west, and this was done by Wadham soon after the train arrived. This was observed by the driver, Mr P.W. Stacey, from under his backout curtain. However, Wadham then received advice from Athelney Signal Box of the approach of the 12.50am ex-Paddington Down newspaper train, which was running eight minutes early. This train had priority, as the GWR would incur financial penalties for its delay, so Wadham returned the relief to main signal No. 3 to 'on' and switched back the points, then asked for 'line clear' from the West Junction signalman for the newspaper train. Having received it, the main line was cleared to allow the Down newspaper train to overtake the express before Norton Fitzwarren.

Having then also obtained 'line clear' for the passenger train to travel down the relief line, the points and signals were set for it to depart towards Norton Fitzwarren too. However, Stacey was given the 'right away' at 3.44am and looking out for a third time was not aware which signal was 'off'. At this point Wadham should have waited for Stacey to blow his whistle before pulling off signal No.10, to allow the driver to acknowledge the change of route but this apparently did not happen. It must have been signal No. 10 for the relief line that was pulled off but Stacey did not realise this and thus blithely headed out on what he thought was the main line. It was not until just seconds before the accident that he realised he was on the relief line, having interpreted the green signals on the main line to Norton Fitzwarren as his, by which time he had passed two successive stop signals at Danger on the relief line. It was only when he saw the five-coach newspaper train overtaking him that his predicament dawned but having no time to react, at 3.47am and travelling at 40-45mph, ran off at the catch points protecting the main line at the end of the Down relief.

The passenger train ploughed straight on, leaving the track and travelling some 140ft beyond the trap points. The derailed locomotive was followed by six of the thirteen coaches in the train, with the first, second and fourth coming to rest foul of the main lines, whilst the third coach telescoped into the tender and the fifth into that. Fortuitously, the newspaper train on the Down main line cleared the point at the junction with the relief line as the accident happened and although hit by flying rivets and ballast, suffered little other damage. However, the guard, on hearing the noise of things hitting his train, applied the emergency brake and the newspaper train stopped at the next signal box, Victory Siding, whereupon it was discovered that the train had suffered minor damage including several broken windows. An amazing escape!

Tragically, there were twenty-six fatalities on the express, including many servicemen and also the fireman, V. Seabridge; another fifty-six were injured out of the 900 passengers on board. Three of the derailed coaches either fouled or were close to fouling the Down D&SR line after the junction. The Up main line had been cleared by the evening of 4th November and the Down line twenty-four hours later.

Had the newspaper train not passed the passenger train just before it derailed, the accident would have surely produced more casualties. The ATC at the Norton relief Down Distant, which would have been at Caution, should have alerted driver Stacey but in the official report he stated that he did not hear the warning bell, so it must have been cancelled by him subconsciously, as the ATC was found to be in working order when subsequently inspected. The official report, by Lieutenant Colonel A.H.L. Mount, gave the sole cause of the accident as an unaccountable lapse of concentration by Mr Stacey, working in blackout conditions on the locomotive, with a late running train caused by a bombing raid on London prior to its departure. Stacey's 'unaccountable lapse' is at least in part explained by the fact that his own house had been bombed the previous evening, which Mount did mention in his report. Poor siting of the signals was another factor, those for the relief line being on the opposite side of the line to normal GWR practice, *i.e.*, on the fireman's side, hence contributing to Stacey reading the wrong signals. It was noted that if the GWR had gone to the expense of siting just one set above the line on a gantry, Stacey's route would have been clear to him, especially in darkness and bad weather. The report also noted, however, that signalman Wadham was not working under any pressure and that even if he changed his mind and made a last minute change of route, he should have made sure that Stacey understood this.

Following the accident, some trains were diverted down the D&SR to Dulverton and thence down the Exe Valley line to reach Exeter. It is understood that Churchward 'Moguls' took the trains along the branch boiler first and then worked tender first down the Exe Valley, despite this being against the rules but these were exceptional circumstances.

Poor driver Stacey, who never forgave himself and told the press "*Don't talk to me, I'm a murderer*", died just over a year later.

1943

The next incident, whilst relatively minor, gives an indication of shunting movements at Dulverton. Mr J. Hall had been a porter there for nearly two years when, at 3.40pm on 21st September 1943, he suffered an injury to his right leg as a wheel on one of the wagons passed over it.

A Taunton to Barnstaple goods had arrived at Dulverton but had been shunted onto the Up line so that a Down passenger train could pass by. There were two wagons to be collected from the Down siding, and Hall had duly attached these during the shunt and then sent the front portion of the train ahead over the points, without realising that the brake handle on the far side of one of them was pinned down. He was on the opposite side of the vehicle when it came to back onto the train and the stationmaster, who was beside him on the barrow crossing at the Barnstaple end of the platforms, remarked about the wagon brake being applied. He immediately stepped forward to release the brake with his shunting pole but the stationmaster, realising that Hall was within 10yds of a dwarf signal, situated centrally in the 6ft 9ins gap between the tracks, called to him to leave the brake alone. Despite this, Hall held onto the pole and as it caught the signal, was thrown over it. The stationmaster rushed to his assistance, dragging him clear of the wheels and thereby saving him from more serious injury. In falling he had hit his head and was unable to remember the incident.

It was concluded that there was no need for Hall to have dealt with the brake at this juncture, as the guard could have done this later, prior to departure. Hall had acted on impulse and was held responsible for the accident. It was also stated that his use of the shunting pole to release the brake was irregular but as the clearance between the signal and the near rail of the Up line was only 2ft 7ins, the result would have been the same if he had used a shorter brake stick instead.

MISHAP AT VENN CROSS 1948

In May 1948, signalman Jim Elson was on duty in Venn Cross Signal Box. He was on the second shift and had been on duty since 1.00pm but it was now about 6.40pm, with the weather clear and dry and the sun beginning to sink in the west.

The 1.30pm goods from Barnstaple GWR to Taunton was running late but had arrived at Venn Cross and was held in the Up platform loop line, the guards van being stood just beyond the point that led to the Up refuge siding. The 6.15pm Taunton to Barnstaple Down service was expected at any minute so shunting of the Up goods was on hold until after the passenger train had cleared the station. Local shunting instructions stated that all Up goods trains requiring to pick up or set down wagons should be set back into the Up refuge siding before commencing shunting. This siding could take twenty-eight wagons and a locomotive, more than adequate for this particular goods train.

On this late spring evening, Jim had been informed that a goods van was to be detached from the front of the goods train and shunted into the yard. The driver was therefore intending to follow instructions and set the train back into the refuge siding, hold the wagons to go forward to Taunton and beyond and pin down the brakes, then detach and draw forward the wagon that was to be shunted across the diamond crossing into the yard.

The passenger train duly arrived in the Down platform loop, thus occupying Jim in his porter's duties.

Once this train had departed west for Morebath, the goods driver was ready to commence shunting. However, whilst Jim had been busy with the passenger train, it appears that the guard, on his own initiative and

Level Crossing
X
VENN CROSS
Goods Shed
SB
Station

ABOVE AND OPPOSITE PAGE TOP: A selection of views of the derailment, with iron filings and fence posts strewn across the running line and the embankment. The final picture shows the breakdown crane at work lifting one of the open wagons back on to the track. ***All Jim Elson***

unaware of the local instructions, had already uncoupled the wagon to be detached. He had assumed the locomotive and wagons would first be drawn forward towards the tunnel and then shunted back into the yard. The reason for his misunderstanding of the situation was possibly because Venn Cross was the only station on the line where a trailing connection from the Up loop led across the Down loop into a Down side goods yard. A section of the 1937 Venn Cross track plan which appears in full in Volume 2 is repeated here to illustrate this, with 'X' marking the point of derailment.

The locomotive reversed to set the goods wagons back into the Up refuge line, giving about fifteen of them a jolt and as they had been uncoupled from the rest of the train, they started to roll back, towards the 1 in 58 gradient. They ran into and along the Up refuge line, with the GWR 'Toad' brake van hitting the buffers, derailing it and injuring the guard (who sustained a damaged pelvis but subsequently recovered). Other wagons came off the rails and spread, amongst other things, their load of iron filings, fence posts and other merchandise (legend has it that local farmers made good use of some of the spilt loads!). The derailed wagons actually just missed the departing passenger train and lay on the signal wire, thus preventing Jim from pulling the Advanced Starting signal (No. 25) back to the 'on' position.

The line was totally blocked by the derailment but the breakdown crane arrived the next day to start the task of clearing up the wagons strewn across the track and services were soon back to normal.

AND ANOTHER MISHAP

Jim Elson was also witness to another minor incident. On this occasion, a Class '55XX' 2-6-2T, which had been shunting in the goods shed at Venn Cross, pulled forwards onto the Down loop, just ahead of the platform where its goods train was waiting, as an Up train was signalled into the Up platform. The 'Prairie' braked to stop ahead of the trap points but its momentum and the slippery rails meant it did not stop when and where the driver expected. With the trap points automatically set to protect the Up line, the locomotive ran off the points and derailed. On this occasion, this was a job for the breakdown train crew and their rerailing jacks rather than the crane, whilst there were no injuries but at least the trap points had served their purpose.

BEES!

The *Daily Telegraph* reported on Tuesday 6th June 1950 that a swarm of bees had invaded Dulverton station and penned the booking office staff and the porters in their offices before being caught!

DULVERTON GOODS DERAILMENT – 1952

The *Somerset County Gazette* reported on 3rd May 1952 that the previous Wednesday afternoon, 30th April, a goods train from Barnstaple to Taunton was derailed at the east end of Dulverton station at the station throat after a brake failure. The engine, 'Mogul' No. 6323, and three wagons came off the track. The 2-6-0 and its tender ploughed into the ballast at the side of the line before coming to rest some distance from the trap points; it was badly damaged. The Up line was blocked for many hours until a breakdown gang from Taunton arrived, working into the early hours of the Thursday morning to repair the damaged rails and put the engine, tender and three goods wagons back onto the track. It was reported that one of the wagons was a horse box and although it contained horses none of them was injured and neither, fortunately, were the driver or fireman.

'Mogul' No. 6323 looking forlorn as it awaits rerailing following the derailment at Dulverton. ***Courtesy Martin Bird***

FIRE!

On 25th October 1952, the *Western Morning News* reported that a hut in the goods yard at Barnstaple Victoria Road caught fire. It contained wood shavings and flames leapt 30ft into the air, severely damaging the hut and a nearby cattle wagon.

FAILURE TO STOP

It was reported on 13th July 1953, in the *Western Morning News*, that the 6.38pm Barnstaple to Taunton train, overshot the buffers in the bay platform (No. 8) at Taunton when it arrived at 8.40pm on the previous Saturday (11th). Several passengers were slightly injured but one sustained concussion and was admitted to hospital. It apparently caused quite a stir at the local cinema in Station Road, 'The Gaiety', as the accident happened at the same time as the climax of the film *Metroscopic*.

DAMAGED POINTS AND DISRUPTION AT VICTORIA ROAD

On Saturday, 6th February 1954, there was a report in the *Western Morning News* of the damage caused on the previous Thursday night by a shunting engine to the points leading into Victoria Road

No. 6398 rests at a drunken angle after coming off the rails at the trap points at the west end of Swimbridge station on 17th August 1956. The view provides a rare glimpse of the end of the loop on the west side of the bridge, with the Up line here occupied by a pair of tool vans that were a part of the Taunton breakdown train. The 0-6-0PT which had brought this train out can be glimpsed at the rear of the goods train, apparently about to draw off the last of the wagons which had remained on the rails. *Courtesy Peter Triggs*

station. This made it impossible for trains to enter or leave, so emergency measures were taken such that passengers from Taunton for Barnstaple were disembarked at Swimbridge, where they were transferred to special buses to complete their journey. Those passengers from Barnstaple were taken by bus to Swimbridge. The last train served by the buses was the 11.20am Barnstaple Junction to Taunton on Friday morning, as just after that the blacksmiths brought in to repair the points completed the job to enable normal service to resume at 12.40pm.

Less than two years later, on 29th March 1954, the *Western Morning News* reported another fire on the railway. The previous day, a strip of undergrowth 300ft long on the embankment bordering Barnstaple Victoria Road station and the loop line to the Junction caught fire. Although the Devon County Fire Service attended with a water tender from Barnstaple and put the fire out by beating, they could not prevent four telegraph poles from being severely damaged and eighteen others slightly damaged.

A Tragedy at Venn Farm

Tragedy struck the Veysey family in the late 1950s, father and son of whom farmed at Venn Farm just west of Nightcott and east of East Anstey. Their farm, like a number on the line, was split by the railway and access across the line was by occupation crossings. On this occasion, Mr John Veysey (the father) was leading his horse and cart across the railway, accompanied by Charlie Quarterly. They had misjudged the time of the train but there was also a strong west wind blowing and this dulled the hearing. As they were crossing the line, a westbound train coming out of Nightcott Tunnel and around the curve could not stop and smashed into the horse, which lashed out killing John Veysey. Sylvia Manley, who had the misfortune to be on board, recalls the jolt which reverberated throughout the short train.

Mishap at Swimbridge in August 1956

Churchward 'Mogul' No. 6398 was derailed on Friday 17th August 1956 at Swimbridge, whilst working the 11.40am Taunton to Barnstaple goods. The locomotive and eight of the wagons, including two loaded coal wagons and two oil wagons, came off the rails at the Barnstaple end of the station on the trap points after running away. Locomotive and tender were off the rails, resulting in the former leaning towards the side of the cutting but still upright, albeit fouling the points and blocking the western approach to the station. A 'Pannier' tank was sent from Taunton with the heavy duty crane lifting equipment to facilitate the rescue. John Howard, of Dulverton S&T department, at this time recalls this incident. It was understood a ganger on a trolley had occupied the section west of the station towards Barnstaple and the trap points were set to reflect this. However, the goods engine driver, anticipating a clear road ahead, failed to stop in time at the red signal and came off at the trap points. It took all weekend to lift the locomotive with the traversing jacks and related equipment, and to clear the line, and repair the signal wires and pointwork.

Ganger Ball, 16th October 1956

Ganger Ball, aged 62, was on the section of track a mile north of Bampton and although not on the D&SR, he was responsible for the section to Dulverton so this mishap is included. He was standing on the front of a hand-trolley being propelled by a motor trolley from the rear, proceeding north to collect a number of old rails. As the ensemble approached a level crossing, Ball indicated to the driver of the motor trolley to slow down but with the gates open, he increased speed instead, causing Ball to fall off and sustain multiple injuries. It was found that Ball was responsible, as he had breached a least two GWR rules, which were still applicable. Namely, standing on the trolley and using the motor trolley to propel the hand trolley.

Victoria Road – May 1959

There was a derailment at Victoria Road in May 1959. During shunting of a goods train, a tank wagon containing 4,000 gallons of petrol came off the rails at the junction of the oil terminal spur and the back road, ending up on its side. The local fire brigade attended and stood by for six hours as petrol was seeping out, whilst it was collected by oil company employees in cans so it did not go to waste. The tank wagon was eventually lifted back on to the track by a visiting crane and normal service was resumed.

The Wrong Coal?

On Saturday 5th October 1963, the 11.15am train from Taunton to Barnstaple with 'Mogul' No. 7337 in charge of three coaches limped into Dulverton at 12.57pm. Having been due to depart at 12.05pm, it was running about forty-four minutes late. There had already been a prolonged stop at Morebath where the fire was thrown out and relit, which accounted for most of the delay and at Dulverton they had no alternative but to repeat the job, especially with the daunting 1 in 58 climb 'up the cutting' ahead. The fire was thrown out onto the ballast and coal from the station coal bunker, adjoining the Up platform, was brought in an old wooden wheelbarrow to the silent locomotive. This coal was meant to be used to keep travelling passengers warm in the station buildings during winter but was 'borrowed' for more immediate use!

The further time lost in relighting the fire at Dulverton amounted to forty-seven minutes, with the train leaving at 1.44pm, ninety-nine minutes late. Unfortunately, the substitute coal did not do the job as the train only managed to crawl up the bank to East Anstey, registering a speed as low as 8mph at times on the climb. However, forward thinking meant that a substitute locomotive had been requested from Barnstaple Junction shed, Ivatt No. 41283, duly arriving at East Anstey ahead of No. 7337, so that as it came to a halt at the East Anstey Home signal, the replacement was attached. Once the Ivatt had piloted the train into East Anstey station, the 'Mogul' was uncoupled from its coaches and shunted into the the goods yard siding, where it was unceremoniously dumped. The Ivatt left East Anstey with its three coach-load at 2.08pm and arrived at Barnstaple at 2.45pm, against a due time of 12.59pm – 106 minutes late, with a total journey time of three and a half hours instead of the one hour forty-four minutes allowed.

The next Up train was due to depart from Barnstaple Junction for Taunton at 2.24pm. It passed the delayed Down train at Swimbridge, with 'Mogul' No. 7317 on a three-coach load running three minutes late. Also, the 1.15pm from Taunton had followed in the wake of the ailing 11.15am and was consequently held in the sections behind it. This later Down train was due to leave Dulverton at 2.06pm, East Anstey at 2.15pm and arrive at Barnstaple at 3.02pm. As for No. 7337, it was later seen at Swimbridge working light on its way slowly back to Barnstaple shed at around 4.30pm. This was an unusual occurrence but what was in the 'Mogul's tender that day? It was clearly not the best South Wales steam coal.

A Near Miss – June 1964

It was reported that a holidaymaker had a '*miraculous escape*', when his car was struck by a goods train on an occupation crossing near Bishops Nympton & Molland station. Mr Hetherington, from Dunfermline, along with his wife and daughters, had been staying at a farm near Molland and were crossing the line to get back to it when

Using a wooden wheelbarrow, coal from the Dulverton station bunker is shovelled aboard No. 7337, as the fireman tries to restore the fire for the to climb up to East Anstey on 5th October 1963. *Michael L. Roach*

the Up goods struck the car and carried it some distance, squashing it '*as if it had been squeezed by a baler*', said one witness, presumably a farmer! The driver was lying across the front seat of the car and had to be cut free by firemen. He was detained in hospital for observation but the incident could have been a lot worse.

ACCIDENT AT WIVELISCOMBE

At an unknown date but probably in the 1950s, a railwayman (possibly a shunter) was helping uncouple some wagons in Wiveliscombe goods yard when he was unfortunately crushed between the buffers and seriously injured. However, he was taken to Taunton by train, where an ambulance was waiting for him to take him to hospital. Despite his bad injuries, he survived.

ALMOST A COLLISION AT DULVERTON

John Nelder, recalled an incident in a letter to the *West Somerset Railway Association Magazine*. Although there is no specific reference to dates, John's uncle, a Mr Smallridge, was the signalman on duty in Dulverton box. The incident involved the use of the auxiliary token machine at the foot of the Down platform.

A train at the Down platform was waiting to head up to East Anstey, with the locomotive taking on water in preparation for departure. Either the driver or the fireman went to the token hut and contacted the signalmen in order to withdraw a token. The East Anstey signalman interpreted this as a reason to withdraw the token for the Up train that was currently in East Anstey station and about to leave, rather than to give the Down train permission to proceed to East Anstey. Meanwhile, the Dulverton signalman switched the points and pulled off the Starter and Advance Starter signals for the Down train to leave. However, their departure was delayed as the refilling of the tender had not been completed and, as luck would have it, the Up train, now well down from East Anstey and presumably approaching the Dulverton Home signal which was still 'on', sounded its whistle, which fortunately the Dulverton signalman heard. At this juncture, he immediately reset the the signals against the Down train and the points at the west end of the station, so the Up train could run safely into the Up platform, which it duly did. A head-on collision was thus narrowly averted.

MISSING TOKENS

Single line operation has been described early in the signalling chapter at the end of Volume 2, in which it was noted that the electric train token played a large part in safe and successful railway operation. However, from time to time, mishaps occured. For instance, tokens could get dropped and lost during the handover between signalman and fireman. Whilst this was a rare occurrence, the probability was increased if there was a short cut taken in the handover. In one such instance, a token on a hoop was lost, only to turn up some weeks later under a carriage at Longsight depot in Manchester!

In another example, a goods train was heading west and, as always, the driver was keen to get a good run at the bank up to Bathealton Tunnel. If the automatic apparatus at Wiveliscombe was not being used, strictly they were supposed come to a halt to effect the handover but crews preferred not to stop, instead carrying out a manual exchange of the token whilst on the move, something which over the years had became common practice all over the railway system. However, here at Wiveliscombe, instead of effecting a simultaneous change of the two tokens, the fireman would instead lob the token for the Milverton/Wiveliscombe section out onto the platform. He would then collect the token for the next section – Wiveliscombe/ Venn Cross – from the signalman further along the platform, who held it up so that the fireman could hook his arm through the hoop as they rattled past and on the train would go. On one occasion all seemed to go well until the train was stopped at Venn Cross, where the signalman asked the fireman what had happened to the Milverton/ Wiveliscombe token, which was apparently nowhere to be seen at the latter station. In fact, it was not found that day and indeed the lineman had to be called to adjust the instruments to allow trains to continue on the Milverton to Wiveliscombe section. It is reported that the token was later found lying on the track at Birmingham Snow Hill!

The only explanation appears to be that somehow the token had hit something on the Down platform and bounced back under the wagons where it then lodged itself and was carried off to pastures new.

A GHOST STORY?

Mystery and myth surrounds Bridge No. 173 on the D&SR, an agricultural occupation overbridge just west of Wiveliscombe. It was referred to locally as 'Lover's Leap', as a number of attempted suicides had apparently occurred at the location. Stories from train crews have suggested that they had seen someone or something falling from the bridge but when the train was stopped for the fireman to look for the object, nothing was found. Indeed, the bridge developed an eerie reputation amongst railwaymen. However, it is easy to see how the poor light of a dusky evening, coupled with the surrounding trees and countryside casting shadows, could confuse those on the footplate, especially on a windy night ...

PICTORIAL INTERLUDE 1

A MASTER PHOTOGRAPHER ON THE D&SR

MICHAEL J. FOX

We are fortunate that numerous talented railway photographers visited the line over the years, from Arthur Halls in the late 1920s, through Roger Sellick in the 1950s, to the likes of Peter Gray, Ron Lumber, Peter Triggs, John Spencer Gilks, Tim Stephens and Peter Barnfield in the 1960s. Amongst these later luminaries was Michael J. Fox, who made several visits to the Somerset end of the line in the early 1960s, seemingly not straying west of Dulverton. Many of his photographs have featured already in this book, as well as the first two volumes but now, by way of an interlude, we present a further selection of some of his best work over the next few pages.

'Mogul' No. 6372 'gets the board' to travel 'up the cutting' (as enginemen referred to it) from Dulverton to East Anstey on 22nd June 1963, as it takes the 4.25pm Taunton departure on to Barnstaple. The Exe Valley train, with Class '14XX' 0-4-2T No. 1421 at the head, simmers in the bay platform. Note the recently whitewashed stones around the flowerbeds on the island platform.

No. 6327 pulls away from Milverton on 12th August 1963 with the 4.20pm Taunton to Barnstaple service.

No. 7303 departs from Wilveliscombe with the 4.03pm Taunton to Barnstaple train on 27th June 1964, past the recently lifted horse dock siding.

No. 7304 looking smart in lined green BR passenger livery at Wiveliscombe with the 4.35pm Taunton to Barnstaple service on 28th August 1961. Just two passengers appear to have got off here on this occasion, unless others were still stranded on the Down platform by the departing train. Dulverton was the only station on the D&SR line that was graced with a footbridge. The line was on a sharp curve through the station and can be seen passing Ashbeers Farm and heading towards Milverton in the right background.

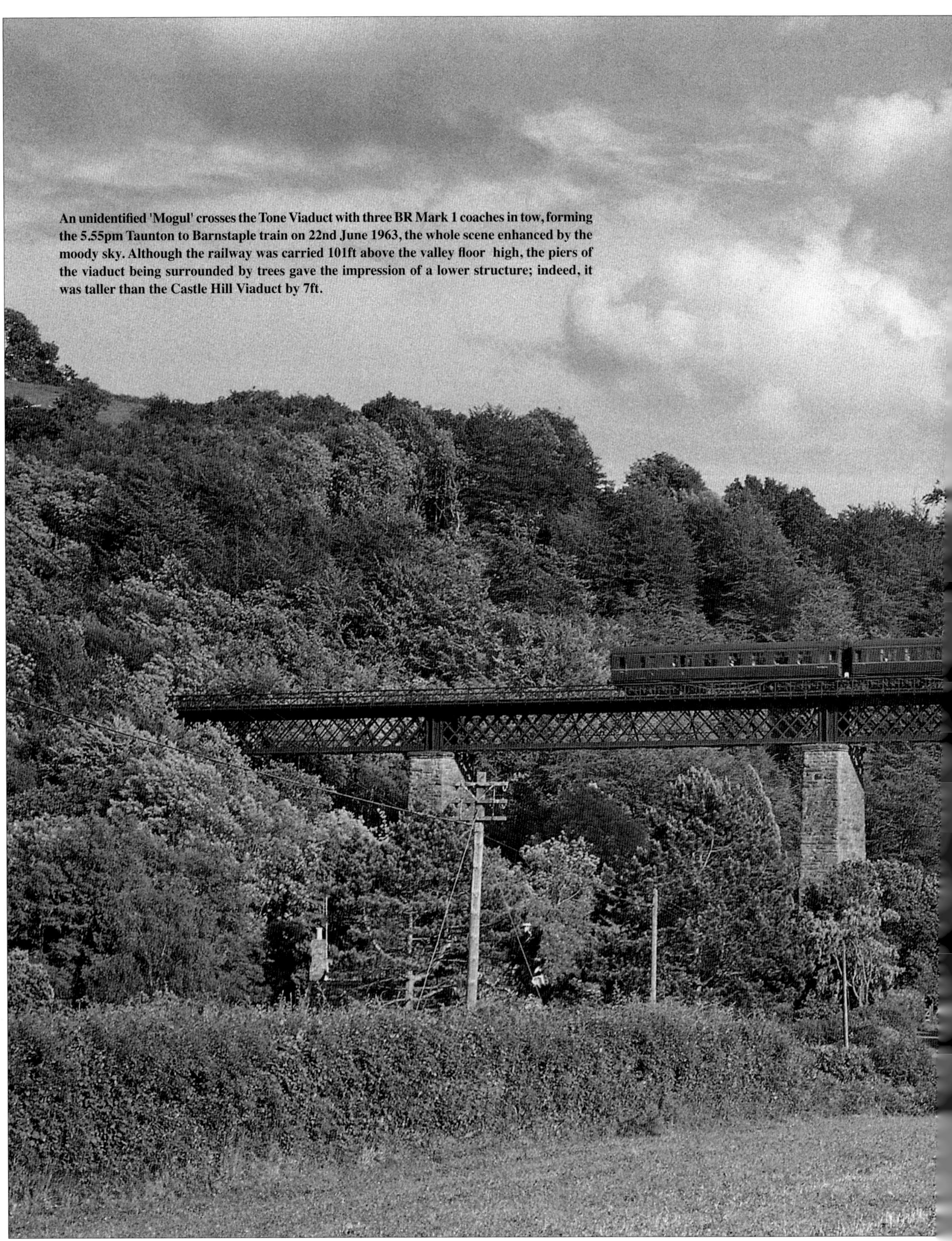

An unidentified 'Mogul' crosses the Tone Viaduct with three BR Mark 1 coaches in tow, forming the 5.55pm Taunton to Barnstaple train on 22nd June 1963, the whole scene enhanced by the moody sky. Although the railway was carried 101ft above the valley floor high, the piers of the viaduct being surrounded by trees gave the impression of a lower structure; indeed, it was taller than the Castle Hill Viaduct by 7ft.

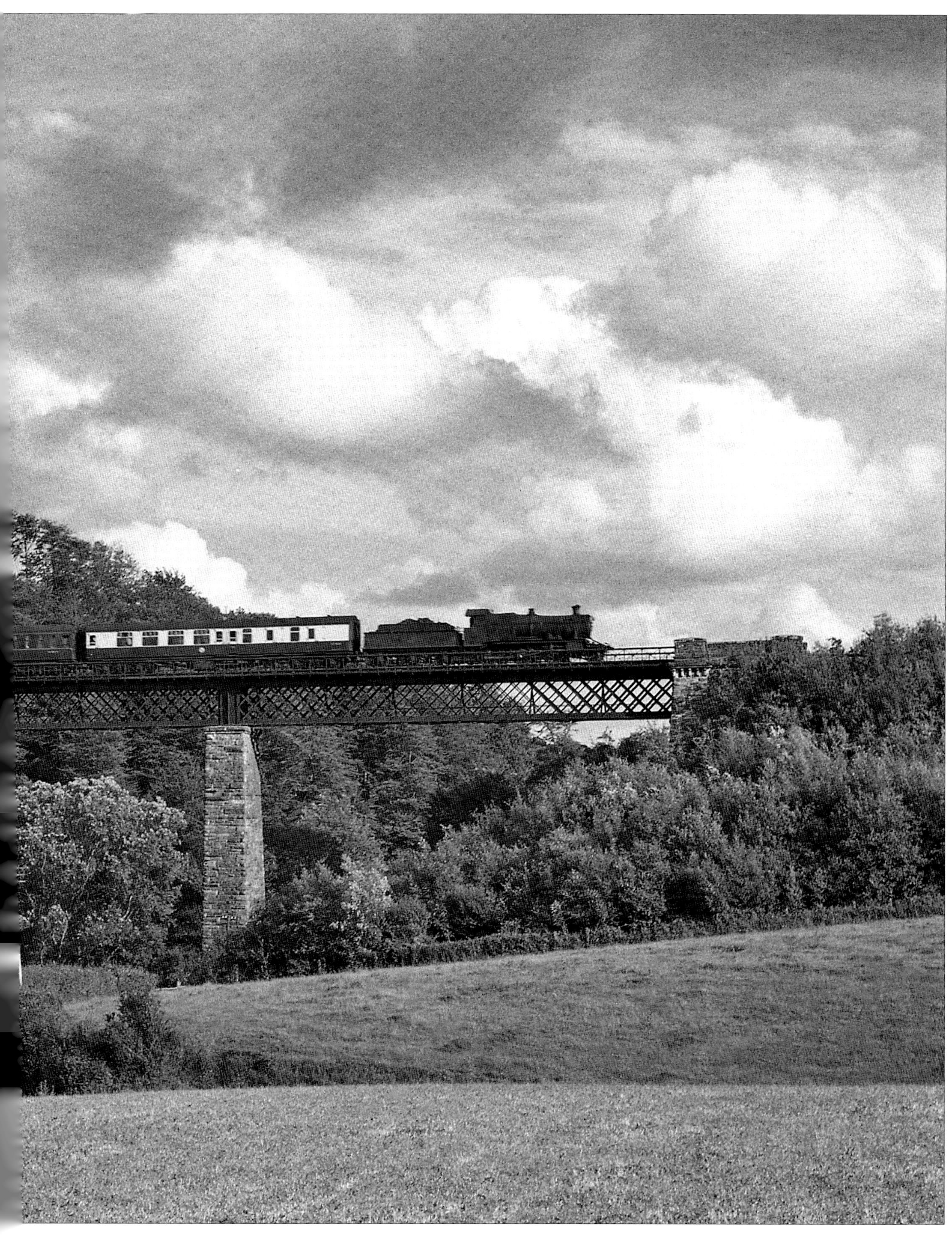

As will be recalled from the previous volume, Michael Fox took a number of photographs at this highly picturesque location, so no apologies for using another one here. Pannier tank No. 9670 ambles over the River Exe bridge just to the east of Dulverton with an Up pick-up goods on 30th August 1961. At this time of year, the ventilated vans are probably laden with locally picked fruit, whilst the steel minerals will be coal empties being returned. Now time for a confession; we inadvertently transposed the captions of this view and the one which appears on page 304 of Volume 2 incorrectly labelled as No. 9670. That should have been identified as No. 5779 crossing the river two days earlier, on 28th August 1961. ***Michael J. Fox, courtesy Rail Archive Stephenson***

RIGHT: Collett Class '14XX' No. 1470 propels the 3.42pm Exe Valley service away from Dulverton on 21st July 1961. The train is about to round the curve prior to crossing the Exe River Bridge on its way to Morebath Junction, Bampton, Tiverton and Exeter St. Davids. The cranes and sheds in the left background are part of Exebridge timber works

BELOW: No. 1421 arriving at Dulverton with the 3.30pm service from Exeter St. Davids on 22nd June 1963, just a few months before closure of the Exe Valley line. Note the pointwork into the yard, with the coal siding furthest right, and also the Bay platform Starting signal so designated with 'BAY' painted on the arm.

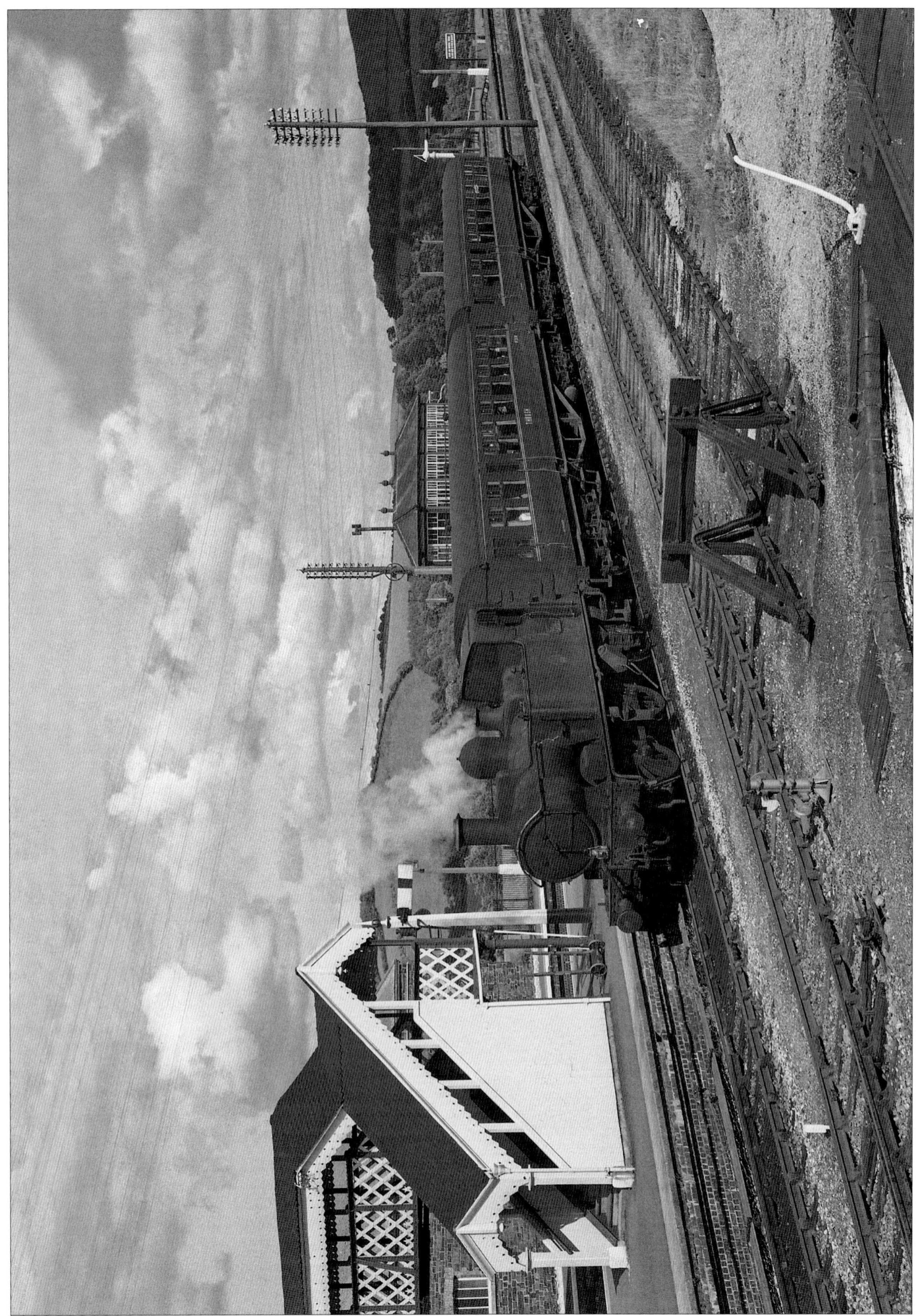

A fine study of No. 1421 in the bay platform at Dulverton after arriving with the 3.30pm train from Exeter st. Davids on 22nd June 1963. Note that one of the auto trailers carries the name *Thrush*. The buffer stops in the foreground were for the goods siding on the Down side, which was used, amongst other things, for exchange traffic between the D&SR and Exe Valley but by this date, there was little or none of that. The ground or shunt signal alongside it, however, looks quite new. In the right foreground is part of the turntable pit and the handle for turning the table.

No. 7304 departs from Dulverton with a four-coach train forming the 5.03pm to Taunton on 21st July 1961. Note the tubular metal post Starting signal to the right, which was a replacement for a wooden square post version around 1957, that was in turn moved to the outside of the goods yard headshunt. The ground or shunt signals – there is another new-ish looking one in the left foreground – were probably installed at the same time. Again there is a clear view of the pointwork in to the bay platform, along with the connection in to the Down goods yard on the left. This was clearly a very warm day and you can almost smell the smoke and lubricating oil from the locomotive and the creosote on the sleepers.

ABOVE: Just over a month later on 28th August 1961 and sister engine (and next in numerical order) No. 7305 departs Dulverton with the 1.17pm Barnstaple to Taunton service. Four coaches and a parcels Brake is a tidy load for this 'Mogul'.

BELOW: From a similar spot, No. 7337 is seen leaving with the three-coach 3.55pm Barnstaple to Taunton train on 22nd June 1963. It is likely that this is the same coaching stock seen on the Tone Viaduct on pages 626-627, working back later that day.

No. 7337 heads away from Dulverton on 27th June 1964 with the 4.03pm Taunton to Barnstaple train, a view taken a few minutes after that on page 178, Volume 1; it had crossed with an Up service seen also just pulling out beyond the footbridge. Note that by this date most of the sidings had been removed, with goods services officially ceasing in the following month.

Above: Stepping back a few moments in time, No. 7337 waits to depart to East Anstey and Barnstaple on 27th June 1964. The viewpoint shows that only the bay platform line remained on the Down side but, despite the imminent closure of goods services here, a collection of ventilated vans can be seen on the back road of the Up side goods yard on the left.

Left: We finish this short interlude with a perfect lineside shot of 'Mogul' No. 6337 as it passes through the arch of the road bridge to the west of Dulverton with the 2.33pm Taunton to Barnstaple service on 28th August 1961. Note the train on this occasion was formed of Bullied coaching stock.

CHAPTER 13

RECOLLECTIONS – LIFE ON THE LINE

Class '45XX' 2-6-2T No. 5504 runs round the goods train which it has just brought into the main platform at Victoria Road. The goods yard is busy with a variety of wagons, including cattle trucks, oil tanks and wooden-bodied opens. The picture is undated but is in the mid-1950s, the station still being open for passengers whilst the 1927-built locomotive was withdrawn in October 1960. ***Courtesy Reg Chamming***

BARNSTAPLE GWR/VICTORIA ROAD

The first part of what is recorded below first appeared in issues of the *Great Western Journal*, from which it is reproduced here with permission, and refers to conversations had with railwaymen who worked at Barnstaple in the 1940s. Following on from that are a series of recollections from people whom I have known or I have met in compiling this book. Most have worked on the railway in some capacity, whilst others remember it fondly. It has been a great joy to meet these individuals, who have been enthusiastic in recounting their stories from an era not that long ago but which is so different from today, whether in terms of railway operation or in life generally. I will let them enlighten you with their recollections.

TRAIN OPERATIONS AT BARNSTAPLE GWR

Trains arriving from Taunton used the main platform (which was called 'No. 1' by the staff) and stopped short of the engine release crossover. Having uncoupled, the locomotive would pull forwards, run round its train and having coupled up to the coaches, would head tender first to Barnstaple Junction via the south loop. The first departure of the day (usually at 6.55am Up to Taunton) was formed of the stock which had arrived on the 8.17pm from Taunton the previous evening. These were placed in the bay platform ahead of another coaching set off the 5.42pm from Taunton. This latter train ran through to Barnstaple Junction and returned with the empty coaching stock to Victoria Road in the evening, to place it at the back of the bay. This set then formed the 8.15am departure (the second departure of the day) to Taunton. Occasionally the stock of the 5.42pm was kept at the Junction.

In the summer months from 1905 until 1939, a number of the through trains to Ilfracombe bypassed the GWR station by traversing the East Chord. This avoided the time consuming and inefficient process of running around the train at GWR and working tender first to Barnstaple Junction.

However, the Down and Up services using the East Chord still connected with the GWR station in the following manner. When the East Chord was opened, a Down train would be brought to a halt at the South Junction Down Starting signal, clear of the points at South Junction. The train was formed in the following order: engine, vehicles for Ilfracombe, other vehicles for Barnstaple Junction, vehicles for Barnstaple GWR. The GWR station master would arrange for an engine, accompanied by a traffic department man, to be waiting at South Junction Down Home signal on the West Chord. The traffic

LEFT: Barnstaple station staff from the *GWR Magazine*, March 1911. After seventeen years here, station master Mr C.A. Withy (centre) had transferred to Leamington Spa on 9th January 1911.

BELOW: This early 1930s photograph from the signal gantry near the engine shed gives almost a driver's eye view of the approach to Barnstaple GWR. An unidentified 'Bulldog' stands outside the shed and there are a rake of coaches parked in the bay platform. *Courtney Card collection, courtesy Ian Huxtable*

department man would divide the train and pilot the local engine to the rear of the Barnstaple portion and couple it on, sending the Ilfracombe portion forwards after attaching the tail lamp. The coaches were then hauled over the West Chord into the GWR terminus. Clearly it was important to ensure that passengers joined the right section of the train and staff at Taunton and Norton Fitzwarren were charged with this responsibility.

Provision was made in service time table for attachments at East Junction, for Up trains that bypassed the GWR station. Ken Barnes recalls coaches being collected at East Junction. In the Up direction, the train from Ilfracombe would traverse the East Chord line and then stop on the Swimbridge side of East Junction, ensuring that it stood clear of the points [*presumably at Starting signal No. 8, 350 yards from the box – see page 435, Volume 2*]. The coaches from the GWR station would be propelled by an engine up to the East Junction Home signal and await the Up train before being attached to it. When the GWR portion was being propelled, a man provided with a horn was required to ride in the leading compartment and to keep a sharp lookout. The Taunton-bound train was then clear to proceed and the propelling engine would run light back to the GWR station. On summer Saturdays, two additional engines would be available at Barnstaple GWR, one to deal with these coaching stock manoeuvres, the other to work additional trains to Ilfracombe.

When it came to goods arrivals, they ran into the main platform road and the locomotive ran around. The locomotive might shunt the goods but on some occasions this was left to another locomotive that had either worked a trip from the Junction or was to take another goods out later. In order to shunt, the goods would be drawn out of the platform line towards South Loop and the 'cuts' of wagons

ABOVE: A selection of staff photographs at Barnstaple GWR from 1930s:
TOP LEFT: A group of happy, mostly station staff pose in front of the running in board.
TOP RIGHT: Courtney Card with Stafford Marshall, left, and an unnamed porter, right, who also appears in the picture top right on the next page.
CENTRE LEFT: Barnstaple yard staff, shunters and footplate crew pose with GWR 'Mogul' No. 4380 circa 1935.
All Courtney Card collection, courtesy Ian Huxtable

RIGHT: The tender first aspect of this 'Mogul' suggests that it has just brought a train round the curve from Barnstaple Junction. The view is undated but is likely to be from the late 1940s, possibly still just in GWR days, so prior to the station being renamed Barnstaple Victoria Road and to the engine shed, visible in the distance, being closed. Note the fine array of advertisements and enamelled signs on the end of the building. ***Jim Elson collection***

A series of photos follows of personnel at Barnstaple Victoria Road in the late 1950s. Unfortunately we do not know who all of the people are but I am grateful to Ann and Malcolm Huxtable for providing some of the names. ***All courtesy Reg Chamming***

TOP LEFT: The signalman poses in front of the box.

CENTRE LEFT: Porter Stafford Marshall looking very smart on his duties.

BOTTOM LEFT: Left to right: Courtney Card (Ann's father), possibly a young booking clerk, Stafford Marshall and another booking clerk (possibly Pat Gisby?), with the station master far right – Mr Payne?

TOP RIGHT: Left to right: head porter, probably an engine driver (based on his clothes) and George Facey. The photograph was taken outside the porters' restroom, with the old gas cooker just visible through the door.

CENTRE RIGHT: Stafford Marshall (right) with an unidentified colleague, outside the porters' rest room.

BOTTOM RIGHT: In the back row, George Facey and Stafford Marshall, with possibly Mr Grigg, the head porter.

RIGHT: The signalman again, inside the box.

Victoria Road in early 1960, with a train bound for the Junction and coaches in the bay. ***James G. Tawse***

detached and allowed to gravitate to the correct sidings. The shunter made the cuts and the porter operated the yard points. Wagons for the oil siding were unofficially 'fly-shunted' into the kick-back siding. Perishable traffic would be on the Bristol goods and shunted to the goods shed for unloading. Lyons tea wagons would be positioned outside of the shed alongside their designated warehouse. Oil wagons would be berthed at the front and back of the back road (depending on the supplier) but the siding would be clear for making up the Bristol goods to depart in the evening. Other wagons would be positioned in the mileage siding, cattle pens and end-dock as appropriate. Wagons for the Southern Region (on the next trip) were usually attached to a brake van in the middle road. The 9.35am Taunton goods would start from the so designated 'carriage siding'. The Taunton afternoon goods was largely made up of empties and was formed wherever convenient.

The make up of the Bristol goods was broadly as follows (from the rear): Brake van, Bristol, Bristol transfers (*e.g.* Wapping Wharf), Bristol mixed, South Wales, Taunton, cattle and engine.

In the 1940s, a stores van would arrive from Swindon and be placed in the bay, with new stores being unloaded and old store items being returned. The wagon would return on the 6.44pm Up service.

The role of Barnstaple Victoria Road as a passenger station passed away on 11th June 1960. This was the last day of the winter service Saturday time table for that year, hence the reason for it to be the 'chosen day'.

Even as early as 1951, a plan had been worked out to redirect all Taunton to Barnstaple trains direct into the Junction by reopening the chord line between East and South Junctions. However, as can be seen, the plan took nearly ten years to implement for some reason. It was perhaps an inevitable step following on from Nationalisation and the reorganisations and amalgamations that took place where Western Region and Southern Region boundaries met. Victoria Road and East and South Junctions were transferred to the control of the Southern Region on 1st January 1958. Closure would remove the inefficient and time wasting process of reversing trains at Victoria Road and provide a more direct connection to the other train services from the Junction. It is debatable whether the Junction's location relative to the town centre was better than that of Victoria Road, as passengers alighting at the former were required to walk over the Taw River bridge to reach the town centre (or await an Ifracombe connecting train and alight at the Town station). One might question the obvious at this point; why was the service not run through to the Town station to terminate there? Admittedly track alterations, and maybe some building work, would have been needed to park the trains on an extended stop over, clearly more difficult in the steam era but with DMUs much more practicable. The continued use of the Taw bridge between the Junction and Town stations and with its maintenance costs would have been prohibitive and may have been the real reason for this truncating of the line at the Junction (albeit this did not occur until the Ilfracombe line was closed in 1970).

So, on 11th June 1960 at 10.06pm, the last train of the day, the 8.25pm from Taunton arrived as it always did and terminated at Victoria Road. On this last occasion, as green 'Mogul' No. 6390 pulled in, it was met by a reasonably sized crowd on the platform and exploding detonators. The 'Mogul' pulled in three freshly painted coaches (Bristol 'B-set' No's 6224/5 and a Brake Composite coach, No. 6913). The 'Mogul' bore a placard '*Farewell. Last passenger train to Barnstaple Victoria Road*'. As the locomotive ran round its train more detonators sounded. It then coupled up to its coaches and with its tender first hauled the rake of three still lit but empty coaches out of Victoria Road, around the curve and up the slight incline towards the Newport cutting and bridge, and out of sight.

Victoria Road became the Southern Region goods station; all sundry goods and general merchandise traffic was concentrated there (Barnstaple Junction at this time, as mentioned elsewhere, dealt with full wagon loads). However, at the time of the last train, there were already signs of 'Southern infiltration' namely, SR green

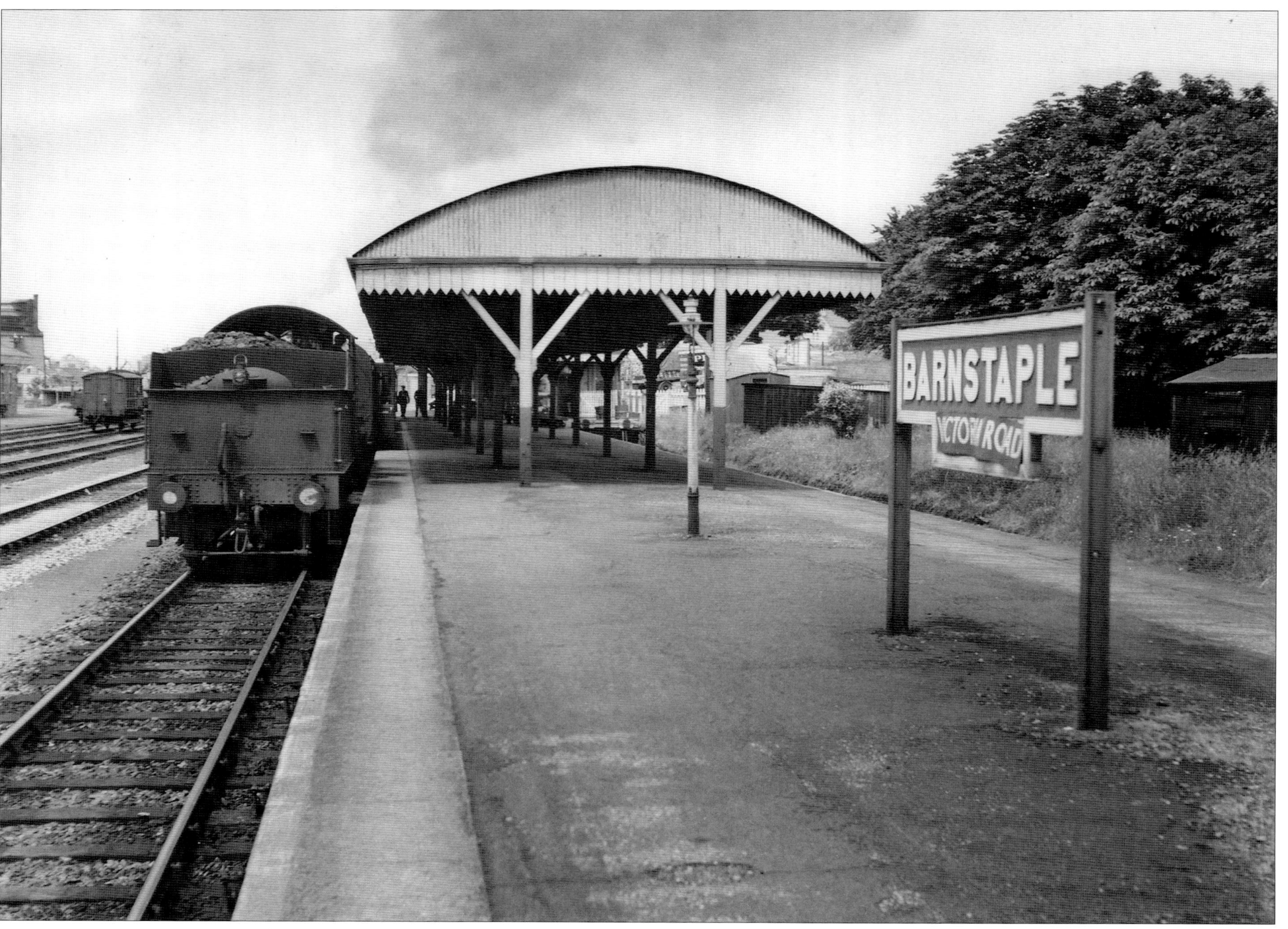

A fine study of Barnstaple Victoria Road on 6th June 1960, with 'Mogul' No. 6309 at the platform on the 10.15am Taunton to Ilfracombe. Victoria Road was added to the station nameboard, which had to be specially extended at the bottom, by BR after Nationalisation but clearly someone had attempted to remove it since the picture on the previous page. *John Spencer Gilks*

A panoramic view of a rather deserted Barnstaple Victoria Road in early June 1960, a few days before the passenger services were withdrawn. ***Peter Barnfield***

goods depot notices and two SR signal department utility vans (No's DS29 and DS162) in the sidings. The diesel shunter retained at Barnstaple Junction was used to shunt the yard and operate the trip workings. There were occasional workings of parcels traffic by North British Class '22's that frequented the Junction and Torrington lines at that time.

The station survived as a goods depot until 5th March 1970. Its closure was precipitated by a dispute after National Carriers Limited (NCL) had taken over the management of the parcels and sundries depot and they commenced using road, not rail transport, between Barnstaple and Exeter on cost grounds. Victoria Road had been the centre for parcels traffic in Barnstaple since 1948 and the role continued until its closure. However, only parcels and sundries were dealt with from 1965, other goods being concentrated at Barnstaple Junction. The former station buildings were used as a store and capacity was expanded by the area covered by the corrugated station canopy being enclosed with corrugated iron covering as can be seen from a variety of photographs of the time. By March 1965 the signal box had been removed but the water crane at the end of the platform remained in place. The track layout changed little except the cattle and carriage sidings (as they were called) were removed by the end of 1966.

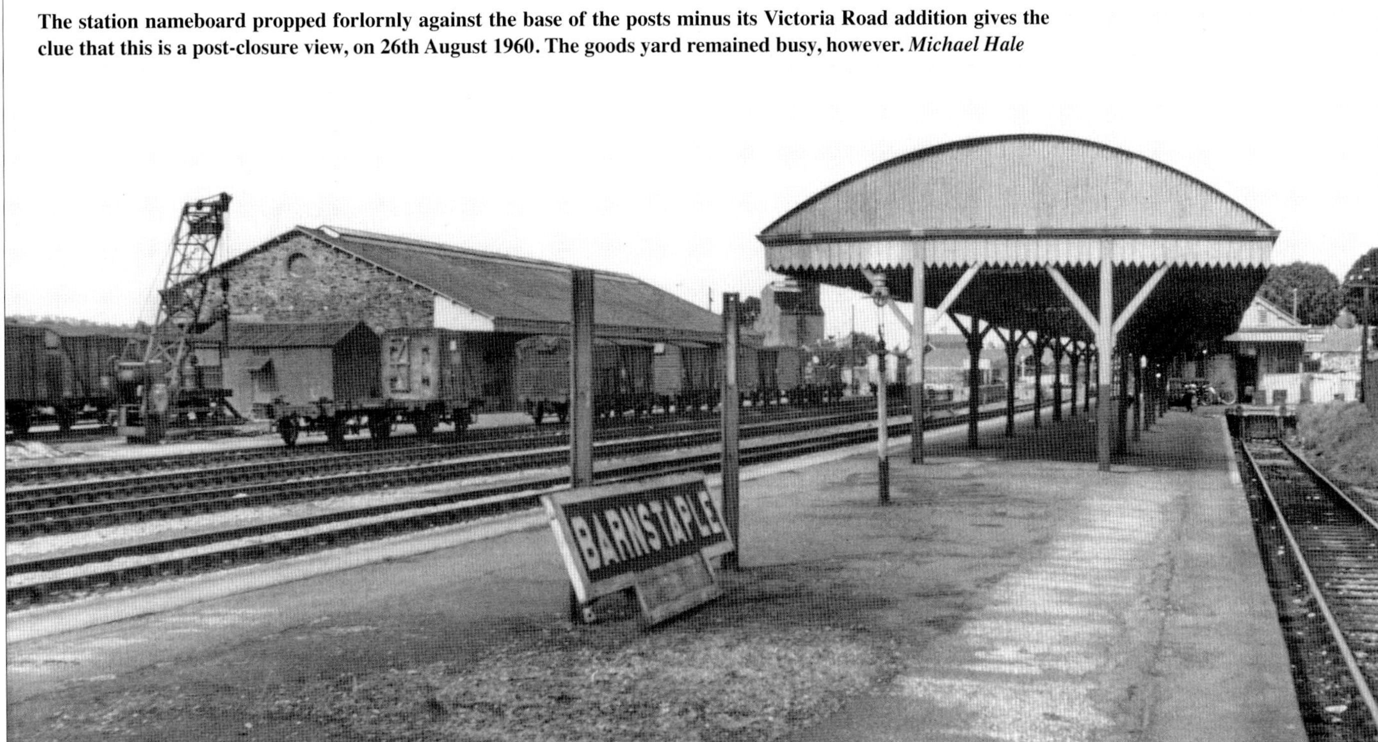

The station nameboard propped forlornly against the base of the posts minus its Victoria Road addition gives the clue that this is a post-closure view, on 26th August 1960. The goods yard remained busy, however. ***Michael Hale***

LEFT: The main platform and the area beneath the station canopy was used for secure and dry goods storage by British Road Services after the cessation of passenger services. Here, pallet loads of sacks occupy the area where passengers once waited; the sacks will be agricultural in nature, filled with either produce, seeds or animal feed. The picture was taken on 27th March 1965, on the occasion of the visit by the 'Exmoor Ranger' rail tour, hence the eager enthusiasts enjoying a last chance to explore the platform. Note the badly sagging canopy at the far end.

BELOW: On the same day, two BRS lorries were parked in the station forecourt, whilst the building now sported a BRS Traffic Office sign. Registration No. AHT 697B is 1964 AEC Mercury which was registered in Norfolk.
Both Michael Messenger

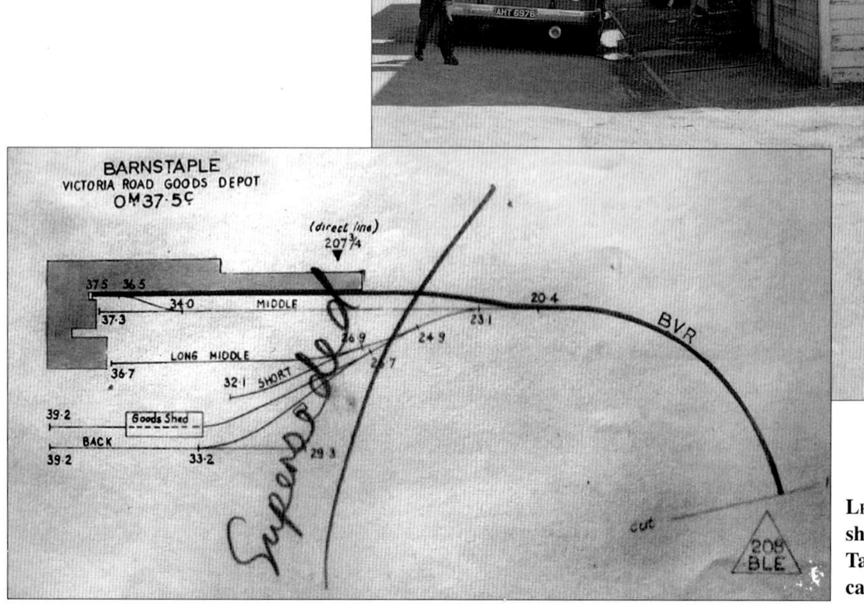

LEFT: A 1966 track diagram for Victoria Road goods depot, showing remaining sidings, from an extract of papers from Taunton Civil Engineers Department; note the cattle and carriage lines had been removed. *Amyas Crump collection*

By the late 1960s the whole area looked run down (see Volume 1, page 193). The corrugated covering on the platform had been removed and the wooden station buildings were soon to be dismantled, whilst the platform line and run round loop, which were still in situ, were out of use; old wooden cable drums litter the track in one photograph from this period.

The line between the Junction and Victoria Road was temporarily closed on 18th December 1967 until after the Christmas holiday period, whilst contractors employed by the town council drilled a tunnel on the embankment section in the Newport area to take a sewer pipe to a new school. BR insisted on a tunnel rather than allow the council to cut away the embankment but this tunnelling resulted in part of the embankment slipping away. This could have created significant delays for freight and parcels deliveries in the North Devon, area as the Victoria Road depot was cut off but, in a foretaste of the near future, a fleet of lorries came to the rescue and the anticipated problems never materialised. Somewhat ironically, the 'cut-and-cover' method was then used to finish the job after the land-slip.

The line between Barnstaple Junction and Victoria Road was officially taken out of use two months after the closure of the goods depot on 30th May 1970.

Barnstaple GWR in the 1930s & '40s

(*The stories below are with permission from* Great Western Journal, *as originally published in No. 42, Spring 2002.*)

The memories of Ted Yeo, Ken Barnes, Walter King and Joe Hugo are shared here covering the period from the late 1930s until just after Nationalisation. Ted, a local man born at Fremington, was a supernumerary porter recruited in 1937. Although initially employed on a non-permanent basis, he was eventually taken on permanently and made a Grade 2 porter. Ken was born at Westbury and joined as an engine cleaner in 1937. He was one of two cleaners at the shed and acted as fireman in the summer of 1939, going to Taunton in 1940 and returning to Barnstaple GWR in 1945. Ken was transferred to the Junction shed in 1951 when the GWR shed closed. Walter started at Barnstaple in 1942 as a lorry van guard (see page 650), having passed an intelligence test in Exeter! He went on to become a shunter at the station and then a goods guard based at Barnstaple Junction. Joe's family originally came from Cornwall but moved to Barnstaple before he was born. He became an engine cleaner in June 1941 after applying for an advertised vacancy. After a brief sojourn at Swindon (late 1941-1943), he returned to Barnstaple at his request in October 1943.

At this time the station master was Mr Tremethick, who lived near the station in Ashleigh Road. He would 'prowl' the station with his hands behind his back supervising the staff. He always had a piece of paper in his hand but the men never knew what the purpose of the paper was! Despite the strict approach of Mr Tremethick, the shed lads used to get Walter King to take their betting slips down to the bookmakers in Tuly Street, Walter doing his best to avoid his boss when running those errands. Tremethick was succeeded by Arthur Payne from Watchet.

Other staff at the passenger station in the late 1930s comprised one booking clerk, one Grade 1 and two Grade 2 porters, and two shunters. The clerk (Mr Haynes) came on duty around 7.00-7.30am. He went home for breakfast and lunch so his shift was spread. During these break times the station master dealt with the clerk's work. The porters covered the platform work, Sid Ash being the Grade 1 porter. He permanently worked the 6.00am to 2.00pm early shift so was responsible for opening the station and booking passengers for the first departure at 6.55am. The Grade 2 porters (Ted Yeo and Ron Farmer) worked alternate weeks of short and long shifts from 7.00am to 2.00pm and 2.00pm to 11.00pm. The shunters, 'Taffy' Wilkins and Len Gregory, covered alternate weeks of 6.00am to 2.00pm and 2.00pm to 10.00pm turns. The early-turn Grade 2 porter and shunter dealt with the Bristol goods (which arrived around 10.00am in the 1940s and 7.00am in the 1950s). Later the porters dealt with cleaning duties and assisted in the parcels office and goods shed. Ted Yeo spent a good deal of his shifts in the parcels office assisting Bill Doble, who

Barnstaple GWR looking towards the buffer stops circa 1930. The coaching stock on view is all clerestory roofed and there is a horse box and box van on the end of the rake stabled on the carriage siding next to the goods yard. The jib just peeping above the wagons on the far left is that of the original 10-ton crane provided here and note the GWR luggage handcart on the right. ***Courtesy, Great Western Railway Society***

LEFT: No. 6358 stands at Barnstaple GWR with a train for Taunton in 1931. Note the Parkend Collieries private owner wagon in the goods yard on the left. Forest of Dean coal was still regularly being delivered to Barnstaple by coasting vessels sailing from Lydney to Rolle's Quay at this time, so it is perhaps a little surprising to see this wagon here. ***Brian Perkes, courtesy Leslie Walker***

BELOW: Much early afternoon activity at Barnstaple Junction on 5th August 1939, a month before war was declared. GWR '45XX' Class 2-6-2T No. 5542 had arrived at 1.38pm with a train from Taunton, which includes a clerestory coach, whilst on the left is the 1.30pm from Ilfracombe which is in the process of being divided. Southern 'N' Class 'Mogul' No. 1858 will take the front three coaches, an ex-L&SWR three coach set, on to Yeoford, whilst the rest of the train will wait for a GWR engine and head for Taunton. ***J.R.W. Kirkby, courtesy Tony Harden***

worked 8.00am to 5.00pm. Ted often opened the office when Bill was off duty. Parcels were delivered with a motor van in later years (driven by Frank Strickland) but in earlier years Charlie Lake used a white horse and van. The porters also dealt with maintaining the signal lamps; on a Friday, the late turn porter had to trek down to the Distant signal and then work back towards the station. The porters assisted with the shunting of the later goods trains and the Grade 1 porter acted as a guard on the transfer trips to and from Barnstaple Junction.

The station signal box was manned by Bill Tanton and Bob Short, who worked alternate weeks of early and late shifts, thereby covering the whole train service. The East and South Loop boxes were opened when required during the summer months (mid-July to September) by relief men, one being Percy Webber.

In the early post-war period, clerks included Ivor Harris, Brian McManus, Mary Huxtable and Vera Barton. Ray Hill was a regular relief clerk. Porters at this time were Percy Bridgeman, Ken Manley, Eric Dymond and Pat Crook. The platform duties were covered in two shifts, 6.00am to 2.00pm and 1.00pm to 9.00pm, the last train being attended by one of the shunters (Walter King or Stan Grigg).

The goods shed was run by chief clerk Jim Elson [*the father of Jim Elson, the signalman at Venn Cross referred to previously in Chapter 12*]. Jim's staff included clerks 'Nobby' Hobbs, Ron Courtney, Jack Ellery, Dorothy Hooper, Olive Parkman (daughter of guard Jack Parkman) and Percy Coles. Uniformed goods staff included foreman Bill Smith, Phil Smaile, checkers Arthur Sluman and James Tucker, porters Pat Woodward, Tom Millard, Bill Pugsley, Jack Gabriel and Ernie Turner. During the year, supernumeraries were employed including Charlie Ratcliff and Jim Jackson. In the post-war years, other goods staff included 'Lofty' Ashton, George Facey, Charlie Gillett, George Shappell, Chris Addams and Bill Jenkins. All goods staff worked from 8.00am to 5.00pm and until midday on Saturdays. Motor drivers included Phil Smaile, Harry Barnes, Bill Crook, Arthur Grant and Arthur Sluman.

On the permanent way side, the gangers based at Barnstaple in the 1940s were Bill Ball and sub-ganger Leonard Dalling senior. Sammy Jewell oiled the pointwork when required. Other men were Joe Hawkins, Fred Cook, Jack Knott and George Yeo. Staff in the early post-war years included Fred Barrett, Bill Holland, 'Taff' Grant, 'Pug' Scrivens and Jack Rippon. These men were responsible for the line between Barnstaple and Swimbridge which they patrolled with a motorised trolley. Joe Hawkins swept the yard on Saturday mornings, all the rubbish going into a natural pit behind the National Benzole Depot. As a concession the men were allowed to take ten old sleepers a

A rather bare looking scene eastwards from the end loading dock, probably soon after the cessation of passenger services in June 1960; note the darker rectangles on the end wall of the station building where posters and time table notice boards had recently been mounted. In the right distance, beyond the rake of wagons, the 'National Benzole' lettering can be made out on the fence of the closed petrol depot. ***Courtesy, Great Western Railway Society***

year at one shilling each, five in the first six months, five in the second.

There were no signal and telegraph staff, as the staff at Dulverton covered the whole area down to Barnstaple (see John Howard's recollections later in this chapter).

In March 1928, one carriage and wagon examiner was based at the GWR terminus. However, by 1942, the two examiners allocated to the terminus, Ken Stevens and Cecil Pritchard, cycled over each morning from the Junction. Walter King recalled the men keeping their tools and equipment in an iron van behind the station building. They came over early in the morning and checked the wheels on the wagons and coaches. On occasion they tapped the wheels of the Bristol goods as it passed the signal box. When vehicles in need of repair were found, they were worked around to the Junction where there was a workshop to carry out the necessary repairs.

On the train crew side, the March 1928 official GWR records show four engines allocated to the shed and five engine drivers and firemen, two cleaners, a chargeman and labourer. In the 1930s and with the intervention of the war, these numbers reduced. The 1946 official document shows three sets of men: drivers Parkhouse, Beer and Saunders, and firemen Barnes, Hugo and Dalling. Fred Beer joined the GWR as an engine cleaner in 1906; he had a spell at Taunton (July 1911-December 1913) but returned to Barnstaple as an experienced fireman and remained at Barnstaple shed, becoming an engineman there in February 1920. Sydney Saunders began his career as a cleaner at Barnstaple in 1917, briefly moving to Severn Tunnel Junction in 1920 as a fireman for five months, then returning to Barnstaple. In 1940 he went back to Severn Tunnel and returned via Taunton (a spell of 3½ years) in June 1944. Jack Parkhouse began his career at Barnstaple in August 1920 and spent virtually all his working life there, becoming a cleaner, fireman and then temporary driver in January 1944, with a permanent upgrade in March 1948. Ivan Dalling started at Taunton as a cleaner in May 1937, transferred to Barnstaple in February 1938 and acted as a fireman during summer 1939. He was promoted to fireman at Taunton and went to Brimscombe and Bristol, returning to Taunton and then Barnstaple in February 1946. Other enginemen recalled include Albert Doran, Fred Burridge, Frank Clement, Fred Edwards and Tommy Phillips. Two passenger guards, three goods guards and one-porter guard were on the payroll in March 1929 reducing to one passenger guard and two porter-guards by 1934. Ted Yeo recalls Ern Vinnecombe covering goods work more than others with Jack Parkman and Courtney Card covering passenger trains. Porter Sid Ash and the shunters covered some of the transfer trips to and from the junction but as referred to above porter-guards such as Bill Chilcott and Bill Turner also did this work.

The station master and possibly a couple of platelayers pose in front of a GWR Third Class coach full of excited schoolboys in the late 1930s/ early 1940s. Nothing is known of the occasion.

LEFT: A 'Mogul' heads tender first along the Barnstaple Branch Railway, with a passenger train from the Junction to Victoria Road that includes an ex-Southern Railway parcels van nearest the engine that will be carrying passenger rated traffic. The picture is looking from Newport Road Bridge and almost hidden by the smoke and steam from the locomotive is an aqueduct which carried a water main over the line. *James G. Tawse*

PAGE RIGHT: Victoria Road looking west across the goods yard circa 1964 but prior to the removal of the carriage and livestock pens sidings in 1966. The viewpoint clearly demonstrates how the platform canopy had been boarded all round by British Road Services to provide additional storage accommodation. The tall building in the background was part of the gas works. *Courtesy, the Lens of Sutton Association*

PASSENGER RATED TRAFFIC AT BARNSTAPLE

Passenger rated parcels traffic peaked during the late 1930s when between 70,000 and 72,000 items were handled each year, an average of around 230 per day (with a six-day week). In 1951, a peak of 136,677 parcels was recorded. Passenger services brought consignments for local shops and took away other commodities, of particular note being the following:

• Gloves – manufactured by Dent Allcroft of Newport Road, Barnstaple, they were shipped to their office in Yeovil.
• Fish arrived regularly for Mac Fisheries in the town.
• Pigeons – these were live pigeons despatched regularly by local clubs. When they were being trained they were taken as far as South Molton and released to fly home.
• Culled rabbits – they were brought to the station by the rabbit merchant Leonard Joslin, who received them from local trappers. It is understood the rabbits went to Sheffield.
• Ferns and greenery – locally cut by travellers, it was brought to the station for the Birmingham market. Consignments went with the rabbits.
• Ice cream – this came from Wall's of Acton, weekly in summer months. Arriving in containers, it was taken to Wall's depot at Vicarage Lawn in the centre of the town for unloading, which took 3-4 hours.
• Strawberries – these were brought for despatch by Ray Norman from the Combe Martin area and sent to Birmingham on the 7.15pm train.
• Yeast – every evening about two tons of yeast was sent by the DCL Company in Boutport Street, Barnstaple to Bristol.
• Mushrooms – these travelled on the 7.15pm parcels vans for the Birmingham markets, having been brought to the station on his 15cwt truck by Colonel Oliver, who owned the Braunton farm which grew them.

Collections and deliveries were carried out by Maurice Strickland in the 1930s, driving a box van. He would go out three times a day, his last round being 2.00pm. Chaplin's limited were goods and parcels agents for the Southern Railway and they dealt with traffic for Bratton Fleming, Lynton and Lynmouth. Other individual carriers from outlying districts would also collect from the station.

GOODS TRAFFIC TO AND FROM BARNSTAPLE

During the 1930s, the total tonnage of goods dealt with fluctuated between 39,000 tons and 44,000 tons per year, at a daily average of 11-12 wagons. In 1938, 28,000 tons of general merchandise (approximately nine wagons per day) were dealt with, which thus accounted for most of the traffic. The total goods tonnage handled peaked during the war years at nearly 72,000 tons in 1944, about twenty 10-ton wagons per day. General merchandise traffic accounted for the bulk of this at around 51,000 tons (14-15 10-ton wagons per day).

There were changes after the war. The 'zonal scheme', implemented from 1st August 1947, saw a concentration of 'smalls' traffic from several local stations, with Barnstaple Victoria Road taking this over from Barnstaple Junction when the scheme under went modifications in 1948 and 1950.

As a result of these zonal schemes, goods traffic rose considerably and in 1951 reached a peak of 124,727 tons (thirty-five 10 ton wagon loads a day). This included livestock handling which, following a pre-war decline, rose to a peak of 1,597 wagons in 1951 (4-5 wagons per day) and remained in excess of 1,000 wagons per year until 1955, when the final decline set in on this traffic.

Most of the livestock traffic originated from the Friday cattle market, the animals being driven on the hoof to the station. In 1938, 266 wagons were despatched (about four per week on average), down from a pre-Second World War peak of 752 (an average of 14/15 per week) in 1930. Most livestock transported was for slaughter. Pigs purchased by a representative of Harris Sausages were sent to their factory in Calne, Wiltshire, whilst others went to Tan-y-Bwlch, Merioneth and the Highbridge Bacon Co. Cattle went to Ystrad Mynach in Glamorgan but some 'store cattle' went to Oxford to a cattle dealer. Cart horses were occasionally despatched for the knackers yard at Martock. The cattle wagons were usually attached to the engine of the Bristol goods so they could be taken off quickly on arrival. Loading took place at the small cattle dock, which had a capacity of four wagons, so when it was busy the loaded ones were removed by locomotive and the next four empties, which were stored ready for loading on the middle road, were gravity shunted alongside the dock.

Based on records from January 1939, smalls/station truck workings were scheduled for despatch each weekday from Bristol, Exeter (via Taunton), Hockley, Plymouth (via the Exe Valley), Smithfield and South Lambeth. All except the Plymouth truck were booked on the Bristol goods. The wagons often contained 'vulnerable' loads such as bottles of whisky, brandy and similar. Other traffic was of a diverse nature. Some wagons went on to the Southern after they had been partially unloaded at the GWR station, as they also contained loads for Bideford, Ilfracombe and other locations. Trucks were returned to Bristol, Exeter (via Dulverton), Paddington, Smithfield and Taunton. These usually worked out on the 2.55pm goods to Taunton. The operation of station trucks was explored further in Chapter 11.

A variety of inwards goods were handled:

• Bananas – these came from Avonmouth, largely for F. Knill & Company, wholesale fruit merchants at The Strand and Maiden Street. They arrived by the van load and were collected by the merchant, with the railway delivering smaller quantities to other traders.

• Tea – this arrived from the Lyons factory at Greenford, West London and was unloaded in the small storage warehouse to the east of the goods shed. Brooke Bond had supplies too, which went into the goods shed for unloading on the deck.

• Confectionery and biscuits – the former was delivered from Fry's of Bristol, the Barnstaple agent, it appears, covering the whole of the South West). The latter came from Huntley & Palmers in Reading, and McVitie & Price in Brentford. They were stored in lock-ups at the Taunton end of the goods shed, having arrived by the van load.

• Flour – Coombes' flour from Avonmouth arrived for the local Co-op.

• Coal – surprisingly, coal tonnages at Barnstaple GWR were never high, with around 3,649 tons delivered in 1938, about 1-2 wagons per day, up from 2,807 tons in 1936, partly due to a new housing development in the Newport area of the town. There were no staithes in the yard, wagons being unloaded straight into trucks. By the 1940s most domestic supplies were dealt with at Barnstaple Junction yard. However, occasional wagons of smelting coal arrived for Thomas Lake, iron founders in Newport Road, as did coal for the local gas works. Prior to the First World War and up until the Second, much house coal had been delivered coastwise to Barnstaple in small vessels trading down the Bristol Channel from Lydney Docks.

• Beer – supplies came from the Starkey, Knight & Ford brewery at Tiverton and from Worthington and Guinness at Park Royal in west London. Vans with barrels worked up the Exe Valley and then got

Goods yard staff remove the pins holding a container securely in place on this flat wagon, prior to using the 6-ton yard crane to lift it on to the road trailer in the background. ***Reg Chamming***

attached to one of the local goods. There were also 'D' containers of bottled beer but these suffered regular breakages and were transferred to road. A two-horse dray collected the barrels from the yard.

• Petroleum – supplies came from Avonmouth (National Benzole petrol arrived on the Bristol goods) and Cattedown, Plymouth (Shell). Both these were dealt with in the 'kick-back' road. Benzole fuel was a concoction of a bi-product of gas, which was collected from local gas works and blended with petrol brought in by rail and then distributed to local garages. Wagons for Pratts (later the Anglo-American Oil Company, then Esso) were dealt with at the end of the back road, where their contents were pumped via an underground pipe to a garage opposite the station. Paraffin was also received and siphoned off to a storage tank below the embankment on the back road. This would then be distributed locally in cans. There was additional in-bound fuel in the 1939-45 period, the RAF based Chivenor pumping it out themselves.

• Bagged cement – arrived from Portland for local builders such as J. Cater & Sons, who made up breeze blocks by mixing the cement with locomotive ash.

• Sugar beet pulp – used as an animal feed, this was returned from the Kidderminster sugar factory in bags and collected through North Devon Farmers based in Tuly Street.

• Animal feed – this was usually supplied by the British Oil & Cake Mills Company (BOCM) to a number of local companies, including Maldram & Jones, seed merchants of Bear Street, Berry & Sons of Tuly Street and North Devon Farmers.

• Fertiliser – this comprised basic slag, sulphate of ammonia and manure. 'Sulfuro' brand fertiliser was sent by a manufacturer in Stonehouse, Plymouth.

• Furniture – arrived in 'D' containers and was distributed by lorry, the empty containers returning later.

Goods outwards showed a similar variety, reflecting the railway's role as a 'common carrier', *i.e.* obliged to transport any goods offered, which was ultimately to lead to the downfall of railborne freight as the road hauliers stole the more lucrative traffics:

• Tar – an occasional traffic from the gas works, the trailer from which would deliver to the end-dock opposite the cattle pens by backing onto it, the contents from the delivery trailer then being pumped into a rail tanker positioned there. It was recalled that these wagons often did not run easily, as their axle boxes were often gummed up.

• Sugar beet – this was despatched in November/December of each year. The lorry effecting delivery to the station would have a special roller floor bottom and handle, enabling it to be backed up to the dock and then tip the beet straight into a waiting rail wagon. Farmers would also deliver their own beet and in later years the produce was taken to Kidderminster for processing.

• Pottery – was despatched in 'D' containers collected from local potters C.H. Brannam of Litchdon Street.

• Wool – was despatched from fellmongers Sanders & Son of Pilton Bridge and Rolle Quay. 'D' containers would be left at the company for loading which the railway company would later collect. The wool could also be packed and shipped in box vans (six bales being loaded upright) or in an open wagon and sheeted. The shipment usually went to Bradford.

• Pelts (sheep skins) – usually loaded into 'D' containers or occasionally dealt with loose from the same supplier as the wool.

• Lace – this was despatched in bales from the Derby Lace factory in Derby Road.

• Timber – this would either be sawn planks sent out in open wagons or logs loaded onto bogie bolster wagons, the wood being supplied by Rawle, Gammon & Baker of Rolle's Quay.

• Pit props – supplied by Chapel & Waldron, these were sent out in open wagons.

• Farm machinery – horse-drawn ploughs, rakes, hoes and similar were manufactured by John Huxtable & Son Ltd at their Alexandria

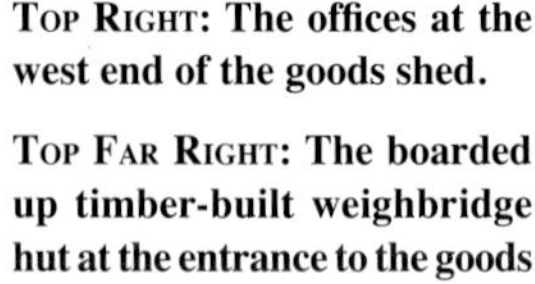

Four views taken around the goods yard in the mid-1970s:

TOP RIGHT: The offices at the west end of the goods shed.

TOP FAR RIGHT: The boarded up timber-built weighbridge hut at the entrance to the goods yard. Note the weighbridge was still in place.

BOTTOM RIGHT: The east end of the goods shed, looking across to the site of the station platform and building, which had been covered over by Eastern Avenue, then recently built.

BOTTOM FAR RIGHT: Another aspect of the west end of the goods shed and offices. Note that the building was still in use by NCL at this time.
All Reg Chamming

A fascinating study at Barnstaple's Castle Quay in the early 1920s, showing unbranded steel barrels being unloaded by hand-operated steam winch from an unidentified steam coaster. The barrels are being lifted out of the ship's hold and on to the load bed of a 5-ton 'C' Type Foden steam waggon of circa 1917, registration No. T-7480 and operated by the Northern Division of Devon County Council, whilst a sister waggon waits to load the next batch behind. It is not known how many of these machines were owned and operated by DCC(ND) but one of them still survives today, registration No. T-8750, fully restored in dark green livery with cream coloured lettering shaded red, which makes regular appearances at steam fayres across the country. Given that these barrels are being collected by DCC vehicles, it might reasonably be speculated that they contain tar for road making perhaps? Barnstaple's situation on the River Taw, which also served other large quays such as Fremington and later Yelland (established in 1955 when East Yelland power station was built), the coasting trade provided regular competition for the railway in this area up until circa 1960. The building on the left housed the Barnstaple Corporation Mains Electricity Department, whilst in the centre background, the roof of the L&SWR Commercial Road Gates Crossing box, which dated from circa 1898. The L&SWR line ran behind the electricity building to pass through Barnstape Town station, just behind and to the left of the photographer. The electricity building has long since been demolished but most of those in the centre background still remain today. *Neil Parkhouse collection*

Works in Alexandra Road and were sent out in open wagons, usually having been loaded by one of the shed cranes. Also, Arthur Thomas despatched corn and turnip drills.

• Reed/thatching – cut reeds for thatching were sent away in open wagons but weighing little were piled high and sheeted, so had to be loaded in the mileage road for the men to be sure that the loads could clear the loading gauge.

• Empty beer bottles – these went back to Tiverton in a loaded 'D' container.

• Furniture – outgoing furniture was despatched in 'D' containers from the manufacturers Elon in Newport Road.

Collection and Delivery of Goods at Barnstaple

Originally, the collection and delivery of goods was by horse and cart, for which the railway had six horses, five for goods and one for parcels. The stables were near the station, just off Victoria Road next to the Rustic Oak Company, so they did not have far to go in the mornings to collect their carts from the goods yard. The horses had gone by the late 1930s.

By 1942, they had been replaced by a fleet of six lorries: one 6-ton and two 3-ton Scammells, a 5-ton AEC, a 3-ton Fordson and a 3-ton Thorneycroft. The heavier Scammell was driven by Arthur Grant and later Arthur Sluman, with Walter King being the van guard (that is responsible for guarding the van but also loading and unloading). Walter would book on at the goods office at 8.00am and he and his driver would collect the already loaded trailer by 8.30am and be on their way delivering around the town centre. The lighter Scammells were driven by Harry Barnes and Phil Smaile and covered the main roads in the town. The AEC and the Thornycroft covered a similar area to the Scammells but the Fordson was assigned to the Country Lorry Service and covered an area bounded by Fremington, Newton Tracey and Filleigh; it was also used for the Newport and Pilton work.

Some of the consignments were not entirely rail-borne. Clay was collected from a pit at Picklington and taken to C.H. Brannam Ltd at their Litchdon Road pottery works. Gloves were also taken from Dent, Allcroft's factory in Newport Road to Pilton for packing, prior to being despatched by rail to their Yeovil head office.

Private carriers such as Chaplin's (later taken over by Pickfords) and those from Bratton Fleming and Combe Martin called at the goods shed. A 3-ton lorry was used on the Lynton run.

There was no garage provided in the railway yard for the lorries, which were therefore left parked overnight up against the goods shed. Maintenance was carried out by Ron Slade, who regularly came over from Tiverton to keep the fleet on the road, or take lorries away if they needed more significant attention.

Barnstaple Petrol Depot

The petrol depot had a staff of six, a manager and five others, who operated under a divisional manager based at Bristol. The exact date of its establishment has not been ascertained but the Anglo-American Oil Company's depot is listed in a *Kelly's Directory* of 1919. The OS maps show that the sidings that served it were already in place, whilst the track plan on page 380 of Volume 2, which shows the oil depot at the end of the kick-back siding as being there in 1902, is now acknowledged to be erroneous in placing it there that early.

The Anglo-American Oil Company, which from 1896 marketed the products of Pratts Oils, established their depot on the opposite side

An enlargement from the aerial view of Barnstaple that appeared in Volume 2, which is now dated a little later as circa 1967, after the removal of two sidings in 1966. In the foreground is the petrol depot, served until 1956 by the short siding which kicked back off the siding running behind the goods shed. Beyond the station, across Victoria Road, can be seen the former Anglo-American depot, by this date under the Esso name, and to the left of that is the gas works. Castle Quay can just be made out, facing out in to the River Taw in the top distance. ***Aerofilms/Historic England***

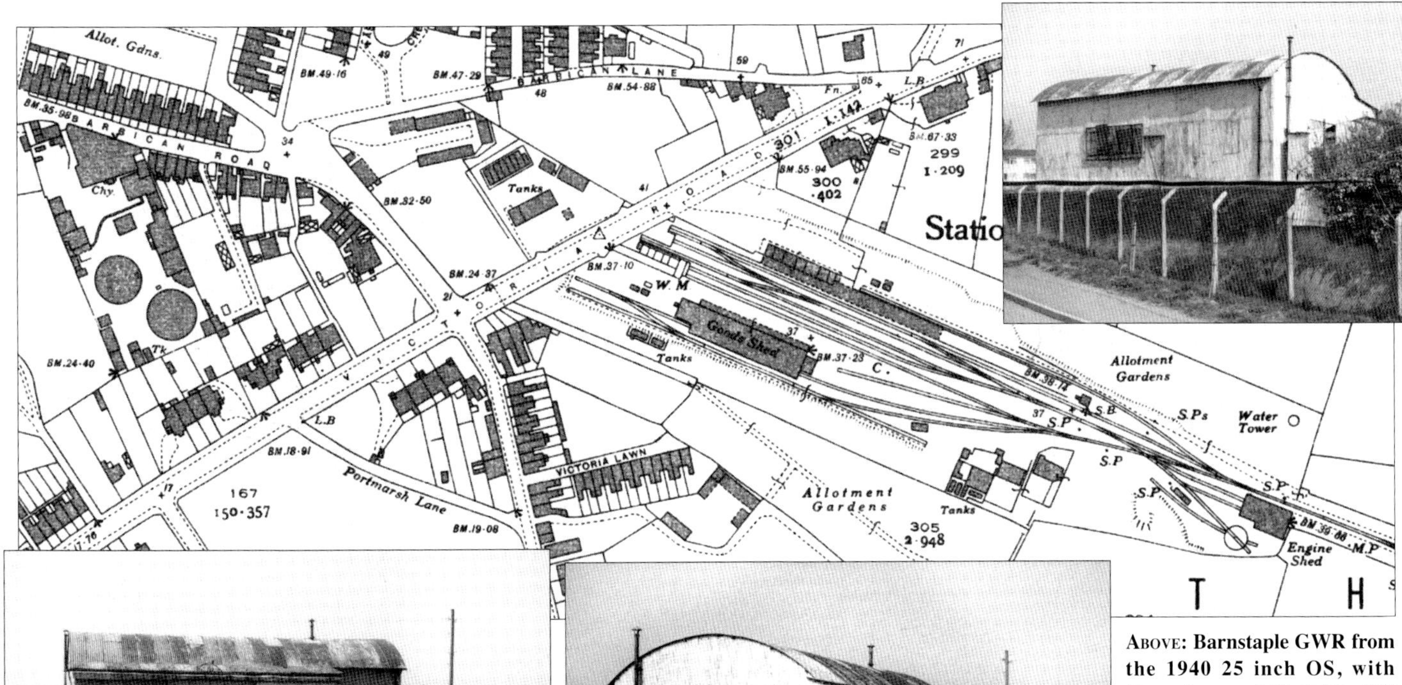

Above: Barnstaple GWR from the 1940 25 inch OS, with the rail-served Shell-Mex/BP petrol depot backing on to the allotments. The Anglo-American depot faced the station, across Victoria Road, its site simply annotated 'Tanks', whilst the gas works, which was never rail connected, can be seen just to the left (west).

Above and Top Right: Three views of the disused oil depot in the mid 1970s showing, from the left, the rail-side with Eastern Avenue in the foreground and the weathered National Benzole lettering still in place on the fence; the depot from the east; the view from Eastern Avenue. Buildings and fence were all constructed of non-flammable corrugated iron sheet. ***All Reg Chamming***

Below: A circa 1965 aerial view of the station, after the still extant petrol depot had closed.

of Victoria Road from the terminus. It grew to become a significant storage facility and distribution depot, being the largest of those at the station. An aerial photograph from the 1950s reveals eleven storage tanks at the depot and even today, long after its closure, the site is occupied, rather appropriately, by an Esso filling station. The Anglo-American Oil Company, which later used 'Esso' as its tradename in place of Pratts, became Esso Petroleum in 1951.

This preserved BP sign at the West Somerset Railway is a smaller version of the large one that adorned the rail side of the petrol depot at Victoria Road (see the picture on page 394, Volume 2).

Shell-Mex Limited was formed in 1921 when Shell Transport & Trading took over the Mexican Eagle Oil & Shipping Company. It later became Shell-Mex & BP Limited under a joint venture company formed in 1932 and had premises at the eastern end of the goods yard, at the end of the kick-back siding. They had around four lorries, which distributed to various garages in the area.

The National Benzole Company Limited was set up in 1919 and established their local distribution depot at the eastern end of the goods yard in the late 1920s. It was one of a number located in the South West of England (others being at Plymouth, Falmouth, Exeter and Taunton) to meet the growing demand for petrol. Deliveries for Barnstaple arrived in tank wagons from Avonmouth, each holding 3,000-5,000 gallons. The petrol was discharged by gravity and then mixed with benzole, a bi-product of coal tar naphtha when it was redistilled with steam and heated with sulphuric acid. It was collected from the local gas works at Barnstaple, Ilfracombe and Bideford, and from the early 1920s was sold as a motor fuel mixed 50:50 with petrol. Authority for the expansion of the National Benzole Depot was given in August 1952 but it is not clear that any work was undertaken. In 1957, the National Benzole Co. became a part of Shell-Mex & BP Ltd but continued its separate trading identity. In the early 1960s, the company was re-branded as National and continued trading until the early 1990s, when the brand was phased out by BP. Barrels of lubricating oil also arrived by rail in open wagons on rare occasions.

The petrol depot closed in 1956 when supplies for Shell started coming in by sea to Yelland. However, the premises survived intact until the early 1960s.

The 1939-1945 War Years

During the Second World War, goods traffic increased, mainly as a consequence of storage depots set up in Barnstaple. Red Cross trains with wounded soldiers bound for a military hospital at Fremington traversed the line, running round at Victoria Road and filling the yard when they did so. With good locomotive coal hard to come by, house coal was used for locomotives, which must have made the jobs of footplate crews much harder. Finally, as D-day was approaching, some troop trains used the East Chord, all done in a secretive manner after dark.

Engine Cleaning Routines

Joe Hugo was a cleaner in 1941. At this time, he recalls there was a 'fire-dropper' on at nights, along with the the early turn cleaner (which is the job Joe initially did when he was only 18 years old) and the chargeman (Joe's father). The cleaners would work alternate weeks from 10.00pm to 6.00am and midnight until 8.00am. There was no night turn on Saturdays because engines were rarely steamed for Sunday duties. Joe would enter the station complex by way of the goods yards gates (climbing over them if they were not open) and walking down to the shed. He remembers there were usually two engines on shed – one being prepared for the 6.55am Up passenger, the other for an early goods working. They carried out the usual disposal work outside the shed, which would include opening the engine's dampers over the ash pit, spraying water through the ash pan to damp down the dust and then raking out. In the winter after re-lighting, they took the engines inside the shed for cleaning but the summer months were busier with extra engines to clean. The cleaners would sometimes be joined by the local policeman, who would be checking the coaches for vagrants and expecting a fry-up of bacon and eggs. The cleaners also had the unenviable task of loading the ash from the pit into wagons for disposal.

Enginemen and Engine Workings

Records of enginemen's rosters and official workings of the 1930s period have not been discovered so reliance is placed on the memories of Joe Hugo and Ken Barnes.

There were four sets of men, the first booking on at 5.10am; they prepared the engine and came off shed at about 6.30am to work the first passenger to Taunton (at 6.55am), which usually departed from the bay platform. The crew worked through to Taunton and on arrival there took the engine on shed, later returning on the 10.35pm departure from Taunton to Barnstaple Junction where, after disposing of their coaches, turning the engine and returning light to the GWR shed at 1.10pm, they booked off.

The second set of men booked on at about 7.30am to take the second engine off shed and then took over the shunting of the morning Bristol goods from the Taunton crew who had brought it in and who would then work back with the second passenger departure at 8.45am. After completing their shunting and working a trip to the Junction and back, the Barnstaple men worked the 9.55am Taunton goods but only for a short distance, switching footplates at Swimbridge with a Taunton crew working the 6.00am Down Taunton goods. On arrival back at the GWR station, the Barnstaple crew would shunt the goods, work another transfer trip to the Junction and book off at about 3.30pm.

The third crew booked on about 10.15am and it is thought they used the third engine to work the 9.50am Ilfracombe to Paddington passenger train. This they took as far as Dulverton, where they changed footplates with Exeter men and worked the Exe Valley auto train to Exeter and back. The Exeter men would work to Taunton and then back to Dulverton, where they would swap again. The Barnstaple crew would then work through to the Junction on a Down passenger to complete their shift.

The fourth set of men booked on at 3.00pm and prepared the engine for the 4.08pm departure to Taunton, which they worked throughout, before going on shed there. They then returned with the last passenger of the day at 8.17pm, due at Barnstaple at 9.56pm.

On arrival they stabled the coaches in the bay overnight and took the engine on shed, booking off at 11.00pm.

By 1941, there were only two locomotives based at Barnstaple, with three sets of men. In the late 1940s for example, the first crew booked on at 5.10am to prepare their engine and as before they then worked the 6.55am to Taunton throughout. They worked back on the 11.00am Taunton to Barnstaple Junction, where they ran round their train and propelled the coaches to the Up main siding on the Bideford line. The engine was turned if necessary and returned light to the GWR shed for the crew to book off at 1.10pm. The crew on this turn sometimes worked a trip down the Exe Valley to keep them familiar with the route in case of diversions.

The second set of men booked on at about midday and prepared the second engine for the late turn men, before then relieving the early crew and using their engine to shunt the yard and form the 2.15pm Taunton goods. They would work this as far as South Molton, where they would change footplates with the Taunton men on the 11.40am Taunton to Barnstaple goods. If that train was running late, the changeover would take place further up the line. On arriving back at the GWR terminus, the goods was sorted, shunted and transfer trips made to and from the Junction. After further shunting the engine returned to shed and the crew booked off at about 8.00pm. This pattern of operation meant that there was an engine change every day at the shed.

The third set of men booked on at about 3.10pm and took the partly prepared second engine to Barnstaple Junction, to collect the coaches from the Up main siding to work the 4.00pm to Taunton; they returned with the 9.10pm from there. On arrival at Barnstaple, the coaches were run around and shunted into the bay for the 6.55am departure the next morning. The engine went on shed and the crew booked off at 11.10pm.

Personal Recollections

Jim Elson

Signalman, Venn Cross – born 21st October 1927, died 5th December 2012

Jim Elson was signalman at Venn Cross in the late 1940s and what follows is a sample of his recollections of life on the Devon & Somerset Railway in the post-war period. He was 18 years of age when he started in 1945 and because he was classified as a 'lad' (under the age of 21) he was on a reduced weekly wage (£9 18s 0d per week then) but, as was the way then, was expected to carry out exactly the same work as his older mate.

At the time, the Venn Cross staff consisted of just a station master and two signalmen sharing the shifts. Being the only station on the line without a porter, the signalman on duty thus frequently had more than his normal job to do.

The first shift signalman came on duty at about 4.20am, in time for the Down Bristol to Barnstaple goods to run through. This shift lasted until 1.00pm and the second shift ran from then until about 11.00pm, after the last train had cleared Wiveliscombe, which was confirmed when the signal box bell rang to indicate 'train out of section' – music to the late-shift signalman's ears and much more so than the bell on the alarm clock that would ring at 3.00-3.30am to wake the first shift signalman. In Jim's case, he would put the alarm clock in a biscuit tin to be sure he woke up and would then get on his push bike and pedal up the hill from Waterrow, where he lived, to Venn Cross station.

Venn Cross signal box in 1947. ***Jim Elson***

The early turn signalman would be busy from the start; there would be three Down freights before 8.00am, one from Bristol and two from Taunton. The Bridgwater auto train would then arrive, having set down various railway workers at stations from Taunton. With the Somerset/Devon border at Venn Cross, this was the limit of Taunton duties, so the auto would then run back to Taunton with paying passengers, mainly school children.

As we have seen from Volumes 1 and 2, Venn Cross was built in a cutting with the majority of the station in Somerset and a short tunnel at the Taunton end. The Up platform had a brick waiting room and behind it, the gents lavatory and a water hand-pump for the station. The grass bank behind the waiting room and platform was a haven for adders on a hot summer's day, so somewhere to avoid. The Down platform had the lamp shed and the signal box, whilst the goods shed and goods yard were also located at the west end on the down side. The main station buildings, comprising the booking office and station master's house, were situated on the top of the bank above the down platform, alongside the main road.

The signalman's regular early morning exercise was to go up the bank to the booking hall to open it up, light the fire, issue tickets and make sure he was back in his box to respond to the neighbouring signalman's bell codes for the next train. When the telephone in the booking hall rang and the station master was not available, again the signalman had to 'hot-foot' it up the bank to answer it; plenty of exercise to keep him fit therefore.

Just after 8.00am, two passenger trains would cross – the 7.24am from Taunton and the 6.55am first train up from Barnstaple, the signalman acting as the porter as well for these and all other passenger trains. This hive of activity would be interspersed with peace and calm, time then for the daily checking and filling of the Tilley lamps that served both the platform and the station buildings. These were in the days before luxuries such as electricity.

Freight movements at Venn Cross were interesting. It was usually the Taunton to South Molton daily goods that stopped to drop off, attach or shunt wagons. If there were wagons to detach from the Down goods for the mileage siding, the locomotive would need to uncouple but only after the guard had secured the brakes and spragged the wheels of some of the wagons. Once this was done, the engine would draw forwards, then run round the train on the Up line and just into the tunnel after the loop points were cleared. These would then be reset for the locomotive to attach itself to the rear of the train and take off the required wagons, which had been deliberately marshalled at the back, reversing once again into the tunnel. It would then shunt them along the Up platform line to the Devon end of the station, accessing the yard via the trailing point along the Up loop and the diamond crossover on the Down loop, to place the wagons in the siding. The locomotive would then have to return the guards van to the rear of the train before itself heading back to the front of the goods to await the signal for the road down the 1 in 58 incline to Morebath. Wagons to be collected from the mileage siding required the above manoeuvres to be carried out in reverse.

Placing of wagons in the goods shed was simpler, requiring the train to be drawn forward clear of the point for that siding on the Down loop. The locomotive would then shunt the required wagons back into the shed, uncouple them and return to its train. Up trains stopping to collect or drop off wagons had first to be placed in the refuge siding before any shunting was carried out. Shunting instructions for Venn Cross can be found on page 289 of Volume 2.

The Down goods would often have a station truck attached just behind the locomotive. This would contain supplies and small goods items for a number on stations on the line, avoiding the need to drop off a separate wagon containing just a few items at each location. When on duty at Venn Cross, Jim was responsible for unloading the sacks, bags and boxes from the station van whilst the train paused at the platform.

On Mondays, the Morebath porter used to arrive to replenish the signal lamps in the Down and Up Distant signals, and also the Down Advanced Starter. If luck was with him, he might manage a lift some of the way on the ganger's trolley but otherwise he was on foot. Thursday was the day for the signalman to replenish the signal lamps at Venn Cross, which had to be carried out whatever the weather, including the extreme conditions Jim experienced in the harsh winter of 1947.

In the evenings the station activity would increase again. When it was required, the 'Rabbiter' from South Molton would arrive at about 7.00pm. Prior to its arrival, the signalman would need to move the crates of rabbits collected locally by trappers from the goods shed on the Down side, over the barrow crossing at the west (Devon) end of the station and on to the Up platform for loading. Jim often moved as many as sixteen crates on the 2-wheeled station barrow, requiring a number of trips across the barrow crossing as he could take only around four crates at a time. One day he was wheeling the barrow a little too close to the Up platform edge and the wheels inadvertently caught the indent where a slight cutaway had been made to enable the overhang of a locomotive to clear the platform whilst taking the point into the yard. The crates spilled over the track but with some speedy work, the track was cleared before the special arrived and the rabbits duly loaded as planned.

The rabbit crates would be loaded into bogie vans, usually a pair of 'Siphons' pulled by a Class '45XX' tank, and this scene would take place at most stations on the line. On arrival at Taunton, the two bogie vans would be attached to the Up Paddington parcels and the cargo would reach its London destination in the early hours of the morning, for distribution to the capital's butchers via Smithfield Market.

Jim relates an occasion that illustrates

ABOVE: A glimpse inside Venn Cross goods shed, with a box van waiting to be loaded in the summer of 1947.

FAR LEFT: Weather extremes at Venn Cross. A view along the Down platform west towards Morebath in the summer of 1948. Note the diamond crossing serving both sidings in the goods yard from the Up line.

LEFT: The same view looking west during the winter of 1947, which is recorded as the snowiest of the 20th century, with snow falling somewhere in the country every day between 22nd January and 17th March.
All Jim Elson

what an unglamorous and dangerous job being a railwayman could be. A Down goods was heading up the 1 in 58 climb to Bathealton Tunnel, which it entered at a slow pace dragging its load behind but before reaching the summit had ground to a halt on wet rails. The guard feared that the train might start running back down the grade to Wiveliscombe so applied the handbrake in his van, but the footplate crew were unaware of this. The fireman stoked up and the driver tried again to get the train moving but, unfortunately, in trying to get a strong head of steam, the driver and fireman were scalded. Eventually, matters sorted themselves out and the train and crew made it to Venn Cross. There they parked the freight in order to return to Taunton on the next Up passenger train as passengers, in order to get to hospital for treatment.

ABOVE: Looking east towards Taunton from the Down platform, showing the neat red brick shelter to a standard GWR design on the Up side. ***Jim Elson***

RIGHT: Ex-Venn Cross signalman Jim Elson outside his home in Taunton in 2010.

There were other, more relaxed, moments befitting that of a country railway. Along large parts of the line, especially west of Dulverton, there were wooded areas running close to the track. It was not unusual for goods trains to stop mid-section to allow the driver or fireman to go in search of bean sticks for his garden or allotment, or collect sticks gathered by gangers. These would then be thrown on top of the tender to transport them. One of the more popular spots for collection was near Castle Hill Tunnel and on one particular occasion, the fireman inadvertently trod on a drainage pit cover in the cess alongside the line. These covers were usually made of metal but this one was wood and was rotten so it collapsed and he ended up to his neck in water!

Jim also recalled an occasion when he had to unload a young calf from a train. Having got it off successfully, he tied it to a lamp post so he could fulfil his other duties and see the train on its way. With a shrill blast on the whistle, the train showed its readiness to depart but it also startled the calf, which broke lose and ran off after the departing train in the direction of Morebath. Jim pursued the animal and managed to chase it off the line but was unable to catch it. As it was getting dark, he left the beast to its own devices, informing the farmer, who should have been at the station to collect it, of the circumstances. The next day Jim spotted the calf content and grazing in a nearby field along with other cows and eventually, although apparently not straight away, the farmer came to collect it.

Jim always had good banter with the drivers, hinting that some were more stubborn than others!

Finally, Jim provided a list of the names of signalmen on the line during his time on the railway:

Milverton.... .... E. Jeans & Gerald Manning
Wiveliscombe.... .... Harold Screech & Harold Elliot
Venn Cross.. .... Jim Elson & J. Waram [?]
Morebath .... F. Hillier & J. Hodge
Morebath Junction.. .... W. Pugh & F. Challis
Dulverton.... .... Arthur Smallridge & K. Alderman
Bishops Nympton & Molland... R. Winter & Mr Wescott
South Molton.... .... Frank Cockram & Mr Gill
Barnstaple ... . Bob Short & Bill Tanton

He could not recall the names of men at East Anstey and Filleigh, or the lady signalman at Swimbridge.

DENIS BENDING

Parcels driver, born 29th June 1929, died 8th March 2008

Denis ('Den') Bending was a parcels delivery driver based at Dulverton station in the late 1950s and early 1960s. He lived at Tiverton, so regularly took the 7.11am Exe Valley train from there to get to Dulverton by 7.42am, in good time for his start at 8.00am.

Den would start the day by loading parcels and non-perishables from the goods shed into his truck, an Austin K2, one of two at the station. When not in use they were covered by canvas sheet, which was clipped down to keep out the worst of the West Somerset weather. Den's responsibilities were to deliver on the Winsford side of the hill, the other truck doing the Anstey side. On Tuesdays and Thursdays, he made deliveries to Winsford and Exford via Bridgetown. On occasion, when required, he ventured as far afield as Simonsbath, some 15 miles from Dulverton station and his return journey would include Withypool, Winsford Hill and Tarr Steps. On the other days of the week he delivered to Brompton Regis, Haddon and Skilgate.

At 8.51am, the Down train from Taunton would have arrived and

Den would be responsible, along with the porters, for collecting the parcels and perishable goods out of the guards compartment; the latter would include, for example, sausages from Calne in Wiltshire and Lyons cakes from London. These goods would be loaded onto a station barrow and then wheeled over the crossing at the north-west end of the station. On one particular occasion, Den and two porters were pushing the barrow across when it got trapped in front a train. They had no time to alert the driver and the train, having been given the road, had begun to pull out of the platform, hitting the barrow and scattering goods over the track. All was not lost, however, as most of the cargo was retrieved and loaded onto the truck for onward delivery, the recipients presumably none the wiser.

Most goods received by train were delivered by truck but some were labelled 'TCF' – 'to be called for'. When the delivery truck needed refuelling there was a hand-cranked diesel pump for the station's use, located opposite the main station buildings, by the galvanised foodstuffs shed on the back road. This diesel tank was refilled by road delivery, not rail.

Den's days were varied and enriched by the wonderful local views he encountered every day on his rounds. Occasionally the unusual happened.

Phil, a Cockney porter, was on duty at Dulverton on a hot summer's day when a Barnstaple-bound train arrived and brought with it a dog (without accompanying owner), which was to be collected from the station later that day. Phil took the dog and rightly tied it up with its lead and left it on its own in the parcels office. However, in unusual surroundings, the dog became agitated and tried to break away from its leash. With one tug it was free from its collar and with the doors of the parcels office, open it escaped. Phil had spotted the escapee and leapt out of his office only to see it running down the platform, past about a dozen passengers and heading for and beyond the signal box. Phil called out "*Stop that dog ... 'tis a parcel!!*" but the passengers were unable to react in time and the animal carried on down the platform, along the line and over the Exe River bridge, ending up at the cottages next to the railway in Exebridge. The dog was later captured and a somewhat relieved Phil took it back into his care until it was eventually collected by its owner.

Percy Belamy was the goods porter and he worked in the office adjoining the goods shed. He lived at Bridgetown and had a stammer, and was in the Home Guard during the war. He was known as 'lucky Percy' as he was a regular winner at local whist drives, so whenever he bought a draw ticket Phil the porter wouldn't bother. Percy travelled from home to the station on a 2-stroke motorcycle, which was quiet and economical, with Percy making it even more so by switching off his engine and gliding the final few yards from the station gate to the goods shed to save petrol.

Den remembered the 'Cornish Riviera' calling at Dulverton on one occasion, when the main line between Tiverton and Exeter was blocked by flooding. The rerouted Down 'Riviera' thus came in to Dulverton from Taunton, where the locomotive ran around before retracing its steps back out to Morebath Junction, down the Exe Valley line via Tiverton to Exeter.

The line was not known for its speed of service and one witty driver played along one day. This particular train had stopped for some reason with the engine near the footbridge. A number of passengers were alighting and crossing over it when the driver (who apparently had a stutter) called up to them and said "*I..I.. dd..don't blame you for...for walking!*".

Den's working day finished about 5.00pm and he would then catch the 5.20pm Exe Valley train back to Tiverton, arriving at 5.45pm and then home to a good and welcome supper prepared by his wife, Vera.

TOP: Portrait of Den Bending in RAF uniform.

ABOVE: The Austin K2 lorry stopped on Winsford Hill, with an unknown youngster in cadet uniform posed in front.

RIGHT: Den and his truck, with snow chains fitted, in the bitter 1963 winter.
All courtesy Vera Bending

JOHN HOWARD,
Signal & Telegraph

John started on the railway at Dulverton station in December 1943 at the age of 14, as a lad porter working on the platforms. His duties at this time included the daily lighting of the platform Tilley lamps, as although there was electricity in Brushford by this time, the GWR had not connected to the local supply. Indeed, it was not until after rail nationalisation in 1948 that the station was supplied with electricity. The oil for this duty was kept in a corrugated iron hut at the north-west end of the station, near the pump house. There were approximately thirty lamps to be lit on the platforms, in the yard and the various offices, and in the signal box. The footbridge had to be lit with hurricane lamps, which were positioned at the base of the bridge, half way up and at the top of the stairs.

After a four-year period of National Service, John returned to Dulverton on 1st January 1950, initially on portering duties. Then Gordon Hooper, who was a lineman (a signal & telegraph engineer) at Dulverton, required an additional lineman who was locally based to help him and John answered the call. This required him to attend the Reading S&T department for four months of training.

Dulverton S&T, which comprised three men in the early 1950s, were responsible for telephones, lock bars, points, signal and track circuits, as well as signal box maintenance between Dulverton and Barnstaple, and from Dulverton to Stoke Cannon. The line between Morebath Junction and Taunton was covered by a separate crew, until closure of the Exe Valley line in 1963 when there was a reallocation of responsibilities. Gordon and a mate took the Dulverton/Barnstaple section and John and Archie Chanter dealt with Dulverton to Norton Fitzwarren.

Their base at Dulverton was the white wooden shed near the horse box dock platform, on the Up side of the line (see Volume 2, page 322), which was about the size of a large car garage. His 48-hour week (which included 4 hours on Saturdays) required him to travel by train to carry out specific and regular examination and maintenance of installations on their section. Every month they would need to walk the full length of this, albeit in phases, to check the instrument panels used by the gangers, which were approximately one mile apart. For example, they would walk from Barnstaple to Filleigh in one phase, leaving other sections for later in the month. Platelayers and gangers were based at Swimbridge, Molland, Bampton (which covered Dulverton – this was Ganger Ball's territory) and Wiveliscombe.

John remembers the two accidents referred to in the previous chapter, the 'Mogul' derailing at Dulverton and the Swimbridge freight derailment. There was a lot of repair work for him and the team to carry out at the latter location.

On a more humorous note, on one occasion a wire signal support stay (known as a 'Y' stay because of its shape) was broken and a telegraph note had to go to Taunton which simply reported 'Y STAY BROKEN', to which the official response was 'Y NOT REPAIR IT THEN'. These stays required some fixing as, once in position, great wrist strength was needed to secure the wire, a job for Gordon Hooper rather than John by his own admission.

Drivers of the early Bristol goods would often state how relieved they were on bursting out of Bathealton Tunnel after a stormy night, that Waterrow Viaduct was still there! He also recalls that gangers would sell surplus sleepers – ten would make half a ton of firewood – and they would charge 1s 2d for each; five good sleepers would build a garden shed. If the ganger liked you then you got a good set of sleepers but if he was not so fond of you he would provide a mass of broken/rotting ones for the price paid.

There was a coal bunker just off the west end of the Up platform, which was originally built as a stone-walled container with no door or roof. A coal wagon would be shunted into the horse box siding along side the bunker and unloaded to replenish the store. This supply of coal was the ration for the season for the booking office and major fireplaces in the buildings. However, the staff would from time to time remove lumps of coal to fuel the S&T hut and porters hut next to the bunker. The station master at the time, Reg Weston, got wise to this and asked for a carpenter to be sent from Taunton to put a roof on the bunker and a lock on the door to restrict the unauthorised removal of coal. The key to the lock was kept in the porters' office but the staff knew this and were then simply able to unlock the door and continue to get their coal supply!

John recalls the newspapers arriving on the first Exe Valley arrival from Exeter. He observed small provisions such as bacon and other perishables arriving on local passenger services, these items being collected by local merchants or delivered by the railway lorries. Most freight for the area arrived on the Taunton to South Molton/Dulverton goods. There would be significant numbers of coal wagons dropped off for Goodlands merchants next to the station. Animal feeds came in by rail and were unloaded from box vans on the back road by the station entrance, where there was a Silcox-Bibbys corrugated iron shed used for storage. Farmers would collect the foodstuffs themselves from the railway. Timber from local woods was loaded from the loading dock on the Down side into open wagons

A deserted scene at the north-west end of Dulverton station in the early 1950s, with the line curving away under the B3222 road bridge towards East Anstey. The corrugated iron hut where the lamp oil was housed can just be made out beyond the stone-built pump house, partially hidden by the Down Starting signal. On the right is the short siding serving the horse dock. ***Joe Moss, courtesy Roger Carpenter***

A Down train heads westwards across the Tone or Waterrow Viaduct having just climbed through the tight bore of Bathealton Tunnel on 20th July 1963. Some drivers, particulary of very early morning trains such as the Bristol goods, confessed to being hugely relieved after a night of very stormy weather to find that the viaduct was still there as they exited the pitch dark tunnel. Two Venn Cross signalmen lived in this vicinity, Jack Upton in a cottage beneath the viaduct and Jim Elson in Waterrow village. *Peter W. Gray*

but sometimes it was just tipped in. Cattle came in from Cutcombe Market to be despatched by train and were originally driven down to the station via Heathpoult Cross and the top road above the Exe Valley but latterly they came by lorry. In busy times there would be special cattle trains run, which could be loaded up to twenty wagons, usually pulled by a pannier tank.

Thursday was wages day and the guard on the 3.30pm train would be responsible for a box in his compartment which stored the cash for the wages, which had to be signed for at each station en route. The station's daily takings were sent up to Taunton on the 9.10am departure from Dulverton. Again the guard would take responsibility for this, as the cash box would be in his compartment with the takings placed in a leather pouch and put into the secure box. Money for the National Provincial Bank branch in Dulverton would arrive in heavy crates by train with little or no security but there were never any incidents. National Provincial was merged into National Westminster in 1970 and under their auspices, the bank, originally opened in 1898, continued in the same premises until 2015 but has now closed.

On another occasion John recalls that a horse box was waiting to be collected by an Up train to go to Taunton and then onwards. The Taunton-bound train pulled in and left but the station workers had forgotten the horse box in its siding. All was not lost, however, and the box was coupled up to the next Exe Valley service for a scenic journey to Exeter before somehow being rerouted on from there to its ultimate destination.

Given his job, John got to know the signalmen well on his section of the line. He recalls Jack Upton at Venn Cross, who lived in a cottage under Waterrow Viaduct, as helpful. Most were characters and happy to make the S&T men cups of tea but a few were just cantankerous and not as hospitable.

John finished working at Dulverton just before the railway closed, watching over the reduction of point work, layout rationalisation and signal boxes being taken out of use from 1963 onwards; he recalls amending signal box diagrams which were sent to Reading. He even recalls getting a bonus for continuing to maintain a point that had been taken out of use. He also remembers that even the DMU service in the final years' was unreliable and they would carry their own oil and diesel just in case they ran out during the journey.

He moved to Swindon for six months to help with the installation of new signalling on the Reading to Bristol main line, working 12-hour days. Although the money was good it was not good for family life, as he had a wife and young son back at Dulverton, so he returned and got a job where he was based at Barnstaple. This required a drive every day to get in but he was rewarded with S&T work on the scenic routes between Barnstaple, Ilfracombe and Torrington. When the D&SR line closed, Gordon Hooper went to work as a car mechanic at the local Carnarvon Garage, which was owned by George Nelder until his death and then run by his widow Kathleen and her stepson Chris (who has provided help with this book). Gordon also drove my school bus in the late 1960s. Archie Chanter, another colleague of John's, joined the family building firm, Radley & Chanter.

Melvyn Baker

Fireman

Melvyn started life at Taunton shed as a cleaner in August 1961 but only did this for ten months before becoming a 'passed cleaner', which meant he could fire locomotives when there was a shortage of men. He progressed to fireman and worked a number of local branch lines from Taunton, including the route to Barnstaple. Set out below are some of his recollections in his own words.

Travelling the Barnstaple Branch – Then & Now

The 5.55pm passenger service in the early 1960s

At that time, I was part of the 'link 3' group of men based at Taunton shed (83B) and this service was part of our 'normal' work for the afternoon shift.

We would book on at about 2.30pm; our first scheduled duty was to work a short goods service to and back from Wellington. However, by the early '60s there was very little traffic on this route and it was not at all unusual for this run to be 'capped' – this was the term used when a working was cancelled owing to a lack of traffic. When this happened, the shed foreman would find us other work in and around the shed to fill in our time – we also had the chance to get an early bit of tea before working the 5.55pm departure!

The loco for this service was always 'prepped' for us by another set of men, taken off shed and coupled to the coaches which were by then already in the Barnstaple bay platform (Platform 3 as it then was). The loco was always a Mogul – either 6372, 7304 with lever reverser, 7326, 7333, or 7337; the latter three locos had a screw reverser and side windows on the cab – as footplate crew, we preferred these as they gave us a lot more protection as we were crossing the open expanses of the edge of Exmoor.

We were able to walk up from the shed to the station at about 5.30pm, relieve the other crew and still have plenty of time to prepare for the journey ahead. So, with the fire readied, all passengers aboard, whistle and green flag given by the guard, away we would go.

The service stopped at all stations on the branch, and we would soon be ticking them off; each station had its own characteristics, but oh how they varied by weather and season. One always stuck in my mind – that was Yeo Mill Halt; this was a station that seemed to be in the middle of nowhere. In the depth of winter, it was by far the worst,

The lonely Yeo Mill Halt, as seen from a passing train on 15th February 1958. Note the spot replacement of rotten planks that had been carried out. ***James G. Tawse***

LEFT: 'Mogul' No. 6337 stands in the bay platform at Taunton with a train for Barnstaple, as the driver checks oil levels prior to departure. The 83B Taunton shedplate can be seen on the smokebox door, the locomotive being allocated there from October 1958 to May 1962 (apart from a month spent at Danygraig in South Wales), which provides a date span for the view. On the right, 'Large Prairie' No. 4157, waiting with a train for Minehead, can narrow this window a little further, being allocated to 83B between August 1956 and September 1961.
The Lens of Sutton Association

RIGHT: A driver's eye view of the route out of the bay platform from the cab of a DMU. However, the picture dates from the late 1960s, after the Barnstaple Branch had closed, so this service was bound for Minehead. Little would have changed from the days of steam, with Taunton to retain its mechanical signal boxes and semaphore signals for another two decades.
Courtesy Roger Carpenter,
The Lens of Sutton Association

LEFT: Having departed, the DMU has joined the Down relief line out of Taunton and is about to head beneath this impressive signal gantry, the route here still being four-track at this date. The road ahead is clear, with both the Home and Distant arms for the Down relief line being 'off'
Courtesy Roger Carpenter,
The Lens of Sutton Association

Above: The first of two photographs taken circa 1960 from the front compartment of an Up train, which give close to a driver's eye view of the line. Here, the train is taking the Up loop at Morebath Junction, with the Exe Valley line curving off to the right. Note the trap and catch points on the Down loop, showing safety was paramount, as well as the array of token apparatus for both routes. *The Lens of Sutton Association*

Above: Entering Morebath, showing the line heading straight and in the distance beginning a short but steep ascent towards Morebath Junction. Again there were trap and catch points here, those on the Up loop visible on the right. Note the pw hut set well back from the line. *The Lens of Sutton Association*

particularly on a night that was cold and dark (as dark as cows' guts, as we would often say). The Halt only had one short platform and that was lit by a single Tilley lamp. On such a nighttime run as this and with no further trains due, we had to stop – whether there were passengers or not – so that our guard could blow out the Tilley lamp.

By now Barnstaple Victoria Road had closed to passenger traffic so our journey would terminate at Barnstaple Junction, around 7.40pm. Once we had arrived, we would quickly uncouple our engine and go 'on-shed'. As this was a Southern shed we, as Western men, were not particularly popular as we didn't dispose of our engines (that is, throw out the fire, clean the smokebox, empty the ash pan, etc). The Western Region was alone in having shed men to do these duties.

There were no services returning along the branch to Taunton at that time of night. So to get home, speed was of the essence to make sure we could travel 'on the cushions' on the last passenger service back to Exeter St. Davids. Once there, it was another mad dash across to Platform 6 to hitch a ride back to Taunton in the brake van of the 'Kensington milk'; and on arrival, we could 'book off' – the end of yet another turn.

In those days, no matter what the duty turn, there was never time to have a set meal break; it was just a case of working it in with the job. As a young fireman, it was a hard way of life but I now look back on my railway life with fond memories of what was a very enjoyable period in my life.

Travelling along the A361 in the 21st century

The Barnstaple Branch is, of course, no more. However, the A 361 'North Devon Link' road from the M5 to Barnstaple is built on some of the former track bed at South Molton and beyond.

Now, some fifty years later, as a courier I travel that road to Barnstaple on a regular basis but I have the creature comforts of an up-to-date van: heating, air-conditioning, radio, the lot. A far cry from the exposure to the elements in the cab of a steam locomotive.

With a 60mph speed limit on most of the road, it is the speed camera van that I am looking out for – no longer the Distant signal for Venn Cross!

Whilst life inevitably moves on, it's nice to think back and reflect on what seems to have been a more relaxed and enjoyable age.

GOODS WORKINGS AND THE 'RUNAWAY TRAIN' – THE 6.04AM SOUTH MOLTON GOODS

The footplate crew

It was 1963 and I was a fireman in Link 3 at Taunton shed (83B). I had by then been promoted from the Link 4 / Chard Branch group of men. In that link, I didn't have a regular driver as my 'mate'; most of the drivers in that link were the older 'green carded' men who were no longer fit enough to be allowed out on the main lines! I found these drivers generally to be a miserable lot and not at all a pleasure to work with. In Link 3 Roy Cross was to become my regular driver.

As a young man, Roy had lived in Martock where his father was the signalman. It is not surprising, therefore, that the young Roy was to follow in his father's footsteps and join the railway as soon as he was able.

He started as a cleaner at Yeovil Pen Mill. If there was no available train for him to get to work – and that was most days, particularly when he was on an 1.00am or 2.00am start – he would cycle all the way from home in Martock to Yeovil. Again, after an 8-hour shift he would regularly cycle back in all winds and weathers; a fair distance to cover on just two wheels. How times and attitudes towards work have changed dramatically in this modern era.

After a few years, he had transferred to Taunton shed but now, if there was no available train, his cycle ride was almost twice as far! Not many people would be that dedicated to their work to do that in this day and age, but in those earlier days, this was not at all uncommon.

Roy progressed through the ranks and by 1963 he was a young driver who had already been promoted from the level of passed fireman.

What a contrast it was to be regularly paired with Roy – work became a lot more enjoyable. We shared a lot of experiences in our time together, both on goods and passenger workings, but one event sticks out above all others – the day of the 'runaway train'.

Goods workings at Taunton

In the early 1960s Taunton had four goods yards:

East Yard Down side – this was used for goods traffic arriving at Taunton for offloading in the goods shed, coal yard and mileage yard;

East Yard Up side – this was the other side of the 'goods avoiding line', which allowed goods traffic to bypass the main station running lines and was at the back of the old postal sorting office at the top of the station approach road. Here, goods traffic going East was marshalled whether it be local traffic to Bridgwater or on to the branches for Chard or Yeovil, or even further afield to Bristol and the north, to Westbury or beyond as far as London.

West Yard – now occupied by the current Post Office's sorting office and other industrial/retail units. This yard was used for marshalling local trains for Wellington or the Minehead or Barnstaple branches.

Fairwater Yard – now used by Network Rail for the High Output Ballast Cleaning Train, etc. This was used for putting off and picking up main line freight. In the final years, Barnstaple Branch goods would start and end here.

All these yards required 'trip working' from Taunton shed as and when needed; five pilot locos were allocated for these tasks.

The whole of the former East Yards, together with the trackbed of the goods avoiding loop line, is now part of a major residential development and what will be a northern inner distribution road for the town.

Taunton turntable out of use

Additional pannier and 'Prairie' tanks were drafted in to Taunton shed in February 1962 because the turntable was taken out of use for repairs and the 'Moguls' could not be turned. Such engines travelling tender first on the branch in the dark of winter would have made it difficult for the driver to see ahead and properly view the signals, so they were parked up at Taunton whilst the tank engines took over. Two Class '45XX' locomotives, No. 5563 from Yeovil and No. 5555 from Exeter, were temporarily transferred to supplement the home engines, No's 4593 and 5554. Also drafted in were BR 'Standard' Class '3' 2-6-2Ts No's 82038, 82041 and 82043, to supplement the home stable of No's 82008, 82030, 82042, 82044.

The 6.04am South Molton Goods

People always ask why this working in the 1960s was known as the 'South Molton Goods', as it was time-tabled to Swimbridge; formerly, in Great Western days, it had been known as the 'Barnstaple Goods' as it worked through to Victoria Road.

However, by the 1960s British Railways had rationalised the routing of freight for Barnstaple and North Devon; traffic was being sent over the former Southern routes via Exeter and Crediton.

As a result, Taunton depot only serviced the daily branch goods as far as South Molton; there we would shunt the yard, fit in our breakfast and, as and when required, take one or two trucks – mainly coal wagons – to either Swimbridge or Filleigh. On our return to South Molton, we would couple up to our train and work our way back up the branch, shunting at each station as required, before finishing in Fairwater Yard. After uncoupling, it was back to Taunton shed light engine to finish the turn.

The 'runaway train'

Most 6.04am turns were uneventful but not on the day of the

Taken from a departing Up train – the Down loop here was signalled for bi-directional working for passenger and staff convenience – this is close to a driver's eye view of the approach to the Down loop at South Molton, similar to that which driver Roy Cross, on the runaway pannier tank, would have had. ***Roger Carpenter, Lens of Sutton Association***

'runaway train'. Nothing at the start of the turn had prepared us for what was to unfold later in the day.

It was a scheduled eight hour shift and I was firing for my regular driver, Roy Cross. As was normal, our loco had already been prepped for us. We were pleasantly surprised to see our rostered loco, pannier No. 9663, ready and waiting and standing on the out-going road in the shed; it was a bright shiny black, as it had only just been out-shopped from Swindon Works after a major overhaul. It was a rare treat indeed, to have a steam loco in such a good condition this late in the Western Region steam era.

After I had had a good and routine check around the locomotive – and, of course, made the early can of tea – we left the shed and passed Taunton West Loop Signal Box and made our way down to West Yard to pick up our train. It was a mixed formation of some eighteen opens and vans. The guard gave us the load weight total and we were soon on our way.

Milverton was the first stop; there we put off one truck of coal and collected one empty 16-ton mineral wagon. Whilst it had been double track from Norton Fitzwarren it became single track from here onwards.

Having collected the single line staff, it was on to Wiveliscombe, where we would exchange it for the one to Venn Cross. At Wiveliscombe, the goods shed was on the Up side, so as was normal practice, we didn't put off or pick up wagons until the return journey.

Now it was up the bank to Bathealton Tunnel, over the Tone Viaduct, still climbing all the way, and on into Venn Cross Tunnel; this had a very low roof. It was quite normal to emerge from the tunnel with the loco covered in yellow sulphur dust; the sulphur fumes and dust had engulfed us through the tunnel and it didn't really bear thinking about what this had been doing to our lungs. There was no way we would have wanted to slip to a stand in such a tunnel and make things worse. Pannier tanks were always very sure footed, as long as they were driven and fired properly; preferably with good Welsh steaming coal on a big fire. With things going well, I was usually able to put the shovel down before we crossed the viaduct and take some respite and sit down most of the way on to South Molton.

We slowed to exchange the staff at Venn Cross and then it was downhill through Morebath and then on to Dulverton. There we put off a few wagons in the goods loop which we were planning to shunt on the return journey.

After another change of staff it was onwards up the 1 in 58 bank to East Anstey (a bit more work for me to do here). Roy had slowed to exchange the staff again at East Anstey, there were no wagons to drop off or collect, before he opened her up to get the train moving downhill to South Molton.

Nothing untoward had happened so far; and there was no inkling of what was to come.

As we gathered speed downhill towards Bishop's Nympton & Molland and thence on to South Molton, Roy closed the regulator in the normal way that all Western men do – open wide and slam shut. Initially, all appeared to be OK … but then we realised that the pannier was still chuffing away. Roy tried several times opening and shutting the regulator but to no avail; he couldn't shut off steam to the cylinders.

Now we knew this was not to be a normal day and that we had a problem!

We were still gathering speed going downhill with what was a loose coupled train. As an emergency measure, Roy put on the steam brake and I wound on the handbrake; we also blew the whistle to alert the guard and got him to apply his brake. We shut all the dampers to cool

Looking west from halfway along the Down platform at South Molton, with the goods yard on the far left; the headshunt was reached by the first point ahead. ***Stuart Blencowe collection***

LEFT: Fireman Melvyn Baker aged 16, leaning out of the cab of No. 7304. Note the automatic token apparatus on the side of the tender. CENTRE: Melvyn in the cab of pannier No. 9647 at Dunster in 1962. RIGHT: Reunited! At home in 2018 with the cabside plate of No. 7304. ***All Melvyn Baker collection***

the fire and to reduce the steam pressure; this worked but, of course, as we had reduced the pressure in the boiler, the steam brake started to lose its effectiveness.

Slowly our speed came down as we approached South Molton. However, as we entered South Molton station with the whistle blowing, we were still moving at a fast walking pace. Looking ahead, we saw that the points at the end of the platform were set for the goods headshunt as normal. In an instant, Roy decided for our own safety that we would both have to jump off on to the platform – so it was a case of "*ready, steady – don't forget the tea can, mate – and JUMP!*" I believe that the guard did the same!

We then ran alongside the train but it ran into the headshunt until it was stopped by the stop blocks. There was no damage to the locomotive or train. Roy and I then climbed back into the cab, threw the fire out and secured the engine. Once the train was 'safe' we contacted Taunton shed to ask for assistance. The locomotive and goods train were left in the headshunt, with Roy and I returning to Taunton on a passenger working and then having to complete various forms to formally report the incident.

Not quite the day we had expected when we signed on for duty but at least we survived uninjured to tell the tale.

Of course, an enquiry was held to determine the cause of the

A pure Great Western scene at Dulverton, although the view is almost certainly in the early days of British Railways; the auto trailer on the left is still in chocolate & cream livery but appears to have a BR 'W' prefix to its number, whilst there is the merest suggestion of a lion & wheel emblem on the side tank of No. 5575. None of the wagons on view appear to carry any 'Big Four' companies insignia but the signal box is still painted in GWR light and dark stone, and note too that it still sports its wooden base. A date of circa 1950 for the picture is therefore likely. ***Courtesy Martin Bird***

accident. The loco was stripped down for a detailed examination; this revealed that a new regulator rod which had been fitted during its recent overhaul at Swindon had failed – it had had a hairline crack in it from its manufacture, which completely broke when the regulator was closed on leaving East Anstey. We, as footplate crew, were exonerated from blame and were thanked for our resourcefulness, expertise and professionalism in minimising the damage!

As a post script, Roy Cross sadly passed away on the 3rd March 2015 aged 88.

BRINDLEY PRUST

Recollections of a Southern driver

Brindley Prust started at Barnstaple Junction as a cleaner in 1942. He progressed through the ranks of steam repairer and ultimately to driver in 1952 and retired in 1971, so all of his railway working life was as a Southern Railway/Southern Region man. His journeys over the D&SR were therefore limited to the occasional trip post-nationalisation, when Southern crews worked selected services, along with the occasional special train.

His most eventful drive of the line was in about 1955 when the circus was in town. Barnstaple had enjoyed the circus for a few days and the entourage was to move away by rail. The train was to have gone to Exeter via the old Southern route but heavy rains had caused flooding in the Taw Valley, meaning that it could only leave via the D&SR.

Brindley came on duty at Barnstaple Junction shed at about 8.00pm, and thought he was to carry out his usual shed shunting and locomotive sorting duties. However, he was told that he had to take the circus train up to Taunton that night. He and his fireman Ray Reid duly left Barnstaple Junction shed with an 'N' Class Maunsell 'Mogul', tender first to go light engine to Victoria Road, where the train and its cargo were stored prior to departure. The locomotive had five tons of coal and 3,500 gallons of water in the tender in preparation for the journey.

On arrival at Victoria Road the locomotive was backed onto the mixture of wagons making up the train stabled in the bay platform. Having coupled up, Brindley then walked back down the train to check the load. He recalls some of the wagons rocking as the animals moved around and seeing elephants in some wagons though the air slots, with them being chained to the floor. All together there was a likelihood the train was about twenty to thirty tons overweight but they had to get to Taunton and they had no time constraint. So with permission from Frank Cox (shed master), they departed after the last Up train and had the D&SR line to themselves.

The train got underway, commencing the climb out of Victoria Road to Swimbridge. Once they had tackled the incline out of South Molton to East Anstey, driver and fireman were glad of the down grade to Dulverton, giving some respite. At Dulverton, the locomotive needed water, as it was already nearly empty. The continued climb to Morebath and Venn Cross meant that more water was needed at Wiveliscombe, so they topped up again there. However, the route from there on to Milverton and thence on to Norton Fitzwarren was relatively straightforward. On reaching Silk Mill, the train was switched to the Up relief line and into a siding to await the Taunton station pilotman to guide it in to the goods dock at Taunton. Having reached the destination, the 'N' Class was detached and taken to Taunton shed for cleaning, servicing, turning and coaling by the former Great Western men. Brindley and his fireman had some tea and a well deserved rest. Once the servicing was complete, Brindley and the 'N' Class returned back light engine overnight to Barnstaple Junction.

Brindley also related the noxious conditions that the drivers and firemen faced when going into the tunnels, especially Bathealton; sulphurous fumes would engulf the cab and the only protection was to wear a handkerchief as a makeshift face mask.

One night in August 1952, Brindley was working a train back from Taunton in torrential rain and having gone into Castle Hill Tunnel, he was unable to tell when they had emerged due to the darkness of the night. As he hit the brakes to go over Castle Hill Viaduct at the required 25mph a load of sludge coal and water washed out of the tender. Brindley gave it no further thought at the time but it transpired it was the night of the heavy rains that brought the Lynton and Lynmouth flood disaster. There was 20ft of water that night pushing against the piers of the viaduct, as the Bray River flooded too!

Brindley sums up the Devon & Somerset line in true Southern driver style: "*It should never 'ave been built – it was a switch-back line and was difficult to drive, with too many catch and trap points. The loops didn't have an inch to spare. The guard didn't dare take his brake off for the gradient would have him rolling back through the catch points and off the rails.*"

A certain degree of Southern bias there perhaps (especially on the loop lengths as they were generous compared to those on the Southern down to Exeter!) but nonetheless a short, very descriptive summary.

Whilst the driver of the Exe Valley auto operates the water crane at the end of the Up platform at Dulverton, the fireman minds the hose, which hangs through the filler cap as No. 1449 takes on water prior to forming the 3.10pm service to Exeter St. Davids on 25th August 1954. This is the crane that Brindley Prust and his driver would have used to fill the tender of their 'Mogul' on their memorable journey up the line with a circus train from Barnstaple circa 1955. ***Mike Esau***

Milverton, where Ron Searle began his career as a lad porter, looking east towards Norton Fitzwarren and Taunton on 8th July 1959. The signalman waits to exchange tokens with the crew of 'Mogul' No. 6375, arriving with the 2.44pm Taunton to Barnstaple train. Built originally as single track, east from here the line was double tracked in 1937-38 all the way to Norton Fitzwarren, the crossover visible just beyond the end of the train, which had formed the east end of the crossing loop, being left in place. ***H.C. Casserley***

RON SEARLE
Signalman

Ron was a signalman at Wiveliscombe. He started with the railway on 13th December 1948 as a lad porter at Milverton. He then did two years National Service, with his job being kept open for him. However, as there was no permanent porter's job available following his return, he accepted a temporary porter's role, which took him to Wellington and Silverton, where he learned his signalling responsibilities. He was at Wiveliscombe from 1955 to 1960, from where he went to Durston, then Norton Fitzwarren and finally Taunton West Junction Signal Box. On being made redundant, he took a temporary job as a guard, before being the last man to operate Silk Mills Signal Box, moving from there on to Tiverton Parkway in 1987, where he spent ten years. He had to retire on his 65th birthday, having completed forty-nine years and three months of service for British Railways.

Ron recalls the South Molton pick-up goods shunting the yard at Wiveliscombe on the way west. This would necessitate the locomotive running round the train via the Up platform and then detaching the wagons for the yard from the rear of the goods train before shunting them in to the sidings. Regular goods inwards would be coal, fertiliser, animal feed and general merchandise, whilst a consignment of Guinness stout would also arrive from time to time. They would get jars to fill up with cider every three weeks/month. On the despatch side would be output from the Hancock Brewery, wool, sugar beet cattle stock and feed potatoes, the wagons being picked up by the

Wiveliscombe looking towards Barnstaple from near the end of the Up platform in the early 1960s, with Ron's signal box in the foreground. The bush in the right foreground is where the house coal for the signal box stove was hidden. It would be replenished from time to time from the tender of a locomotive on an Up train when stopped alongside. ***Courtesy Great Western Study Group***

returning goods along with any empties. There was not much horse traffic at the station in Ron's time but it was usually a trial if there was. When a Down train arrived with the horse box at the front, it would require the locomotive to shunt it onto the Up line from where the wagon had to be propelled manually in to the siding. However, the points would need to be clipped first. It was simpler if the box was on the rear of an Up train, which would just set back into the horse dock siding to drop the wagon off. Ron also remembers special cattle trains being put on for market days.

Ron recalls the Whittaker apparatus being rarely used, as it was a fair walk to the relevant pick up/set down posts for the signalman. On one occasion, he recalled a goods going through but the token exchange with the apparatus failed, the token flying off and later being found in a field. The goods had to stop with the token having 'disappeared', if only temporarily on this occasion (see page 673).

Collett 0-6-0 No. 2268 heads a pick-up goods off the Barnstaple Branch and over the boarded crossing at the west end of Norton Fitzwarren station in the early 1950s. ***Peter Triggs***

Summer Saturday trains in the late 1950s were usually 'full and standing', and trains would struggle on the climb up through Crowford to Wiveliscombe. Down goods trains could run out of steam as they worked up from Milverton if they were not prepared for the climb. Once beyond Wiveliscombe, where the climb got steeper and longer, if a goods train was too heavy it would be split, with some wagons being left in the yard at Wiveliscombe and the first batch taken forwards to Venn Cross, the locomotive then returning for the remainder.

One day the lad porter was asked to temporarily man the signal box whilst the signalman undertook some errands. No trains were due, it was just a watching brief but the task coincided with a thunderstorm, during which the electrical charges in the air caused the bells to ring indiscriminately and lightening to jump from lever to lever!

ERIC STONE

A signalman's story

I am grateful to Mrs Joyce Stone, who let me borrow Eric's booklet of his life on the railways and to include his story here and to reproduce the accompanying photographs from her collection.

Eric was born on 5th March 1938 and started at Wiveliscombe as a junior porter at Easter 1953 at the age of 15. At the time, the stationmaster was Charlie Deverell, with signalmen Harold Elliott and Harold Screetch, lorry driver Reg Williams, goods clerk Arthur Woodgate and two porters, Edgar and Bill Webber (who were not related). Other personnel included a booking clerk and a fourteen-man permanent way gang.

When Eric arrived on his first day for duty and knocked on the signal box door, he was greeted with a "*Who's there?*". He answered politely "*Mr Stone, with a letter from British Railways, to present myself*

ABOVE: Eric takes a rest between trains at Morebath.
BELOW LEFT: An un-named colleague at Morebath Signal Box.
BELOW: Eric (in uniform) and a colleague at Morebath.

to you". The response was terse "*My name is Mr Elliott. I am the signalman in this box. You have called at a very busy time. I have two trains. Stand on the carpet, do not move, as I have to deal with the two trains*". Quite an introduction to life on British Railways!

As junior porter, Eric's jobs were basic. He filled oil lamps for signals weekly on Thursdays, collected milk from local farms and a paper from the shops for the station master, who always checked the racing pages. He would also drive the station lorry with short trips to Arnold & Hancock, the local brewers, and the cider factory. Tuesday was day-old chick day; the farm manager of Auton Dowells brought the chicks down for despatch on the 7.00pm Up train. The 'Rabbiter' was recalled stopping at the station at around 7.30/7.45pm to load rabbits.

Sugar beet from local farms was despatched from Milverton station and the lad porter would be responsible for collating and dealing with documents before despatch.

ABOVE: Venn Cross looking east towards the tunnel mouth from near the signal box circa 1960.

BELOW: looking west circa 1960. The station building and the house that Eric Stone moved in to were at a higher level than the platforms, at the top of the bank on the left; part of the station building can just be seen through the bushes. The path leading down to the platform can be seen part way along. It can be seen that the line was still climbing through the platforms to the summit at the far end.
Both courtesy Great Western Railway Society

Eric did National Service from 1956 until 1958, after which he returned to Wiveliscombe, his job being kept open for him. From lad porter, Eric rose to porter, porter signalman and then signalman (of which there were several classes). He applied for a Grade 4 signalman post at Ilminster box on the Chard Branch. On passing the Rules & Regulations test in 1959 at the age of 21, he became the youngest signalman in the Taunton area at that time.

One day, when travelling home on his BSA Bantam motorbike from his Ilminster duties, he had an accident and the bike was beyond repair but during his period of recuperation, he was upgraded to relief signalman. Having got married in 1960, shortly after the arrival of his first son he spotted that there was a vacancy at Venn Cross station house, one of the railway gang moving to a council house. Eric applied for the tenancy and received a letter of confirmation from Clarence Hawkins, the signalling inspector at Taunton, moving in just before Christmas 1962 at a rent of £1 per week.

At the same time, Eric also took over the role of signalman at Venn Cross. In the winter of 1962-63, when he was on duty at Morebath, the weather was so bad at one time that he was marooned in the box, with snow covering the platforms and surrounding area. On one particular day at this time, an Up goods took between two and three hours to get from Dulverton to Morebath. The driver pushed on to Venn Cross but only managed to get ten yards out of Morebath before coming off the rails. The crew spent three days playing cards and drinking tea in between digging out the train, until they could get back on the rails and proceed. The men also decided there was too much coal on the tender, so they 'borrowed' some, carrying it in every spare bucket at the station to the signal box!

One late spring/early summer, whilst again on duty at Morebath box, a Dulverton to Taunton goods train came to a stand in his section, near Morebath woods. The driver said he had dirty coal so the signalman gave him twenty minutes to stoke up. When the train went past the signal box a while later, there were pea sticks sticking out of the tender, leaving Eric rather suspicious of the 'dirty coal' story!

The drivers of Up goods that had to set back into the refuge siding at Venn Cross to enable a passenger train to pass, had a trick when they had a long wait; they would hang a firebucket on the signal arm (presumably the Home signal, as the refuge only had a ground situated shunt signal). When this signal was pulled off, the bucket would fall to the ground, make a noise and wake up the resting driver and fireman. One would have thought the passing train would have been enough to wake them up but the signal gave an 'early' alarm call.

The 5.00pm train at Morebath brought evening papers for the local village, which would be delivered there and to Shillingford by a Mrs Coggins. On occasion she would bring a slice of cake for the signalman's tea. Eric also recalled the Beatles' special waiting at Venn Cross for twenty minutes in 1964.

Signalmen at branch stations took pride in their signal boxes and spent their time between trains cleaning the brasswork and the floor, which was usually spotless. In good weather they would also tend the station flower beds and at some stations would sell tickets to passengers too.

When Lord Beeching's *The Reshaping of British Railways* report was published, Eric could see his life was going to change. With Morebath box closing, he then only worked Venn Cross box. In 1965, his first wife left him and with redundancy coming following closure of the D&SR in 1966, Eric had to look for a new career. He continued to rent the Venn Cross station house but went to Wellington to work at Fox Brothers and then Taunton Vale Industries. Eric then met Joyce and they married in 1969, whilst in 1971, he got the opportunity to return to his signalman's duties at Whiteball Signal Box, an opportunity he leapt at.

On returning from his Whiteball duties one day, men from the BR Property Board were waiting to see him. They wanted him to vacate the Venn Cross house, as they wanted to sell it and offered him £6,000 as an incentive to leave. With help from a property developer friend, Eric saw an opportunity, so sat tight and started to negotiate with BR. Four years later he bought the station house. He could have bought the tunnel too but sensibly declined as he saw it as a liability rather than an asset. To this day it remains in Network Rail ownership and it is their responsibility to survey it every six years and maintain it.

With Whiteball box closing, Eric went to Crediton and travelled every day from Venn Cross; one hour travelling each way and an eight hour shift did not make for an easy life. So, in 1986, Eric, Joyce and family moved to a house near Crediton signal box and Venn Cross was sold. Eric retired as a signalman in March 1993 at the age of 55 and passed away on 17th March 2004.

Harry Kirkland

Fireman

Harry was evacuated from West Ham in London in 1939 when he was 8 years of age. Initially relocating to Newbury, later in the war years he had been reunited with his family and was based in Taunton, where he still lives. Having trainspotted in his youth at Newbury, he looked to the railways for employment in 1947 at age 16, starting as an engine cleaner at Taunton shed; in 1949 he became a fireman, having passed his test at Swindon. He had fired 245 locomotives by this stage, having filled in to cover for a shortage of fireman at that time, spending his time shunting in the Down goods yard and footplating 'Bulldogs' No. 3443 *Chaffinch* and No. 3444 *Cormorant* on empty coaching stock workings. In his time as a fireman, he worked on the Chard, Yeovil, Minehead and Barnstaple branches but after a relatively short spell on the railways, moved to the South Western Electricity Board in 1954.

Harry's description of his work indicated it was far from easy. The steam locomotive firelighters would arrive at about 10.00pm to commence their preparations and by the time Harry booked on at midnight, the fires would just about be burning. He then had to 'prep', that is clean and make ready, five locomotives for the morning's local services on the branches. This occasionally included cleaning up after fatalities (suicides), a very unpleasant job.

Was there a problem with the Exe Valley auto here at Dulverton on 6th August 1956? The station master has come over to see what is happening, the driver seems to be explaining what the situation is and the fireman, who has been down between No. 6422 and its auto coach coupling up, puts his 'sixpenny'orth' in from track level. All watched – from a safe distance – by an interested passenger. And top right, something has startled the birds! A lovely, everyday study of men at work on a rural railway, always a different pace to life on the main line and no doubt the train departed on time at 1.05pm, for Exeter St. Davids, a short while later, after collecting commuteing passengers alighting from a connecting service from Taunton. ***John Spencer Gilks***

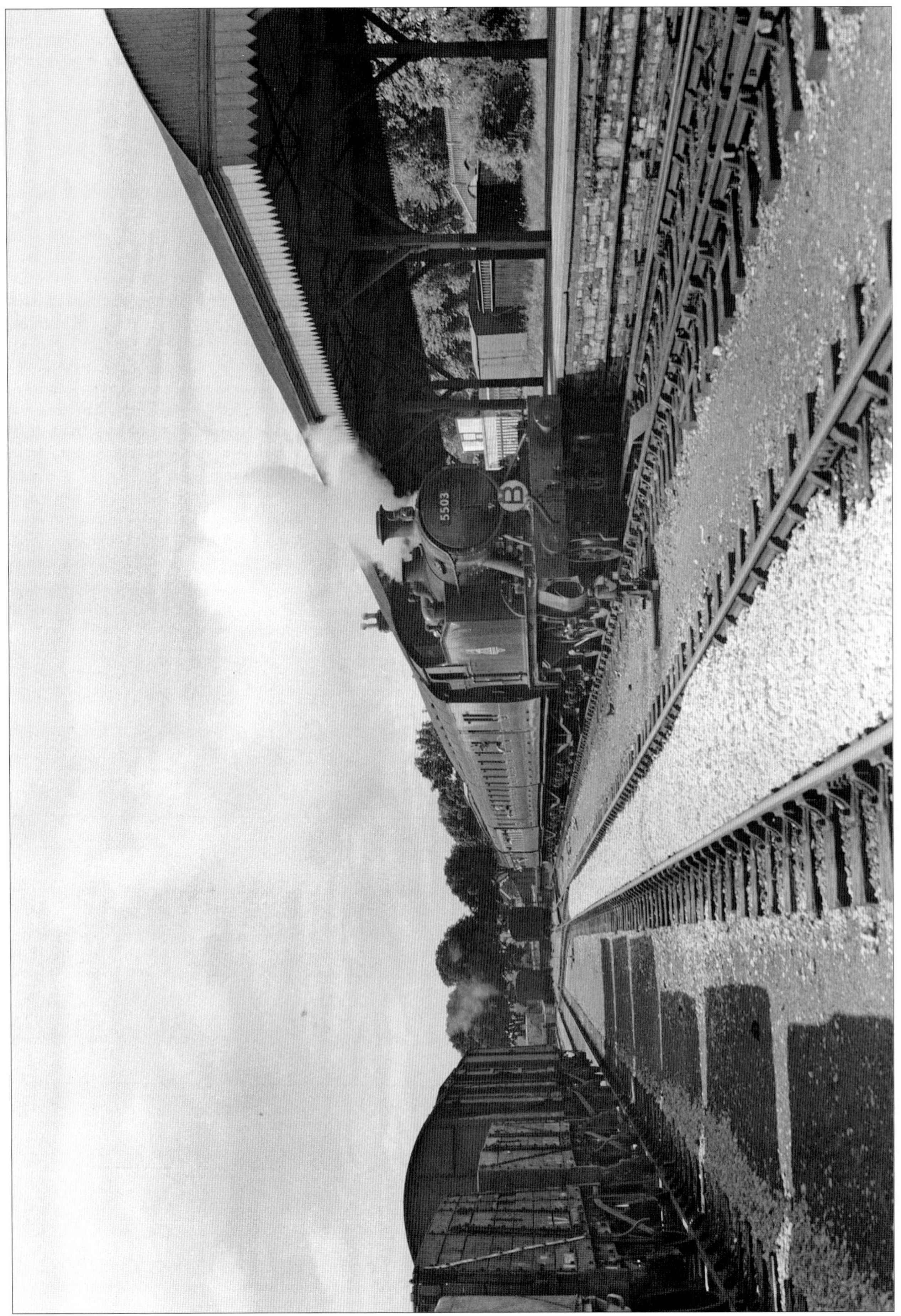

Numerous passengers lean out if the carriage windows to watch the photographer take his picture of Class '45XX' 2-6-2T No. 5503 at Barnstple Victoria Road on 28th July 1951, which was clearly a warm summers day. In the foreground, some fresh ballast has been dropped in place on the run round loop, which will require the attention of the local permanent way gang to spread it out neatly and evenly. *Roger J. Sellick, courtesy National Railway Museum*

As a fireman he regularly worked the pick-up goods along the D&SR. Normal loadings were 10-17 wagons but could reach 25 on occasions. The usual procedure was to drop off wagons on the Down train and pick up wagons on the return Up journey. He described the Barnstaple Branch as '*tough and heavy work with steep inclines*'. The climb up to Bathealton Tunnel was the worst and once inside, the clearance was small. A heavy goods would climb slowly and the swirling exhaust fumes in the tight bore were unpleasant. Footplate crew often soaked their handkerchiefs in water and covered their mouths to avoid the sulphurous and other fumes that could not escape the confines of the tunnel whilst the locomotive passed through. Harry also recalls the occasion when a 'Mogul' stalled in the tunnel and in an effort to restart the crew were scalded by escaping steam. It was indeed a dangerous and unpleasant job at times.

Roger Sellick
Fireman

Roger was based at Taunton shed from 1962 to summer 1965 and was a fireman on the line. He remembers one day trundling along with a train between South Molton and Yeo Mill when the driver received instructions to stop – a passenger had spotted a sheep on its back in the field. The train came to a halt and Roger went down over the embankment to put the animal back on its feet!

Driver and fireman turns meant some travel 'on the cushions'. For instance, on an afternoon turn, they would travel down on the train to Barnstaple Junction and then 'put the train away' for the Barnstaple men – that is stable the stock ready for its next working. They would then turn the locomotive and 'trip' to Victoria Road to shunt, sometimes taking goods wagons. On returning to Barnstaple Junction, they would take a break prior to working the 8.30pm train back to Taunton. If they worked an afternoon Down passenger service, their duties would include taking the locomotive to shed, getting it coaled and watered, and a 'trip' to Victoria Road if required. Goods from Barnstaple at this time would be going down to Exeter. They might have to clean out the engine and make up the fire ready for the next crew. If they worked the 5.55pm Taunton to Barnstaple service, they would leave the carriages in Platform 3 on the far side of the island platform and take the engine to shed. To get back, they would await the 8.25pm Ilfracombe to Exeter train, where they would change onto the Night Mail train to Manchester, alighting at Taunton at 10.50pm to head home.

Pannier tank No. 9635 was not a favourite engine. It had slow injectors, which resulted in no water in the boiler at times, whilst care had to be taken in driving and firing it as, although it would steam, it was inconsistent and temperamental. Roger once went with the engine to Minehead, where it failed and had to be rescued by BR 'Standard' No. 82042. On a trip down to Barnstaple with driver George Edney, they had anthracite in the coal, which required serious work as they had to fill up the firebox at each station to keep going.

Roger recalls working down the line in the afternoons of 1965 with a Type '2' Class 'D63XX' diesel-hydraulic and Brake van or Parcels Brake, for the Torrington milk, as referred to in the goods section

No. 6327 drifts away downhill from Venn Cross with a three-coach Up train on 3rd June 1963. ***Peter W. Gray***

People on a crowded Down platform at Dulverton, many of whom will have arrived here via the Exe Valley auto simmering gently in the bay, start moving in anticipation of the arrival of the Taunton-bound train drawing in behind No. 7304 on 7th September 1962. ***John Spencer Gilks***

of Chapter 11. There was a small reward; they were given a can of milk by the dairy to make their tea and coffee before working back.

Roger was secondman on a Down train, when their 'D63XX' was shunted back to couple up to a Southern set at Taunton but would not buffer up properly. They managed to couple the carriages to the locomotive but Roger thought the train rode like a loose-coupled goods! That was until Venn Cross when Roger adjusted the coupling, it presumably having worked itself loose on that first stage of the journey.

Even in those days, engineering works did not run smoothly. One Sunday, Roger took an engineers train down the branch to decommission Morebath Signal Box but the occupation of the line over-ran by six hours, which meant that his shift expired and he and the driver had to be relieved by another crew.

The South Molton signalman kept chickens (Roger believes their run was behind the goods shed) and the signalman would go and collect the eggs and give them to the guard to take them up the line.

Roger is very complementary about the 'Moguls' he fired – good engines and good work horses that could do anything asked of them. However, he also felt the BR 'Standard' Class '3MT's were excellent and rode very well at speed. In his experience, No. 82044 was the best of the bunch allocated at Taunton. The 'Moguls' had no speedometer so speeds had to be judged by experienced drivers, especially the slow-down to 25mph over the viaducts. Roger was convinced, after going over the viaducts at a controlled 25mph in a D63XX, that the 'Moguls' may have been going a bit faster when they crossed – or was it just the illusion of speed created by being in the cab of the steam locomotive without a clear view ahead that the diesel would provide?

BRIAN SINGH
Fireman

Brian was similarly employed from January 1962 until summer 1965. He went to Southall in the bad winter of 1962-63 to learn his trade where 'he was thrown in at the deep end' and fired long-distance goods trains. By Easter 1963, he was back at Taunton shed and worked the local lines.

He recalls a trip on the 8.05am train from Taunton to Barnstaple Junction, with driver Lionel Cox. On arrival the train was put away and the locomotive sent to the shed for servicing and turning. With some down time until their return trip at 2.24pm, Lionel suggested a visit to the cinema to watch Rock Hudson and Doris Day in *Move Over Darling*, so that's what they did to 'kill' time.

It was not always that relaxing. He remembers an Up passenger working with driver Mervyn Jones where the locomotive was losing steam, the fire was not good and burned with a blue and orange hue. Brian, being sixteen years of age at the time, was inexperienced and relied on the experience of his driver, who decided that he would stop for a 'blow up'. It took ten to fifteen minutes to get the steam up and to get going again but they got so far and then had to stop again. As they came off the the branch onto the main line at Norton Fitzwarren they were losing steam again but Melvyn felt they had enough to get to Taunton; however, he would only lightly touch the brakes as a stop would give them problems. They limped under Staplegrove Bridge and saw a red signal, inching towards it whilst urging it to be pulled 'off'. It stayed resolutely 'on', however, and they had no option but to put the brakes full on and come to a standstill. Then the arm dropped but the engine would not move. The solution was to call for help and a diesel shunter came to the rescue, pulling the train into the station. Brian said this was the only time he had trouble of this nature and it seems it was down to what he and follow railwaymen called 'egglets', not proper Welsh steam coal but probably formed with compacted coal dust and cement to keep them in shape. With the end of steam, drivers and firemen had to make do with whatever quality of coal was provided.

The view from the station forecourt on 1st October 1966, which generations of passengers would have seen as they arrived along the entrance road at Dulverton to catch a train. ***Michael Messenger***

PHILIP COX

Schoolboy

If it was not for his dad, Lionel Cox, who was a driver based at Taunton shed, Phil would have joined the railways for a career. Lionel did not allow it but, nonetheless and unsurprisingly, Phil developed an interest in railways and has a few memories to recall.

His dad was the driver of the train referred to above, which lost a token at Wiveliscombe when it flew into a field but was found. Phil went down to Dulverton in 1964 to visit a friend. On the train back he was recognised by the driver who invited him up onto the footplate of 'Mogul' No. 7332. Despite being only two weeks from withdrawal, the locomotive gave a good account of itself but there seemed to be a few loose parts and plenty of rattling metal!

It was normal for Phil and a friend to take an evening train from Taunton to Milverton, along with their bicycles. On arrival they would then cycle over to Wellington to meet his father on the banking locomotive stationed there for Whiteball duties. On this particular evening it was apparent that something else was coming down the line after they disembarked from the train. So the boys stayed for a while and were rewarded by witnessing Southern Region 'N' Class 'Mogul' No. 31845 trundle past with a permanent way train of Grampus wagons loaded with concrete sleepers. Phil remembers the train stretching from the starting signal to just under the road bridge, where the brake van brought up the rear. Phil also recalled a fireman commenting that on one occasion an un-rebuilt 'West Country' Class did traverse the line from Barnstaple to Taunton. Finally, a North British diesel on at least one occasion travelled down the line to Barnstaple Junction, on to Torrington and Halwill, and into Cornwall. This was a demolition train from Fairwater Yard for the 'Withered Arm' lines.

GORDON BRAY

Lad porter

Gordon was a lad porter for eighteen months between 1948 and 1949 at South Molton. He went to Exeter for his job interview, which included a colour test, being presented with swatches of wool of different colours and being asked to identify the colour. He started on two guineas (42s) per week, which was supplemented by a half-crown 'tip' from the station master for a good job done in polishing the floor in the waiting room.

His jobs were numerous, including cleaning the platforms, the ladies waiting room and toilet, general waiting room and gentlemen's toilet. He also had to light fires in the station master's office and waiting room. All lighting was his responsibility including filling and lighting Tilley lamps (daily in winter). The nine signal lamps were replenished weekly by Gordon, the Distant signals each being over 1,000 yards away from the station. On one occasion he got a lift back from one of the Distant signals on the footplate of a locomotive on a goods train. The spare lamps were kept in the tin shed on the Down platform. On a calm day they were easy to light but on a typical Exmoor windy day it would test the patience. There was a technique to the lighting. If the wick was burning the light would be blown out and the wick trimmed. Once the lamp was placed in its container, it would be re-lit through a hole in the top (about $^{2}/_{3}$in. diameter) with a match. The lid would then be shut gently and then a check through the lens that the light was burning.

Station staff included the station master (Mr Cole in 1948, with Mr Vickery as a temporary) and booking office clerk, signalmen (Frank Gill, Stan Sully and Harry Cockerham in the late 1940s), a parcels clerk and employees in the goods office, and a shunter in the yard (Tommy Everest in 1948). The majority of goods inwards were coal and animal feedstuffs. Gordon recalls bricks being brought in by rail for building the Community College.

Gordon would work 8.00am to 5.00pm and the parcels clerk would come on at 11.00am and work until 8.00pm. Gordon was responsible for parcels duties up to 11.00am, which might involve loading parcels on the George Hotel motor bus that connected the station to the town a mile away with a regular service.

As with other stations on the line, there was a a one-wagon dump of coal at the end of the platform to last the signal box and station one year. On one occasion this coal ran out and Gordon was sent into the goods yard by the parcels clerk to replenish the station supply. The signalman saw him and told him off because the coal he 'borrowed' belonged to the local coal merchant.

On another occasion a bicycle was delivered and the station master proceeded to ride it up and down the platform. A very practical way of dealing with it!

No. 6364 departs East Anstey for Barnstaple on 15th February 1958. Note the velocipede and 4-wheeled flat trolley belonging to the local permanent way gang in the foreground. ***James G. Tawse***

MICHAEL W. BRAY

Lad porter

Michael's story was first published in the 1994 *Exmoor Review* and is summarised here. His passion for railways and all things Great Western was initiated by Mr Yandle, the station master at East Anstey in the summer of 1953 (appointed in 1946). Michael was only sixteen years old at the time and just out of boarding school when he was offered the job of lad porter. He lived at Molland and so had to use his Phillips Vox Populi motorcycle to get to his interview and his job, which earned him £2 19s 1d per week, just enough to cover the hire purchase on his motorcycle!

As lad porter his role was the care and maintenance of all the lamps associated with the station, and there were quite a few. In addition, the signal lamps had to be cleaned, refilled with paraffin and replaced weekly and great care was needed to ensure that the flame was of the right shape and size so it would not blow out. Tuesday was the day for attending to Up signals (those heading towards Taunton) and the 'dummies' (ground or shunting signals); the Down side signals were serviced on Thursdays. The summer walk to the Distant signals, some three quarters of a mile out from the station, was pleasant and enabled strawberries and blackberries which grew on the banks to be picked and eaten! Winter was frequently harsh when, with numb or wet hands, grabbing the metal ladder runs to climb up the signal posts to the lamps was a trial. Tilley lamps lit the offices and waiting rooms and were described as '*troublesome contraptions*' but Michael became adept at fitting a new mantle and making the lamp burn without backstops on the mantle. He was also responsible for the storm lantern type at Yeo Mill Halt, which required frequent attention.

His station duties involved meeting the trains, dealing with passenger enquiries, offloading newspapers from the early train, cleaning offices and waiting rooms, and making sure coal fires were lit and attended to. The goods shed had to be swept out every Friday and help provided loading and unloading wagons in the goods yard. A Levers cattle food store was attached to the goods shed, where their feedstuffs were unloaded from wagons and loaded onto local transport and despatched. Parcels were booked in and invoiced out, there were racks of consignment notes and goods labels, all creating the masses of paperwork for which the GWR (now BR(WR)) was renowned. Michael was given the task of learning more about booking office practices, with returns and requisitions. These returns had to be submitted to the District Operating Superintendent's Office (DOSO) for all items that moved, whether it be a duster or a supply of cotton for cleaning. These required a requisition form to Swindon Stores.

Michael remembers the monthly livestock market that was held in a field adjacent to the station, after which cattle and sheep had to be loaded for despatch. He hated this aspect of the work, because the cattle pens in the yard by the goods shed had to be hosed down and scraped clean. Water for this task was supplied from the gent's toilets and the duty signalman would have to work the hand pump, so Michael could brush and scrape away the trodden in cow-pats! Farmers could park in the station yard on market days for 6d but many were loath to pay and looked for ways to avoid the charge.

As East Anstey was the highest point on the line (at 699ft above sea level), baskets of racing pigeons would arrive for release almost on a daily basis in the summer months. Michael released the birds, watched them circle the station and then set off on their mission to return home. The time of release was marked on the baskets and these were put on the next available train for returning to the owner.

Another special service was the 'Rabbiter', which often ran daily from South Molton to Taunton collecting crates of rabbits on the way. These would make their way to Home Counties markets, such as Slough, Langley and Walton-on-Thames. The local rabbit dealers were Herbie Harris from Yeo Mill and Harold Thorne from Rackenford. Each crate brought in had to be weighed and labelled, and consignment notes made out heralding a busy hour for Michael up to the time of arrival of the train.

The signalmen at the time were Alfie Antell and Melvyn Tarr, who moved to East Anstey in 1947. Alfie lived at West Anstey and rode to work on a motorcycle, whilst Melvyn lived locally at Waddicombe. Michael had a good rapport and working relationship with both men but Melvyn allowed him to operate the box under his supervision; a particularly interesting task when the pannier tank was shunting the daily pick-up goods in the yard or running round its train. On one occasion there was a relief signalman in for Alfie who was away; the relief man came from Sampford Peverell and brought his bike down on the train so he could cycle home after his late shift was over. Once he realised that Michael could operate the box (albeit illegally!), he disappeared on the last Up train, with bike as well, leaving Michael to cross and clear the last two trains of the day and close the box. Fortunately for both employees, the substitution never caused an issue and it would seem the relevant authorities were blissfully unaware of the matter, otherwise no doubt a heavy price would have been paid in terms of dismissal.

In the spring, the goods yard would often contain several wagons of fertiliser or slag. This would be loaded onto the 2-ton Austin lorry that was shared with Dulverton station and driven around the district by Fred Woodley from Tiverton. Michael would sometimes be signed as driver's mate to help distribute and unload at the various farms served. The reward was a cup of tea and a pasty at the Tantivy Café in Dulverton at about 4.30pm and it was Fred's treat for Michael.

Unlike many of the stations on the route, East Anstey was near the village it served and was therefore the centre of village life. The station was a clearing house for local gossip ,and the signalmen and the porter knew most of what was going on; they missed little.

Michael described his days at East Anstey as *"a sheer delight"*, there was always much to do and time never seemed to drag. The camaraderie of his colleagues from the signalmen to the crews, permanent way gang and the S&T staff was evident. However, National Service beckoned and his time with the railway was over in 1955. His story shows how much life revolved around the station and how many people relied on it for employment. Of course this work approach and lifestyle was unsustainable but it served its purpose for many years,

George Facey (as told to Graham Robinson)

Signalman

George was a signalman at Filleigh and recalled on one summer Saturday in the late 1950s or early 1960s, an Ilfracombe-bound train, hauled most likely by a 'Mogul', arriving at the station. As it approached the automatic token exchange equipment, the locomotive rocked slightly causing, the pick-up arm to strike the hoop containing the token instead of collecting it and sending hoop and token flying. The train had to be brought to a rapid and unexpected halt but an extensive search by train crew, station staff and signalman for the missing item was to no avail and extensive delays ensued. About two weeks later, a parcel was received from Manchester which contained the missing hoop and token. It had apparently been found caught up underneath a passenger coach at Longsight depot!

Max Perry

Farmhand

Max Perry remembers the days when he used to work on a farm near Shillingford, where the land was bisected by the railway, between Venn Cross in the Up direction and Down to Morebath. Every day the cows had to cross the line for milking via an occupation crossing and timing was everything, as the gates had to be opened and the cattle transferred before any trains passed through. If an Up train was pulling out of Morebath it could be heard as it prepared for the climb up to Venn Cross. However, the Down trains were the dangerous ones, as they would coast down the bank from Venn Cross and could not be heard. The farmer therefore had to know the time table but this only worked if the trains were more or less on schedule. Max is pleased to report he never personally experienced any scary moments, although he does recall with some sadness the tragedy at Venn Farm, west of Dulverton, recorded earlier in the previous chapter.

In 1967-68, Max had the workmen who were dismantling the railway staying at his house. Woodham Brothers from Barry dismantled the track and signalling infrastructure, whilst Cohens removed the rails and signal cabling, etc. The wooden sleepers were a valuable commodity for local farmers, being collected and stored for future use or used to build sileage pits, barns, or small bridges over streams; even today, many still survive in such uses around the local countryside. However, collecting these sleepers was not a job for everyone, especially on the section between Dulverton and East Anstey. That stretch of line was a haven for adders, so every time a sleeper was moved prior to lifting it was essential to look out for these snakes, which sometimes congregated on the discarded cinders and ballast in large numbers.

Wesley Wyatt

Farmer

Wesley and his family have farmed in the Milverton area for generations. His great great grandfather was a tenant at the time the D&SR was being built and compulsory purchase of agricultural lands in the area was being carried out. Part of the conveyance of land at Hillacre Farm to the D&SR in 1867 is reported and illustrated in Volume 1, page 50.

The farm produced sugar beet, which was delivered up-country to Tewkesbury, and also reed to South Wales, both by rail. Animal feed stuffs were brought in, whilst cattle were taken to the market and then sent on for winter grazing and feeding up before the slaughterhouse beckoned. The station master would visit at Christmas time to thank the farmer and his family for their custom.

Wesley recalls a spark from a steam locomotive catching stubble alight in a cornfield circa 1962-63, the sheaves being burned and the whole of Crowford Hill turned black.

To emphasise the friendliness of the railway to the local community, Wesley would hitch a lift from his fields back to the farmhouse on the ganger's trolley for some of the journey.

There was a dog who, on hearing the train coming, would run down the track and, as if to encourage him, the drivers would sound the whistle.

The Devon & Somerset line was essentially a rural railway, serving largely agricultural communities of which it formed a working part for generations. Here, on 14th July 1962, No. 7337 gallops through farm fields near Wiveliscombe, with the 8.35am Ilfracombe to Manchester train. ***John Spencer Gilks***

RUSSELL DARBYSHIRE

Schoolboy

Russell's parents were at Dipford Manor Farm near Shillingford from 1947 until 1951. He went to school at Kestrels at East Anstey and as a day-boy therefore regularly took the train from Morebath station up to East Anstey. On arrival, the boys would try to avoid Miss Du Boe, their French teacher, who travelled up from Dulverton station on the same train. If they succeeded they would walk back from the station along the top of the cutting and across the fields to the school. If she spotted them she would make them walk with her along the road to the school – a greater distance of course. Despite the family moving to North Curry in 1951, he still went to school there until 1953 but as a border.

Russell refers to it as a 'personable line'. The train would occasionally reverse back into the platform if a regular passenger, running late and just about to miss it, could attract the attention of the crew. The maintenance gang once offered a passenger a trip down the line on the trolley as they had missed their train; perhaps quite sensibly, they opted to wait for the next one.

The children occasionally went into the guard's van to ride the train. On one day there was a coffin in the compartment so, boys being boys, they sat on it. The guard said nothing and the coffin was taken off en route. On the return journey the coffin got loaded again but this time when they attempted to sit on it, they were reprimanded – the body was in there this time!

Russell recalls cattle trucks being picked up at Dulverton and taken to East Anstey where they were detached for the local market, the load usually being Ruby Red cattle or sheep. He also recalls dead rabbits tied to poles, with flies buzzing around them, being loaded into the guards compartment. The rabbit catcher from Petton Cross near Shillingford travelled on a motor bike with a sidecar, which was loaded with his 6ft hazel poles to tie the rabbits to. Milk churns, the large 17-gallon conical variety, were also put on the train in the guards van on a regular basis.

In a more malicious act, Russell remembers an incident where rocks were heaved over the side of the railway bridge at East Anstey but, somewhat fortunitously, nothing untoward ensued as a result.

JOHN MILTON

Farmer

This account is transcribed from tapes held at the Dulverton Heritage Centre and it is with thanks to that organisation that the following is reproduced here.

John Milton was born at Yeo Mill in 1931 and farmed in the area all his life at Partridge Arms Farm. When the railway ran it was essential to his family's needs, both farming and transport. Although his father owned a car as early as the 1930s, perhaps the first in the village, the train was the way to go to the weekly market on Thursdays at South Molton. Indeed it was popular for those passengers using East Anstey and Bishops Nympton & Molland stations as well; the platforms were usually full. Although there were markets at Bampton and Dulverton they were not well attended by those in the South Molton district. Bampton was not so easy to get to by train, requiring a change at Dulverton and a trip down the Exe Valley line. However, for the annual Bampton pony fare, which took place on the last Thursday, in October a special effort was made. The Dulverton market was on a smaller scale to South Molton and not weekly.

The local miller used to collect compounds and meal from East

An undated view of Bishops Nympton & Molland station, albeit taken after the construction of the new signal box in 1937. The layout of the tight knit group of buildings, with signal box, station booking hall and offices, and the goods shed all in a line, was similar to other stations on the line. The brickwork at the front of the waiting room did not match the rest of the building, which was built of stone, so is likely to have been a later infill. The station was the most isloated on the Barnstaple Branch, being, respectively, three miles and two miles from the villages it purported to serve. However, a nearby cattle market ensured that there was a certain amount of traffic. ***Great Western Railway Society***

Anstey goods yard which he would take to the mill.

As the railway ran through John's farm, this meant livestock and equipment had to cross the line by an occupation crossing from time to time. On one such occasion a hay load was crossing the line and a wheel on the cart collapsed. The horse was detached and before the cart could be removed, a train was heard coming up the valley. A farm worker was sent to flag down the approaching train and after he had succeeded, the driver and fireman gave a hand to remove the offending cart. The railway line is now used by John as a farm track and to this day he still stops and looks at the occupation gates just to check whether or not a train is coming.

One favourite pastime in this area in the 1940s was fishing for salmon in the river, which of course took place at night and without the appropriate licences. The river was policed by water bailiffs and they would come out from Barnstaple on the train, usually the 4.00pm from Barnstaple that reached Yeo Mill about 4.55pm. They would get out at East Anstey and walk back to Molland down the river or sometimes down the railway line as this gave a vantage point. Having done his job, the bailiff would return to Barnstaple on the last Down train, around 10.20pm from Molland back to Barnstaple.

From 1943, Yeo Mill and the surrounding area was alive with American soldiers. They arrived by train at Dulverton and East Anstey, from where they were transported on to Molland Moor and Anstey Common for training.

Despite its isolated location, the area did play its part in the war effort beyond housing the troops on the hills, with anti-aircraft batteries and search lights located at strategic points. One was near Yeo Mill and played its part in the defence of the South Wales docks, just across the Bristol channel, which were prone to German bomber attack from time to time. This led to the occasional dogfight in the skies, which resulted in a number of houses and buildings suffering from shrapnel damage, for which the owners were compensated by the Government.

Alan Marshall

Regular passenger

Alan now lives at Ashbrittle, near Bathealton but in his younger days he lived near Bishops Nympton & Molland station and was a regular traveller on the line. On one memorable journey in the early 1960s, the Taunton-bound train ground to a halt just outside Wiveliscombe. A crankshaft had fallen off the locomotive (most likely a run-down 'Mogul') and it was going nowhere. The train was of course delayed, a substitute locomotive being sent out from Taunton to rescue it. The rescue engine dragged the train to Wiveliscombe, where the failed locomotive was unceremoniously dumped in the goods yard.

Alan had an uncle, Mr Greenslade, that lived near Bathealton Tunnel during the Second World War and was a member of the local defence volunteers (LDVs or Home Guard). He and others were well 'armed' with hay picks (basically a two-pronged fork) to defend the tunnel and railway line from German enemy forces. Fortunately for them and other local residents, no attack by German forces came via the D&SR!

Harry Gibbs

Fireman

(courtesy Dulverton Heritage Centre)

Harry was a fireman working out of Taunton shed in the 1950s and 60s. One winter's day he and his mate, Reg Ashton, had just finished work for the day when the shed master at Taunton said "*I want you to take the '73* [meaning a Class '73XX' or 'Mogul'] *to South Molton.*" A locomotive on the 2.30pm Barnstaple to Taunton service had failed and there was concern for the passengers because a blizzard was blowing and the main road was getting impassable. So off they set, with raincoats on and the locomotive sheeted with a canopy to provide some protection from the weather on the footplate, as they were travelling tender first, exposing them to the elements as they headed west.

On arrival at South Molton they were greeted with a muffled cheer. Having backed on the train they whistled and set off on the way back to Taunton, with a goodbye wave from the staff on the platform. Harry said that they could not see the permanent way for snow, it was a 'winter wonderland' all the way. The driving wheels slipped but an application of sand on the rails by the crew (and a prayer, said Harry) saved the day and they got back safely to Taunton.

Another trip resulted in bit more drama. He was on a goods running down the grade from Venn Cross to Morebath when, suddenly, a pack of hounds on the scent came racing across the field and on the line. This was an unfitted goods, with a number of wagons on and consequently, the train was unable to pull up. Tragically, three or four hounds were killed but a number of others ran though the wheels of the wagons unscathed. Naturally all concerned were upset but there was little that could have been done to avoid the mishap.

On working the line, Harry tried not to let the safety steam valve lift, with one exception and that was at Dulverton, as he wanted to get the steam pressure up to climb the 1 in 58 to East Anstey.

People along the line were kindly and the crew would sometimes receive a bag of mushrooms to take home.

TONY 'PRES' SLOLEY

Schoolboy

(Courtesy Dulverton Heritage Centre)

Tony went to school at Huish's, the grammar school in Taunton. Each school day, he along with other boys would gather in Dulverton to be taken by Fred Greenslade's charabanc to the station. The journey was usually eventful; the younger children would be forced to travel in the luggage racks or subjected to other 'tortures', such as being forced to look at light bulbs or being smacked with a ruler. Things that were considered character building in the 1950s and 60s but today would be bullying!

There was a fun side to it; when it snowed up at Venn Cross the boys would jump out of the train, collect snow for snowballs and have snowball fights on the train! One day, a lady was trying to get on at Venn Cross with skis but the train began to pull away before she had managed, so one of the boys hung onto the communication cord. The train stopped but the guard (a regular, Charlie, a rotund gentleman who could not really cope with children) knew who was responsible – or so he thought. He was of course given the wrong name but, to be fair, the perpetrator did later confess to his deed.

ROY YANDELL

Fireman

Roy started as a Link 8 fireman and moved up to Link 4. He occasionally worked the Barnstaple Branch (passenger or goods) but his main duties were on other lines from Taunton shed. He recalls Fred Pavitt, a Taunton driver and a keen gardener for whom he was firing, working a goods down the branch. Whilst shunting at an intermediate station (probably Dulverton), the shunter came up onto the footplate to have a discussion. Fred had spotted some branches on trees near the line that would make ideal bean sticks but the goods had to work on down the line, so there was no respite. On the return working, a bundle of sticks cut and trimmed were waiting on the platform for Fred to load up onto the tender. He lived outside of Taunton though, so he somehow still had to get that large bundle of sticks back home.

DAVID GRAVES

Schoolboy

David's family lived at Huish Champflower and restored a cottage there, somewhat curiously discovering a near hundred year old copy of an 1870 newspaper, from the time when the railway was being built. When living there, he would cycle to Wiveliscombe each day to get the train to Huish's Grammar School in Taunton, leaving his bike at the station. He also had some time at Dulverton when his father ran the shop out at Amory Road/Barns Close. The shop supplied provisions to the goods depot at Dulverton in the snow-filled winter of 1962-63, when it was used as a staging point for RAF helicopters taking these supplies out to farmers up on Exmoor. When at Dulverton, David had a long day getting to and from school. Leaving home at 6.50, he and two others would travel from the town by Stanbury's bus to the station. There they would catch the 7.30am train to Taunton, joining one other boy already on the train from East Anstey, whilst another would get on at Morebath Junction Halt. On the journey, to pass the time, they would amuse themselves by playing the card game whist. On arrival at Taunton, they had a twenty minute walk to the other side of the town to the school. He would frequently have no option but to catch the later train on the way back, not getting home until 7.00pm.

One day, David had an unfortunate practical joke played on him. As he got up at Dulverton to reach his briefcase on the luggage rack, one of the boys pulled his legs from under him. The result was a broken arm and a trip to Minehead hospital! These trips to school meant he had a season ticket, which covered all seven days of the week, so frequently on Saturdays they would go up to Taunton to train spot!

ROGER JOANES

Local resident

Mr Hooper was the post-war station master at Filleigh, a post he held until the early 1950s. Life on the rural railway could be rewarding in a number of ways … sleepers, pea sticks, etc. Also, if a train hit a pheasant, the driver would make a mental note of where they were and on the return trip would slow at the spot to enable the fireman to get down to retrieve the bird. If they were somewhere he was not needed to fire the engine for a while – on a down grade for example – then he would jump into the guards van and rejoin the footplate at the next station!

COURTNEY CARD

Passenger guard

Courtney worked at Barnstaple Victoria Road in the 1950s, as noted earlier in the section on Barnstaple Victoria Road. It is with thanks to Ann, Malcolm and Ian Huxtable that a few of his memories are recorded here. On market day shoppers would come with their pannier baskets, whilst calves were transported in sacks! In the strawberry season it would be 'all hands to the pump' to pack the Combe Martin produce. On occasional Sundays there would be day-excursions, with Bristol, Weston-Super-Mare and Cardiff, and Exeter, Dawlish and Teignmouth via the Exe Valley line being typical destinations. When the Bertram Mills Circus train visited, Courtney recalled it being stabled on the loop line between East and South Junctions.

JONATHAN LOMAS

Local resident

Jonathan recalls a New Year's Eve in Barnstaple in the late 1940s/early 1950s when, with church bells ringing out to herald in the new year, the SR men at the Junction shed and WR men at Victoria Road, not to be left out, blew their engine whistles at one another to create a further cacophony of sound to keep the Barnstaple inhabitants awake! He also recalled 'Echo bridge' between Barnstaple Grammar School and the Taw Bridge on the route to the Junction, so-called by local inhabitants because children would frequently go there to shout under the bridge and listen for the echo.

AND FINALLY, THE LOCAL RAILWAY

Anonymous

The railway served the community and operated at a somewhat relaxed pace. So when on one occasion a regular passenger was spotted running to the halt a bit late, the driver called out "*Don't worry, Missus, us'll wait vor 'ee*". It is a shame that a way of life and the railway that supported it is now sadly gone forever.

Pictorial Interlude 2

The DMU Era – 1964-66

As noted in Chapter 10, steam traction on the D&SR ceased at the end of the summer 1964 time table, after which, with few exceptions, passenger services were handled by diesel units, some as single cars only but the busier trains by DMUs. During 1965, the long distance summer Saturday workings, such as the through trains to and from Ilfracombe, were hauled by North British Class 'D63XX' diesel-hydraulics, as was the through milk train from Torrington which passed along the line in 1965. Goods traffic had ceased in 1964, with the withdrawal of services from all of the remaining intermediate goods yards along the line. Victoria Road of course continued to be serviced from Barnstaple Junction.

This final era on the line has been reasonably well illustrated throughout this series of books, allowing for the fact that many photographers had turned their attentions elsewhere after steam on the line had finished; the Western Region did not fully dispense with steam until the 31st December 1965, whilst elsewhere around the country it was not until August 1968 that BR operated their final steam service. A few did, however, capture some scenes of the DMUs and 'Bubble Cars' during the last two years of the line as it went through its death throes and this second photographic interlude is thus a short tribute to their foresight. It may have been an attempt to make the line profitable by paring the service to a minimum but in reality it was doomed to fail as traffic levels were never likely to rise to a level whereby it would make money, most of the communities en route being just too small, coupled with the fact that most of the stations were poorly sited in relation to them.

As a postscript, we finish this interlude with three photographs showing the very last diesel on the line, the 4-wheeled John Fowler shunter that was used by the contractors during the dismantling of the line in summer 1967.

We begin this interlude with a slightly earlier glimpse of a DMU on the D&SR at Dulverton on 5th October 1963. This rare and interesting view, taken from the departing 6.44am Barnstaple to Taunton train, which had just crossed a Down service still at the platform, shows a DMU in the Exe Valley bay, on what was the last day of passenger services on the Exe Valley line. It is a Swindon Cross Country unit (later Class '120') and is carrying reporting No. 2C87, which was used for this service in its final few months. The presence of a headcode box indicates it is one of the nine units in the second batch – power cars No's 51573-51581 (DMBC) and No's 51582-51891 (DMS), which went into service in 1961 from Tyseley, before being transferred as a block to Laira in April 1962. It rather looks as though Exeter shed had put the unit on the Exe Valley diagram on the last day in place of the auto train, possibly the first time a DMU had been used on the service? Being based at Laira, it would not have been difficult to get the unit to Exeter. Note the rake of cattle wagons along the back siding and the horse box on the right hand end. ***Brian Conyard***

A railcar pauses at Dulverton in May 1965. There are a few passengers and still some luggage to be either loaded or unloaded before the 'bubble car' can continue on its way to Barnstaple Junction. The number of the unit was not recorded but it is one of the twenty Gloucester Railway Carriage & Wagon Company's 1958-built Motor Brake Seconds (the initials MBS can be seen on the left side), in the number series W55000-W55019, which were later designated Class '122' under the TOPS scheme of 1974. The photograph was also used by Pete Barnfield as the basis for his painting which features on page 475. ***Peter Barnfield***

RIGHT: A driver's eye view as two DMUs cross at Bishops Nympton & Molland. The lack of leaves on the trees indicates that this is a winter or early springtime picture but the date is otherwise not known. The DMU we are viewing from is a Birmingham Railway Coach & Wagon Company built unit, with a Swindon-built two-car unit standing in the Down loop on its way to Barnstaple Junction. *Brian Conyard*

BELOW: An unidentified Pressed Steel Ltd 'Bubble Car', built at Linwood in Scotland in 1960, pauses at Bishops Nympton & Molland Down platform whilst on its way to Barnstaple on 16th October 1965. Later designated Class '121', these units were ordered by the Western Region of BR after the successful introduction of the Gloucester RC&W Co. cars. They enjoyed long lives and the last surviving example of the class was in Network Rail use until 2017. A number have been preserved. It is tempting to speculate that the photographer was the only passenger on board on this occasion, given the attention of the Guard: "*Are you ready, Sir, we really ought to be leaving now ...*". *Roger Joanes*

RIGHT: Journey's end rather than beginning! This Derby-built two-car DMU, with trailing car No. W50923 at the near end, had arrived from Barnstaple on 1st October 1966, the last day of passenger services on the D&SR, but had been signalled in to Taunton's Up relief line platform, rather than the usual arrival bay No. 8, to the left of the unit.
Owen Mogg courtesy Peter Triggs

BELOW: A five car DMU made up of a two-car and a three-car set, both built by the Birmingham Railway Carriage & Wagon Company, emerges from Venn Cross Tunnel to enter the Down loop on one of the final trains to head west to Barnstaple on 1st October 1966. The dismantled platform edges at this end of Venn Cross mirrored a practice that was widespread on the railways at this period, apparently carried out to lower the rateable value of a station but which lent them a depressing air. *Michael Messenger*

A few minutes later, the same five-car unit departs Venn Cross on its way to Barnstaple. This service had been strengthened to cater for the number of people wishing to travel on the final day but not all of the trains were so treated, other services as we shall see being operated by two-car units. By this date, only the passing loop remained *in situ* here, the sidings in the goods yard having been lifted. Note the rails for a pw trolley at right angles to the line, which were laid here after the sidings had been lifted. *Michael Messenger*

The same DMU as in the previous photograph, now stopped at South Molton on its way to Barnstaple Junction on 1st October 1966. This was the last day of passenger services on the line, hence the unusually crowded scene on the platform.
Owen Mogg collection, courtesy Peter Triggs

Moments later, the unit heads away westwards from South Molton. The sidings here were still in place but the grass growing through them showed they had not seen any use since goods services had been withdrawn over two years earlier, on 6th July 1964. Note the cast iron water tank hiding behind the trees, a final reminder of the steam age.
Owen Mogg collection, courtesy Peter Triggs

A final spectacular view of the line on the last day, as a two-car BRC&Wagon Co. DMU traverses the 94ft high Castle Hill Viaduct on its way to Barnstaple. If the railway had remained open, this scene could have been almost identical but with a 'Pacer' unit instead – but all a far cry from the B&ER broad gauge 4-4-0s, the Dean 'Bulldogs' and the stalwart Churchward 'Moguls' that gave so much sterling service to the railway for so many years. ***Michael Messenger***

LEFT: To finish, three views of the demolition train which have come to light since publication of the previous two volumes. The train was here just starting its duties, outside of Victoria Road, near the site of the old East Junction signal box and on the long straight stretch towards Landkey. Volume 1 (page 188) refers to No. ED3, the Fowler 0-4-0 diesel that ferried the collection of mainly bogie bolster wagons from the demolition depot established at Dulverton to the railhead. Track lifting started at the Barnstaple end of the line, which was where construction had begun too after the first sod was cut at Hacche Moor, South Molton. The cow was clearly more interested in the photographer.

RIGHT: These very early days of the demolition work would have been in June 1967. The contractors, George Cohen, Sons & Co. of Kettering, had bought the Fowler only the previous year from BR. Built in 1949 for use by the Engineering Department of the London Midland Region, this was to be the Fowler's swansong too; Cohens took it out of service in September 1967 after the contract was completed and cut it up the following year.

LEFT: Looking east up the slope towards Landkey. It would be another couple of months, in August to be precise, when the Fowler plus its train of wagons daily trundled past the foot crossing near Brushford church on its way east, in sight of the author and building on his initial interest in the line, after his failure to travel on or even see the last train on 1st October 1966. The Fowler was not used exclusively on this work, incidentally, the occasional train being handled by a North British 'D63XX' locomotive, one such being witnessed by the author albeit only from a distance.
All Ann & Malcolm Huxtable, courtesy Ian Huxtable

Appendix 16
Locomotive Rosters

Locomotive Turns Summer Saturdays 1953 (Courtesy *Great Western Railway Journal*)

TN 70 43XX	Time	Location	Location	Time
LE	am 3.45	TN shed	Taunton	am 3.50
Goods K (1.50am Bristol)	4.05	Taunton	Barnstaple VR	6.43
Goods K	7.20	Barnstaple VR	Barnstaple Jct	7.25
Goods K	8.00	Barnstaple Jct	Barnstaple VR	8.05
Pass B	8.45	Barnstaple VR	Taunton	10.27
LE	10.30	Taunton	TN shed	10.35
LE	pm 1.45	TN shed SX	Taunton	pm 1.50
Pass B	2.05	Taunton	Barnstaple VR	3.51
Pass B	4.07	Barnstaple VR	Barnstaple Jct	4.12
Goods K	5.08	Barnstaple Jct	Barnstaple VR	5.13
Goods K	5.50	Barnstaple VR	Barnstaple Jct	5.55
Pass B	6.38	Barnstaple Jct	Barnstaple VR	6.43
Pass B	6.53	Barnstaple VR	Taunton	8.38
LE	8.45	Taunton	TN shed	8.50
SO alternative				
LE	pm 12.30	TN shed SO	Taunton	pm 12.35
Pass B (to Ilfracombe)	12.50	Taunton	Barnstaple VR	2.36
LE	3.10	Barnstaple VR	Barnstaple Jct	3.15
LE	3.50	Barnstaple Jct	Barnstaple VR	3.55
Pass A (11.30am Paddington)	4.20	Barnstaple VR	Ilfracombe	5.10
Pass B (to Taunton)	6.50	Ilfracombe	Barnstaple VR	7.42
LE	7.52	Barnstaple VR	Barnstaple shed	7.57
LE (as ordered)	0/0	Barnstaple shed	TN shed	0/0

TN 71 43XX	Time	Location	Location	Time
LE	am 4.40	TN shed FSX	Taunton	am 4.45
Goods K	5.00	Taunton	Barnstaple VR	7.58
Goods K	8.53	Barnstaple VR	Taunton	11.47
LE	11.50	Taunton	TN shed	11.55
LE	am 4.25	TN shed SO	Taunton	am 4.30
Goods K	4.45	Taunton	Barnstaple VR	7.58
LE	8.20	Barnstaple VR	Barnstaple Jct	8.25
LE	8.45	Barnstaple Jct	Barnstaple VR	8.50
Pass A (8.25am Ilfracombe to Manch Exch)	9.27	Barnstaple VR	Taunton	11.00
LE	11.05	Taunton	TN shed	11.10
LE	pm 2.15	TN shed	Taunton	pm 2.20
Pass B	2.35	Taunton	Barnstaple VR	4.32
Pass B	4.40	Barnstaple VR	Barnstaple Jct	4.45
Goods K	5.22	Barnstaple Jct	Barnstaple VR	5.27
Goods K	5.50	Barnstaple VR	Barnstaple Jct	5.55
Pass B	6.38	Barnstaple Jct	Barnstaple VR	6.43
Pass B	6.55	Barnstaple VR	Taunton	8.38
LE	8.45	Taunton	TN shed	8.50

TN 72 43XX	Time	Location	Location	Time
LE	am 5.10	TN shed	Taunton	am 5.15
Goods K	5.30	Taunton	Barnstaple VR	8.26
Goods K	10.40	Barnstaple VR SX	Barnstaple Jct	10.45
Pass B	11.25	Barnstaple Jct	Barnstaple VR	11.30
Pass B	11.36	Barnstaple VR	Taunton	pm 1.04
LE	pm 1.20	Taunton	TN shed	1.25
LE	4.40	TN shed	Taunton	4.45
Pass B	5.00	Taunton	Barnstaple VR	6.36
Pass B	6.50	Barnstaple VR	Barnstaple Jct	6.55
Goods K	7.30	Barnstaple Jct	Barnstaple VR	7.35
Goods K (Bristol)	8.00	Barnstaple VR	Taunton	10.24
LE	10.30	Taunton	TN shed	10.35
SO alternative				
Pass B (8.30am Taunton)	10.26	Barnstaple VR SO	Barnstaple Jct	10.31
Pass B (10.12am Ilfracombe)	11.05	Barnstaple Jct	Barnstaple VR	11.10
Pass B	11.30	Barnstaple VR	Taunton	pm 1.14
LE	pm 1.20	Taunton	TN shed	1.25
LE	4.15	TN shed	Taunton	4.20
Pass B	4.35	Taunton	Barnstaple VR	6.27
Pass B	6.45	Barnstaple VR	Barnstaple Jct	6.50
LE	7.08	Barnstaple Jct	Barnstaple VR	7.13
Goods K (Bristol)	7.30	Barnstaple VR	Taunton	10.24
LE	10.30	Taunton	TN shed	10.35

TN 74 43XX	Time	Location	Location	Time
LE	am 8.10	TN shed	Taunton	am 8.15
Pass B	8.30	Taunton	Barnstaple VR	10.13
Pass B	10.26	Barnstaple VR SX	Barnstaple Jct	10.31
Goods K	11.05	Barnstaple Jct	Barnstaple VR (and shunt)	11.10
Pass B (1.55pm B Jnc)	pm 2.06	Barnstaple VR	Taunton	pm 3.55
LE	4.00	Taunton	TN shed	4.05
LE				
Goods K	am 10.40	Barnstaple VR SO	Barnstaple Jct	am 10.45
Goods K	11.16	Barnstaple Jct	Barnstaple VR (and shunt)	11.21

TN75A 43XX	Time	Location	Location	Time
LE	am 11.20	TN shed	Taunton	am 11.25
Goods K	11.40	Taunton SX	Barnstaple VR	pm 3.38
Goods K	pm 7.03	Barnstaple VR	Barnstaple Jct	7.08
LE	7.13	Barnstaple Jct	Barnstaple shed	7.18
SO alternative				
Goods K	am 11.40	Taunton SO	Barnstaple VR	pm 3.55
LE	pm 7.00	Barnstaple VR	Barnstaple shed	7.05

TN 75B 43XX	TIME	LOCATION	LOCATION	TIME
LE	am 6.28	Barnstaple shed	Barnstaple VR	am 6.33
Pass B	6.55	Barnstaple VR	Taunton	8.31
LE	8.35	Taunton	TN shed	8.40
LE	10.40	TN shed	Taunton	10.45
Pass B	11.00	Taunton	Barnstaple VR	pm 12.37
Pass B	pm 12.43	Barnstaple VR	Barnstaple Jct	12.48
Pass B (to Taunton)	1.55	Barnstaple Jct	Barnstaple VR	2.00
Goods K	2.15	Barnstaple VR	Taunton	5.26
LE	5.30	Taunton	TN shed	5.35

TN77 43XX	TIME	LOCATION	LOCATION	TIME
LE	am 4.40	TN shed FO	Taunton	am 4.45
Goods K	5.00	Taunton	Barnstaple VR	7.58
LE	8.20	Barnstaple VR	Barnstaple shed	8.25
SO				
LE	am 7.10	Barnstaple shed SO	Barnstaple VR	am 7.15
Pass A (5.20am Taunton)	7.22	Barnstaple VR	Ilfracombe	8.25
Pass A (to Cardiff)	9.25	Ilfracombe	Barnstaple VR	10.24
LE	10.47	Barnstaple VR	Barnstaple Jct	10.52
LE	11.35	Barnstaple Jct	Barnstaple VR	11.40
Pass A (10.55am Ilfracombe to B'ham)	11.56	Barnstaple VR	Taunton	pm 1.32
LE	pm 1.40	Taunton	TN shed	1.45
LE	3.16	TN shed	Taunton	3.21
Pass A (10.50am Wolverhampton to Ilfracombe)	3.36	Taunton	Barnstaple VR	5.03
LE	5.08	Barnstaple VR	Barnstaple Jct	5.13
LE	5.45	Barnstaple Jct	Barnstaple VR	5.50
Pass A (5.15pm Ilfracombe)	6.12	Barnstaple VR	Taunton	7.53
LE	7.55	Taunton	TN shed	8.00

TN78 43XX EXETER	TIME	LOCATION	LOCATION	TIME
LE	am 5.00	TN shed SO	Taunton	am 5.05
Pass A (to Ilfracombe)	5.20	Taunton	Barnstaple VR	6.52
Pass A (to Ilfracombe)	7.11	Barnstaple VR	Barnstaple Jct	7.16
LE	8.10	Barnstaple Jct	Barnstaple VR	8.15
Pass B (7.15am Taunton)	9.05	Barnstaple VR	Ilfracombe	9.58
Pass A (to B'ham Snow Hill)	10.55	Ilfracombe	Barnstaple VR	11.49
LE	11.55	Barnstaple VR	Barnstaple Jct	pm 12.00
LE	pm 2.20	Barnstaple Jct	Barnstaple VR	2.25
Pass B	2.55	Barnstaple VR	Ilfracombe	3.56
Pass B (to Taunton)	5.15	Ilfracombe	Barnstaple VR	6.05
LE	6.15	Barnstaple VR	Barnstaple Jct	6.20
LE	7.30	Barnstaple Jct	Barnstaple VR	7.35
Pass B (6.50pm Ilfracombe)	8.00	Barnstaple VR	Taunton	9.38
LE	9.45	Taunton	TN shed	9.50

TN79 43XX NEWTON ABBOT	TIME	LOCATION	LOCATION	TIME
LE	am 6.55	Taunton shed SO	Taunton	am 7.00
Pass B	7.15	Taunton	Barnstaple VR	9.00
LE	9.20	Barnstaple VR	Barnstaple Jct	9.25
LE	9.55	Barnstaple Jct	Barnstaple VR	10.00
Pass A (9.25am Ilfracombe to Cardiff)	10.32	Barnstaple VR	Taunton	12.00
LE	pm 12.05	Taunton	TN shed	pm 12.10
LE	2.06	Taunton shed	Taunton	2.11
Pass A (11.30am Padd to Ilfracombe)	2.26	Taunton	Barnstaple VR	4.11
LE	4.26	Barnstaple VR	Barnstaple Jct	4.31
LE	5.00	Barnstaple Jct	Barnstaple VR	5.05
Pass A (10.50am Wolverhampton)	5.15	Barnstaple VR	Ilfracombe	6.16
Pass B	8.10	Ilfracombe	Barnstaple Jct	8.49
		Turn Engine		
ECS	9.15	Barnstaple Jct	Barnstaple VR	9.20
LE	9.30	Barnstaple VR	TN shed	11.17

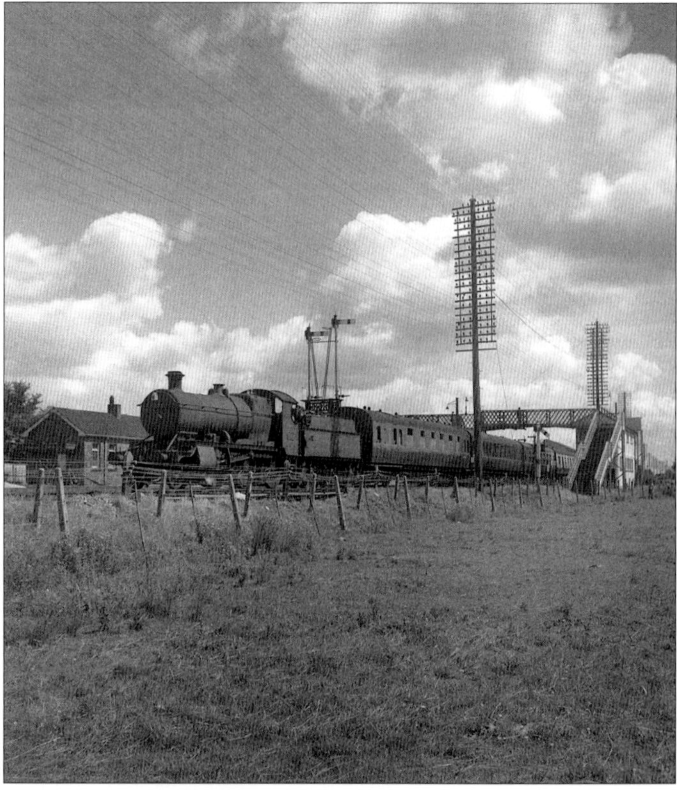

A view from the field adjacent to the railway, as 'Mogul' No. 6372 takes the Barnstaple Branch at Norton Fitzwarren Junction on Saturday 4th August 1962 with what was probably a through train to Ilfracombe. The viewpoint gives just a glimpse of the rear of the signal box, showing that there were windows at the back too. ***Owen Mogg, courtesy Peter Triggs***

Collett '2251' Class Turns in 1953

Turn 61	
Time	Train
7.00am	Taunton to Dulverton goods (arrive 10.23am)
12.05pm	Dulverton to Taunton goods (arrive 2.23pm)
3.30pm	Taunton to Minehead passenger (arrive 4.29pm)
5.10pm	Minehead to Taunton passenger (arrive 6.13pm)
8.10pm	Taunton to Minehead passenger (arrive 9.10pm)
9.20pm	Minehead to Taunton passenger (arrive 10.23pm)
Turn 73	
7.24am	Taunton to Barnstaple passenger (arrive 9.15am)
9.35am	Barnstaple to Taunton goods (arrive 1.28pm)
7.05pm	Taunton to Bristol parcels (arrive 10.00pm)
	Return to Taunton light engine

1955-56 Locomotive Roster

It is interesting to study the roster for engines in the winter 1955-56 period when the line had six Down and seven Up passenger services, and four Down and three Up goods trains. Two pairs of engines each worked three trips between Taunton and Victoria Road daily, each turn being a two-day schedule, one engine ran four sectors and two more turns ran two trips each. A number of turns ran passenger and goods trip workings to Barnstaple Junction. Given that it was the winter time table, there were no through services to Ilfracombe, so that did not need to be accommodated into the workings. A summary of the engine workings are as follows: Turns 70, 71, 72, 74 and 75 were allocated to 'Moguls'.

Turn 70	Time	Train
Day 1	tbc	Down goods
	tbc	Up goods
	5.45pm	Taunton to Barnstaple Jct passenger (arrive 7.37pm)
Day 2	6.55am	Barnstaple VR to Taunton passenger (arrive 8.30am)
	10.15am	Taunton to Barnstaple Jct passenger (arrive 12.10pm)
	2.20pm	(assumed) Up goods Barnstaple to Taunton
Turn 71	Time	Train
Day 1	tbc	Taunton to Barnstaple goods (maybe 11.40am (d) –
		arriving 3.38pm)
	3.58pm	Barnstaple Jct to Taunton passenger (arrive 5.55pm)
	8.25pm	Taunton to Barnstaple Jct passenger
Day 2	8.20am	Barnstaple VR to Taunton passenger (arrive 10.02am)
	12.25pm	Taunton to Barnstaple Jct passenger (arrive 2.20pm)
	5.25pm	Barnstaple VR to Taunton passenger (arrive 7.28pm)
Turn 72	Time	Train
Day 1	tbc	Down goods
	10am	Barnstaple Jct to Taunton passenger (arrive 11.48am)
	4.35pm	Taunton to Barnstaple Jct (arrive 6.25pm)
	7.35pm	Up goods Bristol
Turn 74	Time	Train
Day 1	8.05am	Taunton to Barnstaple Jct (arrive 9.57am)
	1.11pm	Barnstaple Jct to Taunton (arrive 2.56pm)
Turn 75	Time	Train
Day 1	11.30am	(assumed) Down goods Taunton to VR (arrive 3.22pm)
	6.40pm	Barnstaple Jct to Taunton (arrive 8.36pm)

Taunton Locomotive Duties, Summer 1957 (Saturdays Only)

Duty 70 (43XX) Train	Comments
Taunton (d) 4.05am, goods to Barnstaple VR (a) 6.43am, (d) 7.18am, Jct (a) 7.23am	Turns at Jct before next duty
Barnstaple Jct (d) 7.45am, Barnstaple VR (a) 7.50am	
Barnstaple VR (d) 8.05 Ilfracombe (a) 9.04am	6.20 am passenger Taunton to Ilfracombe, then to shed to turn
Ilfracombe (d) 10.12am, Barnstaple VR (a) 11.10am, (d) 11.35am Barnstaple shed (a) 11.40am	Light engine back to Jct (turn)
Barnstaple Jct (d) 12.43pm Taunton (a) 2.29pm	11.50am Ilfracombe to Taunton. Loco off shed at 12.20pm to join train. Loco on shed at Taunton
Taunton (d) 4.35pm Barnstaple Jct (a) 6.42pm	Passenger. Loco to Barnstaple shed to turn
Barnstaple Jct (d) 7.17pm Taunton (a) 9.18pm	Off shed to take 6.30pm Ilfracombe to Taunton
Duty 71 (43XX) Train	**Comments**
Taunton (d) 4.45am goods Barnstaple VR (a)8.20am	Loco departed VR 8.35am to Barnstaple shed (a) 8.40am (turn)
Barnstaple Jct (d) 9.12am passenger VR (a) 9.17am, (d) 9.25am Taunton (a) 11.00am	Off shed at 9am to take forward the 8.25am Ilfracombe departure (to Manchester) from Jct
Taunton (d) 2.26pm passenger Barnstaple VR (a) 4.09pm	Turn at Taunton shed on arrival, off shed at 2.10pm
Barnstaple VR (d) 4.26pm Barnstaple shed (a) 4.31pm	Light engine to shed
Barnstaple shed (d) 5.05pm Barnstaple VR (a) 5.10pm	Light engine to take forward 3.36pm Taunton Down train to Ilfracombe
Barnstaple VR (d) 5.36pm Ilfracombe (a) 6.35pm on 3.36pm Taunton departure	Ilfracombe shed for turning
Ilfracombe (d) 8.00pm passenger to Taunton. Barnstaple Jct (a) 8.39pm	
Barnstaple Jct (d) 9.00pm Barnstaple VR (a) 9.05pm	Light engine Barnstaple VR (d) 9.15 Barnstaple shed (a) 9.20pm
Duty 72 (43XX) Train	**Comments**
Taunton (d) 5.20am Barnstaple Jct passenger (a) 7.16am	Turn loco
Barnstaple Jct (d) 7.45am Taunton (a) 9.31am	Loco to shed to turn
Taunton (d) 12.50pm Barnstaple VR (a) 2.38pm (d) 3.10pm Barnstaple Jct (a) 3.15pm	Turn loco
Barnstaple Jct (d) 3.55pm passenger to Barnstaple VR (a) 4.00pm	Passenger
Barnstaple VR (d) 4.20pm Ilfracombe (a) 5.10pm	Take forward 2.26pm Taunton passenger. Loco turns at Ilfracombe
Ilfracombe (d) 6.30pm passenger Barnstaple Jct (a) 7.09pm	Loco turns at Barnstaple shed
Barnstaple Jct (d) 7.30pm Barnstaple VR (a) 7.35pm (d) 8.00pm Barnstaple VR to Taunton (a) 10.22pm Up goods	Light engine to Victoria Road

TURN 73 (43XX) TRAIN	COMMENTS
Taunton (d) 6.20am passenger Barnstaple VR (a) 7.55am, (d) 8.20am Barnstaple Jct (a) 8.25am	Turn at Jct
Barnstaple Jct (d) 8.45am Barnstaple VR (a) 8.50am (d) 9.05am on 7.15am Taunton passenger, Ilfracombe (a) 9.58am	Light engine Jct to Victoria Road. Ilfracombe turn loco
Ilfracombe (d) 10.55am passenger Barnstaple VR (a) 11.49am	Return light engine to Barnstaple shed Barnstaple VR (d) 11.55am, (a) noon, Barnstaple shed and turn
Barnstaple shed (d) 2.39pm Barnstaple VR (a) 2.44pm	Light engine
Barnstaple VR (d) 3.05pm goods Taunton (a) 7.34pm	Loco then on shed
TURN 77 (43XX) **TRAIN**	**COMMENTS**
Barnstaple Jct (d) 7.29am Ilfracombe (a) 8.14am	Loco off Barnstaple shed 7.10am to take on 5.20am Taunton to Ilfracombe from Barnstaple Jct. Loco turns at Ilfracombe
Ilfracombe (d) 9.25am Barnstaple VR (a) 10.23am	Returns light engine (d) 10.50am Barnstaple VR, Barnstaple Jct (a) 10.55am and turns
Barnstaple Jct (d) 11.30am goods to Barnstaple VR (a) 11.35am	
Barnstaple VR (d)11.56am Taunton (a) 1.30pm	Takes on 10.55am Ilfracombe train, Taunton loco to turn
Taunton (d) 3.36pm Barnstaple VR (a) 5.11pm Barnstaple VR (d) 5.25pm Barnstaple Jct (a) 5.30pm	Loco turns at Junction
Barnstaple Jct (d) 5.55pm Taunton (a) 7.51pm	Takes on 5.10pm Ilfracombe to Taunton

In addition, Barnstaple duty 574 ('N' Class 'Mogul') would work from Barnstaple shed at 2.45pm to reach Victoria Road at 2.50pm, departing at 2.55pm from there with the 12.50pm Taunton to Ilfracombe train (arriving at 3.56pm). It would return later on a passenger train to the Junction.

Barnstaple duty 583 ('M7' Class) would leave the Junction at 5.32pm on a trip goods to Victoria Road arriving 5.37pm. It would leave Victoria Road at 5.48pm on the goods back to the Junction.

Exmouth Junction duty 531 (an 'N' Class 'Mogul') would work from Barnstaple Junction at 10.02am to Victoria Road (arriving at 10.07am) and would leave Victoria Road on the 10.30am departure, the 8.30am Taunton to Ilfracombe service (arriving at 12.28pm). It would work back to Exeter later in the day. This illustrates some of the locomotive changes that took place at Victoria Road rather than Barnstaple Junction, which made for slightly smoother operation, given the reversal that took place at the time with the East Chord out of use.

By summer 1959, the locomotive rosters had changed and in summary, three '43XX' Class locomotives worked a three-four-three trip schedule over a three day period, one engine was on a four-trip day and two others on two trip turns each. The most popular locomotives on the route at this time were '43XX' Class No's 6323, 6337, 6343, 6364, 6372, 6375, 7304, 7305, 7319 and 7337 (ex-9315). As can be seen from the shed listing on page 505, they were Taunton based. At this time Taunton had seven turns for 'Moguls', with ten engines allocated to that shed.

SUMMER 1961

By August 1961, the locomotive turns on summer Saturdays were as follows ('Moguls'). Some of the timings vary slightly from the working time table (only by minutes). Carriage loadings and type are also listed in the notes column.

TN70 (43XX) TRAIN	NOTES
05.20am Taunton to Ilfracombe (arrive 7.58am)	8 WR coaches '63XX' to Ilfracombe (pilot from Barnstaple Jct 'N' Class)
09.22am Ilfracombe to Cardiff (10.06am Barnstaple Jct, 12.10am Taunton)	8 WR coaches. Piloted by 'West Country' Class to Barnstaple Jct
11.30am Paddington to Ilfracombe	6 WR coaches TN70 on at Taunton 2.26pm to Barnstaple Jct (4.18pm) and Ilfracombe (5.10pm)
6.37pm Ilfracombe to Taunton	6 WR coaches. Piloted by 'N' Class to Barnstaple Jct (7.22pm and 9.21pm Taunton)
TN71 (43XX) **TRAIN**	**NOTES**
6.20am Taunton to Ilfracombe (9.04am)	6 WR coaches arrive Barnstaple Jct 8.08am. '43XX' throughout
10.12am Ilfracombe to Wolverhampton	6 WR coaches arrive Barnstaple Jct 10.55am, 1.06pm Taunton. '43XX' to Taunton
10.30 Wolverhampton (3.36pm Taunton) to Ilfracombe (arrive 6.35pm)	6WR coaches arrive Barnstaple Jct 5.36pm. Train from Wolverhampton. '43XX' Taunton to Ilfracombe
8.05pm Ilfracombe to Taunton (arrive 10.30pm)	6WR coaches arrive Barnstaple Jct 8.44pm. '43XX' throughout
TN72 (43XX) **TRAIN**	**NOTES**
7.00am Taunton to Ilfracombe	8 WR coaches arrive Barnstaple Jct 8.45am, Ilfracombe 9.42am. '43XX' throughout
11.00am Ilfracombe to Wolverhampton	8 WR coaches arrive Barnstaple Jct 11.46am, Taunton 1.30pm. '43XX' throughout
4.35pm Taunton to Ilfracombe	4 WR coaches (loco to Barnstaple Jct only 6.37pm)
8.10pm Barnstaple Jct to Taunton	Bristol goods arrive Norton Fitzwarren 10.16pm
TN73 (43XX) **TRAIN**	**NOTES**
8.30am Taunton to Ilfracombe	5 WR coaches arrive Barnstaple Jct 10.33am and Ilfracombe 11.22am. 43XX throughout
12.25pm Ilfracombe to Paddington	5WR coaches arrive Barnstaple Jnc 1.06pm, Taunton 3.07pm. '43XX' Ilfracombe to Taunton
TN 74 (43XX) **TRAIN**	**NOTES**
4.35am Taunton to Victoria Road (arrive 8.31am)	Goods
10.50am Victoria Road to Jct (arrive 11.00am)	Goods trip
11.50am ex-Torrington to Taunton (arrive 2.30pm)	Departs Barnstaple Jct 12.48pm, 3 WR coaches. '43XX' from Jct
6.15pm Taunton to Barnstaple Jct (arrive 8.02pm)	4 WR coaches

TN75 (43XX) TRAIN	NOTES
4.05am Taunton to Barnstaple Jct (arrive 6.39am)	Goods
7.20am trip to Barnstaple VR	Arrive 7.30am
8.50am Barnstaple VR to Barnstaple Jct	Arrive 8.58am. Light engine
8.30am Ilfracombe to Manchester	Takes over at Jct at 9.18am to Taunton (arrive 11.03am) 9 LMR coaches
1.50pm Taunton to Barnstaple Jct (arrive 3.30pm)	5 WR coaches
5.00pm Barnstaple Jct to Taunton (arrive 6.55pm)	5 WR coaches
TN 76 (43XX) – swaps with TN74 on alternate days	
TRAIN	NOTES
7.45am Barnstaple Jct to Taunton (arrive 9.36am)	4 WR coaches. 7.30am off Barnstaple loco shed
12.50pm Taunton to Ilfracombe (arrive 3.56pm, Barnstaple Jct (arrive 3.00pm)	4 WR coaches. '43XX' throughout to Ilfracombe and turn at shed
5.10pm Ilfracombe to Taunton (arrive 7.51pm)	4 WR coaches. '43XX' throughout (Barnstaple Jnc arrive 17.48). On shed at Taunton

TN 77 (43XX) TRAIN	NOTES
6.43am, Barnstaple Jct to Taunton (arrive 8.30am)	3 WR coaches. 6.25am off Barnstaple loco shed
10.25am Taunton to Torrington (Barnstaple Jct arrive 12.16pm)	3 WR coaches. '43XX' as far as Barnstaple. Then to loco shed
2.15pm to Barnstaple VR	Light Engine (arrive 2.23pm)
3.03pm Victoria Road to Taunton (arrives Norton Fitz 7.27pm)	Goods (shunts and stops a lot). To Taunton loco shed
8.40pm Taunton to Barnstaple Jct (arrive 10.24pm)	3 WR Coaches. To Barnstaple loco shed.
TN 78 (43XX) TRAIN	NOTES
10.30am Taunton to Barnstaple VR (SO)	Goods (arrive 2.04pm) shunts and carries on to Jct
3.15pm Barnstaple VR to Barnstaple Jct (arrive 3.25pm)	Goods
3.55pm Barnstaple Jct to Taunton (arrive 6.01pm)	3 WR coaches plus 1 parcels van

'Mogul' No. 7325 at Silk Mills, Norton Fitzwarren, with a long goods train on 29th September 1962. Given its length, it is highly unlikely that this train was off the Barnstaple Branch but the picture is included to show the versatility of these GWR 2-6-0 workhorses. *Owen Mogg, courtesy Peter Triggs*

GWR locomotives were regular visitors to the Southern's terminus at Ilfracombe and at first glance this looks to be an unidentified 'Mogul' heading away from the station at the commencement of the steep 1 in 36 climb up through the Slade Valley to Mortehoe. However, careful inspection of the picture shows more coaches in the platform behind, so the locomotive is probably engaged in shunting stock on a busy summer Saturday. More carriages can be seen to the left of the engine; there were a bank of eight sidings here, laid in specifically to cater for stabling coaching stock during the holiday season, part of the Southern's improvements to the station carried out in the mid to late 1920s. The final part of this work was the provision of the new engine shed, seen here on the right, built of concrete blocks and completed circa 1930. The loss of the railway was to be a blow to the resort's economy. ***Tim Stephens***

APPENDIX 17
THROUGH COACH WORKINGS, SELECTED PERIODS, 1892–1938

1890s

A review of historical records shows that through coaches were a regular feature in July 1892 (this was after the final gauge conversion). The table below summarises the position. Abbreviations used throughout this appendix: compo – composite coach; tri-compo – composite coach comprising First, Second & Third Class accommodation; brake tri-compo – included a brake van/luggage compartment in addition to the passenger accommodation; w – wheels.

DOWN TRAIN	CARRIAGE(S)	DESTINATION	NOTES/RETURN WORKING
9.00am Padd to Penzance	8w tri-compo	Ilfracombe	see 8.35am Plymouth to Padd
11.25am Padd to Paignton	8w compo 8w brake Third	Ilfracombe	11.17am Ilfracombe to Padd
11.45am Padd to Penzance	8w van	Ilfracombe	11.17am Ilfracombe to Padd
1.50pm Padd to Exeter	8w compo	Taunton	Forward on 3.15pm Taunton to Ilfracombe next day. Then back on 11.17am Ilfracombe to Padd
3.00pm Padd to Plymouth	8w Third	Ilfracombe	11.17am Ilfracombe to Padd

UP TRAIN	CARRIAGES	NOTES/DOWN WORKING REF.
8.35am Plymouth to Padd (arr 2.53pm)	8w tri-compo	Leaves Ilfracombe on 7.35am
11.17am Ilfracombe to Padd (arr 6.20pm)	8w brake Third 8w Third 8w compo 8w compo 8w van	Through working

The 11.17am would reach Paddington in 6 hours and 43 minutes.

There was a note that stipulated that if 8-wheeled coaches were not available, then one 8-wheeled coach should be replaced by two 6-wheeled coaches (and three 6-wheelers instead of two 8-wheelers).

In June 1894 there were only two Down trains, each containing one 8 wheeled brake tri-compo as the through coach. These were the 9.00am and 11.45am Paddington to Penzance trains. For the return workings, the coaches were attached at Taunton to the 8.45am and 10.50am Plymouth to Paddington trains. The service was stepped up again for the summer period from July 1894, with a similar pattern to the 1892 table above and the 11.17am Ilfracombe to Paddington reinstated. In the winter period starting in October 1894 there were no through coaches.

June 1895 saw the introduction of one coach Down (an 8-wheeled brake tri-compo) on the 11.45 am Paddington to Penzance, this working back from Ilfracombe on the 9.15am train the next day to be attached to the 10.45 Plymouth to Paddington, arriving at 6.00pm.

The summer of 1895 (July, August, September) again restored three Down sets of through coaches, along with the coach detached off the 1.35pm Paddington to Exeter at Taunton to work forwards to Ilfracombe the next day. Of the six coaches that worked Down, five worked back on the 11.17am from Ilfracombe, the other being attached to the 8.45am from Plymouth at Taunton as before . However, by this time the van (on the 11.45am Paddington to Penzance previously) no longer worked down.

Throughout 1896 the workings were usually an 8-wheeled brake tri-compo Down on the 11.45am Paddington to Penzance, working back on an early Ilfracombe train (the 9.15am or 10.05am) to be attached to the 10.45am Plymouth to Paddington (which by this time was designated a 'Mail train'). The records for summer 1896 were unavailable for review.

This was certainly the case in July, August and September of 1897, when three Down trains provided through coaches. The 1.35pm Paddington to Exeter carried an 8-wheeled Third as far as Swindon, where it was detached and worked to Ilfracombe on local services (see below). This coach and four others would work back on the 11.17am from Ilfracombe to Paddington service, which train was now designated 'Mail'.

There were no through coaches in the early part of 1898. The summer period restored the usual workings and the movements of the 8-wheeled Third off the 1.35pm Paddington to Exeter are revealed. Having been detached off the train it was worked at 5.15pm on the Swindon to Bristol, then the next day the 4.25pm Bristol to Taunton and on the 7.20pm from Taunton to Barnstaple.

In the summer period of 1898, there were six Down through coaches to Ilfracombe (from Taunton) and six Up from Ilfracombe (to Taunton). The 11.17am departure from Ilfracombe was the through Paddington service. This continued to comprise five coaches formed from four Down workings. Two of the Down trains were 'fast' in the sense that they did not stop at all stations and traversed the line in 100 minutes (the 3.15pm off Taunton) and 94 minutes (the 6.55pm off Taunton). The latter train's through coach arrived at Ilfracombe at 9.29pm.

There were three sets of through coaches to Taunton in the October period but no through train to Paddington.

In 1899 there were no through coaches until the July to September period. There were three separate Down through coach workings and the usual 11.17am Up train from Ilfracombe. Through coaches ceased again after September for the winter period. For the August Bank Holiday of this year (5th), the 1.35pm ex-Weymouth train was noted to be extended from Chippenham to Swindon, to relieve the 11.17am Ilfracombe to Paddington train on this section of the line.

1900

In 1900 itself there were no through coaches on the line until the July, August, September period. The coaches ran as follows.

DOWN TRAIN	CARRIAGES	DESTINATION	NOTES/RETURN WORKING
9.00am Padd to Penzance (Mail)	8w bk tri-compo 8w bk Third (4 comp)	Ilfracombe	Returns on 7.20am Ilfracombe Returns on 11.17am Ilfracombe to Padd
11.30 Padd to Kingswear	8w compo 8w bk Third (5 comp)	Ilfracombe	Both return on 11.17am Ilfracombe to Padd
3.00pm Padd to Plymouth	8w bk tri-compo	Ilfracombe	Returns on 11.17am Ilfracombe to Padd

UP TRAIN	CARRIAGES	NOTES/DOWN WORKING REF.
8.30am Plymouth to Padd	8w bk tri-compo	7.20am Ilfracombe to Taunton attached at Taunton
11.17am Ilfracombe to Padd (arr 6.15pm)	8w bk Third (5 comp) 8w compo 8w bk tri-compo 8w Third 8w bk Third (4 comp)	The 8w Third travels locally from Swindon to Ilfracombe having come off the 2.35pm Padd departure

1901

The pattern of through coaches in 1901 was similar. However, the two coaches on the 9.00am Paddington departure made up part of the 11.17am Ilfracombe to Paddington next day return working. It was the 8-wheeled brake tri-compo off the 3.00pm Paddington to Plymouth that worked from Taunton to Ilfracombe, returning from Ilfracombe at 7.20am the next day to join the 8.30am Plymouth to Paddington at Taunton.

1902

This year registered the first slip coach working at Taunton for the Barnstaple line. The through coaches still only ran in the three main summer months, the details of which are set out below.

The slip coach worked back to Taunton from Ilfracombe on a local service. It was then attached to the 11.42am ex-Newton Abbott Up service at and slipped at Reading.

The notes associated with the through coach workings show that, on certain Saturdays, the 11.20am Ilfracombe to Paddington service would be divided from Weston-Super-Mare to Bristol.

DOWN TRAIN	CARRIAGES	DESTINATION	NOTES/RETURN WORKING
9.00am Padd to Penzance	8w luggage body tri-compo 8w bk Third (4 comp)	Ilfracombe	Both return on 11.20am Ilfracombe to Padd
11.35am Padd to Kingswear	8w tri-compo (slip) 8w tri-compo (luggage body)	Ilfracombe	Both coaches were slipped at Taunton to work forward to Ilfracombe
1.10pm Padd to Plymouth	8w compo	Newton Abb	Works to Ilfracombe to return on 11.20am following day
	8w compo	Taunton	This works to Ilfracombe the next day to return on 11.20am
3.00pm Padd to Plymouth	8w bk tri-compo	Ilfracombe	Works back on 7.20am Ilfracombe to Taunton joining 8.30am Plymouth to Padd

UP TRAIN	CARRIAGES	NOTES/DOWN WORKING REF.
11.20am Ilfracombe to Padd (arr 6.10pm)	8w bk Third (4 comp) 8w tri-compo (luggage body)	First two off 9.00am Padd
	8w compo	From Newton Abbott
	8w tri-compo (luggage body) 8w bk Third (4 comp)	Non-slip coach off 11.35am Down. Slip coach works back as above (page 693)

1903

In 1903 the through coaches only ran in July, August and September

DOWN TRAIN	CARRIAGES	DESTINATION	NOTES/RETURN WORKING
9.00am Padd to Plymouth (Mail)	8w bk tri-compo 8w bk Third (4 comp)	Ilfracombe	Both returning on 12.10pm Ilfracombe to Padd
11.35am Padd to Kingswear	8w slip tri-compo 8w slip tri-compo	Ilfracombe	SCW8. See slip working notes below SCW30. Attached at Bath to slip at Taunton
1.10pm Padd to Plymouth	8w bk tri-compo	Taunton	Works forward to Ilfracombe on 7.06pm from Taunton to return on 12.10pm Ilfracombe to Padd next day
3.03pm Padd to Plymouth	8w bk tri-compo	Ilfracombe	Returns 7.20am Ilfracombe to Taunton and then to Padd

UP TRAIN	CARRIAGES	NOTES/DOWN WORKING REF.
12.10pm Ilfracombe to Padd (arr 6.40pm)	8w bk tri-compo 8w bk Third (3 comp)	Ilfracombe to Birkenhead (down from Birkenhead at 8.55am previous day)
	8w bk Third (4 comp) 8w bk tri-compo 8w bk tri-compo	

As indicated on page 534, 1889 recorded the first occasion of through coaches working from somewhere other than London but these were suspended until resumed in 1903. On the Down journey, Birkenhead coaches worked forward from Crewe on the 9.35am to Kingswear and were detached at Taunton. The return working had the coaches detached at Bristol, where they went forwards on the 4.10pm Bristol to Crewe.

The through coach workings were complicated by the slip coach workings, which are summarised in the table at the bottom of the page. As can be seen, the movements were quite involved and coach working 30/39 managed a scenic tour around the network.

1904

In 1904, the through coaches were modified slightly, largely impacting on the slip coach workings. The slips now employed on these services were double-ended.

DOWN TRAIN	CARRIAGES	DESTINATION	NOTES/RETURN WORKING
9.00 Padd to Plymouth (mail)	8w bk compo 8w bk Third (5 comp)	Ilfracombe	Both return on 12.15pm Ilfracombe to Padd
11.35 Padd to Kingswear	8w tri-compo (slip) 8w compo (2/3)	Ilfracombe	Slipped at Taunton (see slip coach working) Returns on 12.15pm Ilfracombe to Taunton
3.03pm Padd to	8w bk tri-compo	Ilfracombe	7.20am Ilfracombe to Padd return

UP TRAIN	CARRIAGES	NOTES/DOWN WORKING REF.
8.30am Plymouth to Padd	8w bk tri-compo	Taken off at Bristol and taken forward on 12.05pm Bristol to Padd
10.50am Kingswear to Padd	8w tri-compo (slip)	See slip coach working. Ilfracombe to Reading
12.15pm Ilfracombe to Padd	8w bk tri-compo	Ilfracombe to Birkenhead
	8w bk Third	Ilfracombe to Birkenhead
	8w compo 2/3 8w compo 8w bk Third (5 comp)	

The Birkenhead coaches arrived at Taunton on the 9.37am Crewe to Plymouth. On the return they were taken off at Taunton and added to the 8.30am Penzance to Crewe.

The slip coach workings were much simplified from the previous year:

SLIP COACH 3	SLIP COACH 8
11.35am Paddington to Kingswear.	9.15am Ilfracombe to Taunton
Slipped at Taunton	1.00pm Taunton to Reading (slip)
3.21pm Taunton to Ilfracombe.	4.05pm Reading to Paddington
Next day working Slip Coach 8	

From October 1904 there was one through coach working. A slip coach on the 11.35am Paddington to Kingswear was detached at Taunton and went to Ilfracombe on the 3.57pm (note re-timing). It returned the next day to Taunton and was attached to the 10.50am Kingswear to Paddington, to be slipped at Reading (as SC3 and SC8 above).

1905

In 1905 there was a through coach (a brake tri-composite) on the 12.25pm Paddington to Penzance, which ran through to Ilfracombe in May and June. This returned the next day on the 9.15am Ilfracombe to Taunton, to be attached to the 10.46 Kingswear to Paddington (where it arrived at 4.30pm).

The July, August, September holiday period saw one major change, being the first through train of coaches – the 10.15am Paddington to Ilfracombe. This was made up as shown in the table overleaf (note coaches without reference to the number of wheels will be 8-wheeled vehicles).

In the Up direction, shown in the second part of the table overleaf, there was an 11.00am Barnstaple to Paddington (due at 4.30pm), in addition to the 12.17pm Ilfracombe to Paddington. The make up of both these trains also follows overleaf, with the Barnstaple Up service shown first.

SLIP COACH 8	SLIP COACH 30	SLIP COACH 39 (NEXT DAY SCW 30)
11.35 Padd to Taunton (slip)	9.02am Swindon to Didcot (slip) on 6.25am ex-Hereford	7.20am Barnstaple to Taunton
3.16pm Taunton to Ilfracombe	9.40am Didcot to Oxford	2.53pm Taunton (attached to 12.10pm from Ilfra) to Didcot (slip)
Next day	11.15am Oxford to Bath	5.57pm Didcot to Oxford
7.20am Ilfracombe to Taunton	1.42pm Bath to Taunton	7.25pm Oxford to Reading
1pm Taunton to Reading (slip)	3.16pm Taunton to Ilfracombe	back to SCW 30 next day
4.05pm Reading to Padd	7.25pm Ilfracombe to Barnstaple	

Down – 10.15am Paddington to Ilfracombe			
Carriage	From	To	Return
Corridor LB	Padd	Minehead	10.15am Minehead
Tri-compo	Padd	Minehead	10.15am Minehead
Third	Taunton	Ilfracombe	8.00am Ilfracombe to Taunton
Third	Padd	Ilfracombe	12.17pm Ilfracombe
Compo	Padd	Ilfracombe	12.17pm Ilfracombe
Van	Padd	Ilfracombe	12.17pm Ilfracombe
Bk tri-compo	Padd	Barnstaple	1.05pm Barnstaple
Compo 6w	Taunton	Barnstaple	8.50am Barnstaple
Third 6w	Taunton	Barnstaple	8.50am Barnstaple
Van 6w	Taunton	Barnstaple	8.50am Barnstaple
Tri-compo (slip)	Padd	Bridgwater	SCW 13
Tri-compo (slip)	Padd	Bath	SCW 41
Up – 11.00am Barnstaple to Paddington			
Carriage	From	To	Return
Bk tri-compo	Ilfracombe	Manch'r	8.35am Manch'r
Bk Third	Ilfracombe	Padd	7.30am Padd
Compo	Ilfracombe	Padd	8.10pm Padd
Compo (2&3)	Barnstaple	Padd	11.35am Padd
Compo	Barnstaple	Padd	11.35am Padd
Bk Third (5c)	Barnstaple	Padd	11.35am Padd
Corr tri-compo	Minehead	Padd	10.15am Padd
Van 6-wheel	Minehead	Padd	12.25pm Padd
Tri-compo	Taunton	Reading	SCW 8
Bk tri-compo	Kingswear	Reading	6.30pm Padd

The coach bound for Manchester was detached at Bristol and transferred to the 10.46am from Kingswear to Crewe and a coach (destined for Reading) taken off this train and attached to the Barnstaple train. The compo (2/3) was slipped at Taunton on the way down with the slip tri-compo (slip coach working 3).

The 12.17pm departure from Ilfracombe (due to arrive at Paddington at 6.15pm) was made up as follows.

Up – 12.17pm Ilfracombe to Paddington			
Carriage	From	To	Return
Bk Third (3c)	Ilfracombe	Birk'head	8.15am Birkenhead
Bk tri-compo	Ilfracombe	Birk'head	8.15am Birkenhead
Bk Third	Minehead	Padd	7.45pm Padd
Compo	Minehead	Padd	7.45pm Padd
Compo (SO)	Taunton	Padd	4.15pm Padd FO
Third	Ilfracombe	Padd	10.15am Padd
Compo	Ilfracombe	Padd	10.15am Padd
Van	Ilfracombe	Padd	10.15am Padd
Bk tri-compo	Barnstaple	Padd	10.15am Padd
Bk tri-compo	Barnstaple	Liverpool	7.05pm Liverpool

It is curious to see a through working to/from Liverpool. This coach was transferred off at Taunton and onwards at 3.08pm on the Taunton to Crewe service, along with the Birkenhead-bound coaches. These came down on the 9.37am Crewe to Plymouth. The Minehead coaches left Paddington for Didcot and then Swindon, then Bristol and then Taunton.

There was one other through coach (a brake tri-compo), which worked down on the 3.03pm Paddington to Taunton, thence on to Ilfracombe and back the next day on the 8.00am Ilfracombe to Taunton, then on to Paddington to arrive at 3.12pm.

The 10.58am Leicester to Taunton train brought a brake Third from Swindon to Ilfracombe, which would work forward to Ilfracombe on the 3.58pm Taunton departure.

In October 1905, the slip coaches did not run, whilst there was one through coach (a brake tri-compo) to Ilfracombe on the 12.25pm Paddington to Penzance, which returned the next day at 9.15am to Taunton and then on to Paddington.

1906

In the May/June period of 1906, the 12.25pm Paddington to Penzance took a brake tri-compo for Ilfracombe. It returned the following day on the 9.15am from Ilfracombe to Taunton, then attached on the 10.45am Kingswear to Crewe as far as Bristol, where it was attached on the 2.10pm Bristol to Paddington service.

The July, August and September period of 1906 had an interesting mix of through coaches. The 10.15am Paddington to Ilfracombe commenced on 14th July and comprised as below.

Down – 10.15am Paddington to Ilfracombe			
Carriage	From	To	Return
Bk tri-Compo	Padd	Minehead	
Third	Taunton	Ilfracombe	8am Ilfracombe
Third	Padd	Ilfracombe	12.17pm Ilfracombe to Padd
Compo	Padd	Ilfracombe	12.17pm Ilfracombe to Padd
Van	Padd	Ilfracombe	12.17pm Ilfracombe to Padd
LB tri-compo	Padd	Barnstaple	1.05pm Barnstaple
Compo 6w	Taunton	Barnstaple	8.45am Barnstaple
Bk Third 6w	Taunton	Barnstaple	8.45am Barnstaple

The 11.35am Paddington to Penzance train had a slip tri-compo from Bath to Ilfracombe, which was slipped at Taunton (SCW 30A). The 11.40am to Kingswear had a slip tri-compo (SCW3) and a compo (2/3) for Ilfracombe. The latter worked back on the 11.00am Barnstaple service. The 10.57am Leicester service had a van Third and a compo attached at Swindon at 1.32pm to Ilfracombe; these worked back on the 9.55am Ilfracombe to Paddington. The 3.30pm Paddington to Penzance had a slip tri-compo to Ilfracombe (SCW40A).

In the up direction the trains comprised the 11.00am Barnstaple to Paddington (arriving at 4.30pm) and the 12.17pm Ilfracombe to Paddington (arriving 5.38pm), made up as below.

Up – 11.00am Barnstaple to Paddington			
Carriage	From	To	Return
Van Third	Ilfracombe	Padd	Down – 10.58am Leicester
Compo	Ilfracombe	Padd	Down – 10.58am Leicester
Tri-compo (slip)	Ilfracombe	Padd	SCW3
Compo 2/3	Barnstaple	Padd	11.40am Padd Down
Compo	Barnstaple	Padd	1.18pm Padd Down
Van Third (5 comp)	Barnstaple	Padd	1.18pm Padd Down
Bk tri-compo	Minehead	Padd	
Van	Minehead	Padd	
Tri-compo (slip)	Taunton	Reading	SCW8
Bk tri-compo	Kingswear	Reading	attached at Bristol
Up – 12.17pm Ilfracombe to Paddington			
Carriage	From	To	Return
Bk tri-compo	Barnstaple	Manch'ter	3.50pm Manch'ter
Van Third (3 comp)	Ilfracombe	Birk'head	9.25am Birk'head
Bk tri-compo	Ilfracombe	Birk'head	9.25am Birk'head
LB tri-compo	Minehead	Padd	10.15am Padd
Third	Ilfracombe	Padd	10.15am Padd
Compo	Ilfracombe	Padd	10.15am Padd
Van	Ilfracombe	Padd	10.15am Padd
LB tri-compo	Barnstaple	Padd	10.15am Padd
Bk tri-compo (70ft)	Taunton	Padd	11.40am Padd
Van Third	Weymouth	Padd	
Compo	Weymouth	Padd	
Tri-compo (slip)	Weymouth	Savernake	

The Manchester and Birkenhead coaches went forwards on the 3.01pm Taunton to Crewe (both the Manchester and Birkenhead-bound brakes had the brake end leading).

There was a brake tri-compo on the 1.15pm Crewe to Plymouth train, which ran from Bristol at 5.00pm to Taunton, thence on the 6.10pm Taunton to Barnstaple; it would return the next day at 1.05pm from Barnstaple.

The slip coach workings in the period are summarised as below.

SCW3	From	To
11.40am	Paddington	Taunton
2.23pm	Taunton	Ilfracombe
(next day) 9.55am	Ilfracombe	Paddington
SCW8*	From	To
8.00am	Ilfracombe	Paddington
12.50pm	Taunton (11.00am Barnstaple)	Reading
4.15pm†	Reading	Paddington
*(40A previous day); † This was a double ended slip		

SCW30A	From	To
9.53am	Reading	Bath (2/7-13/7)
10.15am	Paddington	Bath (commence 14/7)
12.13pm	Bath	Bristol
1.10pm	Bristol (on 11.35am Cardiff)	Taunton (slip)
2.23pm	Taunton	Ilfracombe
1.25pm (next day)	Ilfracombe	Taunton (slip)
4.10pm	Taunton	Paddington
SCW40A	From	To
3.30pm	Paddington	Taunton (slip)
6.10pm	Taunton	Ilfracombe

In October 1906 the slip workings were as shown below; SCW68, formed of a single-ended slip of 8ft 6ins stock, became SCW69 the following day.

SCW68	From	To	Note
10.30am Limited	Padd	Penzance	Tri-compo slipped at Taunton to go to Ilfracombe at 1.24pm
SCW69	From	To	
9.15am	Ilfracombe	Taunton	
1.18pm	Taunton	Bristol (10.40am Kingswear to Bristol)	
2.10pm	Bristol	Padd	

1907

In January 1907, the 10.30am Paddington to Penzance ('The Limited') took a tri-compo slip coach for Ilfracombe (SCW 68). This returned the following day (as SCW69) on the 7.30am Barnstaple to Taunton, thence Taunton to Bristol (on the 10.46am Kingswear to Crewe) and back to Paddington on the 2.10pm from Bristol. This continued in May and June but once into the summer period (July to September), through coach activity substantially increased. Key trains are summarised below.

Down – 10.15am Paddington to Ilfracombe			
Carriage	From	To	Return
Bk tri-compo	Padd	Minehead	10.45am Minehead to Padd
Third 6w	Taunton	Ilfracombe	8.00am Ilfracombe to Taunton
Third	Padd	Ilfracombe	12.17pm Ilfracombe to Padd
Compo	Padd	Ilfracombe	12.17pm Ilfracombe to Padd
Van	Padd	Ilfracombe	12.17pm Ilfracombe to Padd
LB tri-compo	Padd	Barnstaple	1.5pm Barnstaple to Padd
Slip tri-compo	Padd	Bridgwater	SCW15
Slip tri-compo	Padd	Bath	SCW29

SCW29 is relevant because it travelled from Bath to Ilfracombe behind the 11.35am Cardiff to Penzance and was slipped at Taunton. The 11.50am Paddington to Kingswear had a slip tri-compo, a dining car and a van Third, all from Paddington to Ilfracombe and slipped at Taunton. This was the first example of a dining car travelling through, being worked from Ilfracombe to Barnstaple at 6.15pm and returning the next day on the 1.05pm Barnstaple to Paddington. The 3.30pm Paddington to Penzance would contain a slip tri-compo (SCW53) for Ilfracombe.

Up – 10.58 Barnstaple to Paddington (due 4.30pm)			
Carriage	From	To	Return
Van Third	Barnstaple	Padd	1.20pm Padd
Compo	Barnstaple	Padd	1.20pm Padd
Van third	Barnstaple	Padd	11.30am Padd
Tri-compo (slip)	Ilfracombe	Padd	SCW49
Bk tri-compo	Ilfracombe	Padd	9.00am Padd
Van Third	Ilfracombe	Padd	1.20pm Padd
Bk tri-compo	Minehaed	Padd	10.15am Padd
Tri-compo (slip)	Taunton	Reading	SCW10
Van	Paignton	Reading	1.00pm Padd
Bk tri-compo	Paignton	Reading	1.00pm Padd

In the next table, it is worth noting the routing of the Birkenhead coach. The brake tri-compo was put on the 3.05pm Paddington to Birkenhead at Shrewsbury. On the way down to the West Country, it departed Birkenhead at 9.15am, was then attached to the Crewe to Plymouth train at Shrewsbury and taken off at Taunton.

Up – 12.17pm Ilfracombe to Paddington (due 5.42pm)			
Bk tri-compo	Ilfracombe	Manchester	3.50pm Manchester
Bk tri-compo	Ilfracombe	Birkenhead	9.15am Birkenhead
Bk tri-compo	Minehead	Padd	7.30am Padd
Compo	Ilfracombe	Padd	10.15am Padd
Third	Ilfracombe	Padd	10.15am Padd
Dining Car*	Barnstaple	Padd	11.53am Padd
LB tri-Compo	Barnstaple	Padd	10.15am Padd
Van	Ilfracombe	Padd	10.15am Padd
Compo	Weymouth	Padd	1.20pm Padd
Van Third	Weymouth	Padd	1.20pm Padd
Tri-compo (slip)	Weymouth	Savernake	1.20pm Padd (SCW37)
*1907 is believed to be the first year in which a dining car was sent through to Ilfracombe.			

The slip coach workings in the period relevant to the line were as shown below.

SCW10 (53 previous day)	From	To
8.00am	Ilfracombe	Taunton
12.58pm	Taunton	Bristol
2.10pm	Bristol	Reading (slip)
4.15pm	Reading	Padd
SCW29	From	To
10.15am	Paddington	Bath (slip)
12.15pm	Bath	Bristol
1.10pm	Bristol	Taunton (slip)
2.40pm	Taunton	Ilfracombe
SCW35 (29 previous day)	From	To
1.20pm	Ilfracombe	Taunton
4.10pm	Taunton	Padd
SCW49 (3 previous day)	From	To
9.55am	Ilfracombe	Padd
SCW3	From	To
11.50am	Paddington	Taunton
2.04pm	Taunton	Ilfracombe
SCW53	From	To
3.30pm	Paddington	Taunton (slip)
6.17pm	Taunton	Ilfracombe

Most slips were designated as 8ft 6ins stock but SCW53 and SCW 10 were designated for double-ended slip coaches.

In the October 1907 period, the through services were provided by slip coaches. The 10.30am Paddington to Penzance ('The Cornish Riviera Limited'), had two single-ended slip coaches for Ilfracombe (SCW69), leaving Taunton at 1.18pm. The return working (SCW70) was the following day, leaving Ilfracombe at 9.15am for Taunton, to pick up the 1.08pm Taunton departure to Bristol (the Paignton to Crewe service). At Bristol they were transferred onto the 2.10pm Bristol to Paddington service.

1908

In 1908, the GWR ran a 'flagship' express from Wolverhampton to Penzance, which commenced on 1st July of that year. When it arrived at Bristol Temple Meads, a slip coach was added for Ilfracombe. Departing Temple Meads at 1.10pm, once the coach had been slipped at Taunton it went forward to Ilfracombe on the 2.40pm stopping service. In the winter months, however, the slip coach was for Taunton only. The Ilfracombe slip was continued in 1909 and beyond to the summer of 1914. However, by summer of 1916, with services affected by the First World War, the slip coach only went from Bristol to Taunton and only on Saturdays. The Wolverhampton to Penzance services were withdrawn in the 1916-17 time table and when they resumed in 1919 there was no Ilfracombe portion. However, by the summer of 1920, the 10.40am Wolverhampton to Penzance had the slip coach for Ilfracombe added at Bristol again.

In May and June 1908, the 10.30am Paddington to Penzance (the CRL) had First and Third slip coaches slipped at Taunton for Ilfracombe, going forward on the 1.18pm from there as SCW69. These were singled ended slips (8ft 6ins stock) and they returned as SCW 70, on the 9.15 Ilfracombe to Taunton service. Leaving there on the 1.08pm from Taunton to Bristol (the 11.02am service from Paignton), they then joined the 2.10pm Bristol to Paddington.

On Mondays and Saturdays only, there was a Third Class coach which went down to Barnstaple on the 4.15pm Paddington to Plymouth, returning from Barnstaple at 10.56am and also being attached to the 11.02am from Paignton for the return working.

In July, August and September 1908 (commencing on 11th July) the following formations were used.

DOWN – 10.15AM PADDINGTON TO ILFRACOMBE			
CARRIAGE	FROM	TO	RETURN
Bk tri-compo	Padd	Minehead	10.45am Minehead (4.30pm Padd)
Third 6w	Taunton	Ilfracombe	8am Ilfracombe to Taunton
Third	Padd	Ilfracombe	12.17pm Ilfracombe to Padd (arrive 5.42pm)
Compo	Padd	Ilfracombe	12.17pm Ilfracombe to Padd (arrive 5.42pm)
Van	Padd	Ilfracombe	12.17pm Ilfracombe to Padd (arrive 5.42pm)
LB tri-compo	Padd	Barnstaple	1.05pm Barnstaple to Padd (arrive 5.42pm)
Bk Third 6w	Taunton	Barnstaple	
Slip	Padd	Bridgwater	
Slip	Padd	Bath	

As for May and June above, the 10.30am from Paddington had a double ended slip coach (SCW69 and 70 for the return).

The 10.00am Wolverhampton to Penzance had one slip (First and Third) from Bristol to Ilfracombe from 10th July onwards, with it being slipped at Taunton and thence forwards on the 2.40pm Taunton to Ilfracombe (SCW35). It returned as SCW75 the next day on the 1.20pm Ilfracombe to Taunton, then the 4.10pm Taunton to Paddington, as far as Bristol.

The 11.50am Paddington to Kingswear had a 56ft slip coach (First and Third – SCW3), dining car, compo (First and Third) and a 57ft van Third. All four were slipped at Taunton for Ilfracombe, going forwards on the 2.40pm to Ilfracombe. The slip coach became SCW77 the next day (see below) and the dining coach also returned on the next day, on the 1.05pm Barnstaple to Paddington (arriving 5.42pm). The other two coaches worked back from Ilfracombe to Barnstaple at 6.15pm the same day they arrived, thence to work forwards the following day at 10.56am from Barnstaple, arriving at Paddington at 4.30pm.

The 3.30pm Paddington to Penzance had a slip (First and Third) for Ilfracombe (SCW53), which returned on the 8.00am Ilfracombe to Taunton, then to Bristol, then to Reading and finally Reading to Paddington as SCW10.

UP – 10.56AM BARNSTAPLE TO PADDINGTON			
CARRIAGE	FROM	TO	RETURN
Van Third	Barnstaple	Padd	11.50am Padd
Compo	Barnstaple	Padd	1.20pm Padd to Swindon, 5.03pm Swindon to Taunton, 7.57am Taunton to Barnstaple next day.
Van Third	Barnstaple	Padd	1.20pm Padd
Slip (First/Third)	Ilfracombe	Padd	SCW77 (SCW No. 3 Down). Leaves Ilfracombe 9.55am
Bk tri-compo	Ilfracombe	Padd	9.00am Padd to Kingswear. Kingswear 7.20pm to Taunton. 4.35pm Taunton to Ilfracombe. Next day 9.55am Ilfracombe to Barnstaple and attached to this train for onwards working.
Van Third	Ilfracombe	Padd	Works down via Didcot, Bristol, Weston, Taunton and on 4.25pm to Ilfracombe. Leaves there at 9.55am next day
Bk tri-compo	Minehead	Padd	
Slip (First/Third)	Taunton	Reading	SCW10
Compo	Paignton	Reading	
Van Third	Paignton	Reading	

The return of SCW69 was SCW70 and it worked 8.00am from Ilfracombe to Taunton, then Taunton to Bristol and Bristol to Reading.

UP – 12.17PM ILFRACOMBE TO PADDINGTON (DUE 5.42PM)			
CARRIAGE	FROM	TO	RETURN
Bk tri-compo	Ilfracombe	Manch'ter	3.50pm Manch'ter (prior day). Off at Taunton 3.08pm departure
Bk tri-compo	Ilfracombe	Bristol	Worked down as 7.45am Bristol/ Yatton/Taunton. 4.20pm Taunton to Ilfracombe
Bk Tri-compo	Minehead	Padd	
Compo	Ilfracombe	Padd	10.15am Padd
Third	Ilfracombe	Padd	10.15am Padd
Dining car	Barnstaple	Padd	11.50am Padd
LB tri-compo	Barnstaple	Padd	10.15am Padd
Van	Ilfracombe	Padd	10.15am Padd
Compo	Weymouth	Padd	
Van Third	Weymouth	Padd	
Slip (First/Second)	Weymouth	Savernake	SCW37

SCW75 (slip First/Third) was attached at Taunton to the 11.05 Penzance to Paddington.

In October 1908, the 10.30am Paddington to Penzance had SCW69, an 8ft 6ins single ended slip, which was worked to Ilfracombe at 1.24pm from Taunton. The return was SCW70, being the 9.15am Ilfracombe to Taunton and 1.00pm Taunton to Bristol, thence the 2.10pm Bristol to Paddington.

1909

In May and June, 'The Limited' still had SCW69 as above in October 1908 (with SCW70 returning as before).

In July August and September, the volume of through coaches increased again. The 10.15am Paddington to Ilfracombe and SCW69 was formed and ran as before.

The 10.54am Leicester to Taunton at this time comprised a brake compo from Leeds to Ilfracombe, formed of Great Central Railway stock. It returned the next day on the 12.17pm from Ilfracombe and onwards from Taunton at 3.08pm. In addition on the 10.54am, there was a brake compo from Wolverhampton to Ilfracombe which was attached at Bristol (off the 11.47am from Wolverhampton), going forward on the 4.20pm from Taunton. It returned on the 8.00am Ilfracombe to Taunton and then on the 11.10am Taunton to Paddington, where it was removed at Bristol to go forwards on the Weston to Wolverhampton service. The third carriage on this train was a brake compo from Halifax, that worked back from Ilfracombe the next day on the 12.17pm departure to Paddington and on the 3.08pm train from Taunton to Leicester.

The 10.50am Paddington to Kingswear had the following consist for the branch, all three being slipped at Taunton and being taken forward on the 2.40pm to Ilfracombe

CARRIAGE	FROM	TO	RETURN
Bk compo (slip)	Padd	Ilfracombe	SCW3
Dining car	Padd	Ilfracombe	1.05pm Barnstaple (Padd 5.42pm)
Van Third	Padd	Ilfracombe	10.56am Barnstaple to Padd (4.40pm arrival). 6.15pm Ilfracombe to Barnstaple prior day

The 3.20pm Paddington to Penzance had a brake compo for Ilfracombe (SCW53).

Both the 10.56am Barnstaple to Paddington and the 12.17pm Ilfracombe to Paddington services were broadly the same as 1908 but the brake compos to Halifax and Leeds referred to above were added instead of the Bristol and Manchester through coaches.

On the slip coach workings, SCW3 (an 8ft 6ins slip) went down on the 11.50am departure from Paddington, was slipped at Taunton and went forwards to Ilfracombe on the 2.40pm departure from there. The return working the next day was SCW70, being on the 9.55am Ilfracombe to Paddington.

SCW10 worked the 8.00am Ilfracombe to Taunton, 12.58pm Taunton to Bristol, 2.10pm Bristol to Reading (slipped) and then the 4.15pm Reading to Paddington (double ended 8ft 6ins slip). The previous diagram was SCW69 – or 53 depending on the time of year. Slip coach SCW 69 would be on the 10.30am Paddington departure Down and then on the 1.24pm Taunton to Ilfracombe. SCW53 was a complex diagram for the return, departing

Paddington at 3.30pm and slipped at Taunton to go to Ilfracombe. It then involved SCW75 and 34.

In October 1909 the 10.30am 'The CR Limited' from Paddington had SCW7 for Ilfracombe, which went onwards from Taunton at 1.24pm and returned as SCW8 on the 9.15am Ilfracombe to Taunton.

1910

In May and June, the diagrams SCW7 and SCW8 remained as above. This was the only through coach in this period but continued through the summer months July, August and September) in addition to those mentioned below.

The 10.15am Ilfracombe to Paddington commenced from 16th July and was broadly similar in its consist to the two previous years, as was the 10.56am Barnstaple to Paddington.

The 10.50am Paddington to Kingswear comprised a 56ft slip coach (SCW5), a 57ft dining car and a van Third for Ilfracombe, all being slipped at Taunton.

Down – 10.54am Leicester to Taunton		
Carriage	From	Notes
Bk compo	Leeds	(GCR stock)
Bk compo	Halifax	
Bk compo	Wolverhampton	Attached at Bristol as before

The first two went forward on the 3.08pm departure, the third by the 4.20pm.

The brake compo from Halifax (with brake end leading) returned along with the Leeds coach on the 12.17 Ilfracombe to Paddington, coming off at Taunton and onto the 3.08pm departure.

The 3.30pm Paddington to Penzance had SCW17 for Ilfracombe, whilst the 11.00am Penzance to Paddington collected SCW48, from Ilfracombe to Paddington, at Taunton.

SCW5 and SCW8 were two day diagrams with coaches No's 7101 and 7102 working continuously for a period.

In October, the services reverted to the one through slip coach. the 10.30am Paddington departure (SCW7, a 57ft coach) being attached to the 1.24pm Taunton to Ilfracombe. The return working SCW8 was via the 9.50am Ilfracombe to Taunton, then to Bristol and on the 2.10pm Bristol to Paddington. Slips No's 7089, 7100, 7101 and 7102 were regulars.

The through coach workings book also had a note at this time:

'A large number of carriages have had the lower step-boards removed for working over the L&SWR between Barnstaple and Ilfracombe, and these must be made use of for working in the Ilfracombe service. In the event of other coaches having to be used, the lower step-boards must be taken off prior to the commencement of the journey.'

1911

From May to 9th July, SCW7 and SCW8 were the only through Down and Up coaches. This continued during the summer period, supplemented by other services as set out below.

From 10th July, the 10.15am and 10.50am Paddington departures were broadly as before. The 10.54am Leicester to Taunton still had the Leeds and Halifax through coaches but by this time, Great Western and Great Central stock was alternated day by day.

The 3.30pm Paddington departure had SCW42 to Ilfracombe.

The 11.00am (note slight re-timing) Barnstaple to Paddington (arriving at 4.30pm) had a similar consist to prior years but now included a brake compo lavatory coach instead of a brake tri-compo; this is the first evidence of such a coach being used. It came down the previous day on the 9.00am Paddington to Kingswear service to Taunton, where it worked to Ilfracombe at 4.30pm. It returned from Ilfracombe to Barnstaple at 9.48am the next day for the 11.00am service.

The 12.17pm Ilfracombe to Paddington continued as for 1908 above. The 11.00am Penzance to Paddington collected SCW35 from Ilfracombe to return it to London.

In October, the through coaches reverted to the 10.30am ex-Paddington (SCW7).

There was special excursion on Saturday 23rd December 1911 from Paddington to Exeter, departing 2.30pm and arriving at Taunton at 6.35 pm, to which there was a special train connection to Barnstaple at 6.50pm. There was a return special from Ilfracombe leaving at 9.48am on Tuesday 26th December. Other specials ran that week.

Slip coach workings are summarised below.

Slip Coach	Train	Notes
SCW5 (8 previous day)	11.30am Padd to Taunton (slipped)	Single ended 57ft, 7101, 7102 gangway end to trail from London
	2.40pm Taunton to Ilfracombe	SCW8 next day
SCW8	9.48am Ilfracombe to Padd	SCW5 next day
SCW6 (7 previous day and 10th-14th July, 42 15th July onwards)	8.00am Ilfracombe to Taunton	57ft coach
	12.58pm Taunton to Reading	Slipped at Reading
	4.13pm Reading to Padd	SCW7 next day
SCW7	10.30am Padd to Penzance	Slipped at Taunton
	1.24pm Taunton to Ilfracombe	
SCW42 (from 15th July)	3.30pm Padd	Slipped at Taunton, 57ft
	6.17pm Taunton to Ilfracombe	SCW6 next day
SCW35	1.18pm Ilfracombe to Taunton	
	4.10pm Taunton to Padd	SCW48 next day (no T/B working)

The SCW8 (Down) and SCW7 (Up) slip coaches worked as before, being the only through service in the period to 20th July.

1912

From 1912, the 10.35am Paddington to Ilfracombe service ran but comprised a different formation, as below.

Down – 10.35am Paddington to Ilfracombe			
Carriage	From	To	Return
Van	Padd	Minehead	10.46am Minehead next day (arrive 4.20pm)
Bk compo	Padd	Minehead	1.05pm Minehead next day (arrive 5.40pm)
Van Third (57ft)	Padd	Ilfracombe	12.17pm Ilfracombe
Compo (57ft)	Padd	Ilfracombe	12.17pm Ilfracombe
Van Third (57ft)	Padd	Ilfracombe	12.17pm Ilfracombe
Bk compo	Padd	Barnstaple	1.08pm Barnstaple to Padd (arrive 5.40pm)
Bk Third (6w)	Taunton	Barnstaple	
Slip	Padd	Weymouth	

The 11.50am Paddington to Kingswear carried a 57ft slip coach (SCW5), a dining car and a van Third (VT1), all being slipped at Taunton and going forwards on the 2.40pm to Ilfracombe, arriving at 5.08pm. The dining car returned to Barnstaple on an L&SWR service at 6.18pm and then worked to Barnstaple GWR to have its gas replenished by the cordon wagon at that station (*see Volume 1, page 135*).

The 10.58am Leicester to Taunton service at this time had a van Third and brake compo from Halifax to Ilfracombe, which returned the following day on the 12.17pm from Ilfracombe.

Up – 11.00am Barnstaple to Paddington (arriving 4.30pm)			
Carriage	From	To	Return
Van Third (57ft)	Barnstaple	Padd	11.50am Padd
Compo	Barnstaple	Padd	7.50am Padd
Slip (57ft)	Ilfracombe	Padd	SCW8 double ended
Bk compo lav	Ilfracombe	Padd	9.00am Padd to Kingswear
Van Third	Ilfracombe	Padd	3.30pm Padd

Four coaches were added at Taunton, two from Minehead and two from Taunton itself, whilst a further two from Paignton were added at Bristol.

Up – 12.17pm Ilfracombe to Paddington			
Carriage	From	To	Return
Bk compo	Minehead	Padd	
Bk compo	Barnstaple	Padd	10.35am Padd
Dining	Barnstaple	Padd	11.50am Padd
Van Third	Ilfracombe	Padd	10.35am Padd
Compo	Ilfracombe	Padd	10.35am Padd
Van Third	Ilfracombe	Padd	10.35am Padd
GCR bk compo	Ilfracombe	Halifax	10.58am Leicester
GCR van Third	Ilfracombe	Halifax	10.58am Leicester

Four coaches were added to this service at Westbury.

From October, a 57ft slip came off the 10.30am Paddington to Penzance and went forward on the 1.24pm from Taunton to Ilfracombe. The return was on the 9.40am from Ilfracombe to Taunton.

There was the following reference to the 10.35am Paddington to Ilfracombe service:

'Towels to be changed before arrival at Taunton by travelling collector and lavatories replenished with water at Taunton. Collector to have 30 spare towels before leaving Paddington. Supply to be replenished at Ilfracombe for the 12.17pm return from Ilfracombe.'

1913

The pattern of through coaches for this year was similar to 1912. However, it was noted that on 26th July 1913 (and 1st August), the 10.35am Paddington to Ilfracombe train was to be divided at Taunton. This was because, on these two days, the 7.50am Paddington to Reading train was extended to Ilfracombe by adding the stock from it to the 10.35am at Reading. This longer than normal train then ran to Taunton where it was divided to run to Ilfracombe in two parts. It must have made for a very long day for many of the passengers, forced to wait at Reading and then again at Taunton for their carriages to be taken on.

1914

The 10.30am ex-Paddington continued to have the slip coach for lfracombe.

The summer period covered 12th July to 30th September. By this time roof label boards should be on the 10.35am Paddington to Ilfracombe.

The 9.00am Paddington to Kingswear, 10.35am Paddington to Ilfracombe and the 12.00pm Paddington to Kingswear ran as before with coaches for Ilfracombe.

Up – 9.50am Ilfracombe to Paddington			
Carriage	From	To	Return
Third	Bristol	Padd	
Compo	Bristol	Padd	
Van	Minehead	Padd	
Bk compo	Minehead	Padd	
Bk compo	Minehead	Padd	
Dining car	Taunton	Padd	
Van Third	Barnstaple	Padd	Not noted
Compo	Barnstaple	Padd	7.50am Padd
Van Third	Ilfracombe	Padd	3.30pm Padd
Bk compo	Ilfracombe	Padd	9am Padd
Slip (SCW5)	Ilfracombe	Padd	SCW5 12.00pm Padd and 2.40pm Taunton to Ilfracombe
Slip	Ilfracombe	Reading	SCW41

SCW5 was a single ended slip, 57ft stock, slotted coaches, No's 6962 or 6963 or 6964. The gangway end had to trail from London.

There were no Halifax through coaches at this time.

The Ilfracombe to Paddington train was re-timed from 12.17pm to 12.10pm but its consist was largely the same as prior years.

From October, the through coach was on the 10.30am from Paddington as before (SCW7).

1921

From 11th July, the Down workings included the through coaches shown below.

Down – 9.25am Paddington to Kingswear			
Carriage	From	To	Return
57ft slip	Padd	Ilfracombe	SCW28
57ft bk compo	Padd	Ilfracombe	11.45am Ilfracombe to Padd
Down – 12 noon Paddington to Kingswear			
57ft buffet van Third	Padd	Ilfracombe	11.45am Ilfracombe to Padd
57ft compo (2 comps)	Padd	Ilfracombe	11.45am Ilfracombe to Padd
57ft bk compo	Padd	Ilfracombe	11.45am Ilfracombe to Padd
Down – 2.00pm Paddington to Penzance			
57ft buffet van Third	Padd	Ilfracombe	9.20am Ilfracombe to Padd
57ft compo	Padd	Ilfracombe	9.20am Ilfracombe to Padd
Down – 4.00pm Paddington to Plymouth			
Bk compo	Padd	Barnstaple	12.40pm Barnstaple to Padd
Slip	Padd	Barnstaple	SCW1

Up – 9.20am Ilfracombe to Paddington			
Carriage	From	To	Return
Bk compo	Bath	Padd	
70ft van Third	Minehead	Padd	
70ft compo	Minehead	Padd	
57ft bk compo	Ilfracombe	Padd	
57ft compo	Ilfracombe	Padd	
57ft buffet third	Ilfracombe	Padd	
70ft van third	Barnstaple Jct	Padd	See below
70ft third	Barnstaple Jct	Padd	See below
70ft compo	Barnstaple Jct	Padd	See below
70ft van third	Barnstaple Jct	Padd	See below
Slip	Barnstaple GWR	Reading	SCW 2

The 70ft coaches that worked back from Barnstaple had a similarly interesting Down journey to that in 1920. They would leave as and remain as a 'set'. Departing on the 1.50pm Paddington to Penzance, they would work through to Penzance and then back on the 8.00am Penzance to Plymouth, thence on the 2.20pm Penzance to Newton Abbot, the 5.10pm Newton Abbot to Exeter, the 9.20pm Exeter to Taunton and the next day Taunton to Barnstaple Junction, in readiness for the 9.20am ex-Ilfracombe.

Up – 11.45am Ilfracombe to Paddington (arriving 5.30pm)			
Carriage	From	To	Return
Bk compo	Ilfracombe	Padd	12 noon ex-Padd
Compo	Ilfracombe	Padd	12 noon ex-Padd
Buffet van Third	Ilfracombe	Padd	12 noon ex-Padd
Bk compo	Ilfracombe	Padd	9.25am ex-Padd
Slip	Barnstaple GWR	Padd	4.00pm ex-Padd
Slip	Minehead	Padd	
Compo	Weymouth	Padd	
Slip	Weymouth	Padd	

Note that at this time SCW1 and SCW2 were double-ended slips. The two buffet cars (on the 9.20am and the 11.45am) were in constant use on both trains carrying them.

By October (3rd onwards), the 10.30am from Paddington had a 57ft slip coach for Ilfracombe. The 9.30am Ilfracombe to Paddington comprised similar stock to the 9.20am above but with the buffet added at Taunton.

1922

From 10th July, two of the Down trains included the following.

Down – 9.15am Paddington to Kingswear			
Carriage	From	To	Return
57ft van Third	Padd	Ilfracombe	9.30am Ilfracombe to Padd
			(arrive 4.05pm)
57ft compo (4 comps)	Padd	Ilfracombe	9.30am Ilfracombe to Padd
			(arrive 4.05pm)
57ft buffet van Third	Padd	Ilfracombe	9.30am Ilfracombe to Padd
			(arrive 4.05pm)

Down – 12.05pm Paddington to Taunton (arriving 2.55pm)			
Carriage	From	To	Return
57ft van Third	Padd	Ilfracombe	11.45am Ilfracombe to Padd (arriving 5.30pm)
57ft Third	Padd	Ilfracombe	11.45am Ilfracombe to Padd (arriving 5.30pm)
57ft buffet	Padd	Ilfracombe	11.45am Ilfracombe to Padd (arriving 5.30pm)
57ft compo (4 comps)	Padd	Ilfracombe	11.45am Ilfracombe to Padd (arriving 5.30pm)
57ft van Third	Padd	Ilfracombe	11.45am Ilfracombe to Padd (arriving 5.30pm)
60ft compo	Padd	Barnstaple	12.40pm Barnstaple to Padd (arriving 5.30pm)
60ft van Third	Padd	Barnstaple	12.40pm Barnstaple to Padd (arriving 5.30pm)

The 11.15am Paddington to Taunton service had a 57ft brake compo that travelled from Paddington to Weston, then back to Bristol at 7.20pm, then Bristol to Bath at 8.30am the next day and then on the 10.10am Bath to go forward to Ilfracombe.

The 2.00pm Paddington to Penzance had a 57ft brake compo that came off at Taunton to go to Ilfracombe and returned on the 3.00pm train from Ilfracombe the next day.

Up – 9.30am Ilfracombe to Paddington (arriving 4.05pm)			
Carriage	From	To	Return
Bk compo	Bath	Padd	
70ft van Third	Minehead	Padd	
70ft compo	Minehead	Padd	
60ft Third	Minehead	Padd	
57ft bk compo	Ilfracombe	Manch'ter	11.42am Crewe
57ft buffet van Third	Ilfracombe	Padd	9.15am ex-Padd
57ft compo	Ilfracombe	Padd	9.15am ex-Padd
51ft van Third	Ilfracombe	Padd	9.15am ex-Padd
Van Third	Barnstaple Jct	Padd	12.00pm ex-Padd
Compo	Barnstaple Jct	Padd	12.00pm ex-Padd
Van Third	Barnstaple Jct	Padd	12.00pm ex-Padd
Slip	Barnstaple GWR	Reading	SCW2

The three coaches on the 12 noon departure from Paddington worked back from Penzance to Plymouth at 4.15pm the next day, then the 9.15pm Plymouth to Newton Abbot and the 1.23am Newton Abbot to Taunton, thence on the 8.00am Taunton to Barnstaple Junction, to return straight away at 10.27am as above.

Up – 11.45am Ilfracombe to Paddington (arriving 5.30pm)			
Carriage	From	To	Return
57ft van Third	Ilfracombe	Padd	12.05pm ex-Padd
57ft compo (4 comps)	Ilfracombe	Padd	12.05pm ex-Padd
57ft buffet car	Ilfracombe	Padd	12.05pm ex-Padd
57ft Third	Ilfracombe	Padd	12.05pm ex-Padd
57ft van Third	Ilfracombe	Padd	12.05pm ex-Padd
57ft bk compo	Ilfracombe	Padd	11.15am ex-Padd
Van Third	Barnstaple	Padd	12.05pm ex-Padd
Compo	Barnstaple	Padd	12.05pm ex-Padd
70ft compo First	Minehead	Padd	
70ft van Third	Minehead	Padd	
Third	Weymouth	Padd	
Slip	Weymouth	Padd	

The 4.10pm Plymouth North Road took a brake compo from Ilfracombe to Paddington from Taunton (this working Down on the 2.00pm ex-Paddington). The 57ft brake compo from Manchester to Ilfracombe was attached to the 11.42am Crewe to Plymouth service and returned on the 10.25am Plymouth to Crewe, being attached at Taunton. The 10.10am Bath to Plymouth North Road had a brake compo from Bath to Ilfracombe. SCW2 ran as follows: 8.00am Taunton to Barnstaple GWR, then 10.30am Barnstaple to Reading (slipped), then forward on the 4.17pm Reading to Paddington. This was a double ended slip. It became SCW1 the next day, working Paddington to Bridgwater (slipped) and then from Bridgwater to Taunton.

In October, the arrangements were as follows. The 10.30am Paddington to Penzance had a 57ft slip coach for Ilfracombe (SCW36), which would go forward on the 1.10pm Taunton to Ilfracombe. The next day, as SCW37, it returned on the 9.30am Ilfracombe to Paddington.

On the 10.30pm Paddington to Penzance on weekdays (but not Saturdays), a van travelled down for Barnstaple, on the 8.00am Taunton to Barnstaple. It laid over until the 6.00pm Barnstaple to Taunton departure, where it was then attached to the 10.10pm Taunton to Paddington service. The 6.35pm Birmingham to Taunton (due at 10.39pm) contained a van for Barnstaple, which went forward at 8.00am and again returned on the 6.00pm Barnstaple to Taunton service, thence on the 11.00pm Taunton to Birmingham train.

Horses were not to be conveyed on the 9.30am Ilfracombe to Paddington service, nor the 8.55am Barnstaple to Taunton.

1923

From 9th July, the 9.15am Paddington to Kingswear ran as in 1922 but the buffet van Third was replaced by a van Third. The 12.05pm Paddington now ran to Plymouth (not Taunton). The 57ft coaches were replaced by 60ft versions and the 57ft buffet replaced by a 60ft dining car and a 70ft brake compo, which ran as far as Barnstaple (returning on the 11.00am departure the next day).

The 3.30pm Paddington to Plymouth had a 60ft slip (SCW9) and 60ft brake compo from Paddington to Ilfracombe, which returned on the 12.40pm Barnstaple to Paddington.

The 10.25pm Paddington to Penzance had a van from Paddington to Ilfracombe. This went forward at 8.00am from Taunton and returned at 4.25pm from Ilfracombe to Taunton, then on the 8.50pm from Taunton to Paddington.

Up – 9.30am Ilfracombe to Paddington			
Carriage	From	To	Return
70ft bk compo	Bath	Padd	
60ft bk compo	Ilfracombe	Manch'ter	Down 10.32am ex-Crewe. Thur/Mon/Sat only
60ft van Third	Ilfracombe	Padd	9.15am ex-Padd
60ft compo	Ilfracombe	Padd	9.15am ex-Padd
60ft Third	Ilfracombe	Padd	9.15am ex-Padd
60ft van Third	Ilfracombe	Padd	2.00pm Padd to Penzance
60ft compo	Ilfracombe	Padd	2.00pm Padd to Penzance
60ft Third	Ilfracombe	Padd	2.00pm Padd to Penzance
60ft van Third	Ilfracombe	Padd	2.00pm Padd to Penzance
70ft bk compo	Barnstaple	Padd	2.00pm Padd to Penzance
70ft van Third	Minehead	Padd	
70ft compo	Minehead	Padd	
70ft Third	Minehead	Padd	
Slip	Minehead	Reading	

The 2.00pm ex-Paddington coaches worked to Penzance, then on the 8.00am Penzance to Plymouth, Plymouth (12.35pm) to Newton Abbot, then 3.07pm Newton Abbot to Taunton and on the 6.08pm Taunton to Ilfracombe ready for the next day return.

From 1st October, the 10.30am Paddington to Penzance had the 60ft single-ended gangway slip (No's 6962, 6963 or 6964) running diagram SCW43 to Ilfracombe, going forward at 1.15pm and returning on the 9.30am Ilfracombe to Paddington (see below). The 10.25pm carried the brake van from Paddington to Ilfracombe, which worked back later the following day to join the 4.15pm Plymouth to Paddington service at Taunton.

Up – 9.30am Ilfracombe to Paddington			
Carriage	From	To	Return
70ft bk compo	Bath	Padd	
70ft slip	Bath	Padd	SCW7
60ft van Third	Ilfracombe	Padd	10.45am ex-Padd
60ft compo	Ilfracombe	Padd	10.45am ex-Padd
60ft third	Ilfracombe	Padd	10.45am ex-Padd
60ft van third	Ilfracombe	Padd	10.45am ex-Padd
60ft slip	Ilfracombe	Padd	SCW44
70ft bk compo	Minehead	Padd	
70ft slip	Minehead	Reading	

The four Ilfracombe coaches off the 10.45am Paddington firstly travelled to Swindon, then on the 1.20pm Swindon to Yatton, then 2.05pm Yatton to Taunton and then on the 5.25pm Taunton to Ilfracombe.

1924

From 14th July	
Down – 9.00am Paddington to Kingswear	
Vehicle	**Working**
60ft Third 60ft compo (4 comps) 60ft Van Third	Padd to Ilfracombe (all returning on 9.15am Ilfracombe to Padd next day, arr. 4.05pm)
Down – 12.05pm Paddington to Plymouth	
60ft van Third 60ft Third 60ft dining car 60ft compo (4 comps) 60ft van Third	All 60ft stock Padd to Ilfracombe returning on 11.40 am Ilfracombe to Padd next day (arr 5.30pm)
70ft bk compo	Padd to Barnstaple GWR. Returning 10.20am Barnstaple to Padd (arr 4.05pm)
Down – 3.30pm Paddington to Falmouth	
60ft slip	Padd to Ilfracombe SCW10
70ft bk compo	Padd to Barnstaple GWR. Returns on 12.35pm Barnstaple to Padd (arr 5.30pm)
Down – 10.25pm Paddington to Penzance	
Van	Padd to Ilfracombe. 8.00am Taunton to Ilfracombe. 4.25pm Ilfracombe to Taunton, then 8.50pm Taunton to Padd (arr 2.35am)
Up – 9.15am Ilfracombe to Paddington (arr 4.05pm)	
70ft bk compo	Bath to Padd
57ft Bk	Ilfracombe to Manchester (10.32am Crewe)
60ft van Third	Ilfracombe to Padd. 9.00am Padd Down
60ft compo (4 comps)	Ditto
60ft Third	Ditto
60ft van Third	10.00pm Padd to Plymouth
60ft compo	7.10am Plymouth to Taunton
60ft van Third	Down working 6.08pm Taunton to Ilfracombe
70ft bk compo	Barnstaple to Padd (12.05pm Padd Down)
70ft van Third 70ft compo 70ft Third	Minehead to Paddington (all below)
70ft slip	Minehead to Reading SCW16
Up – 11.40am Ilfracombe to Paddington (via Lavington)	
60ft van Third 60ft compo (4 comps) 60ft dining car 60ft Third 60ft van Third	Ilfracombe to Padd (from 12.05pm Padd above)
70ft bk compo	Barnstaple to Padd (3.30pm Padd Down)
70ft van Third	Minehead to Padd
70ft compo	Minehead to Padd
Compo (3 comps)	Weymouth to Padd
Van Third	Weymouth to Padd
Up – 1.30pm Penzance to Paddington	
60ft bk compo	Ilfracombe to Padd (1.30pm Down)
Up – 10.05am Plymouth to Crewe	
60ft bk compo	Ilfracombe to Manchester (10.32am Down)

Slip No.	Train
SCW10 60ft double ended slip	3.30pm Padd to Taunton, onwards at 6.08pm to Ilfracombe
SCW 11 (next day)	8.00am Ilfracombe to Barnstaple Jct 10.28 Barnstaple Jct to GWR 10.50 Barnstaple GWR to Taunton 6.18pm Taunton to Newbury 8.15pm Newbury to Reading 9.30pm Reading to Paddington

From 22nd September Down – 10.30am Paddington to Penzance	
Vehicle	**Working**
60ft slip	Padd to Ilfracombe SCW5. This was likely to be one of No's 6962, 6963 or 6964
Down – 10.25pm Paddington to Penzance	
Van	Padd to Ilfracombe, forward on 8.00am Taunton to Ilfracombe

1925

From 13th July	
Down – 9.00am Paddington to Kingswear	
Vehicle	**Working**
60ft Third 60ft compo (4 comps) 60ft van Third	Padd to Ilfracombe (all returning on 9.55am Ilfracombe to Padd next day (arr 4.05pm)
Down – 12.05pm Paddington to Plymouth (weekdays)	
60ft van Third 60ft Third 60ft dining car 60ft compo (4 comps) 60ft van Third	All 60ft Padd to Ilfracombe returning on 12.00pm Ilfracombe to Padd next day (arr 5.30pm)
70ft bk compo	Padd to Barnstaple GWR. Returning 12.45pm Barnstaple to Padd (arr 5.30pm)
Down – 12.05pm Paddington to Ilfracombe (Saturdays only)	
60ft van Third 60ft Third 60ft dining car 60ft compo (4 comps) 60ft compo 60ft Third 60ft Third	Returns (Mondays only) 12.00pm Ilfracombe to Padd
60ft van Third	MO 12.45pm Barnstaple to Padd
70ft bk compo	MO 12.45pm Barnstaple to Padd
Down – 3.30pm Paddington to Falmouth	
60ft slip	Padd to Ilfracombe SCW12, 6.08pm Taunton to Ilfracombe. Return SCW32 3.25pm Ilfracombe to Taunton as SCW11 above
Down – 10.25pm Paddington to Penzance	
Van	W/Th/FO Padd to Barnstaple. 8.00am Taunton to Barnstaple. M/Th/FO back 4.35pm Ilfracombe to Taunton then 8.40pm Taunton to Padd (arr 2.40am)
Up – 9.55am Ilfracombe to Paddington (arr 4.05pm)	
70ft bk compo	Bath to Padd
60ft bk compo	Ilfracombe to Manchester (10.32am Crewe)
60ft van Third	Ilfracombe to Padd. 9.00am Padd Down
60ft compo (4 comps)	Ditto
60ft Third	Ditto
60ft van Third	9.50am Padd to Plymouth
60ft compo	9.50am Padd to Plymouth
60ft van Third	9.50am Padd to Plymouth
70ft van Third	Minehead to Paddington
70ft compo	Minehead to Paddington
70ft slip	Minehead to Reading SCW17
Up – 12.00pm Ilfracombe to Paddington (arr 5.30pm)	
60ft van Third 60ft compo (4 comps) 60ft dining car 60ft Third 60ft van Third	Ilfracombe to Padd (from 12.05pm Padd above)
70ft bk compo	Barnstaple to Padd
70ft van Third	Minehead to Padd
70ft compo	Minehead to Padd
Compo (4 comps)	Weymouth to Padd
Van Third	Weymouth to Padd
Down – 10.32am Crewe to Truro	
60ft bk compo	Manchester to Ilfracombe
Down – 10.50am Wolverhampton to Ilfracombe Saturdays only (arr 5.05pm)	
60ft van Third 60ft Third 60ft compo 60ft van Third	Wolverhampton to Ilfracombe
Bk compo	Wolverhampton to Barnstaple
Van Third Third Compo Third Van Third	Wolverhampton to Taunton (return 6.35pm T-W)

No balanced return. First indication of a Wolverhampton through train.

Down – 6.35pm Birmingham to Taunton	
Van (MX)	Birmingham to Barnstaple Jct. 8am Taunton to Barnstaple. Returns 5.55pm Barnstaple Jct to Taunton and 11.00pm Taunton to Birmingham

If there was to be a division of trains, then the 9.55am to Paddington would be preceded by an additional train departing from Ilfracombe at 9.38am, to convey traffic for Paddington only. It would stop at all stations to Barnstaple GWR (arrive 10.28, depart 10.40) and then only South Molton, Dulverton and Taunton. It was routed via Somerton and Lavington.

From 21st September	
Down – 10.30am Paddington to Penzance	
Vehicle	**Working**
60ft slip	Padd to Ilfracombe SCW33
Down – 1.30pm Paddington to Penzance	
60ft bk compo	Padd to Ilfracombe (back on 2.46pm Taunton to Padd next day)
Up – 9.55am Ilfracombe to Paddington	
70ft bk compo 60ft slip 60ft van Third 60ft compo 60ft van Third Dining car 70ft bk compo 70ft slip	Bath to Padd Ilfracombe to Padd SCW34 B Jct to Padd (Down 9.50am Padd to Plymouth) 4.20pm Plymouth to Taunton 8.00am Taunton to Barnstaple Jct Taunton to Padd Minehead to Padd Minehead to Reading
Down – 6.35pm Birmingham to Taunton	
Van (MX)	Birmingham to Barnstaple (Down on 8.00am Taunton to Barnstaple, 6.10pm Barnstaple back)
Down – 10.25pm Paddington to Ilfracombe	
Bk Van	Padd to Ilfracombe (forward on 8.00am Taunton to Barnstaple. Back 4.33pm Ilfracombe to Taunton and Taunton at 8.43pm to Padd)

1937-38

Winter period 27th September 1937 to 3rd July 1938

Down – 9.00am Paddington to Paignton (24th Dec. to 14th April)	
Vehicle	**Working**
60ft Third 60ft bk compo	Padd to Ilfracombe Padd to Ilfracombe
Down – 10.30am Paddington to Penzance	
60ft slip	Padd to Ilfracombe (must be one of No's 6962, 6963 or 6964). SCW15 (non-gangwayed stock)
Down – 1.30pm Paddington to Penzance	
60ft bk compo	Padd to Ilfracombe (brake end trailing). Returns on 9.50am Ilfracombe to Padd
Up – 9.50am Ilfracombe to Paddington	
60ft slip 60ft bk compo 70ft van Third 70ft compo 70ft van Third	SCW16 (see above – non-gangwayed) Ilfracombe to Padd, Down on 1.30pm above Barnstaple Jct to Padd (6.30pm Down SX – all below) Suns Down 9.50pm, stock works to Plymouth and back up to Taunton and to Barnstaple
Up – 11.00am Ilfracombe to Paddington SO commencing 25th June 1938	
60ft van Third 60ft Third 60ft compo 60ft van Third	Ilfracombe to Padd (brake end leading) Ilfracombe to Padd Ilfracombe to Padd Ilfracombe to Padd (brake end trailing)
This train would be joined by five coaches from Minehead at Taunton	
Down – 10.25pm Paddington to Plymouth (Millbay) Parcels	
Siphon G	Padd to Barnstaple, 7.50am Taunton to Barnstaple, return 8.40pm off Taunton to Padd (SX)

There were no cross country through coaches in this period, so this would necessitate passengers changing at Taunton for the Barnstaple Branch and Ilfracombe.

Slip Coach workings are summarised as below.

SCW	Train
15	10.30am Padd to Taunton (day 1), slip
15	1.10pm Taunton to Ilfracombe (on local service)
16	9.50am Ilfracombe to Padd (next day, then reverts to 15)

60ft single-ended slip coaches No's 6962, 6963 and 6964 were designated for the Barnstaple Branch.

1938

4th July 1938 to 25th September 1938

12.20am Paddington to Kingswear (SO from 23rd July)		
Stock	**Working**	**Balance**
60ft Third 60ft compo 60ft van Third (bk end trailing)	Padd-Ilfra	9.50am Ilfracombe to Manch'ter (SO)
Down – 1.35am Paddington to Penzance		
60ft van Third	Padd-Penz	12.02pm Taunton to Ilfracombe SX,
(bk end trailing)		12.08pm Taunton to Ilfracombe SO, 9.50am Ilfracombe to Padd SX, 11.00am Ilfracombe to Padd SO
Down – 9.00am Paddington to Paignton (SX)		
60ft bk compo	Padd-Ilfra	9.50am Ilfracombe to Padd (MSX),
 60ft dining car 60ft bk compo (bk end trailing)		11.00am Ilfracombe to Padd (SO) 12.47pm Barnstaple to Padd (MX) 12.47pm Barnstaple to Padd (MX)
Down – 9.00am Paddington to Paignton (SO)		
Bk compo	Padd-Ilfra	9.50am Ilfracombe to Padd (MO)
Dining car Bk compo	Padd-Barnst Padd-Barnst	12.47pm Barnstaple to Padd (MO) 12.47pm Barnstaple to Padd (MO)
Down – 9.35am Paddington to Minehead (SO)		
60ft bk compo	Padd-Ilfra	9.50am Ilfracombe to Padd (MO)
(bk end leading) 3x 60ft Thirds 60ft dining car 60ft bk compo (bk end trailing)		 9.50am Ilfracombe to Padd (MO) 12.47pm Barnstaple to Padd (MO) 12.47pm Barnstaple to Padd (MO)
Down – 12.05pm Paddington to Ilfracombe (FO until 9th September)		
60ft van Third	Taunton-Ilfra	
(bk end leading) 60ft Third 60ft compo 60ft van Third (bk end trailing)	 Padd-Ilfra Padd-Ilfra Padd-Ilfra	 To be used to assist in forming 9.50am Ilfracombe to Manchester (SO)
Other stock attached included six coaches for Minehead		
Down – 12.06pm Paddington to Ilfracombe (SO until 10th September)		
3x 60ft Thirds	Padd-Ilfra	12 noon Ilfracombe to Padd (MO)
60ft van Third (bk end leading) 60ft compo 60ft van Third (bk end trailing)		
other stock attached included 6 coaches for Minehead		
Down – 12.10pm Paddington to Plymouth (SO)		
60ft van Third	Padd-Taunton	12 noon Ilfracombe to Padd (MO)
(bk end leading) 60ft compo 60ft van Third (bk end trailing)		
other stock attached included 2 coaches for Minehead		
Down – 1.40pm Paddington to Penzance (SX)		
60ft bk compo	Padd-Ilfra	12 noon Ilfracombe to Padd (MX)
(bk end trailing)		
Down – 2.15pm Paddington to Minehead (SO)		
2x Thirds	Padd-Ilfra	12 noon Ilfracombe to Padd (MO)
Brake compo		
Down – 3.30pm Paddington to Penzance		

60ft bk compo	Padd-Ilfra	3.16pm Ilfracombe to Padd
Down – 9.50pm Paddington to Penzance		
60ft van Third (bk end leading)	Padd-Ply (N Rd)	12 noon Ilfracombe to Padd (MWX)

The 9.50pm from Paddington to Penzance on Sundays contained a 60ft compo, which travelled to Plymouth and then returned to work the 4.32pm Taunton to Ilfracombe service (on Tuesdays only). In addition, a 60ft van Third (brake end trailing) travelled to Plymouth but was worked to Ilfracombe and attached to the 12 noon Ilfracombe to Paddington on Wednesdays only.

Up – 12.15pm Minehead to Paddington (SO)		
Stock	**Working**	**Balance**
Bk Compo (bk end trailing)	Ilfra-Padd	9.00am Padd (MO)
60ft Third		
60ft van Third (bk end leading)		1.55am Padd (MO)
60ft compo		
60-ft Third	Minehd-Padd	
60ft van Third (bk end trailing)	joins at Taunton	
Up – 9.50am Ilfracombe to Paddington (SX)		
60ft van Third (bk end leading)	Ilfra-Padd	1.35pm Padd (MX)
60ft compo		
60ft Third		
60ft van Third (bk end trailing)		
Bk compo	Barnst-Padd	9.00am Padd (MSX), 9.35am Padd (SO)
Up – 12 noon Ilfracombe to Paddington		
60ft bk compo	Ilfra-Padd	1.40pm Padd (SX), 2.15pm (SO)
60ft van Third (bk end leading)		9.50pm Padd (FSX)
60ft compo		12.06pm Padd (SO)
60ft van Third (bk end trailing)		9.50pm Sun
Dining car	Barnst-Padd	9.05am Padd SX)
Bk compo		9.35am (SO)
Up – 1.30 Penzance to Paddington		
60ft bk compo	Ilfra-Padd	3.30pm Padd

Up – 6.15pm Plymouth to Paddington (SX)		
Stock	**Working**	**Balance**
Bk van	Ilfra-Padd (4.45pm Ilfra-Taunton)	6.35pm SX
PLA van (FO)	Ilfra-Manch'ter (4.45pm Ilfra- Taunton)	
Up – 4.25pm Plymouth to Paddington (SO)		
PLA van	Ilfra-Padd (5.00pm Ilfra-Taunton)	
PLA van	Ilfra-Bristol (5.00pm Ilfra-Taunton)	
There were no equivalent Up workings on Sundays		
Down – 11.55am Crewe to Plymouth via Newport		
GWR dining car	Manch'ter-Plymouth	9.50am Ilfra-Manch (SO)
Up – 5.00pm Penzance to Crewe via Newport		
GWR PLA van	(FO) Ilfra-Manch'ter (attached Bristol from 6.15pm Plymouth)	
Up – 9.50am Ilfracombe to Manchester (SO)		
Van Third	Ilfra-Manch'ter	
4x Thirds		
Compo		
Van Third (Bk end leading)		
Dining car	Barnst-Manch'ter	11.55am Crewe (Sun)
Bk Compo		
All GWR stock – a brake compo was attached at Cardiff to Manchester		
Down – 10.40am Wolverhampton to Ilfracombe (SO, via St. Philip's Marsh)		
Bk compo (bk end leading)	Wolve-Ilfra	
3x Thirds		
Compo		
Van Third (bk end trailing)		
Three coaches for Minehead were also attached to this train)		

There were no slip coach workings in the summer period.

Acknowledgement goes to Brian Morgan for providing the relevant through coach information from which the 1937-38 analysis has been produced.

A photograph from the first coach of the 11.05am (Saturdays Only) Ilfracombe to Wolverhampton train on 29th August 1964, as 'Mogul' No. 6326 leads it across the wrought iron girder spans of the River Taw bridge, carrying the Ilfracombe Branch over the water from Barnstaple Town to Barnstaple Junction. The tightness of the curve coupled with the narrowness of the bridge shows why coach lengths on this line were limited, whilst certain GWR locomotives had to have ther steps cut back to avoid fouling the girders. *Tim Stephens*

APPENDIX 18
CARRIAGE WORKINGS SUMMARY 1954-55

The carriage workings from Barnstaple Junction for normal weekday services in the 1954 summer period were as below.

TRAIN	STOCK	OTHER WORKING
11.25am Taunton	4 WR set	8.30am Taunton (10.31 arr)
1.10pm Torrington	3 WR set 1 PMV (4)	11.00am Taunton (12.48 arr)
1.55pm Taunton	3 lav set	8.53am Torrington (9.23 arr)
4.00pm Taunton	3 WR set	2.47pm Torrington (2.22 arr)
5.15pm Ilfracombe	4 WR set FX 7 LM coaches FO	2.05pm Taunton (4.12 arr)
6.38pm Taunton	4 WR set	5.45pm Ilfracombe (6.28 arr)
8.55pm Taunton	3 WR set FX	6.15pm Taunton (8.11 arr)
	2 WR set FO	
Berthed MO	3 lav set	5.00pm Taunton (6.55 arr)

The Saturdays only summary for Barnstaple Junction was as below.

TRAIN	STOCK	PRIOR WORKING
6.30am Ilfracombe	4 WR corridors	6.20am BVR (6.25 arr)
7.22am Ilfracombe	6 WR corridors	5.20am Taunton (7.16 arr)
9.13am Ilfracombe	6 WR corridors	7.15am Taunton (9.10 arr)
10.36am Ilfracombe	4 WR corridors 2-set (63/75, com 4/9)	8.30am Taunton (10.31 arr) 9.00am Ilfracombe (9.40 arr)
11.05am Taunton	4 WR corridors	10.12am Ilfracombe (10.55 arr)
11.44am B'ham SH	6 WR corridors	10.55am Ilfracombe (11.40 arr)
1.28pm Torrington	2 cor set (com 11/9) 4 WR corridors	11.55am Torrington (12.25 arr) 11.00am Taunton (12.52 arr)
1.55pm Taunton	3 lav set	12.35pm Torrington (1.18 arr) until 28/8
3.09pm Ilfracombe	6 WR corridors	12.50pm Taunton (3.00 arr)
4.00pm Taunton*	4 WR corridors	2.47pm Torrington (3.20 arr)
4.28pm Ilfracombe (until 11/9)	6 WR corridors	2.26pm Taunton (4.25 arr)
5.30pm Ilfracombe (until 4/9)	6 WR corridors	3.36pm Taunton (5.20 arr)
6.00pm Taunton	6 WR corridors	5.15pm Ilfracombe (5.54 arr)
6.55pm Ilfracombe	3 lav set	4.35pm Taunton (6.50 arr)
8.55pm Taunton (11/9 and 18/9 only)	3 WR corridors	6.15pm Taunton (8.11 arr)
9.15pm Barnstaple VR (until 4/9)	3 WR corridors	6.15pm Taunton (8.11 arr)
Berthed	4 WR corridors	2.35pm Taunton (4.45 arr)
*Saturdays excepted this was an 'N' Class duty; Saturdays only it was booked for a 'T9'.		

The Saturdays only summary for Ilfracombe, which gives an indication of stock movements along the D&SR in the summer of 1954 was as below.

TRAIN	STOCK	PRIOR WORKING
8.25am Bristol (until 26/6) 8.25am Manchester Exchange (from 3/7)	7 LM corridors	Berthed (worked down FO 5.15pm Barns Jct, 5.56 arr)
9.25am Cardiff	4 WR corridors until 10/7 and from 4/9. 9 WR corridors 17/7 to 28/8	5.20am Taunton (8.12 arr)
10.12am Taunton	4 WR corridors	6.20am VR (7.14 arr). 'M7' duty
10.55am B'ham SH	6 WR corridors	7.15am Taunton (9.58 arr)
5.15pm Taunton (until 11/9)	6 WR corridors	12.50pm Taunton (3.56 arr)
5.45pm Taunton	4 WR corridors	8.30am Taunton (11.18 arr)
6.50pm Taunton (until 4/9)	6 WR corridors	3.36pm Taunton (6.16 arr)
8.45pm Barns Jct	6 WR corridors	4.35pm Taunton (7.37 arr)

In the winter period 1954-55, there were six Up and six Down trains. The 6.55am was the first Up departure from Victoria Road, whilst the first Down train was the 8.05am from Taunton, arriving at 9.50pm.

Carriage workings on summer Saturdays in 1955 were as below.

TRAIN	FORMATION	DOWN WORKING
8.25am Ilfra-Manch	7 LM corridors	Berthed overnight Ilfra
9.25am Ilfra-Cardiff	6 WR corridors	5.20am Taunt-Ilfra (8.12 arr)
10.12am Ilfra-Taunt	4 WR corridors	6.20am Taunt-Ilfra (9.01 arr)
10.55am Ilfra-Wolve	6 WR corridors	7.15am Taunt-Ilfra (9.58 arr)
5.10pm Ilfra-Taunt	4 WR corridors	12.50pm Taunt-Ilfra (3.56 arr)
5.45pm Ilfra-B Jct	4 WR corridors (+ 2 Thirds)	8.30am Taunt-Ilfra (11.18 arr) (off a Waterloo service)
6.30pm Ilfra-Taunt	6 WR corridors	2.26pm Taunt-Ilfra (5.10 arr)
8.00pm Ilfra-Taunt	6 WR corridors	3.36pm Taunt-Ilfra (6.16 arr)
8.45pm Ilfra-B Jct	4 WR corridors	4.35pm Taunt-Ilfra (7.37 arr)

In the winter of 1955 the coaching stock formations and their respective train workings are set out below:

TRAIN	SET	FORMATION
06.55am BVR-Taunton	77	B set plus brake compo
08.05am Taunton-BJ	81 plus 82 attached	van Second, Second, brake compo (81) plus 82 (van Second) plus brake van & milk van attached
08.20am BVR-Taunton	79	van Second, Second, brake compo
10.00am BJ-Taunton	76	van Second, Second, brake compo
10.15am Taunton-BJ	75	B set plus brake compo (& stores
		van Tuesdays only)
12.25pm Taunton-BJ	77	B set plus brake compo
1.11pm BJ-Taunton	81	van Second, Second, brake compo
3.58pm BJ-Taunton	75	B set plus brake compo
4.35pm Taunton-BJ	81	van Second, Second, brake compo
5.25pm BVR-Taunton	82	van Second plus brake van
5.45pm Taunton-BJ	79	van Second, Second, brake compo
6.40pm BJ-Taunton	77	B set plus brake compo & milk van
8.25pm Taunton-BJ	75	B set plus brake compo

It will be noted that there was a long turnaround time of the stock sets 75, 76, 77 and 81 at Barnstaple Junction. This was because each set made a return trip to Torrington under Southern motive power, most likely an Ivatt 2-6-2 tank.

In view of the unbalanced passenger workings, the 5.25pm being an extra Up train, the stock for this service (set 82) was added to the 8.05am Down passenger from Taunton to Barnstaple Junction. The additional brake van also included was off the 10.18pm (previous day) Paddington to Penzance service, where it was detached at Taunton. The return working at 5.25pm back to Taunton enabled the brake van to return to London on the 3.45pm Penzance departure. The milk van, which was also worked down on the 8.05am Taunton service, also made its way from Paddington on the prior day on the 10.18pm departure. However, it then worked its way to Torrington for milk churn collection before returning back to Barnstaple Junction to be added to the 6.40pm departure to Taunton, where it too was attached to the 3.45pm Penzance to Paddington service.

Based on a traffic survey conducted on 11th August 1956 (arguably one of the busiest summer Saturdays ever), there was a relief service from Ilfracombe departing at 7.30am to Birmingham Snow Hill. This appears to have been supplemented by a further train from Taunton to Birmingham, at 1.32pm from Taunton, in addition to the usual time-tabled service leaving Ilfracombe at 10.55am. In the Down direction, the 10.50am departure from Wolverhampton to Minehead and Ilfracombe consisted of twelve coaches before the split at Taunton.

APPENDIX 19
TRAIN SURVEY 1962-65

The tables below have been summarised, with permission, from the RCTS publication *Western Change – Summer Saturdays in the West 1957-1995* by Paul Chancellor.

TAUNTON 28TH JULY 1962

TIME	TRAIN	LOCO	COMMENTS
arr 11.08am	8.35am Ilfra-Manch'ter 1M14	6327	Minehead portion added, 6327 replaced by 5958
arr 11.39am	Barnstaple-Taunton	6372	
dep 11.59am	Taunton-Barnstaple	7326	
arr 12.57pm	Barnstaple[1]-Cardiff	7337	added to 12.05pm from Minehead forward with D812
arr 1.44pm	Ilfra-Wolve	7333	added to 12.45pm from Minehead forward with 1006
dep 2.16pm	Taunton-Ilfracombe	6327	
arr 2.56pm	Barnstaple-Taunton	7304	
dep 3.12pm	10.55am Wolve-Ilfra	7337	D7016 removed at Taunton
arr 5.41pm	Barnstaple-Taunton	6327	
dep 5.57pm	Taunton-Barnstaple	7333	

1. Most likely the 10.12am Ilfracombe to Cardiff
Note: All 'Moguls' used at this time were allocated to Taunton shed (83B)

TAUNTON 27TH JULY 1963

TIME	TRAIN	LOCO	COMMENTS
arr 11.11am	Barnstaple[1]-Manch 1M14	6327	Minehead portion added forward at 11.19am by 4993
dep 11.25am	Taunton-Barnstaple	6372	
arr 11.43am	Barnstaple-Taunton	7333	
arr 12.58pm	Barnstaple[2]-Cardiff	7326	Added to 12.05pm from Minehead, forward at 14.07pm by 5963. Delayed due to failure at Minehead
dep 1.13pm	Wolve-Barnstaple	7333	Arrival behind 7019, Minehead portion split off
arr 1.44pm	Ilfra-Wolve	7337	Added to 12.45pm Minehead to Wolve, forward at 14.31pm by 6904
dep 2.08pm	8.50m Swansea-Ilfra	6327	Arrival behind D7043, Minehead portion split off
arr 3.07pm	Barnstaple-Taunton	41276	Departed 3.15pm as ECS
dep 4.31pm	Taunton-Barnstaple	7326	
arr 5.47pm	Barnstaple-Taunton	6372	
dep 5.58pm	Taunton-Barnstaple	7337	

1. Most likely the 8.35am Ilfracombe departure
2. Most likely the 10.12am Ilfracombe to Cardiff
Note: All 'Moguls' were allocated to Taunton shed (83B), No. 41276 was allocated to Barnstaple Junction (82E).

Ganger Ball on his trolley (see pages 621 and 657), between Morebath Junction and Bampton on the Exe Valley line. *Jim Elson collection*

TAUNTON 25TH JULY 1964

TIME	TRAIN	LOCO	COMMENTS
arr 10.23am	Ilfra-Taunton	6345	departed ECS at 10.33am
arr 10.41am	Ilfra-Manch 1M90	D6335	Ilfracombe portion added to Exmouth to Manch'ter, dep 10.53am behind D7038
dep 11.26am	Taunton-Ilfra	6363	
arr 11.47am	Ilfra-Taunton	31406	ex-Southern 'N' Class
dep 12.17pm	Taunton-Ilfra	D6335	carried headcode 1C77
arr 12.58pm	Ilfra-Cardiff 1T33	7306	added to 12.05 Minehead to Cardiff, dep 13.30pm behind D7075
arr 1.11pm	Llanelli-Ilfra 1C58	31406	took over from D7004, dep 13.31pm
arr 1.45pm	Ilfra-Wolve 1M35	D6329	added to Minehead to Wolve dep 13.58pm behind D7004
arr 3.01pm	Ilfra-Taunton	7303	departing 3.09pm ECS
dep 4.24pm	Taunton-Barnstaple	7306	
arr 5.38pm	Barnstaple-Taunton	6363	
dep 5.45pm	Taunton-Barnstaple	7337	

It is worth noting that Class '22' North British diesels worked the branch this year on the inter-regional and local services, along with the usual '43XX' Class 'Moguls' which were being phased out. The references to 'Hymeks' are merely for completeness in their working of main line trains and the Minehead Branch portion of the inter-regional services. No evidence, photographic or otherwise, has been found of 'Hymeks' working the line. All 'Moguls' with the exception of No. 7306, allocated to Severn Tunnel Junction (86E), were Taunton engines. 'N' Class No. 31406 was allocated to Exmouth Junction (83D), whilst the North British diesels were allocated to Newton Abbot (83A).

TAUNTON 21ST AUGUST 1965

TIME	TRAIN	LOCO	COMMENTS
arr 10.13am	07.55am Ilfra-Manch'ter 1M14	D6331	Combined with 09.18am Exmouth-Manch'ter, dep 10.46am behind D7038
dep 11.20am	Taunton-Ilfra 2C87	DMU	
arr 11.37am	09.25am Ilfra-Taunton	DMU	on arrival departed ECS at 11.44am
arr 12.56pm	10.20am Ilfra-Cardiff	D6333	Combined with 12.17pm Minehead-Cardiff, dep 13.29pm behind D7002
dep 1.14pm	8.00am Wolve-Ilfra/ Minehead 1V53	D6331	D7012 arrived 12.56pm, replaced by D6331 on Ilfra portion, D6347 to Minehead
arr 1.33pm	11.10am Ilfra-Wolve 1M35	D6348	Combined with 12.40pm Minehead-Wolve dep 1.54pm behind D7087
dep 1.35pm	10.50am Cardiff-Ilfra/Minehead 1C59	D6333	D7052 brought train in at 1.21pm. D6333 took Ilfra portion, D7003 to Minehead
arr 2.20pm	11.45am Ilfra-Taunton 2C84	DMU	
dep 4.00pm	11.45am Ilfra-Taunton 2C84	DMU	
arr 5.38pm	3.10pm Ilfra-Taunton 2C84	DMU	

In this period there were three Down and two Up trains between Ilfracombe and Paddington. These ran via Exeter and did not travel down the D&SR. There was no steam on the line by this stage. The diesels were allocated to Newton Abbot, with the exception of D6348 which was a Laira engine (84A).

APPENDIX 20
9.55AM ILFRACOMBE-PADDINGTON SERVICE, DAILY MINUTES LOST, AUGUST 1930

This table summarises the progress of the 9.55am Ilfracombe to Paddington train in August 1930, by way of an example. *Courtesy National Archives*

DATE	MINUTES LATE								MINUTES LOST								
AUG.	BARNSTAPLE JCT	TAUNTON	HIGHBRIDGE/ WESTON	CASTLE CARY/ BRISTOL	SWINDON	WESTBURY/ STEVENTON	READING	PADDINGTON	TAUNTON	READING	EXETER DIVISION	BRISTOL DIVISION	ENGINE	SIGNALS	ENGINEERING	EXCEPTIONAL	REMARKS
1	/	7	7	/	12	12	10	10						25	2		
2	6	17	19	13	32	28	35	40						36	2	2	Stop Reading
3	Sunday																
4	not run																
5	4	6	4	2	2	2	5	/	3					5		3	Stop Reading
6	/	5	52	36	37	36	37	35	2					13		46	Derailment Dunball
7	10	25	25	13	14	11	9	6	5					16	2		
8	1	7	7	/	6	3	2	/						17	3		
9	10	23	23	23	25	25	28	30	8		2	2		8			
10	Sunday																
11	/	7	7	3	8	6	5	2	7	2				9	2		
12	/	10	9	/	/	/	/	/	10					3			
13	/	/	/	/	/	/	/	/						3	1		
14	3	/	9	/	/	/	/	/						11	2		
15	/	8	8	/	/	/	/	/						14			
16	2	16	16	12	27	26	31	30				1	3	36	3		
17	Sunday																
18	/	/	/	/	5	5	3	/						9			
19	/	8	8	/	/	/	/	/	8						2		
20	/	10	10	/	/	/	/	/	10								
21	/	14	17	3	7	5	2	/						25	2	3	Handle not turned
22	/	/	/	/	/	/	3	/						3	2	3	
23	/	10	12	12		14	12	10	1		5			8	2		
24	Sunday																
25	/	/	/	/	6	4	6	1		2		2		6	2		
26	/	2	/		3	3	/	/	2					5	3		
27	/	4	3	/	/	/	/	/	4					7	2		
28	/	7		/	2	/	/	/	7					3	2		
29	8	4	/	2	5	5	4	2	4					6	3		
30	/	6	6	8	15	11	10	15	3		3			19			
31	Sunday																

Appendix 21
Summary of Passenger Countings, Review of Passenger Services at Selected Dates 1915-37

The following information was extracted from passenger traffic returns (Third Class only).

1913 – week commencing 15th September
In the Down direction, the 7.57am and 12.10pm from Taunton had the highest average number of passengers – 148 and 115 respectively at South Molton. Friday was the busiest day of the week, most likely due to Barnstaple market, with 379 and 351 passengers counted on these two trains at South Molton.

In the Up direction, the 2.20pm, 3.02pm and 6.33pm Friday Barnstaple departures had the highest loadings, with 600 counted on the 6.33pm train. The first Barnstaple departure, the 7.32am, was lightly loaded at the start, with an average of 12 passengers, but numbers picked up by Milverton, reflecting regular travellers to Taunton. The 8.50am departure was well patronised, with an average of 46 passengers leaving Barnstaple and 73 on the train at Milverton. The 12.17pm Ilfracombe to Paddington service was modestly loaded on the Barnstaple (only) portion, with an average of 21 passengers, but was well patronised at Taunton (average 116).

1920 – week commencing 12th January
The average figures for the week were boosted by extra passengers on the Saturday, the 5.00pm Down train being well patronised with 191 passengers. However, there was a broad consistency of passengers in the Down direction on most trains, most days of the week.

In the Up direction, the 8.50am Barnstaple to Taunton was well patronised at Milverton, especially on the Saturday (142 passengers), and the 4.00pm Up service was the most heavily loaded through the week, with an average of 62 passengers leaving Barnstaple, 78 at Dulverton and 71 at Milverton.

1925 – week commencing 5th October
In the Down direction, the most popular trains were the 1.15pm and 5.20pm Taunton to Ilfracombe. A large number of passengers had disembarked before Dulverton on the 5.20pm, an average of 89 at Taunton being depleted to 25 at Dulverton and 20 at South Molton. Mondays, Fridays and Saturdays were the busiest days.

In the Up direction, the number of passengers present by Milverton on the first two Up trains is apparent, an average of 50 and 55 respectively. The 2.50pm Ilfracombe to Taunton was the most popular departure from Barnstaple for numbers leaving that station, averaging 37). Friday was the busiest day, with 122 leaving Barnstaple on the 2.50pm.

1929 – week commencing 29th April
The 4.30pm Taunton to Barnstaple Junction was the most popular, with Monday, Thursday, Friday and Saturday enjoying good loadings, an average of 120 passengers leaving Taunton.

In the Up direction, the 3.52pm Barnstaple Junction to Taunton was the busiest with an average of 45 but especially on the Friday (126 passengers).

1932 – week commencing 2nd May
The 4.33pm Taunton to Ilfracombe was the most patronised, with an average of 81 at Taunton. Tuesday 3rd May providing the highest loadings of the week – Taunton 150, Dulverton 110 and South Molton 100. There is a consistent theme of only a few passengers taking these trains from Barnstaple GWR onwards.

The Up trains in this period were consistently loaded. The first Up train at 6.55am had an average of only 8 and 9 passengers as far as East Anstey but an average of 53 at Milverton.

1932 – week commencing 7th November
The 4.33pm to Ilfracombe had the highest average number of passengers on departure from Taunton at 64 but an average of only 10 left Barnstaple GWR.

In the Up direction, the 3.55pm Barnstaple Junction to Taunton service was the most patronised of all trains from Barnstaple, with Friday and Saturday providing the highest passenger numbers.

1935 – week commencing 27th May
The 8.17pm Taunton to Barnstaple train had an average of 153 passengers. However, totals of 220, 300 and 304 passengers were recorded on the Thursday, Friday and Saturday on departure from Taunton, reducing to 78, 75 and 45 by Dulverton. The earlier part of the week on this train was quiet by comparison.

In the Up direction, the 1.40pm Ilfracombe to Taunton boasted an average of 32 passengers on departure from Barnstaple, which was the highest. There was also a relief train added in the evening, departing Barnstaple at 8.45pm on the Thursday, Friday and Saturday.

1935 – week commencing 11th November
The highest average number of passengers leaving Taunton was on the 4.30pm to Ilfracombe. It is curious to see that the 8.17pm Taunton to Barnstaple was the heaviest loaded of all trains from Taunton (120) but there were no passengers on it at Dulverton, although 16 were then recorded at South Molton.

The Up trains in this period had consistent but modest loadings, with only one train from Barnstaple having more than 20 passengers on average on departure. This was the 3.58pm Barnstaple Junction departure, which was boosted by a loading of 69 passengers on the Friday.

1937 – week commencing 1st November
Average passenger numbers were not that spectacular for the week in either direction. The highest average of 58 was counted at Taunton on the 4.30pm to Ilfracombe but only 9 left Barnstaple GWR to venture further north-west.

In the Up direction, Milverton consistently provided good passenger loadings on all trains every day of the week, except the 5.40pm from Barnstaple. Other average loadings did not exceed 25 at all stations except Barnstaple, which had 29 on the 3.58pm Barnstaple Junction to Taunton, which was boosted by a total of 68 passengers on the Friday.

The table overleaf gives the passenger numbers per day for the stations on the branch for all Down and Up trains for the week of 1st-6th November 1937.

The prospective traveller's view of Wiveliscombe station, from the forecourt, probably in the late 1950s. Note the white-washed brickwork. *Jim Elson collection*

TABLE 1: MONDAY 1ST-SATURDAY 6TH NOVEMBER 1937							
THIRD CLASS ONLY							
STATION	MON	TUES	WED	THUR	FRI	SAT	AVE
Down – 7.50am Taunton-Barnstaple Jct							
Taunton	46	47	61	64	52	22	49
Dulverton	18	7	22	19	33	14	19
South Molton	16	11	15	18	36	8	17
Barnstaple	4	3	1	4	4	3	3
Down – 10.35am Taunton-Barnstaple Jct							
Taunton	21	12	15	16	12	14	15
Dulverton	13	10	16	15	10	12	13
South Molton	13	18	11	12	18	8	13
Barnstaple	4	4	4	2	0	17	4
Down – 1.10pm Taunton-Barnstaple Jct							
Taunton	20	21	14	29	10	18	19
Dulverton	19	23	13	20	12	32	19
South Molton	18	23	18	10	20	54	24
Barnstaple	6	10	3	4	4	10	6
Down – 1.35pm Taunton-Wiveliscombe ThSO							
Taunton				0		8	4
Milverton							
Down – 4.30pm Taunton-Ilfracombe							
Taunton	75	61	51	53	60	47	58
Dulverton	33	37	20	22	36	31	29
South Molton	35	32	22	24	29	30	29
Barnstaple	10	10	10	6	6	14	9
Down – 5.40pm Taunton-Barnstaple Jct							
Taunton	24	28	16	22	25	19	22
Dulverton	9	7	8	4	10	8	8
South Molton	12	3	6	4	6	9	7
Barnstaple	4	0	1	3	4	6	3
Down – 8.17pm Taunton-Barnstaple							
Taunton	36	12	30	32	24	109	41
Dulverton	19	9	14	15	10	20	14
South Molton	20	11	9	12	10	13	11
Down – 11.05pm Taunton-Wiveliscombe (SO)							
Taunton						54	54
Milverton						44	44
Up – 6.55 Barnstaple-Taunton							
Barnstaple	17	11	9	9	8	8	10
East Anstey	21	4	3	5	8	13	9
Milverton	52	42	48	49	50	20	43
Up – 8.45 Barnstaple-Taunton							
Barnstaple	28	14	12	19	11	8	15
East Anstey	21	24	16	15	15	13	15
Milverton	43	26	18	26	18	31	27
Up – 1.40 Barnstaple Jct-Taunton							
Barnstaple	15	16	9	16	23	22	17
Dulverton	33	17	14	13	22	27	21
Up – 2.05 Wiveliscombe-Taunton ThSO							
Milverton				10		34	22
Up – 3.58 Barnstaple Jct-Taunton							
Barnstaple	19	16	19	35	68	15	29
East Anstey	35	17	19	21	31	14	23
Milverton	74	65	60	65	79	106	64
Up – 5.40 Barnstaple Jct-Taunton							
Barnstaple	12	5	7	10	22	38	16
East Anstey	17	5	7	6	9	18	10
Milverton	9	8	6	9	7	27	9
Up – 8.35 Barnstaple-South Molton							
Barnstaple						19	19

ABBREVIATIONS FOR TABLE RIGHT

G – Goods station; P – Passenger and Parcels station; F – Furniture vans, carriages, portable engines and machines on wheels; L – Livestock; H – Horse boxes and prize cattle vans; C – Carriages by passenger train

APPENDIX 22
MISCELLANEOUS INFORMATION ABOUT THE BARNSTAPLE BRANCH

LOCATIONS OF 'SOUND WHISTLE' BOARDS

LOCATION (BETWEEN)	UP/DOWN TRAINS	MILEAGE
Milverton and Norton Fitzwarren	Up	167 miles 8 chains
Wiveliscombe and Milverton	Up	171 miles 15 chains
Venn Cross and Morebath	Down	179 miles 22 chains
East Anstey and Dulverton	Up	187 miles 15 chains

STATIONS AT WHICH LOOSE SCREW COUPLINGS ARE KEPT (1947)

STATION	NO. OF TYPE A COUPLINGS	NO. OF TYPE B COUPLINGS
Milverton		1
Dulverton	1	1
Filleigh		1
Barnstaple		2

Loose screw couplings are provided as above and if required at adjoining stations they may be obtained on application. They are to be returned to the station from which they have been obtained without delay.

CROSSING OF THE RAILWAY BY ELECTRIC POWER LINES (1947)

MILEAGE	NEAR	BETWEEN	SUPPLY CO	TELEPHONE
170m 42½c	Milverton	Milverton & Wiveliscombe	Wellington & District Elec Co	Wellington 144
172m 15½c	Wiveliscombe	Milverton & Wiveliscombe	Wellington & District Elec Co	Wellington 144
172m 68¼c 172m 73c 172m 75c	Wiveliscombe	Wiveliscombe & Venn Cross	Wellington & District Elec Co	Wellington 144
184m 46½c	Dulverton	Dulverton & East Anstey	Exe Valley Electric Co	South Molton 43
201m 57½c	Filleigh	Filleigh & Swimbridge	Exe Valley Electric Co	South Molton 43
204m 6c	Swimbridge	Swimbridge & Barnstaple	Bideford & District Elec Supply Co	Bideford 160

The permanent way inspectors duties in 1947 indicated that Taunton to Barnstaple branch inspectors were responsible for the branch and the Exe Valley – Morebath Junction to Tiverton (exclusive) and the Tiverton Branch – Tiverton Junction (exclusive) to Tiverton (exclusive).

SAMPLE FARES: BARNSTAPLE TO PADDINGTON

YEAR	ORDINARY SINGLE (1ST)	ORDINARY SINGLE (3RD)	MONTHLY RETURN (1ST)	MONTHLY RETURN (3RD)
1901	34s 6d	17s 3d*	60s 6d	37s 10d
1947	54s 11d	32s 11d	66s 2d	44s 1d
1955	41s 2d	27s 5d		
1958	47s 0d	31s 4d		

*There was a 2nd Class fare at this time of 21s 6d

In 1904 the Railway Clearing House published a handbook of stations showing the facilities available throughout the country. The relevant entries for the stations on the D&SR were as follows:

STATION	G	P	F	L	H	C	CRANE POWER
Milverton	X	X		X			1 ton 10cwt
Wiveliscombe	X	X	X	X	X	X	2 tons
Venn Cross	X	X		X			2 tons
Morebath	X	X		X			2 tons
Morebath Jct	-	-	-	-	-	-	-
Dulverton	X	X	X	X	X	X	5 tons
East Anstey	X	X		X			2 tons
Yeo Mill	-	-	-	-	-	-	-
Bishops N&M	X	X		X			2 tons
South Molton	X	X	X	X	X	X	2 tons
Filleigh	X	X	X	X	X	X	2 tons
Swimbridge	X	X		X			2 tons
Barnstaple	X	X	X	X	X	X	10 tons

Appendix 23
Summary of Minor Accidents 1921-39

Most of the following are minor accidents, taken from the *GWR Accident Register* for selected years, but give a flavour of the everyday dangers that existed on the railway. They are the reported dates, not necessarily that on which the accident or incident occurred.

Date	Location	Event/incident
1921		
1 Feb.	Barnstaple	Horse injured outside station
10 Feb.	Btw Wivey/Venn C	Engine failure
14 Feb.	Venn Cross	Wagon on fire
24 Feb.	South Molton	Porter-signalman Shattock injured
22 Mar.	Barnstaple	Foreman Parkman injured
28 Mar.	Barnstaple	Shunter Brooks injured
28 May	Wiveliscombe	Goods guard Carpenter
17 June	Barnstaple	Mr Gould injured
29 June	Molland and SM	Telephone 'bont' 12 on fire
28 July	Btw E Anstey/Dulv	Heifer killed (Follet claim)
29 July	Btw VC/Morebath	ETS irregularity
29 July	Filleigh	Passenger train parting
3 Sept.	Wiveliscombe	Train staff irregularity
9 Sept.	Barnstaple Bay	Coach derailed
10 Sept.	Wiveliscombe	Wagon derailed
5 Nov.	Btw SM/BN&M	Engine failure
3 Dec.	Wiveliscombe	Bullock killed on line
1924		
2 April	Dulverton	R. Stevens injured
13 June	Wiveliscombe	Ballast washed away
4 July	Morebath	Reverend Buller injured
7 July	Barnstaple	Casper Ward suicide
17 Sept.	Barnstaple Jct	Pilot working
14 Oct.	South Molton	Pw E. Glanville hurt
1 Dec.	Wiveliscombe	Tunnel, threatened landslide
1925		
21 Jan.	Barnstaple Jct	Engine derailed
13 Jan.	Wiveliscombe	Land slip
5 Mar.	South Molton	G.M. Bell fell
11 May	South Molton	Goods porter P. Ball hurt
16 June	Wiveliscombe	Lamb killed
3 Nov.	Dulverton	Passenger guard Pedlar taken ill
26 Nov.	Dulverton	Lad porter Balin hurt (on 23/9/1923)
1 Dec.	South Molton	Engine derailed
1 Dec.	Dulverton	Station master Wakley hurt
14 Dec.	Filleigh	Hound killed
1926		
4 Feb.	Dulverton	Derailment
1 Mar.	East Anstey	Lamb killed on line
20 Mar.	Milverton	Ford lorry damaged
12 May	Dulverton	Porter Jeffries strained groin
22 May	East Anstey	Wagon on fire
31 Aug.	Dulverton	Mr Pile, injured leg
11 Sept.	Milverton	Mrs Palfrey, strained leg
22 Sept.	Barnstaple	Foreman Parkman, cut elbow
15 Nov.	Barnstaple	Mr Cann, broken ribs
22 Nov.	Dulverton	Engine derailed
8 Dec.	Barnstaple	Haulier White, crushed finger
1927		
11 Feb.	South Molton	Engine derailed
8 July	Barnstaple	Lad porter Phillips, toe crushed
1 Sept.	Dulverton	Lorry damaged shunting
13 Oct.	Barnstaple	Guard Walker and unknown boy injured
27 Nov.	Dulverton	Signalman Smallridge, thigh injury
21 Dec.	Barnstaple	Mr Thomas' steam waggon struck by door of SR wagon
1929		
18 Jan.	South Molton	Engine fouls brake van
13 April	Barnstaple	Porter Preston, foot injured
24 April	Barnstaple	Motor driver Ashton, big toe bruised
4 May	Barnstaple	Shunter Brooks, rupture/ Porter Belcher, toe injured
20 May	Dulverton	Miss Harrison, eyebrow bruises
21 May	Dulverton	Train passes signal at danger
24 May	Wiveliscombe	Engine derailed
7 June	BN&Molland	Lamb killed; Mr Cole's
16 Sept.	Barnstaple	Van-man Squire injured
20 Sept.	Btw VC/Wivey	Horse box derailed
23 Sept.	Dulverton	Master Courtney, finger squeezed
28 Oct.	Morebath Jct	Train staff left behind
19 Nov.	Milverton	Hon J.H. Watson's vehicle damaged
1935		
8 Jan.	Dulverton	Mrs Thomas & child/Mr Tarr killed (page 616)
4 Mar.	Dulverton	Driver Northcote injured
29 Mar.	Swimbridge	Guard Walker injured
14 Sept.	Barnstaple	Horse box derailed
7 Oct.	East Anstey	Mr Jones, injured left hand
12 Oct.	South Molton	Collision with lorry
25 Oct.	SM (Chittleham)	Driver Gardner fell off motor lorry
13 Nov.	Barnstaple	Loader Marshall, injured hand

Note: There was an entry under Dulverton: '*Stafford Bridge Mr Madge killed*'. This may be miscategorised but is noted here for completeness.

Below follows a sample from some years not recorded above to give a further flavour of the mundane to the bizarre incidents that afflicted the railway.

Date	Location	Event/incident
1923		
10 Sept.	South Molton	9.30am Ilfracombe parted
1928		
21 Jan.	Barnstaple	Foden steam waggon damaged
28 April	Molland	Wagons derailed
16 Nov.	Btw Wivey/Venn C	Landslip (gales in S. Wales & West of England)
1930		
10 Oct.	Filleigh	Coach derailed
31 Oct.	Barnstaple	Goods porter T. Preston, leg fracture
1932		
15 Jan.	Dulverton	1.25am ex-Bristol goods struck barrow
11 Aug.	Dulverton	Mat in coach on fire
31 Oct.	Dulverton	Driver Northcott, sprained right ankle
1933		
6 Jan.	Btw Venn C/Wivey	Collision between trolley and 9.30am ex-Barnstaple goods
1 Nov.	Dulverton	10.05am passenger train overran signal
12 Feb.	Dulverton	Driver Manley injured right elbow
1934		
7 Dec.	Wiveliscombe	Land slide
1936		
24 July	Wiveliscombe	Rails bent
1937		
11 April	Dulverton	Engine derailed
31 May	Dulverton	Empty tks [tanks?] off Up SM goods derailed
3 Dec.	Filleigh	landslide – Up loop blocked
1938		
15 Jan.	South Molton	Brake van derailed
22 Aug.	Barnstaple S Jct	Mr R.C. Scillithe, abrasions to forehead
7 Sept.	Dulverton	1.15am Bristol Down goods derailed
4 Oct.	Barnstaple	Engine off 5.40pm Barnstaple failed
1939		
30 July	Swimbridge	C. Wadham (passenger guard), injury to hand
30 Sept.	Fileigh	Trucks off 9.55am goods ran away
27 Nov.	Dulverton	Brake van derailed

APPENDIX 24
STAFF MATTERS (1876) AND STAFF CHANGES 1904-63

This information has been extracted from a review of the *Great Western Railway Magazine* each month for the year concerned. Note that the month shown is when it was recorded, not necessarily the date of the actual move. This does not purport to be a comprehensive staff summary or of staff moves, merely an extract from what was reported to the *GWR Magazine* in the years summarised below; indeed, I may have missed some but have tried to make it as comprehensive as possible. Some names also appear more than once, as they moved around. Not all job descriptions are listed. However, what is set out below shows how people progressed and where they moved to, often not far as would be expected in the era covered.

Before embarking on the staff summaries and transfers, the table below is a summary of weekly pay for drivers and firemen at Barnstaple shed on 1st Jan. 1876.

DRIVER	PAY	FIREMAN	PAY
H. Frost	7s	W. Dodge	3s 9d
A. Williams	6s 3d	F. Humphrey	3s
C. Panis	6s 3d	W. Johns	3s
J. Green	7s	W. Squire	3s
J. Braund	7s	T. Tucker	3s 6d
		S. Perry	3s 6d

MONTH	NAME	TRANSFER
1901		
Sept.	A.W.C. Boon	Parcel porter Minehead. Appointed station master Venn Cross
1904		
July	W.H. Heard	Brakesman. Appointed goods guard Barnstaple
July	W. Fursdon	Brakesman. Appointed goods guard Barnstaple
July	F.W. Battrick	Shunter, Barnstaple appointed brakesman
1905 – No records available		
1906		
June	F.W. Walker	Barnstaple to Minehead Passenger Dept
June	S.J. Stanbury	Tiverton Jct to Barnstaple Passenger Dept
June	A.E. Rhodes	Swimbridge to Bridgwater
June	H. Trott	Taunton to Swimbridge as signal porter
Oct.	S.J. Yandle	Station master at Filleigh to Williton
Oct.	A. Tout	Ticket collector Durston to Filleigh as station master
1907		
April	W.C. Greenaway	Fitter Bristol to Barnstaple as chargehand
Sept.	W.J. Court	Wiveliscombe signalman to Taunton
Oct.	W.E. Davies	Venn Cross to Morebath as signal porter
	S.H. Fogwill	Morebath to Stoke Cannon as signalman
Nov.	A. Laskey	Wellington to Barnstaple as foreman
1908		
Jan.	R.C. Burleigh	Barnstaple to Taunton
	H.O. Ridler	Taunton to Barnstaple
Feb.	W.T. Withers	Stogumber to Milverton as signal porter
April	W.C. Hutchings	Highbridge to Barnstaple as brakesman
Aug.	C.H. Brooks	Wiveliscombe to Taunton
	W. Coles	Clerk Teignmouth to Wiveliscombe
Nov.	S.T. Stanbury	Clerk Dulverton to Taunton
1909		
Feb.	H. Galpin	Porter Wiveliscombe to Morebath as signal porter
May	L. Carpenter	Lustleigh to Bishops Nympton & Molland as signal porter
July	H. Jones	Clerk Barnstaple to Taunton
	W.G. Grigg	Clerk Chard to Barnstaple
	W. Coles	Clerk South Molton to Chard
Sept.	M.J. Hayman	Porter Longdown to Milverton as signal porter
	F.C. Smith	Signal porter Dunster to Wiveliscombe as signalman
Oct.	J. Adams	Chief goods clerk Barnstaple to Watchet as station master
	S.J. Stanbury	Clerk Barnstaple to Exeter
Dec.	C. Pyke	Clerk Ilfracombe to Barnstaple
1910		
Jan.	C.H. Brooks	Clerk Exeter to South Molton
Feb.	C.E. Blackmore	Relief signalman at Exeter to South Molton as station master
April	G.W. Pitman	Porter Wiveliscombe to Dunball as signal porter
June	H.J. Court	Signalman Heathfield to Dulverton
	W.W. Tucker	Signalman Morebath Jct to Heathfield
	T. Ellacott	Signalman Chard to Morebath Jct
July	H.J. Court	Signalman Dulverton to Exeter City Basin Junction
Aug.	C.H. Brooks	South Molton to Exeter
	J. Ball	Dulverton to Tiverton
	W.P. Matthews	Barnstaple to Paignton
	G.H. Heath	Appointed 3rd Class fireman from shunting fireman (at Barnstaple)
Nov.	T. Ellacott	Signalman Morebath Jct to Torre
	F.W. Nix	Signal porter Brent Knoll to Morebath Jct as signalman
	G. Snell	Signal porter South Molton to Dulverton as signalman
Dec.	J.C.W. Symons	Signalman Dulverton to Newton Abbot
1911		
Jan.	G. Pyke	Clerk Barnstaple to Chard
	H. Trott	Signal porter Swimbridge to Morebath Jct as signalman
Feb.	C.H.A. Withy	Station master Barnstaple to Leamington
	F.C. Smith	Signalman Wiveliscombe to Bleadon & Uphill
	A.R. Birch	Signal porter Bishops Lydeard to Wiveliscombe as signalman
Mar.	H.J. Kerch	Station master Goring & Streatley to Barnstaple as station master
April	A.J. Cridland	Porter Cadleigh to East Anstey as signal porter
May	W.J. Mitchell	Porter Barnstaple to Norton Fitzwarren as sectional lampman
June	A. Tout	Station master Filleigh to Milverton
Aug.	G.A. Bloomfield	Wiveliscombe to Exeter
	G.H. Foster	South Molton to Taunton
	W.J. Staddon	Porter Bishops Nympton & Molland to Thornfalcon as signal porter
	C. Paul	Ganger Milverton retired
Sept.	S. Brice	Packer Venn Cross retired
	J. Seldon	Ganger South Molton to Milverton
Oct.	A.R. Birch	Wiveliscombe to Wellington as signalman
Nov.	E.W. Davies	Signal porter Morebath to Bampton as signalman
1912		
Jan.	G.R. Pope	Signal porter Filleigh to Newton Abbot as signalman
	F.T. Clement	Engine cleaner to 3rd Class fireman (Barnstaple to Pontypool Road)
	J.H. Murray	Engine cleaner to 3rd Class fireman (Barnstaple to Llantrisant)
Feb.	W. Bawden	Leading packer South Molton retired
Mar.	F.D.S. Drake	Signal porter Bovey Tracy to Wiveliscombe as signalman
	J. Vickery	Parcel porter Barnstaple to Newton Abbot as parcel foreman
April	P. Nichols	Porter Dulverton to Brent Knoll as parcel porter
July	W.H. Rabjohns	Clerk South Molton to Ilminster
	A.E. Taylor	Signal porter Dulverton to Wiveliscombe as signalman
Aug.	W.G. Gigg	Clerk Barnstaple to Taunton
	W.J. Hutchings	Porter shunter Barnstaple to Brixham as foreman
	A.E. Taylor	Signalman Wiveliscombe to Bampton

	W.G. Court	Signal porter Bampton to Wiveliscombe as signalman
Sept.	J. Ball	Clerk Tiverton to South Molton
	G.D.R. Ward	South Molton to Tiverton
	G.A. Bloomfield	Exeter to Barnstaple
	P.W. Peacock	First group fireman to engineman (3rd group) at Barnstaple
	A.J. Hayward	Barnstaple to Taunton
Oct.	W. Yandle	Leading packer Barnstaple to Morebath as ganger
	H. Butt	Ganger Morebath to Cullompton
	S.J. Smale	Packer Barnstaple appointed leading packer
	A.E. Doran	2nd group fireman promoted to 1st group fireman at Barnstaple
Nov.	W. Hull	Porter shunter Barnstaple to Taunton as shunter
	W.H. Winter	Porter Hele & Bradninch to Barnstaple as porter shunter
1913		
Jan.	H.O. Ridler	Barnstaple to Exeter (DSO)
	R. White	Exeter (DSO) to Barnstaple
Feb.	H. Galpin	Signal porter Morebath to Wiveliscombe as signalman
April	J. Ball	Clerk South Molton to Tiverton Junction
	F.J. Chamy	Clerk Exeter to Barnstaple
	G.A. Bloomfield	Bampton to Brixham
	R.J. Coombes	Paignton to Filleigh as station master
	T. Lidstone	Porter Mortonhampstead to South Molton as checker
	H.W. Dare	Checker South Molton to Tiverton Jct as foreman
	A. Webber	Packer Bishops Nympton & Molland appointed leading packer
	F. Sully	Morebath to Bampton leading packer
May	H.W. Wood	Clerk Barnstaple to Taunton
	H.C. Sabine	Clerk Dulverton to Cullompton
	R.F. Hurford	Clerk Cullompton to Dulverton
July	W.G. Stone	Porter guard Tiverton Jct to Barnstaple as foreman
Aug.	W.H.G. Wakley	Goods clerk Barnstaple to South Molton as station master
	W.L. Lile	Paignton to Barnstaple
	C.T. Lloyd	Paignton to Barnstaple
Sept.	J .Brend	Signal porter Wivelscombe to Newton Abbot goods yard as signalman
Nov.	G.W. Pitman	Signal porter Dulverton to Newton Abbot as signalman
Dec.	C.H. Brooks	Clerk Barnstaple to Exeter
	W.H. Winter	Porter shunter Barnstaple to Exeter as shunter
	W.C. Greenaway	Fitter Barnstaple to Yeovil as chargeman

DSO = District Supervisor's office

1914		
Jan.	J. Parsons	Packer Morebath to Bampton as leading packer
Mar.	C.C. Harris	Signalman East Anstey to Silverton
	W.W. Langford	Signal porter Tiverton Jct to East Anstey as signalman
	C.E. Davey	Signal porter Trusham to Venn Cross as signalman
	W.J. Tooze	Signal porter Morebath to Dulverton as signaman
April	F.J. Channing	Clerk Barnstaple to Taunton
	A.S. Thorne	Clerk Torre to Barnstaple
	H. Galpin	Signalman Wiveliscombe to Starcross
May	P.W. Gammon	Signalman Molland to Bleadon & Uphill
	R.C. Boxer	Porter shunter Barnstaple to Newton Abbot as shunter
	S.W. Sampson	Signal porter Chard to Venn Cross as signalman
Aug.	H.A. Payne	Clerk Dulverton to Exeter
	S.A. Cole	Clerk Barnstaple to Torre
	A.R. Way	Clerk Torre to Dulverton
	C.E. Blackmore	Station master Morebath to Bishops Lydeard
	W.R. Hensley	Checker Watchet to Morebath as station master
	F.G. Boobyer	Signalman Filleigh to Stoneycombe
	C. Hancock	Signal porter Chard to Filleigh as signalman
	J. Pedler	Signalman Swimbridge to Kingskerswell
	F. Telling	Signal porter Morebath to Swimbridge as signalman
Oct.	W.E. Clarke	Signalman Morebath Jct to Dawlish
	W.O. Job	Signalman Bishops Lydeard to Morebath Jct
	C. Hooper	Packer Tiverton to Dulverton as leading packer
Nov.	H.A. Payne	Clerk Exeter to Barnstaple
	A.G. Harris	Clerk Newton Abbot to Barnstaple
	C.W. Franklin	Clerk Kingswear to Barnstaple
Dec.	M. Pike	Signal porter Dulverton to Blue Anchor as signalman
1915		
Jan.	H.S. Lee	Porter Dulverton to Brent Knoll as parcel porter
	H.F. Vowden	Signal porter Chard to Venn Cross as signalman
April	P.J.C. Bailey	Clerk Taunton to Dulverton
	C.T. Lloyd	Clerk Dulverton to Taunton
	J. Harvey	Porter shunter Barnstaple to Newton Abbot as shunter
May	S.R. Reed	Clerk South Molton to Teignmouth
	C.W. Franklin	Clerk Barnstaple to Chard
	S.H. Quick	Parcel porter Minehead to Venn Cross as station master
	W.H. Fursdon	Signalman Christow to Wiveliscombe as checker
	W.W. Willis	Signal porter Bishops Lydeard to Filleigh as signalman
June	H.A. Payne	Clerk Barnstaple to South Molton
July	W.S. Gibbs	Clerk Minehead to Barnstaple
	J. Crowle	Passenge guard Barnstaple to Exeter
Aug.	P.J.C. Bailey	Clerk Dulverton to Taunton
	S.R. Reed	Clerk Teignmouth to Dulverton
Sept.	A.R. Way	Clerk Dulverton to Bampton
	P.J. Coles	Clerk Ilminster to Dulverton
	J.E. Bartlett	Leading packer South Molton to Tiverton as ganger
	W.J. Ball	Packer Venn Cross to South Molton as leading packer
Oct.	S.H. Brooks	Clerk Minehead to Barnstaple
	R.S. Bale	Clerk Barnstaple to Tiverton
	E.W. Evans	Wiveliscombe to Aberbeeg as brakesman
1916		
Jan.	W.S. Gibbs	Clerk Barnstaple to Exeter
	J. Hawkes	Clerk Torre to Barnstaple
	H.J. Screech	Signal porter Buckfastleigh to Wiveliscombe as signalman
Feb.	A. Cole	Porter shunter Barnstaple to Chard as checker
Mar.	A.R. Way	Clerk Barnstaple to Hele & Bradninch
April	C.E. Lockyear	Clerk Dulverton to Barnstaple
	S.H. Brooks	Clerk Barnstaple to Dawlish
May	C.H. Morgan	Clerk Torre to South Molton
1917		
Jan.	C.H. Morgan	Clerk South Molton to Totnes
Feb.	W.J. Penwarden	Clerk South Molton to Tiverton
	C.H. Drake	Clerk Tiverton to South Molton
May	C.H. Drake	Clerk South Molton to Tiverton
	J.K. Hawkes	Clerk Barnstaple to Hele & Bradninch
July	W.J. Ashton	Parcel porter Barnstaple to Torre
Sept.	P.S.R. Park	Barnstaple to Paignton
Oct.	C. Criddle	Leading packer Wiveliscombe to Tiverton as ganger
Nov.	L.W. Ricard	Kingswear to Dulverton
	L.G. Hooper	Dulverton to Kingswear
Dec.	W.J. Stenner	Signalman Taunton to Morebath as station master
1918		
Feb.	H.R. Bourne	Clerk South Molton to Torre
Mar.	P. Nicholls	Porter guard Hemyock to Wiveliscombe as checker
May	P.J. Cole	Clerk Dulverton to South Molton
June	J. Lock	Packer at South Molton retired
	A. Webber	Leading packer at Bishops Nympton & Molland to Martock as ganger
Sept.	R. Hayes	South Molton to Totnes
1919		
Feb.	S. Evans	Station master Dulverton to Maiden Newton
	W.H.G. Wakley	Station master South Molton to Dulverton
	W.F. Laskey	Goods clerk Minehead to South Molton as station master
Mar.	R.W. Rickards	Clerk Dulverton to Dawlish
	J.C. Pleace	Clerk Tiverton to Dulverton
	W.G. Stone	Foreman Barnstaple to Tiverton Junction
	C. Jennings	Packer Milverton retired

April	P.J. Cole	Clerk South Molton to Tiverton
	P. Sully	Signal porter Dulverton to Christow as signalman
	T. Ousley	Signal porter Chard to Milverton as signalman
	H.G. Elliott	Signalman Wiveliscombe to Tiverton Junction
May	F.C. Challice	Bampton to Venn Cross as signalman
	A.B. Smallridge	Signalman Milverton to Dulverton
	F. Telling	Signalman Swimbridge to Taunton as brakesman
	W.F. Hapgood	Thorverton to Milverton as signalman
June	C.J. Webber	Clerk Barnstaple to Tiverton
	F.A. Gill	Signalman South Molton to Filleigh
	P.J. Cole	Clerk Tiverton to South Molton
July	S.R. Telling	Signalman Molland to Heathfield
	H.L. Acreman	Silverton to Swimbridge as signalman
	G.H. Oakwell	Signalman Watchet to East Anstey
Aug.	H.S. Kench	Station master Barnstaple to Wednesbury
	H.S. Stone	Bishops Lydeard to Milverton as signalman
	H.C.W. Hopkins	Paignton to Molland as signalman
Sept.	J. Gordon-Hogg	Station master Minehead to Barnstaple
Oct.	H.C.W. Hopkins	Signalman Molland to Heathfield
	H. Chown	Barnstaple to Wiveliscombe as leading packer
	C. Chown	Swimbridge to Bishops N&M as leading packer
1920		
Feb.	W. Cook	Packer retired
May	C.E. Lockyer	Clerk to Barnstaple
June	F. Vowles	Bishops N&M to Kingskerswell as station master
	F.W. Nichols	Brixham to Barnstaple as passenger guard
	R.J. Coombes	Filleigh to East Anstey as station master
	I.C.W. Symons	Newton Abbot to Filleigh as station master
July	J. Vickery	Newton Abbot to Bishops N&M as station master
Aug.	C.E. Lockyer	Barnstaple to Torquay as booking clerk
	W.F. Ridgway	Churston to Morebath as signalman
	L.W. Rendell	Minehead to Barnstaple as working foreman
Nov.	J. Chubb	Bovey Tracy to Swimbridge as station master
	R.H. Lydon	Dulverton to Exeter as goods guard
	R.J. Coombes	East Anstey to Ashburton as station master
	J. Sledge	Exeter St Thomas to East Anstey as station master
Dec.	W.W. Langford	Signalman East Anstey to Tiverton Junction
	S.H. Crook	South Molton to Kingswear as shunter
	E.W. Biffin	Signalman Wiveliscombe to Exeter St. Thomas
1921		
Jan.	W.C. Shattock	Minehead to South Molton as porter signalman
	F. Brooks	South Molton to East Anstey as signalman
May	R.E. Cole	Stogumber to Filleigh as porter signalman
June	E.J. Sleeman	Signalman Buckfastleigh to Venn Cross
	H.T. Langdon	Venn Cross to Heathfield as signalman
	S.J. Smale	Barnstaple to Bishops N&M as ganger
July	J.C. Pleace	Dulverton to Exeter (DTMO)
	L.F. Nickels	Clerk Minehead to Dulverton
	L.J. Hill	Silverton to Dulverton as parcels porter
	A.G. Routley	Clerk South Molton to Torquay

DTMO = District Traffic Manager's Office

1922		
Jan.	J.H. Margetts	Exeter DTMO to Morebath as station master
	W.W. Vickery	Clerk Torre to Barnstaple
April		*pages missing in journal reviewed*
June	A.S. Thorne	Clerk Barnstaple to Exeter
Sept.	H.E.T. Cornish	Clerk South Molton to Bridgwater (goods)
Nov.	A.J. Veysey	Signalman Longdown to Venn Cross
	F.C. Challice	Signalman Venn Cross to Martock
1923		
Jan.	G.H. Bibbings	Paignton to Barnstaple working foreman
	J. Adams	Watchet to Barnstaple as Station Master
Mar.	F.C. Carpenter	Goods guard Taunton to Barnstaple
May	C.J. Stuckley	Chard to East Anstey signalman
	G.H. Oakwell	Signalman East Anstey to Bridgwater
	W. Hancock	Kingskerswell to Venn Cross as signalman
June	T. Floyd	South Molton retired
July	F.C. Carpenter	Goods guard Barnstaple to Taunton
	W.F. Haywood	Signalman Milverton to Langport West
	J.F. Lyddon	Goods guard Taunton to Barnstaple
Sept.	W.H. Ridgway	Signalman Morebath to Langport West
	E. Ball	Uffculm to South Molton as goods porter
	A.J. Veysey	Signalman Venn Cross to Bridgwater
	J.S. Passmore	Williton to Venn Cross as signalman
	W.R. Howell	Cadeleigh to Venn Cross as signalman
Oct.	C.R. Lee	Clerk Barnstaple to Exeter
	L.C. Russell	Clerk Ilminster to Barnstaple
Dec.	A.J. Chubb	Bramford Speke station master to Filleigh
	F. Barwick	Clerk Dulverton to Hele & Bradninch
	I.C.W. Symons	Filleigh to Exminster station master
	S.S. Morrall	Clerk Hele & Bradninch to Wiveliscombe
	P. Nicholls	Checker Wiveliscombe to Barnstaple
1924		
Jan.	F. Burridge	Driver locomotive/carriage department Barnstaple. Commendation for exceptionally meritorious action
Feb.	L.C. Russell	Clerk Barnstaple to Ilminster
	W.H. Drake	Kingswear to Swimbridge as signalman
	H.L. Acreman	Swimbridge to Starcross as signalman
	R.S. Boyce	Clerk Teignmouth to Barnstaple
Mar.	F. Langford	Signalman Morebath to Tiverton
April	L.J. Upham	Churston to Venn Cross as signalman
	J. Sledge	East Anstey to Burlescombe as station master
	G. Soper	Signalman Newton Abbot to Swimbridge
	J.H. Eckhart	Signalman Swimbridge to Newton Abbot
	G. Pursey	Station master Up Exe to East Anstey
	J. Passmore	Signalman Venn Cross to Morebath
	C.W. Gardner	Porter signalman Wiveliscombe to Churston
May	G. MItchell	Chard to East Anstey as signalman
	C.J. Stuckey	Signalman East Anstey to Swimbridge
	W. Lugg	Signalman Milverton to Trusham
	W.H. Drake	Signalman Swimbridge to Newton Abbot
June	F. Brooks	Signalman East Anstey to Teignmouth
	F.A. Gill	Signalman Filleigh to South Molton
	A.G. Gill	Signalman Hatch to Filleigh
	W.C. Shattock	Signalman South Molton to Milverton
Aug.	L.F. Nickels	Clerk Dulverton to Taunton
	F.T. Barwick	Clerk Ilminster to South Molton
	S.A. Keitch	Clerk South Molton to Taunton
Dec.	F. Trood	Durston to Swimbridge as station master
	J. Chubb	Station master Swimbridge to Hemyock
1925		
Feb.	G.W. Bibbings	Barnstaple to Bridgwater as yard foreman
	F. Puckett	Signalman Keinton Mandeville to Barnstaple
Aug.	R.E. Cole	Signalman Filleigh to Crowcombe
	A.E. Bending	Langport West to Filleigh as signalman
	W.E. Kemp	Clerk Paignton to Barnstaple
Sept.	H.S. Lewis	Clerk Barnstaple to Tiverton Junction
Nov.	F. Puckett	Signalman Barnstaple to Durston
Dec.	J.H. Margetts	Morebath to Exeter (DTMO) as relief clerk
1926		
Feb.	T. Way	Signalman Blue Anchor to Swimbridge
	H.C. Govett	Clerk Dawlish to Wiveliscombe
	J. Boyles	Station master Langport East to Swimbridge
	J.W. Balsdon	Station master Longdown to East Anstey
	F.T. Trood	Station master Swimbridge to Morebath
	G. Soper	Signalman Swimbridge to Barnstaple
April	R.E.J. Weston	Clerk Dulverton to Stourbridge Town
	I.H.P. Pressick	Clerk Tiverton Junction to Dulverton
Sept.	H.C. Govett	Clerk Wiveliscombe to Minehead
Oct.	W.W. Vickery	Clerk Barnstaple to Minehead
	L.R. Wellington	Clerk Churston to South Molton
	F.T. Barwick	Clerk South Molton to Barnstaple
1927		
Mar.	J. Boyles	Station master Swimbridge to Culmstock
April	F.C. Burrow	Brixham to Dulverton as shunter
	H. Cockram	Station master Culmstock to Swimbridge
May	J.S. Matthews	Station master Charlton Mackrell to Dulverton
June	R. Vickery	Clerk Dulverton to Moretonhampstead

	L.J. Hill	Signalman East Anstey to Tiverton Jct
	A.G. Gill	Signalman Filleigh to Washford
	C.A.L. Reeves	Clerk Hemyock to Dulverton
July	W.G. Yandell	Dunball to East Anstey as signalman
Aug.	H.S. Stone	Signalman Milverton to Exminster
Sept.	H.E. Cornish	Clerk Barnstaple to Exeter DTMO
	W.G. Yandell	Signalman East Anstey to Teignmouth
	V.E.H. Fenner	Clerk Wiveliscombe to Chard
	H. Chown	Wiveliscombe to Venn Cross as ganger
Oct.	A.H.S.O. Penny	Chard to East Anstey as signalman
	A.E. Bending	Signalman Filleigh to Milverton
	R.H. Underhill	Long Sutton & Pitney to Filleigh as signalman
Dec.	H.S. Cornelius	Clerk Wiveliscombe to Dawlish
1928		
Jan.	F.J. Underhill	Signalman Filleigh to Northolt Junction
	W.O. Cudmore	Clerk Minehead to Barnstaple
Feb.	T.G. Honeywill	Langport West to Filleigh as signalman
April	A.E. Bending	Signalman Milverton to Bridgwater
	C.J. Stuckey	Signalman Swimbridge to Milverton
	W.J. Tanton	Tiverton Jct to Swimbridge as signalman
May	J. Boyles	Station master Culmstock to Wiveliscombe
	C.A.C. Reeves	Clerk Dulverton to Exeter DTMO
	D.C. Croker	Clerk Exeter to Dulverton
June	W.O. Cudmore	Clerk Barnstaple to Minehead
	F.J. Lyddon	Guard Barnstaple to Newton Abbot
Sept.	J.H. Connibeer	Station master Crowcombe to Swimbridge
	J. Blackmore	Dunball to East Anstey as Signalman
	G. Mitchell	Signalman East Anstey to Tiverton Jct
	H. Cockram	Station master Swimbridge to Uffculme
Nov.	J. Ellery	Clerk Barnstaple to Cullompton
	W.G.C. Hooper	Clerk Torre to Barnstaple
	J. Northcombe	Ganger Swimbridge retired
Dec.	G.D. Miller	Signalman Bishops N&M to Cullompton
	F. Winter	Signalman Cadeleigh to Bishops N&M
	DC Croker	Clerk Dulverton to Tiverton
	ER Woollatt	Clerk Tiverton to Dulverton
1929		
Jan.	S.R. Hawkins	Clerk Dawlish to Barnstaple
Feb.	P. Nicholls	Barnstaple to Brixham passenger guard
	T. Seldon	Swimbridge appointed ganger
April	S.R. Hawkins	Clerk Barnstaple to Tiverton
May	F.T. Willmott	Goods guard Barnstaple to Exeter
Sept.	W.G.C. Hooper	Clerk Barnstaple to Torre
	C.E. Vellacott	Bishops N&M to Venn Cross as sub-ganger
Oct.	J. Ellery	Clerk Cullompton to Barnstaple
	A.M. Taylor	Clerk Wiveliscombe to Tiverton
	W. Venn	Engineering department Barnstaple retired
Nov.	R.G. Salter	Ilminster to South Molton as motor driver
	A.H. Barnes	Carter Martock to Barnstaple
Dec.	A.M. Taylor	Clerk Tiverton to Wiveliscombe
	W.G.C. Hooper	Clerk Torre to Barnstaple
1930		
Feb.	H.E.T. Cornish	Clerk Barnstaple to Wellington
	J. Harvey	Barnstaple to Exeter as passenger Guard
	W.J. Fisher	Barnstaple to Hele & Bradninch as checker
	E.R. Wollatt	Clerk Dulverton to Lambourne
	P.H. Strickland	Checker Hele & Bradninch to Barnstaple
	R. Vickery	Clerk Mortonhampstead to Dulverton
	R.J. Berry	Clerk Taunton to Wiveliscombe
	A.M. Taylor	Clerk Wiveliscombe to Mortonhampstead
May	W.C. Humphries	Signalman Barnstaple to Taunton
	E.A. Hexter	Dunball to Filleigh as signalman

An easy load of three coaches for 'Mogul' No. 7304 as it climbs Allerford Bank, just beyond Norton Fitzwarren, with a stopping service to Barnstaple Junction on Saturday b13th July 1963. It is still possible to see the occasional locomotive and item of rolling stock on this section, as the track has been reinstated for a short distance by the West Somerset Railway. However, the gradient is now less of an incline, as some of the bank was removed in making the chord line that now occupies the old trackbed (see Volume 1 page 195-199). *Owen Mogg, courtesy Peter Triggs*

	T.G. Honeywill	Signalman Filleigh to Tiverton Junction
	F.J. Evans	Minehead to Dulverton as motor driver
	R.G. Short	Minehead to Barnstaple as signalman
June	R.J. Berry	Clerk Wiveliscombe to Taunton
	C. Burston	Morebath to Venn Cross as ganger
July	E.A. Hexter	Signalman Filleigh to Martock
	T.W. Webber	Paignton to Filleigh as signalman
Aug.	J. Kingdon	Barnstaple to Swimbridge as ganger
Sept.	W.G.C. Hooper	Clerk Barnstaple to Torre
	F.O. Nicholls	Passenger guard Barnstaple to Newton Abbot
Dec.	A. Ball	South Molton to Dulverton as sub-ganger
1931		
May	R.G.T. Churchill	Station Master Longdown to Swimbridge
June	H. Belcher	Barnstaple to Dulverton as motor driver
	J.S. Vellacott	Motor driver Dulverton to Langport West
Oct.	W.E. Kemp	Clerk Barnstaple to Martock
	H.E.T. Cornish	Clerk Martock to Barnstaple
	A.R. Way	Clerk Torre to Barnstaple
Dec.	M.HB. Brownley	Clerk Dulverton to Somerton
1932		
Jan.	R.G. Sadler	Motor driver South Molton to Taunton
June	G. Coles	Dulverton Engineering department retired
July	A.R. Symonds	Dulverton to Exeter (shed staff)
Aug.	A.L. Saunders	Station master Bampton to Dulverton
	J.S. Matthews	Station master Dulverton to Norton Fitzwarren
Sept.	W.L. Kelly	Exeter to South Molton as motor driver
Oct.	J.S. Vellacott	Motor driver South Molton to Taunton
1933		
April	F.E. Manley	Hele & Bradninch to Dulverton as motor driver
June	D.H. Terry	Clerk Dulverton to South Lambeth (goods)
Dec.	R. Hayes	Clerk Exeter to South Molton
1934		
May	A. McDonald	Bridgwater to South Molton as motor driver
	A.J. Parkhouse	Barnstaple to Swindon engine cleaner to fireman
June	J.B. Gould	Fireman Barnstaple to Laira
	T.W.M. Phillips	Fireman Aberbeeg to Barnstaple
July	R.S. Boyce	Clerk Barnstaple to Taunton
Aug.	A. Ball	South Molton to Bampton as sub-ganger
Sept.	G.H. Guard	Clerk Barnstaple to Tiverton
	H.E. Tout	South Molton to Mattock as leading parcel porter
	H. Chidgey	Parcel porter Wellington to South Molton
Nov.	H. Chidgey	South Molton to Swimbridge as station master
	M.V. Southerton	Station Master Swimbridge to Hatch
Dec.	H.G. Beer	Barnstaple to South Molton as parcel porter
	F.J. Lightfoot	Exeter to Barnstaple as porter guard
	G.H. Guard	Clerk Tiverton to South Molton
	S.J. Lock	Clerk Wellington to Wiveliscombe
1935		
Jan.	H.J. Gardner	Crowcombe to South Molton as motor driver
	W.I. Kelly	Motor driver South Molton to Tiverton
	E.Y. Webber	Shed staff Barnstaple to Taunton
Feb.	E. Spencer	Station master Athelney to South Molton
	P.G. Tremethick	Station master Langport West to Barnstaple
Mar.	H.W. Wood	Station master Bishops N&M to Hemyock
	S.J. Dodswell	Clerk Paignton to Barnstaple
April	F.C. Wyatt	Tiverton Jct to Bishops N&M as station master
May	C.J. Lightfoot	Barnstaple to Exeter as parcel porter
	O.J. Thomas	Taunton to Wiveliscombe as motor driver
	A.J. Cornell	Wellington to Barnstaple as porter guard
July	F.J. Ebeworthy	Shunter Barnstaple to Exeter
	I.A. Eckhart	Kingswear to Dulverton as motor driver
Aug.	I. Gregory	Shunter Wellington to Barnstaple
Nov.	T.J. Emery	Carriage & Wagon staff Barnstaple to Exeter
1936		
Feb.	E.J. Taylor	Barnstaple to Wellington as parcel porter
	J. Caryl	Sampford Peverell to Barnstaple as porter guard
	J.S. Dinham	Wiveliscombe to Brixham as checker
Mar.	F.C. Denmead	Tiverton Junction to Wiveliscombe as carter
	E. Lewis	Cleaner Barnstaple promoted to fireman to Bristol
June	H.W. Burnett	Wiveliscombe to Stogumber as grade 1 porter
July	A.J. Chubb	Station master Filleigh to Athelney
Aug.	S.R.B. Sledge	Fireman appointed driver at Barnstaple
Sept.	J. Caryl	Barnstaple to Exeter as leading parcel porter
	W.J. Tanton	Signalman Swimbridge to Barnstaple
Oct.	G. Soper	Signalman Barnstaple to Cullompton
Nov.	W. Marshall	Barnstaple to Paignton as carter
	W.R. Hitt	Signalman Exeter to Swimbridge
	J.R. Stockham	Uffculme to Wiveliscombe as porter signalman
	R.G. May	Wiveliscombe to Exeter as signalman
	S.R.B. Sledge	Driver Barnstaple to Severn Tunnel Junction
	C.E.C. Richings	Fireman Barnstaple to Chippenham
Dec.	W.A.E. Salter	Trusham to Barnstaple as porter guard
1937		
Jan.	T. Pavey	Ashton to Barnstaple as shunter
Feb.	A.L. Twigg	Barnstaple to Ashton as grade 1 porter
	T.J. Brooks	Barnstaple to Tiverton Junction as goods guard
	W.F. Collier	Dulverton to Chard as grade 1 porter
	C.J. Stephenson	Kingswear to Barnstaple as carter
	A.J. Palmer	Minehead to Wiveliscombe as carter
	F.C. Denmead	Wiveliscombe to Tiverton Jct as motor driver
Mar.	T. Millard	Charlton Mackrell to Barnstaple as carter
April	P.A. Pope	Driver Barnstaple to Taunton
	W.G. Ritchie	Fireman Barnstaple to Taunton
	D.A. Yeo	Cleaner Barnstaple promoted to fireman at Severn Tunnel Junction
May	I.G. Hooper	Wellington to Filleigh as station master
June	A.S.L. Stredwick	Clerk Barnstaple to Wellington
	T. Pavey	Shunter Barnstaple to Taunton
	W.J. Moore	Ide to Bishops N&M as station master
July	C.K. Spencer	Clerk Wiveliscombe to Cullompton
Aug.	F. Male	Langport West to Morebath as signalman
	J. Passmore	Signalman Morebath to Exminster
	J.R. Stockham	Porter signalman Wiveliscombe to Langport West
Nov.	I. Hall	Dulverton to Sampford Peverell as grade 1 porter
1938		
Jan.	W.H. Priter	Signalman Filleigh to Kingskerswell
	J.R. Stockham	Langport West to Filleigh as signalman
April	J.D. Totterdell	Engine cleaner Barnstaple to Salisbury as fireman
May	A.R. Way	Clerk Barnstaple to Exeter (DSO)
	S.J. Elson	Chudleigh to Barnstaple as chief goods clerk
	J.M. Laver	Dulverton to Chard as grade 1 porter
	C.H. Drew	Langport West to Filleigh as signalman
June	W.A.E. Salter	Barnstaple to Torre as parcel porter
	A.J. Cornel	Barnstaple to Exeter as parcel porter
	H. Durman	Chard to Barnstaple as porter guard
July	A.W. Chilcott	Dunball to Barnstaple as porter guard
Nov.	A. Ball	Appointed ganger at Bishops N&M
	T. Perrett	Appointed patrolman at Milverton
1939		
Feb.	H.E. Cornish	Clerk Barnstaple to Dawlish
	W.J. Parry	Signalman East Anstey to Athelney
	W.R. Hitt	Signalman Swimbridge to East Anstey
	L.R. Wellington	Clerk Tiverton to Barnstaple
Mar.	W.A. Hayman	Brixham to Swimbridge as signalman
May	H. Durman	Barnstaple to Newton Abbot as parcel porter
	H.E.G. Butcher	Signalman Longdown to Morebath
	W. Hancock	Signalman Morebath to Teignmouth
	S. Cornish	Torre to Barnstaple as porter guard
June	H.C. Card	Barnstaple to Long Sutton & Pitney as grade 1 porter
	J. Ellery	Barnstaple to Hemyock as station master
	J.S. Hodge	Keinton Mandeville to Morebath as signalman
July	H.E.G. Butler	Signalman Morebath to Exeter St Thomas
Aug.	S.R. Cornish	Barnstaple to Exeter as parcel porter
	J.M. Laver	Chard to Barnstaple as porter guard
Sept.	A.E. Lang	Carriage cleaner Barnstaple to Swindon
Oct.	H.J. Gardner	South Molton to Taunton as cloakroom attendant
Nov.	C.H. Howard	Churston to Wiveliscombe as loader
	E.A. Antell	Dulverton to South Molton as motor driver

	H. Townsend	Wiveliscombe to Hatch as porter signalman
Dec.	J.N. Sloman	Driver Barnstaple to Andover
	F.T. Clement	Driver Barnstaple to Chippenham
	T.W.M. Phillips	Fireman Barnstaple to Chippenham

1940

Jan.	J.L. Lockyer	Paignton to Wiveliscombe as station master
	K.R. Barnes	Cleaner Barnstaple to Banbury as fireman
Mar.	R.S. Boyce	Clerk South Molton to Ilminster
May	F.T. Barwick	Clerk Barnstaple to South Molton
	E.E.J. Reed	Signalman Exeter to Milverton
	P.J. Cole	Clerk South Molton to Barnstaple
Oct.	A.W. Chilcott	Barnstaple to Paignton as parcel porter
	E.A. Hexter	Signalman Martock to Dulverton
Nov.	G.H. Guard	Clerk Barnstaple to South Molton
	W.C. Dinham	Signalman Dulverton to Durston
Dec.	C. Card	Long Sutton & Pitney to Barnstaple as porter guard

1941

Jan.	S. Sanders	Fireman Barnstaple to Severn Tunnel Jct as driver
Mar.	J.G. Polyblank	Clerk Brixham to South Molton
	K.W. Jeffries	Fireman Barnstaple to Reading
April	C.H. Drew	Signalman Filleigh to Martock
	S.J. Yendell	Keinton Mandeville to Filleigh as signalman
July	H.R. Lee	Cleaner Barnstaple to Westbury as fireman
Sept.	R. Vickery	Clerk Dulverton to South Molton
	M.J. Hull	Clerk Minehead to Barnstaple

1942

Jan.	R.S. Chidgey	Wiveliscombe to Taunton as shunter
Feb.	R. Hayes	Clerk Barnstaple to Exeter
May	M.J. Hull	Clerk Barnstaple to Norton Fitzwarren
Sept.	J.D. Totterdale	Fireman Barnstaple to Westbury

1943 (limited returns for Exeter Division for this year)

June	H.T. Townsend	Signalman Filleigh to Dawlish Warren
	R. Vickery	Clerk South Molton to Ilminster
July	W.A. Hayman	Signalman Swimbridge to Dawlish Warren
Aug.	W.E. Howell	Signalman Venn Cross to Norton Fitzwarren
Nov.	A.E. Cummins	Ashton to Venn Cross as signalman

1944

Feb.	P.G. Tremethick	Station master Barnstaple to Teignmouth
	W.J. Moore	Station master Bishops N&M to Williton
	A.E. Cummins	Venn Cross to Bishops N&M as station master
	H.A. Payne	Station master Watchet to Barnstaple
Mar.	J.A. Parkhouse	Fireman Barnstaple to driver
April	T. Preston	Barnstaple appointed signalman Swimbridge
	J.E. Picket	Clerk Dulverton to Chard
	E.J. Reed	Milverton appointed signalman Brixham
	M.E. Jeans	Montacute to Milverton as station master
July	A.H. Thornton	Ashton to Filleigh as signalman
	S.E. Oak	Barnstaple to Exeter as passenger shunter
	I.J. Harris	Clerk Chard to Barnstaple
	J. Herridge	Dulverton to Filleigh as signalman
	S.J. Yandell	Signalman Filleigh to Bovey Tracey
	L. Glanville	Hele & Bradninch to Barnstaple as grade 1 porter
	F.W. Spurdle	Newton Abbot to Filleigh as station master
Oct.	L. Glanville	Signalman Barnstaple to Thorverton
	R.B. Coles	Signalman Chard to Filleigh
	A.J. Finch	Porter Dartmouth to Barnstaple
	J. Herridge	Signalman Filleigh to Burlescombe
Nov.	F. Male	Signalman Morebath to Dawlish
	F.C. Hillier	Appointed signalman

1945

April	A.J. Finch	Barnstaple to Exeter as signalman
	E.H. Symis	Chard to Milverton as signalman
Aug.	R.B. Coles	Signalman Filleigh to Starcross
	E.H. Symis	Signalman Milverton to Burlescombe
Oct.	J. Blackmore	Signalman East Anstey to Torre
Nov.	S.A. Cole	Station master Dunster to South Molton
	W.C. Mortifee	S&T Dulverton to Taunton as temporary labourer

1946

Feb.	A.J. Yandall	Signalman Bishops Lydeard to East Anstey as station master
	A.W. Chivers	Exeter District relief signalman to Filleigh as station master
	F.W. Spurdle	Station master Filleigh to Burlescombe
	F. Edwards	Driver Barnstaple to Taunton
April	K. Grinter	Signalman Milverton to Burlescombe
	W.T. Hutchings	Swimbridge to Exeter relief signalman
July	R.E. Garland	Filleigh to Newton Abbot as shunter
Oct.	A.J. Dalling	South Molton to Taunton as goods shunter
Dec.	H.C. Hillier	Signalman Morebath to Chard

1947

Jan.	E.H. Alderman	Filleigh appointed signalman
	A. Loweys	Station master Montacute to Wiveliscombe
	J.L. Lockyer	Station master Wiveliscombe to Hele & Bradninch
April	W.R. Hitt	Signalman East Anstey to Exeter St. Thomas (City Basin Jct)
May	R.G. Peacock	Signalman Filleigh to Swimbridge
June	H.E. Beer	South Molton to Newton Abbot as passenger guard
July	M.L. Tarr	Signalman Minehead to East Anstey
	F.G. Gliddens	Dulverton to Cinderford as assistant lineman (S&T)
Nov.	J. Legg	Signalman Cadleigh to Dulverton
	G.A. Hexter	Signalman Dulverton to Durston (Creech Jct)

1948 (now employees of British Railways, Western Region)

Mar.	L.H.T. Preston	Appointed motor driver Barnstaple
April	G.E. Taylor	Taunton to Dulverton as assistant lineman (S&T)
May	R.W.P. Farmer	Appointed loader at Barnstaple
	P.J. Bearman	Brixham to Filleigh as signalman
	E.E. Jeans	Appointed signalman Milverton
June	R.W.P. Farmer	Appointed motor parcel vanman at Barnstaple
July	L. Perryman	Appointed loader at Barnstaple
	R.W. Turner	Appointed parcel porter Filleigh
Aug.	F.T. Barwick	Clerk Barnstaple to South Molton
Sept.	H.C. Card	Appointed leading parcel porter Barnstaple
	H. Durman	Chard to Barnstaple as passenger guard
Oct.	E.E. Jeans	Milverton, passed WR signal exams with merit (415/500)
	N.J. Elson*	Venn Cross passed signalling exams (278/500)
	D.S. Hawkins	Milverton passed signalling exams (278/500)
	F.C. Hillier	Signalman Morebath to Dulverton
	A.L. Lewington	Driver Exeter to Barnstaple
Nov.	A. Hutter	Appointed signalman Morebath
Dec.	W. Marshall	Appointed ticket collector Barnstaple

* See recollections Chapter 13

1949

Jan.	T. Preston	Appointed checker Barnstaple
Feb.	G. Crook	Appointed grade 1 porter Barnstaple
	A.W. Chivers	Station master Filleigh to Charlton Mackrell
May	A.E. Ashton	Appointed loader Barnstaple
June	S.A. Cole	Station master South Molton to Newport (DSO as relief)
	J.L. Willis	Station master Uffculme to South Molton
July	J. Crossman	Wiveliscombe to Taunton as goods shunter
Dec.	H. Durman	Passenger guard Barnstaple to Newton Abbot
	S.A. Grigg	Barnstaple to South Molton as goods checker
	J.L. Willis	South Molton to Exeter (DSO as relief station master)
	N.J. Elson*	Venn Cross appointed relief signalman (Exeter SO) at Taunton
	H. Milford	Newton Abbot to Barnstaple as passenger guard

*See recollections Chapter 13

1950

Jan.	A.E. Ashton	Appointed motor driver Barnstaple
	H.V. Pennington	Dulverton to Plymouth as assistant lineman (S&T)
Feb.	P.G. Smale	Appointed goods foreman Barnstaple
	J.H. Tucker	Appointed loader at Barnstaple
April	G.W. Hooper	Appointed lineman at Dulverton
May	F.H.W. Adlam	Signalman Milverton to Stoke Cannon crossing box
June	L. Gregory	Appointed goods guard Barnstaple
	D.J. Bending*	Silverton to Tiverton as goods porter
July	W. Kelso	Appointed goods shunter Barnstaple

	W.J. Glass	Wellington to Milverton as signalman
Aug.	W.J. Glass	Signalman Milverton to Taunton West Loop box
Sept.	G.E. Manning	Dunball to Milverton as signalman

*See recollections Chapter 13

1951

Jan.	W.E. Wilkins	Barnstaple (VR) to Barnstaple Jct as goods shunter
Feb.	H.J. King	Appointed goods shunter at Barnstaple
Mar.	D.S. Hawkins	Signaman Filleigh to Wellington (Poole Siding)
April	G.R. Vowden	Signalman Filleigh to Bovey Tracey
June	R.F. Delve	Appointed signalman at Filleigh from Barnstaple Jct
	H.S. Darch	Dulverton to Taunton as goods shunter
July	F. Green	Venn Cross appointed traffic regulator Exeter (Cowley Bridge Jct)
Aug.	D.J. Tree	Dulverton passed station accounting exams (286/500)
	D.L.G. Dymond	Barnstaple passed station accounting exams (321/500)
	M.I. Tarr	East Anstey passed station accounting exams (344/500)
	H.C. Card	Barnstaple passed station accounting exams (329/500)
Sept.	F.E.J. Pill	Newton Abbot to Venn Cross as station master
	S.J. Elson	Clerk Barnstaple (VR) to St. Austell
Oct.	D.O. Jones	Station Master appointed relief station master (Exeter DSO) at Okehampton
Nov.	G. Crook	Appointed goods shunter at Barnstaple VR
Dec.	C.A. Adams	Porter Barnstaple to South Molton as motor driver

1952

Feb.	A.E. Cummins	Station master Bishops N&M to Venn Cross
	G.S. Cook	Station master Bovey Tracey to South Molton
April	H.W. Luscombe	Signalman Newton Abbot to Bishops N&M as station master
June	W.J. Sweetland	Newton Abbot to Barnstaple as general foreman
July	H. Milford	Passenger guard Barnstaple VR to Exeter
	E.E. Jeans	Signalman Milverton to Wellington
Aug.	W.J. Short	Ticket collector Barnstaple Jct to Barnstaple VR as passenger guard
	G.E. Manning	Signalman Milverton to Norton Fitzwarren
	D.S. Hawkins	Signalman Wellington to Milverton
Sept.	T.J.E. Milum	Barnstaple VR passed station accounting exams (Passenger & Parcels – 347/500)
	A. Chalk	Barnstaple VR to Umberleigh as porter signalman
	K.J. Marney	Dunball to Milverton as signalman

1953

Jan.	J. Moore	Motor driver Newton Abbot to Barnstaple VR
May	D.F.H. Cocks	Clerk Barnstaple VR to Braunton
	D.J. Bending*	Motor driver Cullompton to Dulverton
	E.W. Pyke	Motor driver Dulverton to Bridgend
June	H.W. Luscombe	Bishops N&M to Exeter as station inspector
	D.G. May	Clerk Barnstaple VR to Exeter (DSO)
Aug.	W. Kelso	Barnstaple Jct to Barnstaple VR as leading porter
	L.R. Slade	Barnstaple Jct to Barnstaple VR as ganger
	W.E. Dymond	Barnstaple VR to Barnstaple Jct as porter guard
	R.O. Tooley	Dulverton appointed relief station master Exeter (DSO)
Sept.	I. Jones	Clerk Barnstaple VR to Exeter (DSO) as railway service representative
Oct.	H.W. Searle	Station master Somerton to Dulverton
	C.L .Young	Clerk South Molton to Barnstaple VR
	F. Sedon	Milverton to Dunster as ganger
Dec.	F.T. Barwick	South Molton signalling exam success (295/500)
	G.S. Cook	South Molton signalling exam success (279/500)
	D.J. Tree	Clerk Dulverton to Tiverton

*See recollections Chapter 13

1954

Jan.	J.A. Mehew	Barnstaple VR porter to South Molton as leading goods porter
Feb.	S.A. Grigg	Checker South Molton to Barnstaple VR
Mar.	K.J. Marney	Milverton to Exeter (DOSO), Taunton as relief signalman
April	J.F. Baker	Signalman Bishops Lydeard to Milverton
	J. Moore	Barnstaple VR porter to Fremington as leading goods porter
	N.R. Seldon	Porter South Molton to Stratford-on-Avon as motor driver
July	W.J. Howard*	Dulverton, appointed lineman (S&T)
Aug.	K.J.H. Crook	Signalman Filleigh to Swimbridge
	J.F. Baker	Milverton to Exeter (DOSO), Taunton as relief signalman
	R.G. Peacock	Signalman Swimbridge to Churston
Sept.	R.F. Delve	Filleigh to DOSO Exeter as relief signalman
	G.S. Cook	South Molton to Torquay as chief booking clerk
	H.S. Belew	Barnstaple Jct to Milverton as signalman
	R.J. Squire	Hele & Bradninch to Filleigh as signalman
Oct.	D.W. Colwill	Clerk Barnstaple VR to Chilcompton as station master
Nov.	R. Pearce	Barnstaple Jct to Filleigh as signalman

*See recollections Chapter 13
DOSO = District Operating Superintendent's Office

1955

Jan.	F. Ide	Exeter to East Anstey as station master
Feb.	F. McDonough	South Molton passed signalling exams (329/500)
	G.S. Cook	South Molton passed signalling exams (291/500)
Mar.	P.E. Bridgman	Barnstaple VR appointed leading porter signalman Umberleigh
	G. Waldron	Porter Barnstaple VR to Yeoford
April	W.G. Crook	Signalman Swimbridge to Braunton
May	C.M. Sage	Dunball appointed signalman Filleigh
	R.J. Squire	Signalman Filleigh to Sampford Peverell
July	D.J. Dunn	Dulverton passed station accounting (Passenger & Parcels) exams (368/500)
	R.A. Prideaux	Porter Barnstaple VR to Ilfracombe
	F.M. Short	South Molton clerk to Exeter
	D.J. Smale	Barnstaple VR lad porter to Exeter MPD
Aug.	G.H. Burgess	Clerk Barnstaple VR to Mortonhampstead
	M. McManus	Clerk Barnstaple VR to Dulverton
	J.H. Rice	Clerk Dulverton to Exeter goods
Sept.	F. Ide	East Anstey to Exeter Central as clerk
Dec.	T.G. Honeywill	Exeter DOSO to East Anstey as station master

1956

Feb.	T.G. Honeywill	East Anstey to Taunton as inspector (traffic regulator)
April	P. Hazel	Dulverton to Wiveliscombe as leading goods porter
	C. Shute	Signalman Exeter to Barnstaple Jct
	L.J. Norman	Porter Barnstaple VR to Barnstaple Jct
Aug.	J.A. Mehew	South Molton appointed head goods shunter Okehampton
	P.J. Crook	Porter Bideford to Barnstaple VR
Sept.	R.A. Beer	Exam success, lengthman Bishops N&M
	R.B. Coles	Station master East Anstey to Stourbridge Jct as station inspector
	G.H. Alderman	Exeter DOSO to Dulverton as signalman
	R.H. Wilkey	Clerk Barnstaple VR to Slough
	E. Webber	Wiveliscombe appointed district relief porter Exeter DOSO, Taunton
Nov.	C.T.W. Samways	Clerk Taunton to East Anstey as station master
	C.T.W. Samways	East Anstey station master to Somerton
	P.A.J. May	Silverton to Wiveliscombe as signalman

1957

April	R.W.H. Searle	Silverton to Wiveliscombe as signalman
	J.E. Davies	Swimbridge to Sampford Peverell as signalman
	T.J.E. Milum	Clerk Barnstaple VR to Worcester DCMO
	B. McManus	Clerk Dulverton to Barnstaple VR
May	P.J. Collins	Clerk Barnstaple VR to Fremington
June	C.M. German	East Anstey to Burlescombe as signalman
	A.S. Grant	Motor driver Barnstaple VR to supervisory foreman
July	C.H. Horrell	Motor driver Bideford to Barnstaple VR
	J. Norman	Bishops N&M to sub-ganger
Aug.	C. Gillett	Barnstaple VR to Barnstaple Jct as goods guard
Sept.	W.C. Rollins	Exam success, lengthman Bishops N&M
Oct.	M.J.R. Johnstone	Bideford to Barnstaple VR as head shunter goods
	H.E. Tout	Bishops N&M to Taunton as station inspector (rest day relief)
	L.G. Dalling	To ganger at Barnstaple Jct

Dec.	E.M. Richardson	Motor driver Barnstaple VR to Ilfracombe
1958		
Jan.	F.R. Pugh	Chief goods clerk Barnstaple VR to Swindon goods
	P. Wallis	Dulverton signalling exam success (296/500)
	H. Pearce	Filleigh signalling exam success (251/500)
Feb.	E. Webber	Exeter DOSO (Taunton) to Wiveliscombe as signalman
	R.G. Lane	Exeter St. Davids to Bishops N& M as station master
	N.A. Wilkins	Porter Dulverton to Wiveliscombe as motor driver
	S.G. Sully	Motor driver South Molton to Morebath Jct as signalman
Mar.	J.W. Horrell	Porter Barnstaple VR to South Molton as motor driver
Sept.	K.J.H. Crook	Swimbridge to district relief signalman Exeter DOSO (Dulverton)
Oct.	F.R. Barrett	Signalman Filleigh to Swimbridge
Nov.	D.L. Eckhart	Taunton goods to South Molton
Dec.	R.G. Lane	Bishops N&M to Newton Abbot as yard inspector
	S.W. Porter	Station master East Anstey to Grampound Road
	E.J. Stone*	Wiveliscombe to Morebath as porter signalman

*See recollections Chapter 13

1959		
Jan.	S.W. Porter	East Anstey signalling exam success (377/500)
	B.H. Willey	Morebath to Porter signalman
	E.J. Stone*	Morebath to Ilminster as signalman
Feb.	A.V.C. Burnett†	Dunball to Morebath as signalman
	C.H. Drew	Exeter St. Davids to East Anstey as station master
Mar.	P.W. Hutchings	Morebath to Durston as leading porter
April	J.L.A. Swallow	Porter East Anstey to Taunton
May	W.G. Franks	Exeter DOSO (Taunton) to East Anstey as signalman
	B.H. Willey	Morebath to Keinton Mandeville as leading porter signalman
Oct.	R. Pearce	Signalman Filleigh to South Molton
Dec.	M.J. Piper	Newton Abbot to Filleigh as signalman
	R.E. Cole	Station master Swimbridge to Thorverton

*See recollections Chapter 13.

†See Chapter 9 Signalling, Volume 2

1960		
Jan.	R. Pearce	South Molton signalling exam success (322/500)
April	E. Pedley	East Anstey to signalman
	R. Pearce	Signalman South Molton to Starcross
June	S.G. Sully	Bampton/Morebath Jct to South Molton as signalman
	D. Branch	Newton Abbot to East Anstey as signalman
	D.J. Bending*	Dulverton exam success goods station working (326/500)
Sept.	D. Branch	East Anstey to Exeter St. Thomas as signalman
	M.J. Piper	Filleigh to Exeter St. Thomas as signalman
	F.R. Sampson	Swimbridge to Filleigh as signalman
Oct.	M.J. Burgess	To East Anstey as signalman
	W.E. Ackroyd	Wellington to Wiveliscombe as motor driver

*See recollections Chapter 13

Skirting the edges of Exmoor, the line was always subject to the vicissitudes of the weather, as we have seen in this volume. Here at Dulverton in 1964, a shaft of sunlight breaks through the rain clouds as an unknown 'Mogul', wreathed in cluds of steam, starts away for Barnstaple. There is little sign of any other activity in the picture, whilst the nameboard looks bare, shorn of its 'Change for the Exe Valley Line' lettering. ***Hugh Davies***

1961		
Jan.	N.J. Elson	Creech St. Michael to Morebath as signalman
	A. Hutter	Morebath to Dulverton as signalman
	W.G. Mitchell	South Molton promoted to signalman
Feb.	D.S. Eckhart	South Molton signalling exam success (324/500)
April	R.H. Watson	Tiverton Jct to Morebath Jct as signalman
	H.V. Sparkes	Wellington to Wiveliscombe as motor driver
May	E.H. Alderman	Dulverton to Tiverton as signalman
	O.J. Elliott	Filleigh promoted to signalman
June	E.A. Antell	Signalman East Anstey retiring
July	W.G. Hooper	Dulverton promoted to ganger
	F. Hawkins	Wiveliscombe promoted to ganger
Aug.	C.C. Grant	Swimbridge promoted to ganger
Oct.	N.J. Elson	Morebath signalling exam success 376/500
	C.M. German	Durston to Dulverton as signalman
Nov.	C.H. Drew	East Anstey to DTSO Exeter as relief station master
Dec.	R. Wescott	Signalman Bishops N&M retirement (24/9/61)
1962		
Jan.	D.W.A. Nation	Dulverton promotion to motor driver
April	M.J. Burgess	East Anstey to Sampford Peverell as signalman
	S.G. Lee	South Molton promotion to motor driver
May	T. Preston	Checker at Barnstaple retired
	C.M. German	Dulverton to Durston as signalman
June	D.E. Shaddick	Filleigh to South Molton as leading porter
Aug.	A. Timperley	Exeter DSO to Wiveliscombe as signalman
	A.J. Daniels	Morebath Jct to signalman
	J.C. Pearman	Newton Abbot to East Anstey as signalman
	A.L. Chubb	South Molton to Paignton as senior porter
	R.W.H. Searle	Wiveliscombe to Dulverton as signalman
	W.C.R. Webber	Wiveliscombe to Milverton as signalman
Sept.	D.S. Hawkins	Milverton to Wellington as signalman
	R.H. Watson	Morebath Jct to Exeter DSO as relief signalman
Oct.	J.C. Pearman	East Anstey signalling exam success (392/500)
	D. Cockram	South Molton signalling exam success (326/500)
Dec.	T.S. Gait	East Anstey to Filleigh as signalman
1963		
Jan.	G.S. Bennett	Taunton to Venn Cross as signalman
Feb.	A.V.C. Burnett	Signalman Morebath to Dulverton
	M.H.K. Mervin	Taunton to Morebath as signalman
April	F.L. Sampson	Filleigh to Swimbridge as signalman
	S.W. Branfield	Venn Cross to Durston as signalman
	H.V. Sparkes	Wiveliscombe to Wellington as motor driver (parcels)
	H. Wyatt	Wiveliscombe to Wellington as motor driver (goods)
May	R.J. Pearce	Watchet to Wiveliscombe as senior checker
June	G.S.S. Sampson	Barnstaple VR to Yeoford as shunter (goods)
	D.E. Shaddick	South Molton to Filleigh as signalman
	F.R. Barrett	Swimbridge to Stoke Cannon Crossing as signalman

'Bulldog' No. 3377 *Penzance* near Castle Hill, with a Down train that has just cleared the viaduct probably in the late 1920s. Originally No. 3429 when initially allocated to Plymouth depot in May 1903, the engine was to have its nameplates removed in August 1930, so the view is clearly prior to that happening. Its was withdrawn from Worcester shed in March 1951, having travelled 1,343,891 miles. *Arthur Halls, courtesy National Railway Museum*

INDEX
TO ALL THREE VOLUMES

No. 7333 comes off the Barnstaple Branch at Norton Fitzwarren with a three coach train from Barnstaple Junction to Taunton on Saturday 22nd June 1963. Note the Railway Hotel behind the train and the stock stabled in the siding alongside the Minehead Branch. ***Owen Mogg, courtesy Peter Triggs***

BELOW: An overall view of Wiveliscombe on 8th February 1964. In the left foreground is the point for the horse box siding, which was clearly not seeing much use by this date. *Peter W. Gray*

This photograph featured in Volume 2 but was used quite small, so merits re-using here as a suitable endpiece. On 22nd August 1964, an unidentified 'Mogul' heads west between Wiveliscombe and South Molton with the 7.00am service from Taunton to Barnstaple Junction. ***Tim Stephens***

THE
TAUNTON TO BARNSTAPLE LINE
A HISTORY OF THE DEVON & SOMERSET RAILWAY

VOLUME 1:
FROM CONCEPTION TO DEMISE

FREDDIE HUXTABLE

232 pages, gloss art paper
colour laminated board covers
ISBN 9781911038 15 3
Price £25 (+ £4 p&p)

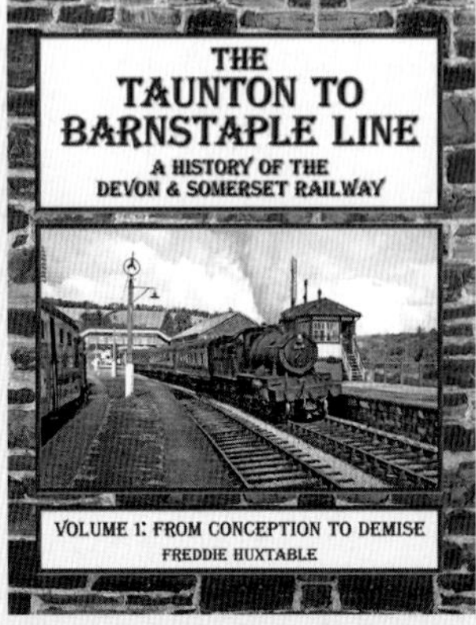

CONTENTS

THE
TAUNTON TO BARNSTAPLE LINE
A HISTORY OF THE DEVON & SOMERSET RAILWAY

VOLUME 2:
THE ROUTE, STATIONS AND SIGNALLING

FREDDIE HUXTABLE

236 pages, gloss art paper
colour laminated board covers
ISBN 9781911038 31 3
Price £25 (+ £4 p&p)

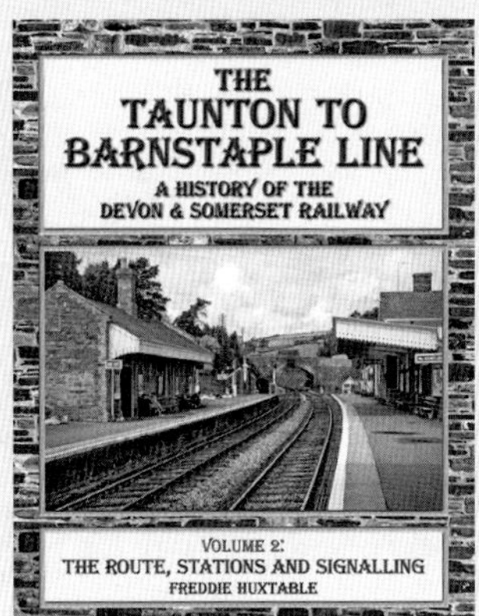

CONTENTS

NTRACT DRAWING N-

DEVON & SOMI

CASTLEHIL

SC

ELEVATION OF FRONT

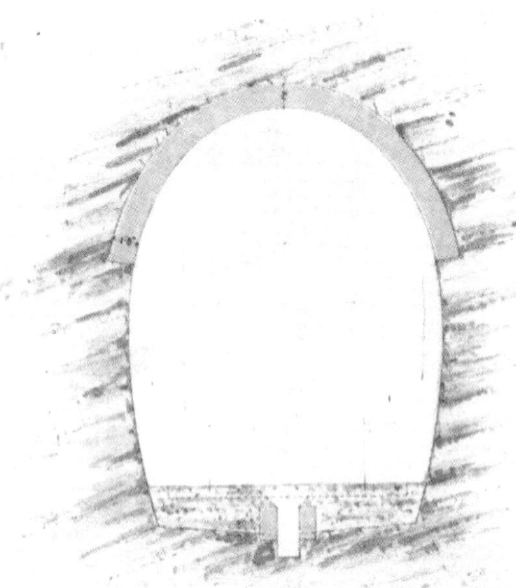

SECTION SHEWING ROOF LINING

LONGITUDINAL SECTION

TO BE RETURN
ENGINEER'S PLA
G.W.R. PADDI

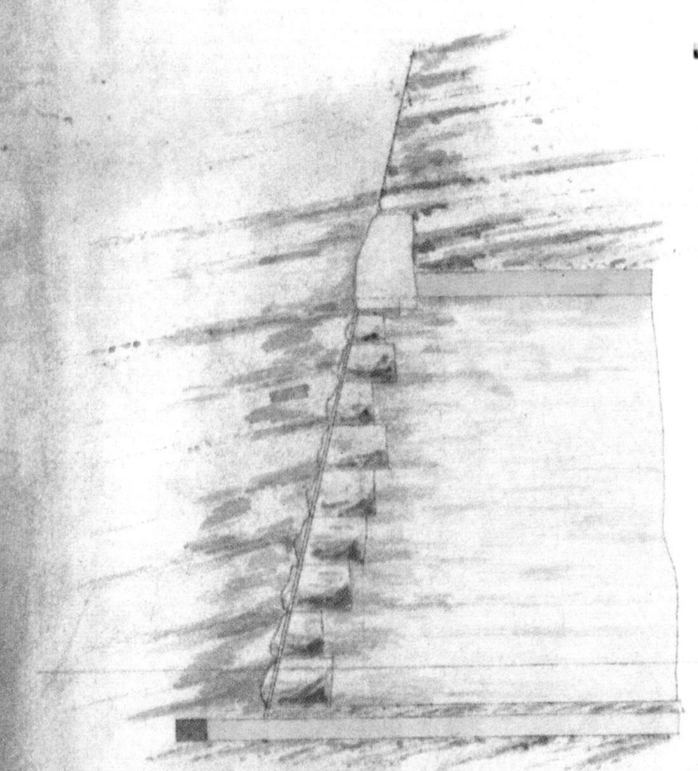

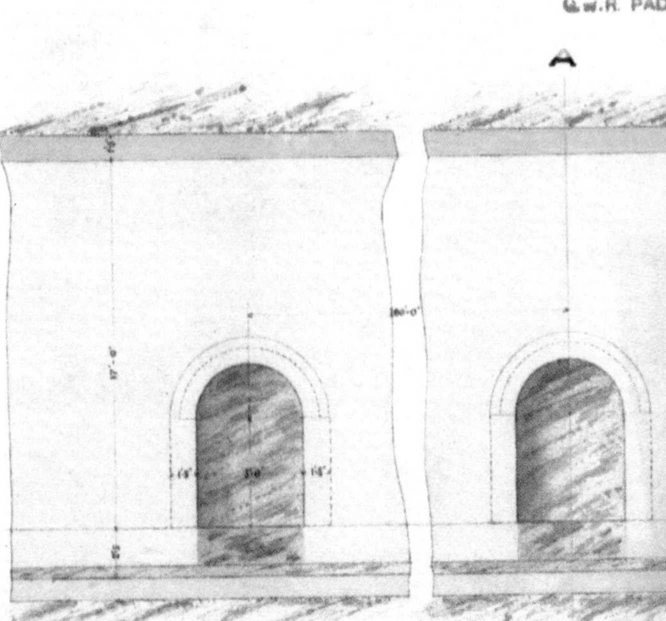

Introduction

This publication is partly a piece of original historical research and in part an opportunity to present hitherto unpublished photographs.

Eastleigh Locomotive Works has played a most important role in the economy of the area since 1910 and this serves as a tribute to the people involved in the construction and rebuilding of 425 locomotives which emerged between 1910 and 1961.

One of the locomotive[illegible] built in 1927, is now back in the confines of the Works undergoing a major overhaul after being rescued by the Eastleigh Railway Preservation Society. Approximately 50p from the sale of each book will be going towards the project and we hope that what follows is an accurate record of what was built at Eastleigh.

Gavin Bowie

The Authors

Eric Forge, who is now in his eighties and living in Beverley, East Yorkshire, was one of the men responsible for the modernisation of the Locomotive Works between 1929 and 1938, began a regrettably short-lived railway museum there in 1937 and has had a lifelong enthusiasm for steam locomotives.

Colin Asprey is the third generation of a railway family in Eastleigh. He is one of the dedicated group of volunteers involved with the restoration of No. 828 and is a draughtsman at the Works.

Gavin Bowie is responsible for social and industrial history at the Hampshire County Museum as well as for co-ordinating a joint Hampshire County Council/Eastleigh Borough Council project to create a museum in Eastleigh.

Contents

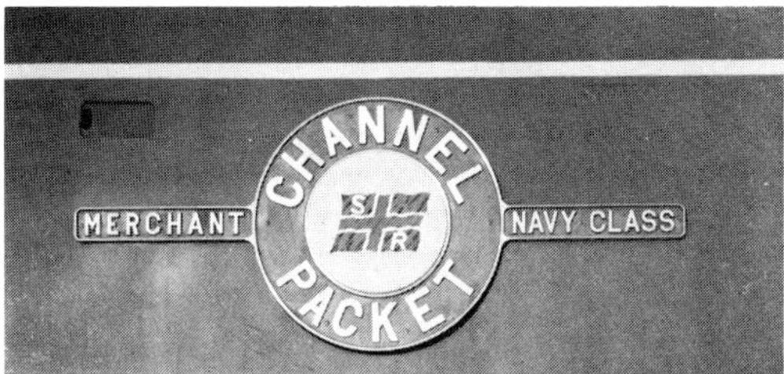

Left-hand side nameplate and centre coupled wheel of No. 21C1 *Channel Packet* built March 1941.

Acknowledgements

This book is based largely on Eric Forge's photographic collection and archives. Additional information and photographs were supplied by Harry Frith, Les Elsey, John Marshall, John Bell, David Parfitt, Richard Drew and other members of the Eastleigh Railway Preservation Society. The original photographs were copied by Trevor Evans of the Hampshire County Museum Service, many of them being taken by Mr. A. Major, photographer at the Works, 1910-1948.

Published by

Kingfisher Railway Productions

188 Bitterne Road, Southampton SO2 4BE
Tel. (0703) 222032

Historical Background

'Eastleie' (sic) is mentioned in the Domesday Book, but this spot of publicity does not seem to have done the place much good as for the next 700 years it made little or no impact on the world at large. Even when postal services were introduced it was known as 'Eastleigh — near Bishopstoke', and the first railway station there bore the name of Bishopstoke, not Eastleigh.

At the end of the 19th century, however, all this was to change.

The London and South Western Railway originally established their engineering headquarters in the Nine Elms district of London, and there they remained for about fifty years, a locomotive works and a carriage works, producing and repairing the locomotives and carriages of the system. Towards the end of the century the old LSWR expanded rapidly and the original works were no longer capable of supplying the service needed. In particular, the Carriage Works, owing to the constricted space between the various shops, could not produce a modern carriage of some 60 feet over the buffers. It seemed to the Directors that the only solution would be to build a completely new works elsewhere on the system, and it was realised that this ought to be nearer 'the centre of gravity' of the railway. It was obviously uneconomic to have a works right at one end of the line involving a great deal of unproductive mileage to bring the rolling stock in for repairs.

No doubt the minute books of the Board of Directors of the time would show the arguments over the new site, but it appears there emerged a short list of two, Andover and Eastleigh. Land was available and relatively cheap in both places, both were about the same distance from each end of the system, but which?

Now the South Western system had been spreading like a fungus over the counties of the south west and west of England, and in the spread Eastleigh had become a focal point for traffic. It was on the direct main line to Southampton and Bournemouth, and at that time, via Eastleigh, the only south west route to Portsmouth. A line connecting Eastleigh to Salisbury gave a valuable link between the south west and west. From Brighton, Portsmouth, Bourne-

Aerial view of Eastleigh Locomotive Works. The Carriage & Wagon Works, which preceded the Locomotive Works from Nine Elms in London by 19 years, may be seen at the top of the picture.

mouth and Southampton, through routes were possible and through trains were run via Eastleigh to all parts of the west and, via the Great Western connection at Basingstoke, to the Midlands and the north of England.

Eastleigh emerged as the obvious choice, and to Eastleigh in 1890, the London and South Western Railway Company moved their entire carriage building operations to a new works erected on the east side of the Southampton main line.

The Carriage Works had not left Nine Elms long before fresh pressure was exerted on the old establishment — this time it was external, arising from the need by the Traffic Department to widen the approach lines to Waterloo. This could only be done by actually pulling down those shops in the Locomotive Works which abutted on the arches bearing the running tracks. So, in 1909, the Locomotive Works started on the same road which their brethren, the Carriage Works, had taken earlier. Now Eastleigh was really on the map. It is worth remembering that Dugald Drummond (of whom more later) had it in mind that he would hold Board Meetings at Eastleigh and thereby wield more influence out of the confines of London!

With the Carriage Works employing some 1500 men and the Locomotive Works engaging another 1100, housing became quite a problem. The Carriage Works problem had been solved by builders erecting a 'grid-iron' of brick-built terraced houses on the three-up and three-down principle, centred on Southampton Road and spreading over the fields to the north and west. Incidentally, it is worth recording that in order to help with the problem of over crowding, most of these houses were provided with an extra cooking range in the middle downstairs room, so two families could share one house without undue inconvenience. This foresight did not extend to the provision of two bathrooms (there was not even one!). The single lavatory was in the backyard and only approachable via the back kitchen. With the setting up of the Locomotive Works, the railway company erected a row of quite good houses on land lying between the Locomotive Works and the Running Shed known as 'Company's Cottages'. These were actually equipped with bathrooms (to keep coals in according to the older residents of the less favoured houses!). The road was known as Campbell Road to the postal authorities, and 'Spike Island' to everyone else.

In 1910 the Carriage Works were under the Carriage and Wagon Superintendent, one Surrey Warner, literally a giant of a man, with A. H. Shepherd as his Works Manager. The design of the stock came under W. H. Beckley. On the other side of the station dwelt the Locomotive Superintendent, the redoutable Dugald Drummond (a Scot), whose Works Manager was Robert Urie (another Scot), and whose engine designs were the responsibility of yet another Scot, James Hunter. It was under Hunter that the South Western produced what may be regarded as their finest design of 4-4-0 wheel arrangement, the 'D15' class.

Eastleigh's steam locomotive building history can hardly be said to have begun spectacularly, as the first locomotives to appear from the new works were two very small engines of the 0-4-0 tank type (class 'S14'). These were a development of earlier Drummond products designed for working with single coaches on the so-called 'Rail Motors'. Like their predecessors, they were not a success and were sold to the War Office.

Then followed the second half of the second batch of Drummond four-cylinder 4-6-0s (class 'P14'). Six had already been built at Nine Elms — they had been failures and their brethren were no better. In spite of being fitted throughout with piston valves they did little or no express work and went to the scrap heap unworked, unhonoured, unsung and unsuperheated!

Undaunted by his early failures Drummond persisted with the four-cylinder arrangement and in 1912 designed another version known affectionately as the 'Paddleboxes' (class 'T14') owing to their enormous splashers over the driving wheels. These locomotives were primarily designed for the less hilly Bournemouth route. Had it not been for the fact that Drummond abandoned the massive boilers of the earlier models in favour of a much smaller steam-raising unit, they might have been very successful. As it was, they had a tendency to run short of steam on the long hauls from London to Basingstoke and the reverse runs from Southampton.

Also from Eastleigh at about this time came another batch of ten suburban and local traffic 0-4-4 tank engines (class 'M7') which were very sound engines of their type. One (No. 126) had the doubtful distinction of receiving an Eastleigh superheater.

Now Eastleigh was to produce Drummond's 'swan song', the 'D15' class, a fine 4-4-0 tender locomotive. Drummond had already brought out a very successful locomotive of this type known as the 'T9' class or 'Greyhounds'. This had been expanded in time to appear as the 'L12', with a bigger boiler and cylinders, but now the final development, the 'D15', was to prove the most brilliant of all his designs. This time he combined an adequate boiler with large cylinders, and inside Walschaerts valve gear driving outside admission piston valves. The result was most satisfactory, as these locomotives proved themselves capable of handling the heaviest trains that the Company put on the Bournemouth run without undue strain. They were Drummond's 'swan song' because his tragic death in 1912 occurred before the batch were all in service.

His death also put a stop to a further four-cylinder project; a 'T14' with smaller diameter wheels was on the drawing board but Urie had no time for his predecessor's unusual four-cylinder designs!

So Drummond did not live long to enjoy his new Works, and Robert Urie took over as Superintendent, with Hunter as his Works Manager. On the design side the responsibility fell to Thomas Finlayson (yet another Scot!). There is no need here to detail all the changes that occurred under Urie as they have all been described many times in the technical press. It can be summed up by saying that everything that Drummond stood for, Urie scrapped. Four cylinders gave way to two, frames and bearings were strengthened, and the combination of steam dryer, feed water heater in the tender, cross water tubes in the firebox, and a duplex feed pump were all consigned to the scrap heap. The result was perhaps the strongest and most reliable locomotive ever to run on British metals, the 'H15'.

It was indeed a tragedy for Urie that the First World War began so soon after his appointment, because it meant a gap of four years in which no new locomotives appeared from Eastleigh. It was not until 1918 that his first real express locomotive, the 'N15' class, was seen. By 1922 his career had terminated, and that time left little scope for any great further innovations in design. Perhaps the original Urie conception was innovative enough, because although his design was the essence of simplicity, its appearance was quite revolutionary by the then modern standards. It was once said that if locomotive designers had given as much care to the design of the cylinders as they did to the splashers, Britain might have had better locomotives. In those days splasher design varied from the sublime to the ridiculous, the latter being epitomised by the Drummond 'Paddleboxes'. Urie had no time for any superfluous decoration on his locomotives, and it was only after a long struggle that he consented to have the stark outline of his stovepipe chimney relieved by a small rim!

With Urie then came a complete change in Eastleigh locomotive production and design. The 'H15' class of mixed traffic locomotives were not glamorous even to the enthusiast, but they were new and to the South Western, revolutionary. At about the same time Urie took Drummond's class 'E14', four-cylinder locomotive No. 335 and gave it what was officially described as a 're-build'. Actually it was nothing of the sort, except for accountancy purposes, as the only parts of the original Drummond locomotive retained were the boiler and the bogiewheel centres. Otherwise it was simply another 'H15'. As hardworking and reliable locomotives, Urie's products soon made their mark. The first 'H15', No. 486, which went into service just before the outbreak of the First World War, did not come back into the Works for a general repair until the war was over!

Machine Shop, looking north from the Boiler Shop end, soon after after the opening of the Works. Points of note are four Erecting Shop bays on extreme right, overhead gantry crane rail, bottom left-hand corner with a component for a class 'P14' locomotive and also extensive use of overhead pulleys and belts to drive the various machine tools.

The 'N15' class of express locomotives were followed by a series of similar ones, the 'S15' class, with 5 feet 7 inch diameter driving wheels for goods work. As these had a lower pitched boiler they gave scope for an even more aggressive stovepipe chimney, and, in spite of their small wheels, they were frequently to be seen in the summer rush traffic hauling express trains.

'Hi-cycle' drilling and tapping for boiler stays. The Boiler Shop, June 1936, chargehand Ken Yeates uppermost, left-hand side.

Pouring molten metal in the Iron Foundry. In the background, *left to right* are W. Lewis, ?, Henry Clift, Geordie? and Ted Ansell, and in the foreground, *left to right* are Charlie Smith and Works Manager E. A. Turbett. c. 1946-48.

Assembling a cylinder mould in the Iron Foundry. *Left to right*, Ted Ansell, Henry Clift and W. Lewis. c. 1946-48.

Urie was responsible for two more outstanding designs. A new hump shunting yard had been laid down at Feltham and a new locomotive was required to heave the long goods trains over the humps for sorting. For this purpose Eastleigh produced four large 4-8-0 tank engines ('G16' class) made largely out of standard parts and with large, 22 inch diameter cylinders giving them a very high tractive effort. Alongside these were produced five similar tank engines ('H16' class), but with a 4-6-2 wheel arrangement; these were intended for working transfer trips between Feltham and the corresponding yards of other railway company lines in the London area. It is an interesting point that whereas the 8-coupled tank engines were painted in the LSWR standard dark green for goods locomotives, their brothers of the 6-coupled variety were given a passenger finish, although for many years the only passenger duties they performed were on the special trains for Ascot Races.

Eastleigh was well in the forefront in the application and development of the superheater. Urie, after making trials with the Robinson and Schmidt designs on his 'H15' class during 1914, finally produced the 'Eastleigh' pattern and fitted it on all his larger locomotives as well as on a number of Drummond rebuilds. It was a dreadful piece of work (ask any fitter who had to work on one) and, soon after the grouping in 1923, was replaced by the simpler and more efficient Maunsell design.

As the senior of the three Mechanical Engineers at the time of grouping, Urie was offered the post of Chief Mechanical Engineer of the newly formed Southern group, but at the time he was 68 years old and decided to decline the offer and make way for a younger man.

R. E. L. Maunsell from Ashford took over and the Scottish dynasty (Beattie-Adams-Drummond-Urie) was replaced by an Irish one! In the old days it was said that an in-coming Chief Mechanical Engineer always designed his first engine as completely different from those of his predecessor as possible in order to make his presence felt, but Maunsell did the opposite. His engineering instinct told him that the basic Urie design was sound in every respect, and, with some modifications to bring it into line with modern developments, he adopted it. Maunsell faced a difficult social problem when he took over the Southern. The South Western was the biggest system with the newest Works. They rightly thought a lot of themselves compared with their humbler neighbours, and could be forgiven for wondering why they should have inflicted on them a Chief from a third rate line like the South Eastern! They were to learn better! The Brighton people had no opinions, or if they had, they were not expressed!

Maunsell quickly established himself. He produced a modified class 'N15' express passenger locomotive into which he incorporated his own design of superheater. Other batches (746-755; 448-457; 793-806) soon followed the first ten (736-745). All the N15s, whether built by Urie or Maunsell, were later named and known as the 'King Arthur' class. The 'King Arthurs' followed a steady pattern with but few modifications. Tail rods were fitted to some, but abandoned (Urie had done the same), a crosshead pump for vacuum maintenance was fitted for a time, but later abandoned, and tenders varied.

In August, 1926, in the middle of the work on the 'N15' class, a four-cylinder locomotive, the pioneer *Lord Nelson*, was produced. The fifteen 'Nelsons' which followed were a mixed class. They embodied the unusual feature of a 135 degree crank setting, giving eight exhaust impulses per revolution. This idea had been tried before on the North Staffordshire Railway but not followed up. Although good locomotives, it was always felt that they should do better, so one was fitted with smaller wheels (No. 859), one had a larger boiler with a combustion chamber on the lines of the Great Northern Pacifics (No. 857), one had an extended boiler (No. 860), and one had its crank converted to the normal 90 degree setting (No. 865). Later they were to have redesigned front ends and Lemaitre blastpipes, but by the time that happened they were no longer 'top link' locomotives and had no real chance to show whether any real improvement had been obtained. The basic task for which this locomotive had been designed was the formidable one of coping with the ever increasing loads of the Dover boat trains. In themselves the loads of these trains were not unduly excessive, the northern lines handled much heavier sets, nor was the speed asked for out of this world. The difficulty lay in the nature of the route between Victoria and Dover, starting with a complicated exit through the south London suburbs, inhibiting any fast running for a start, followed by the need to cope with the ups and downs of the Kentish North and South Downs. It is interesting to conjecture whether if the Dover route had been as kind as the route to Bournemouth, a 'Nelson' would have been required at all.

By now the Southern locomotives were showing signs of very mixed parentage. Maunsell's technical staff had been drawn from various sources — James Clayton, his personal assistant, came from Derby (hence the cab design), Pearson and Holcroft from Swindon (top feed, regulator in the smokebox, and taper boiler), and Tom Finlayson, the Chief Draughtsman and a dour Scot, was still at Eastleigh to preserve the South Western influence, and to restrain what Maunsell himself once described as his 'Celtic impetuosity'. It was a great team which produced some great locomotives.

Our review now leads us on a few years from the grouping. At Eastleigh, Hunter had retired from the position of Works Manager; he had stayed on for a time but was always a draughtsman at heart and never very happy under his rather impatient new chief. His place was taken by Eyre Turbett, another Irishman! Turbett's impact on Eastleigh was prodigious and a book could be written about what happened to the Works from 1929 onwards. He had worked with Maunsell previously at Richborough when the latter was Chief Mechanical Engineer to the whole of the British Railways during the First World War, and later had acquired much engineering experience world wide. He came to Eastleigh not so much as a breath of fresh air, but rather as a typhoon!

Eastleigh Locomotive Works had for some years rested on its laurels, as it were. When the Works moved from London the Directors made it clear that there would be little money available for new plant, and they would have to make do with what machinery they already had. In one way this was no bad thing. It made the high standard of hand fitting, for which Eastleigh was pre-eminent, even more necessary than it might otherwise have been, but it was undoubtedly tedious, time consuming, and thereby uneconomic under modern conditions. Turbett altered this without lowering any standards. Many old restrictive practices flew out of the door as fast as new plant flew in! The major improvement he brought about was the installation in the Iron Foundry of a first ever (in railway service) continuous casting plant. This plant, made in France, sent out repetitive casting, such as brake blocks, electrical pickup shoes, and wagon and carriage axleboxes, to the Fettling Shop in hitherto unheard of quantities. Much new machinery was installed in the Machine Shop and the Brass Finishing Shop, and a new technique of 'hi-cycle' drilling and tapping was introduced to the Boiler Shop. The chemical laboratory was transferred from Ashford. Many other modern techniques, such as flux testing for flaws (with the accompanying welding under strict supervision), saved the company many thousands of pounds in the recovery of expensive components that would otherwise have been scrapped.

Between 1929 and 1939 Eastleigh reached a peak of efficiency and performance. A steady stream of new locomotives emerged from the Erecting Shop, and the schedule for a complete general repair was reduced to 18 days for a 4-coupled locomotive and 21 days for a 6-coupled locomotive without any lavish expenditure on flow systems as were alleged to have been practiced in other works such as Crewe. At the same time detailed work processes were brought under critical review. In this respect Ashford had undoubtedly been ahead of Eastleigh ever since Maunsell's arrival at the former works, but in 1929 one of the draughtsmen from the Ashford Process Office was transferred to Eastleigh to set up a similar establishment there. As a result of this an elaborate programme of jigging and tooling was implemented to obtain the maximum advantage from the new plant.

Whilst at Ashford, Maunsell had experimented successfully with three-cylinder arrangements, producing the 'N' and 'U' class 2-6-0 locomotives. He was apparently sufficiently satisfied with this arrangement to adopt it for his next express locomotive which took the form of a large 4-4-0. Thus was born the 'V', or 'Schools' class and the Eastleigh stable found it had produced yet another thoroughbred winner. Forty were built at Eastleigh between 1930 and 1935. They were undoubtedly the great success of the era as they went everywhere and did everything well. Twenty were later fitted with Lemaitre exhaust and large diameter chimneys by Bulleid.

Finally came the 'Q' Class. The most modern 0-6-0 that the system possessed for working medium goods trains dated back to 1899 and it was felt that something more modern was now needed. The result was an unexciting looking engine (it is difficult to make an 0-6-0 look exciting), but it was a powerful machine of substantial dimensions with the unusual arrangement of outside admission piston valves and inside cylinders and motion.

At length, in 1937, came the unwelcome news that Maunsell was to retire. He had been in bad health for some years and had undergone at least one serious operation, and to everyone's sincere regret, he went. Maunsell had come to Eastleigh very much a stranger and somewhat under suspicion — one could almost hear the old die-hards saying 'can any good thing come out of Ashford?' But it was not long before he lived that down. Essentially a fair man himself, he dealt with his men fairly, and they responded. They came to realise that any case of injustice that was brought to his notice would be quickly sorted out. He ended his career as popular at Eastleigh as he was in his 'home' works. Naturally, speculation as to his successor was rife. Many at Eastleigh hoped that Turbett would get the job — he seemed to most people the natural choice — but for some reason he was passed over. The choice of the Directors fell upon O. V. S. Bulleid, the Carriage and Wagon Superintendent of the London and North Eastern Railway, and protégé of Sir Nigel Gresley, the Chief Mechanical Engineer of the same company.

The good people of Eastleigh who thought they had seen some innovations were soon to experience new surprises. It started in the Carriage Works with a batch of Buffet Cars which appeared after a prolonged and painful gestation with thick pile carpets on the floor and silk tapestry upholstery on the chairs. It was perhaps unfortunate that the first of these cars were allocated to the Portsmouth line and were rostered on the last trains taking sailors back to 'Pompey' after a night in London! It was not long before the cars had to be refurbished in a less exotic style. These were followed by some 'Tavern Cars' where customers found compensation for the complete lack of windows in the provision of a lavish 'pub' sign on the outside.

Bulleid was an enthusiastic supporter of steam and indeed was said to have set back the progress of electrification on the Southern Railway by at least 20 years. He wanted to create a new image for steam propulsion and, that he managed to produce a brand new Pacific design during the dark years of 1940 and 1941, was a remarkable achievement. The 'Merchant Navy' class had their real fill of innovations and were radically different from normal Southern Railway practice. Bulleid's own design of chain driven valve gear enclosed in an oil bath, high 280p.s.i. boiler pressure, all-steel welded fireboxes with Nicholson thermic syphons, fancy Bulleid-Firth-Brown Boxpok cast wheels, and electric lighting provided by a steam turbine, were a few of the avant garde features, the whole being covered with what was then termed an 'air-smoothed' slab-sided, sheet metal casing.

There were a number of teething problems with such an original and unusual design, particularly the unusual valve gear which was designed to reduce maintenance compared with orthodox ones, but was actually more troublesome and expensive. Most of the engine crews regarded the 'Merchant Navys' as free steaming locomotives, if less reliable than might have been hoped. They were certainly extremely powerful, with a capacity to handle anything that was hitched behind them, but were heavy on coal, and were something of a fitter's nightmare. These large Pacifics were irreverently known in some circles as 'Flannel Jackets'. They were followed by a smaller and lighter counterpart named after Battle of Britain aircraft, squadrons and personalities and West Country towns. Eastleigh built the 'Merchant Navy' series (21C1-10; 21C11-20; 35021-30), and

The naming ceremony of No. 21C1 *Channel Packet* in the Works Yard, 10th March 1941 by Lt. Col. T. Moore-Brabazon, later Lord Brabazon. Note the Tin Hats and Gas Masks carried by some men, the Dining Hall in the background and the Time Office on the right of the photograph.

six of the 'West Country' class. The others were turned out by the revitalised Brighton Works.

Just as the building of the 'Merchant Navy' class was a remarkable achievement in one way, so the rebuilding of the class was in another. It was remarkable that so complete a rebuild of an entire class should have been undertaken between 1956 and 1959, the declining years of steam on British Railways. It became an orthodox locomotive produced by R. G. Jarvis who led the British Railways design team at Brighton. The air-smoothed casing was removed, the enclosed valve gear was replaced by three sets of conventional Walschaerts gear, most of Bulleid's avant garde features were discarded and other features added which gave the class a family likeness to the B.R. 'Brittania' Pacifics. The rebuilt 'Merchant Navys' proved to be both outstanding and economical performers, much beloved by the maintenance men. Sixty of the 'West Country' and 'Battle of Britain' class were rebuilt in a similar way at Eastleigh between 1957 and 1961, the last being 'West Country' class No. 34104 *Bere Alston* which was outshopped in May 1961.

Two other Bulleid designs should be mentioned, as Eastleigh Works provided some parts for them, though the locomotives were erected elsewhere. Hence Eastleigh provided the motion works and some of the boilers for Bulleid's 'Q1' class 0-6-0 goods engines built at Ashford and Brighton in 1942. The Works also built the motion work, brake gear, boilers, and other parts for the novel and controversial 'Leader' class between 1948 and 1950. On these, the locomotive and tender were mounted on two six-wheeled bogies with a driver's cab at each end. Each bogie had a 3-cylinder arrangement with sleeve valves. The boiler had a conventional barrel, but an arrangement of four thermic syphons in the firebox made it possible to dispense almost entirely with boiler stays. The construction of five locomotives started at Brighton in 1949, but only one, No. 36001, actually entered trial service. The trials were based at Eastleigh during the summer of 1950. So many major flaws were apparent in the design, that the project was abandoned at the end of the year, and the locomotive was dismantled at Eastleigh in 1951.

The glamour of a locomotive works such as Eastleigh is usually measured by the shiny, new, and exciting locomotives they produce, but that was a small part of their total activity. By far the greater percentage of their effort lay in the continuous repair and rebuilding of existing types which usually returned to their place of birth every 75,000 miles or 18 months. A 'general', as it was called, was a most comprehensive repair. The locomotive was lifted off its wheels which went away to the wheel shop, the boiler was lifted and went to the boiler shop, and all detail such as valves, motion links, connecting rods and similar parts went to the fitting shop until what was left of the locomotive lay on jacks, stripped to its bare frames. Eventually all these parts returned refurbished and were duly re-assembled. For the whole of this process, a time of 21 days was allowed. As there were always some twenty or thirty locomotives in at any one time, it can be seen how much of the Works' time was absorbed in this very necessary work.

In addition to repairs, there were nearly always cases of rebuilding and modification going on. Amongst the principle rebuilds were the old Drummond four-cylinder jobs which were completely rebuilt as described earlier, the conversion of seven out of the twenty 'River' 'K' class tank engines to tender engines during 1928, and, similarly, the seven L.B. & S.C.R. Baltic 'L' class tanks which were converted to the 'N15X' class between the end of 1934 and spring of 1936.

In the 1930s much work, and a good deal of amusement, was generated by the experiments undertaken to counteract the down draught of exhaust steam over the driver's cab. This was a real menace, and came about largely because of the greater efficiency of steam in the cylinders which led to the exhaust steam emerging at a much lower pressure than formerly. Unfortunately the problem was tackled at the wrong end first. Many experiments had as their object the forcing upwards of the exhaust steam which took the form of peculiar shovel-like attachments to the chimney both fore and aft. These had no effect whatever on the exhaust. They also tried fitting a blower ring around the top of the chimney of the same pattern as that used on the blastpipe to boost the fire. This one was very amusing as the engine could be seen spouting live steam from the ring into the high heavens with the exhaust flowing past the jets as if they were not there! Ultimately the solution came from Germany. A vacuum was being formed under the boiler by the spreading of the air displaced by the smokebox in the passage along the track. This was actually sucking the steam down. A pair of side sheets, now known as smoke deflectors, prevented this spread and the exhaust steam was then free to rise as it was meant to do. The problem was solved. All locomotives with short chimneys were fitted with a modification of the German device as they passed through the Works.

In the course of one of his earlier visits to Eastleigh, Maunsell made the statement that he was so impressed with the standard of workmanship that he wanted to see as many as possible of his new locomotives built there. This objective he saw fulfilled. Apart from the thirty 'N15' class built by North British Locomotive Company in 1925, no new locomotives were henceforth ordered from outside contractors.

Those 'N15s' were built elsewhere because the Southern Railway had been more heavily used during the First World War and received less maintenance than any other railway. A backlog arose and the Works could not clear it in a reasonable time. A decision, actually detrimental to Eastleigh, to put the locomotive building out to contract was taken. From long experience a skilled locomotive fitter learnt to know exactly how to 'bed' in an axlebox to suit a particular type of locomotive, the same applied to nearly all fitting jobs. The outside locomotive contractors had none of Eastleigh's expertise on the 'N15' class, it was just another job to them and, because they were working against a price, short cuts were taken. In some cases the axleboxes of the North British 'N15s', the 'Scotch Arthurs', did not stand up to being hauled dead from Scotland and had to put into Crewe to be re-metalled. In the case of later locomotives, the first thing Eastleigh did on receipt of them was to lift them and re-line the boxes. Much of the boiler work was also below the standard normally required.

The years 1961-67 saw an upheaval in the pattern of work at Eastleigh Locomotive Works. Nationwide, a programme of rationalisation of British Railways workshops took place with some famous works such as Darlington (the 'birthplace' of the steam locomotive) disappearing, and other large works, such as Swindon, losing their carriage works. Eastleigh was no exception, for in 1967 the Carriage Works was closed down and transferred to the Locomotive Works. By this time the Locomotive Works had been reduced to one half-bay in the 4-bay Erecting Shop. The decline in steam locomotive work was due to two factors — the hasty implementation of the 1955 Modernisation Plan, which foresaw the end of steam by 1967 and, to a lesser extent, the effect of the 1962 Beeching Plan which axed feeder branch lines and made many small engines redundant. Work began on the provision of a diesel repair shop in 1958 and was completed in June 1959.

On the steam side, repairs of familiar classes as well as most of the British Rail standard range, continued in the early 1960s. Unfamiliar locomotives came from Ashford, which had changed over to wagon building, and, as Swindon stopped repairing steam locomotives, Western Region 0-6-0 pannier tanks came to Eastleigh for repair. Locomotives also came from Brighton, which had closed in 1957, and 8F 2-8-0 goods engines and 2P tanks arrived from the London Midland Region. There were various restoration jobs — some were put into full working order and others were merely given a 'cosmetic' job. Locomotive scrapping started in earnest. Finally, on the 3rd of October, 1966, rebuilt 'Battle of Britain' class No. 34089, *602 Squadron* was outshopped as officially the last steam locomotive repaired at Eastleigh Locomotive Works. It was seen off by Valerie Singleton of the television programme 'Blue Peter'. Now somewhere in the BBC archives there is another piece of Eastleigh's history!

The completion of electrification through to Bournemouth meant the end of steam working out of Eastleigh. On Saturday, the 9th of July, 1967, locomotives steamed out of the Running Shed for Salisbury and thence to either Woodham Brothers Yard at Barry, where some gained a reprieve, or to Cashmore's at Newport where they did not! The last batch included 'West Country' No. 34104 *Bere Alston* which was not only the last steam locomotive to be built at Eastleigh (April, 1950), but also the last to be rebuilt (May, 1961) — this is supposed to be just a coincidence, but will we ever really know for sure?

When this photograph was taken, in May 1961, it was the occasion of the last rebuild of a Bulleid pacific 'West Country' class 4-6-0, in this case No. 34104 *Bere Alston. Left to Right, Back Row:* H. Frith, ?, J. Miller, H. Riley, A. Bintcliffe, H. Pendry, R. Lewis, C. Matthews, A. West, G. Watts, A. Folland, C. Sharpe, G. Giles, J. Bentley, F. Ryan, E. Martin, G. Robey, E. Thorne, L. Bishop, T. Wood, G. Fenn, A. Graham, L. Griffen, A. Clare, G. Barrett, L. Smith, C. Spicer, R. Cramer, H. Fletcher and F. Riley. *Front Row:* G. Woodman, G. King, F. Janaway, R. Heal, S. Stone, ?, F. Service, R. Bolton, D. Dyson, L. Beasley, E. Harvey, I. Weekes, F. Hutchinson and L. Legg.

List of Steam Locomotives Built or Rebuilt at Eastleigh, 1910-1961

Locomotive Number LSWR SR	British Rail	Building Date	Withdrawal Date	Notes
DRUMMOND CLASS 'S14', 0-4-0T				
101		Sept. 1910	May 1917	Sold to War Office
147		Sept. 1910	May 1917	Sold to War Office
DRUMMOND CLASS 'P14', 4-6-0				
448		Dec. 1910	Jan. 1925	
449		Dec. 1910	Oct. 1927	ES Converted to 135 degree cranks
450		Jan. 1911	Jan. 1925	
451		Feb. 1911	Jan. 1925	
452		Feb. 1911	Jan. 1925	

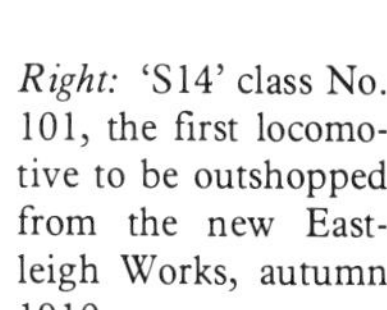

Right: 'S14' class No. 101, the first locomotive to be outshopped from the new Eastleigh Works, autumn 1910.

Below: Another fine example of a Drummond locomotive — No. 449 as rebuilt by Urie with Eastleigh superheater and 135 deg. crank settings, c. 1919.

Locomotive Number LSWR SR	British Rail	Building Date	Withdrawal Date	Notes
DRUMMOND CLASS 'T14', 4-6-0 —		Popularly known as 'Paddleboxes' because of their enormous splashers; 4 cylinders with 15in. diameter/26in. stroke; Walschaerts valve gear; driving wheels 6ft. 7in. diameter; ten in class.		
443	30443	Apr. 1911	May 1949	ES Dec. 1915; MS Oct. 1929; rebuilt July 1931
444	30444	May 1911	Feb. 1950	ES July 1917; MS Mar. 1931; rebuilt Mar. 1931
445	30445	June 1911	Nov. 1948	ES Jan. 1915; MS Mar. 1931; rebuilt Mar. 1931
446	30446	July 1911	Apr. 1951	ES Nov. 1915; MS Oct. 1929; rebuilt Aug. 1931
447	30447	July 1911	Dec. 1949	ES Mar. 1917; MS Sept. 1930; rebuilt Sept. 1930

The very unusual lines of Mr Drummond's 'T14' class, nicknamed the 'Paddleboxes', are very visible in this view of No. 443 in April 1911.
Cyril Saunders Collection

DRUMMOND CLASS 'M7', 0-4-0T				
125	30125	Aug. 1911	Dec. 1962	
126		Sept. 1911	May 1937	ES
127	30127	Oct. 1911	Nov. 1963	
128	30128	Nov. 1911	Jan. 1961	
129	30129	Nov. 1911	Nov. 1963	
131	30131	Nov. 1911	Nov. 1962	
328	30328	Nov. 1911	Mar. 1963	
479	30479	Nov. 1911	Apr. 1961	
480	30480	Nov. 1911	May 1964	
481	30481	Nov. 1911	May 1959	
DRUMMOND CLASS 'T14', 4-6-0 (cont.)				
458		Jan. 1912	Oct. 1940	ES Sept. 1915; MS Nov. 1930; rebuilt Jan. 1931; destroyed in Blitz, Nine Elms
459		June 1912	Nov. 1948	ES May, 1917; MS Jan. 1931; rebuilt Jan. 1931
460	30460	Feb. 1912	Nov. 1948	ES Sept. 1916; MS Apr. 1930; rebuilt Apr. 1930
461	30461	Apr. 1912	June 1951	ES Mar. 1918; MS June 1931; rebuilt June 1931
462	30462	May 1912	Feb. 1950	ES Dec. 1917; MS Aug. 1930; rebuilt Aug. 1930

Drummond class 'T14' No. 461 as rebuilt by Urie with 'all over' splasher, c. 1918.

In B.R. livery and fitted for 'push-pull' working, and standing at Eastleigh shed on 4th October 1952, is 'M7' class 0-4-4 No. 30128. *L. Elsey*

Looking very elegant outside the Eastleigh No. 1 Bay Erecting Shop, is 'D15' class No. 465. Note the fairing around the smokebox and LSWR coat of arms on the splasher which are clearly visible. The locomotive is seen here as outshopped in 1912.

Locomotive Number LSWR SR	British Rail	Building Date	Withdrawal Date	Notes
DRUMMOND CLASS 'D15', 4-4-0				
463	30463	Apr. 1912	Dec. 1951	ES Oct. 1916; MS Feb. 1926
464	30464	May 1912	Sept. 1954	ES May 1915; MS Apr. 1926
465	30465	July 1912	Jan. 1956	ES Oct. 1915; MS Sept. 1926
466	30466	July 1912	Aug. 1952	ES Mar. 1916; MS Feb. 1926

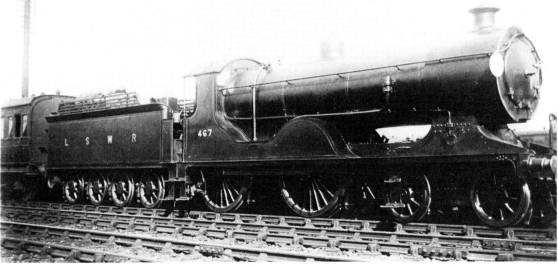

Totally different from its earlier built sister, No. 467 poses at Eastleigh station in 1917.

Locomotive Number LSWR SR	Locomotive Number British Rail	Building Date	Withdrawal Date	Notes

DRUMMOND CLASS 'D15' — Drummond design, built under Urie.

LSWR SR	British Rail	Building Date	Withdrawal Date	Notes
467	30467	Aug. 1912	Sept. 1955	ES Apr. 1917; MS Aug. 1925
468	30468	Sept. 1912	Jan. 1952	ES July 1916; MS Feb. 1926
469	30469	Oct. 1912	Dec. 1951	ES Dec. 1916; MS Dec. 1925
470	30470	Nov. 1912	Dec. 1952	ES June 1917; MS Aug. 1925; Oil fired in 1921 and 1926
471	30471	Dec. 1912	Feb. 1954	ES Sept. 1917; MS May 1926
472	30472	Jan. 1913	Jan. 1952	ES Feb. 1916; MS June 1926

Some thirty-five years later we see 'D15' class No. 30467, now in B.R. livery, at the back of Eastleigh shed on 6th September 1952.

L. Elsey

URIE CLASS 'H15', 4-6-0 — Mixed traffic; 2 cylinders of 21in. diameter/28in. stroke; Walschaerts valve gear; driving wheels 6ft. diameter, twenty six in class including rebuilds; boiler interchangeable with S15.

LSWR SR	British Rail	Building Date	Withdrawal Date	Notes
486	30486	Jan. 1914	June 1959	RS Jan. 1914; MS Mar. 1930
487	30487	Feb. 1914	Nov. 1957	ES Feb. 1914; MS May 1929
482	30482	Mar. 1914	May 1959	SS Mar. 1914; MS Oct. 1934
483	30483	Apr. 1914	June 1957	SS Apr. 1914; MS Sept. 1929
488	30488	Apr. 1914	Apr. 1959	RS Apr. 1914; MS Mar. 1928
484	30484	May 1914	May 1959	SS May 1914; MS Jan. 1931
489	30489	June 1914	Jan. 1961	RS June 1914; MS Mar. 1932
485	30485	June 1914	Apr. 1955	SS June 1914; MS July 1928
490	30490	July 1914	June 1955	ES Dec. 1919; MS May 1929
491	30491	July 1914	Jan. 1961	ES Oct. 1917; MS June 1927; taper boiler fitted June 1929
335	30335	Jan. 1915	June 1959	MS Dec. 1929; rebuilt from Drummond 'E14' class

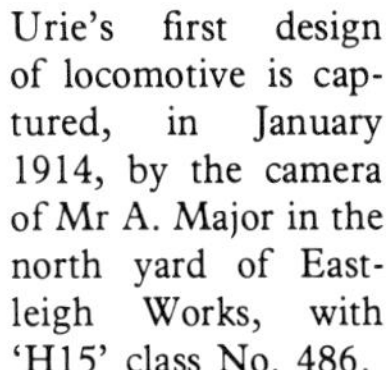
Urie's first design of locomotive is captured, in January 1914, by the camera of Mr A. Major in the north yard of Eastleigh Works, with 'H15' class No. 486.

Urie 'H15' No. 335 rebuilt from the solitary Drummond 'E14' class. This view was taken during the winter of 1914-15.

Left: Urie 'H15' class No. E488 showing large smokebox and small, 'squat', chimney. About this time, after the grouping in 1923, the locomotive number was carried on the tender (a practice continued until 1938-39) and prefix 'E' added for Eastleigh built locomotives. To facilitate the interchangeability of tenders, numbers once again reverted to the cabside. Photograph c. 1935.

Opposite page top: The first Urie 'N15' class No. 736, as completed in September 1918. This express passenger class was known as the 'King Arthur' class and No. 736 was later named *Excalibur* when John Elliott was appointed Public Relations Officer of the Southern Railway by Herbert Walker (later Sir Herbert Walker).

Opposite page bottom: A 'King Arthur' No. 737 with an oil tank in the tender and adapted for oil firing in 1921.

Locomotive Number LSWR SR	British Rail	Building Date	Withdrawal Date	Notes
URIE CLASS 'N15', 4-6-0 — Express passenger; commonly known as the 'King Arthur' class; 2 cylinders of 20.5in. diameter/28in. stroke; driving wheels 6ft. 7in., seventy four in class; taper boiler; other parts exchangeable with the 'H15'.				
736	30736	Sept. 1918	Nov. 1956	*Excalibur*; MS Sept. 1930; 21in. diameter cylinder, Sept. 1928, Lemaitre exhaust, large diameter chimney
737	30737	Oct. 1918	June 1956	*King Uther*; MS June 1929; 21in. diameter cylinder, June 1928; oil fired 1921 and 1926, Lemaitre exhaust, large diameter chimney
738	30738	Dec. 1918	Mar. 1958	*King Pellinore*; MS Mar. 1930; 21in. diameter cylinder, Mar. 1930
739	30739	Feb. 1919	May 1957	*King Leodegrance*; MS Apr. 1930; 21in. diameter cylinder, Oct. 1928; oil fired 1921 and 1926
740	30740	Apr. 1919	Dec. 1955	*Merlin*; MS Dec. 1929; 21in. diameter cylinder, Nov. 1925
741	30741	May 1919	Feb. 1956	*Joyous Gard*; MS Feb. 1929; 21in. diameter cylinder, Feb. 1925, Lemaitre exhaust, large diameter chimney
742	30742	June 1919	Feb. 1957	*Camelot*; MS Aug. 1930; 21in. diameter cylinder, June 1930
743	30743	Aug. 1919	Oct. 1955	*Lyonnesse*; MS May 1930; 21in. diameter cylinder, June 1930
744	30744	Sept. 1919	Jan. 1956	*Maid of Astolat*; MS Jan. 1930; 21in. diameter cylinder, Oct. 1928
745	30745	Nov. 1919	Feb. 1956	*Tintagel*; MS -/1931; 21in. diameter cylinder, May 1930

Locomotive Number LSWR SR	British Rail	Building Date	Withdrawal Date	Notes
URIE CLASS 'S15', 4-6-0 — Goods locomotive, 2 cylinders of 21in. diameter/28in. stroke; driving wheels 5ft. 7in.; forty five in class including Maunsell variety; boiler interchangeable with the 'H15'.				
497	30497	Mar. 1920	July 1963	MS Feb. 1928
498	30498	Apr. 1920	June 1963	MS Feb. 1930
499	30499	May 1920	Jan. 1964	MS June 1931
500	30500	May 1920	June 1963	MS Oct. 1930
501	30501	June 1920	June 1963	MS Aug. 1931
502	30502	July 1920	Dec. 1962	MS May 1930
503	30503	Aug. 1920	June 1963	MS May 1931
504	30504	Sept.1920	Nov. 1962	MS Jan. 1929
505	30505	Oct. 1920	Nov. 1962	MS Dec. 1931
506	30506	Oct. 1920	Jan. 1964	MS Feb. 1930
507	30507	Nov. 1920	Dec. 1963	MS Jan. 1932
508	30508	Dec. 1920	Nov. 1963	MS Aug. 1929
509	30509	Dec. 1920	July 1963	MS Apr. 1929
510	30510	Jan. 1921	June 1963	MS Feb. 1931
511	30511	Jan. 1921	July 1963	MS Nov. 1930
512	30512	Feb. 1921	Mar. 1964	MS Aug. 1931
513	30513	Mar. 1921	Mar. 1963	MS May 1930
514	30514	Mar. 1921	July 1963	MS May 1931
515	30515	Apr. 1921	July 1963	MS Sept. 1931; Oil fired 1921 and 1926
496	30496	May 1921	Jan. 1963	MS Sept. 1927

As built in 1920 we find Urie 'S15' No. 498 with stovepipe chimney, later replaced by Maunsell's version, and with raised section at the front of the running plate.

A shunting engine of the 'G16' class 4-8-0T No. 492 as completed in July 1921.

Locomotive Number LSWR SR	British Rail	Building Date	Withdrawal Date	Notes
URIE CLASS 'G16', 4-8-0T				
492	30492	July 1921	Jan. 1959	MS May 1930
493	30493	July 1921	Nov. 1959	MS July 1931
494	30494	Aug. 1921	Dec. 1962	MS Dec. 1929
495	30495	Aug. 1921	Dec. 1962	MS Mar. 1930
URIE CLASS 'H16', 4-6-2T				
516	30516	Nov. 1921	Nov. 1962	MS Aug. 1929
517	30517	Nov. 1921	Dec. 1962	MS May 1929
518	30518	Dec. 1921	Nov. 1962	MS Mar. 1929
519	30519	Jan. 1922	Nov. 1962	MS Dec. 1928
520	30520	Feb. 1922	Nov. 1962	MS Dec. 1929

Catching the camera, and proud to be part of the photograph, are these two men on their 'H16' class No. 519 as completed in January 1922.

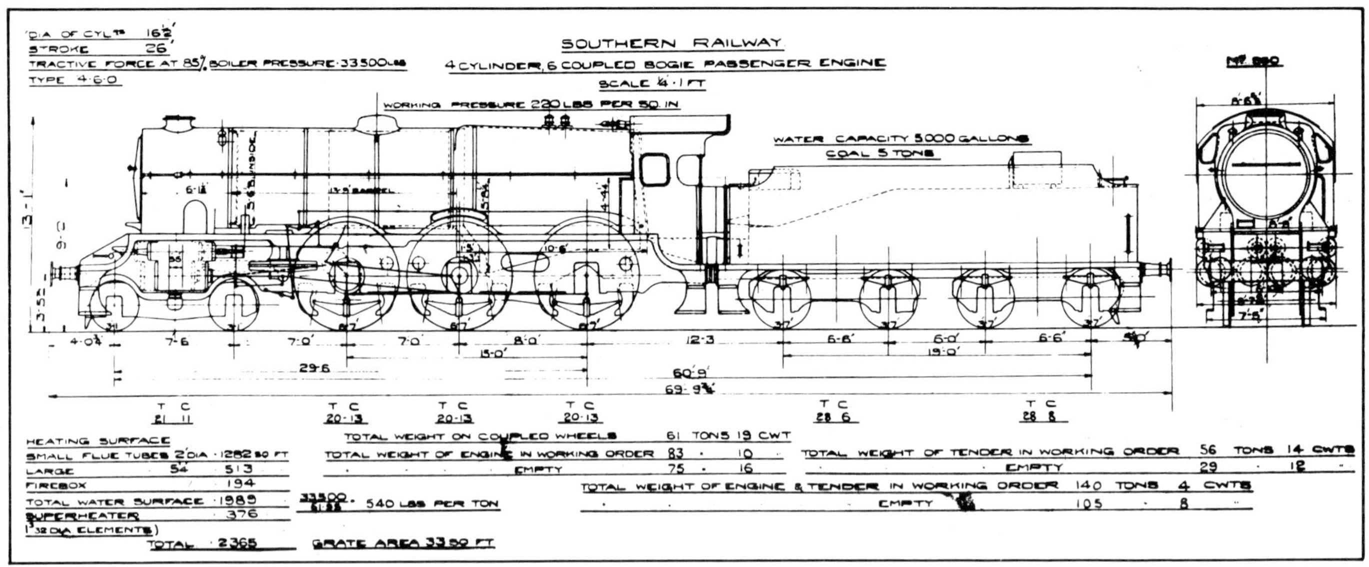

A fine example of the very best that Eastleigh produced in Southern Railway days. In 1926 4-6-0 'Lord Nelson' class No. E850 is photographed in Eastleigh locomotive works yard, and named *Lord Nelson*. To this day it is still used on railtours and maintains all the very best in looks and sounds.

'Lord Nelson' Class No. 30859 Lord Hood.

Locomotive Number LSWR SR	British Rail	Building Date	Withdrawal Date	Notes
URIE CLASS 'N15', 4-6-0 (cont.)				
746	30746	June 1922	Oct. 1955	MS Jan. 1929; *Pendragon*
747	30747	July 1922	Oct. 1956	MS Nov. 1930; *Elaine*
748	30748	Aug. 1922	Sept. 1957	MS Nov. 1929; *Vivien*
749	30749	Sept. 1922	June 1957	MS Dec. 1928; *Iseult*
750	30750	Oct. 1922	July 1957	MS Feb. 1930; *Morgan le Fay*
751	30751	Nov. 1922	June 1957	MS June 1929; *Etarre*
752	30752	Dec. 1922	Dec. 1955	MS Sept. 1930; *Linette*, Lemaitre exhaust, large diameter chimney
753	30753	Jan. 1923	Mar. 1957	MS June 1929; *Melisande*
754	30754	Feb. 1923	Jan. 1953	MS Jan. 1930; *The Green Knight*
755	30755	Mar. 1923	May 1957	MS Mar. 1929; *The Red Knight*, Lemaitre exhaust, large diameter chimney
MAUNSELL CLASS 'H15', 4-6-0 (cont.)				
E473	30473	Feb. 1924	July 1959	MS Nov.1931
E474	30474	Feb. 1924	Apr. 1960	MS June 1931
E475	30475	Mar. 1924	Dec. 1961	MS June 1930
E476	30476	Apr. 1924	Dec. 1961	MS Jan. 1929
E477	30477	May 1924	June 1959	MS Dec. 1929
E478	30478	June 1924	Mar. 1959	MS May 1930
E521	30521	July 1924	Dec. 1961	MS Sept. 1929
E522	30522	July 1924	Sept. 1961	MS Apr. 1929
E523	30523	Sept. 1924	Dec. 1961	MS July 1929
E524	30524	Sept. 1924	Feb. 1961	MS
E330	30330	Oct. 1924	May 1957	Rebuilt from Drummond Class 'F13'
E331	30331	Nov. 1924	Mar. 1961	Rebuilt from Drummond Class 'F13'
E332	30332	Dec. 1924	Oct. 1956	Rebuilt from Drummond Class 'F13'
E333	30333	Dec. 1924	Oct. 1958	Rebuilt from Drummond Class 'F13'
E334	30334	Jan. 1925	June 1958	Rebuilt from Drummond Class 'F13'

A Maunsell-approved Urie design with 'H15' class No. E473 as built in 1924. Of interest is the pump under the crossbars, which was later dispensed with.

Locomotive Number LSWR SR	British Rail	Building Date	Withdrawal Date	Notes
MAUNSELL CLASS 'N15', (cont.) —		The naming of the 'N15s' began with *King Arthur*, No. 453, in 1925, thus numbers 736-745 and 746-755 were named retrospectively; thirty 'N15s' were built by the North British Locomotive Company in 1925 and were known as the 'Scotch Arthurs' Nos. 793-806 fitted with 6-wheel tenders.		
E453	30453	Feb. 1925	July 1961	*King Arthur*
E454	30454	Mar. 1925	Nov. 1958	*Queen Guinevere*
E455	30455	Mar. 1925	Apr. 1959	*Sir Launcelot*
E456	30456	Apr. 1925	May 1960	*Sir Galahad*
E457	30457	Apr. 1925	May 1961	*Sir Bedivere*
E448	30448	May 1925	Aug. 1960	*Sir Tristram*
E449	30449	June 1925	Dec. 1959	*Sir Torre*
E450	30450	June 1925	Sept. 1960	*Sir Kay*
E451	30451	June 1925	June 1962	*Sir Lamorak*
E452	30452	July 1925	Aug. 1959	*Sir Meliagrance*
E793	30793	Mar. 1926	Aug. 1962	*Sir Ontzlake*
E794	30794	Mar. 1926	Aug. 1960	*Sir Ector de Maris*
E795	30795	Apr. 1926	July 1962	*Sir Dinadan*
E796	30796	May 1926	Feb. 1962	*Sir Dodinas le Savage*
E797	30797	June 1926	June 1959	*Sir Blamor de Ganis*
E798	30798	June 1926	June 1962	*Sir Hectimere*
E799	30799	July 1926	Feb. 1961	*Sir Ironside*
MAUNSELL CLASS 'LN', 4-6-0 —		Express passenger; known as the 'Lord Nelson' class; 4 cylinders of 16.5in. diameter/26in. stroke; cranks set at 135 degrees except No. 865; driving wheels 6ft. 7in. in diameter except No. 859; sixteen in class.		
E850	30850	Aug. 1926	Aug. 1962	*Lord Nelson*

One of the 'N15' 'King Arthur' class locomotives, No. E451 *Sir Lamorak*, with shelter surrounding the smokebox front end containing equipment for testing performance.

Locomotive Number LSWR SR	British Rail	Building Date	Withdrawal Date	Notes
MAUNSELL CLASS 'N15' (cont.)				
E800	30800	Sept. 1926	Aug. 1961	*Sir Meleaus de Lile*
E801	30801	Oct. 1926	Apr. 1959	*Sir Meliot de Logres*
E802	30802	Oct. 1926	July 1961	*Sir Durnore*
E803	30803	Oct. 1926	July 1961	*Sir Harry le Fise Lake*
E804	30804	Dec. 1926	Feb. 1962	*Sir Cador of Cornwall*
E805	30805	Jan. 1927	Nov. 1959	*Sir Constantine*
E806	30806	Jan. 1927	Apr. 1961	*Sir Galleron*
CLASS 'S15', (cont.)				
E823	30823	Mar. 1927	Nov. 1964	
E824	30824	Mar. 1927	Sept. 1965	
E825	30825	Apr. 1927	Jan. 1964	
E826	30826	May 1927	Dec. 1962	
E827	30827	June 1927	Jan. 1964	
E828	30828	July 1927	Jan. 1964	
E829	30829	July 1927	Nov. 1963	
E830	30830	Aug. 1927	July 1964	
E831	30831	Sept. 1927	Nov. 1963	
E832	30832	Oct. 1927	Jan. 1964	
E833	30833	Nov. 1927	May 1965	
E834	30834	Nov. 1927	Nov. 1964	
E835	30835	Dec. 1927	Nov. 1964	
E836	30836	Dec. 1927	June 1964	
E837	30837	Jan. 1928	Sept. 1965	

Maunsell class 'S15' No. E825, without smoke deflectors, but with snifting valves behind the chimney, as built in 1927.

Eastleigh's very own S15 No. 30828 speeds up the main line with a Salisbury to Waterloo train in May 1960. *The Late Derek Cross*

Locomotive Number LSWR SR	British Rail	Building Date	Withdrawal Date	Notes
MAUNSELL 'U' CLASS, 2-6-0 – Originally twenty 'River' class 'K', 2-6-4T, built under Maunsell at Ashford for SE&CR, 1917; twenty rebuilt, seven at Eastleigh, as tender engines; 2 cylinders with 19in. diameter/28 in. stroke; driving wheels 6ft. diameter; prefixed 'A' from Jan. 1923 until June, 1931.				
A790	31790	June 1928	May 1965	*River Avon*
A793	31793	June 1928	May 1964	*River Ouse*
A794	31794	June 1928	June 1963	*River Rother*
A795	31795	June 1928	June 1966	*River Medway*
A791	31791	July 1928	June 1966	*River Adur*
A792	31792	July 1928	Sept. 1964	*River Arun*
A796	31796	July 1928	Jan. 1964	*River Stour*

A rebuilt 'River' class No. 31792 in British Rail days. On rebuilding, the 'River' class names were lost and therefore the 'U' class of locomotives remained unnamed for life.
John Marshall

MAUNSELL 'LN' CLASS, 4-6-0

LSWR SR	British Rail	Building Date	Withdrawal Date	Notes
E851	30851	June 1928	Dec. 1961	*Sir Francis Drake*
E852	30852	July 1928	Feb. 1962	*Sir Walter Raleigh*
E853	30853	Sept. 1928	Mar. 1962	*Sir Richard Grenville*
E854	30854	Oct. 1928	Sept. 1961	*Howard of Effingham*
E855	30855	Nov. 1928	Sept. 1961	*Robert Blake*
E856	30856	Nov. 1928	Sept. 1962	*Lord St. Vincent*
E857	30857	Dec. 1928	Sept. 1962	*Lord Howe*; large diameter boiler, no Belpaire firebox
E858	30858	Jan. 1929	Aug. 1961	*Lord Duncan*
E859	30859	Mar. 1929	Dec. 1961	*Lord Hood*; 6ft. 3in. wheels
E860	30860	Apr. 1929	Aug. 1962	*Lord Hawke*; Longer boiler
E861	30861	Sept. 1929	Oct. 1962	*Lord Anson*
E862	30862	Oct. 1929	Oct. 1962	*Lord Collingwood*; Kylchap blastpipe & double chimney
E863	30863	Oct. 1929	Feb. 1962	*Lord Rodney*
E864	30864	Nov. 1929	Jan. 1962	*Sir Martin Frobisher*
E865	30865	Nov. 1929	May 1961	*Sir John Hawkins*; 90 deg. cranks, Kylchap blastpipe & double chimney without capuchon

'Lord Nelson' class No. E857 *Lord Howe* with large diameter boiler, without Belpaire firebox and fitted with experimental smoke deflectors, c. 1929.

Locomotive Number LSWR SR	British Rail	Building Date	Withdrawal Date	Notes
MAUNSELL CLASS, 'V' 4-4-0 — Light express passenger; known as the 'Schools' class; 3 cylinders of 16.5in. diameter/26in. stroke; driving wheels 6ft. 7in. in diameter; forty in class, twenty modified.				
E900	30900	Mar. 1930	Feb. 1962	*Eton*
E901	30901	Mar. 1930	Dec. 1962	*Winchester*; Lemaitre exhaust; large diameter chimney
E902	30902	Apr. 1930	Dec. 1962	*Wellington*; Lemaitre exhaust; large diameter chimney
E903	30903	Apr. 1930	Dec. 1962	*Charterhouse*
E904	30904	May 1930	July 1961	*Lancing*
E905	30905	May 1930	Dec. 1962	*Tonbridge*
E906	30906	June 1930	Dec. 1962	*Sherborne*
E907	30907	July 1930	June 1961	*Dulwich*; Lemaitre exhaust; large diameter chimney
E908	30908	July 1930	Sept. 1961	*Westminster*
E909	30909	July 1930	Feb. 1962	*St. Paul's*; Lemaitre exhaust; large diameter chimney

Left: The Southern's answer to streamlining c. 1938. A 'Schools' class locomotive, No. 935, is disguised and renumbered 999 with wooden mock-up air smoothed casing with a touch of the Bulleid un-rebuilt design, and 'Sunny South Sam' emblem adorning the smokebox door; a slogan of the times.

Below: As completed in March 1930, Maunsell class 'V', No. E900 *Eton*. This example ran with an unmodified front end, apart from the addition of smoke deflectors, and was the most powerful 4-4-0 in Europe.

Locomotive Number LSWR SR	British Rail	Building Date	Withdrawal Date	Notes
MAUNSELL 'U1'CLASS, 2-6-0 —		Similar to the 'U' class; 3 cylinders of 16in. diameter/28in. stroke; twenty one in class (No. A890 was the only one of the class built at Ashford as a 2-6-4T in 1926).		
A891	31891	Jan. 1931	Apr. 1963	
A892	31892	Jan. 1931	Nov. 1962	
A893	31893	Feb. 1931	Dec. 1962	
A894	31894	Feb. 1931	Dec. 1962	
A895	31895	Mar. 1931	Dec. 1962	
A896	31896	Mar. 1931	Dec. 1962	
A897	31897	Mar. 1931	Nov. 1962	
A898	31898	Apr. 1931	Dec. 1962	
A899	31899	Apr. 1931	Dec. 1962	
A900	31900	May 1931	Dec. 1962	
1901	31901	June 1931	June 1963	
1902	31902	July 1931	Dec. 1962	
1903	31903	July 1931	Dec. 1962	
1904	31904	July 1931	Nov. 1962	
1905	31905	Aug. 1931	Dec. 1962	
1906	31906	Sept. 1931	Dec. 1962	
1907	31907	Sept. 1931	Dec. 1962	
1908	31908	Oct. 1931	Dec. 1962	
1909	31909	Oct. 1931	Dec. 1962	
1910	31910	Nov. 1931	July 1963	
MAUNSELL 'W' CLASS, 2-6-4T —		Transfer freight traffic; 3 cylinders with 16.5in. diameter/28in. stroke; driving wheels 5ft. 6in. in diameter; fifteen in class with five built at Eastleigh and ten at Ashford.		
1911	31911	Jan. 1932	Oct. 1963	
1912	31912	Jan. 1932	Aug. 1964	
1913	31913	Jan. 1932	Mar. 1964	
1914	31914	Jan. 1932	Aug. 1964	
1915	31915	Feb. 1932	Oct. 1963	

During the depression years of the early 1930s the workload was spread over the system, resulting in Ashford's designs being built at Eastleigh. One of these, a 'U1' class No. 31895, is seen in later British Rail livery at Ashford on 18th May 1951.

L. Elsey

One of the five Maunsell 2-6-4T 'W' class, No. 31911, in the livery of British Rail, at Eastleigh shed in the early 1960s. A building date of January 1932 started this first short class.

G. W. Morrison

All forty in the class of 'Schools' built were named after English Public Schools. This fine study of a locomotive, No. 923 *Uppingham* carried this name for a very short time as the school objected to its name being carried on a railway locomotive, and it was therefore re-named *Bradfield*. Cabside and tender are slanted to give increased clearance through the narrow tunnels of the Hastings line.

Locomotive Number LSWR SR	British Rail	Building Date	Withdrawal Date	Notes
MAUNSELL CLASS 'V' (cont.)				
910	30910	Nov. 1932	Nov. 1961	*Merchant Taylors*
911	30911	Dec. 1932	Dec. 1962	*Dover*
912	30912	Dec. 1932	Nov. 1962	*Downside*
913	30913	Dec. 1932	Jan. 1962	*Christ's Hospital*; Lemaitre exhaust; large diameter chimney
914	30914	Dec. 1932	July 1961	*Eastbourne*; Lemaitre exhaust; large diameter chimney
915	30915	May 1933	Dec. 1962	*Brighton*; Lemaitre exhaust; large diameter chimney
916	30916	May 1933	Dec. 1962	*Whitgift*
917	30917	June 1933	Nov. 1962	*Ardingly*; Lemaitre exhaust; large diameter chimney
918	30918	June 1933	Oct. 1961	*Hurstpierpoint*; Lemaitre exhaust; large diameter chimney
919	30919	June 1933	Jan. 1961	*Harrow*; Lemaitre exhaust; large diameter chimney
920	30920	Oct. 1933	Nov. 1961	*Rugby*; Lemaitre exhaust; large diameter chimney
921	30921	Nov. 1933	Dec. 1962	*Shrewsbury*; Lemaitre exhaust. large diameter chimney
922	30922	Dec. 1933	Nov. 1961	*Marlborough*
923	30923	Dec. 1933	Dec. 1962	*Uppingham*, renamed *Bradfield*
924	30924	Dec. 1933	Jan. 1962	*Haileybury*; Lemaitre exhaust; large diameter chimney
925	30925	Apr. 1934	Dec. 1962	*Cheltenham*
926	30926	May 1934	Dec. 1962	*Repton*
927	30927	June 1934	Jan. 1961	*Clifton*
928	30928	June 1934	Nov. 1962	*Stowe*
929	30929	July 1934	Dec. 1962	*Malvern*; Lemaitre exhaust; large diameter chimney
930	30930	Dec. 1934	Dec. 1962	*Radley*; Lemaitre exhaust; large diameter chimney
931	30931	Dec. 1934	Sept. 1961	*King's Wimbledon*; Lemaitre exhaust; large diameter chimney
932	30932	Feb. 1935	Jan. 1961	*Blundell's*
933	30933	Feb. 1935	Nov. 1961	*King's Canterbury*; Lemaitre exhaust; large diameter chimney
934	30934	Mar. 1935	Dec. 1962	*St. Lawrence*
935	30935	May 1935	Dec. 1962	*Sevenoaks;* streamlined as No. '999'; Lemaitre exhaust; large diameter chimney
936	30936	June 1935	Dec. 1962	*Cranleigh*
937	30937	June 1935	Dec. 1962	*Epsom*
938	30938	July 1935	July 1961	*St. Olave's*
939	30939	July 1935	July 1961	*Leatherhead*; Lemaitre exhaust; large diameter chimney

'N15X' CLASS, 4-6-0 – Known as the 'Remembrance' class; originally built at Brighton as Baltic tanks under L. B. Billinton of LB&SCR; rebuilt at Eastleigh as tender engines; 2 cylinders of 21in. diameter/28in. stroke; driving wheels 6ft. 9in. in diameter; seven in class.

LSWR SR	British Rail	Building Date	Withdrawal Date	Notes
2329	32329	Dec. 1934	July 1956	*Stephenson*
2327	32327	Apr. 1935	Jan. 1956	*Trevithick*, originally named *Charles C. Macrae*
2333	32333	June 1935	Apr. 1956	*Remembrance*, kept original name as World War One memorial engine of the LB&SCR
2330	32330	Sept. 1935	Aug. 1955	*Cudworth*
2332	32332	Nov. 1935	Jan. 1956	*Stroudley*
2328	32328	Feb. 1936	Jan. 1955	*Hackworth*
2331	32331	Apr. 1936	Jan. 1956	*Beattie*

Locomotive Number LSWR SR	British Rail	Building Date	Withdrawal Date	Notes
MAUNSELL CLASS 'S15', (cont.)				
838	30838	May 1936	Sept. 1965	
839	30839	May 1936	Sept. 1965	
840	30840	June 1936	Sept. 1964	
841	30841	July 1936	Jan. 1964	
842	30842	Aug. 1936	Sept. 1965	
843	30843	Sept. 1936	Sept. 1964	
844	30844	Oct. 1936	June 1964	
845	30845	Oct. 1936	July 1963	
846	30846	Nov. 1936	Jan. 1963	
847	30847	Dec. 1936	Jan. 1964	

The first of the last batch of 4-6-0 locomotives designed by Maunsell. Outshopped in passenger green lined livery, No. 838 of the 'S15' class as built in May 1936. Some of this '800' series were supplied with six-wheeled tenders.

'N15X', No. 2333 *Remembrance* as rebuilt from a 'Baltic' tank in June 1935. Known affectionately as the 'Remembrance' class and originally built at Brighton. *O. J. Morris/F. S. Birch Collection*

Locomotive Number LSWR SR	British Rail	Building Date	Withdrawal Date	Notes
MAUNSELL 'Q' CLASS, 0-6-0				Goods engine; 2 cylinders of 19in. diameter/26in. stroke; Stephenson's valve gear; driving wheels 5ft. 1in. dia.; twenty in class, modified by Bulleid with large diameter chimney and multiple jet blastpipe
530	30530	Jan. 1938	Dec. 1964	
531	30531	June 1938	July 1964	
532	30532	June 1938	Jan. 1964	
533	30533	July 1938	Mar. 1963	
534	30534	Sept. 1938	Dec. 1962	
535	30535	Sept. 1938	Apr. 1965	
536	30536	Oct. 1938	Jan. 1964	
537	30537	Oct. 1938	Dec. 1962	
538	30538	Nov. 1938	July 1963	
539	30539	Dec. 1938	Jan. 1963	
540	30540	Jan. 1939	Nov. 1962	
541	30541	Jan. 1939	Nov. 1964	
542	30542	Mar. 1939	Dec. 1964	
543	30543	Mar. 1939	Dec. 1964	
544	30544	Apr. 1939	Jan. 1964	
545	30545	June 1939	Apr. 1965	
546	30546	June 1939	May 1964	
547	30547	July 1939	Jan. 1964	
548	30548	Aug. 1939	Mar. 1965	
549	30549	Sept. 1939	July 1963	

Above: The final design of Maunsell on the Southern Railway did not materialise until after his retirement. In 1938 the first of the 'Q' class appeared, a locomotive for freight working. Here we see No. 534 as built at Eastleigh.
O. J. Morris/F. S. Birch Collection

Right: Modification to the 'Q' class took place, and when photographed in September 1950, No. 30530's alterations by Bulleid are visible, namely large diameter chimney and Lemâitre exhaust.
L. Elsey

Locomotive Number				
LSWR SR	**British Rail**	**Building Date**	**Withdrawal Date**	**Notes**
BULLEID CLASS 'MN', 4-6-2 —	'Merchant Navy' class; express passenger; 3 cylinders, 18in. diameter/24in. stroke; Bulleid valve gear; 6ft. 2in. driving wheels; thirty in class; rebuilt as orthodox locomotives.			
21C-1	35001	Feb. 1941	Nov. 1964	*Channel Packet*, rebuilt Aug. 1959
21C-2	35002	June 1941	Feb. 1964	*Union Castle*, rebuilt May 1958
21C-3	35003	Sept. 1941	July 1967	*Royal Mail*, rebuilt Sept. 1959
21C-4	35004	Oct. 1941	Oct. 1965	*Cunard White Star*, rebuilt July 1958
21C-5	35005	Dec. 1941	Oct. 1965	*Canadian Pacific*, temporarily fitted with mechanical stoker; rebuilt June 1959
21C-6	35006	Dec. 1941	Aug. 1964	*Peninsular and Oriental S. N. Co.* rebuilt Oct. 1959
21C-7	35007	June 1942	July 1967	*Aberdeen Commonwealth*, rebuilt May 1958
21C-8	35008	June 1942	July 1967	*Orient Line*, rebuilt May 1957
21C-9	35009	July 1942	Sept. 1964	*Shaw Savill*, rebuilt Mar. 1957
21C-10	35010	Aug. 1942	Sept. 1966	*Blue Star*, rebuilt Jan. 1957

Probably what O. V. Bulleid will best be remembered for, 21C1 *Channel Packet*, as built in February 1941 and before any minor modifications altered its appearance. Points of note are the 'horseshoe' 'Southern' plate on the smokebox door, cast brass number plates at the front end and cabside, with a 'Southern' plate on the tender. These embellishments were confined to the first two locomotives of the class, thereafter the numbers and lettering were painted on in 'sunshine' gold characters.

Locomotive Number LMSR	British Rail	Building Date	Withdrawal Date	Notes
CLASS '8F', 2-8-0 — Designed by W. A. Stanier for LM&SR, therefore having LM&SR numbers, 23 in batch				
8600	48600	Dec. 1942	Nov. 1966	Built for Ministry of War Transport during World War Two. Railway Works at Brighton, Ashford and Swindon also built batches.
8601	48601	Jan. 1943	June 1965	
8602	48602	Apr. 1943	July 1967	
8603	48603	Apr. 1943	June 1967	
8604	48604	June 1943	May 1967	
8605	48605	July 1943	Aug. 1966	
8606	48606	Aug. 1943	Aug. 1966	
8607	48607	Sept. 1943	Aug. 1965	
8608	48608	Sept. 1943	Feb. 1966	
8609	48609	Oct. 1943	Jan. 1968	
8650	48650	Oct. 1943	Aug. 1967	
8651	48651	Oct. 1943	Nov. 1966	
8652	48652	Oct. 1943	June 1968	
8653	48653	Oct. 1943	Aug. 1965	
8654	48654	Nov. 1943	Oct. 1964	
8655	48655	Nov. 1943	Aug. 1967	
8656	48656	Nov. 1943	Aug. 1965	
8657	48657	Nov. 1943	Oct. 1964	
8658	48658	Nov. 1943	July 1965	
8659	48659	Dec. 1943	May 1966	
8660	48660	Dec. 1943	July 1965	
8661	48661	June 1944	Sept. 1965	
8662	48662	June 1944	Nov. 1966	

To the design of W. A. Stanier, a new name to Eastleigh, came the LMS class of locomotive known as the '8F'. These were constructed during the last war and built for the War Department; our example here is of No. 48660 in British Rail days at Bath Green Park. *John Marshall*

Locomotive Number LSWR SR	British Rail	Building Date	Withdrawal Date	Notes
BULLEID CLASS 'MN', 4-6-2, (cont.)				
21C-11	35011	Dec. 1944	Feb. 1966	*General Steam Navigation*, rebuilt July 1959
21C-12	35012	Dec. 1944	Apr. 1967	*United States Lines*, rebuilt Feb. 1957
21C-13	35013	Feb. 1945	July 1967	*Blue Funnel*, rebuilt May 1956
21C-14	35014	Feb. 1945	Mar. 1967	*Nederland Line*, rebuilt July 1956
21C-15	35015	Mar. 1945	Feb. 1964	*Rotterdam Lloyd*, rebuilt June 1958
21C-16	35016	Mar. 1945	Aug. 1965	*Elders Fyffes*, rebuilt Apr. 1957
21C-17	35017	Apr. 1945	July 1966	*Belgian Marine*, rebuilt Mar. 1957
21C-18	35018	May 1945	Aug. 1964	*British India Line*, rebuilt Feb. 1956
21C-19	35019	June 1945	Sept. 1965	*French Line C. G. T.*, rebuilt May 1959, Giesel ejector and single chimney fitted, 1948-50
21C-20	35020	June 1945	Feb. 1965	*Bibby Line*, rebuilt Apr. 1956
	35021	Sept. 1948	Aug. 1965	*New Zealand Line*, rebuilt June 1959
	35022	Oct. 1948	May 1966	*Holland America Line*, rebuilt June 1956
	35023	Nov. 1948	July 1967	*Holland Afrika Line*, rebuilt Feb.1957
	35024	Nov. 1948	Jan. 1965	*East Asiatic Company*, rebuilt May 1959
	35025	Nov. 1948	Sept. 1964	*Brocklebank Line*, rebuilt Dec. 1956
	35026	Dec. 1948	Mar. 1967	*Lamport and Holt Line*, rebuilt Jan. 1957
	35027	Dec. 1948	Sept. 1966	*Port Line*, rebuilt May 1957
	35028	Dec. 1948	July 1967	*Clan Line*, rebuilt Oct. 1959
	35029	Feb. 1949	Sept. 1966	*Ellerman Lines*, rebuilt Sept. 1959
	35030	Apr. 1949	July 1967	*Elder-Dempster Lines*, rebuilt Apr. 1958

The last of the second batch of 'Merchant Navy' class locomotives, No. 21C20 *Bibby Line*, at the far end of number three bay Erecting Shop, c. May 1945. *J. Bell*

Cab view of a 'Merchant Navy' class locomotive. Driver's position is on the left-hand side and the Fireman's on the right. Of note is the 'Butterfly'-type of firehole doors and drawbar (centre bottom) for coupling to the tender.

Locomotive Number LSWR SR	British Rail	Building Date	Withdrawal Date	Notes
BULLEID 'WC' & 'BB' CLASS, 4-6-2 — Known as 'West Country' or 'Battle of Britain' class; 3 cylinders, 16⅜in. diameter/24in. stroke; Bulleid valve gear; 6ft. 2in. driving wheels; one hundred and ten in class, six built in Eastleigh, one hundred and four built in Brighton; sixty rebuilt at Eastleigh as orthodox locomotives — listed according to rebuild date at Eastleigh.				
	34095	Oct. 1949	July 1967	WC *Brentor*, rebuilt Jan. 1961
	34097	Nov. 1949	Apr. 1966	WC *Holsworthy*, rebuilt Mar. 1961
	34099	Dec. 1949	Nov. 1964	WC *Lynmouth*
	34101	Jan. 1950	Nov. 1966	WC *Hartland*, rebuilt Sept. 1960
	34102	Feb. 1950	July 1967	WC *Lapford*
	34104	Apr. 1950	June 1967	WC *Bere Alston*, rebuilt May 1961; last locomotive built at Eastleigh

'West Country' class No. 34102 *Lapford*, photographed on 20th August 1955 at Eastleigh Running Shed, and newly outshopped in British Rail livery. This was one of only six built in Eastleigh Works and the last un-rebuilt to be withdrawn from B.R. service in 1967. *L. Elsey*

West Country/Battle of Britain Class Locomotives Rebuilt at Eastleigh

Locomotive Number LSWR SR	British Rail	Rebuild Date	Withdrawal Date	Notes
21C-105	34005	June 1957	Oct. 1966	WC *Barnstaple*, originally built at Brighton, July 1945
21C-103	34003	Sept. 1957	Sept. 1964	WC *Plymouth*, originally built at Brighton, June 1945
21C-127	34027	Sept. 1957	Aug. 1964	WC *Taw Valley*, originally built at Brighton, Apr. 1946
21C-113	34013	Oct. 1957	July 1967	WC *Okehampton*, originally built at Brighton, Oct. 1945

21C-125	34025	Oct. 1957	July 1967	WC *Whimple*, originally built at Brighton, Mar. 1946
21C-101	34001	Nov. 1957	July 1967	WC *Exeter*, originally built at Brighton, June 1945
21C-117	34017	Nov. 1957	Oct. 1966	WC *Ilfracombe*, originally built at Brighton, Dec. 1945
21C-121	34021	Dec. 1957	July 1967	WC *Dartmoor*, originally built at Brighton, Jan. 1946
21C-122	34022	Dec. 1957	Apr. 1965	WC *Exmoor*, originally built at Brighton, Jan. 1946
21C-112	34012	Jan. 1958	Dec. 1966	WC *Launceston*, originally built at Brighton, Oct. 1945
21C-104	34004	Feb. 1958	July 1967	WC *Yeovil*, originally built at Brighton, July 1945
21C-126	34026	Feb. 1958	Sept. 1966	WC *Yes Tor*, originally built at Brighton, June 1946
21C-114	34014	Mar. 1958	Mar. 1965	WC *Budleigh Salterton*, originally built at Brighton, Nov. 1945
21C-116	34016	Mar. 1958	June 1964	WC *Bodmin*, originally built at Brighton, Nov. 1945
21C-128	34028	Mar. 1958	May 1964	WC *Eddystone*, originally built at Brighton, May 1946
21C-137	34037	Mar. 1958	July 1967	WC *Clovelly*, originally built at Brighton, Aug. 1946
21C-150	34050	Aug. 1958	Aug. 1965	BB *Royal Observer Corps*, originally built at Brighton, Dec. 1946
21C-118	34018	Sept. 1958	July 1967	WC *Axminster*, originally built at Brighton, Dec. 1945
21C-152	34052	Sept. 1958	July 1967	BB *Lord Dowding*, originally built at Brighton, Dec. 1946
21C-145	34045	Oct. 1958	June 1964	WC *Ottery St. Mary*, originally built at Brighton, Oct. 1946
21C-131	34031	Nov. 1958	Feb. 1965	WC *Torrington*, originally built at Brighton, June 1946
21C-147	34047	Nov. 1958	June 1967	WC *Callington*, originally built at Brighton, Nov. 1946
21C-153	34053	Nov. 1958	Oct. 1965	BB *Sir Keith Park*, originally built at Brighton, Jan. 1947
21C-129	34029	Dec. 1958	Sept. 1964	WC *Lundy*, originally built at Brighton, May 1946
21C-110	34010	Jan. 1959	Mar. 1965	WC *Sidmouth*, originally built at Brighton, Sept. 1945
21C-139	34039	Jan. 1959	May 1965	WC *Boscastle*, originally built at Brighton, Sept. 1946
21C-142	34042	Jan. 1959	Oct. 1965	WC *Dorchester*, originally built at Brighton, Oct. 1946
21C-146	34046	Feb. 1959	Oct. 1965	WC *Braunton*, originally built at Brighton, Nov. 1946
21C-148	34048	Mar. 1959	May 1966	WC *Crediton*, originally built at Brighton, Nov. 1946
21C-162	34062	Mar. 1959	July 1964	BB *17 Squadron*, originally built at Brighton, May 1947
21C-159	34059	Mar. 1960	May 1966	BB *Sir Archibald Sinclair*, originally built at Brighton, Apr. 1947
	34082	Apr. 1960	May 1966	BB *615 Squadron*, originally built at Brighton, Sept. 1948
	34088	Apr. 1960	Mar. 1967	BB *213 Squadron*, originally built at Brighton, Dec. 1948
21C-144	34044	May 1960	Mar. 1965	WC *Woolacombe*, originally built at Brighton, Oct. 1946
	34071	May 1960	Apr. 1964	BB *601 Squadron*, originally built at Brighton, Apr. 1948
	34093	June 1960	July 1967	WC *Saunton*, originally built at Brighton, Sept. 1949
	34085	June 1960	Sept. 1965	BB *501 Squadron*, originally built at Brighton, Nov. 1948

Locomotive Number LSWR SR	British Rail	Rebuild Date	Withdrawal Date	Notes
21C-108	34008	July 1960	July 1967	WC *Padstow*, originally built at Brighton, Sept. 1945
	34077	July 1960	Mar. 1967	BB *603 Squadron*, originally built at Brighton, July 1948
21C-134	34034	Aug. 1960	July 1967	WC *Honiton*, originally built at Brighton, July 1946
	34090	Aug. 1960	July 1967	BB *Sir Eustace Missenden, Southern Railway*, originally built at Brighton, Feb. 1949
21C-136	34036	Sept. 1960	July 1967	WC *Westward Ho*, originally built at Brighton, July 1946
21C-132	34032	Oct. 1960	Oct. 1966	WC *Camelford*, originally built at Brighton, June 1946
21C-140	34040	Oct. 1960	July 1967	WC *Crewkerne*, originally built at Brighton, Sept. 1946
	34100	Oct. 1960	July 1967	WC *Appledore*, originally built at Brighton, Dec. 1949
21C-158	34058	Nov. 1960	Oct. 1964	BB *Sir Frederick Pile*, originally built at Brighton, Apr. 1947
21C-160	34060	Nov. 1960	July 1967	BB *25 Squadron*, originally built at Brighton, Apr. 1947
	34089	Nov. 1960	July 1967	BB *602 Squadron*, originally built at Brighton, Dec. 1948
21C-156	34056	Dec. 1960	May 1967	BB *Croydon*, originally built at Brighton, Feb. 1947
	34087	Dec. 1960	July 1967	BB *145 Squadron*, originally built at Brighton, Dec. 1948
21C-109	34009	Jan. 1961	Oct. 1966	WC *Lyme Regis*, originally built at Brighton, Sept. 1945
21C-124	34024	Feb. 1961	July 1967	WC *Tamar Valley*, originally built at Brighton, Feb. 1946
	34098	Feb. 1961	July 1967	WC *Templecombe*, originally built at Brighton, Dec. 1949
	34109	Mar. 1961	Sept. 1964	BB *Sir Trafford Leigh Mallory*, originally built at Brighton, May 1950
	34096	Mar. 1961	Sept. 1964	WC *Trevone*, originally built at Brighton, Nov. 1949
	34108	Mar. 1961	July 1967	WC *Wincanton*, originally built at Brighton, Apr. 1950

ABBREVIATIONS

ES Eastleigh Superheater
MS Maunsell Superheater
RS Robinson Superheater
SS Schmidt Superheater

NOTES Between May and June 1931 the 'A', 'B' and 'E' prefixes were dropped from the numbers and the following number system was introduced.

Western Section (formerly LSWR) — O or nothing
Eastern Section (formerly SE&CR) — 1000 added
Central Section (formerly LB&SCR) — 2000 added

Preserved Eastleigh Built and Rebuilt Steam Locomotives

Class	Number	Name	Owner	Location
S15	30499		Urie S15 Preservation Group	Mid-Hants Railway
S15	30506		Urie S15 Preservation Group	Mid-Hants Railway
Q	30541		Maunsell Locomotive Society	Bluebell Railway, Sussex
S15	30825			Barry, South Wales
S15	30828		Eastleigh Railway Pres. Society	Eastleigh, Hants
S15	30830		Barry Steam Loco. Action Group	Barry, South Wales
S15	30841	*Greene King*	Essex Locomotive Society	North York Moors Railway
S15	30847		Maunsell Locomotive Society	Bluebell Railway, Sussex
LN	30850	*Lord Nelson*	National Railway Museum	York/Steamtown, Carnforth
V	30925	*Cheltenham*	National Railway Museum	York
V	30926	*Repton*	Steamtown	Scranton, Penn., USA
V	30928	*Stowe*	Montagu Ventures	Bluebell Railway, Sussex
WC*	34010	*Sidmouth*	Privately owned	North York Moors Railway
WC*	34016	*Bodmin*	Privately owned	Mid-Hants Railway
WC*	34027	*Taw Valley*	Privately owned	Bury, Lancs.
WC*	34028	*Eddystone*	Ashford Railway Trust	Barry, South Wales
WC*	34039	*Boscastle*	M. J. Tawse	Great Central Railway, Loughborough
WC*	34046	*Braunton*	Ashford Railway Trust	Barry, South Wales
BB*	34053	*Sir Keith Park*	C. Timms	Barry, South Wales
BB*	34058	*Sir Frederick Pile*	C. Timms	Barry, South Wales
BB*	34059	*Sir Archibald Sinclair*	Bluebell Railway	Bluebell Railway, Sussex
WC+	34101	*Hartland*	Shaws Metal Supplies, Derby	Peak Park Railway
MN+	35005	*Canadian Pacific*	Steamtown, Carnforth	Carnforth, Lancs.
MN+	35006	*Peninsular & Oriental S. N. Co.*	P&OSN Co. Society	Toddington, Glos.
MN+	35009	*Shaw Savill*	(unclaimed)	Barry, South Wales
MN+	35010	*Blue Star*	(IA) Engineman's Group	Barry, South Wales
MN+	35011	*General Steam Navigation*	Southern Locomotive Action Group	Barry, South Wales
MN+	35018	*British India Line*	Privately owned	Mid-Hants Railway
MN+	35022	*Holland America Line*	Southern Steam Trust, Swanage	Barry, South Wales
MN+	35025	*Brocklebank Line*	Brocklebank Society	Barry, South Wales
MN+	35027	*Port Line*	Swindon & Cricklade Railway	Blunsdon, Swindon
MN+	35028	*Clan Line*	Merchant Navy Loco. Pres. Society	Bulmers Yard, Hereford

NOTES

* — Rebuilt, but not originally built at Eastleigh.
\+ — Built and rebuilt at Eastleigh.
None of the Eastleigh 'West Countrys' survive as built.
No. 35029, *Ellerman Lines* sectionalised at National Railway Museum, York.
No. 30825 has no boiler.
No. 30841 as named after its private purchase.

Bibliography

Arthurs, Nelson and Schools at Work, S. C. Townroe — Ian Allan
Bulleid Locomotives, B. Haresnape — Ian Allan
Maunsell S15s, P. Cooper — Kingfisher Railway Productions

The Merchant Navy in its final form. No. 35028 *Clan Line* takes on water at Southampton Central station in 1965. *Clan Line* was the last in the class to be rebuilt and survived until the end of steam on the Southern in July 1967; indeed it is still to be seen now on special main line trains, mainly in the north of England.

F. R. Sherlock